Evlyn Griffith
april 28, 1989

CHAPLIN
and American Culture

The Evolution of a Star Image

Charles J. Maland

PRINCETON UNIVERSITY PRESS

Princeton, New Jersey

Frontispiece: Charlie's trademarks. Courtesy Wisconsin Center
for Film and Theater Research, Madison

This book has been composed in Linotron Baskerville text
and Helvetica Bold display type.

Clothbound editions of Princeton University Press books are printed
on acid-free paper, and binding materials are chosen for
strength and durability. Paperbacks, although satisfactory
for personal collections, are not usually suitable
for library rebinding

Printed in the United States of America by Princeton University Press,
Princeton, New Jersey

Library of Congress Cataloging-in-Publication Data

Maland, Charles J.
Chaplin and American culture : the evolution of a
star image / Charles J. Maland.
p.   cm.
Bibliography: p.
Includes index.
ISBN 0-691-09440-3 (alk. paper)
1. Chaplin, Charlie, 1889–1977. 2. Comedians—United
States—Biography. 3. Motion picture producers
and directors—United States—Biography. 4. Celebrities—
United States. 5. United States—Civilization—20th
century. 6. Fame. I. Title.

PN2287.C5M264 1989
791.43'028'0924—dc19
[B] 88-20916

To Nancy—again
To Jonathan
and
To the memory of
Marvin Felheim

Contents

CONTENTS

CONTENTS

Illustrations

CREDITS

In the following list, the numerals are the figure numbers. Any items not credited are from private collections.

Acme News pictures, 20, 21

Emporia Gazette, 11

IBM Corporation, 34, 35

Frank Interlandi, 30

Rollin Kirby, 12

Liberty, 13

London Daily Herald, 29

Motion Picture Magazine, 1, 2, 3, 4, 5, 6

New York Herald Tribune, 7

Joanna T. Steichen, 10

Tribune Media Services (*Chicago Tribune*),
    22, 28, 31

United Artists, 9, 14, 15, 16, 17, 18, 24, 25, 26, 27

Washington Evening Star, 19

Wisconsin Center for Film and Theater Research,
    frontispiece, 20

Wide World Photo (Associated Press), 23

Preface

Sometimes accidents of history divide lives into eerily symmetrical parts.

Such was surely the case with Charles Spencer Chaplin, whose place in American culture was marked by four twenty-year milestones. In 1912 the young English music-hall comedian, then unknown to most Americans, arrived in New York on the SS *Oceanic* for his second Canadian and U.S. tour.[1] Twenty years later, this same Charles Chaplin, now the world's most famous movie star, returned to the United States following a sixteen-month world trip. From the Thames to Tokyo, from Berlin to Bali, Chaplin had been celebrated by court and commoner alike. In 1952, however, two days after Chaplin and his family had set sail for Europe, the U.S. attorney general's office announced that Chaplin's reentry permit had been revoked and that if he wished to return to the United States, he would have to prove his political and moral worth. Chaplin chose exile, settling in Switzerland. Yet twenty years after he left the United States in this climate of hostility, he returned as a conquering (or at least semi-rehabilitated) hero, acclaimed by some during this 1972 visit as the greatest genius the movies had ever known. Americans apparently sought to restore Chaplin to his preeminent position of stardom in recompense for a previous generation's vilifications.

This fluctuating public reputation suggested by Chaplin's trips to and from America every twenty years is grounded in an intriguing relationship, one between Charles Chaplin—a complex, talented, and often enigmatic man—and the United States—a country that during Chaplin's residence moved fitfully and somewhat reluctantly into the world community. Although the London-born Chaplin was indelibly shaped by a Victorian world view and the performance tradition of English music halls, he also lived in the United States for nearly forty years, established himself as a star working in the American film industry, and learned that his success and failure were closely tied to his relationship with American culture.

Although many books and countless articles have been written about Chaplin, none has concentrated primarily on explaining the relationship between Chaplin and the United States.[2] This study seeks to fill that gap by tracing the dynamic interplay between Chaplin and American culture from 1913 to the 1980s and by focusing particularly on Chaplin's star image, which rose so quickly early in his career, fell so dramatically in the 1940s and 1950s, and then rose again from the 1960s on.

In carrying out this goal, the book embraces both a major and a minor theme. The major theme contends that a Chaplin *star image*, fashioned by Chaplin himself, by certain ideological and signifying practices within the film industry, by the press, and by representatives of other social institutions, was established and then evolved in American culture from World War I to the present. The star image consists of the complex and shifting set of meanings, attitudes, and mental pictures associated in the public mind with a recognized motion-picture performer—both the real person and the persona he or she plays in films. Thus Chaplin's star image consists of the changing qualities and traits associated with Charles Spencer Chaplin and the changing qualities and traits associated with the characters Chaplin played in his films, particularly his Charlie persona.[3] The book traces the complex evolution of that star image in the United States and the dynamic relationship between Chaplin and American culture. On the one hand, it focuses on how Chaplin, through his actions, words, and films, contributed to his star image. On the other, it explores how American society—through the activities of reviewers, press publicists, editorialists, moralists and censorship groups, governmental agencies, and intellectuals—helped to make Chaplin a star, to sustain that stardom, gradually to politicize it, and eventually, by the early 1950s, to nearly destroy his star image. Subsequently, the book traces how that image was reconstituted in the 1960s and especially in the 1970s, when it once again took on positive, though sometimes different, associations, allowing Chaplin and his film to experience a revival.

The minor, yet closely related, theme holds that the shifts in Chaplin's star image are intimately related to historical developments in the United States between World War I and the present. These developments include both internal advances in the film industry, like the transition to sound, and external political and social events, like the on-set of the Great Depression and the Cold War.[4] The consideration of such historical factors illuminates the study of Chaplin's star image by showing not only how these developments affected Chaplin but also how they influenced the standards and character of critical discourse through which the reviewers, critics, and general audience responded to him and his work.

A few words about method indicate how these themes are developed. The notion of stardom, as Richard Dyer has noted in *Stars*, his excellent inquiry into stardom, may be examined from two different, though related, perspectives. An ideological or sociological approach focuses on stardom as a dominant and probably symptomatic characteristic of modern society. A textual or semiotic approach concentrates on stardom as a part of the way films create meaning. The two approaches, Dyer argues, are interdependent. One can understand the social significance of stars only if one understands how their meaning or signification is realized in films (and in newspapers, magazines, advertisements, and other media texts that publicize or comment on them). Conversely, since all texts are created in contexts, and since a star image changes over time, the textual approach to the study of stardom must be informed by a contextual approach sensitive to historical change.[5]

What is the apparatus by which stars are created and sustained in a culture? Dyer observes that in the second decade of this century certain well-defined institutional practices that helped build and maintain stars grew up within the American film industry. In particular, the star image emerges from the interplay of four kinds of media texts already evident in that period. First, the films themselves create a cumulative and evolving star image: in a star's films one can discern continuities and variations in costume, gesture, narrative concerns, and character development. Second, studio promotional materials concerning the stars and their films—sent to fan magazines, journalists, and movie-theater owners—contribute to the star image. Third, publicity—"What the press finds out" about stars—helps fashion their image. As Dyer notes, publicity seems, but may not be, more "authentic" than promotion. Finally, criticism and commentary on the stars and their films, from daily newspaper reviews to critical biographies, also play a part. This book examines all four kinds of texts—films, promotion, publicity, and commentary—in exploring the growth of Chaplin's star image.[6]

As we shall see, Chaplin, functioning within this flux of surrounding media texts, managed to obtain an unusual amount of control over the production and distribution of his films because of the rapid and unprecedented popularity of his early work. Consequently, by the 1920s he had managed to gain control over his star image to a degree almost unheard of in the American film industry in the 1920s, 1930s, and 1940s. This control included the promotion of, and often even the publicity about, his life and films. (By the mid-1920s he was so popular that he could select who would interview him and in what circumstances.) Yet in the 1930s and especially in the 1940s he began to lose control over what Dyer terms the publicity about his films. In addition, commentary about Chaplin and his films became much more divided during that same period, as the filmmaker struggled with the technological challenge of sound and with the place of political issues in his films. This inability to control the press response to him and his work eventually damaged Chaplin's star image by linking it to moral and political activities that alienated large and sometimes vocal segments of the American public.

An examination of how a star image evolves also benefits from the work of Hans Robert Jauss, probably the most historically oriented of the literary reception theorists. In his essay "Literary History as a Challenge to Literary Theory," Jauss criticizes in particular two assumptions of traditional literary history: that an objective and eternal truth can be discovered in texts and that texts rather unproblematically represent or reflect the historical reality from which they emerge. As an alternative, Jauss proposes that literary history should be "methodologically grounded and written anew," based on "an aesthetics of reception and influence." For Jauss, literary works (and for our purposes, narrative feature films) have no intrinsic history and meaning except to the extent that successive audiences respond to them.[7] Thus the history of a body of works by a writer or by a filmmaker like Chaplin must take into account the background against which the work first appeared; the "horizon of expectations" against which it was experienced by its audience; the response (critical and otherwise) that it generated; and the changes that appeared in succeeding works, due partly to responses the artist received from other artists, from reviewers, from other sectors of the intelligentsia, and from the audience at large. If we keep in mind that the "horizon of expectations" of the audience is influenced by broad social and political factors in addition to more purely aesthetic ones, this model of reception helps clarify how an artist's career unfolds temporally and how a culture's response to an artist's work is cumulative, shifting, and multifaceted.[8]

THIS BOOK is divided into five parts. Part One, "To the Top," traces the process by which Chaplin first became a star and then managed to sustain that stardom through 1919. Part Two, "At the Top: Charlie and the 1920s," concentrates on Chaplin's star image from 1920 until the release of *City Lights* (1931). Part Three, "The Challenge of Progressive Politics," treats the period between the stock market crash and

World War II, when three factors had an especially powerful impact on Chaplin's relationship with American Culture: the pressure on Chaplin to make dialogue films, the Great Depression, and the rise of fascism. If Chaplin's star image reached its height of popularity in the 1920s and 1930s, it became politicized and plummeted to its nadir in the late 1940s and early 1950s. Part Four, "Unraveling," examines the decline of Chaplin's star image in America between 1942 and 1952, and his response to that decline. Part Five, "The Exile and America," discusses the guarded restoration of Chaplin's star image from the mid-1950s to the present. An epilogue tracing the way Chaplin's Charlie persona has become "commodified" in the 1980s, particularly in the highly successful advertisement campaign for IBM microcomputers, concludes the study.

The contours of this project support the belief that the most illuminating historical criticism and analysis, exemplified by Edmund Wilson's work on Dickens, is a criticism that shows the artist as a human being grounded in a particular time and place, struggling to understand self and society and to embody that understanding in the work of art. It is a criticism rarely practiced on a filmmaker, for few who have worked in the dominant film industry have ever managed the creative control that Chaplin enjoyed for most of his career. Yet the lives and work of these few artists who, like Chaplin, have functioned successfully in the cinema can sustain such an examination. F. O. Matthiessen's suggestive comment in *American Renaissance* that the work of artists is "the most sensitive index to cultural history," since artists can articulate only what they are and what they have been made "by the society of which (they are) a willing or unwilling part," undergirds this approach to Chaplin.9 If what follows illuminates the dynamic interplay between Chaplin and American culture, it will have achieved what it set out to do.

Knoxville, Tennessee
May 1988

Acknowledgments

The assistance, generosity, and friendship of many people and institutions have helped bring this book into being. Although it is impossible to list everyone who influenced this work, I acknowledge the following with pleasure.

Thanks first to John Mitchell and Ron Palosaari, who in the late 1960s convinced me that the movies were an art, industry, and social force worth examining.

The University of Tennessee has supported this book in a number of ways. A summer research grant from the Graduate School assisted initial research efforts. Later grants from the John C. Hodges Fund in the English Department also sustained my work, as did Joseph Trahern, department head during the time I was working on the book. I also thank the graduate and undergraduate students in my course on Chaplin and American Culture; their probing of and enthusiasm for Chaplin's work helped me think about the subject that gradually transformed itself into this book.

A number of archives, libraries, and other institutions provided me with invaluable information and generous assistance as I prepared this study. They include the University of Tennessee Libraries and especially Director Don Hunt, Judy Webster, Angie LeClercq, and the reference and interlibrary loan staffs; the British Film Institute Library, London; Barbara Humphreys and Emily Sieger of the Motion Picture Section of the Library of Congress, Washington, D.C., Charles Silver of the Museum of Modern Art Film Department, New York; three collections in the New York Public Library system—the Lincoln Center Library (Billy Rose Collection), the Main Library, and the Newspaper Library; the Wisconsin Center for Film and Theater Research, Madison; and the American Film Institute Library, Beverly Hills. The U.S. government provided me with its files on Chaplin following my Freedom of Information Act request. IBM Corporation generously provided information about its personal computer advertising campaign featuring Charlie.

ACKNOWLEDGMENTS

I benefited constantly from the work of three Chaplin scholars, in particular. David Robinson's fine biography provided information from Chaplin's papers that is available nowhere else. The bibliographies of Timothy Lyons and Wes Gehring were of great assistance, as was their encouragement through correspondence. I thank these three scholars for their painstaking work.

Various others offered important counsel at key stages of the project or read and commented on the manuscript. For their assistance, I would like to thank Neal Gabler, Michael Lofaro, John Raeburn, Robert Ray, and Janet Staiger. At Princeton University Press, Joanna Hitchcock provided generous support for the project early on, as did Marilyn Campbell. Elizabeth Gretz helped me to avoid factual errors and stylistic lapses through her careful copyediting.

Special thanks go to three people: to Nancy Klein Maland, whose support for and assistance on this project have been, as with my previous work, unfailing; to Jonathan Maland, who is three years younger than the idea for this book and thus had to live with it since infancy (thank goodness he likes Charlie!); and to the late Marvin Felheim, whose dedication to teaching and scholarship was an inspiration to generations of students, not least those of us in the American Culture Program at the University of Michigan in the early 1970s. Grateful for the vital and indispensable contributions each of these three people have made to me, I am pleased to dedicate this book to them.

Abbreviations

BRC Billy Rose Collection, Lincoln Center Branch, New York Public Library, New York

CHC David Bordwell, Janet Staiger, and Kristin Thompson, *The Classical Hollywood Cinema: Film Style and Mode of Production to 1960* (New York: Columbia University Press, 1985)

CHLA David Robinson, *Chaplin: His Life and Art* (New York: McGraw-Hill, 1985)

MA Charles Spencer Chaplin, *My Autobiography* (New York: Simon and Schuster, 1964)

NYT *New York Times*

RLC Robinson Locke Collection, in the Billy Rose Collection, Lincoln Center Branch, New York Public Library, New York

SAC special agent in charge (FBI)

UAC United Artists Collection, Wisconsin Center for Film and Theater Research, Wisconsin State Historical Library, Madison

ONE

To the Top

1

Chaplin, the Early Films, and
the Rise to Stardom

The Rough-Edged Diamond:
Charlie at Keystone

On 12 May 1913 Alf Reeves, manager of a Fred Karno music-hall company touring in America, received a telegram at the Nixon Theater in Philadelphia:

> IS THERE A MAN NAMED CHAFFIN IN YOUR COMPANY OR SOMETHING LIKE THAT STOP IF SO WILL HE COMMUNICATE WITH KESSEL AND BAUMAN 24 LONGACRE BUILDING BROADWAY NEW YORK

Reeves, suspecting that the telegram must be referring to one of his featured players, Charles Chaplin, showed it to him. When Chaplin learned that the Longacre Building primarily housed legal offices, he surmised that he had inherited some money and immediately arranged a trip to New York City. But he soon learned otherwise. Adam Kessel, Jr., and Charles O. Bauman were owners of the New York Motion Pictures Company. The telegram had been sent by Mack Sennett, head of one of their subsidiaries—a film production company in Los Angeles called Keystone. Sennett had seen Chaplin perform in 1911 at the American Music Hall and thought that Chaplin might do as a replacement for Ford Sterling, a leading Keystone comedian who was threatening to leave. Though Chaplin had no previous experience in film, he was lured to accept the offer by a princely salary: $150 weekly for three months, raised to $175 weekly for the rest of the year. Before joining Keystone, however, Chaplin had to complete his Karno tour. After his last performance, in Kansas City on November 28, an eager yet anxious Chaplin parted with his Karno associates and took a train to California. Little did he know that within three years he would be one of the most famed and highly paid men in America.[1]

Chaplin arrived in Los Angeles at a propitious time in the development of the American film industry. Though motion pictures had been projected in America since 1896, the movie industry did not experience its first significant growth until the nickelodeon boom of

1906–1907.[2] In an attempt to cash in on the enormous potential profits offered by this expansion, a group of manufacturers of motion-picture technology, headed by Thomas Edison, formed the Motion Picture Patents Company. By controlling nearly all of the key patents on motion-picture film, cameras, and projectors, the Trust—as the group was popularly known—kept tight control on the industry for several years. But a group of renegade production companies, including Keystone, emerged and by 1912 had formed a strong and organized independent movement. These Independents gradually began to weaken the hegemony of the Trust, and this in turn laid the groundwork for the ascendance of the studio system in the late 1910s and the 1920s.[3]

Chaplin's timing was fortunate because in the previous several years, the film industry, groping toward the star system that would later dominate it, had begun to market films by featuring particular actors. Thanks partly to the stability created by the Trust after its foundation in 1908, the industry was able, in the words of one scholar, "to turn investment away from patent litigation and into product development." Actors were one aspect of production that quickly received attention. (I use the term "actors" to refer to both men and women.) As early as February 1910, an author in *Nickelodeon* noted that movie audiences were demanding "a better acquaintance with those they see upon the screen," and by 1912—the year before Chaplin's arrival on the Keystone lot—a "star system" was beginning to establish itself. Although the film industry was starting to standardize its technology and method of telling stories, the star system provided a way for one company to differentiate its product from that of other companies.[4]

But Chaplin did not become a full-fledged star immediately. In fact, it would probably be more accurate to say that although he gained a considerable following among moviegoers during his year at Keystone, he did not actually become a star until after he signed with a new company, Essanay, in early 1915.

The construction of the star image did begin at Keystone, however, primarily as a result of the films rather than promotion of them or publicity and commentary about them. Chaplin appeared in thirty-five films for Keystone in 1914. The first, *Making a Living*, was released on February 2; the last, *His Prehistoric Past*, on December 7. Although most of the films were one-reelers (about ten minutes long), several were only about five minutes, and one, *Tillie's Punctured Romance*, featuring Marie Dressler, took up six reels. Chaplin appeared in his "tramp" or "Charlie" costume very early—in his second film, *Kid*

*Auto Races at Venice.*⁵ By his twelfth film, *Caught in a Cabaret*, he had finally persuaded Sennett to let him co-direct (with Mabel Normand, his costar). Chaplin then went on to direct or co-direct (with Mabel Normand, four more times) twenty of his last twenty-three films at Keystone. The year was a frenetic, educational one for Chaplin. He learned moviemaking by doing.

A look at some characteristics of the Keystone films, particularly of the persona Chaplin played, indicates the kind of star image that Chaplin began to develop during his year there. That image was shaped in part by the studio in which Chaplin worked: Sennett's studio was famous for its iconoclastic nose-thumbing at propriety and its frantic Keystone cop chases. Chaplin himself, accustomed to the more polished acting and pantomime of the English music hall, felt uneasy with the hectic, broad Keystone style (MA, pp. 147–50). Even though he began to differentiate himself through the creation of a character and to achieve some level of independence by directing his own films, Chaplin still created a persona that was tempered by the Keystone stamp.

Generalizing about Chaplin's persona at Keystone is nearly impossible, largely because he was much less conscious of the character he played (and less able to control that persona, given his position as Sennett's employee) than he became in later years. Though viewers today associate Chaplin's screen persona with a distinct outfit and props— derby and cane, tight-fitting coat and baggy pants, floppy shoes—this costume was not his trademark during the early Keystone days. In his first film Chaplin played a dandy; he wore a top hat, a double-breasted frock coat, and a monocle, and he sported a handlebar mustache. In *Mabel at the Wheel*, his tenth Keystone film, he wore a top hat, long overcoat, black gloves, spats, and a goatee. Even after he began directing himself, Chaplin's costume varied. The top hat appeared again, for example, in *Mabel's Married Life* (his nineteenth Keystone film). Sometimes his occupation in a film determined his clothing: coatless, Chaplin wore a waiter's apron over his vest in *Caught in a Cabaret*. As the Keystone year passed, however, the costume became more conventional. By his final Keystone, the Charlie persona must have been widely known to a growing audience, for in that film—*His Prehistoric Past*—Charlie wore his derby and big shoes with his caveman's skins, which suggests that the derby and shoes were already trademark enough.

Much has been written about the essential appeal of Charlie's costume and character, and these discussions often revolve around conceptions of contrast that Chaplin, in his autobiography, recalled using when trying to describe his new character to Sennett after piecing together the costume: "You know this fellow is many-sided, a tramp, a gentleman, a poet, a dreamer, a lonely fellow, always hopeful of romance and adventure. He would have you believe he is a scientist, a musician, a duke, a polo player. However, he is not above picking up cigarette butts or robbing a baby of its candy. And, of course, if the situation warrants it, he will kick a lady in the rear—but only in extreme anger" (MA, p. 144). In writing this passage Chaplin was either disingenuous or forgetful, because such a multifaceted and complex conception of Charlie's character was not apparent during the Keystone year. In fact, it would be relatively accurate to say that Chaplin's description would fit his Keystone persona well if the first half were deleted and the second half—about picking up cigarette butts, stealing candy from babies, and kicking ladies—were emphasized.

The Charlie persona that emerged from the Keystone films was often mean, crude, and brutish. Examples from the films abound. In *Between Showers*, for example, Charlie pokes Ford Sterling in the backside with an umbrella and thumbs his nose to a cop. In *A Film Johnnie*, he gets ejected from a movie theater for disruptive behavior, and in *Mabel at the Wheel*, he sticks a pin in Mabel's thigh and her boyfriend's buttocks. As a waiter in *Caught in a Cabaret*, he dusts off some food with a dirty rag, then drops the food on the floor, steps on it, puts it back on the plate, and serves it. As a dentist's odd-job man in *Laughing Gas*, he hits a man on the mouth with a brick, causing the man to spit out a mouthful of teeth. In the same film, he poses as a dentist and clambers onto a woman in the chair; when she resists, he pulls the woman's nose with a forceps and kisses her. Though the Keystone films also contain a number of the graceful and clever comic touches that would become a Chaplin trademark, the humor in these films is generally broad and sometimes bawdy slapstick. The gentle and tender character apparent in later Chaplin films—*City Lights*, for example—is at this point nowhere to be found.

Given this screen persona, what evidence exists in the press that Chaplin was becoming a name to reckon with in the film industry? One way to approach this question is to examine how representative film magazines of the day recognized Charlie (or Chaplin) in their reviews of films he appeared in. *Moving Picture World* reviewed at least seventeen of Chaplin's Keystones, and its varying levels of awareness of Chaplin suggest the degree to which he was becoming known while at Keystone. Without naming him specifically, the magazine noted his performance in its review of Chaplin's first Keystone, *Making a Living*: "The clever player who takes the role of a nervy and very shifty sharper in this picture is a comedian of the first water, who acts like one of Nature's own naturals."[6] There were no references to Chaplin in March or April. In a May issue, however, a review of *Caught in a Cabaret* stated, "Charles Chaplin was the leading funmaker" (9 May 1914: 821). This mention would suggest that Chaplin's name was becoming familiar, but that may not have been true: in a number of later reviews, Chaplin's name was misspelled. The review of *Mabel's Married Life* states, "Charles Chapman and Mabel Normand are at their best" (27 June 1914: 65). In a review of *Recreation*, the name is misspelled "Chaplain" (29 August 1914: 1242), and in the September 19 and 26 issues, the spelling reverts to "Chapman." By the time *Those Love Pangs* was reviewed in October, *Moving Picture World* had finally learned to spell Chaplin's name correctly (17 October 1914: 337). Even then, however, reviews suggest that he was not as established and settled a performer as Mabel Normand or Mack Swain. Note the review of *His Musical Career*: "Chas Chaplin and Ambrose disport themselves in this number as a pair of piano movers" (14 November 1914: 932). Ambrose was the name of the character Mack Swain played in the Keystone films at that time; reviewers and apparently audiences regularly referred to Ambrose and to Mabel, but Chaplin had not yet become known as Charlie or the tramp or the little fellow, at least not until near the end of his year at Keystone.

A similar indication that Chaplin's popularity began to grow near the end of this year comes from *Motion Picture Magazine*. The periodical featured a regular section called "Green Room Jottings," which consisted of one- or two-sentence references to people, primarily actors, in the movie business. The first reference to Chaplin appeared in the August 1914 "Jottings," in which readers learned that "Charles Chaplin (Keystone) has been an 'actor man' for sixteen years, yet he is now only twenty-four years young."[7] That same issue contained a rather bizarre caricature of Chaplin on a page with nine other figures, including Ford Sterling, John Barrymore, and—the largest in size— V. A. Potel, the "Funny Man at G. M. Anderson's Essanay Camp" (p. 131). The Chaplin sketch showed him with brawny shoulders, barrel chest, bulging biceps, and tiny waist and legs, a bulldog at his side (see Figure 1). To George Edwards, the artist, Chaplin seemed to suggest a young athlete or acrobat. Mustache, derby, and cane played no part in his star image here.

In its October 1914 issue *Motion Picture Magazine* announced the results of its "Great Player Contest," in which over eleven million ballots had ostensibly been cast by readers before the cutoff date of August 20. Earle Williams, Clara K. Young, and Mary Pickford topped the list

CHAPLIN

1. Cartoon from August 1914,
before Chaplin became
identified as Charlie.

of the one hundred leading vote getters. Mabel Normand, in fortieth place, was the highest-ranking Keystone star; the name of Charles Chaplin did not appear (p. 128). In the December issue another caricature of Chaplin appeared, this time in baggy pants, tight coat, and top hat, and carrying a cane (p. 130); in addition, there was a full-page collage containing five pictures of Chaplin's face in closeup. This was significantly more attention than he had received in the August issue.

The January issue provided a stark contrast to the "Great Player Contest" of the previous October, for in it, the results of the "Great Cast Contest" were announced (p. 126). The contest featured twelve categories, including leading man, leading woman, old man, old woman, villain, and so on. In the male comedian category, Charles Chaplin came out on top, accumulating 10,390 votes and edging out John Bunny, in second place with 9,510 votes. Even more striking, perhaps, is the fact that only Mary Maurice, who won the "old woman" category, received more votes than Chaplin. Since voting took place during the third week in November, it is apparent that by the last months of the Keystone period, Chaplin's films had become very popular. The "Great Cast Contest" was also held the following year, and by November of 1915, Chaplin had garnered 1.9 million votes, with Ford Sterling a distant second at 1.4 million votes (p. 124). Even if we are skeptical of the numbers and the voting procedures, the fact remains that by late 1914, readers of the magazine were learning about Chaplin in terms that were full of praise.

These two magazines do give us a good general picture of how Chaplin's reputation began to grow during 1914, but it is important to make a distinction here between Charlie and Chaplin. Evidence suggests that Chaplin's screen persona did become popular with viewers by the end of the Keystone period. But Chaplin himself had not yet become a star: there was little discussion in the press of the man who was responsible for the creation of the character. Recalling in 1916 his experiences near the end of his Keystone contract, Chaplin wrote: "It was odd, walking up and down the streets, eating in cafes, hearing Charlie Chaplin talked about, seeing Charlie Chaplin on every hand and never being recognized as Charlie Chaplin. I had a feeling that all the world was crosseyed, or that I was a disembodied spirit. But that did not last long."[8] Up to the end of the Keystone period, then, the star image of "Charlie Chaplin" revolved almost entirely around a character on the movie screen.

One does not really become a star until publicists and journalists focus on and the audience gets interested in the personality of the actor behind the mask, and it seems likely that Sennett and Keystone, realizing how popular Chaplin was becoming and how high his salary demands might go when it was time to renew his contract, were careful not to exploit the private life of the performer. Despite their efforts, when Chaplin's contract ran out at the end of 1914, other studios became interested in signing him up. Nineteen-fifteen was to be the year in which Chaplin would become a bona fide movie star.

"Chaplinitis": Charlie at Essanay

As Chaplin's Keystone contract neared its end, Mack Sennett had to decide what he and his associates would be willing to pay to keep Chaplin on. Sennett knew that audiences around America were lining up to see the Charlie films, but Chaplin did, too. Chaplin himself remembered asking Sennett to increase his salary to $1,000 per week, a request Sennett denied, protesting that even *he* did not make that much money (MA, p. 159). After Chaplin and Keystone failed to come to terms, Chaplin signed a one-year contract with Essanay on 2 January 1915. The terms included a $10,000 bonus for signing and $1,250 per week. The first of three large and increasingly publicized contracts for Chaplin, it ushered in a remarkable twelve months for the actor— the year of what one writer called a national case of "Chaplinitis."[9]

Chaplin's stardom grew during the Essanay period partly because

9

the persona he had begun to create the year before became in 1915 part of a widespread craze not unlike the Davy Crockett phenomenon of the mid-1950s. Of course, Chaplin's Essanay films (thirteen released in 1915), all of which featured Charlie, contributed to the enthusiasm. (The new dimensions added to the persona during this period will be discussed in the following section.) In addition, however, the Charlie persona was proliferating throughout American culture. Manifestations of this included advertisers' use of Chaplin's character to sell toys and other paraphernalia, imitators of Chaplin, and cartoons about Chaplin.

Throughout 1915 and particularly in the last half of the year, Chaplin's name or Charlie's picture was used to sell all sorts of products. *Motion Picture Magazine* ran a picture of Charlie in its July issue to help advertise its August issue, which concluded its article on Chaplin (p. 171). The July issue also offered a free portrait of Chaplin in his Charlie costume to anyone who ordered a back issue of the magazine (p. 177). The September issue contained an advertisement by the Kirkham Company headed "Charlie Chaplin's Surprise—the Funniest Novelty Ever" (p. 159). Though it was not entirely clear exactly what the novelty was, for ten cents a Chaplin fan could find out. By the October issue, the Fisher Novelty Company was offering a "Charlie Chaplin Squirt Ring" for fifteen cents; a picture of Charlie with derby and mustache topped the ring (p. 164). By the December issue, the Nuidea Company was offering a "Charlie Chaplin Outfit," consisting of a Charlie Chaplin mustache, an imitation gold tooth, a $1,000 bankroll of stage money, and a medallion coin with a "life-like image" of Charlie on it—all for only a dime plus two cents postage (p. 158). The fact that entrepreneurs were appropriating the Charlie persona to merchandise their wares stresses how popular that persona had become.

It has been said that imitation is the sincerest form of flattery. If that is the case, Chaplin was flattered by an overwhelming number of Americans in 1915. Evidence of such imitation appeared frequently in the popular press. In June, *Motion Picture Magazine* reported that "the Chaplin mustache is spreading—not the mustache, but its popularity." The same month, the *Cleveland Plain Dealer* reported that "Cleveland has been getting so full of imitators of Charlie Chaplin that the management of Luna Park decided to offer a prize to the best imitator and out they flocked." (A young man named Leslie T. Hope, later known as Bob Hope, won one such competition in Cleveland.) Indeed, Chaplin look-alike competitions were thriving throughout the country; the

New York World reported in mid-July 1915 that over thirty theaters in the city were sponsoring Chaplin amateur nights.[10]

Chaplin imitations went well beyond amateur night at the local movie house and were found on the screen itself. In the film industry this imitation was not primarily a form of flattery. Rather, like the advertisements, it aimed at cashing in on the success of Charlie. In 1915 film actors imitating Chaplin abounded. The most prominent—and possibly the most blatantly exploitative—was Billie Ritchie, who had also worked for Karno, preceding Chaplin in a Karno sketch called "The Mumming Birds." Though Ritchie went so far as to accuse Chaplin of imitating *him*, he was really quite shameless in copying Chaplin's costume and even his plots: for example, two weeks after Chaplin's *Work* was released, Ritchie came out with *The Curse of Work*.[11] Another Chaplin imitator, Steve Duros, who was hired by theater owners in Columbus, Ohio, to dress like Charlie and walk the streets, was featured in a November issue of *Motion Picture Magazine*.[12]

Cartoons were the third manifestation of the national case of Chaplinitis. These were the first in a long line of cartoons, editorial and otherwise, that attested over the years to Chaplin's star status and reflected the press's various reactions to him. At least as early as April 1915, there appeared a regular comic strip entitled "Charlie Chaplin's Comic Capers."[13] More important for the purposes of this discussion are the single-frame cartoons alluding to Charlie. Sketches of Charlie—and also of Chaplin—began to be printed regularly in the fan magazines after the first few months of 1915. One of the most important and interesting appeared in *Motion Picture Magazine* (June 1915: 152). Headed "Charles Chaplin, Essanay Mirth Provoker," it presented a mini-biography of Chaplin himself (see Figure 2), distinguishing between the filmic persona and the man behind the mustache. It slotted Chaplin in the typical rags-to-riches category so central to the American success myth: "From a penniless immigrant stranded in New York—to a small-time comedy acrobat—to the highest paid movie actor—is the story of Chaplin's rapid rise to success." Small matter that the description bore little relation to reality; it made good copy and began to factor Chaplin the man into the calculus of the Chaplin star image.

Another cartoon, featuring a sketch of Charlie only, raised some questions about the whole Chaplin phenomenon. The August 1915 issue of *Motion Picture Magazine* commented on Chaplin's huge salary in what appeared to be negative terms. (see Figure 3). Here Charlie was sneering at someone—his competitors? Keystone? the audi-

The caption and labels within the image include: "HE DESERTED KEY STONE FOR ESSANAY", "FROM A PENNILESS IMMIGRANT STRANDED IN NEW YORK—", "CHARLES CHAPLIN ESSANAY MIRTH PROVOKER", "YOU'RE ALL RIGHT, CHARLIE! HEE! HEE! YOU'RE ALL RIGHT, YOU LITTLE RASCAL!", "—TO A SMALL-TIME COMEDY ACROBAT—", "—TO THE HIGHEST PAID MOVIE ACTOR—", "—IS THE STORY OF CHAPLIN'S RAPID RISE TO SUCCESS", "THE WHOLE WORLD ENJOYS CHAPLIN COMEDY—"

2. Chaplin, the success story, June 1915.

ence?—while doggedly protecting his bag of money labeled "Highest Salary."

Yet another cartoon commented on Charlie's popularity without presenting the Chaplin star image. The *Cleveland Leader* of 17 May 1915 showed two boys standing outside a movie theater. One of them, alluding to the world war, asked, "Jimmie, would you rather be the President or the Kaiser?" Jimmie replied, "Aw Fudge—I'd ten thousand times rather be Charley Chaplin."

The Chaplin phenomenon, two other cartoons suggest, was also creating cultural divisions. The first, from *Motion Picture Magazine* (October 1915: 148) showed how the Chaplin star image was fostering a generation gap: a child becomes convinced of his uncle's astonishing ignorance when the uncle has to ask who Charlie Chaplin is (see Figure 4). The second, though appearing in the April 1917 issue of *Motion Picture Magazine* (p. 129), after the first tidal wave of Chaplinitis, reflected a problem that began to be much discussed in 1915 and 1916. The cartoon shows a Sunday morning Bible class, in which a young boy sits daydreaming about Charlie (see Figure 5); though it does not editorialize against the boy (in fact, the apearance of the red-nosed genteel teacher makes her seem as much the target of satire as the boy), a number of Americans would have seen the cartoon as an accurate expression of the threat to decency and morality posed by the whole Chaplin phenomenon.

If Chaplin's star image was spread by films, advertisements, imitators, and cartoons, it was also extended in 1915 by articles about the man himself, a topic not discussed during the Keystone period. As the author of "Chaplinitis" put it, after Chaplin signed the Essanay contract, "the world went mad. From New York to San Francisco, from Maine to California, came the staccato tapping of the telegraph key. 'Who is this man Chaplin? What are his ambitions? What's his theory of humor? Is he married, or single? How does he like American life? Does he eat eggs for breakfast? Is he conceited?' The newspapers wanted to know; the country demanded information."[14] The country's appetite for learning more about the funny little man in the movies was for a time insatiable.

What picture of Chaplin the man emerged from the profiles of him in 1915? Richard Dyer has suggested that the American success myth, which holds that the society is so open that anyone can rise to the top,[15] is frequently associated with stars: they become symbols of the myth. If closely examined, the 1915 articles on Chaplin together draw a portrait of the man entirely consistent with Dyer's observation.

Chaplin's humble beginnings and his personal quality of humility are stressed. "Unknown a few months ago," one article stated, Chaplin "is now said to be the highest salaried funny man in the film world." He has, continued the article, a "violet-like reluctance" to talk about himself. "There's nothing worth while talking about," it quotes Chaplin as saying. "I am no one—just a plain fellow." A second essay called him "a little Englishman, quiet, unassuming." Yet another article reinforced that view: "Personally he is said to be extremely modest, retiring, declining to assume he has accomplished much worth making a fuss about." Though Chaplin the man later would be described as being dominated by hubris, the early Chaplin was termed humble.[16]

This humility, according to one article, was "one of the best things that can be said about anybody and one of the real proofs of greatness." Greatness, or extraordinary talent or ability, was the second characteristic of Chaplin's stressed. The author of "Chaplinitis" was one of the first writers to call Chaplin a "genius" at his work, though as time passed that term came to be regularly associated with Chaplin's star image. "Once in every century," the article commented, "a man is born who is able to color and influence his world." In the twentieth

3. Controversy over Chaplin's Essanay
salary, August 1915.

century, "Charles Chaplin is doing it with pantomime and personality." The genius and greatness attributed to Chaplin were, according to one of the articles, "proof that talent will come to the top despite adverse circumstances."[17] The assumptions about humility and greatness embedded in the profiles of Chaplin enabled a generation raised on Horatio Alger novels to feel secure that its attitude toward success had again been proven in the real world.

Thanks to the national bout with "Chaplinitis," a Chaplin star image, combining the persona created in the films with the man who created it, was firmly anchored in the United States by the end of 1915 (see Figure 6). The man was portrayed as humble and unassuming, yet imbued with greatness. The persona, while immensely popular, was nevertheless in a state of flux. If the crude and mischievous persona from the Keystone era had helped to initiate Chaplin's stardom, it also met with resistance in certain sectors of American culture.

The Genteel Tradition and the
"Vulgar" Charlie

Not everyone was caught up in the Chaplin craze. In fact, a significant minority found Chaplin's films a social menace. Because the individual voices raised against Chaplin represented larger social forces, it is necessary, in order to put his dilemma in context, to say a few words about the broader social canvas.

14

American historians, taking a cue from George Santayana's famous essay, "The Genteel Tradition in American Philosophy," have looked upon the first two decades of this century as a time in which the Genteel Tradition gradually lost its dominance.[18] Briefly, the Genteel Tradition was a segment of society that emerged in America in the nineteenth century after the growth of a democratic ethos and the appearance of a new business class had displaced the traditional elite from positions of wealth and power. These displaced elites—the American "gentility"—placed high value on refined manners, a polished and elegant life style, and cultivation of the high arts. They came to perceive themselves as the custodians of American culture, at least in part to compensate for their eroding economic and social status.

Leaders of the American gentility felt that because theirs was an enlightened minority which understood and appreciated culture, it must, in Charles Alexander's words, "try to elevate the national mind by promoting the creative spirit and love of beauty," even as it struggled to keep beauty from being corrupted by the uncomprehending masses and the philistine new rich.[19] One of its most cherished assumptions about art was that it had an essential moral dimension: art should teach proper moral conduct.

Proponents of the Genteel Tradition regarded the movies with mixed feelings. On the one hand, the movies seemed to belong to the "uncomprehending masses"—those who had no appreciation for "real" art or culture. On the other hand, since the movies communicated so powerfully to so many people, some saw film as a great opportunity for educating the masses, if only the proper hands could gain control of the medium. This dual view is encapsulated in a comment from an essay in *The Outlook* in early 1914, about the same time that Chaplin's first film was being released: "The very potency of the motion picture for degrading taste and morals is the measure of its powers for enlightenment." If the movies could be properly regulated, another spokesman argued, they could ideally function as "a grand social worker," enabling the genteel elite to spread its values to others lower on the social scale and hence to extend its social control.[20] As the popularity of movies with working- and middle-class Americans continued to grow, genteel custodians of culture thus began to criticize what they perceived as the danger of movies and to urge reform.

As we have noted, the character Chaplin played in his Keystone films was often abrasive and crude, however funny. Such a character was a likely target of genteel critics, particularly given Chaplin's mass popularity. A 1914 review of *The Property Man* in *Moving Picture World* indicates the dilemma some observers faced: "Some of the funniest

15

WILLIE—I just saw Charlie Chaplin.
UNCLE—Charlie Chaplin? Who is he?
WILLIE—What? Dont you know who Charlie Chaplin is?
Gosh, what ignorance!

THE SUNDAY MORNING BIBLE CLASS

4 (*left*). Chaplinitis and the generation gap, October 1915.

5 (*right*). Charlie competes with Sunday School, April 1917.

things in the picture are vulgar," wrote the critic. "They are too vulgar to describe; but are too funny to pass for vulgarity when only seen."[21]

Although this commentator was generous enough to allow that Chaplin was funny despite his vulgarity—it would be difficult for a movie reviewer to react otherwise—more genteel observers were not so tolerant. One attack on Chaplin by a custodian of culture appeared in a 1915 letter to the editor of the *New Orleans American*.[22] The purpose of the letter, in its author's words, was "to justify the stand taken by so many of the better class and better educated people in New Orleans, who find that the [Chaplin] films are not worth going to see." Why were the films unworthy? The writer pulled no punches: because of the "grotesque and vulgar antics of that product of the slums of Whitecastle." Instead of debasing public taste by presenting the low comedy of Chaplin and his ilk, the author urged, theater owners should present more inspiring programs: travel films, filmed opera, and adaptations of classic novels, poems, and plays.

Others, including religious leaders, joined in the anti-Chaplin chorus. A headline in the *Detroit News* indicates the form such criticism often took: "Low Grade Persons Only Like Charlie Chaplin and Mary Pickford, Says Pastor."[23] The article gave an account of the denunciations of these two movie stars by a prominent Detroit minister. Reactions like this one give an idea of the threat that moralists believed Chaplin's Keystone persona posed to genteel moral standards.

How did Chaplin respond to these criticisms? "The New Charlie Chaplin," a 1916 article in *Motion Picture Magazine*, suggests not only that Chaplin was aware of these challenges to his popularity but also that he was consciously beginning to shift and mold his star image in

16

response to them.[24] The article is J. B. Hirsch's account of a meeting between Chaplin and W. W. Barrett, a member of the executive staff of the National Board of Censorship. This organization, formed in 1909 to encourage "quality" movies and safeguard the public from immorality in films, arranged for a representative to meet with Chaplin and discuss with him the content and future of his movies. The article presents a dramatic account of how the Genteel Tradition put pressure on filmmakers; it also shows how Chaplin's star image was beginning to evolve.

According to Hirsch's article, Barrett visited Chaplin not only because the National Board was concerned about some questionable aspects of Chaplin's movies but also because its members believed that there were "great possibilities in the comedian's future work, both as a helpful influence in the community and as a factor in the artistic development of the Motion Picture" (p. 115). In the essay, Chaplin defended himself against charges of vulgarity: "It is because of my music-hall training and experiences that I . . . work into my acting little threads of vulgarisms." Linking his humor to a venerable tradition, Chaplin added, "This Elizabethan style of humor, this crude form of farce and slapstick comedy . . . was due entirely to my early environment, and I am now trying to steer clear from this sort of humor and adapt myself to a more subtle and finer shade of acting" (pp. 115, 117). The essay portrays Chaplin as apparently contrite, or at least as being careful not to antagonize a group that could limit his popularity.

This "new Charlie Chaplin," wrote Hirsch, has "burst the tawdry chrysalis of the . . . English music-hall manner" in favor of "a new fame, to be built on the basis of a more delicate art that will not countenance the broad sallies his old technique demanded" (p. 115). The essay recounts one of the first recorded instances of Chaplin's conflicts with pressure groups in America, conflicts that were to become more frequent as his career progressed. In this early example, Chaplin bowed to the pressure group and assured it that he would evolve as an artist in directions that would prove suitable to the National Board of Censorship and to the American public. At a time when the middle classes were beginning to attend movies in ever increasing numbers, the Chaplin described in the article was thinking about altering the character of his movies to make them more palatable to this larger audience.[25]

This essay is also interesting because it shows how Chaplin's star image was changing after he had been in the limelight for over a year. The picture of Chaplin that accompanies the article—"as he appears in real life," according to the caption—portrays a youthful-looking, handsome man wearing a dinner jacket and bow tie and gazing seriously at the viewer. The text reinforces the image. Barrett found Chaplin to be quite different from his film persona: "a neat and stylishly dressed young man; as charming and affable a boy . . . as anyone would wish to meet." In a list of features that corresponds in several ways to the list of qualities Richard Dyer associates with stardom, Hirsch describes Chaplin as a "hard worker, who writes, acts, produces and manages; an unusually intelligent man, modest, not in the least affected by his great popularity, and very keen, businesslike and thrifty—not at all like the usual actor of the 'get-rich-quick' variety." (Chaplin's thriftiness, even stinginess in certain respects, did not fit the star pattern of conspicuous consumption; it nonetheless was consistent with the Horatio Alger tradition and a quality often associated with his star image throughout his career.) Finally, Barrett saw in Chaplin an ambitious artist: "He has shaped for himself the slogan 'Art for Art's sake,' and he has dreams of unmeasured possibilities for the future of the films—all from an artistic point of view" (p. 115).

This new view of Chaplin as the unaffected yet serious artist appeared in another 1916 article, "The Real Charlie Chaplin," by Stanley W. Todd.[26] Todd claimed that those interested in knowing Chaplin rather than Charlie are "certain to encounter some surprises" (p. 41). According to Todd, Chaplin was known to his friends "as a serious-minded young fellow whose accession to affluence has not spoiled his democracy or ambitions." Chaplin also constantly sought to improve himself, telling Todd that "no man or woman should be satisfied with having won a fortune or fame in one line of work. I expect to be at it fifty years from now" (p. 44). This affirmation of hard work was a cardinal virtue of the Genteel Tradition, as was another of Chaplin's qualities reported in Todd's article: interest in high culture and the fine arts. Todd told his readers that Chaplin had read Shakespeare "from beginning to end" and was familiar with "the works of George Eliot and other noted writers" (p. 44). Chaplin, who had little formal education, was already compensating for that lack by talking with the press about his intellectual aspirations, and the press dutifully reported them.

These articles portray a star concerned about cleaning up his image and presenting a picture of his private life that would make him acceptable even to genteel Americans. The potentially damaging clash between the American gentility and the "vulgar" persona created by Chaplin was partly averted when the man behind the persona began to present himself as a hard-working, serious, aspiring artist. But there was another significant element in this new view of Chaplin: the films

6. Chaplin's star image, blending person and persona, became firmly
defined in the Essanay period. This sketch appeared
in November 1915.

he made during the Essanay period, from early 1915 to early 1916. How did they portray Charlie in this period when the American gentility was attacking the vulgarity of Chaplin's films?

Romance and Pathos: The "Refining" of Charlie

The Essanay films contributed to this "new" star image. Chaplin made fourteen films at Essanay: the first in the company's Chicago studios; the next five in G. M. Anderson's ill-equipped Niles studios, near San Francisco; and the remainder in Hollywood. The first seven were released within three months; thereafter, Chaplin slowed his work pace and made about one film a month. Although no neat progression from film to film is apparent, Chaplin clearly did try out new ideas, some of which broadened the appeal of his films, during this period.

At first, however, Chaplin seemed to be repeating himself. As Theodore Huff points out, a number of the Essanays resemble the Keystones. *A Night Out* treats the comic misadventures of two drunks and is in much the same vein as *The Rounders*. *In the Park* and *By the Sea* both show the flirtatious and slightly lecherous Charlie being chased by a policeman, as did a number of the Keystone films, including *Twenty Minutes of Love*. *The Champion* is a boxing story similar to that in *The Knockout*, though *The Champion* was more successful at the box office, while both *Work* and *Shanghaied* continue the slapstick comedy prominent in Keystone movies. Reaching back even earlier than the Keystone films, *A Night in the Show* draws from an old Karno sketch entitled, "A Night in an English Music Hall."

Despite these continuities, Chaplin also changed during the Essanay period. The most significant alteration was in the portrayal of Charlie's relationships with the heroines of the films. During the Keystone period, Charlie was most often at odds with women, at least in part because of the feisty screen persona of Mabel Normand, who often appeared opposite Chaplin. A fairly typical example is *Getting Acquainted*, in which Charlie, unhappily married to a demanding wife, flirts with the wife of another man until a policeman breaks up the affair.

Beginning with his second Essanay film, however, Chaplin was paired with a new actress, Edna Purviance, who was to remain his leading lady through his first United Artists film, *A Woman of Paris* (1923). For several reasons, the heroines in Chaplin's films began to change, as did Charlie's relationships with them. First, Purviance's appearance and demeanor—more youthful, passive, rounded, delicate, and innocent than Normand's—prompted a shift toward a gentler interaction between Charlie and the heroine. Second, Chaplin and Purviance themselves began to develop a relationship outside of work almost immediately after she began to act in his films. Chaplin tells us in his autobiography that after they had moved to Los Angeles (immediately after making *The Tramp*), they dined nearly every night at the Los Angeles Athletic Club, where Chaplin had rented an apartment (MA, p. 204). As would often happen during his career, Chaplin's feelings for other people worked themselves into the characterizations and narratives of his films. Third, Chaplin's awareness of criticism from genteel quarters also encouraged him to think about altering his films to broaden their appeal; one way to accomplish this was to idealize the heroine and involve Charlie in a romance with her. Fourth, the switch from one- to two-reel films gave Chaplin the opportunity to develop Charlie's relationship with another character more fully. Finally, as film historians have shown, signifying practices in the film industry were changing. In the movement from primitive to classical Hollywood in the early 1910s, the goals and desires of central characters began to structure film narratives. One of the most common of these desires was for a romantic relationship.[27]

The shift in Chaplin's portrayal of women and of Charlie during the Essanay period occurred gradually. In several of the early Essanay films, the portrayal of women is indistinguishable from that in the Keystones. Women are either objects of Charlie's lust, targets of his antics, or inconsequential to the narrative. In *A Night Out*, for example, Edna's husband discovers her in bed with a drunken, sleeping Charlie. Though Charlie does give Edna a discreet kiss at the end of *The Champion*, her role is not important in the film. Charlie's involvement with women in both *In the Park* and *By the Sea* consists almost entirely of his attempts to pursue the wives or sweethearts of other men. And Edna's part as the maid in *Work* is relatively unimportant. In these films, Charlie is often as irreverent and "vulgar" as he was at Keystone. *Variety's* review of *Work*, Chaplin's eighth Essanay, was similar to the kind of criticism he often received in his Keystone days: "The Essanay release of the Charlie Chaplin picture for this week is *Work* in two reels. It is the usual Chaplin work of late, mussy, messy and dirty." Charging that "the Censor Board is passing matter in the Chaplin films that could not possibly get by in other pictures," the reviewer joined the genteel chorus of Chaplin critics.[28]

By the time *Work* was released, however, Chaplin had already begun displaying an emergent gentility and greater attention to characterization in his work, although sometimes these were only brief moments in otherwise knockabout films. In *A Jitney Elopement*, for example, Chaplin used an iris out (a circular lab effect that closes down to emphasize a detail) when Charlie sniffs a flower under Edna's window, just after we learn that Edna is being made to marry someone else against her wishes. The use of the flower and the attempt at pathos both foreshadowed aspects of Chaplin's work that would recur often, most notably in the final shots of *City Lights*. The moment provided one of the first examples of Charlie's stretching to do something different and more serious in his work, though it was not at all sustained in this particular film.

Chaplin's next film, *The Tramp*, concentrated more on trying to achieve pathos. It, along with *The Bank*, represented Chaplin's most careful attempts to move in directions that would make his films more acceptable to genteel audiences. The two films share several elements. First, Charlie still exhibits some of the cruelty and "vulgarity" he had become known for during the Keystone period, usually while working with other men. Second, Charlie becomes romantically attracted to the character played by Edna Purviance. Third, after Charlie's feelings become known, the audience learns that Edna already has a suitor—larger, more handsome, or of a higher social class than Charlie. Fourth, Charlie becomes caught between social groups and opts to side with Edna. Finally, Charlie's hopes are dashed when he learns that his relationship with Edna will not succeed, and he thus evokes pathos.

The sympathy both films elicit, as well as the romanticizing of women in them, gives them a more gentle quality, more breadth of feeling, than the Keystone films. Largely because of this shifting treatment of women and Charlie's relationship to them, Chaplin's films began to appeal to a broader audience.

Why was this so? The appeal stemmed in part from a portrayal of the underside of romantic relationships in a patriarchal society. If we use Janice Radway's definition of patriarchy as "a social system where women are constituted only in and by their relationships with more powerful men," Chaplin's tales of Charlie's pure and unrequited love for a woman take on added significance. Some men in his audience could identify and empathize with his *failures* in love: in a society that was becoming increasingly bureaucratized and hierarchical, losing a woman to a man of higher status or wealth was not an uncommon experience for men. Similarly, women could identify with Charlie's tenderness toward his beloved, even his renunciation. Radway has recently found through interviews with female readers of romance novels that tenderness is among the masculine qualities they prize most.[29]

Charlie's reticence and complete devotion once he falls in love project tenderness at the start of the relationship but prove heartrending when he realizes he must renounce his love. Although in later films Chaplin handles his romantic relationships and pathos more effectively, it is important to reiterate here that Chaplin's romances increased his appeal to men who had been rejected in love because of inadequate wealth, prestige, or power; to women who admired his tender and nurturing spirit; and to viewers with genteel sensibilities for whom the romance helped to negate the "vulgarity" that worried them.

In addition to romance and pathos, *The Tramp* and *The Bank* contain yet another similarity that reinforced a value dear to the Genteel Tradition. In both films Charlie feels deeply discouraged but shakes off that discouragement with an energetic resilience. The final shots of both show Charlie walking in long shot away from the camera, which emphasizes the depth of the frame and Charlie's isolation; he then springs forward with a sprightly step, straightening and walking off as if renewed. Though it is difficult to describe the movement adequately, its effect is clear: Charlie will not let his disappointment overwhelm him. He will move on with as much vitality and inventiveness as before, accepting a contingent universe in which suffering is a part of life. This determination to go on in spite of the odds, in spite of travail and disappointment, was a cardinal value of the Genteel Tradition. Even if Charlie did not always act with propriety, this quality endeared him to respectable audiences as much as did any other.

Thus, elements of Chaplin's films during the Essanay period made them more palatable to his genteel opposition. The films show a learning filmmaker cautiously moving in directions that deepened his work and broadened its audience appeal. Chaplin seems to have been conscious of the new directions he was taking and concerned about whether the experiment was working. When Charles McGuirk left Chaplin after a day on the set, Chaplin called after him: "Say, did you see *The Tramp*? I know I took an awful chance. But did it get across?"[30] For an increasing number of viewers, it did.

Chaplin also showed an increasing tendency to include other "serious" elements in these films, the most prominent of which was a clear depiction of class conflict and difference. In *Work* the class differences between Charlie and Edna on the one hand and the owners of the home on the other are particulary clear, just as in *The Bank*. Charlie and his janitor friend stand in contrast to the bank owners and other wealthy bank patrons. *Police*, the final Essanay film, contains an interesting satire on reformers: in it, a do-gooder tries to move Charlie

23

toward righteousness and ends up stealing his watch. The same film interestingly shows Charlie caught between the law and the lawless, as he would be again in later films, including *The Pilgrim* and *Modern Times*. John McCabe tells us that during the final months of his Essanay contract Chaplin began working on a film called *Life* (never finished) that would draw on his own painful childhood experiences and "show the tragicomic world of flophouses, grimy alleys, and living 'on the beg.' "[31]

By the end of the Essanay period Chaplin's star image was composed of the softening, more romantic Charlie and the serious, hard-working, ambitious, and modest young filmmaker who aspired to high art. A new, more serious Chaplin was emerging, one who asked film writer Terry Ramsaye to refer to him as Charles, not Charlie.[32] The young music-hall comedian had been vaulted to fame in Hollywood. He also had faced the genteel moralists of America and had begun to make films that, in certain ways, were more palatable to them. But his Essanay days were approaching an end, and new challenges, both aesthetic and cultural, were to confront him as he moved to a new studio and America moved toward more active involvement in World War I.

2

The Perils of Popularity

Chaplin's Star Image in the
Mutual Period

On the evening of 20 February 1916 Chaplin, visiting New York for contract negotiations after fulfilling his Essanay contract, attended a benefit concert at the New York Hippodrome. Asked to appear on the stage and direct a Sousa march, he agreed. Though his performance initially received only perfunctory applause, when he briefly imitated Charlie's walk on the third curtain call, the audience erupted. This reaffirmation of his stardom could not have hurt Chaplin as he entered serious negotiations with John R. Freuler of the Mutual Film Corporation. Reaching an agreement on the 25th, the two parties signed the staggering contract on February 27. It required Chaplin to make twelve comic films. In return, Chaplin would receive $10,000 per week and a $150,000 bonus for signing.[1] Remembering the atmosphere of those days in his autobiography, Chaplin wrote: "Like an avalanche, money and success came with increasing momentum; it was all bewildering, frightening—but wonderful" (MA, p. 174).

About this same time Chaplin unknowingly became involved in the first of a series of autobiographical books that would eventually contribute to his star image. Nearly a year earlier, during the Chaplinitis craze, Rose Wilder Lane of the *San Francisco Bulletin* had interviewed him for a series of biographical articles. The pieces, padded with colorful but invented details, subsequently appeared in the *Bulletin*, and by July 1916 Bobbs-Merrill Publishers wired Chaplin for pictures to supplement a book about his life, a reprint of Lane's series, to be titled *Charlie Chaplin's Own Story.*

The book contained, among other details, highly unflattering pictures of Chaplin's father and some early Chaplin employers. Consequently, Chaplin's lawyer, Nathan Burkan, began proceedings to prevent publication. The publisher countered by offering Chaplin authorship, with "editorial assistance" by Lane, as well as 5 percent of the sales price. When Chaplin continued to refuse, Lane wrote Chaplin that the "publicity value of the book" was very high, but all efforts to persuade him were fruitless. Although a few advance copies of the book did leak out, by December 1916 Bobbs-Merrill agreed that the book would not be sold without Chaplin's approval. This never came, and therefore Chaplin's first "autobiography" never saw the light of day or significantly affected his star image.[2]

Before this controversy, however, Chaplin began at Mutual, and released his first comedy in the middle of May. By October 1917 his twelfth film, *The Adventurer*, was finished. The eighteen-month period was a remarkably prolific and creative one for Chaplin. He had both the time and the creative independence to make films as he wished, and it paid off. Some critics look back on this as Chaplin's most successful period—Theodore Huff calls 1916–1917 "Chaplin's most fertile years, his most sustained creative period"—and Chaplin himself remembered the Mutual years as "the happiest period of my career."[3]

Nevertheless, from the time he signed his huge Mutual contract, Chaplin generated some resentment, much of which revolved around questions of high salary and worth, in the popular press. Granted, the American success ethic presumes that the talented rise to the top and deserve the rewards they win, and the rise of movie stars to the top has been framed in terms of the traditional American success story from the beginning of the star system. But $670,000? Some were skeptical, much as today some question the salaries paid to top professional athletes.

This general resentment over huge salaries for movie stars was reflected in Alfred A. Cohn's article in *Photoplay*, which, though published the month after Chaplin signed his Mutual contract, seems to have been written before Chaplin signed with Mutual.[4] Titled "What They Really Get—NOW," the piece argued essentially that the star salaries were grossly inflated in an era of unemployment, concern about the instability threatened by the war in Europe, and other worrisome economic trends. Cohn mentions Chaplin specifically, and argues that the comedian's $175,000 earnings in 1916 were unreasonably high. If Cohn considered the Essanay salary exorbitant, what would he have thought about the Mutual agreement?

The attitude of another journalist (and probably of many of his readers) toward Chaplin's new salary appeared in the May 1916 issue of *Photoplay*. Titled "C. Chaplin: Millionaire-Elect," it compared statistics to inform readers about Chaplin's accumulating wealth. According to the essay, except for John Hayes Hammond, president of U.S. Steel, "Chaplin's salary is likely the biggest salary grabbed off by any public person outside of royalty."[5] Compared to the public sector, Chaplin's salary represented 17 percent of the total salaries paid to 96 senators and 435 representatives of the U.S. Congress, and 93 percent of the Senate's payroll alone. If the nine Supreme Court justices pooled their earnings, the combined total would amount to 19.5 percent of Chaplin's salary. The author's resentment is clear from the tone of the article; note the use of "grabbed off" instead of "earned" in the quotation above. But he also reflected a tension in American cultural values. If the talented rise to the top, and if, in a business like the movie industry, the star's films make a profit despite the huge salary paid out, isn't the star entitled to what he or she can earn in the marketplace? Such at least was the author's conclusion: though the size of the salary might seem "wildly extravagant," it did fall "into its proper relation in the scale of receipts and disbursements when the profits made out of Chaplin pictures [were] considered."

Chaplin seems about this time to have become more sensitive to the importance of good publicity. In July he told a reporter that "publicity is one of the most essential things in the career of a man, whatever his profession, whose popularity depends in no small way upon keeping himself before the public." It was the press, Chaplin continued, that sustained the "spark of interest" that the public has for the performer.[6] This concern about the importance of publicity helped keep Chaplin at the forefront of the public imagination after the signing of the Mutual contract, even though the faddishness, imitations, and commercialization of the Charlie persona waned compared to the heady days of mid-1915. As we shall see in subsequent chapters, Chaplin's attitude toward the press and his willingness to cultivate it varied considerably throughout his career. By 1953 he blamed much of his problematic situation on a hostile press and claimed it had always treated him badly. During the Mutual years, however, the facts suggest otherwise.

One of the most notable developments in Chaplin's star image in this period was the growing tendency in the press to treat Chaplin not just as a movie star and director but also as a serious artist, something highly unusual in the upstart, brash medium of motion pictures. The tendency, as we saw in Chapter 1, was established in the January 1916 article in *Motion Picture Magazine* by J. B. Hirsch, "The New Charlie Chaplin." But perhaps more important in helping Chaplin gain intellectual legitimacy was an article in the venerable *Harper's Weekly* by the prominent stage actress Minnie Maddern Fiske in May 1916.[7] Though Chaplin had begun to claim early on—partly to compensate for his lack of formal education—that he read the classics and was interested in the life of the mind, it was an important breakthrough for Chaplin's reputation to have an established artist praise him in a prominent national magazine, where serious critical attention was much more significant for his star image than yet another article in a movie fan magazine.

Fiske opened her brief essay by asserting that "a constantly increasing body of cultured, artistic people are beginning to regard . . . Charles Chaplin as an extraordinary artist, as well as a comic genius." The universal popularity of Chaplin's films, she said, required critics to account for the basis of his success. This could be located in "the old, familiar secret of inexhaustible imagination, governed by the unfailing precision of a perfect technique."

Significantly, Fiske challenged genteel critics (and many readers of *Harper's*, one suspects) over the issue of Chaplin's alleged "vulgarity." The point was moot, she argued. "Chaplin is vulgar," she admitted, but "there is vulgarity in the comedies of Aristophanes, and in those of Plautus and Terence and the Elizabethans, not excluding Shakespeare. Rabelais is vulgar, Fielding and Smollett and Swift are vulgar. . . . Vulgarity and distinguished art can exist together." And they did in Chaplin's work. Although Chaplin had to function within the trying context of an art still in its infancy, he had done well and would do better: "Those of us who believe that Charles Chaplin is essentially a great comic artist look forward to fine achievements. . . . [W]e are confident that he will attain the artistic stature to which it seems he is entitled." The praise was surely gratifying to Chaplin; he repaid it when, in his autobiography, he called the "ebullient, humorous and intelligent" Fiske one of the American actresses he most admired (MA, p. 261). Even more important for the growth of Chaplin's star image, the article informed the custodians of culture that Chaplin was a name worth taking into account in discussions of important American artists.

A similar defense of Chaplin appeared in another prestigious but more recently established journal of opinion, *New Republic*. When its first issue appeared in November 1914, it described itself as "A Journal of Opinion which seeks to meet the challenge of a new time." Politically liberal and culturally sympathetic to the attack on the Genteel Tradition in the arts, *New Republic* represented a younger and considerably different constituency than *Harper's*. Yet it, too, stamped its approval on Chaplin in Harvey O'Higgins's "Charlie Chaplin's Art," published in early 1917.[8] An American writing from Europe, O'Higgins noted that "Chaplin is as preeminent a favorite in Paris . . . as he is here." Chaplin's films, he argued, had "become more and more delicate and finished" than they had been in the early Keystone period. It is significant that he also defended Chaplin's art as a democratic art, much as cultural nationalists like Van Wyck Brooks, writing in the pages of the same magazine, were simultaneously calling for a revitalization of American literature and culture. To O'Higgins, Chaplin was "an example of how the best can be the most successful, of how a real talent can triumph over the most appalling limitations put upon its expression, and of how the popular eye can recognize such a talent without the aid of pundits of culture and even in spite of their anathemas" (all quotes p. 18). In writings like those of Fiske and O'Higgins, Chaplin began to establish a clientele among the American intelligentsia, a following that became more pronounced in the 1920s and that he sustained through much of his career.

The Further "Refining" of Charlie

When O'Higgins noted that Chaplin's films were becoming more "delicate and finished," he might also have added "more serious." During the Mutual period Chaplin continued to explore the more serious issues in his comedies that he had begun in such Essanay films as *The Bank* and *Police*, and in the unfinished *Life*. One Chaplin critic, Wes Gehring, has even argued that in the Mutual period one can discover "a consistent, viable political stance in Chaplin's work," which Gehring aligns with the American Progressive movement. To defend this thesis, he notes that in eleven of his twelve Mutual films Chaplin focused on five different issues important to the Progressives: "urban corruption; the plight of the urban poor; the idle rich . . . ; elitism; and alcohol." Although this argument is sometimes strained—as when a film like *One A.M.* is read as "a comic nightmare" and a "commentary on the misuse of alcohol"—it is clear that in his films Chaplin often represented class divisions or the squalid conditions of urban poverty that corresponded to the same reality in American society in his day. As Joris Ivens has observed, in some of Chaplin's films "the real feeling of human misery in filthy surroundings was completely communicated."[9]

Yet the Mutual films were by no means tracts. There is no consistent political thread weaving through their fabric, and though the Progressive issues Gehring mentions form a backdrop in the films, they are never the primary focus of narrative concern. The attempts of middle-class elites to instruct and control the behavior of the urban lower classes—efforts that are identified by American historians as a central strand of American Progressivism—are not central in the Chaplin Mutuals. Indeed, at times the middle-class reformers, like the preacher at the opening of *Easy Street*, are satirical targets rather than sympathetically treated figures.

I would argue that the Mutual films generally are unified by placing Charlie in a particular setting and creating comedy through his interactions with objects (like escalators or alarm clocks) and people (like those he waits on in *The Rink*) in the settings. Chaplin the director also continues in many of these films to develop romantic relationships between Charlie and Edna, though the endings do not always lead to Charlie's failure in love, as occurred in *The Bank*. To get a sense of Chaplin's achievements and handling of Charlie in this period, we can focus on three of the "serious" Mutual films: *The Vagabond*, *Easy Street*, and *The Immigrant*, the third, ninth, and eleventh of Chaplin's Mutuals. The three films have at least one thing in common: in each of the three Charlie and the characters played by Edna Purviance—a gypsy waif, a social worker, and a freshly arrived American immigrant—are united in the end.

In *The Vagabond*, Charlie plays an itinerant street musician who falls in love with the Edna character, who has been captured by a brutal gypsy (Eric Campbell). Though Charlie and Edna manage to escape midway through the film, the plot is complicated when a painter seeking inspiration "discovers" Edna as she walks through the woods and asks to paint her portrait. He does, and she begins to be attracted to the talented artist. Returning to the wagon, where Charlie has been fixing a meal, Edna showers all her attentions on the artist, a scene even more somber because of the elaborate and careful preparations Charlie has made as his way of showing his affection to Edna. The pangs of unrequited love are captured most effectively in a medium two-shot of Edna and Charlie that lasts about fourteen seconds—an unusually long take in the early Chaplin films. In it, as Edna on the right of the frame looks longingly after the departing artist, Charlie glances slowly back and forth between the artist and Edna's reaction. After the artist leaves to arrange for his portrait of Edna to be exhibited, Charlie pathetically and ineffectually tries to compete with his rival by sketching his own picture of her. The film moves toward its resolution by drawing on a plot device from nineteenth-century novels: Edna turns out to be the stolen child of a wealthy woman, who comes in a limousine to claim Edna after discovering her identity when the painting is displayed. Learning of the situation, Charlie politely gives a genteel handshake to Edna's mother, tenderly embraces Edna, and magnanimously shakes hands with the artist. The film appears to be heading toward an ending similar to *The Tramp* and *The Bank*: the car drives off, leaving Charlie alone. Facing the camera, he somberly leans against the wagon, then tries to move forward with his sprightly resilient walk. But he fails. Turning away, he drags himself back to the wagon and leans with his forehead on his forearm in the most moving shot of the film.

Where could Chaplin go from here? If Charlie's sheer will to overcome disappointment failed to work as it had worked in earlier films, how could the story end? Walter Kerr tells us that a sequence was originally planned in which Charlie committed suicide by jumping in a pond, but Chaplin realized that such a scene would never do.[10] Instead, Edna has a change of heart and orders the chauffeur to turn around. As Charlie sits on the wagon steps, head in hands, the car returns, Edna hustles Charlie into it, and everyone leaves together. Chaplin tempers the film's strong sense of isolation and the pain of rejection through the conventional, classical Hollywood closed ending.

The importance of the quest for romantic love in Chaplin's films from the Mutual period on cannot be minimized if we are to understand their immense and lasting popularity. Had Chaplin stayed within the framework of Keystone slapstick, he would never have survived in Hollywood as long as he did: either audiences would have tired of the persona or Chaplin would have exhausted the creative pantomimic spark he had honed in the British musical halls, or both. But by adding to comedy the element of romantic love, whether requited or not, Chaplin tapped deeply into one source of what has made narrative art popular for centuries.

Though feminist critics have persuasively argued that this myth of romantic love can be a powerful cultural tool to justify, manage, and perpetuate a patriarchal society, in Chaplin's films, romance functions somewhat differently. In general, Charlie's social class and physical strength are inferior to his male rivals. Neither a Heathcliff nor a Rhett Butler, Charlie never sweeps a woman off her feet with his appearance; he's tender and vulnerable. The relationship between Charlie and his heroine is therefore always tentative, not based on qualities traditionally associated with masculinity: strength, physical attractiveness, and wealth. If women are commonly dominated by men in the myth of romance, Charlie himself is also threatened by those same men, and moviegoers who have experienced some form of domination in their lives (this includes nearly all moviegoers), find the conflicts of romance depicted in Chaplin's films very real indeed. The question of how romance functions in the Chaplin films will recur, but suffice it to say here that by the time Chaplin made *The Vagabond*, he was already working creatively within the tradition of romance and adapting it to his own aesthetic uses.[11]

The importance of romance in Chaplin's Mutual films can also be seen by looking briefly at *Easy Street* and *The Immigrant*. These two films also demonstrate that it is nearly impossible to find a consistent political and social perspective in the Chaplin Mutual films. In *Easy Street* Charlie falls in love with a social reformer working at an urban mission; to win her approval he becomes a policeman and helps rid a decrepit neighborhood of a domineering bully. After saving the reformer from a drug fiend, Charlie ends up winning her affections and establishing himself as a respected and somewhat genteel authority figure in the community—the neighborhood cop. In contrast to the position of authority he earned in *Easy Street*, Charlie, like Edna, is a jobless newcomer arriving in America in *The Immigrant*. This film includes a scene in a restaurant that is extremely funny, partly because neither Charlie nor Edna has the money to pay for the food they have ordered. Only an artist, who admires Edna's beauty and offers her money to pose, saves them from a dire fate. At the end of this film, Charlie is pulling Edna into the office of a justice of the peace to get married, despite their tenuous financial condition. Though the couple achieved a kind of respectable gentility at the end of *Easy Street* and still remains in urban poverty at the close of *The Immigrant*, the romance between Charlie and Edna is a constant in the two films, as are a somber social background and Charlie's skill at generating humor through his interactions with objects and people. The Mutual period is clearly a maturing and creative one for Chaplin.

That maturation process reached its first flowering in *A Dog's Life*, Chaplin's first film for First National Exhibitors Circuit, the company he signed with after completing his Mutual contract. Chaplin had agreed upon terms with First National on 17 June 1917, amid another splash of publicity. Even though Mutual had offered Chaplin a million dollars to make twelve more comedies, Chaplin resisted, commissioning his brother Sydney to enter into negotiations with the newly formed First National, headed by J. D. Williams. First National was composed of a group of prominent theater owners in larger cities who wanted to combat the growing influence of producer Adolph Zukor. They planned to do so by signing up popular stars who would make films that First National could distribute. They offered Chaplin a million dollars, plus a bonus of $75,000 upon signing, to make eight comedies, with Chaplin himself bearing the production costs. First National would pay Chaplin $125,000 as he began each comedy; if the comedy ended up longer than two reels, Chaplin would receive $15,000 for each additional reel after the film was completed. Though the contract was not as lucrative as his Mutual contract, it offered

Chaplin more creative control over the films he made and more time to make them than he had experienced at Mutual.

The whole signing was pervaded by a businesslike aura. General Manager Williams of First National told reporters about his company's expectations: "The whole idea of the contract is to do away with quantity and substitute quality. Chaplin has pledged himself to establish a reputation for perfect pictures. He fully realizes that the production of unsatisfactory comedies at this time would cost him anywhere from a quarter million to a half million dollars on his next contract."[12] But, the press reported, Chaplin had no intention of making films that lost money. As he told an interviewer a few months earlier, making movies was a tremendous responsibility: "I get depressed thinking of it. You see, it's like this. I should hate to think that my pictures weren't making money for the firm releasing them. My pride couldn't stand that."[13]

Surely Chaplin held up his end of the bargain with *A Dog's Life*. Released in April 1918, it was a three-reel film, about 50 percent longer than any of his Mutuals, and though it might be fair to call it his most ambitious offering to that time, it continued developing some of the characteristics of the "serious" Mutuals discussed above. Like a number of the Mutuals, its background was one of urban poverty. It, too, presented a romance between Charlie and Edna. But it also was more self-conscious, with a more sophisticated thematic and structural unity. In his autobiography Chaplin recalled that with *A Dog's Life* he "was beginning to think of comedy in a structural sense" and that the central motif that unified his structure was "paralleling the life of a dog with that of a tramp" (MA, p. 209). Indeed, the title is perfectly appropriate, for it plays on the clichéd metaphor—"it's a dog's life"—which suggests how difficult human existence is. The film makes the metaphor concrete by showing the travails of Charlie and a dog named Scraps.[14]

From the film's opening Chaplin uses visual and narrative parallels to connect Charlie and Scraps. When we first see Charlie, he is lying asleep outdoors against a fence, his prone body near the bottom of the frame, head facing left. The first shot of Scraps is graphically almost identical: he, too, is asleep outdoors, curled in a pail at the lower part of the frame, his head also facing left. At the beginning of the film Charlie is disturbed by a policeman who chases him away; the same policeman frightens Scraps a few moments later. After Charlie awakens, he wanders into an employment agency and is taken advantage of by other job seekers; when Scraps starts his day, a pack of dogs attacks him. Following these parallels, Charlie and Scraps meet as

Charlie saves Scraps from the pack, a gesture Scraps returns later in the film by digging up a wallet filled with money for Charlie.

If Charlie and Scraps are living a dog's life, so is Edna. Consistent with the film's focus, Edna finds herself thrust into a system of exploitation—the sexual exploitation of a dance hall. Edna first appears singing a slow and melancholy song that contrasts starkly to the frenetic dances of the other performers. After the song, the hall owner orders her to flirt with the male customers and do whatever is necessary to make him some money. When she refuses, she's fired—out on the streets like Charlie. Fortunately, Charlie has been enriched by Scraps's discovery of the wallet just before Edna is let go, and he befriends her with the same tenderness and gentle affection that he had shown in some of his earlier films and that he would show again in most of the later Charlie features. And as with *The Vagabond*, *The Immigrant*, and *Easy Street*, Charlie and Edna are united at the end. The plot device of the discovered money enables Charlie, Edna, and Scraps to settle down on a little farm, their escape from the dog's life of urban poverty.

An important Chaplin film, *A Dog's Life* reiterated several tendencies evident in the Mutual films, particularly the romance between Charlie and Edna, and the "serious" theme underlying the comedy. It solidified the persona of the increasingly complex Charlie. It reinforced the tendency of the press to present Chaplin as a serious artist. And it pointed forward to later Chaplin films in two particularly significant ways. The relationship between Charlie and Scraps looks almost like a trial run of the one between Charlie and the kid in *The Kid* (1920). And the ending of the film, in which a brightly lit rural setting provides an oasis in the desert of urban difficulties, anticipates a number of films in which a pastoral setting or a "folk" world offers some characters a vision of hope and serenity in contrast to the harsh urban world. This pastoral world is especially noticeable at the ending of *A Woman of Paris*, in the Austerlich countryside in *The Great Dictator*, and in Henri Verdoux's country home in *Monsieur Verdoux*, but one can also detect it in a different form in the blind girl's apartment in *City Lights* and in the daydream shared by Charlie and the gamin in *Modern Times*. This tendency to juxtapose two sets of values in the films would by the 1940s profoundly affect Chaplin's star image, because the contrasts began to imply distinct social and political commitments. For the time being, however, the creative freedom offered by the First National contract enabled Chaplin to move toward greater flexibility and complexity in his films. With *A Dog's Life* he moved forward confidently in developing his art and created films that ensured the continuity and growth of his star image.

Chaplin the "Slacker"?

Despite these shifts in his films, however, Chaplin's reputation continued to face challenges. Though he seemed to be overcoming charges of vulgarity and greediness as he made his First National films, another began to rear its head: the question of Chaplin's military status during World War I. When the war broke out in Europe in August 1914, Chaplin was midway through his first year at Keystone, and the conflict seemed distant to him, as it did to most Americans. He was not yet particularly well known, and American neutrality was strongly established. Few Americans were concerned about the relationship between a British movie actor and his country far across the ocean.

But that situation changed as Chaplin's fame grew, as the United States moved away from neutrality, and as the movie industry's role in the war effort entered public debate. In tracing how and when the country moved from neutrality to involvement, one might note that after the war broke out in Europe, the United States imported a number of German films, like *Behind German Lines* and *The German Side of the War*, presenting the German perspective on the war; such films were shown in American theaters as late as 1916. Beginning with the sinking of the British liner *Lusitania* in May 1915, however, tolerance for such German films—indeed for Germany itself—diminished. Despite official government disapproval, films urging preparedness or even celebrating the British war effort began to appear. For example, *The Battle Cry of Peace* (1915), director J. Stuart Blackton later recalled, "was propaganda for the United States to enter the war. . . . It was against the administration because at that time Mr. Wilson was arguing for neutrality and peace." The shift from a neutralist or pacifist attitude to a pro-involvement view developed inexorably in America between 1915 and April 1917, when the United States entered the war. By that time, in the words of one film historian, the transition "to out-and-out pro-war passion was already complete."[15]

After America joined the Allies, government legislation helped suppress pacifism and encourage pro-war sentiment. The Espionage Act of 15 June 1917 set maximum fines of $10,000 and twenty years' imprisonment for anyone who interfered with the draft or encouraged disloyalty. The Espionage Act of May 1918 extended these penalties to cover a wide variety of activities, including obstructing the sale of

U.S. bonds or speaking critically about the government, Constitution, or flag of the United States.

Simultaneously, the government sought to build morale through the Committee on Public Information, headed by George Creel. Established by an act of Congress in May 1917, it sought through various means, including movies, to influence public opinion in favor of the American war effort, both at home and abroad.[16]

Within this context, it is not surprising that Chaplin's attitude toward the war and his military status became an issue. As a prominent movie star from 1915 on and as a young British male eligible for the draft, Chaplin inevitably drew the attention of some citizens. As early as his Keystone days, Chaplin began to be criticized in England for not being in uniform and fighting for his country. In addition to receiving threatening letters, some enclosing white feathers (a symbol of "slackers" during World War I), Chaplin was also the target of occasional public attacks. In an effort to defuse the antagonism he had aroused, Chaplin contributed money to the British cause.

When it became known that his 1916 Mutual contract contained a clause that forbade him from leaving the United States without company permission, however, Chaplin received another barrage of criticism from the British press.[17] One newspaper account reported in June 1916 that signs were beginning to appear at some British movie theaters reading, "No Chaplin Here," protesting Chaplin's lack of involvement in the British war effort.[18]

After America entered the war, publicity about and criticism of Chaplin's nonparticipation became more widespread in the United States. Theodore Huff writes that Chaplin received thousands of letters at his studio, many of them abusive, demanding that he enlist. *Variety* reported two months after the U.S. entry that not only was Chaplin being called a "slacker" by his fellow citizens but he was also being observed by U.S. government officials who had been told that Chaplin had refused a British War Office demand that he return to England. The article reported that the Secret Service was keeping Chaplin under surveillance because he had reportedly told someone about plans to move to South America, bringing along his assets in gold.[19]

Such public charges, regardless of their veracity, were clearly a threat to Chaplin's star image. Partly to stem the tide, Chaplin's studio released a press announcement saying that Chaplin had registered for the selective service draft in Los Angeles on June 5. According to stories, he actually visited the recruiting station but was rejected for being underweight.[20]

Not everyone attacked Chaplin for failing to enlist. In fact, some quoted in the press felt that Chaplin would be much more useful to the war effort making movies. In July 1917 the *New York Telegraph* reported on an article in a British magazine that demanded Chaplin join up, thus demonstrating his pride in his British origins. The reporter for the *Telegraph* objected: Wasn't Chaplin able to communicate to many more people by making movies or even by making public appearances in support of the British cause than by fighting in the trenches?[21] Many soldiers agreed with him. A wounded British officer told an American audience in 1918 that Chaplin "made us laugh when it often seemed that nothing else could. And I for one hope that the authorities will realize he is of far greater value as a gloom chaser than as a fighter." After hearing such testimony from many sources, Chaplin used the same argument when he wrote to a British correspondent early in 1918: "I only wish that I could join the English army and fight for my mother country. But I have received so many letters from soldiers at the front, as well as civilians, asking me to continue making pictures that I have come to the conclusion that my work lies here in Los Angeles. At the same time, if any country thinks it needs me in the trenches more than soldiers need my pictures, I am ready to go."[22]

Chaplin was never drafted, but his letter makes clear that he took seriously the questions about his involvement. Just as he and the press had earlier "cleaned up" his image when confronted by genteel critics, here he used the press to help manage the war controversy.

If the press helped Chaplin avoid the image of slacker, it also helped him establish the image of patriot. In early 1918 the U.S. government announced the third Liberty Loan Drive for April and May, aimed at raising $3 billion to support the war effort. Chaplin was invited to join a large group of speakers, including several movie stars, who would encourage groups gathered in large cities to purchase bonds. He agreed and made a number of appearances in the Northeast and the South in April.

As might be expected, his appearances drew huge crowds and raised large amounts of money; his participation also solidified and even enhanced his star image. He began in Washington, D.C., to help open the drive. On the first anniversary of America's entry into the war, April 6, he appeared with Douglas Fairbanks, Mary Pickford, and Marie Dressler, parading down Pennsylvania Avenue before huge crowds, after which each star was assigned to a large booth on the White House ellipse to take Liberty Loan subscriptions. The newspapers said the next day that Chaplin and Fairbanks had to run through the crowds to get to their booths after the parade. Mary Pickford was delayed 45 minutes trying to get to hers. Over $3 million in Liberty bonds were reported sold.[23]

From Washington Chaplin moved to New York, perhaps his most spectacular appearance on the tour. The New York rally took place at noon on April 8, on the steps of the U.S. Sub-Treasury Building, at the corner of Broad and Wall streets, in the center of the financial district. At least 20,000 people gathered to see Chaplin and Fairbanks. One newspaper reported Chaplin's brief speech. "Now listen, I have never made a speech before in my life," Chaplin began to a cheering and laughing crowd,

> but I believe I can make one now. You people out there—I want you to forget all about percentages in this third Liberty Loan. Human life is at stake and no one ought to worry about what rate of interest the bonds are going to bring or what he can make by purchasing them. Money is needed—money to support the great army and navy of Uncle Sam. This very minute the Germans occupy a position of advantage, and we have to get the dollars. It ought to go over so that we can drive that old devil, the Kaiser, out of France.

Fairbanks followed with a brief speech, and the celebration concluded with Fairbanks lifting Chaplin aloft, who in turn raised a derby into the air (see Figure 7). The audience loved it.[24]

After New York Chaplin took a southern swing while Fairbanks and Pickford took a northern route. On the tour Chaplin spoke to large crowds in Richmond, Virginia; Lexington, Kentucky; Macon and Atlanta, Georgia; Nashville and Memphis, Tennessee; and finally New Orleans. The pattern was nearly the same everywhere: Chaplin would be met by large crowds at the train station. He would appear at large auditoriums (Atlanta and Nashville) or even outdoors in parks (Memphis and New Orleans) to give brief impassioned speeches about buying bonds to support the war. Finally, to help entertain the audiences and hasten the pace of selling, he would perform some "Charlie antics."

According to the prominently placed newspaper accounts, Chaplin was a hit with the crowds and successful as a bond seller. An Atlanta reporter judged Chaplin's April 17 speech as "excellent and effective," then described the pandemonium that broke loose when Chaplin did his Charlie walk.[25] In Nashville Chaplin filled Ryman Auditorium on April 18; thousands had to be turned away. After appearing at Overton Park in Memphis on a cold, damp day, Chaplin was ordered to bed by a doctor.[26] He soon went on to New Orleans where, Huff records, a former government official demanded to be listed above the "vulgar" movie comedian on posters. He was, and drew an audience of 400; Chaplin drew 40,000.[27] By April 30 Chaplin was back in New York, leading a rally at City Hall Park that raised well over $100,000, and then concluded his efforts with a brief address at the Astor Hotel on May 1. By May 3 he was on his way back to California after the long and exhausting tour.[28]

Besides supporting the war effort through the Liberty Loan tour, Chaplin also bought $350,000 worth of Liberty bonds during the first three drives and made two films about the war.[29] The first, titled *The Bond* and sponsored by the Liberty Loan Committee, is a brief film encouraging people to buy bonds. It is an allegory showing how the bonds of marriage, love, and friendship are capable of creating a powerful mallet strong enough to knock out the Kaiser. The Liberty Loan Committee distributed it without charge throughout the country.

More substantial was *Shoulder Arms*, Chaplin's second film for First National and one of the most remembered American entertainment films dealing with World War I. The film opens in boot camp, where Charlie, in uniform, tries to adapt himself to military discipline and training, not always successfully. Charlie moves to the trenches, then volunteers for a special mission that enables him to meet Edna, playing a French peasant girl who embodies the fate of "poor France." Together they concoct a scheme and capture a large group of German soldiers—or so it seems. Chaplin ends the film as he ended *The Bank*: Charlie wakes from his dreams of accomplishment. All the action and comedy had taken place in his mind as he slept after an exhausting day in boot camp.

In some ways *Shoulder Arms* was a departure for Chaplin. It was the longest movie he had directed up to that time, and it contained more action, particularly in the final reel, than was common for a Chaplin film. In addition, the film is interesting for the way it places Charlie in a typical war situation. Unlike many of the Hollywood films of the day, it did not portray the Germans as "vicious Huns" or go out of its way to stir up hatred. The German soldiers are for the most part non-entities, though one leader is a comic butt because of his tiny stature and authoritarian treatment of his troops, and another lustful leader threatens Edna. Chaplin's aim was rather to use comedy and a gentle tenderness to appeal to his audience. Incidents in the boot camp, as when Charlie tries to march and handle a rifle, and in the trenches, as when he launches a Limburger cheese grenade or floats in the flooded dugout bedroom, provide good examples of Chaplin's comic imagination at work. The most poignant scene comes when Charlie, after

7. Chaplin and Fairbanks on Wall Street during
Liberty Loan Drive, April 1918.

receiving no mail during mail call, looks over the shoulder of another
soldier reading his mail. Though we don't see the contents of the letter, we know what they are by watching the shifting emotions at play
on Charlie's face as he reads along. This is a shot that surely touched
soldiers abroad and their loved ones at home as they sought a few
moments of respite from the strain of the war.

It is unlikely, however, that the film had much direct effect on soldier morale, because it was not completed until late October 1918,
only a couple of weeks before the Armistice was signed. Nevertheless,
Chaplin's contribution to the war effort was significant: not only did
he lend his celebrity status and his energies toward raising large
amounts of money (and indeed contributing sizable sums of his own),
but he also through this and earlier films provided pleasure and re-
minders of home for soldiers abroad who saw them. Blackton, writing
for *Photoplay* in June 1918, described Chaplin's effect on the soldiers.

"It was my impression," Blackton wrote concerning a visit to the trenches, "that the buoyancy of the American soldier even during the dark days of the war was in large part due to the diverting influence of the motion picture." The most important and popular of the diversions, he added, were the films of Charlie Chaplin.[30] Many would doubtless have agreed with critic Julian Johnson's assessment that "in a shrapnel-smashed world, Mr. Chaplin is today the greatest single lightener of the iron burden" wrought by the war.[31]

In response to the significant social challenge to his popularity posed by the issue of his war involvement, Chaplin supported the dominant attitudes in American society of his day, thus sustaining and even enhancing his star image. Though in his autobiography he remembers the war as a time of "barbarism" in which a "religion of war" brought on "an avalanche of mad destruction and brutal slaughter," his behavior in 1918 was suitable, even exemplary, to the vast majority of Americans who supported the war effort (MA, pp. 213, 218). The ultimate short-term result added the characteristic of patriotism to the Chaplin star image. In later years, when his conflicts with certain pockets of the American public and press led him to be branded as a dangerous threat to the country, few remembered these days of Chaplin's contributions to the U.S. war effort. For the time being, however, the image of Chaplin as slacker had been turned aside.

The First Marriage and Divorce

The huge crowds Chaplin drew during the Liberty Loan tour reaffirmed his status as a leading movie star. That stardom, as the fan magazines were fond of pointing out, made the young, handsome Chaplin one of the country's most eligible bachelors. Up to this point, Chaplin's relationships with women had not played a large part in the public perception of his star image. Between 1918 and 1920, however, that changed. In relatively rapid succession the twenty-nine-year-old Chaplin met a seventeen-year-old movie actress, married her after learning of her pregnancy, and divorced her. The first of Chaplin's four marriages and three divorces, this experience caused Chaplin personal pain and created another distressing public conflict for him, making 1919 and 1920 two of the most trying years—both privately and professionally—in his young life.

Because Chaplin's relationships with women increasingly came to affect his star image, it will be useful to say a few words about the basis of his attitudes toward women. Chaplin's attraction to particularly young women and his unstable relationships with the first two women

41

he married seems rooted in his earlier personal experience. Without being unduly psychological, one might note that Chaplin's parents separated when he was very young, partly due to his father's alcoholism. Chaplin and his half brother Sydney remained with their mother for a time but were forced into the Lambeth workhouse in 1896 when their mother became unable to support them. David Auerbach has reasonably suggested that the vulnerable seven-year-old Chaplin felt betrayed by his mother, deprived of her love and support when he needed it most. At the same time he came to feel some guilt about being unable to help her then or in the subsequent decade, when she was in and out of sanitariums. Auerbach hypothesizes that this ambivalence led to Chaplin's tendency to view women in two opposite ways: as ideal, romantic young beauties or as threatening viragos.[32] In his relationships with women, he was irresistibly drawn to those who fit his conception of the former.

This attraction was solidified in his mind through his relationship with Hetty Kelly, which he dwells on at some length in his autobiography. Chaplin was nineteen and a relatively successful music-hall comedian in England when he met Kelly, a fifteen-year-old dancer in a troupe appearing on the same bill as Chaplin. Captivated by her youthful beauty, Chaplin first arranged to meet her on a Sunday afternoon. Both shy, they went for strolls several times, but when Chaplin impulsively mentioned marriage, Kelly drew back and they stopped seeing one another. Chaplin later wrote that "the episode was but a childish infatuation to her, but to me it was the beginning of a spiritual development, a reaching out for beauty." In another context, he added: "Although I had met her but five times . . . that brief encounter affected me for a long time."[33]

Chaplin seems never to have gotten over Kelly. When he was in New York for the signing of his Mutual contract, after experiencing for the first time the attentions of rabid movie fans on his train trip from California, he learned that Kelly was in New York visiting a friend (in the intervening years she had married a wealthy American). Feeling a paradoxical loneliness amid all the attention, Chaplin stole away from his hotel and walked to the building where she was staying, too shy to call but hoping he would meet her going into or coming out of the building. He didn't.

Later, on his trip to London in 1921, he hoped he would be able to see her but was shocked to learn that she had died. The one meeting he had really desired on the trip was denied him.[34] This experience of unrequited love seems to have shaped an image of the ideal woman—young, beautiful, almost ethereal—in Chaplin's mind, which drew him to women whose appearance matched it yet made it impossible for any woman to live up to his demands and expectations.

Such, at least, was the pattern played out in Chaplin's relationship with young Mildred Harris, a movie actress whom Chaplin had first met at a party given by Samuel Goldwyn in mid-1918. Harris was only seventeen at the time, already an experienced movie actress, having appeared in films since 1914. As Chaplin tells it, she pursued him, asking for a ride home as he prepared to leave the party. They began to see one another—"dinners, dances, moonlit nights and ocean drives"—and in October Harris told Chaplin she believed she was pregnant. On the 23rd of that month they were married in a quiet ceremony in Los Angeles.[35]

The marriage was probably doomed from the start. Chaplin remembers feeling ambivalent about the entire situation. On the one hand he felt that the "union had no vital basis"; on the other, "now that I was married I wanted to be and wanted the marriage to be a success." But for a number of reasons the relationship never had a chance. Chaplin became upset about a contract Harris signed with Louis B. Mayer, and the couple argued about her career. (Though Chaplin claimed that she didn't obtain favorable terms in the contract, he may also have felt threatened by a working spouse.) And Chaplin, perceiving himself as something of an intellectual, felt that she was too simple for him. Perhaps most damaging to the relationship was the death of their child in July 1919; it lived only three days. In Chaplin's words, this loss "began the withering of our marriage" (MA, pp. 237–39). By the fall of 1919 the couple had separated, Chaplin moving back into the Los Angeles Athletic Club.

Despite the separation the Chaplins—Mildred at least—tried to keep up appearances. In January 1920 she told a newspaper reporter that "I intend to have a happy home and realize that the trouble with most love affairs after marriage is that the romance dies out and is supplanted by commonplace things. I am determined that this should never be."[36] But her hopes were in vain. In April the newspapers reported a fight between Chaplin and Mayer in a Los Angeles restaurant. Apparently Chaplin had taken offense when Mayer suggested that Chaplin's settlement offer to his wife was embarrassingly small. On August 3 the *New York Times* reported that Harris's lawyers had filed divorce papers for her on the basis of cruelty. The next day they printed a clarification. Harris, who was then visiting New York, had expressed surprise when she learned the papers had been filed. She also told reporters that the charges would be "mental cruelty" and denied any reports that Chaplin had been physically violent with her.[37]

The divorce was finally granted in November 1920, with Harris winning a settlement of $100,000 and some community property.

How did the press respond? Since the marriage and divorce of one of Hollywood's biggest stars would seem to be a "perfect" story, one would expect it to be plastered on the front pages of newspapers across the country. But such was not the case. The press seemed unusually restrained and discreet in its reporting of the first Chaplin divorce. The *New York Times* carried one story in March on the Chaplins' domestic troubles (on page 10), two stories in August—the first on the filing of the divorce, the second something of a retraction (both on page 14)—and failed even to report the divorce settlement, even though Chaplin was in New York City when the divorce was granted.

The *Times* was also sympathetic to Chaplin when it editorialized on August 11 concerning the filing of the divorce. The editorial quoted Harris's allegation that Chaplin ignored her by taking long, contemplative walks, even in the rain. According to Harris, "the harder it rained, the longer he walked and harder he thought." The editorialist treated the charge as absurd and, though finding such a tendency rare in Hollywood, defended Chaplin's right to think. "If thought on the part of a movie artist has such devastating consequences," the editorial concluded rhetorically, "what would happen if movie audiences started to think?"[38]

For the most part this gentle treatment was typical of how the press handled the situation. As personally painful as the whole relationship was for Chaplin and Harris, they were not, except for the ridicule Harris suffered in the *Times* editorial, as victimized by the press as Chaplin would be in 1927 and 1928 during his second divorce and even more so during the Joan Barry affair in the 1940s.

Why was this? One important reason relates to the state of Chaplin's star image, which in 1918 and 1919 contained fewer negative connotations and contradictions than it would later. American culture associated Chaplin first with the irreverent, funny, sympathetic, and increasingly romantic Charlie. They next pictured Chaplin himself as an aspiring, talented, and still relatively humble filmmaker. A crucial third reason is that Chaplin, after the Liberty Loan tour, was associated with patriotism and with supporting dominant opinions. With such positive qualities linked to the star image, a divorce seemed like an unfortunate anomaly. Though the breakup would later be considered a more serious and negative element of Chaplin's star image, the press and the public in 1919 thought it forgivable. For the most part an aura of magic still surrounded Chaplin's star image.

Troubles at First National

But what happened to Chaplin's film career between the time he met Harris and the time he divorced her? What kind of films did he make? If the press was relatively quiet about his divorce, what did they write about him generally? The two "Harris years" were for Chaplin artistically distracted, if not arid, years. Though the press continued to portray Chaplin the man as an intriguing and serious artist, significant numbers of film reviewers and commentators were displeased with the two films he made during this period, and there was even speculation that Chaplin's greatness might be on the wane.

The two films were *Sunnyside* and *A Day's Pleasure* (released in June and November 1919), which Chaplin worked on from about the time he married Harris until the time they separated. In addition to the pressures of the relationship, several other factors made it difficult for Chaplin to concentrate on his work. First, Chaplin had to worry about expenses for his new film studio, begun in November 1917 and completed three months later. Building his own studio was one of Chaplin's shrewdest acts of foresight, enabling him to control his productions and own the rights to his films, an independence almost unheard of in Hollywood, before or after. Nonetheless, it cost him a lot of money and considerable anxiety.

Second, Chaplin was beginning to be restive, chafing at the bonds imposed by the First National contract. He had hoped to honor his eight-picture contract in no more than eighteen months, but by the time that period had elapsed, he had completed only two films. The agreement seemed even more constricting because in early 1919 Chaplin entered into negotiations with D. W. Griffith, Douglas Fairbanks, Mary Pickford, and William S. Hart (who later withdrew) to form a company, United Artists, that would distribute films they each independently produced. As will be discussed in more detail in Chapter 3, since film companies like Adolph Zukor's Paramount were beginning to integrate film production, distribution, and exhibition in single organizations, Chaplin and the other prominent film figures feared that competition for their talents, and thus the amount of money they could command for their services, could drop precipitously. In April the United Artists' contracts of incorporation were signed, an event that for Chaplin made finishing his six remaining First National films seem even more onerous. When First National executives refused to renegotiate his contract (both *A Dog's Life* and *Shoulder Arms* had done very well at the box office, and Chaplin hoped for more favorable terms), the ruthless attitude of the executives,

Chaplin wrote, "embittered me" and "impeded the progress of my work" (MA, p. 224). All these concerns made it hard for Chaplin to work fruitfully on his films.

The pressures show in the films. *Sunnyside* displeased critics when it was released and generally continued to do so long after. The film is poorly structured by the standards of the classical Hollywood cinema that were then solidifying. In the middle of a film about Charlie's difficulties as a hotel employee, for example, Charlie gets bumped on the head and has a dream about dancing through a sylvan forest with some wood nymphs. With no apparent connection to the narrative, the scene seems nothing more than an homage by Chaplin to Nijinsky, whom Chaplin had met some time earlier.

Despite this structural weakness, *Sunnyside* is at times interesting thematically.[39] A central element of the film is its criticism of small-town hypocrisy. The opening shot irises out to a long shot of the church in the village of Sunnyside early on a Sunday morning, then irises in and back out to a sign, "Love Thy Neighbor," hanging over the bed of the hotel owner, Charlie's boss. Except for time spent piously reading his Bible, this ostensibly religious man spends the entire film unceremoniously kicking Charlie in the hindside. He never exhibits the behavior urged by the sign over his bed. It is significant that Chaplin's attack came out the same year as Sherwood Anderson's *Winesburg, Ohio*, and the year before Sinclair Lewis's *Main Street*, both assaults on what the authors saw as twisted and hypocritical lives lived in small-town America. Chaplin's social criticism in this early 1919 film was at times uncharacteristically harsh, given his previous films.

Also interesting is *Sunnyside*'s half-hearted romance. Ever since Edna Purviance had joined Chaplin early in his Essanay period, some element of romance had become commonplace in his films. But the romance in *Sunnyside* is handled so cynically that a viewer is tempted to read it autobiographically.[40] Chaplin's quest for love in earlier films like *The Bank* or *The Vagabond* seems to have worn thin after his relationship with Harris had ended in marriage: when he introduces Edna as the somewhat foolish farmer's daughter in *Sunnyside*, he does so with the perfunctory title, "And Now, the Romance." Though he does attempt to achieve some pathos later in the film, when Charlie unsuccessfully tries to imitate the dress and manners of the city slicker who dominates Edna's attentions—reminiscent of the way he tried to sketch Edna after the artist painted her in *The Vagabond*—the romance is hard-edged, tinged with a bitter cynicism uncommon in Chaplin's previous films. To critics and audiences used to his earlier work, *Sunnyside* was an unwelcome departure.

A Day's Pleasure was also received harshly. Like *Sunnyside*, it has no real romance. Instead, Charlie plays a married man taking his wife and two boys—both of whom wear Chaplinesque derbies—for a day of what they hope will be pleasure. Their hopes are in vain, of course. The film consists of three sequences: starting the car, riding on a boat, and driving home. Chaplin seems to have begun by trying to create a comedy that would draw sustenance from the increasing popularity of automobile driving in America ("Everybody's doing it," one title says). But inspiration and vitality are absent. Except for a few amusing moments, as when Charlie tries to set up a deck chair or when he escapes from a puddle of tar by stepping out of his shoes and into a policeman's fallen hat, the film is flat and even, at times, mean spirited. Charlie uses a plump woman for a gangplank when he scurries on the boat, and tries to fish her out of the water with a sharply hooked pole. In one of the few instances of racial stereotyping in his films, Chaplin has the black trombonist in the boat's band roll his eyes in the worst minstrel tradition, then puts him in whiteface to suggest the musician's nausea. In a fight with another seasick man on the boat, Charlie is as cruel as he was in his Keystone era, ending his fight with several strategically aimed punches to the man's groin.

The typical critical response to these two films was summed up by one film magazine when it wrote that "*Sunnyside* was anything but sunny. *A Day's Pleasure* was certainly not a pleasure." *Variety*, long a relatively reliable litmus test for the popularity of films and filmmakers, was also hard on both the films. *Sunnyside* suggested that the Chaplin comic well "was running dry," for at no time was it "up to the Chaplin standard." Nor did *A Day's Pleasure* "measure up to the standard of his old offerings." Instead, it was "just a series of episodes, padded to the extreme."[41] In two years Chaplin, working at a much slower pace than he (and his fans) had grown used to, had completed only two short and relatively unsuccessful films while competitors like Buster Keaton and Harold Lloyd were appearing frequently in comic shorts. A star needs to stay in the public eye if he is to maintain his position of stardom, and Chaplin had not consistently done so through new films during these years.

Nevertheless, though his reviews were bad, not all of his press between 1918 and the start of 1920 was so harsh. In fact, Chaplin's star image stayed as high as it did during that time more because of promotion and publicity about Chaplin himself than because of his films. The two most important essays praising Chaplin appeared in *Ladies' Home Journal*, in August 1918, and the following month in *Photoplay*.

The first article, "Mr. Charles Spencer Chaplin: The Man You Don't

Know," was written by Rob Wagner, a former teacher and artist who became Chaplin's publicity man during World War I. Clearly intent on promoting Chaplin, the piece turns the comedian into something of a saint. The "real Chaplin" loves and is loved by children, according to Wagner, and is a versatile creative genius at filmmaking, the maker of "essentially one-man pictures." He is an aesthete who responds deeply to music. He is intellectual, an "omniverous reader" whose "tastes run to philosophy and the modern English realists." He works tremendously hard when engaged on a film, "yet for the fame that comes with them he cares very little." To top it all off, despite the fortune he has made, "the modesty of his material wants are strongly expressed in his personal life." The Chaplin portrayed by this article— one of the first profiles of Chaplin to appear in a large circulation, national mass magazine—shines in his devotion to art, his unparalleled creative versatility, and his limited material desires.[42]

A second, equally complimentary profile was the article in *Photoplay* by Julian Johnson, one of the best of early movie writers. The title and subtitle of the essay, based on some discussions Johnson and Chaplin had at a Los Angeles restaurant, suggest its main purpose: "Charles, Not Charlie: Concerning a serious-minded man whose screen personality is better known than any other being in the world."[43] Johnson sought to cut through all the contradictory information about Chaplin appearing in the popular press. To do so, he writes, one must begin by distinguishing clearly between Chaplin the man and Charlie the movie character.

The article paints a sympathetic and admirable portrait of the "real" Charles Spencer Chaplin. According to Johnson, Charles dislikes crowds, largely because the only emotion he sees on the faces is curiosity, nothing that can lead to serious interchange between humans. He dresses conservatively, with "the unostentatious attire of good breeding." He is a cautious businessman whose "charities are carefully chosen." Though Chaplin has little formal education, he is rapidly becoming a man of culture. He "talks with the clean, well-bred speech of an Englishman," and his studio is the "most artistic" ever built in Hollywood.

These qualities, writes Johnson, reflect "the innate taste and refinement of a man slowly rising to self-won culture after early vicissitudes and almost no schooling." This "innate taste" is moving Chaplin toward an interest in more serious, ambitious films. "The serious bits in all of his plays are the episodes he likes most," writes Johnson, Chaplin's favorite being the episode in *The Bank* in which Charlie discovers the bouquet he had given Edna tossed into a wastebasket. "In the ensuing bit of almost motionless pantomime," writes Johnson in a comment that typifies the desire of some critics to raise Chaplin's aesthetic standing, "Chaplin struck a note of tragedy which in its depth and universality was really Shakespearean."[44]

One factor contributing to this perspective of Chaplin as a serious and talented artist was the degree to which Chaplin was beginning to entertain and be entertained by famous artists and other figures from around the world, many of them more anxious to meet the famous comedian than he was to meet them. In his autobiography Chaplin describes at considerable length his meetings during this period with Pavlova, Nijinsky, Paderewski, pianist Leopold Godowsky, Jascha Heifetz, Lord and Lady Mountbatten, Constance Collier, and Sir Herbert Beerbohm Tree. Chaplin was internationally recognized and in demand. By associating with artists and other notables, he was apparently legitimizing his own status as an important artist, particularly since many of them sought out the great Chaplin rather than vice versa.

Other articles, and indeed the comedian himself, echoed this tendency to view Chaplin as a serious artist. *Moving Picture World* carried an article that stressed how much attention Chaplin was getting in a wide variety of magazines. It claimed that only the Kaiser and President Wilson had received more attention than Chaplin in the public press over the previous two years. Furthermore, a wide number of "high brow" journals like the *New Republic*, *New Statesman*, *Century*, and *Smart Set* were praising Chaplin's work.[45] Chaplin himself, during a visit to New York City on the Liberty Loan tour, told a reporter that he was a "high-lowbrow," an artist interested in both serious and popular art. While there, he added, he hoped very much to see the production of Ibsen's play *A Doll's House*.[46] Film writer Elsie Codd, after visiting Chaplin on the set of *Sunnyside*, reported that Chaplin was interested in writing a screenplay on a "deep psychological problem." She added: "I have never seen a man more intensely *alive*."[47]

Chaplin also fostered this image by writing an article that appeared in *American Magazine* in November 1918. In "What People Laugh At," Chaplin wrote as a comic theorist, seeking to explain the sources of his comedy. Though some of the essay deals with examples of how he got ideas for films by observing the world around him, in other sections Chaplin makes pithy observations about comedy and human experience, as when he writes: "Restraint is a great word, not only for actors but for everybody to remember. Restraint of tempers, appetites, desires, bad habits, and so on [is valuable to cultivate]."[48] The unschooled music-hall comedian had become a somber comic theorist in barely five years.

At the turn of the decade, however, two articles questioned whether the recent failed films or the positive profiles were more important to the star image. *Theater Magazine* published an article in late 1919 that asked, "Is the Charlie Chaplin Vogue Passing?" A genteel attack on Chaplin written in a huffy tone, the author recalled that two years earlier it "would have been deemed treasonable to cast the smallest of critical stones at Chaplin." Ascribing Chaplin's success to simple repetition, the critic charged that "the appeal of every Chaplin picture is to the lowest human instincts," a familiar charge of genteel critics since the Keystone days. To this, the essay added that the Chaplin comedies were based on "the psychological principle that pain is diverting" and that their appeal was "an extremely unintellectual one." "I strenuously object to incompetent persons styling Charles Chaplin a great artist," the essay concluded, "when he's nothing of the sort."[49]

Another piece, this one more sympathetic despite the concerns it raised, appeared in early 1920. The April issue of *Photoplay* opened with "A Letter to a Genius," addressed to Chaplin, on its title page. After registering its disappointment over Chaplin's films since *Shoulder Arms*, the letter concluded (perhaps "implored" might be a better word): "We are not commanding nor advising nor even criticizing; we speak because we need you—because you made this turbulent God's marble a better thing to live on—because since you have been out of sorts the world has gone lame and happiness has moved away. Come back, Charlie!"[50] Such a statement suggested how profoundly Chaplin's work in the 1910s had affected moviegoers. Despite the conflicts over the alleged vulgarity in Chaplin's films, despite his huge salaries, despite the war controversy, despite his divorce and the two weak films made as his marriage was dissolving, Chaplin's star image still evoked hope from his followers.

As the decade ended, then, Chaplin's star image had already begun to evolve. Initially it was based almost entirely on the character of Charlie, which first appeared in the Keystone years. There Charlie had been crude, at times cruel, and often very funny. During the Essanay contract, however, and even more during the Mutual years, Charlie tempered that cruelty and became known for both his amusing antics and, increasingly, his yearnings for romance and friendship with an idealized woman. Though he was nearly always vulnerable both physically and fiscally, he maintained his dignity and the purity of his desires.

But beginning with the Essanay years, the real person, Charles

Spencer Chaplin, began to figure into the equation of his star image. Most of the press first portrayed him as the modest and talented beneficiary of American opportunity, a kind of Horatio Alger hero with comic talents. Later, as doubts and misgivings were raised about his huge salaries or his war involvement or his divorce, the press in general came to Chaplin's defense and portrayed him not just as the modest man of success but as the serious, ambitious, and versatile artist. At the end of this period, even the term "genius" surfaced.

By 1920, contradictions and strains already characterized the star image. Charlie was often penniless; Chaplin was an enterprising man making millions. Charlie's ardor for Edna was intense and unyielding; Chaplin's marriage quickly disintegrated. Charlie often mixed with the down and out; Chaplin mixed with the rich and famous. Yet despite these conflicts and tensions, by the end of the decade, Chaplin had found many defenders in the press who hoped he would regain the artistic form he had seemed to lose in *Sunnyside* and *A Day's Pleasure*. As the 1920s were beginning and his divorce settlement was being worked out, Chaplin himself was feverishly engrossed in a new film about Charlie, an orphan, and a cold world that challenged them both. Much of his future, in the coming decade and beyond, depended on it.

TWO

**At the Top: Charlie
and the 1920s**

3

From *The Kid* to *The Gold Rush*

Finishing Up at First National

As we have seen, Chaplin's rise in 1914 and 1915 was meteoric. But the history of stardom in America is filled with stories of stars and celebrities whose popularity lasted a few years, a few months, or even a few weeks. As Chaplin himself found during 1919, when his marriage was breaking up and his creative juices seemed to stop flowing, patience and fidelity were not virtues possessed by all of the moviegoing public. Sustaining his star image was no easy task.

Yet Chaplin managed to maintain his popularity in the first half of the 1920s, and he did so by managing his star image—both his comic persona and the way he presented himself to the press—in a much more sophisticated way than observers have sometimes granted. Through his films, his writings, his dealings with the press, and even his interactions with a branch of the young intelligentsia, Chaplin solidified his status in the 1920s as the world's premiere comic film performer and director.

One crucial way a star image is sustained is, of course, through films. For most stars the personae they play contribute centrally to their star images. In Chaplin's case, however, because he not only acted in films but also wrote and directed them, the films are important to his star image both in respect to the Charlie character and to the kind of filmmaker and artist Chaplin was perceived to be. Charlie seemed less warm and romantic in *Sunnyside* and *A Day's Pleasure*, but the artist implied by the films also seemed less skilled and ambitious. Both changes threatened his star image. Yet in Chaplin's next film, *The Kid* (1920), as well as in two of the remaining three films on his First National contract (*The Idle Class* and *The Pilgrim*), Chaplin managed to resurrect and deepen Charlie while implicitly presenting Chaplin as a renewed filmmaker.

The renewal began with *The Kid*. In his autobiography Chaplin recalled telling a friend that as *The Kid* developed, he was beginning to blend "slapstick with sentiment" (MA, p. 235). More accurately, Chap-

55

lin returned in *The Kid* to the mixture of comedy and pathos evident in films like *The Vagabond* and *The Bank* but entirely absent in *A Day's Pleasure*. Chaplin apparently realized that the sentiment was one of the sources of popularity of his films. Furthermore, he added other characteristics to the film, including some pointed social criticism and some "artistic" stylistic devices, that helped viewers and critics to see the film as a stunning artistic achievement.

The opening title emphasized what Chaplin was after: "A comedy with a smile—and perhaps a tear." The narrative structure was simple. A woman, abandoned by the artist who fathered her child, leaves the infant in a luxurious car outside a mansion, hoping he will be offered the life she cannot provide. The car is stolen and the child abandoned again, only to be discovered by Charlie, who decides to heed the note left with the child, which asks the finder to love and care for the "orphan." Five years pass. The baby is now "the kid," who breaks windows so his adoptive father can make a living by repairing them. Their scenes together display a deep bond of affection. When the central conflict arises—a threat by county officials to take the child away from Charlie because of his poverty and humble setting—the effect is striking and generates the most powerful moments of pathos in the movie. Though the officials initially fail, Charlie and the child are forced to go into hiding. The child's birth mother, who has become a wealthy and successful actress and has subsequently devoted herself to charity work in the slums, learns the boy's true identity when she is shown the note she originally pinned on his blanket. She offers a reward for his return, and an unscrupulous flophouse owner steals the child from Charlie. Falling asleep on his doorstep after an exhausting search for the boy, Charlie dreams of heaven (a much more integrated dream sequence than was found in *Sunnyside*). There an initial social harmony quickly degenerates due to jealousy and envy. Awakened by an apparently hostile policeman, Charlie is dragged to a car, then taken to the elegant home of the mother/actress. He and the kid are reunited.

The Kid is important to Chaplin's star image partly because of its vivid portrayal of cruel people and venal social institutions that make it difficult for the poor but noble Charlie to survive. The ironic opening scene shows the mother, whose "only sin is motherhood," being turned out of the charity hospital, babe in arms. The bars of the gate she passes through visually equate the hospital with a prison. Shortly thereafter, Chaplin cuts to the callous father, apparently an artist, who accidentally knocks a picture of his former lover into a fireplace, retrieves it, then matter-of-factly tosses it back to be burned.[1] Parallel to the hospital is the county orphan asylum, which on the advice of a "country doctor" who treats the child, decides that he would be better off in an orphanage than with Charlie who has nurtured him from infancy. Those living in the Victorian urban squalor of Charlie's neighborhood also exhibit cruelty. The kid gets accosted by a neighborhood bully, and when the kid seems to be getting the upper hand, the bully's monstrous brother threatens to attack Charlie. Later, it is the flophouse owner who kidnaps the boy to collect a $1000 reward.

The film portrays a bleak social background, and the method of the film is one that would increasingly characterize Chaplin's work: it juxtaposes two moral universes, a negative one associated with various ills of society and a positive one embodied in Charlie and his closest relationships. In contrast to the harsh and uncaring society in this film are the woman, the kid, and Charlie. The reference to the charity hospital in the first scene is an important one, for the film's positive moral universe is related to charity in two senses. One definition of charity, providing help or relief to the poor, is acted out by the mother. Although she achieves success as an actress quickly, she is not corrupted by wealth. In fact, as one title puts it, for her charity is not a "duty" but a "joy."

In developing her character, Chaplin at least twice used stylistic devices that helped identify him as a "serious" filmmaker. In the first scene Chaplin associates the mother with Christ through a nondiegetic insert: as she walks away from the hospital, Chaplin cuts to an image of Christ carrying the cross up Calvary.[2] Even before Eisenstein, Chaplin was experimenting with intellectual montage. Second, some prints of the film emphasize the mother's goodness with a shot of her standing with her infant outside a church as a young woman and older man come outside in their wedding procession. Though the mother is unmarried, the church window behind her creates a halolike effect around her head.[3] Such attention to style and symbol helped foster the "serious" image that Chaplin was seeking to convey.

Charlie's relationship with the child exhibits a second kind of charity: the feeling of benevolence and good will toward another. Throughout the film, in both comic and sentimental scenes, Charlie and the kid demonstrate their deep emotional bond. When Charlie cares for the infant in his comic improvised nursery, when the two perfect their window-breaking and repairing service, even when Charlie cleans his boy's face or the boy cooks for his father, we see how close they have become.

Their bond is the central human tie in the film, and the dramatic climax occurs when the asylum director, his driver, and a policeman forceably separate Charlie and the kid. This climax is heightened through the use of film style in several ways. One medium shot of the child backed into a corner makes him look almost like a trapped animal. A medium two-shot of the boy and Charlie embracing, bleary-eyed Charlie looking into the camera, captures the intensity of their bond. After the two are separated, Chaplin cross-cuts between the child in the back of the asylum truck and Charlie being restrained in his apartment: the boy imploringly reaches out his arms and mouths the words, "I want my daddy, oh please." Their deep bond is indestructible, and it is a bitter social irony that the officials believe their brand of charity, the same kind that ignominiously turned the child's mother out of the hospital at the opening of the film, will be more humane than the one already animating the relationship between the kid and Charlie.

Chaplin's dream sequence, effectively integrated in the narrative, provided another indication of Chaplin as "serious" filmmaker. The dream follows the boy's separation from Charlie; in it, Charlie imagines a limited view of heaven, set entirely in the street outside his flat but cheerfully painted and garlanded. The inhabitants are Charlie's neighbors, dressed in white and sporting wings. They fly, including even a little dog, play harps, and dance in the streets, but the utopia cannot last. Three devils slip by a sleeping guardian at the pearly gates and enter to plant seeds of discord. One devil tempts a dark-haired young beauty (played by Lita Gray, who would become the second Mrs. Chaplin in 1924) to "vamp" Charlie, entices Charlie to pursue her, then prods her "sweetheart"—who happens to be none other than the monstrous bully whose younger brother picked the fight with the kid—into jealousy. A fight ensues, a winged policeman intercedes, and when Charlie tries to fly away, the policeman shoots him down. Not only does the scene provide some comic relief, but it also closes off Charlie's escape: evil exists even in his dreams of heaven.

The ending is a tentatively happy one: although the kid and Charlie are reunited through the other charitable character, the woman, the conclusion is not as closed as film viewers in the 1920s were accustomed to. Rather, its tentativeness is similar to the close of *City Lights*. Dragged by a policeman to a luxurious car, Charlie is driven to the woman's home, which resembles the house in front of which she abandoned her infant in the opening scenes of the film. As the policeman leads Charlie to the front door, the boy accompanies his mother out to greet him. He embraces Charlie, which cements the central relationship of the film. But then, as Charlie, the kid, and the mother step into the entry and close the door, the camera remains discreetly outside and Chaplin fades to darkness. Just how the relationship among the three will work itself out remains a mystery. Charity in both senses is affirmed in the film, but the presence of evil in the world, even in the world of dreams, makes any overly optimistic inference about the conclusion uncertain at best.

Response to Chaplin's blend of slapstick, sentiment, and serious art was striking, among both the public and the critics. The film, according to one source, grossed around $2.5 million, with Chaplin's share over $1 million. Robinson, who had access to Chaplin's records, says that Chaplin convinced First National to advance him $1.5 million and to pay him 50 percent of the net after the advance was recovered. By 1924 the film had played in fifty countries around the globe. Such success enabled Chaplin to retain the financial security he had built up in his three previous contracts, despite the fact that *The Kid* cost him over $500,000 to make.[4]

Critics also responded positively to the film. The thoughtful reviewer for *Exceptional Photoplays* suggested that Chaplin "can bring tears or laughter to the largest audience in the world with less apparent effort than any other actor on the screen." During an era when the values of genteel Americans were being challenged, the reviewer defends Chaplin from the charge of being "very lowbrow, very vulgar, very unesthetic." Rather, he says, Chaplin's slapstick is rooted in a venerable tradition, of the sort that appeared in Aristophanes, Cervantes, Shakespeare, and Goethe. *The Kid* is "a criticism of life" and a celebration of the kid and his father's love: "it is the charm of their relation against egotism and unconcern of the rest of the world which makes the picture so fascinating."[5] Typical of a number of reviews, this one stresses that Chaplin the artist was doing much more than just making another comedy.

In the *New Republic* Francis Hackett called *The Kid* a "triumph," a film of "integrity." In contrast to the typically low standards of Hollywood, he added, Chaplin's "wisdom, his sincerity, his integrity . . . should go some way to revolutionize motion picture production in this country. From an industry *The Kid* raises production to an art."[6] The review underlines how Chaplin's star image was beginning to be contrasted to, and placed on an aesthetic level above, regular Hollywood films. The *New York Times* and *Variety* also praised the film, and *Theatre Magazine* wrote that the film "certainly outdoes in humor and the special brand of Chaplin pathos, anything this popular film star has yet produced."[7] This blend of comedy and pathos was already becoming a firmly fixed characteristic of the Chaplin films, so much so that viewers were easily noticing and even expecting it.

Chaplin completed his First National contract by making *The Idle*

Class, *Pay Day*, and *The Pilgrim*. Of the three, *Pay Day* did the least to enhance his star image. A potboiling blend of *One A.M.* and *The Rounders*, focusing on Charlie's drinking and his escape from a domineering wife, the film seems done simply to help fulfill the burdensome First National obligation. The fact that it took him only thirty working days to complete the film, about the same pace he had used at Essanay, helps confirm this suspicion.[8]

Both *The Idle Class* and *The Pilgrim*, however, show Chaplin seriously engaged in defining his central persona. In *The Idle Class*, furthermore, he drew on autobiographical elements, just as he had in *The Kid*, only here the personal content referred to more recent events than the childhood memories fueling the earlier film. Chaplin worked on *The Idle Class* after returning from the premiere of *The Kid* in New York, where he was feted by the wealthy and constantly surrounded by adoring fans whenever he was out in public. In the film, Chaplin plays two roles: the familiar Charlie and an isolated wealthy drunkard, Mr. Charles.[9] The film's title refers to both characters: one's idleness contributes to his poverty, the other's idleness results from his prosperity. The wealthy man, unlike Chaplin, is an alcoholic. Yet similar to Chaplin after his divorce, he is lonely, a part of but somewhat alienated from high society, and estranged from his wife.

In contrast, Charlie, though a down-and-out underdog, is nevertheless a dreamer. This is most evident in Charlie's daydream, which hearkens back to his wish-fulfillment dreams in *The Bank* and *Shoulder Arms*. The dream comes after Charlie sees the rich man's wife gallop past on a runaway horse. In rapid succession, Charlie imagines saving the woman, falling in love with her, marrying her, and fathering her children—a respectable, middle-class dream for such a social outcast, and an obvious wish fulfillment that also points forward to *The Gold Rush*. Unsurprisingly, though, Charlie awakens quickly. Later he does for a time romance the rich man's wife at a costume party, where his regular clothing constitutes his costume. He is soon on the run again, however, when the husband escapes from his suit-of-armor costume, and Charlie's true identity is uncovered. Before he leaves, Charlie gives a parting kick to the hindside of the wife's wealthy father. If the real Charles is now wealthy, polished, and somewhat isolated, the persona Charlie can still thumb his nose at the upper classes from the underside of society.

Following *The Idle Class* Chaplin, who had worked almost constantly since arriving on the Keystone lot in 1913, took a European trip and wrote a book on his travels, *My Trip Abroad*, to be discussed later in this chapter. Back in America, he ground out the indifferent *Pay Day*, and then turned to *The Pilgrim*. In a departure from his regular practice, Chaplin worked from a written script and completed the film more quickly than was his custom: forty-five working days. Finished in September 1922 and released in January 1923, *The Pilgrim* was a four-reeler that First National accepted as the final two films of his contract.[10] Like *The Idle Class*, *The Pilgrim* shows a serious Chaplin at work exploring the contours of his comic persona.

In it, as in *The Kid*, Charlie plays a social pariah whose intuitive goodness opposes the flaws of respectable society, a contrast generating satire on genteel piety attuned to the zeitgeist of the 1920s. As the film opens, Charlie has escaped from prison (an allusion to breaking free from the First National contract?) and steals a minister's clothing: Charlie becomes a chaplain. After he takes a train to Devil's Gulch, Texas, where a new minister has been expected, the film follows Charlie's comic misadventures at the train station, a church service, a genteel home, and a saloon, where Charlie retrieves some money stolen from his host family. The story ends when the town sheriff, appreciating Charlie's honesty in returning the money, sets him free along the Texas–Mexico border.

In addition to the comedy arising from Charlie's struggles to act like a minister (you can take Charlie out of prison, but you can't take the prison out of Charlie), the narrative creates humor through its satire of the small town. In contrast to the idealized, white-picket-fence image that M-G-M would later exploit in the Andy Hardy series, Chaplin's small town is much more similar to those described by American writers who "revolted against the village" in the first decades of the twentieth century: writers like Edwin Arlington Robinson, Edgar Lee Masters, Sherwood Anderson, and Sinclair Lewis.[11] Two examples should suffice. While walking to church with the deacon, Charlie discovers that the apparently temperate deacon keeps a bottle of whiskey in his back pocket. Later, when visiting the Brown family (Edna Purviance plays their daughter in her final leading comic role for Chaplin), Charlie the minister is accosted by the small son of a couple who arrive for a brief visit. The little rogue jabs people with a knitting needle, rains a barrage of punches on Charlie and his own father, pours fishbowl water on Charlie, and plasters his father's face with a sticky sheet of flypaper. When his parents leave the room, the urchin tries to follow Charlie into the kitchen and gets a swift kick in the rear. In many of the Keystone and Essanay films, Charlie had used the kick gratuitously, which alienated some viewers, but here the kick is underplayed and justified by the narrative. We clearly side with Charlie as he tries to defend himself against the behavior of the uncontrolled child.

As in *The Kid*, Charlie's morality is clearly underlined in the film. He is attracted to Edna, but his romance is cut short when an acquaintance from prison weasels himself an invitation to spend the night at the Brown residence and steals their savings. Selflessly, Charlie recovers the money and returns it to the Browns, but his cover has been blown. The sheriff, who cannot avert his eyes, must arrest Charlie the wanted escapee, but he hasn't the heart to lock up a person who has performed such an act of kindness and virtue. He therefore takes Charlie to the Texas–Mexico border and suggests that he pick some flowers across the border (and outside the sheriff's jurisdiction). Puzzled for a time about the strange request, Charlie finally understands. Standing in Mexico, he lifts his eyes and raises his arms to the skies in a gesture of freedom. Immediately, he's caught in an outlaw gun battle. Scampering back to the American side, Charlie wavers indecisively. Where should he go? Texas, offering social order and the Brown's daughter, is impossible because he will be returned to prison. Mexico, tempting him with freedom, is lawless and anarchic. In the final shot, a fitting conclusion to Chaplin's First National years, Charlie waddles away from the camera, one foot on each side of the border. There is no easy and comfortable spot for Chaplin's Charlie to plant himself. In like manner, Chaplin himself, after an increasingly rich and self-consciously creative period at First National, was now at a crossroads, finally ready to embark on independent production. But in what direction and to what end?

Interviews and Writings in the Early 1920s

If Chaplin's films during these final years at First National contributed to his star image, so did the interviews he granted and his own writings. One of the first interviews of Chaplin after his divorce from Mildred Harris in November 1920 was also one of the most important, for it presented an image of Chaplin the serious artist to a culturally influential audience and reinforced the serious undertones evident in films like *A Dog's Life*, *Sunnyside*, and *The Kid* (the latter released two months after the interview).

The title of the interview captured its thrust: "The Hamlet-Like Nature of Charlie Chaplin."[12] Conducted by Benjamin De Casseres, the interview has a tone and substance that would have been almost unthinkable just three years earlier, when Chaplin was still working at the frenetic pace of nearly a film a month. It is an interview given by someone who is becoming used to constant attention and adulation yet is not particularly satisfied with the situation. Similarly, it is an interview with someone impatient with the role of funny man and drawn instead to the world of ideas and a dark view of life.

Near the opening of the interview, De Casseres outlined the contours of his picture of Chaplin: "In many hours' easy conversational talk with Chaplin I discovered a spirit of a very rare vintage—a poet, an esthete; a dynamic and ultra-advanced thinker; a man with a thousand surprising facets; a man of many accomplishments; a man infinitely sad and melancholy; a man as delicate as violin strings that register the world-wail and the world-melody; a Puck, a Hamlet, an Ariel—and a Voltaire." In the interchange that follows, Chaplin's comments suggest that he was increasingly becoming interested in ideas. Though he had very little schooling and as late as age thirteen could barely read or write, Chaplin had begun to feel the need to educate himself as early as his first trip to America (MA, p. 123). This lack of formal education bothered Chaplin: he once wrote that "I wanted to know not for the love of knowledge but as a defense against the world's contempt for the ignorant." Although Raoul Sobel and David Francis are probably accurate when they argue that Chaplin's grasp of ideas was superficial, Chaplin apparently began to read more, after he slowed his working pace, and would then allude in interviews to the authors and works he was encountering, which gave an aura of high art to his image and his films.[13] At a time when the movies were struggling for respectability (and a broader audience), this was shrewd of Chaplin, as well as potentially profitable. By presenting himself as interested in ideas, he was differentiating his star image from that of competitors like Buster Keaton or Harold Lloyd (see Figure 8).

In this interview Chaplin displayed his learning several times. He talks of his dissatisfaction at being pressured into the role of Charlie: "Solitude is the only relief. The dream-world is then the great reality; the real world an illusion. I go to my library and live with the great abstract thinkers—Spinoza, Schopenhauer, Nietzsche and Walter Pater." He also indicated a desire "to retire to some Italian lake with my beloved violin, my Shelley and Keats, and live under an assumed name a life purely imaginative and intellectual."

In addition, Chaplin stresses his stardom by mentioning celebrities he has encountered, like Caruso and Heifetz. A little rankled that Caruso had called him the "Caruso of the Movies"—and more rankled at waiting in Caruso's dressing room for attention from the great tenor— Chaplin tells the interviewer that he called Caruso the "Chaplin of the

Operatic Stage." When Heifetz dined at Chaplin's house, according to the interview, Chaplin played "a bit of Bach" for him. By mentioning how he mingled and even showed up leading artists from other arts, Chaplin sought to reaffirm his status as star.

The interview also presented a relatively common notion about stardom: that it's lonely at the top. At times, Chaplin told De Casseres, "I am oppressed . . . . by what is known among the Romantics as world-weariness." Later, asked about what it felt like to rocket from poverty to wealth, Chaplin replied, "Nothing fails like success. I mean by that that money never satisfied a spiritual or intellectual need. . . . I doubt whether a rich man ever has a real friend—for how when one is fixed for life in this world's goods can one tell friend, enemy or fawner? I always understand poor artists; rich ones always seem to me a contradiction in terms." Such comments cumulatively draw the star closer to the stargazers by suggesting that despite the star's privileged status, his life is still beset with problems and difficulties.

While this *Times* interview did much to present Chaplin as a serious, popular, and at times melancholy artist, Chaplin's most detailed "advertisement for himself" was his account of his 1921 European journey, *My Trip Abroad*.[14] The trip itself lasted from September 4 to October 18, with stopovers in New York City both before and after. He traveled to London, to Paris (twice), and to Berlin. Chaplin's account was mainly dictated to a young newsman, Monta Bell, during the return by train from New York to Los Angeles. In general, the book recounts his activities while on the trip, and though at times repetitious, it provides another interesting picture of Chaplin's presentation of himself early in the 1920s. The fact that it was first published as a series of articles in *Photoplay* before being sold in book form meant both that Chaplin was paid twice for his efforts and that a wider readership was ensured.

The book reiterated some of the star characteristics evident in the 1920 *Times* interview and added others. It first gives a vivid picture of how wearing it was to be surrounded constantly by people. Early in the trip, before leaving New York City, Chaplin writes of putting on his "prop" smile for reporters and crowds as a way to survive the constant attention: this is another picture of the paradoxical loneliness of the star that he had alluded to in the *Times* interview.

Another aspect of *My Trip Abroad* is its definition of Chaplin's stardom by listing the celebrities he met while on his trip. He tells of meeting Carl Sandburg in Chicago; Max Eastman, Douglas Fairbanks, and Mary Pickford in New York; H. G. Wells, J. M. Barrie, and Nathan Burke in England; Waldo Frank, Sir Phillip Sassoon, and Dudley Field

8. Chaplin in 1920—the image of the serious
artist begins to establish itself.

Malone in Paris; and many others. In addition, Chaplin claims to have
either turned down or been afraid to go to affairs attended by George
Bernard Shaw or Lloyd George.

But more evident in this book than in any earlier work is Chaplin's
interest in politics and the direction of his political sympathies. Although Chaplin's only extensive political involvements before his 1921
trip had been the Liberty Loan tour and the making of *Shoulder Arms*,
both of which showed Chaplin reaffirming the opinions dominant in
the United States, *My Trip Abroad* shows Chaplin flirting with or at
least open to the leftist political ideas that would later become closely
associated with his star image.

One indication of this is Chaplin's reference to Soviet Russia in the
book. The first mention comes when a reporter asks him if he is a
Bolshevik. Chaplin's answer: "I am an artist. I am interested in life.
Bolshevism is a new phase of life. I must be interested in it" (p. 8).
When reporters continue to badger him about Bolshevism, Lenin, and
Russia, Chaplin backs off, telling them, "I am an artist, not a politi-
cian," almost precisely the defense he would use in 1947 when the
opening of *Monsieur Verdoux* stirred up considerable controversy (p.

45). Later in the book he wrote that if given the opportunity, he would like to meet Trotsky and Lenin. Perhaps because he had had dinner with Max Eastman and some of his other leftist friends just before leaving for his trip, Chaplin had socialism, Russia, and the Bolshevik Revolution on his mind and wasn't afraid to tell reporters or inform readers of his book about these political encounters or thoughts.

Chaplin's comments about Bolshevism and their impact on his star image in 1920 and 1921 must be understood in the context of the Red Scare of 1919 and 1920. While the October 1917 Bolshevik Revolution in Russia raised the hopes of socialists throughout Europe and America, it also raised fears and generated negative reaction among those Americans who perceived socialist ideology to be a threat to their wealth and status or a challenge to American individualism. Though public and private propaganda during World War I was aimed primarily at Germany, after the end of the war cultural hatreds and anxieties were refocused by conservative attacks against radicalism, specifically the "Red menace." Several bombings in 1919, including one in the front of Attorney General A. Mitchell Palmer's home, intensified these fears and were attributed to the "Reds." In late 1919 the United States government deported over 250 alien residents to the Soviet Union, even though most had committed no offense and were not Communists. On New Year's Day in 1920, Palmer orchestrated a nationwide raid of radicals (many of whom were American citizens and avowed non-Communists) that led to the arrest of some 6,000 people. Despite the systematic violation of the civil rights of those arrested, few spoke out against Palmer's tactics.[15] Chaplin's openness about what Bolshevism represented probably sounded dangerous to many Americans who either actively participated in or passively acquiesced to attacks on the "Red menace."

In addition to this series of references to Bolshevism, Chaplin offers a more general picture of his political sympathies in a number of places in his book. These remarks form one of the book's most interesting dimensions, showing Chaplin grappling with a central and extremely unusual life experience: his meteoric rise from relative poverty to extreme wealth, his shift from lower to upper class, and the effect of this on his view of the world. Throughout *My Trip Abroad* Chaplin consistently reveals a social consciousness and a sympathy for the lower class, particularly those who are suffering most.

For example, describing his days on the ship, Chaplin tells of attempting to play cricket with some of the ship's crew and becoming upset when the first-class passengers crowd in to gawk at the movie star. His subsequent arrival in London and particularly his visit back to his old neighborhood make Chaplin reflect on the poverty out of which he arose. At one point he indicates that he wishes he could do something to solve a social problem like unemployment (p. 49). At another he writes sympathetically about encountering a blind man he had known as a child on the streets of London. At yet another, when his cousin Aubrey points out that a passing truck driver is a fallen aristocrat, Chaplin replies that the fall is probably for the best. The truck driver, in Chaplin's view, is a "true aristocrat," part of the "real elite, not the Blue Book variety," because he now is "loving adventure, . . . doing something all the time, and loving the doing" (p. 142). In these instances, as well as in his comments on the death penalty and prison reform (p. 152), Chaplin exhibits a sympathy for the outcasts of society, a populist skepticism about the wealthy, and an awareness of social problems affecting the poor.

The conclusion suggests that Chaplin wishes to leave his reader with an image of his genuine social concern. His final thoughts relate to his desire for world disarmament, and he quotes Tennyson:

> When shall all men's good
> Be each man's rule and universal peace
> Shine like a shaft of light across the land,
> And like a lane of beams athwart the sea?

Such an allusion, despite the slight misquotation, not only stresses Chaplin's social conscience; it also reiterates his desire to be considered a learned man. Both were strong characteristics of the star image he was projecting in the first half of the 1920s.

Two other documents from 1922 reiterate Chaplin's image in this era: an interview in *Literary Digest* and an article by Chaplin, "In Defense of Myself," in *Collier's*.[16] In the interview, Chaplin attacks the British class system: he knew, the interviewer tells us, "that the very people who were clamoring and beseeching him to their tables and receptions would not before have given him a considered glance. . . . They wanted to see, not him, but the symbol of success." Chaplin also talked to his interviewer of "his bitter youth and his loneliness and his struggles" and seemed to the interviewer "the loneliest, saddest man I ever knew." This invites comparison with the image of the lonely husband Chaplin played in *The Idle Class* and supports the contention that Chaplin was at this point working more often in an autobiographical vein than he had in his earlier years.

"In Defense of Myself," besides giving an interesting and perceptive discussion of his screen persona's essence and its appeal to the movie audience, stresses the seriousness of "quality comedy" (and hence the seriousness of Chaplin the artist). Genuine and lasting humor, Chaplin writes, goes beyond "broad and slapstick kind of comedy":

> The true spirit of humor does not revolve about physical mishaps or even incongruities of dress and behavior. These may be the outward paraphernalia of humor, like the motley of the fool, but humor itself is woven deeper into the fabric of life. I began to look upon humor as a kind of gentle and benevolent custodian of the mind which prevents one from being overwhelmed and driven to the point of insanity by the apparent seriousness of life.

Thus the star image of Chaplin in the early 1920s, forged by the interplay of Charlie's role in films like *The Kid* and Chaplin's writings and interviews, blended a number of themes: humor, populism, social and political awareness, serious aesthetic and intellectual aspirations, and a loneliness engendered by a popularity that made intimate human contact almost impossible. In his next two films Chaplin moved a long way toward solidifying this star image and asserting his position as the preeminent artist in the American film industry.

Branching Out: *A Woman of Paris*

After completing his First National contract, Chaplin was finally able to contemplate his first film for United Artists, the distributing company he had formed with Fairbanks, Pickford, and Griffith in 1919. And as those thoughts began to shape into firmer plans, Chaplin startled his partners: his new film would not be a comedy but rather a sophisticated romantic melodrama, and would star not Chaplin but rather Edna Purviance and Adolphe Menjou. The result, *A Woman of Paris*, was released in October 1923. Before examining this film, however, it is important to discuss Chaplin's economic situation as he moved into independent production at United Artists, for this presented him with both constraints and opportunities and had a bearing on the development of his star image.

As we have already seen, Chaplin became a wealthy and famous star in part because he had the good luck to enter the film industry just as companies were beginning to market their films by emphasizing the actors who appeared in them. From 1913 to 1919 the star system institutionalized itself, and Chaplin, like Pickford and Fairbanks, was a prime beneficiary of that shift. However, by late 1918 two companies, Adolph Zukor's Paramount Pictures and the First National Exhibitors Circuit, had gained considerable control over the distribution of movies. Paramount, a distributing company, signed contracts with a number of production companies (e.g., Famous Players–Lasky) that gave it exclusive rights to distribute their pictures and then required theater owners to rent its films in large blocks. First National, an association of theater owners, had formed partly to counter Paramount's growing power; it hoped to obtain outstanding films made by independent producers for their member theaters. In addition to signing Chaplin to his million-dollar contract for eight films, First National made a similar agreement with Mary Pickford.[17]

United Artists arose in early 1919 when, at a January convention of the First National Exhibitors Circuit in Los Angeles, rumors began flying about an impending mammoth merger in the industry. According to an account in *Moving Picture World*, one such story was that "First National is going to form a combination with Famous Players [a Paramount production branch], Artcraft, Goldwyn, Metro, Fox, and after that they'll tell the stars just where to get off in the matter of salary."[18] Any such merger of Paramount and First National was certain to constitute a threat to the salaries of Chaplin and other big stars. Significantly, Chaplin himself attended the convention to ask the First National directors for extra funds for production costs, since both *A Dog's Life* and *Shoulder Arms* were longer than the two-reel films for which he had contracted.[19] When he was turned down, even treated with indifference, he and his brother Sydney decided that something must be done. On January 14 Chaplin held a meeting at his house with Fairbanks, William S. Hart, Griffith, and a representative for Pickford, who was ill. By the next afternoon, all had become signatories to the articles of agreement that established the United Artists' Association.[20]

In essence, United Artists, by distributing collectively the films Fairbanks, Pickford, Hart, Griffith, and Chaplin would independently produce, was designed to protect the independence that they had managed to attain in the film industry. (Hart, though involved in the planning stages, withdrew and remained at Famous Players–Lasky when offered $200,000 per film.)[21] Though Fairbanks, Pickford, and Griffith had all begun releasing films through United Artists by 1920—with some other producers joining them—Chaplin was tied to his First National contract through the release of *The Pilgrim* in 1923. As film historians have shown, Chaplin's years at First National were key years in the consolidation of the American film industry, during which three important shifts were occurring: studio production began to dominate the market; producers began to wrest creative control from directors, resulting in a "central producer" mode of production; and principles of scientific management and systematic division of labor became commonplace in the production of movies.[22]

The dimensions of Chaplin's emerging star image that stressed his serious side and his concern for high art were cultivated at least in part to counter this trend of "assembly-line "movie production and to differentiate his "product" and those of others at United Artists from the films made by the major studios. Chaplin had this in mind when, in February 1923, he, along with Pickford, Fairbanks, Harold Lloyd, and Griffith, signed what they told reporters was a "declaration of independence from producers and exhibitors of 'machine-made' films." In a joint statement, the filmmakers warned that the powerful corporate combinations "will dwarf the artistic growth of the motion picture." They also claimed a desire "to protect the independent producer and the independent exhibitor against these commercial combinations."[23] In this case, as well as later in his career, Chaplin's use of the press to emphasize an aspect of his star image—his individual artistic vision—stemmed at least in part from distinct economic motivations.

Since United Artists lost money in each of its first three full years of operation (1920–1922) and since Paramount and First National had if anything increased their strength in the market, the success of this declaration of independence and the links with independent exhibitors were crucial if Chaplin and his colleagues were to survive in the competitive marketplace and still retain creative and financial control over their films. It was in this context that Chaplin contemplated his first film for United Artists.

Chaplin's writings and interviews in 1922 indicate that he was becoming restless with comedies featuring Charlie. As early as 1920 he told an interviewer that his "world-weariness" was partly "a reaction from my innate sense of humor, disgust of the character that circumstances has forced me to create."[24] He also was interested in directing a film that would star Edna Purviance, who was becoming less appropriate in appearance for the ingenue type that Chaplin liked in his comedies as a romantic companion for Charlie. Thus, when Peggy Hopkins Joyce, with whom Chaplin had a brief affair in 1922, suggested a film based on Henri Letellier, a wealthy Parisian bon vivant, Chaplin began working on a film called *Public Opinion*. It would star Purviance and, in the Letellier part, Adolphe Menjou, who reportedly resembled him.[25] From this germ grew *A Woman of Paris*, which more than any other film established Chaplin's reputation as a serious film director and artist quite apart from his performing talents.

Chaplin stresses his artistic concerns in the opening titles, which contain a statement warning viewers that he will not appear in the film and that it is the first "serious drama" he has written and produced. He also sets the tone by subtitling the film "a drama of fate." What

follows is a simple narrative, focusing on Marie St. Claire (Edna Purviance), Jean Millet (Carl Miller), and Pierre Revel (Adolphe Menjou).
Marie and Jean, from the same village in France, have decided to leave
for Paris and marry despite the objections of their fathers. When
Jean's father is suddenly stricken ill, eventually dying, Jean misses his
appointment to leave with Marie on the train. Marie, however, believes
he has rejected her. A year passes and we learn that Marie has become
the kept woman of Pierre Revel, a wealthy and eligible Parisian bachelor. Her life with Pierre is one of pleasure and luxury, but she begins
to reevaluate their relationship when Pierre announces his upcoming
marriage of convenience and when she accidentally meets Jean, who
has moved to Paris with his mother and is eking out a living as a
painter. He proposes, though his mother disapproves, and the remainder of the film traces Marie's attempts to choose between luxury
or marriage, while fate conspires to keep her from realizing happiness. Ultimately, Jean's misapprehension about Marie's feelings leads
him to suicide. The stricken Marie renounces her life with Pierre and,
after reconciling with Jean's mother, retires with her to the countryside, where they dedicate their lives to the care of orphans.

In many ways, the film is most un-Chaplinesque, at least as reviewers, critics, and audiences had come to define that term from his previous films. Probably the most important shifts are the film's general
lack of broad comedy and its restrained acting style. Discussing the
film with an interviewer, Chaplin stressed his concern for such restraint: "In real life great emotions are repressed. There are no such
great emotional splurges as we often see on the stage and on the
screen. . . . It is this realism that is worthwhile striving for—a realism
that will portray emotions intelligently and at the same time keep the
audience interested in the story."[26] Perhaps the best example of underplayed emotion in the film comes when Jean's mother learns of her
son's death. Instead of broad and uncontrolled grief, Chaplin sought,
and actress Lydia Knott achieved, a stunned numbness—the kind of
formal feeling that, wrote Emily Dickinson, follows great pain.[27]

The restraint and subtlety of acting is combined with a more ex-
pressive use of film style. Early in the film Chaplin shows the influence
of German Expressionism, as looming shadows of both fathers pre-
cede them when they first appear. He uses the interplay of light and
shadow again at the train station, a device frequently noted by the reviewers. In that scene Chaplin presents Marie in a medium shot, and,
as her eyes blur with grief after surmising that Jean has abandoned
her, the shadows of a moving train pass by her. She walks toward the
camera and passes to the right of it in closeup: Chaplin implies the

existence of the fateful train to Paris without once showing it. Two other subtle uses of film style are the cutaway to a close-up of a smoking pipe lying on the carpet, indicating to viewers the incapacitation or death of Jean's father, and Jean's discovery of a man's shirt collar in Marie's dresser, a visual suggestion of Pierre's frequent presence in her apartment. Chaplin also managed to titillate audiences without unduly offending censors when he showed the feet and lower legs of a woman being "unwrapped" at a Latin Quarter party and when, by framing the masseur and keeping Marie's body just below the bottom of the frame, he presented a nearly nude Marie getting a massage. Although the narrative is linear and quite simple, Chaplin tells the story with a kind of visual sophistication that was rarely evident in his earlier films.

Despite the lack of sustained comedy in the film and the more sophisticated use of film style, *A Woman of Paris* does resemble some of Chaplin's earlier comic narratives—*The Kid*, most obviously—in the way it contrasts two distinctly different ways of life, both of which embody moral universes that generate narrative conflict. The two perspectives in *A Woman of Paris* represent the urban haves and have-nots, a contrast that Chaplin would return to in a later comedy, *City Lights*. The urban haves are represented by Pierre, Marie (after she becomes his mistress), and their acquaintances. The urban have-nots are represented by Jean and his mother after they move to Paris, where he has become a talented but struggling painter. Throughout the film Chaplin skillfully uses mise-en-scène,[28] particularly sets (Marie's apartment versus Jean's) and costumes (Pierre's versus Jean's; Marie's versus Jean's mother's) to juxtapose the two worlds.

This contrast, particularly the one between Pierre and Jean, poses the central question of the film: will Marie favor Pierre or Jean, after Jean again declares his love for Marie? As one title puts it: "In the mind of Marie St. Clair is the problem—marriage or luxury." Costume becomes important here, for the Marie whom Jean loves is the one he knew before they went to Paris. She poses for him wearing a long, white, low-cut dress and a feathery hat; Jean, however, paints her in the dark, high-necked dress and subdued hat she was wearing the night they were to have left for Paris. Significantly, when Marie agrees to reconcile with Pierre after Jean has temporarily come between them, she puts on the same costume, and she is wearing it when Jean commits suicide in despair after he believes he has been rejected by Marie.

Whereas the earlier Chaplin films that posed moral contrasts usually drew a clear melodramatic line between good (Charlie) and evil (the wealthy, the physically imposing, the snobbish, etc.), that line is fuzzier here. Jean's dedication to art and his basic decency are beyond question, but his strained relationship with his father and later, his mother, keep us from identifying him exclusively with good. And though Marie's "friends" Paulette and Fifi surely suggest that the wealthy are hypocritical, dishonest, and spiteful in their dealings with one another, Pierre's charm, love of the good life, and tolerance of Marie keep us from fully identifying him with evil. After the climactic event of the film—Jean's suicide at the base of the nude statue in the café's entrance—Marie reconciles with Jean's mother. They are bound by their mutual grief. The closing scene, which is introduced by the title, "Time heals, and experience teaches that the secret of happiness is in service to others," reminds one of the affirmation of charity in *The Kid*. Marie and Jean's mother have dedicated themselves to running a small orphanage in a bucolic rural setting, ninety kilometers from Paris.

By the end of the film, the meaning of Chaplin's subtitle, "a drama of fate," is clear. At several crucial points in the narrative pure coincidence or accident conspire to keep Jean and Marie apart. The death of Jean's father just as Jean prepares to leave with Marie to Paris constitutes the first. The second comes when Jean's mother arrives home unexpectedly, just in time to overhear Jean propose marriage to Marie. Then the tables are turned when Marie, coming to visit Jean unannounced, overhears Jean tell his mother that the proposal came at a moment of weakness and that he would never marry Marie, even though we know he really feels differently. Fate even seems to lend a hand in the final shots of the film. Pierre, riding with a friend back toward Paris and telling him he doesn't know what has happened to Marie St. Clair, drives past a horse-drawn cart traveling in the other direction. Though Pierre is unaware of it, Marie is riding in the cart with one of her orphan children. Thus she passes her former lover, though neither is aware of it. The feeling that humans are victims of fate pervades the film.

A Woman of Paris is also interesting because of the submerged autobiography in the film. Just as he had in *The Kid*, Chaplin used his personal experience in constructing the narrative. But whereas *The Kid* was informed primarily by childhood experiences and memories, *A Woman of Paris*, like *The Idle Class*, drew on dilemmas Chaplin was undergoing as a private man and public celebrity after he had become widely known and admired.[29] This tendency to express sides of his personality through the characters of his films became increasingly common in Chaplin's films from the time his United Artists period began until its culmination in *Limelight*, the most obviously autobiographical of Chaplin's films.

Although the autobiography may be more buried in *A Woman of Paris*, it is nevertheless there.[30] Chaplin claims in his autobiography that he made the film partly because he was still interested in Edna Purviance's career, even though they had become "emotionally estranged" shortly before Chaplin's first marriage (MA, p. 296). In some ways, Marie's story is Edna's. Edna came from a rural area—Lovecraft, Paradise Valley, Nevada—and agreed to come to a big city, Los Angeles, with a budding young artist, the twenty-six-year-old Chaplin, in 1915. Later, after Chaplin's fame had grown, she, like Marie, became the mistress of a wealthy man (Chaplin) whose engagement to another woman (Mildred Harris) she read about in the newspapers. The central difference between Marie and Edna is that Marie breaks free of Pierre while Edna remained on Chaplin's payroll for the rest of her life (MA, p. 496).

As these parallels suggest, Chaplin projected himself into two characters in the film: the struggling dedicated artist, Jean, and the wealthy cosmopolitan cynic, Pierre. Much of the complexity of the film, and its refusal to move into a tempting melodramatic mold, stems from the fact that Chaplin apparently felt drawn toward both of the characters, which left him unable to commit himself fully to either. One of Chaplin's dedications in the early 1920s was to movies as art—indeed, he would not have risked making a film like *A Woman of Paris* if he had not had aspirations toward serious art. That dedication drew him toward Jean, even though Jean's case was weakened when Chaplin cast a rather weak actor—at least in comparison to Adolphe Menjou—in Jean's role. On the other hand, Chaplin himself was increasingly cast in the role of celebrity and bon vivant in the early 1920s, particularly after his European tour. He no longer had to seek out other celebrities: they sought him. It is evident that Chaplin invested some of his own experience in Pierre, and the way he is presented in the film, in part due to Adolphe Menjou's engaging performance, makes it clear that Chaplin found it impossible to condemn a man that the conventions of melodrama would surely have cast in the role of villain. This autobiographical subtext of *A Woman of Paris*, though not much apparent to viewers and critics in 1923, casts important light on how Chaplin, consciously or unconsciously, was drawing on his own experience as he sought to establish himself as a serious artist in his first genuinely independent feature-length production. It is probably fair to suggest that Chaplin even projected himself into Marie's character in the scene in which Pierre tries to console the melancholy

Marie by telling her that she has everything. Marie's answer, "Not everything," underscores the hints in Chaplin's writings in the early 1920s that his life, despite his fame and fortune, was less than satisfactory.

Nevertheless, Chaplin's desire to be recognized as a serious artist and director in *A Woman of Paris* was certainly satisfied, at least as far as critics and reviewers were concerned. The *New York Times* reviewer wrote on the day after the film opened that it "fascinated an interesting and curious throng last night at the Lyric Theater." To this reviewer Chaplin proved himself to be "a bold, resourceful, imaginative, ingenious, careful, studious, and daring artist."[31] The following Sunday the *Times* again praised the production: "mostly it is the detail to which much studious thought and attention has been given, that is responsible for the great charm of this unusually fine production."[32]

Other reviewers were equally enthusiastic. In the *New York Herald Tribune*, for example, Harriette Underhill wrote, "we could say volumes and write columns, but the few words to which we are limited seem inadequate, no matter how we choose them. Charles Chaplin is a great artist!" And the film, Underhill added, was "the perfect motion picture."[33] Robert Sherwood held that Chaplin "proves to the satisfaction of everyone that he is the first genius of the silent drama."[34] One of the few hesitancies expressed, somewhat amusingly, appeared in *Photoplay*. Warning its readers that the film was "for the sophisticated rather than for a strictly family audience," *Photoplay's* reviewer suggested that "any fifteen-year-old child who appreciates it should be taken home and spanked." Though the reviewer believed that the film was not "great," it did prove that Chaplin "is one of the greatest of all directors."[35] Even the *New Republic's* demanding Stark Young, who the previous year had called on Chaplin to become more ambitious in developing his art, praised *A Woman of Paris*: "not a great drama, this Woman of Paris, but for these forward achievements of Mr. Chaplin's an exciting spot on the horizon."[36]

These reviews failed to note any autobiographical elements in the work, perhaps because *A Woman of Paris* was such a departure from Chaplin's previous films that its obvious differences drew the attention of reviewers. Viewers of Chaplin films in 1923 had been led to expect a comedy that featured Charlie and included both romance and pathos. There had also been some indication, through Chaplin's interviews in the early 1920s and *My Trip Abroad*, that Chaplin was becoming a restive funny man, concerned with issues more serious than slapstick. To the extent that audiences and reviewers were aware of this, *A Woman of Paris* helped include Chaplin the serious intellect and talented director within his star image.

Because of viewers' expectations about Chaplin as a comic film-maker, however, it was almost inevitable that the film would not become a box-office hit. Nevertheless, it seemed to fool *Variety*, the trade publication whose reviews sought in part to gauge box-office potential. The *Variety* reviewer, calling it "a serious sincere effort" and "a candidate for honors and dollars entirely independent of the drawing power Chaplin built up in other fields," raved about the film. Judging Chaplin "a new genius both as a producer and director," the reviewer thought the film "a cinch for the biggest houses."[37] This enthusiasm was not entirely realized. Domestically, the film grossed $634,000, which was surely higher than the gross for a run-of-the-mill studio picture but about the same as the *least* successful United Artists films of Griffith, Pickford, and Fairbanks up through 1923.[38]

So Chaplin made his point and firmly established himself among critics and more sophisticated viewers as a serious and ambitious artist, without suffering too much financially. Yet by the time the film opened, he was telling people that *A Woman of Paris* was an experiment, a deviation from the kind of films that had made him and would keep him an independently wealthy man. In an interview appearing the Sunday after *A Woman of Paris* opened, Chaplin stated that "unless my feelings undergo a marked change, I am going right back to comedy—back to one of the kind of films with which the public identifies me."[39] He reiterated this intention to return to comedy to a group of school children in Detroit a week later, and by the spring of 1924 he had begun production on a full-length feature comedy/romance/epic.[40]

Creating an Epic: *The Gold Rush*

"This is the picture that I want to be remembered by," Chaplin stated on one of the newspaper advertisements provided in the pressbook for *The Gold Rush*.[41] Surely Chaplin had great ambitions for the film, which he hoped would surpass even *The Kid* as a serious comedy featuring Charlie as the central character. After *A Woman of Paris* had established him as a serious director and producer, Chaplin's next step was to outdo any of his comic competitors—Harold Lloyd, Harry Langdon, and Buster Keaton, among others—in the creation of a full-length feature comedy. And he did. Starting to shoot in February 1924, Chaplin completed in fourteen months a ten-reel feature film, longer than any of his competitors' films to that time. After the August

1925 release of *The Gold Rush*, Chaplin reached the height of his reputation up to that time as a film artist and comic performer for American film viewers. Besides the film itself, Chaplin's skill as a publicist and purveyor to the press of particular star qualities helped him to achieve this fame.

The film, of course, accounts for some of his popularity. Chaplin remembers telling himself that his "next film must be an epic" as he cast about for ideas after completing *A Woman of Paris* (MA, p. 303). He also labeled his next work a "dramatic comedy" in the film's promotional material. These comments are entirely appropriate, for the resulting film returns to and in some ways surpasses in effectiveness the characteristics that audiences of Chaplin's films had come to expect in his work: "serious" concerns, comedy, and pathos.

The epic elements of the film relate partly to the film's unlikely source: the Donner party disaster, in which a group of pioneers was snowbound while trying to cross the Sierra Nevadas in 1846 and 1847. According to C. F. McGlashlin's *The Story of the Donner Party*, a book that Chaplin most likely read, only forty-eight of the ninety survived, some of them resorting to cannibalism.[42] This tenacious human struggle to overcome the threats of nature provided one epic conflict at the foundation of *The Gold Rush*. The fact that Chaplin did considerable location shooting in Truckee, California, near the Donner party statue, emphasizes this source of the film's epic stature.[43]

But Chaplin did not set the film in California in the 1840s. Rather, perhaps influenced by some stereoscopic slides he had seen at the home of Douglas Fairbanks, he made the Klondike in 1898, during the height of the gold mania that drew many dreamers, entrepreneurs, and get-rich-quick schemers to Alaska in search of their fortunes, the setting. Significantly Chaplin, living in the middle of the consumption-oriented 1920s, rooted his film in a time equally known for its materialism. The fact that *The Gold Rush* appeared in the same year as two literary works that explored the abiding, almost pathological lure of wealth and success in America—*The Great Gatsby* and *An American Tragedy*—and just a year after Erich von Stroheim's *Greed*, suggests that a number of artists were perceiving and responding to the same cultural currents. And by setting his film during a gold rush, Chaplin enriched its epic and metaphorical possibilities.

However, after the opening shots, which show hundreds of fortune hunters laboring slowly up the Chilkoot Pass—one of them collapsing of exhaustion and ignored by his compatriots—the film does not really have much of an epic scope. On the contrary: after this opening, the cast of characters, except for a large group of extras and bit characters at the dance hall, is really quite small. It consists principally of Charlie, Big Jim (his fellow prospector), Black Larsen (a villain who dies midway through the film), Georgia (a dance-hall girl who falls in love with Charlie), and Jack (a rival to Charlie for Georgia's affections). Through the interactions of this smaller cast of characters arise both the comedy and the dramatic pathos, both of which were familiar to Chaplin fans.

In creating the comedy, Chaplin drew once again on his pantomimic skills honed in the English music halls. Anything he ever did in film is equalled by a number of his comic routines here, particularly Charlie's attempts to escape the sights of the shotgun that Jim and Black Larsen struggle over; the boiled shoe Thanksgiving dinner, replete with spaghetti shoestrings; and the "Oceana Roll" that Charlie performs for Georgia and his other dinner guests in his dream. In a final scene, the cabin set—a raised stage that rested on a fulcrum and tipped back and forth through the use of a pulley system—generates the comic climax. The cabin is ostensibly blown to the edge of a precipice, after which it tilts back and forth depending on which side Charlie and Jim are standing.[44]

But it may be the pathos generated by the relationship between Georgia and Charlie that constituted the film's most lasting contribution to the shaping of Chaplin's comic persona and his persistent appeal to viewers. In *The Gold Rush* Charlie is not like what Joan Mellen has called the "Big Bad Wolves" of American movies: the typical masculine stereotype of a strong, attractive, self-confident, and engaging man, represented in *The Gold Rush* by Jack.[45] Rather, Charlie is physically unimposing, even somewhat ridiculous in appearance, and often bumbling. Edgar Morin perceptively notes that in contrast to the typical romantic hero in movies, the comic hero portrayed so convincingly by Chaplin relates to women in quite a different manner. Whereas the relationship between the typical hero and women is sexual, the relationship between the comic hero and women is desexualized. Yet, says Morin, the comic hero is often in love: "his love is sublime because it is not founded on sexual domination and appropriation: it is a total gift of himself, like infantile or canine love." Though the comic hero may not seem to have as much to give, he is willing to give it all.[46]

In *The Gold Rush* Chaplin's idealized love for Georgia—his yearning for human intimacy and his contrasting fear of isolation—is symbolized by an important prop, a picture of Georgia. He initially gets the torn picture from the floor of the dance hall shortly after he first sees her. Later we learn, as does Georgia, that Charlie keeps it under the pillow of his bed. Even after he has struck it rich near the end of the film, Charlie retains the picture, now framed on a side table in his sleeping quarters. The film suggests that human fulfillment comes not from riches but ultimately from close human ties.[47]

This need for close bonds with others and the difficulty of achieving them lead directly to the two scenes of most profound pathos in *The Gold Rush*. They occur close to one another, three-quarters of the way through the film. The first comes on New Year's Eve, traditionally a time when people gather with friends to reflect on the past and look toward the future. Charlie, having invited the dance-hall girls to dine with him, has worked hard to earn some money to prepare a feast for them. They're late, but Chaplin dissolves from a shot of a table empty except for Charlie to one of the table surrounded by the women. Charlie entertains his guests with the Oceana Roll, but as he finishes and is being congratulated, Chaplin again dissolves to Charlie asleep at the otherwise empty table. The warmth of the crowded frame shifts to the coldness of the nearly empty one, and elicits strong empathy from the viewer. As in *The Bank*, *Shoulder Arms*, and *The Idle Class*, Charlie's accomplishments take place only in his dreams. But here, because of the situation and the characterization, the effect is deeper and richer than in the earlier films.

Only a few moments after this scene, the second prominent situation of pathos appears. Noticing that it is nearly midnight and his party a failure, the despairing Charlie makes his way to the dance hall. Just as he reaches the building, Chaplin frames Charlie in an extremely powerful way: he stands in the frigid winter air, alone, outside a window, while inside the dance hall people embrace, celebrate, and collectively ring in the new year. Literally an outsider looking in, Charlie is both spatially and psychologically distant from the festive crowd. The effect of these two scenes must be experienced to be fully apprehended.

The final scene of *The Gold Rush*, superficially a happy ending and arguably forced, fashioned with the box office in mind, is actually much more aesthetically complex than it first appears. After Charlie and Jim find their gold, they become millionaires and are leaving the Klondike on a ship. Jim seems happy after striking it rich, but Charlie still seems empty and incomplete without Georgia. For reporters, Charlie changes back into his prospecting clothes. He tumbles down a stairway to find himself at Georgia's feet, and—when she thinks he is a stowaway—is protected by her. They whisper, apparently decide to marry, and are being photographed by a newspaperman as the film ends.

This final scene does give the audience its "happy ending," realizing the romance Charlie has desired. But it is more complicated in two ways. First, Chaplin was again working in submerged autobiography. Like Charlie, Chaplin went from rags to riches in an extremely short time, finding his gold mine in the movie industry. Just as Charlie had to get into his old clothes at the end of the film to satisfy reporters and win Georgia, so Chaplin had to get into his tramp costume to satisfy movie audiences. Also like Charlie, Chaplin often found himself a lonely, isolated man, both before he struck it rich (notably in the Hetty Kelly incident) and after. The pressbook for *The Gold Rush* shows that Chaplin was conscious of the parallels between Charlie and himself: one proposed newspaper headline reads "Chaplin Comedy an Autobiography: The Material Success of Charlie Chaplin at Last Has Never Satisfied His Soul."[48] With one marriage failed and the second marriage already on the rocks, as will be discussed in Chapter 4, the melancholic Chaplin must have yearned for a relationship of trust and mutual affection shorn of role playing and status, though his desire for control in his dealings with others made it hard for him to achieve such a relationship.

The film's ending is also more complicated by Chaplin's self-referential look at what he was doing in his role as film director and producer. At the very end of the original version of the film, Charlie and Georgia are posing for the photographer. Just before the picture is snapped, however, Charlie turns and kisses Georgia. In a title, the photographer replies: "Oh! You've spoilt the picture." If we take the photographer to be the filmmaker's spokesman, we see Chaplin the self-conscious director telling alert viewers that he knows the happy ending, the embrace, and the kiss in one sense "spoil" the film: after all the hunger, brutality, and cruelty in the film narrative, a coincidental gold strike and even more coincidental reconciliation of lovers seems implausible if not contradictory. Yes, it is, Chaplin hints in his conclusion, and like Murnau's *The Last Laugh* a year earlier, a happy ending is subtly undercut by a self-referential gesture.[49]

The Gold Rush works as epic, as comedy, as conveyer of dramatic pathos, as submerged autobiography, and as self-referential exploration of happy endings. Charlie had surely endeared himself to a large mass audience and added to Chaplin's star status. But the promotion of the film, the most elaborate and systematic effort Chaplin had overseen to that time, also contributed to his star image and suggests how Chaplin sought to shape that image in the mid-1920s.

To place the promotion of *The Gold Rush* in context, a few words should be said about advertising in the film industry. Film historians have shown that advertising became important early. Advertising was important to the development of the film industry not simply because it directed people to individual films but also because it helped set up the ground rules for what was acceptable and even expected in film production. In the first decade of the century, film production companies like Edison advertised to distributors and exhibitors by using catalogues that listed and "pitched" their films. By the next decade, fan magazines emphasizing stars appeared on the scene. As the studio system began to establish itself, studios set up publicity departments, which in turn provided newspaper reviewers and theater owners with information like pressbooks that would help advertise locally. According to one film historian, the early catalogue advertisements "exhibit many of the exchange-values the industry has consistently promoted as the qualities in their films: novelty, specific popular genres, brand names, 'realism,' authenticity, spectacle, stars, and certain creators of the product whose skills as artists were considered acknowledged."[50] If we can add to this list a tendency to hyperbolize the qualities of a particular star or story or set design, we have a pretty good idea of the kind and degree of characteristics which were typically emphasized in advertisements for Hollywood films. With this list in mind, the promotion for *The Gold Rush* seems in many ways typical, in a few ways unusual.

Perhaps the most important piece of promotion literature for *The Gold Rush* was the program prepared for the film's opening at Grauman's Chinese Theater.[51] Besides listing the events that preceded the feature—which included an overture by Grauman's Egyptian Orchestra, with Julius K. Johnson at the "Mighty Egyptian Organ," and a "Festival of Dancing Ice Skaters"—the text of the program gives an idea of Chaplin's artistic reputation as he wished to project it. Hyperbole is used to stress Chaplin's apparently unique talent for movies: "Chaplin was the biggest man on the lot from the time he made his first comedy." A variation on that theme—and one that Chaplin and his publicists often referred to throughout the 1920s after his association with United Artists began—was the assertion that his films were more serious and of much higher quality than the typical studio-made film. As opposed to the "factory system of movies," *The Gold Rush* "was never restricted by definite schedule or time clock methods, but inspired by Chaplin with a passion for perfection as his only taskmaster." Chaplin's being is invested with a kind of transcendence: "Within a short time after his entry into pictures directors complained to the powers-to-be [*sic*] that Chaplin wanted his own way and could not 'take direction.' It was great talent trying to assert itself and climb out of the embryo into the uniform of the greatest actor in the world. He was conscious of ability in his soul, as great talent ever is." Finally, expanding some of the publicity statements that accompanied *A Woman of Paris*, the program emphasizes how painstakingly Chaplin works and how much money he has been willing to spend to make films that satisfy his artistic genius. Syd Grauman writes that on the day he visited the set, only three set-ups were completed, though each was "shot at least twenty times." A section called "What Was Used in Making" employs numbers to express the epic scope of the film: 500 workmen used 239,577 board feet of lumber, 2,000 feet of garden hose, and 7,000 feet of rope. The snow was simulated by using 285 tons of salt, 100 barrels of flour, and four carloads of confetti for blizzards. In Richard Dyer's terms, to be a star, one must be portrayed as extraordinary, and the program stresses this dimension of Chaplin through its emphasis on star, novelty, and spectacle.

The pressbook, assembled by a United Artists publicity staff under the guidance of Chaplin and his own staff to help exhibitors promote the film, reiterates many of these themes (see Figure 9). One of the proposed headlines to pass on to newspapers was "Opening Scenes Cost $50,000," which uses budget figures to sell the film, a ploy with which contemporary film viewers are familiar. Two more—"One Man Power in Chaplin Picture" and "*The Gold Rush* Is Chaplin's Greatest"— implied that Chaplin's name alone sold tickets, as indeed it did by 1925. The pressbook suggested that exhibitors encourage the sponsorship of a Chaplin walking contest for children, and it included a number of telegrams of congratulation from Hollywood luminaries like Fairbanks, Pickford, William Hart, and Norma Talmadge (all of whom had been or were associated with United Artists). Among the other telegrams was an interesting tribute from rival Buster Keaton, who called the film "the most impressive comedy ever made." The pressbook even carried reviews and articles that could be signed by the newspaper's movie reviewer. One, describing a visit to the Chaplin's set, was modestly headed, "Chaplin's Genius Supreme on Set in Famous Studio." If anything, the pressbook was even more extreme than the program in promoting the film and stressing Chaplin's genius. And though the promotion for *The Gold Rush* emphasized a number of the same qualities found in other Hollywood advertising, it was helping to shape and reinforce a distinct star image for Chaplin: the independent, even solitary creative genius, admired by the greats of the industry, who was willing to spend whatever money and effort necessary to achieve perfection in his films.

Some of the reviews of the film, one in particular, were as enthu-

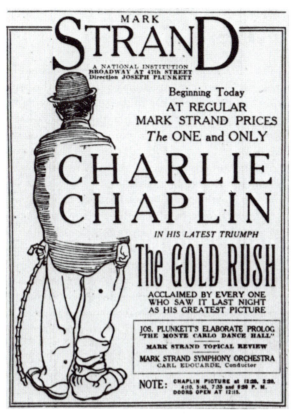

9. The long-familiar Charlie helps advertise
The Gold Rush in 1925.

siastic as the promotion material. In its prerelease review of the film, *Variety* was extravagant: "*The Gold Rush* is a distinct triumph for Charlie Chaplin from both artistic and commercial standpoints, and is a picture sure to create a veritable riot at theater box offices. It is the greatest and most elaborate comedy ever filmed and will stand for years to come as the biggest hit in its field, just as *The Birth of a Nation* still withstands its many competitors in the dramatic field."[52] If such a review seemed too good to be true from the box-office weathervane of trade journals, it was. A month later, at the New York opening of the film, *Variety* reviewed the film again, this time more circumspectly. *The Gold Rush* "may have impressed Chaplin's friends on the coast to that degree," the New York reviewer wrote, "but as shown at the Strand, New York, it does not live up to the rave from the west. It's just a good Chaplin comedy." Despite these qualifications, however, the reviewer adds that "in any kind of show, it will draw a heavy gross."[53]

Ivan St. Johns in *Photoplay* followed the line established by the second *Variety* review: "That it is a great development in the comedy field, or that it brings a new comedy era to the screen certainly is not true. It is simply ten reels of a very good Chaplin comedy, which ought to be enough for anybody, but it is no more."[54] In the *New York Times* Mordaunt Hall judged the film "by all means Chaplin's supreme effort, as back of the ludicrous touches there is a truth, a glimpse into the disappointments of Chaplin's early life."[55]

Two points are worth noting here. First, as Hall's comment suggests, some observers were beginning to see hints of Chaplin's autobiography woven into the fabric of his films, a blending that helped his star image in the 1920s but hindered him later on. Second, the reviews show that Chaplin was becoming so highly regarded by the reviewers that their role was not to judge whether his films were good enough to recommend but rather to decide where on the spectrum of Chaplin's greatness a particular film belonged. Like the promotion and the film itself, the reviews of *The Gold Rush* showed a star at the height of his popularity.

Cultivating the Intelligentsia

As well as making films that were consistently successful with mass audiences and daily newspaper reviewers, Chaplin also managed by the mid-1920s to do something no other Hollywood star had: win the respect of American intellectuals. This occurred during a period of literary renaissance in America, which Malcolm Cowley would later call the "second flowering" of American literature. It was stimulated in part by a lively group of literary, political, and cultural magazines— like the *Dial*, the *New Republic*, and *Vanity Fair*—the most important of which were centered in New York City. As Chaplin's fame enabled him to make contacts there, his relationships with some of these intellectuals, as well as their friendships among themselves, eventually led to frequent praise for Chaplin in their articles and books as the first and only important American screen artist. Public kudos from such circles gave Chaplin's star image a legitimacy among the intelligentsia rarely attained by an American filmmaker before the studio system broke up. A look at the activities and writings of Max Eastman, Waldo Frank, Stark Young, Gilbert Seldes, Edmund Wilson, and John Peale Bishop demonstrates the dynamics that enabled Chaplin to become a darling of the younger and generally antigenteel intellectuals in the 1920s.[56]

The best place to start is the fall of 1919, an unhappy time in Chaplin's life: his infant son had died in July after living only three days, his marriage with Mildred Harris was unraveling, and he was feeling oppressed by his First National contract (*A Day's Pleasure* would be released in December). For some reason he decided to attend a political lecture by Max Eastman in the Philharmonic Auditorium. Eastman was, in his own words, "about the only Socialist agitator who had opposed the World War and supported the Russian revolution, and yet managed to stay out of jail."[57] After the lecture, Chaplin visited Eastman backstage, praised his "restraint," contributed a modest $25 to his magazine, the *Liberator*, and invited him to dinner. Their friendship grew, and they remained good friends until Eastman's politics turned to the right in the late 1930s and the 1940s.

This friendship helped Chaplin meet other Greenwich Village intellectuals when he took a trip to New York City in November 1920 (MA, p. 247). Perhaps partly because his divorce had just become final and work on *The Kid* was nearly completed, Chaplin was ready to make new acquaintances. He visited the editorial offices of *Vanity Fair*, where he met, among others, its young managing editor, Edmund Wilson. On the same trip, he began to encounter a number of other young intellectuals and artists, including some of the Provincetown Players. In his autobiography Chaplin also recalled meeting on this visit both critic Waldo Frank (who had already written on him—not entirely positively) and poet Hart Crane (who later wrote a poem, "Chaplinesque," inspired by *The Kid*) (MA, p. 248). All in all, Chaplin's 1920 visit provided the film star with a nucleus of intellectual acquaintances who helped advance his career through their writings and their influence on others throughout the decade and after.[58]

Although Eastman later wrote a good deal about Chaplin, sometimes repeating his stories of their acquaintance from book to book, he did not write much on Chaplin in the 1920s.[59] Eastman's influence was more personal, for in addition to the interactions already noted, Chaplin also visited Eastman in New York City on his way to and from Europe in 1921, referring to him in *My Trip Abroad* as "one of my best friends."[60]

Waldo Frank wrote considerably about Chaplin both before and after he met the comedian, but more positively after he had met Chaplin personally. Frank, six years younger than Eastman and nearly the same age as Chaplin, had earned an M.A. from Yale and was the founder and editor of the *Seven Arts* in its short (1916–1917) but influential life. His first reference to Chaplin was in a *Seven Arts* article in 1917, "Valedictory to a Theatrical Season." He wrote: "Chaplin is an extremely brilliant clown but also an unhealthy one," a comment that sounds much like those the genteel critics of Chaplin's "vulgarity" were making at much the same time. Later, in *Our America* (1919) Frank made similar observations, acclaiming Chaplin as "our most significant and most authentic dramatic artist" but objecting to the "sophistications in Chaplin's work that are not healthy."[61]

Yet meeting the star seemed to make people revise their negative opinion of him. Chaplin recalls his 1920 meeting with Frank in his autobiography, calling him "the first to write seriously about me" and adding, "naturally, we became very good friends" (MA, p. 248), a comment that underlines Chaplin's tendency to surround himself with admirers. Frank also remembers the meeting and recalls that Chaplin thanked him for his positive comments in *Our America*; in Frank's view, Chaplin was grateful to have a "highbrow" take his work seriously. After they became personally acquainted, Frank's writings strongly defended Chaplin the artist. When he reprinted his 1917 essay in *Salvos* (1924), Frank appended a note: "The injustice which this essay does to Mr. Chaplin by a total disregard for the pure aesthetic virtue of his art, I have righted. . . . Mr. Chaplin's art is far from unhealthy. His art is indeed a symbol of health in a complexly morbid world."[62] Frank had begun to identify the comic world created by Chaplin as a viable alternative to the materialism of American culture.

The next year Frank published his first piece focused entirely on Chaplin, the essay that contributed most of any by Frank to Chaplin's star image. Titled "Funny-Legs," it appeared in the first volume of the *New Yorker*, a new magazine aimed at a sophisticated urban audience. The article stressed Chaplin's worldwide fame: Frank reported that when Chaplin visited a circus in Paris while on his European tour, the audience feverishly chanted, "Charlot!" In addition to remarking on "the intellectuals of New York and Paris [who turned Chaplin's] stunts into logarithmic mazes as if he were Einstein," Frank portrayed Chaplin as an enigmatic, questing genius. He recounted a long evening spent discussing Schopenhauer and Spinoza with Chaplin. Sometime during the night, according to Frank, Chaplin reflected on his dissatisfactions in spite of his fame: "I don't know . . . I may retire. I may study Sanskrit." Chaplin is a man of masks, in Frank's view, a man of many faces and possibilities, who is trying to find answers to life. His quests leave him "lost in a world of which he is the king, and which he does not love and which distrusts him, knowing him different from it."[63] The essay provides an admiring, penetrating personal view of

Chaplin and stresses, among other qualities, Chaplin's melancholia and his interest in the life of the mind.

Another intellectual to take Chaplin's work seriously in this period was Stark Young (b. 1881), a native Mississippian who earned an M.A. from Columbia University in 1902 and who taught literature at the universities of Mississippi and Texas and Amherst College from 1904 to 1921. Thereafter, he moved to New York City and served on the editorial staffs of *Theater Arts Monthly* and the *New Republic*, where he was drama critic. Young was a demanding and fastidious critic with classical tastes, yet in 1922 he published an open letter to Chaplin, "Dear Mr. Chaplin," in the *New Republic*, which praised Chaplin's achievements, particularly his comic persona ("You have created one of the great clowns of all time") and his acting style ("The greatest actor in English you are easily. You have a technique completely finished").[64]

Yet Young's letter was not simply a tribute to Chaplin's brilliance; it also urged Chaplin to become more ambitious, to "go on to a larger field." Because Chaplin was such a gifted artist, Young suggested, he should break out of the "one thing" he had so far done—silent comedies—and do *Liliom* or *He Who Gets Slapped* or *Peer Gynt*. Or even better, Young advised Chaplin, "You could do new things written by you or for you, things in which you would use your full endowment, comic and otherwise." Like Frank, Young observed an unfulfilled yearning in the mask of Charlie, "a poetry and a music and a poignancy that eats into you." Tap that in your art, Young advised, and you will satisfy that most demanding of critics: yourself. Written after profiles of Chaplin that, as we have seen, portrayed Chaplin as the lonely and "Hamlet-like" artist, this article not only helped legitimate Chaplin as an important artist to *New Republic* readers but also helped to reinforce that dimension of Chaplin's star image that portrayed him as a serious, ambitious, and versatile artist.

Young's praise apparently did not fall on deaf ears. Shortly after the open letter was published, Chaplin began *A Woman of Paris*. When visiting New York City for the opening of that film, Chaplin asked Young to dinner, in part to thank him for his praise and in part, it seems, to seek more positive publicity about his new film. Young came away from the dinner even more impressed with Chaplin than before. In a letter to Julian Huxley, he rhapsodized: "A very remarkable person, as well as an extraordinary artist. Talks amazingly. . . . I found him a very congenial mind . . . the most interesting person I have seen in a long time except Duse."[65] As we have seen, Young did subsequently praise *A Woman of Paris*. Despite their divergent political opinions—

Young later became a contributor to the famous Southern Agrarian manifesto, *I'll Take My Stand*—Chaplin always remained high in Young's esteem.

Another admirer of Chaplin, though from a perspective quite different from Young's, was Gilbert Seldes (b. 1893). A contemporary and friend of Edmund Wilson (b. 1895) and John Peale Bishop (b. 1899), Seldes was a Phi Beta Kappa graduate of Harvard University in 1914, a correspondent during World War I, and an editor for the *Dial* from 1920 to 1923. Most important for our purposes, Seldes was the author of the first sustained examination and defense of American popular culture, *The Seven Lively Arts* (1924).[66] Like Frank, Seldes was interested in what moved the "real America," and he sought to discover this in a variety of American popular entertainments: ragtime, jazz, Ziegfeld productions, the satire of Mr. Dooley and Ring Lardner, circus clowns, popular dance, and even Krazy Kat comic strips. Unlike high culture, Seldes argued, these popular amusements did not seek to uplift or express the sublime and tragic. Nevertheless, in their desire to entertain, they often were as imaginative and as stimulating as high culture. And one of the most imaginative and stimulating of popular artists in America was Chaplin.

Seldes treated Chaplin briefly in his book's first chapter, which focused on the Keystone films. But his central examination of Chaplin's art appeared in Chapter 3, " 'I Am Here Today': Charlie Chaplin." Seldes found it miraculous that "a figure wholly in the tradition of the great clowns," which required "creative energy, freshness, inventiveness, change," should arise in the 1910s and 1920s in America, "for neither the time nor the country in which Charlie works is exceptionally favorable to such a phenomenon" (p. 41). Like many young American intellectuals coming to maturity during or after World War I, Seldes, by defending Chaplin against charges of vulgarity, was challenging what he perceived as the outmoded values of his genteel elders.

Demonstrating his awareness of the French admiration for Chaplin, Seldes distinguished between the person, Charlie Chaplin, and the mask, Charlot, just as Frank did in his *New Yorker* essay the following year. (Both Seldes and Frank lived in France for periods in the early 1920s, and they probably helped transmit the French influence on the American intellectual acceptance of Chaplin.) The name Charlot, wrote Seldes, "will serve for that figure on the screen, the created image which is, and at the same time is more than Charlie Chaplin, and is less" (p. 43). Beginning as a comic persona familiar to children, then to "the people," after which he became "universally known and admired" with films like *The Bank* and *Shoulder Arms*, Chaplin finally was considered, after *The Kid*, as a "great artist," not just a comic persona. For Seldes, as for many others after him, the making of *The Kid* marked a new stage in the development of Chaplin the artist.

Yet Seldes especially admired early films like *The Pawnshop*. Unlike Young, Seldes urged Chaplin to continue in the vein of comic vitality that he established in the short films: "the surest way to be wrong about Charlie is to forget the Keystones" (p. 52). In fact, Seldes took a direct and extended swipe at Young's open letter to Chaplin in his own essay. To Young's suggestion that Chaplin appeal to "a more cultured audience," Seldes responded: "Oh Lord! these are the phrases which are offered as bribes to the one man who has destroyed the world and created it in his own image" (p. 53). Rather than having Chaplin become serious and develop his "literary" side, Seldes, referring to the French name for Charlie, urged him to remember the early Charlot, the one announced by the billboards outside the nickel movie theaters: "I am here today." To Seldes, this terse phrase constituted "the beginning before time and the end without end of his wisdom and his loveliness" (p. 54). Thus, as well as praising Chaplin's artistry in the 1920s, Seldes celebrated the comic inventiveness of the early Charlot.

One of Seldes's intellectual compatriots in the early 1920s was Edmund Wilson. Though Wilson is known to us today as the magisterial man of letters who authored monuments like *Axel's Castle* and who generally abhorred popular culture, he was also an early advocate of Chaplin. Wilson first publicly discussed Chaplin in a review of *The Seven Lively Arts*. The review may partly have been a favor to Seldes, who once got Wilson a job as press agent for the Swedish Ballet when it was visiting the United States.[67] Not long after, Seldes sent a copy of *The Seven Lively Arts* to Wilson, who—without giving up his disdain for much popular art—wrote a fairly positive review of the book, calling it "a valuable and enormously entertaining book on the vulgar arts."[68]

Shortly after reviewing Seldes's book, Wilson did meet Chaplin again, thanks to his job with the Swedish Ballet. In February 1924 Wilson, having written a comic ballet for the troupe, traveled to California to try to persuade Chaplin to appear in it. Wilson visited the set of *The Gold Rush*, and talked with Chaplin there and then again at his home. Though Chaplin seemed amused at Wilson's ballet, later published as *Cronkhite's Clocks*, he "explained that he always had to do everything himself, invent and play his own character." Wilson came away from the experience impressed: "[Chaplin] was good mannered and perfectly natural. . . . When one talked to him, one found that his instant reactions were as fresh, as authentically personal, as those of a poet

like E. E. Cummings."[69] Wilson admired Chaplin for his creative independence, something Wilson himself always sought.

The following year Wilson wrote his only extended piece on Chaplin, a review of *The Gold Rush* for the *New Republic*.[70] Wilson began by
noting that gags were the most important part of silent film comedy
and by giving examples of gags from the films of Keaton, Lloyd, and
Fairbanks. But the only comedian, he wrote, "doing anything really
distinguished with this comedy of gags is, of course, Charlie Chaplin."
To Wilson, Chaplin's ability to extend gags through the use of situation and pantomime—as in the tilting cabin scene of *The Gold Rush*—
constituted one of his central artistic accomplishments. Wilson also
praised Chaplin for his creation of "deliberately ironic or pathetic situations," but, in his characteristically probing manner, suggested that
the "straight situations and the gags rather jar together." Although
Wilson was accurate in noting that "Chaplin has gained in reputation
with the critics and the sophisticated public," he was probably less accurate when he suggested that he was losing some of his original popular audience: *The Gold Rush* was a great popular success, grossing
over $4 million in its first several years, giving Chaplin $2 million in
profits, United Artists $1 million.[71]

Wilson was prescient, however, when he suggested that Chaplin's
films, when compared with those of Lloyd or Keaton, *looked* old-fashioned, even more so than old-fashioned movies. To Wilson, Chaplin's
gift was "primarily the actor's, not the artist's or director's." Particularly after sound was introduced in Hollywood and Chaplin continued
to make nondialogue films, reviewers frequently pointed out that even
given Chaplin's enormous gift with pantomime, his films were stylisti-
cally primitive. Although Wilson's charge did not become a widely
shared part of Chaplin's star image for some time, it is an early expression of an idea that would later plague Chaplin as he attempted to
sustain his star image in the 1940s and 1950s.

Despite his reservations, however, Wilson concluded that Chaplin's
recent comedies, like *The Kid* and *The Gold Rush*, "with their gags and
their overtones of tragedy, their adventures half absurd, half realistic,
their mythical hero, now a figure of poetry, now a type out of the
funny papers, represent the height of his achievement." Thus the man
whose reputation as a discriminating reviewer and critic was growing
bestowed his critical approval on Chaplin.

Chaplin's reputation among the young intellectual elite in America
is also evidenced in the writings of John Peale Bishop, a classmate of
Wilson's at Princeton who also knew Seldes. An editor of *Vanity Fair*
for a time, Bishop was primarily known in the 1920s and 1930s as a

critic of contemporary literature. He wrote two thoughtful essays on movies in the mid-1920s, however—reflecting the growing legitimacy of movies as a subject of aesthetic discourse—and Chaplin figured in both of them.

The first, "The Movies as an Art: *The Last Laugh*," appeared in *Vanity Fair* in June 1925, a few months before the opening of *The Gold Rush*.[72] The essay is structured as a dialogue between a screenwriter and a critic, and the debate suggests something about the divergent attitudes toward the movies in America at the time. Intellectuals were beginning to admit that the German Expressionists and, later, Soviets like Eisenstein were capable of making genuinely artistic films while American studio films were simply light or vulgar entertainments. In fact, it is probably fair to say that the regular reviewing of movies in the more intellectual journals—almost unheard of in the mid-1920s but commonplace by the mid-1930s—resulted in part from these kinds of foreign films, which differed in varying degrees from the standard Hollywood product. They seemed to such writers more challenging, visually "artistic," and complex than American films.[73]

In Bishop's essay, the critic defended the more elitist position—that only foreign films like *The Last Laugh* can genuinely be considered art—while the screenwriter defended American films. Notably, however, the screenwriter often used Chaplin as an example of the best in American movies, and even the critic had positive comments on Chaplin's work. When the critic praised the visual economy of *The Last Laugh*, the screenwriter replied that Chaplin's films, even his early ones, were also "virtually without titles." Even though the critic thought *The Last Laugh* superior to any Chaplin film, he admitted that the best of Chaplin's work possessed a "comic poetry" in a high vein.

Bishop's other essay, "Sex Appeal in the Movies," which appeared in the *New Republic* in 1927, countered the notion that sex appeal sells movies. He argued that, on the contrary, the actors who had managed to remain popular for a considerable time in the movies were those who projected characters that were not particularly sexual. Though Bishop mentioned Pickford, Keaton, and others, he spent more time discussing Chaplin. The crux of his remarks were that if the Chaplin persona was in love, the woman he loved remained "mysterious and remote," and if he was married, as in *Pay Day*, the persona interacted with his wife like a "capricious little boy doing his best to arrange things amicably with a severe parent." Though his analysis was convincing, more important here is the implicit status Chaplin had assumed by November 1927. At one point Bishop referred to Chaplin's "middle period," after the Mutual films but before *A Woman of Paris*,

10. Portrait of Chaplin in 1925 by photographer Edward Steichen; reprinted by permission of Joanna T. Steichen. Print courtesy International Museum of Photography, George Eastman House, Rochester.

and he also stated, almost as if it were a given that no one would argue about, that Chaplin "alone of all the actors of the screen actually arrives at creating a separate world." The assumption of the essay, one that Chaplin surely relished, was that Chaplin was the unquestioned king of comedy in Hollywood and the premiere actor in the movie industry.

If we collect these treatments of Chaplin by Frank, Young, Seldes, Wilson, and Bishop, we can see that Wilson was accurate when he observed in 1925 that Chaplin's reputation among critics and more sophisticated movie viewers had grown considerably in the first half of the decade. Out of Frank's divided view of Chaplin emerged—after Frank met and became friendly with the star—a glowing, almost reverent picture of the melancholy film artist. His meeting with Stark Young at a critical time—the New York City release of *A Woman of Paris*—earned Chaplin a well-placed friend who remained a devoted admirer for the rest of his life. Chaplin's meetings with Wilson; Seldes's defense of popular art, particularly Chaplin's; and the mutual friendship of Wilson, Seldes, and Bishop helped Chaplin get critical attention from these three intellectuals. These were by no means the only American intellectuals to write on Chaplin in the early and mid-1920s, nor did they always agree on what constituted his central artistic contributions. What is important is that they discussed his work seriously and thus gave Chaplin's star image an artistic status higher than any other American film artist of the era. Photographs of Chaplin by prominent photographers only reinforced this status (see Figure 10).

Chaplin's star image had solidifed. Though Charlie still constituted an important part of that image, he had become more than a slapstick anarchist: he was also associated with romantic, often unrequited, yearnings and the pathos engendered by loneliness, suffering, or rejection. In addition, especially after *My Trip Abroad*, *The Kid*, and *A Woman of Paris*, Chaplin the man began to figure prominently in the star image. This man had artistic and intellectual aspirations, he at times worked his own experiences into his films (especially his experiences of childhood suffering and adult loneliness), and he was willing to take risks like *A Woman of Paris* to demonstrate that his creative versatility extended beyond performance. The success of *The Gold Rush* and the positive attention of the intelligentsia (thanks in part to Chaplin's personal charm and even calculated shrewdness) underlined Chaplin's growing reputation in the mid-1920s as the foremost star and serious film artist in Hollywood.

4

Struggling through the Twenties

Chaplin and Lita Grey

In his autobiography Chaplin says that while in New York City for the premiere of *The Gold Rush*, he had an unexplained "collapse" that so frightened him he wanted to make out a will (MA, p. 305). Though he recovered quickly, the collapse was symbolically apt, for it ushered in a difficult half decade for Chaplin the star. The period, in Chaplin's own words, "was one of great professional prosperity but also of private grief."[1] Between 1925 and the release of *City Lights* (1931), Chaplin suffered through a second divorce and serious tax problems, struggled with the aesthetic challenge of sound films, and witnessed the onset of the Great Depression. All posed challenges to what seemed in 1925 to be Chaplin's unassailable public reputation.

The second divorce provided the first test for Chaplin's star image. Following his divorce from Mildred Harris, Chaplin's private life in the early 1920s generated little negative publicity. Nearly everyone who knew Chaplin in these years and wrote about him testified that he was an extremely engaging, charming, and magnetic personality. This, combined with the star status he had achieved in the film industry and the fact that he was again a bachelor, made him very attractive to women. Between 1921 and 1924 his name was linked with a number of women, among them Peggy Hopkins Joyce (the original "Gold digger"), Claire Sheridan (the sculptor and cousin of Winston Churchill), and Pola Negri (the movie star).[2] As might be expected, the fan magazines and newspaper syndicates were interested in these relationships, and some sources even alleged that Sheridan and Negri were both engaged to Chaplin at one time or another in the early 1920s.

However, Chaplin's relationship with Lillita McMurray—whose stage name was Lita Grey—was probably the most wrenching, destructive, and unfortunate relationship he had with a woman in his life. The circumstances of their marriage in November 1924 and their subsequent divorce, which became official in August 1927, not only caused both of them extreme mental grief and anguish but also posed Chaplin with the first serious threat to his star image since his rise to preeminent stardom. Furthermore, it planted some of the seeds of acrimony among the public that would grow and later blossom when his reputation was seriously sagging in the 1940s.

Telling the full story of the courtship, marriage, separation, and divorce of Chaplin and Grey is an impossible task. Chaplin does not mention Grey by name in his autobiography, where he disposes of their entire relationship tersely: "During the filming of *The Gold Rush* I married for the second time. Because we have two grown sons of whom I am very fond, I will not go into any details. For two years we were married and tried to make a go of it, but it was hopeless and ended in a great deal of bitterness" (MA, p. 305).

Lita Grey, however, discusses their relationship in great detail, using fourteen of the twenty-two chapters of her memoirs to explain from her point of view how their relationship developed from the time she visited Chaplin's studio in hopes of getting the lead in *The Gold Rush* until the divorce settlement. Any account will necessarily be tinged by the fact that only one side of the story has been told.

Despite this, it is possible to outline what occurred and to describe in particular the tremendous strain Chaplin experienced for a variety of reasons in January and February of 1927. Grey first met Chaplin through a neighbor, Chuck Riesner, who served as Chaplin's assistant director in the early 1920s. Through Riesner, the twelve-year-old Lillita got a job as an extra in *The Kid*. Chaplin was so impressed by her appearance that he soon cast her as the angel temptress in the heaven sequence of the film. A short time later, Lillita and her mother played brief roles as maids in *The Idle Class*. Early in 1924 Grey auditioned and won the role of Georgia in *The Gold Rush*. She signed a contract in March. Chaplin was attracted to her, a feeling that she reciprocated, and by the fall of 1924 she was pregnant with Chaplin's child. In November they were married in Enpalme, Mexico. That same month Chaplin announced that Georgia Hale had replaced Grey in *The Gold Rush*, for Lita wished to devote full time to her new role as Chaplin's wife. Charles Chaplin, Jr., was born on 5 May 1925, though Chaplin managed to keep the birth a secret until it was announced (with an altered birth certificate, according to Grey) on June 28.[3] Though the marriage began intolerably, according to Grey, she and Chaplin had a brief period of rapprochement after the birth of the baby. By the summer of 1925 she was again pregnant, and gave birth on 30 March 1926 to their second son, Sydney, named for Chaplin's half brother.

In the spring and summer of 1926 the marriage deteriorated. Grey writes that Chaplin would take her to an occasional party or premiere "for appearances' sake," but otherwise would have virtually nothing to do with her or their sons: with *The Circus* well under way, he apparently was completely absorbed by it, as he tended to be in the midst of a film production. Grey, finding the situation hopeless, asked Chaplin for a divorce in the fall. Chaplin told her to take a vacation to think things over, which she did, sailing for Hawaii with her mother and oldest son in November. Upon returning, she decided to separate immediately, and on December 2 newspapers reported in front-page stories that Chaplin's wife had left him and had taken their children with her. A day later, they reported that the split had been declared permanent and that Grey asked for $1 million in alimony payments.[4]

In January 1927 the Chaplin divorce case became a national controversy. On January 10 Grey's lawyer and uncle, Edwin McMurray, filed a divorce complaint against Chaplin, Chaplin's studio, United Artists, Alf Reeves (Chaplin's business manager), and a number of banks that held Chaplin's assets. Grey's uncle wrote the complaint without letting her see it until just before it was filed. Though her most damaging complaints were included in the document, she says in her memoirs that a number of them were also "cleverly, shockingly enlarged upon or distorted." By January 12 copies of the complaint were being sold on the street corners of Los Angeles. As Grey observed, "by the liberal standards of the 1960's, phrases like these might seem comparatively tame. But in 1927 such words as 'abnormal,' 'unnatural,' 'degenerate' and 'indecent'—especially as applied to the world-beloved Charlie Chaplin—struck several million sensation seekers with bombshell force."[5] The Chaplin image was under siege.

In addition to the divorce complaint, Chaplin was also worried at the time about an unauthorized biography of him, written by a former employee, Jim Tully, who had worked for Chaplin for eighteen months during the production of *The Gold Rush*. One of the reasons Chaplin left for New York City in January was to visit the offices of *Pictorial Review*, which had announced that the four-part Chaplin profile would appear from January through April. If his pleas to halt publication fell on deaf ears, Chaplin was prepared to use his considerable legal means—once successful with *Charlie Chaplin's Own Story* in 1916—to prevent dissemination of the series. After learning of the articles and worrying about how the possibly negative publicity would affect the impending divorce, Chaplin's lawyers sued Tully on January 8, then sought an injunction against *Pictorial Review* on January 14 to prevent publication of the remaining issues. On February 3 the courts refused to issue the injunction, and the articles were published as scheduled under the title, "Charlie Chaplin: His *Real* Life Story."[6]

If the divorce complaint and unauthorized biography were not

11. "The Gold Rush": Cartoonist William Cargill
dramatizes Chaplin's plight over divorce and tax
problems, January 1927. Reprinted by
permission of *Emporia Gazette*.

enough, Chaplin learned shortly after arriving in New York City that
federal tax authorities were claiming he owed a huge sum in back
taxes. The *New York Times* reported on January 18 that government
tax officials, like Lita Grey's lawyers, were seeking a lien against Chaplin's assets, in this case to ensure payment of back taxes. On the 22nd
the government claimed that Chaplin owed $1.135 million in personal
income taxes, going back as far as 1918. Chaplin's money was placed
into receivership by January 20. Not until January 28 was he able to
free any of his New York funds, but that same day the government
filed another lien, this one against United Artists. The financial pressures on the independent filmmaker, with both his wife and the government claiming over a million dollars, must have been overwhelming. Although the tax problem dropped out of the news (Chaplin
didn't settle with the government until 10 February 1928), coming as
it did in the middle of the divorce controversy, it surely added to the
strain.[7] The cartoon that originally appeared in the *Emporia Gazette*
suggests graphically how Chaplin must have felt in this rush for his
gold (see Figure 11).

On January 16 Chaplin's doctor reported that Chaplin was "suffering from a serious nervous breakdown."[8] With his funds placed in receivership and charges of abnormality emanating from certain quarters, the Chaplin story remained hot and constant news throughout January and into February. Thereafter, occasional stories continued to appear through the summer, with Chaplin's answer to the divorce complaint and his counter-complaint reported on June 3, and Grey's answer to Chaplin's cross-complaint covered on July 2. After all the buildup by the press in January, the coverage of settlement itself was relatively quiet. On August 22, Lita Grey—who had been seeking $1.25 million—was awarded $825,000: $625,000 for herself, plus a $100,000 trust fund for each son. Chaplin was ordered to pay Grey $375,000 immediately, $100,000 a year in 1928 and 1929, and $50,000 in 1930. He was also ordered to pay $10,000 in expenses to Grey for the separation period, $22,000 receivers' costs, $2,100 court costs, and $1,000 per month for the children for five years while the trust funds were being set up. Chaplin himself was not in the courtroom when the decision was announced.[9] For the next four months, Chaplin's name was barely mentioned in the *New York Times*. It must have been a relief.

Mixed Reviews: The Press and the
Second Divorce

How did the public and press handle this separation and divorce? Despite Chaplin's enormous popularity, he had often been charged with "vulgarity" earlier in his career by genteel Americans. In the 1920s, despite a relatively broad political consensus, American life was characterized by deep cultural divisions, as manifested by such controversial issues as Prohibition, immigration restriction, and the Scopes trial. Such issues all embodied splits in American culture: traditionalism versus modernism, rural versus urban values, fundamentalist religious versus secular viewpoints, and nativist versus cultural pluralist perspectives. Although Chaplin's popularity was widespread, traditionalists who supported Prohibition, favored immigration restriction, and opposed the teaching of evolution in the schools could find much to criticize about Chaplin. The "puritanism" that Van Wyck Brooks and other cultural critics denounced in the 1910s and 1920s may have been misnamed; however, there is no doubt that conservative moralists, fueled by the Fatty Arbuckle scandal in 1921 and the unsolved death of William Desmond Taylor in 1922, were as concerned about the possible harmful effects of movies in the 1920s as they had been in the preceding decade. Such individuals were not likely to forgive Chaplin his indiscretions simply because he was a famous star.

The incident that stimulated the most debate and denunciation of Chaplin was Grey's divorce complaint, filed January 10. Even as staid and conservative a newspaper as the *Chicago Tribune* reported on the spectacular details with glee. They reprinted what Grey allegedly heard Chaplin tell his entourage on his wedding night: "Well, boys, this is better than the penitentiary but it won't last long." They quoted Grey's claim that she was a "virtuous and innocent girl" when she was engaged to Chaplin. They reported that Grey accused Chaplin of "soliciting, urging, and demanding throughout their entire married life, that the defendant submit to acts which were revolting and degrading; shocking to her sensibilities and abhorrent to her conception of decency." And they wrote that, according to Grey, Chaplin had withheld support for the Chaplin babies since November 30 except for paying one milk bill of $27 and had not even visited the children at Christmas.[10]

The first wave of public response to these allegations was critical of Chaplin. His alleged failure to provide food for his children presented a concrete image that drove women's clubs around the country into action. A spokesperson for one such group told reporters: "If Chaplin thinks he can starve his child-wife into submission, he is reckoning without the women of Hollywood. Thirty women, representing twenty clubs, met Thursday, and we already have begun to raise money to properly feed and care for Mrs. Chaplin's little boys."[11] Among other reactions in the first days after the complaint was filed, the mayor of Quebec banned all posters and advertisements for Chaplin films. He stated that he would have banned the films, too, but could not because the local censorship board was responsible for that. The next day, the La Salle, Illinois, League of Women Voters called for a ban on Chaplin films; the mayor of Seattle asked his censorship board to rule on banning Chaplin's films; and the mayor of Lynn, Massachusetts, ordered that no Chaplin films were to be shown while the divorce proceedings were going on.[12] Another example of the public outcry was a letter to a film columnist a week after the story broke. Mrs. R. T. Niles wrote to protest an article defending Chaplin. She charged that Chaplin "has an unfortunate habit of getting himself mixed up with young women whom he subsequently marries—probably to keep out of prison or from being deported." She concluded, "Is this man to be permitted to run riot for the rest of his life amid the foolish little girls of this country?"[13]

But Chaplin also had his defenders, both among the public and in the press (see Figure 12). A few days after the first criticisms from women's clubs, the Miami Beach Women's Club publicly asked Miami theater owners not to ban Chaplin's films but instead to play as many of them as possible in a gesture of support for Chaplin. Their spokesperson, Mrs. Clayton Sedgwick Cooper, said her group aimed to counteract "silly agitation which women's clubs have taken in regard to Chaplin's pictures." The same day that the city of Pasadena banned Chaplin's films, the Theater Owners Chamber of Commerce praised his talents as a filmmaker. At the end of January a letter to the editor of the *New York Herald Tribune* added a defense of Chaplin. Its author, Alice Carpenter, wrote: "There is no one, man or woman, in the movie world who has done more to lift the pictures to a high plane, or who deserves to a greater extent the loyal sympathy and support of our people than Mr. Chaplin, now suffering from the unbalanced actions of a willful girl." In February, the Motion Picture Theater Owners of America, meeting in New York City, passed a resolution praising Chaplin, and the Green Room Club of New York City presented him with a gold plaque honoring his talents.[14]

The motivations for these defenses of Chaplin are not always clear, but several seem likely. On the one hand, the defense by the Miami Beach Women's Club could be seen as a liberal response to the conservative moralism of those women's clubs who urged the banning of Chaplin's films. On the other, their position could also be seen as simply a variation of conservative moralism, but one that defended Chaplin because it was his wife's fault that the marriage had foundered. For the theater owners, the motivations were clearer: Chaplin's films drew well and made them money. If Chaplin were discredited as Arbuckle had been several years earlier, one of their most dependable box-office draws would be lost.

Beginning with some early pieces on the editorial pages, the press also defended Chaplin. On January 15, the *New York Morning Telegraph* ran an editorial, "The Chaplin Films," defending Chaplin and criticizing the bans on his films. "The public must hear the full story if it is inclined to meddle in the personal marital problems of a movie star," the editor declared, adding that "the masses seem to relish scandal when it invades the movie lot or struts back stage." It backed New York City mayor Jimmy Walker's refusal to ban Chaplin films. About the same time, the editorial page of the *New York Telegraph* commented approvingly on Will Hays's refusal to step into the controversy: "What is gained," it asked, "by rushing into print with attacks on anyone before that person has had his day in court, or, at least, [been] given an opportunity to tell his story for public analysis?"[15]

A number of journalists who had earlier written positively about Chaplin's films also supported him in print. Among them was Har-

WHAT REMAINS UNTOUCHED

12. Cartoonist Rollin Kirby in *Theatre Arts* defends Chaplin the artist during the 1927 divorce publicity.

riette Underhill, film columnist for the *New York Herald Tribune*. Shortly after the divorce story broke, she wrote a column praising Chaplin's filmmaking talents: "The reason everyone has loved Charlie Chaplin's pictures is because his soul *is* photographed. Charles Chaplin is a superior soul. He is filled with ideals. . . . He is a public benefactor and he belongs to his public. Mr. Chaplin never should marry. He probably realizes this himself." Though her column was not really a commentary on the divorce case, it did urge readers to keep cool heads and not to prejudge it. Underhill's piece generated considerable reader response, including the castigation by Mrs. Niles cited above and a number of defenses of Chaplin, some of which were printed in the column the following week.[16]

The trade magazines and columnists also came to his defense. *Moving Picture World*, in "The Spotlight Turns Yellow," gave a telling subtitle to its article: "Reformers for hire are only eager to seize on Chaplin, but the world will judge him as an artist and a victim." The essay defends Chaplin as an idealist and lover of beauty, writing hopefully that Chaplin "was, and is, wistful and very human. So we think that the public will be fair simply because it likes Chaplin."[17] H. L. Mencken, that boisterous observer of the American scene, apparently enjoyed the public's display of fickleness, for he wrote in a *Baltimore Sun* column that "the very morons who worshipped Charlie Chaplin six weeks ago now prepare to dance around the stake while he is burned."[18] Mencken was no particular admirer of either Chaplin or the movies, but he found his cynical view of the American "booboisie" reinforced in its denunciations of Chaplin.

Not surprisingly, the *New Yorker* also defended Chaplin in Ralph Barton's satiric "Picking on Charlie Chaplin." In the essay Barton wrote that Chaplin

> is probably more important than anybody else on earth. . . . What other man on earth has been loved, respected and admired, at the same time, by French intellectuals, isolated Esquimaux, Iowa Babbits, jazz-maddened New Yorkers, Bulgarian peasants, Scotch Presbyterians, New Guinea cannibals, German scientists, English statesmen, real estate brokers, dentists, kindergarten teachers, and the entire race of artists? The fellow is, let us admit it with a befitting hysteria, unique in history.[19]

Much as Chaplin's comic films were used to justify his failure to serve as a soldier in World War I, Chaplin's star status here is used to excuse his marital problems. A similar defense of Chaplin appeared in a cartoon printed in *Liberty* magazine (see Figure 13). It accused Lita Grey of cultivating the women's clubs and manipulating the press to exaggerate how difficult her life had become after separating from Chaplin.

Artists and intellectuals generally rose in defense of Chaplin, which suggests something of the split then evident in American culture between conservative moralists and a more cosmopolitan, educated, and urban audience that felt the attacks simply reinforced Brooks's view of the "puritanism" endemic in American culture. One might add that French intellectuals were also vocal in expressing their opinions in fa-

IT WILL ALL COME OUT OF THE ALIMONY. Mrs. Charles Spencer Chaplin poses for a few photographs in the kitchen with the baby, to show the palpitating public how she has been obliged to take up menial duties while waiting for her husband to come across.

13. *Liberty* cartoon (1927) satirizes Chaplin's wife, the women's clubs, and the press during the second divorce.

vor of Chaplin, perhaps even more actively than American intellectuals: the *Boston Evening Transcript* carried an article, "Paris Still Pays Honor to 'Charlot,' " which described organized efforts by French intellectuals to defend Chaplin.[20]

Tully's articles, which appeared during and immediately after the greatest publicity surrounding the divorce, also contributed to Chaplin's star image. Although it is difficult to say whether Chaplin's fears about the articles were justified, he did have some reason to be uneasy, for he had fired Tully when he refused to delete some passages uncomplimentary to Chaplin from a book he was about to publish. Perhaps suspecting that the articles would be a vindictive retaliation for the firing, and knowing that due to the separation and pending divorce, publicity was imminent, Chaplin felt he had no alternative but to seek to halt publication.

However, the articles themselves, which appeared between January and April 1927 in *Pictorial Review*, are neither denunciation nor hagiography; both critics and defenders of Chaplin found support for their positions in them. The first installment, while containing praise, also included more negative passages than the other three. Take, for instance, this description: "Complex and weirdly strange, a rider of stormy moods, he is a complex human riddle that even a Havelock Ellis might never solve" (Jan., p. 8). This installment also called Chaplin "notoriously close with money" and completely unwilling to acknowledge any influence of others on his acting style and comic persona (Jan., p. 29). Chaplin only visited his mother "a few times in as many years" after he brought her to California in 1921, Tully wrote, a charge disputed by Lita Grey in her book. And in one final, cutting passage, Tully, who presented himself as a man of common stock but superior aesthetic taste, wrote that Chaplin is "plentifully supplied with the littleness of big men" (Jan., p. 30).

But in the subsequent issues, and even in certain details of the January piece, Chaplin was portrayed more positively. From the first, Tully portrayed Chaplin as physically attractive and engaging, even magnetic, at social occasions. In the February article, Tully wrote that Chaplin often liked to "chatter on philosophical and sociological subjects" with him, that he could be the "most ingratiating of men," that he was capable of strong pity and kindness, and that he was a brilliant artist completely absorbed in his work (Feb., pp. 19–20). The March issue reiterated Chaplin's pity for the down and out, his artistry, and his enormous capacity for work as it recounted shooting on location in Truckee for *The Gold Rush*. And in the brief final installment, Tully called Chaplin "one of the two greatest men in motion pictures"—the other was James Cruze, director of *The Covered Wagon* (Apr., p. 104).

Compared to the nearly idolatrous picture of Chaplin that had dominated the early 1920s, Tully's was probably more balanced and reasonable. In fact, it appears that the public and press were generally split in their response to the divorce case. Even though we lack Chaplin's version of his relationship with Grey, it seems on balance that he emerged from the whole incident with much less damage to his star image than one might have expected. This may have to do at least in part with the dynamics of stardom. A man as wealthy as Chaplin was able to spend considerable money on his defense. More subtly, however, a star's fans are interested not just in his films but also in his private life: as Richard Dyer has suggested, one of the central concerns of fan magazines is "the *problems* of love."[21] Following this line of argument, the movie fan, by empathizing with the difficulties the star has in searching for personal happiness and love, adds another level to the identification with the star that began with his or her presentation in the movies. The press's treatment of Chaplin's divorce case may even, paradoxically, have enabled some of his fans to identify more strongly with Chaplin by allowing them vicariously to share the burdens of the "real" person. In any case, viewed with hindsight, Chaplin's reputation foundered surprisingly little in 1927 because of the press coverage surrounding his divorce difficulties. Although his marriage with Lita Grey was over, Chaplin's honeymoon with the American public was apparently continuing. After his struggles with taxes, Tully, and Grey, Chaplin had to return his attention to the film that was well under way when the problems began.

The Burdens of Being Funny:
The Circus

Shortly after the opening of *The Gold Rush* in August 1925, Chaplin was back at work, planning another film. His choice of subject was crucial. On the one hand, in only one of his two previous films had his Charlie persona appeared. Chaplin's Olympian status among critics, as well as his own aspirations, encouraged him to follow Stark Young's advice from 1922 and take on something new and more ambitious. On the other hand, *The Gold Rush* had done far better at the box office than had *A Woman of Paris*, and Chaplin was both jealous enough of his independence and shrewd enough to know that keeping the Charlie persona at the center of his films would be an economically sound decision.

Chaplin was thus pulled in two directions about his new project: should he stick with Charlie or abandon him? In November an article in the *New York Times* commented on Chaplin's plans. It reported that Chaplin had toyed with the idea of making a film called *The Suicide Club* but had discarded that idea in favor of another film—contents unknown—called *The Dandy*. After completing that film, Chaplin would make *The Clown*, in which Charlie would appear in the costume of a circus clown except for his shoes, cane, and bowler. "This story," continued the article, "was described as another dramatic comedy, and in its method something after the style of *The Gold Rush*, except that it was to have a tragic ending—the funmaker impersonated by Chaplin is supposed to die in the tanbark while the spectators are applauding the comic pantomime."[22] These descriptions suggest that Chaplin was compromising by planning one non-Charlie film, then a second featuring a close relative of Charlie.

As it turned out, however, Chaplin returned more quickly than the *Times* article suggested he would to the formula that succeeded in *The Gold Rush*. *The Dandy* disappeared into the rapidly filling bin of discarded Chaplin ideas and projects, and *The Clown* evolved into *The*

Circus. The tragic ending of *The Clown* was deferred (it sounds much like the conclusion of Chaplin's 1952 film, *Limelight*). And instead of being disguised as a circus clown, Charlie looks quite familiar in *The Circus*, clad in much the same way he appeared in most scenes of *The Gold Rush* and in many earlier Charlie comedies.

For some reason, reviewers suggested when the film was released that *The Circus* (1928) was somewhat archaic. In the *New York Times*, Mordaunt Hall praised it and noted that it was "more like his earlier films than either *The Kid* or *The Gold Rush*."[23] In the *New Republic* Chaplin's old friend Young used almost the same phrasing, calling *The Circus* "purer in the old-style Chaplin than *The Kid* or *The Gold Rush*."[24] It is true that some gags recall those of earlier Chaplin films, as when Charlie quickly gulps down a baby's hot dog when his father is not looking, reminiscent of the lunch wagon scene in *A Dog's Life.*

Nevertheless, in *The Circus* Chaplin also very carefully builds on the success of *The Gold Rush* by following the narrative structure and the essential blend of comedy and pathos he had established in this earlier film. One could almost say that Chaplin was self-consciously creating his own genre, one that ensured his popularity and respect among a diverse audience and sustained his star image.

Consider the similarities between *The Gold Rush* and *The Circus*. In both films the central character is Charlie, dressed the same in nearly every scene. In both works Charlie is thrust into a new social situation—the Klondike, a circus—in which he must learn to function. In both settings human beings exhibit cruelty to others. In *The Gold Rush* both Black Larsen and Jack cause problems for Charlie; in *The Circus* the circus owner is an unreasonable and often cruel character.

Both films develop a romance between Charlie and a heroine that creates joy and sorrow, and here they are especially similar. Charlie's joyous enthusiasm in Hank's cabin in *The Gold Rush*—he jumps around, swings from the rafters, and beats the feathers out of a pillow when Georgia accepts his invitation to a New Year's Eve dinner—is analogous to the scene in *The Circus* when Charlie dances gleefully after he believes that Merna loves him. Both films also create moments of pathos that stem from Charlie's unrequited love. The pathos that arises in *The Gold Rush* when Charlie wakes up from his dream of a successful party with Georgia, followed by his walk to the dance hall and his isolated look into the window at the others' celebration, functions in much the same way, albeit more powerfully, as the scene in *The Circus* in which Charlie overhears Merna tell the fortune-teller that she is in love with Rex, the tightrope walker. Chaplin shows Charlie's reaction in medium close-up, followed by a long shot of Charlie alone in the dressing room. The isolation of Charlie in the frame recalls the similar isolation when Charlie stands alone outside of the Monte Carlo dance hall in *The Gold Rush*.

Both films also frequently use animals to generate comedy. *The Gold Rush* uses bears, dogs, and a mule, and for a time Big Jim even imagines Charlie to be a chicken. In *The Circus*, Charlie often has an intransigent circus mule chasing him. He swallows a horse pill whole trying to blow it through a tube into a horse's throat. He has a comic scene when locked in with a lion, a circumstance exacerbated by a barking dog outside the cage. And in the comic climax of the film, monkeys clamber all over Charlie as he tries to walk the tightrope.

This final scene suggests yet another similarity. In both films, the final long *comic* scene places Charlie in extreme danger, either balancing tenuously in a cabin at the edge of a precipice or walking a tightrope, high above the circus crowd, when he doesn't really know how. Taken collectively, these similarities in the areas of central character, setting, handling of romance, use of animals to generate comedy, and climactic comic scenes suggest that however different the films are in other ways, they possess a very similar structure, one with which Chaplin's approving audience was becoming familiar and with which Chaplin's star image was becoming associated.

There are, of course, dissimilarities in the two films. (A central dynamic of popular cinema generally is the equipoise between similarity and differentiation from film to film.) One of the most prominent differences lies in the conclusions. Most simply, in *The Gold Rush* Charlie gets the girl and in *The Circus*, he does not. More precisely, he realizes in *The Circus* that he is not right for Merna and that Rex is, so he sacrifices his own desires for the well-being of the other two. The final shots of *The Circus* contrast significantly to the final shots of *The Gold Rush*. At the end of *The Circus*, Charlie picks up a torn paper with a star on it that had once been the center of the hoop Merna jumped through in the film's first shot. He looks at it, apparently musing on how transitory stardom is (even he himself had been a star "funny man" in the circus for a time). He then crumples it into a ball, begins walking away from the camera, tosses the ball into the air, and kicks it sideways as it falls toward the ground. After a few heavily burdened steps, he takes a sprightly bounce, much like at the end of *The Tramp*, and walks away from the camera with renewed resolve. One of Charlie's increasingly central characteristics—his ability to endure pain and grief without letting it destroy him—is revealed in this final scene. A social outsider, Charlie nevertheless does not let disappointments destroy his affirmation of life.

However different from the final scene of *The Gold Rush*, this conclusion does resemble the ending of that film in its hints of self-referentiality. Viewed from the perspective of Chaplin's unhappy second marriage, the angry divorce proceedings, and other problems that confronted Chaplin as he was working on the film (among them the pressure to follow *The Gold Rush* with another worthy of his reputation), Charlie's act of crumpling up and discarding the star suggests that Chaplin himself was at times doubtful that the pressures of stardom were healthy for him or his art. The ending of *The Circus* thus employs self-referentiality much as the ending of *The Gold Rush* does.[25]

The Circus is also self-referential in the sense of alluding to one's autobiography. Chaplin explores the contradictions of his own being in ways that recall *A Woman of Paris*. A number of people who knew Chaplin in the mid-1920s have noted how variable his moods were. Tully, in his *Pictorial Review* articles, for example, wrote that Chaplin had "moods that change like early March weather in his native England."[26] Lita Grey stressed the doubleness of the Charles Spencer Chaplin she knew: "I saw him in every conceivable mood, from the peak of elation to the nadir of prolonged depression. I was witness to his compassion and his cruelty, to his explosive rages and about-face kindness, to his wisdom and his ignorance, to his limitless ability to love and his incredible insensitivities."[27]

Doubleness in *The Circus* is expressed primarily through Charlie and the ringmaster, Chaplin's shadow self. Charlie expresses the joyous, resilient, amusing, compassionate side of Chaplin. We have already seen Chaplin's compassion for the poor and down and out expressed in *My Trip Abroad*. Tully also recalls that when he was "a hungry writer with more ambition than capacity," Chaplin gave him a hundred dollars that had helped him a great deal.[28] Though self-sacrifice was not a new trait of Charlie's in *The Circus*, his sacrifice of his own love for Merna's happiness, a decision that dooms him to a loneliness that Chaplin himself had experienced, was an act crucial to Charlie's character and crucial, too, one could argue, to Chaplin's best self-image.

If this image of a charitable, compassionate, self-sacrificing Charlie was not new, what *was* relatively new in *The Circus* was Chaplin's willingness to confront the harsher side of his being. As one critic has shrewdly noted, the ringmaster in *The Circus* is the first in a long line of shadow selves that appear in later Chaplin films. Allan Garcia played the ringmaster, who resembles a number of other Chaplin characters, including the millionaire in *City Lights* and the factory owner in *Modern Times* (the latter also played by Garcia). The ringmaster's costume in *The Circus*, which consists of a top hat, riding boots, jodhpurs, and a whip, is similar to the costumes worn by the Hynkel character in *The Great Dictator* and by Calvero when he does his "flea act" in *Limelight*. And the ringmaster's cruelty is not unlike the darker side of Monsieur Verdoux in the film of that title.[29]

The ringmaster is like Chaplin both professionally and personally. Professionally, his comic enterprise, the circus, functions as a metaphor for another comic enterprise, the movie studio concerned with making Chaplinesque comedies. Many accounts of Chaplin on the set stress his complete control and his desire for perfection; in Tully's words, "Never did a despot dominate a country as Chaplin rules his studio."[30] Like Chaplin, the ringmaster is a demanding perfectionist: in the tryout he is constantly directing his clowns. In fact, his first line in the film, spoken to Merna—"you missed the hoop again"—mirrors Chaplin's tendency to control his set completely and to make sure a shot was perfect before moving on.

But the ringmaster also resembles Chaplin's darker personal side. The character denies his daughter food because she fails to perform up to his expectations. Later in the film he physically abuses her, and he summarily fires a group of men working under him when they seek higher pay. Although we only have Lita Grey's version of their marriage and divorce, if her account is at all accurate, Chaplin was at times incredibly cruel to his second wife from the day they were married— or perhaps even from the day he learned she was pregnant. Although the ringmaster does reluctantly approve of his daughter's marriage ex post facto—perhaps an acknowledgment by Chaplin that his own darker side could be brightened—he exhibits a human cruelty that Chaplin seemed to be discovering both in himself and in others as he struggled through some of his difficulties in the mid-1920s. This would become an increasing concern as he observed the human sufferings of the Depression and World War II.

These autobiographical links were not frequently drawn by critics of *The Circus* in 1928. However, Tully's charges about Chaplin's moodiness and despotism and more generally circulating stories about Chaplin's perfectionism did have some effect on his star image. Comments like Tully's transferred a potentially noxious germ to the body of Chaplin's star image, but for the time, at least, the illness remained latent. Not until the 1940s did the germ, in combination with others, come to infect the entire star image. On the other hand, the stories of Chaplin's perfectionism could be, and in the 1920s were, read more positively, as the true indication of Chaplin's demanding genius. As long as the resulting films were satisfying to audiences, his high standards were generally considered a positive quality.

How did *The Circus* fare with the critics and the public? *The Circus* did very well with both groups. Surveying the reviews, *Literary Digest* gathered the impression that Chaplin's "critical admirers are killing the fatted calf to celebrate his return to his own field of pure clown-ing."[31] Critic Robert Sherwood had high praise for Chaplin: "Chaplin doesn't have to play *Hamlet*. He doesn't have to play any part created by any other genius from Shakespeare down." Countering those who thought Chaplin should abandon Charlie for more serious subjects, Sherwood, echoing comments by Seldes earlier in the decade, wrote that Charlie "is just as important, just as true, as all the melancholy princes who ever discovered that there is something rotten in Den-mark."[32] To Alexander Bakshy, writing in the *Nation*, Chaplin was "again at his very best" in *The Circus*, and Young, in spite of some res-ervations about Chaplin's makeup and the handling of pathos in the film, also found the film a triumph.[33]

The critical reception of the film suggests that the expectations Chaplin had raised through his previous films were well satisfied by *The Circus*. More and more, it seemed that Chaplin was forming his own genre. Or, to put it another way, he was establishing an aesthetic contract with his audience, promising them a consistent central char-acter, a romance tinged with pathos, inventive humor, and some seri-ous themes or concerns (often, like many Hollywood films, based on moral contrasts rooted in individual characters) underlying the work. In exchange, viewers offered their dollars for tickets and their critical adulation. To them, Chaplin satisfied his end of the aesthetic contract in *The Circus*.

The film also did well at the box office, nearly as well as *The Gold Rush*. The United Artists balance sheets of domestic film rentals through the end of 1931 show that *The Gold Rush* had accumulated $2.15 million in rentals, while *The Circus* had garnered $1.82 million.[34] For some reason, Chaplin later did not remember *The Circus* as very successful, perhaps because he associated the making of it with an un-pleasant period of his life. His attitude is suggested by the fact that he did not revive the film until 1969 (*The Gold Rush* was revived much earlier, in 1942) and that he mentions it only once in his autobiogra-phy, and then only in the context of his mother's final illness (MA, p. 288). It is too bad that *The Circus* has faded from public consciousness, for it is a fascinating film that shows Chaplin dealing successfully with interesting thematic material. It is also historically significant as the last film Chaplin had the luxury of making in the silent era.

Charlie and the Threat
of the Talkies

Two events of almost equally cataclysmic effect took place during the time that Chaplin was at work on his next film, *City Lights*. First, the interest in talking films, generated by public enthusiasm for *Don Juan* (1926), *The Jazz Singer* (1927), and other films using Warner's Vitaphone and Fox's Movietone systems, led nearly the entire film industry to transform to sound film production and exhibition between the spring of 1928 and the end of the decade.[35] Second, in October 1929 the crash of the stock market diminished or wiped out the assets of many Americans and eventually led to an economic depression of such magnitude that by 1933 a quarter to a third of the nonfarm work force in the United States was unemployed. Both the internal factor, the technological development of sound, and the external factor, the national economic catastrophe of the depression, had far-reaching effects not only on the American film industry but also on Chaplin's evolving star image.

However, only the challenge of sound films significantly affected *City Lights*. The plot contours of *City Lights* were laid out well before the crash. Talking with *Times* reviewer Mordaunt Hall in July 1929, Chaplin said that the central characters in the film were Charlie, a blind girl, and a wealthy "Jekyll and Hyde inebriate" who when drunk, recognized Charlie, but otherwise did not—exactly the central dramatis personae and situation of the completed film.[36] Though the depression subsequently had a profound effect on Chaplin's film, life, relationship to his audience, and even to some extent on the way his films were approached by critics—as will be related in upcoming chapters—*City Lights* is not a film of the depression but rather a film of the 1920s.

Though the crash had no large effect on *City Lights*, it can be documented that the threat of sound films clearly did challenge and worry Chaplin. Less than six months after *The Jazz Singer* premiered and three months after *The Circus* opened, a nervous group at United Artists, including Chaplin, Griffith, Pickford, Fairbanks, Norma Talmadge, and Barrymore, gathered in one of the studio bungalows and waited to let their fans hear they had voices. They were all participating in a special radio broadcast called the Dodge Brothers Hour, broadcast both to fifty-five NBC radio affiliates nationwide and to a number of movie theaters in the larger cities throughout the United States. Though the program included music by the Paul Whiteman Orchestra and a pitch for the new six-cylinder Dodge by the president of Dodge Motors, most listeners had tuned in to hear the voices of their favorite silent movie stars. Talmadge gave a short discourse on fashion, Griffith spoke about love, Fairbanks gave a typically optimistic pep talk to America's youth, and Chaplin—what else?—told a couple of jokes.[37]

To the extent that the silent stars considered this a test of their abilities to survive in the increasingly popular medium of talking films, the reports of the broadcast had to be worrisome. *Variety* solicited the comments of movie-theater owners around the country about how their audiences responded to the radio hookup that had interrupted their regular programs. Their responses were almost uniformly sobering. The Boston audience started "the razz" within ten minutes and forced the owner to go back to the regularly scheduled movies. A number of theaters reported that their business was off. None felt it was up. A Baltimore theater owner probably voiced the consensus among owners and much of the audience when he told the *Variety* reporter that he felt it was a mistake to take audiences behind the scenes and let them listen to entertainers "whose talents are essentially visual."[38]

"Entertainers whose talents are essentially visual." If Chaplin read these words or heard them reported by his staff, as he most likely did, they must have unsettled him. Although the theater owners had no specific criticism of Chaplin's performance in their summaries of audience response, neither did they have any praise, while they did for John Barrymore. More significantly, a *Variety* reporter who talked with Chaplin after the broadcast wrote "that he nearly died while doing it, through mike fright, and was worried as to how he did."[39] This was not Chaplin's first encounter with radio: a few years earlier he had broadcast on New York's WOR. Afterward, he told the studio director that he was so certain he had lost "about nine pounds" that he would be willing to sign a statement to that effect.[40] If Chaplin participated in the Dodge broadcast as a way to try out his voice with a movie audience without having to risk the large investment of a film, there is little doubt that this helped discourage him from adding dialogue to his next picture.

The threat of sound was a vexing one for Chaplin, for although *The Circus* did well at the box office, he was still confronted with considerable financial pressures. Not only did his divorce settlement require him to come up with $825,000 in several payments through 1930, but his income tax dispute with the federal government was finally settled the month before the broadcast, and not in his favor. The settlement required $1,670,000 of Chaplin: $1,073,000 in personal income taxes and the rest in corporate taxes from the Charles Chaplin Film Corporation.[41] In deciding whether to accept or reject dialogue in his next film, Chaplin had economic considerations in mind.

It was not an easy decision, for Chaplin halted activity and postponed production during the spring and summer of 1928 to think about it.[42] By October, however, he had cast Virginia Cherrill in the role of the blind girl, and by the spring of 1929 he was ready to cast his lot as a partial aesthetic conservative: though he would not resist recorded sound tracks per se, he would resist pressure to have his characters, particularly Charlie, speak. The clearest evidence of Chaplin's growing resolve to resist dialogue appeared in "Charlie Chaplin Attacks the Talkies," which appeared in *Motion Picture Magazine* in May 1929. When asked about his attitude toward talkies, Chaplin replied to the interviewer, "You can tell 'em I loathe them." Chaplin's other comments elaborated on this theme:

They are spoiling the oldest art in the world, the art of pantomime.

They are ruining the great beauty of silence.

They are defeating the meaning of the screen, the appeal that has created the star system, the fan system, the vast popularity of the whole—the appeal of beauty.[43]

A couple of months later, in the midst of production, Chaplin told Mordaunt Hall that he might have "an incidental song, the patter of dancing feet, now and again the tones of a trombone or a cornet and the inevitable synchronized musical score" but that he would not have sound effects or dialogue. Hall, who had talked with Chaplin about sound in 1928, found that Chaplin "was even more strongly opposed to giving shadows a voice" than he had been the year before.[44] Though Chaplin would include a musical score ("music, like pictures, is a universal language," he told the *Motion Picture* interviewer), sound effects, and especially dialogue, were out.

Chaplin decided to resist dialogue in his next film for several reasons. First, since the foreign revenues on Chaplin's films were even larger than the domestic grosses, having Charlie speak English would mean partially cutting him off from non–English speaking audiences. Second, many intellectuals, both American and European, sharply criticized talking films on aesthetic grounds and praised the artistry that arose from the limitations of silent film style. Given the primitive quality of the first silent films and the beauty of the best films made in the late silent period, their resistance was understandable. And given Chaplin's concern for support from the intelligentsia, his decision to resist dialogue made sense.[45] Third, Chaplin had already shown that he was nervous about using his voice in public and uncertain about associating his voice with the Charlie persona: since Charlie's essential appeal resulted from his pantomime, Chaplin logically surmised that making Charlie a talking as well as a miming character could undercut his appeal.

Probably the most important reason that Chaplin decided to resist spoken dialogue in *City Lights*—and also a key reason for his continuing popularity through *Modern Times* in 1936—was that he was shrewd enough to know that he had in his previous films established what we have called an "aesthetic contract" with his audience. Central to the nature of Hollywood films from the 1910s to the present is the notion of story types or genres. Though the term "genre" is a thorny one, genre critics have usefully suggested that audiences of popular films often prefer films that are a blend of convention and innovation, standardization and differentiation: the audience responds first to convention (established and familiar characters, themes, actions, and iconography) and then looks for something fresh or interesting to take place within that conventional structure.[46]

As the above comparison of *The Circus* and *The Gold Rush* demonstrated, Chaplin had by the late 1920s created a kind of personal genre (not unlike what Hitchcock did later in another vein) consisting of the central comic persona, a romance, pantomimic comedy, situations of pathos leading to empathy for that comic persona, and a contrast in value systems or moral perspectives. Although Chaplin's personal genre must be understood as fitting comfortably within the contours of 1920s "persona comedy" (Lloyd, Keaton, Langdon, etc.) and the narrative conventions of classical Hollywood cinema, it was also distinctive enough, especially because of the Charlie persona, to be perceived as identifiably different and attractive by viewers. And because Chaplin, unlike other Hollywood movie comedians, owned his studio, he had the luxury after the introduction of sound of deciding the extent to which he would continue making films within his personal genre. It became clear to him that having Charlie talk would violate a central tenet of Chaplin's aesthetic contract: Charlie the silent, pantomimic character capable of evoking both laughter and tears.

Though Chaplin had decided firmly by 1929 that *City Lights* would be a nondialogue film, production history was troubled. Sound films came more and more to dominate the industry in 1929 and 1930, and the top-grossing film of 1930 was *Animal Crackers*, a dialogue comedy starring that most un-Chaplinesque group (except perhaps Harpo), the Marx Brothers. During this time Chaplin, who had become an ever more meticulous and deliberate perfectionist on the set and was sometimes even irregular about coming to the studio at all, had an extremely difficult time working consistently. Going over the shooting schedule in some of Chaplin's papers recently made available, Kevin Brownlow noted that in the first 534 working days after shooting of

City Lights began, shooting took place on only 166 days: the others were "off" days, even though the cast and crew were on the set and being paid. Such details suggest that Chaplin's decision to stay with nondialogue films caused him considerable anxiety.[47] The technological change was posing a distinct threat to the star image.

Farewell to the Twenties:
City Lights

Once the troubled shooting schedule and the scoring of *City Lights* (1931) were completed, however, its promotion campaign, the completed film itself, and its critical reviews all suggest that Chaplin fulfilled his aesthetic contract with his audience and preserved his star image in a remarkably effective way. The pressbook prepared for *City Lights* skillfully sought to reinforce the image of Charlie and of Chaplin's films that had been built up through *The Circus*. One full-page ad was headed, "The King of Comedy in the Supreme Laugh Sensation of the Century."[48] It stressed that Chaplin would continue to offer comedy and pathos: the film, it claimed, "plays on your funny bone and the heart strings." Since part of Chaplin's star image emphasized his versatility and complete creative control, one headline showed how that control was extended in the sound era: "Chaplin Writes Songs in Film." Promotion headlines also stressed Chaplin's negative response to talkies: "Comedian Defies Movie Trend in Making *City Lights*: Thinks It His Best." Another headline made bold claims: "*City Lights* Is Expected to Change Trend of Film World. . . . Movie Prophets Predict Avalanche of Talkless Pictures as a Result" (the prophets were wrong). While these two headlines sought to present Chaplin as an aesthetic purist, they also hinted at the aesthetic conservatism that would later become an important element of his star image and that damaged it for many people.

Somewhat uncharacteristically, at least compared to the promotion campaigns for *The Gold Rush* and *The Circus*, the pressbook contained an article about Chaplin's personal life. It was headed, "Tennis and Running Keep Chaplin Healthy." Perhaps the promoters wanted the audience to know that Chaplin was still fit and robust despite his age. Pictures and sketches in the pressbook, some of which were later included in Chaplin's *My Life in Pictures* (pp. 236–37), stressed the familiar costume, mustache, and manner of the old Charlie. Time may have passed, the promotion material seemed to say, but Chaplin has stayed the same, except that he has added musical composition to his varied and considerable talents.

Though no full analysis of *City Lights* is possible in this limited space (Molyneaux's book provides a close reading), it is useful to highlight three characteristics of the film. First, the film fulfills Chaplin's aesthetic contract—that is, it continues the familiar development of Chaplin's comic/romantic/pathetic narratives that his audience had become familiar and pleased with in his previous two comic feature films. Second, Chaplin again works submerged autobiography into *City Lights*, much as he had in some previous films from *The Kid* on. And third, *City Lights* shows Chaplin as a cultural critic, casting a critical eye on urban American culture in the 1920s from the perspective of the Victorian world view that so profoundly shaped his sensibility.

We noted earlier that film genres, including Chaplin's "personal genre," consist of "regularized variety": the interplay of repetition and variation. *City Lights* exhibits many of the narrative and comic conventions of *The Gold Rush* and *The Circus* and also adds variations, thus honoring the contract Chaplin had made with his audience. Charlie again appears at the center of the film with his familiar costume and demeanor. As in the other two films, he is apparently not gainfully employed (he does work for a time, but not very successfully). He falls in love with a beautiful woman, which leads to comic and pathetic situations, both of which are related to one of the film's innovations— the woman is blind. Comedy results when she unknowingly tosses water in his face or winds the yarn of his underwear into a ball; probably the most powerful pathos comes when Charlie is released from prison: alone, haggard, and penniless. To a lesser extent than the other films, animals help create comic situations, as when the elephants pass by the street-cleaning Charlie.

There are also variations from *The Gold Rush* and *The Circus* in *City Lights*. Largely because of the film's urban setting, humor comes more than usual from Charlie's interactions with people, at times in elegant settings. Like the other two films, Chaplin sets up alternative moral universes, each representing a set of cultural values, but in *City Lights* this is handled somewhat differently. In the previous two films, Charlie represented the "good" values, Black Larsen and the ringmaster the "evil" values. In *City Lights*, however, Charlie moves back and forth between two worlds: the upper-class luxury of the millionaire and the urban, almost folk world of the flower girl and her grandmother. Charlie acts with charity in both worlds, but the film also morally affirms the flower girl's world and criticizes the millionaire's. The ending of *City Lights*, like the endings of the previous two films, concentrates on the outcome of the relationship between Charlie and the girl. However, whereas Charlie is united with Georgia in *The Gold Rush* and sacrifices his love for Merna in *The Circus*, in *City Lights* Chaplin leaves the relationship between the flower girl and Charlie (and the audience itself) poised in a delicate and sublimely indecisive manner, leading to what for several reasons is one of the most memorable endings in movie history. Using innovation within the boundaries of convention, Chaplin fulfills his audience's expectations.

A second characteristic of *City Lights* is the continuation of submerged autobiography that Chaplin began working into his films during the 1920s. The two worlds that Charlie moves between—the urban poor and the urban wealthy—equate with the two worlds that Chaplin experienced at different periods of his life: his poverty during his London childhood and his later wealth. The plain and simple mise-en-scène of the flower girl's apartment recalls Jean's apartment in *A Woman of Paris*, just as the luxurious mise-en-scène that surrounds the millionaire in *City Lights* resembles the life of Pierre and Marie in Paris. Chaplin was familiar with both worlds. Even more specifically autobiographical are the similarities between Chaplin the man and the millionaire in the film.[49] Both the millionaire's extremely erratic behavior, a key element of the plot and theme, and his ability to dominate a party resemble the vital yet moody and almost schizophrenic Chaplin of the mid-1920s, described by Tully and Grey in their accounts of Chaplin. Since Chaplin does not portray the millionaire as sympathetically as he did Pierre in *A Woman of Paris*, it may be that his awareness of his behavior during his second marriage made him more critical of this melancholy and occasionally cruel side of his own being. His apparent consciousness of that behavior, as well as his longing for the almost pastoral Victorian world of the flower girl and her mother, help give *City Lights* a decidedly personal resonance.

In addition to these autobiographical implications, *City Lights* contains serious criticism of American urban life. This characteristic of the film perpetuates a dimension of the Chaplin star image that began to emerge in the early 1920s: the serious artist concerned with more than just providing laughs. If *The Pilgrim* was a less systematic and developed critique of the small town, in *City Lights* Chaplin turned his attention to what he saw as the disturbing quality of life in prosperous urban America. Although it is not apparently set in the depression, *City Lights* might fruitfully be paired with F. Scott Fitzgerald's short story, "Babylon Revisited," for both of these 1931 works directly or obliquely take a searching look at the glittering way of life of wealthy Americans in the Jazz Age and find it lacking.

Although Chaplin had from early in his career shown a sympathy for the dispossessed and had even occasionally, as in *The Immigrant* or

The Pilgrim, satirically attacked society, *City Lights* begins a series of four films (through *Monsieur Verdoux*) in which sober cultural or political concerns increasingly dominate the narratives while the comedy becomes less central. As cultural criticism, *City Lights* is thematically quite direct: it presents Chaplin's response to the social world in which he had moved in the 1920s—the world of the urban upper class—and contrasts it to an idealized urban folk world, rooted in Chaplin's memory, which serves as the film's moral alternative to the superficiality, rootlessness, and moral emptiness of the urban upper classes.

It is important to note, however, that this theme is subtly developed: although Chaplin had satiric aims in the film, he took pains not to be too topical. Chaplin's images do not attack city life overtly or polemically; rather, the film presents a subtler denunciation.[50] The fact that neither the city nor the central characters are ever specifically named (the characters are simply called the girl, the millionaire, and the tramp) gives the film a broader mythic appeal, as opposed, for example, to a work like *The Grapes of Wrath*, which is securely rooted in a specific time and place.[51] Using this more general approach, *City Lights* nevertheless is Chaplin's somber commentary on the 1920s, the decade of his greatest success, his pinnacle of stardom.

The film's opening shot emphasizes its overriding concern with modern urban life: behind the words "City Lights," which are formed by bright lights, a city landscape bustles with rushing people and passing vehicles, accompanied by a jazz theme. The sound track early identifies the city as American: in the opening statue-dedication sequence, characters come to attention when the "Star-Spangled Banner" is played—even Charlie, whose pants are skewered by the sword of one of the statues. That scene also sets up a contrast between the city respectables and the disreputables like Charlie. The respectables are represented by the mayor, a woman's club spokesperson, and the sculptor responsible for the ridiculous public statuary that is being dedicated. Their voices are approximated by a kazoo; Chaplin uses the aural device to satirize them (from the start, *City Lights* is never a silent film) and to contrast them with Charlie.

After the opening two scenes set up Charlie's character and his alienation from much of urban society, Chaplin moves toward the central contrast in the film: in the third and fifth scenes he introduces the other two key figures in the movie, the flower girl and the millionaire.[52] The girl lives in a simple second-story apartment with her grandmother. Apparently lit by natural light, it has sparse furnishings, though some of them, including the canary and the potted flowers on the window sill, derive from nature. A central possession in the home is the family album, which Charlie looks at and describes to the flower girl: it associates her way of life with family unity and social tradition. Significantly, this warm and fulfilling way of life is also threatened by the city. Charlie accidentally learns midway through the film that the flower girl and her grandmother are in danger of being evicted because they do not have enough money to pay their rent.

In contrast, the millionaire moves through the glamour and glitter of the Jazz Age. If the flower is the central image associated with the girl's world, money is the millionaire's key image. His home is sumptuously decorated, and in the evenings, during parties, illuminated artificially. Its elaborate furnishings contrast to the simplicity of the girl's, both in quantity and in splendor. Structurally parallel to the girl's cherished photograph album is the millionaire's picture of his estranged wife, which he tosses to the floor after looking at it early in the film. (As we have seen, being estranged from a wife was hardly unusual for Chaplin, as well.) In contrast to the sedate yet struggling world of the flower girl, the millionaire is constantly active (giving parties or going to night clubs) frequently suicidal (particularly when drunk), and apparently made of money, for he never seems to worry about it. If the flower girl's world is one in which human relationships are important and human compassion is lasting, the millionaire's world is one of short-term and superficial human relationships: significantly, it is only when he's drunk that the millionaire knows and is generous to Charlie. His life alternates between frenetic activity and despair.

This contrast between the two worlds provides the basic rhythm of the plot, which alternates between pathos and comedy. The flower girl's world is a passive one: Charlie must visit her for that plot strand to progress. This element of the story—his kindness to her, her misapprehension that Charlie is wealthy, and the development of their romance—leads to the central moments of pathos in the film. On the other hand, the primary comic scenes arise either from Charlie's interactions with the millionaire or from his attempts to make money for the girl's operation by taking jobs: the waterfront scene, the nightclub scene, the party scene, and the boxing scene. This is the more active world and the source of most of the film's comedy.

But amid the humor, Chaplin weaves a satirical critique of the millionaire. A man alone, the millionaire flings away the picture of his estranged wife. The night club and party scenes, as well as his trip to Europe, show him as a man constantly on the move but going nowhere. His drinking is presented as a desire for escape, yet ultimately it only leads him back to suicidal thoughts. The contradiction of his generosity to Charlie when drunk and indignant rejection of him when sober is more than a narrative device to further the plot and generate comedy; the contradiction is Chaplin's comment on the superficiality of the millionaire's world and the emptiness of his values.

The flower girl's world serves as a counterpoint in Chaplin's cultural critique. We have already noted that her life is associated with simplicity, nature, and poverty. It is a world that the millionaire knows nothing about; the glare of the city lights blind him to the sufferings of the less fortunate. It is true that, as one critic suggests, *City Lights* endorses the flower girl's "more remote, gratifying and likable folk world."[53] But were it not for Charlie's good fortune and concern for the flower girl, she and her grandmother would be turned out on the streets for failing to pay their rent. The good are victimized and nearly powerless in this film; the flawed are powerful and oblivious.

After presenting the urban upper-class world as gaudy, prosperous, and superficially appealing, yet morally hollow at the core, Chaplin offers the flower girl a choice in the famous, inconclusive conclusion of *City Lights*. Charlie, just released from prison, where he had served a term for stealing the money that enabled the girl to pay her rent and to get the operation that restored her sight, is as bedraggled in costume, makeup, and manner as his audience had ever seen him. After harassment from two pea-shooting newsboys, Charlie trudges by the floral shop run by the now-prosperous flower girl and her grandmother. Looking through her store window, the girl observes him picking up a wilted flower by the curb but, never having seen him, does not know who he is. Their eyes meet, and the flower girl, taking pity on him, offers him money—the central image of the millionaire's world. Charlie refuses and, painfully aware of his appearance, tries to scurry by. The flower girl comes outside the door and offers him a flower. Their hands meet, and through her sensitive touch she realizes that Charlie is her benefactor. "You?" she says in a title. Charlie replies in anticipation, "You can see now?" Their exchange invites us to reflect on the double meaning of "see"—to visualize and to understand—for the flower girl sees through her eyes but understands through her touch. An indescribable expression of wonder, disappointment, and gratitude, complicated by tears blurring in her eyes, covers the flower girl's face, but Chaplin cuts back to a close-up of Charlie. Is his expression anticipation? Hopelessness? Bittersweet recognition of the absurdity of life? Happiness? Before it is clear, the shot fades out.

Chaplin leaves his audience suspended. He has presented the world of a millionaire who is not only unhappy but even mean-spirited. He has also shown a tramp and blind flower girl from another world who are charitable and, for most of the film at least, victimized. Then at the conclusion Chaplin twists the plot and gives the flower girl a choice. Will she opt for the appealing yet hollow world of the millionaire, the world of money, the world of the prosperous 1920s that her restored sight has made a possibility? Or will she return, like the woman of Paris, to the world from whence she came, the world of flowers, the world where charity leads to self-sacrifice and lasting human ties? We will never know, and one of the reasons this scene is so emotionally powerful is that Chaplin himself knew the attractions of both worlds and, though wanting ideally to choose the flower world, knew that he sometimes chose the other. Some of our most powerful and penetrating cultural criticism in narrative art arises when the creator confronts commonly shared dilemmas that he feels deeply in his own being. *City Lights* is just such a work, and by posing the alternatives so effectively, Chaplin was continuing to foster his image as a serious comedian.

How did the public and critics react to the film and to a filmmaker whose work had not appeared on the screen for three long years? The public evidently responded very positively. When *City Lights* opened at the Cohan Theater in New York City, it initially played continuously from 9 A.M. through a midnight show every night but Sunday. It grossed over a half-million dollars at this one theater during its twelve-week run. Another indicator of how well *City Lights* did comes from the United Artists' corporate records: by the end of 1931, the ledgers reveal, *City Lights* had already accumulated more domestic rentals than *The Circus* and over 90 percent of the domestic rentals that *The Gold Rush* had garnered since 1925.[54] These results, one might add, came during the depths of the depression.

The press was for the most part even more enthusiastic. Paul Rotha wrote in his first edition of *The Film Till Now* that *City Lights* had more advance publicity than any film in history up to that time. If the *New York Times* coverage was typical, he may be right: Mordaunt Hall was doing articles on *City Lights* as early as July and August 1929, and as the opening approached, the *Times* gave Chaplin prominent space in two Sunday issues in January. The newspaper reviews were generally raves. Typical was Hall's, titled "Chaplin Hilarious in *City Lights*," which described the audience's enthusiasm on opening night, praised the boxing scene and the ending, and summed up: "It was a joyous evening. Mr. Chaplin's shadow has grown no less."[55] The *Herald Tribune* was equally enthusiastic, calling the picture "a very brilliant film, a genuinely hilarious comedy which shows the Great Man of the Cinema

in his happiest and most characteristic moods." *City Lights* was, the reviewer wrote, "a magnificent comedy" that blended "hilarity with pathos" so skillfully that it deserved to be called "an historic comedy."[56]
Chaplin had, for this reviewer at least, fulfilled his aesthetic contract.

Some of the reviewers in the weeklies or monthlies, including Chaplin's advocate Seldes, also thought the film superb. Writing in the *New
Republic*, Seldes found it "beyond question" that Chaplin had "created
one of his masterpieces." It is, he wrote, "magnificently organized,
deeply thought out and felt, and communicated with an unflagging
energy and a masterly technique." Accurately noting the film's alter-
nation between comedy and romance—another staple of Chaplin's
personal genre—Seldes too singled out the ending as especially effective, as "infinitely sad and altogether appropriate. For in this picture
Chaplin has not for a moment suggested that our laughter hides our
tears; only that at the end of our laughter, there will be nothing but
tears for the gayest of us."[57]

Thus, despite all the uncertainty Chaplin had shown during the
production of the film, as well as the bravado he had exhibited in defending the nondialogue, pantomimic film in the years before its release, *City Lights* joined the long line of Chaplin star vehicles. There
was little indication that Chaplin's star had fallen, even though the industry had transformed itself to talking films and the nation itself was
in the throes of the depression.

There were storm clouds on the horizon, however. Some respon-
dents, although a decided minority, had reservations about *City Lights*
and Chaplin's future. *Variety* issued one warning. Though acknowledging that Chaplin "is still the consummate pantomimist," *Variety*
thought that Chaplin might suffer a little by sticking with nondialogue
films. "There will always be room for Chaplin," they admitted, but
sound films will likely "make him slightly less important in the general
public eye as time goes on." As the quality of sound films improved,
Variety suggested between the lines, Chaplin was in danger of making
himself an anachronism.[58] This was a criticism that Chaplin would
have to, and did, confront in his next film, *Modern Times* (1936).

But perhaps the most negative (as well as most prophetic) review of
City Lights came from an old defender of Chaplin, Alexander Bakshy,
whose review, "Charlie Chaplin Falters," appeared in the *Nation*. Re-
sisting the "fervent acclaim" given the film, Bakshy judged it "the fee-
blest of his longer pictures," and for a very specific reason: Chaplin
was trying too hard to be serious and evoke pity. Chaplin's comic character—"a round peg in a square hole"—could generate pity by itself,
wrote Bakshy, which made a sentimental plot unnecessary and even

counterproductive. "Chaplin's growing seriousness, his desire to be more than a mere comedian," Bakshy objected, has "deceived him into holding sentiment more precious than fun."[59] Thoughout the 1920s, large numbers of Americans had come to perceive Chaplin as a serious, even brilliant artist. That Chaplin aspired to fill this role is evident from his films of the period. That it had become a distinct part of his star image is evident from Bakshy's comment. As the depression deepened, however, and as Chaplin prepared to leave for a world tour following the opening of *City Lights*, his dual perception of himself as a serious cultural critic and as a comedian were about to become a central issue in his art and life. And as it did so, his star image continued its evolution.

THREE

**The Challenge of
Progressive
Politics**

5

The Depression, the World Tour,
and *Modern Times*

A Comedian Sees—and Comments
on—the World

Chaplin's film career after *City Lights*, particularly the evolution of his star image, is explicable only if one keeps in mind the historical circumstances in which Chaplin made his films and the cultural climate in which critics and audiences responded to them. Andrew Sarris spoke persuasively and well several years ago when he lamented the tendency "to look at Chaplin's entire career as a single slab of personal achievement and thus to flatten out the temporal perspective by which each of the films was viewed at the time." If we are able to flesh out rather than flatten out this temporal perspective, we should have a much firmer conception of how and why Chaplin's star image evolved, particularly after he began to face the challenge of progressive politics.[1]

If *City Lights* is best considered Chaplin's postscript on the 1920s, his world tour in 1931 and 1932 was his introduction to the depression, to the political debates it engendered, and to the challenges it posed to him as a filmmaker and world-renowned public figure. The tour reiterated both to him and to the world that his status as an artist and celebrity was undiminished, but it also vividly demonstrated to him how widespread the effects of the depression were and encouraged him to comment on political and economic affairs, something he did both on his tour and in his account of it, *A Comedian Sees the World* (1933). In the years following his return, Chaplin witnessed the depths of the American depression, the election of Franklin D. Roosevelt and the passage of his first New Deal policies, Upton Sinclair's 1934 EPIC (End Poverty in California) campaign, and the growing conflict between the producers and aspiring unionists in Hollywood. Within this national and local context, he conceived and filmed *Modern Times*, which both before and after its release generated a great deal of controversy concerning its social and political implications.

Chaplin's world tour, which began the same month that *City Lights* opened in New York City and lasted fifteen months, was an experience that modified his world view and affected his subsequent career. He wrote extensively about the trip, publishing his reflections both in a high circulation magazine and later as a book, and this too affected the American star image of Chaplin as a celebrity. The trip itself, the press's coverage of it, and Chaplin's account of it provide a basis for understanding Chaplin's next film and constitute a starting point for the politicization of Chaplin's star image.

Like his European tour in 1921, Chaplin drew huge crowds on his 1931 trip whenever his arrival in a new city was made public. Unlike the previous journey, however, Chaplin spent considerable time in various locations and saw much of the world. His itinerary included England, Germany, France (Paris, Normandy, Nice), Austria, Italy (Venice and Rome), Spain, Switzerland (St. Moritz), Ceylon, Singapore, Java, Bali, and Japan.[2]

Though short reports about his tour were carried relatively frequently in the American press, probably the most publicized incident occurred in early May, when Chaplin was charged with refusing to participate in a command performance for the King of England.[3] Chaplin quickly denied the allegations. He stated that he had only been asked by a music-hall manager to appear in a charity program and, refusing, had sent a $1,000 check for the benefit fund instead (the same amount he earned in his last two years in England before going to America). The incident clearly raised Chaplin's ire, as his comments indicate: "They say I have a duty to England. I wonder just what that duty is? No one wanted me or cared for me in England seventeen years ago. I had to go to America for my chance, and I got it there. Only then did England take the slightest interest in me." Such a comment delighted American cartoonists and editorialists, for it reaffirmed the dearly held myth of America as the land of opportunity.[4]

In the same press conference Chaplin also commented on public affairs in what was, up to this point in his career, an unusually candid and testy way: "Patriotism is the greatest insanity the world has ever suffered. I have been all over Europe in the last few months. Patriotism is rampant everywhere, and the result is going to be another war. I hope they send the old men to the front the next time, for it is the old men who are the real criminals in Europe today."[5] Although such a comment was unlikely to antagonize many in the early 1930s—in both Europe and America the memory of World War I was as strong as the isolationist desire to avoid another one—such overt political comments by a movie star could easily jeopardize his status in another context. Evidence suggests that during his trip Chaplin became increasingly willing to comment on political and economic issues.

128

This is in part because Chaplin met even more prominent political figures and commentators on this trip than in 1921. If one only goes through *A Comedian Sees the World*, the list that can be compiled of such people is impressive.[6] In England he met and talked with Ramsay MacDonald, Lloyd George, Winston Churchill (the present, past, and future prime ministers), Gandhi, George Bernard Shaw, H. G. Wells, Aldous Huxley, Sir Phillip Sassoon, and many members of Parliament. In Germany he dined with members of the Reichstag and the nephew of the Kaiser. In France he met the permanent secretary of the French Cabinet. In Belgium he was decorated by the King—and so on through the trip. It is apparent that political affairs were more on his mind in this trip than in the previous one.

In fact, a close examination of *A Comedian Sees the World* reveals the star image Chaplin sought to present in the early 1930s. One of the first themes in the memoir is Chaplin's awareness of being a celebrity and his skill at coping with that fact. At one point Chaplin warns his readers that "the tourist's opinions of countries he visits are usually in error, especially a celebrity's, who sees things through a glamour of excitement." Reading of the crowds Chaplin had to wade through at nearly every stop on the tour, one knows clearly what he means. The constant attention of the press is another indication of Chaplin's celebrity status, but Chaplin, referring to the press's behavior after he had visited MacDonald, shows how he has learned to deal with it: "I have a technique now for such interviews. I usually answer in monosyllables, and to foolish questions just smile."[7] The persona of this memoir is a celebrity who has, despite becoming weary of and exhausted from the constant adulation, become able to function within its structure.

The book's political references are perhaps its most interesting dimension. Chaplin wrote of his vague longings to help the underprivileged in *My Trip Abroad*, but specific references to political affairs were relatively rare in that book in comparison with *A Comedian Sees the World*. Here, Chaplin frequently records his political discussions with the powerful and prominent and often offers his prescriptions for the economic dislocations of the depression. Probably the most detailed is his account of a speech he gave at a dinner given by Lady Astor that included members of each political party in Parliament. Speakers were asked what they would do if given the power of a Mussolini to help England in its present situation. Chaplin spoke first and proposed, among other changes, the following:

1. Reduce the government
2. Create a government Bureau of Economics that would control prices, interests, and profits
3. Amalgamate England's colonies "into an economic unity"

4. Support "internationalism, world cooperation of trade, the abolition of the gold standard"
5. Reduce hours of labor and provide a "comfortable amount" to all men and women over twenty-one
6. "Stand for private enterprise so far as it would not deter the progress or well-being of the majority"[8]

While the list is something of a hodgepodge—the first two points, for example, seem contradictory—it gives some idea of Chaplin's thinking about the depression in the early part of his trip.

Later interchanges provide more insight into Chaplin's politics. At a "dialectic evening" with Winston Churchill and some young members of Parliament, Chaplin responded to criticism of Gandhi by saying that "Gandhis or Lenins do not start revolutions. They are forced up by the masses and usually voice the want of the people." He also added, however, "I believe we should go with evolution to avoid revolution, and there's every evidence that the world needs a drastic change." In Berlin, Chaplin's comments to Albert Einstein about the necessity for fewer working hours, more printing of money, and price controls prompted Einstein's famous statement, "You're not a comedian, you're an economist." Meeting with Gandhi in London's East End, Chaplin queried him about his opposition to machine technology and defended the machine as a way to provide modern man with more leisure.[9] Though it would be difficult to reconcile all of Chaplin's political comments in the memoir, most are consistent with the core "progressive" beliefs that, according to Richard Pells, were shared among the American Left between the Progressive Era and World War II: faith in the capacity to reform people by affecting their technological and social environment; admiration for organizational efficiency; and a yearning to harmonize liberty and art with technological progress and community participation.[10]

Two tangential political themes in the book are especially relevant here: Chaplin's attitude toward America and his comments on the relationship between his art and politics. Within the decade, people would be charging that Chaplin had only scorn for his adopted country. The memoir, however, presents a mixed picture of the United States. Some details are critical. While visiting the south of France, Chaplin encountered a number of American expatriates and recounted their inability to live in America because of its "prohibition and Blue Laws and all the don'ts of organized puritanisms." For a man who had been hounded by certain sectors of the population during his 1927 divorce, such a perspective was not surprising. Later, Chaplin commented indirectly on conditions in America when he mentioned

130

meeting two young Americans who, to avoid living unemployed back home, had settled in Bali, where the amount of five dollars a day was perfectly adequate to live on. Describing his return to the United States, however, Chaplin is more positive. He writes at the end of his memoir that America's "youthful spirit born of prosperity and success has worn off and in its place there are a maturity and sobriety." (The first half of this comment seems quite consistent with the central concerns of *City Lights*.) In his closing paragraph Chaplin reports his feeling "that in America lies the hope of the whole world. For whatever takes place in the transition of this epoch-making time, America will be equal to it."[11]

Chaplin's attitude toward art and its relationship to politics is important because, as we shall see, artists were increasingly being pressured by critics and by some of the public to be "socially conscious" in their art during the early years of the depression. For the most part, Chaplin's comments on the subject in his memoir suggest that he was opposed to the notion of "socially conscious art." The subject comes up both directly, as in a reference to a meeting with George Bernard Shaw, and indirectly.

Recounting the meeting with Shaw, Chaplin wrote that he admired Shaw's intellect but was uncomfortable with his view "that all art should be propaganda." Chaplin's view was quite different, for he preferred "to think the object of art is to intensify feeling, color or sound." This intensification "gives a fuller range to the art in expressing life, in spite of the moral aspect of it."[12] Although the distinctions are not especially sharp in this formulation, it does seem that Chaplin did not, at this point in his career, believe that art should be aimed primarily at providing moral or political instruction to its audience.

Other comments from the memoir support this position. In discussing his unrequited love affair with Hetty Kelly, Chaplin connects art with love. For him that failed affair "was the beginning of a spiritual development, a reaching out for beauty," and the "beautiful" was consistently linked with the creation of art. If we think of the pathos that stems from unrequited or jeopardized love in his films, we get a fuller understanding of what he means by art's intensification of feeling and art's relationship to love. At another point, while visiting Italy, he was impressed by the comment of an Italian: "Art is the treatment applied to work, and has nothing to do with subject matter." Chaplin here stresses the importance of style over subject matter. Finally, as he nears the end of his book, he makes an offhand remark about the remarkably ritualized Japanese tea ceremony: "To the practical western world the tea ceremony might seem quaint and trivial. Yet if we consider the highest object of life is the pursuit of the beautiful, what is more rational than applying it to the commonplace?"[13] Life at its best, Chaplin is arguing in this passage, aspires toward art, and art itself is concerned much more with style than with content. What is so remarkable about these comments is that Chaplin was quickly confronted with other views as the 1930s wore on, and his next three films showed an increasing concern with subject matter or content, sometimes so overtly that Chaplin began to be attacked for his inadequate, primitive style and didactic messages. But at the time he wrote this memoir, Chaplin leaned toward a more aesthetic than sociological view of art.

All in all, *A Comedian Sees the World* gives us a vivid picture of Chaplin at his height as a celebrity to that point, confronted for the first time in a serious way with the strains engendered by the depression. Because the press coverage of the tour concentrated on the famous people Chaplin met and talked with, Chaplin's star image afterward was even more sterling than before. Instead of simply being known as a major figure in world cinema, he began to be rated by some as one of the most important people in the world. A feature in the *New York Times* from January 1932—even before Chaplin completed his trip— gives an idea of how important a public figure he had become in the press and, by extension, in many sectors of the public imagination.

The article, "Ten Men Who Stand as Symbols," discusses ten people whose "personalities have caught the imagination of mankind": the Prince of Wales, Mussolini, Stalin, the Pope, Henry Ford, Gandhi, Charles Lindbergh, Albert Einstein, George Bernard Shaw, and Chaplin. These "Decemviri of Individuality" were important, argued the author, because each person had enabled people to visualize something that was important to humanity. The two artists of the group, Chaplin and Shaw, were both "rebels against routine." Chaplin's particular appeal, according to the author, was the ability of his comic persona to reconcile disparities in human class, manners, and personality. He was "the highbrow who happens to be a hobo, the duke who was only born a dustman, the utterly genteel who is utterly shabby." Significantly, the author seemed to blend Chaplin and Charlie: Chaplin himself was something of a dustman turned duke in his private life, and the description also relates to oppositions in Charlie's character. Here Chaplin's star image overtly blends the man and his filmic creation, something that later—particularly in a film like *Monsieur Verdoux*—would seriously damage his reputation. Nevertheless, the article aimed not to bury Chaplin but to praise him: "as Homer was a father of poetry, so is 'Charlie' a father of laughter." Chaplin was "the standard by which others are estimated."[14]

High tributes to Chaplin were common in the early 1930s, and he was often grouped with celebrities in the press. For example, a *Vanity Fair* page from the early 1930s, featuring celebrities who played the violin, pictured Mussolini, Upton Sinclair, Einstein, and Chaplin. When a newspaper ran an article called "Distorted Faces of Celebrities," it included caricatures of the faces of Ramsay MacDonald, Lloyd George, and Chaplin.[15] In these instances Chaplin was associated with politicians but not necessarily with politics. Though he mixed with world political leaders on his world tour—the first time that Chaplin met frequently with politicians—his own political views were generally not a focus of articles in the early 1930s, even though he was beginning to make more public comments about social issues than he had previously. From the mid-1930s on, however, his political views did interest the press, and they eventually became an inextricable part of his star image.

Critics, Artists, and
Depression America

The period between Chaplin's return to the United States in 1932 and the release of *Modern Times* in 1936 was absolutely crucial to the evolution of his star image. During this period Chaplin, like many other artists, began to feel more pointedly the challenge of progressive politics.

Chaplin returned from his world tour in May 1932 to an America approaching the depths of the depression. Since President Herbert Hoover had taken office in 1929, industrial production had declined more than half. At the start of the summer of 1932, according to *Iron Age*, steel plants were running at 12 percent capacity, with no immediate improvement in sight. Industrial construction, falling from $949 million to $74 million in three years, had nearly halted. Unemployment estimates for nonfarm jobs ranged from a quarter to a third of the work force, many of whom had no source of income or relief. In parts of Los Angeles not far from Hollywood, people unable to pay their utility bills were cooking on wood fires outside their apartments. As many as two million people, whose plight was soon to be documented in Warner Brothers' *Wild Boys of the Road*, were wandering around the country in search of work or sometimes just a warm meal.[16]

The presidential primaries were already in full swing when Chaplin returned. A couple of weeks earlier, in the California Democratic primary, Speaker of the House John Nance Gardner from Texas, aided by newspaper magnate William Randolph Hearst (a Chaplin acquaintance), had run well ahead of the favorite, New York governor Franklin D. Roosevelt. However, at the June Democratic national convention in Chicago, the patrician Roosevelt marshaled enough support to win the nomination in the fourth roll call. Flying to Chicago to address the convention, Roosevelt pledged "a new deal for the American people." Roosevelt ran a relatively moderate campaign—far too moderate for many leftists—and won a landslide victory. He captured every state south and west of Pennsylvania and accumulated a 472–59 margin in the electoral college.[17]

Though Roosevelt came into office in early 1933 with no firm or ideologically based plan for pulling the country out of the depression, he did begin dramatically. Within his first two weeks he had engineered a "bank holiday" that closed and helped restore confidence in banks. He had proposed and persuaded Congress to pass strong economic measures that included budget cuts, and he had recommended that Congress end Prohibition. After his first, famed "Hundred Days," Roosevelt and a sympathetic Congress had begun to lay the groundwork for the New Deal and to reassure many Americans that the country was not in ruins. When Congress passed a second group of laws in 1935, including the Social Security Act and the Wagner Act, Roosevelt garnered even more support, and in November 1936—nine months after the opening of *Modern Times*—he easily won reelection. From a mood of despair the country had moved in four years to a mood of cautious optimism. And though the irate "economic royalists" who were Roosevelt's target in the 1936 campaign may not have admitted it at the time, his policies helped to save a tottering capitalist system.[18]

Hollywood felt the effects of the depression much as many other parts of the country did. Within the movie colony itself, the movement of political sentiment to the left was more belated and never quite as widespread as it was among artists centered in New York City and its environs. This was due in part to the fact that the depression affected the movie industry more gradually than it hit heavy industry or construction: it was easier for a person to scrape up a dime for a movie ticket during hard times than it was for an investor to finance a skyscraper. By 1932, however, the film industry too was struggling. Estimates suggest that attendance had dropped to sixty million tickets a week from eighty million in 1929. Paramount, which had made $18 million in 1930 and $6 million in 1931, had a $21 million deficit in 1932. The next year it went into backruptcy, Fox underwent reorganization, and RKO was placed in receivership. The depression had reached the movies.[19]

Political activity in Hollywood was in part stimulated by actions the movie producers took at almost precisely the time Roosevelt called the bank holiday. At a meeting of the executives of the Motion Picture Producers and Distributors Association (MPPDA), the producers agreed on March 9 to impose a blanket wage cut on employees. On March 12 one of the only strong unions in Hollywood, IATSE (International Alliance of Theatrical Stage Employees, which covered electricians, engineers, grips, and the musicians' union), refused the cut, which led to the closing of the studios on March 13. The producers hurriedly met with members of the IATSE and ironed out an agreement acceptable to both nonunion and union employees. The IATSE members emerged united and strong, providing a model for unorganized groups like the screenwriters. Union organizing thereafter became an important political activity in Hollywood.[20]

The 1934 gubernatorial campaign in California provided another political focus for Hollywood. That year, over 700,000 workers in California, half of them in Los Angeles County, were unemployed, and strife between citrus growers and migrant workers was rampant. Socialist Upton Sinclair, famed for his muckraking novel *The Jungle* (1907), decided to run for governor under the EPIC (End Poverty in California) campaign and won the Democratic party nomination in late August. Prominent businessmen, including many studio chiefs, were appalled at the prospect of trying to conduct business in a state with a socialist governor. The studio executives were particularly worried because a year earlier, in a curious book done with the cooperation of studio chief William Fox (*Upton Sinclair Presents William Fox*), Sinclair had advocated either national ownership or at least firm federal regulation of the movie industry.

The studio heads worked hard to defeat Sinclair. Besides making and distributing deceptive anti-Sinclair newsreels, they publicly threatened to move to Florida if Sinclair were elected. Sinclair in response mockingly told audiences that if the studios moved to Florida, a bite on the nose of a starlet by a vicious Florida mosquito could cost a studio $50,000 per day in lost production costs. And even if they did move, said Sinclair, he might just "put the state into making pictures . . . I'll ask Charlie Chaplin to run part of the show."[21]

The studios' anti-Sinclair tactics spawned a leftist counter-offensive in Hollywood. Dorothy Thompson and Gene Fowler, among others, combined with writers from around the state to found the California Authors' League for Sinclair. Chaplin was one of the Hollywood figures who supported Sinclair, partly because of personal acquaintance. Chaplin had known him for some time: in his autobiography, Chaplin later wrote that his interest in socialism stemmed from his acquaintance with Sinclair (MA, p. 350), and Sinclair had even submitted a script to Chaplin called *The Hypnotist* in 1918, though nothing had come of it. Recalling the EPIC campaign in his autobiography, Sinclair wrote that Chaplin agreed to speak at a Sinclair rally in Hollywood, though no firm evidence exists that the speech ever took place. Nevertheless, it does seem clear that Chaplin supported Sinclair's candidacy. Active support for Sinclair was for many Hollywood figures a first taste of political involvement, and often not the last. Even though Sinclair eventually lost by some 230,000 votes (a third-party candidate split the vote on the left), the EPIC campaign served as an early event in the politicization of Hollywood that would increase considerably in the late 1930s.[22]

The economic breakdown of the early 1930s and the ensuing political controversies had a powerful impact on many American artists and intellectuals. Perhaps the earliest and most profound effects were to weaken what Malcolm Cowley in *Exile's Return* termed the "religion of art," so widely held by expatriate artists in the 1920s, and to heighten the awareness of artists and intellectuals concerning the social and political dilemmas of the age. With the effects of the depression so vividly apparent in the cities where many of the artists and intellectuals gathered, this growth of political consciousness is no surprise.[23]

However, merely being conscious of the social and political currents of the age was not enough for many. Artists and intellectuals were pressured, particularly by the Left, to exercise their awareness by treating social realities in their work and identifying explicitly with the interests of the dispossessed. The attack on playwright/novelist Thornton Wilder by *New Masses* critic Mike Gold in 1930 provides a vivid and famous picture of such pressure. Reviewing four novels and a volume of plays by Wilder in the *New Republic*, Gold accused Wilder of creating "an historical junkshop" of a world, with characters brooding over their "little lavender tragedies" with "tender irony." Because Wilder had no guiding social philosophy, except perhaps an outdated and socially irrelevant "Anglo-Catholicism," asserted Gold, he spoke for the values of the leisure classes: "the air of good breeding, the decorum, priestliness, glossy high finish as against intrinsic qualities, conspicuous inutility, caste feeling, love of the archaic." In contrast, Gold urged authors to depict a real world where the working class struggled with real social problems, and to write from an ideological perspective sympathetic to workers and attuned to a Marxist view of history and the class struggle.[24]

Gold's interest in the relationship between art and reality from a leftist perspective gradually became shared by a number of American intellectuals, including some film critics and reviewers. Myron Lounsbury, in his history of American film criticism before World War II, identified two varieties of film criticism—the "social radical" and the "modern liberal"—affected by these leftist pressures in the 1930s. Social radical criticism, which appeared in such periodicals as *Experimental Cinema*, *New Theater*, and *New Masses*, was closer to Gold's perspective, more overtly supportive of radical social change and the place of the cinema as a mass art to encourage it. The modern liberal approach, which appeared in such journals as the *Nation* and the *New Republic*, shared the social radical's assumption that cinema reflects and shapes the values of its audiences, but tended to support more gradual social reform. The modern liberal critic likewise approved of films that attempted to grapple with the realities of contemporary life in its narrative.[25] Although social radical criticism in the early 1930s was more likely to denounce American capitalism (and Hollywood as an expression of it) in the early 1930s, the two strains of American film criticism became more similar after the beginning of the Popular Front period and the achievements of the New Deal in the mid-1930s. Both groups encouraged filmmakers like Chaplin to make his films more politically relevant to the problems of the age and to show his commitment in a time of social turmoil.

Some of the most accomplished social radical film criticism in the early 1930s was written by Harry Alan Potamkin. Born in 1900, Potamkin began a career in the 1920s as a poet but became a devoted writer on film after experiencing the vitality of French film culture during a trip to Paris in 1926. Though his writings on film in the late 1920s reveal an aestheticism characteristic of that era, the stock market crash and the onset of the depression, as well as the example of Soviet films that were beginning to be shown in the West in the late 1920s as an alternative to Hollywood, shifted Potamkin's focus. In the words of Lewis Jacobs, Potamkin's criticism in the 1930s "was generated by a social consciousness that responded to the crisis of the Depression with a critical approach that was sociological, tempered by a Marxist viewpoint. The compulsion to 'change the world' linked Potamkin's aesthetic sensibility with political and economic insights into a synthesis that directed his criticism in the last years leftward, toward social reform."[26] From around 1930 until his untimely death in 1933, Potamkin wrote a vigorous and challenging social/ideological criticism whose assumptions became widespread in the leftist press in the middle and latter part of the decade.

Potamkin's assumption that movies should grapple with the realities of the depression shaped his comments on Chaplin. In a 1931 essay on the growth of film criticism in the United States, he criticized Seldes and others like him who in the 1920s created a "cult of Charlie Chaplin which has never allowed a decent study of a man of talent who has not realized the great work that might have been expected of him." A 1932 essay expressed his view of Chaplin's weakness more explicitly. There Potamkin, challenging the critical consensus of the 1920s, objected to the "overdose of maudlin pathos" in Chaplin's previous three films. For Potamkin *City Lights* peaked in the opening scenes, then abandoned its serious concerns: "Its major motif, the relation between the millionaire and 'the classic hobo,' becomes subsidiary to the minor motif of the blind girl and Chaplin. The author-director-producer-star has weakened. He has fallen very far beneath the indications of *The Kid*, its social satire, its insistence on the major relationship, as against the formula romantic relationship."[27] In this view, Chaplin had abdicated his responsibility to concentrate on serious social concerns like the extremes of wealth and poverty and had focused instead on the wish fulfillment of romance and the emotional balm of pathos.

A similar analysis of Chaplin's work was advanced in 1934 by another social radical critic, Lorenzo Turrent Rozas. His essay, "Charlie Chaplin's Decline," originally published in Spanish in a Mexican Communist literary monthly, appeared in *Living Age* in June 1934. This was during the difficult period when Chaplin was working on the screenplay for *Modern Times*, four months before shooting began. It is not unlikely that Chaplin, accustomed to lavish praise of his films, looked carefully at an article in a popular magazine that argued his reputation was sliding. In the essay Rozas criticized *The Gold Rush* in much the same terms that Potamkin had used in objecting to *City Lights*. Rozas admitted that *The Gold Rush* was "one of the harshest criticisms ever made of capitalism in its last stage," but he nevertheless charged that the romantic ending was an evasion and salve for audiences.

Although generally praising the criticism of a corrupt society implicit in *The Gold Rush* and other Chaplin films, Rozas argued that Chaplin, like Kropotkin, was an anarchist, a position that led one "inexorably to defeat" because the anarchist "finally becomes involved with the society he repudiates." Rozas, expressing the Marxist view of the stages of economic development, held that "Chaplin and his art triumphed in the boom days of Yankee capitalism," but with the onset of the depression, Chaplin became "an accomplice of capitalism." At present, he continued, Chaplin was "in his decadence—alone, seated in the limited arena of his art. He explores the horizon. There is no road for him to follow. To insist on the old one is impossible, and to go where the workers are now marching is also impossible. To do that he would have to throw away the ballast of his millions."[28] Believing it unlikely that Chaplin would choose the "road of Marx and Lenin," Rozas charged that in hard times Chaplin's films were really harmful, because they "disorientate and confuse men who are struggling for the final victory of the disinherited." Like Potamkin, Rozas thought that Chaplin's commitments to pathos and to the individuality of the Charlie character weakened his art in the changed political and economic climate. Both critics implicitly suggested that a movement in the direction of social realism and overt commitment to radical politics would be useful and enriching to Chaplin's art. Their work was part of the broader challenge of progressive politics that confronted Chaplin and many other artists in the period.

Although building an airtight case of influence is difficult, there is evidence that suggests Chaplin was influenced by social radical criticism. In his autobiography, Chaplin wrote that as he cast about for a new film idea after returning from his world tour, "I was depressed by the remark of a young critic who said that *City Lights* was very good, but that it verged on the sentimental, and that in my future films I should try to approximate realism. I found myself agreeing with him" (MA, p. 383). It is not unlikely that the "young critic" Chaplin spoke of was either Potamkin or Rozas.

Direct influence or not, it is indisputable that many artists felt widespread pressures in the early and mid-1930s to demonstrate their social and political commitments in their works. Because of the temper of the times, it is also understandable from a psychological as well as a political and social perspective why so many artists, even many in Hollywood by the mid- and late 1930s, devoted themselves to political causes. In the 1930s, identification with some social or political group helped to mitigate alienation in a period of economic distress. It also protected one from being charged with outmoded individualism, lack of sympathy for common people, or aestheticism. For an artist like Chaplin, who knew loneliness and was already sympathetic to the dispossessed, this political climate was, as we shall see, ineluctably affecting.[29]

Chaplin's Public Politics
before 1936

What political views were associated with Chaplin's star image before the depression? Looking at the period before the crash, it is fair to say that although Chaplin mixed with a number of political leftists in his travels, he really had little active political involvement, and the press did not frequently discuss that dimension of his star image.

The issue did, however, occasionally arise before 1929. Recall Chaplin's statement to the press during his 1921 European tour that as an artist interested in life, he must be interested in Bolshevism. Before leaving on that trip, he had held a press conference at the Ritz-Carlton Hotel in New York. There a surprised reporter found that Chaplin was interested in social problems like "government ownership of railroads, socialism, unemployment, and the relations of capital and labor." Doubting the "soundness" of Chaplin's opinions but not his "sincerity," the skeptical reporter quoted rather moderate comments by Chaplin. For example, Chaplin urged that management must cooperate with labor if the country was to be prosperous. The reporter's surprise indicates that he did not expect Chaplin to comment on politics, particularly from a leftist perspective: it was not a part of his star image in the early 1920s.[30]

This early indication of social awareness and the politics of what John Diggins has called the American "lyrical left" probably stems both from Chaplin's own sympathy for social outcasts and from his associations with artists he met in Los Angeles and New York. Besides meeting Upton Sinclair in the late 1910s, Chaplin also became acquainted about the same time with two men who edited leftist magazines: Max Eastman, editor of the *Liberator*, as discussed in Chapter 3, and Frank Harris, editor of *Pearson's*. He met the Englishman Harris in New York at the end of 1920. Eastman and Harris, different in many ways, were both socialists at the time, and both had publicly opposed American involvement in World War I. Chaplin made small contributions to each magazine, after a personal solicitation by Eastman and a published appeal in Harris's magazine. Although Eastman remained a friend at least until his politics moved to the right (by the 1950s he was writing for William F. Buckley's *National Review*), he felt Chaplin's political views superficial: "Charlie liked radical ideas; he liked to talk about transforming the world; but he didn't like to pay for the talk, much less the transformation." These comments were written after Eastman had become more conservative, but it is probably true that Chaplin's politics were not firmly formed in the 1910s and 1920s: he may have been drawn, after the fact, to those who opposed World War I, but he himself had actively supported American involvement by raising money for war bonds and by making *The Bond* and *Shoulder Arms*, activities that both supported the system and helped to build his public image. These actions were more firmly associated with Chaplin's star image before the crash than any fixed political positions.[31]

By the time he finished his 1931–1932 tour, however, Chaplin was beginning to speak out more often on political affairs, and reporters found them newsworthy. Stopping in Vancouver at the end of his journey on 13 June 1932, Chaplin held a press conference. There, echoing Einstein's recent comments to him, he told reporters, "I am reputedly a comedian but after seeing the financial conditions of the world I have decided I am as much an economist as financiers are comedians." Chaplin was joining a growing chorus of critics who would have agreed with his view that these financiers "would have to take less profit" if economic conditions were to improve.[32]

Chaplin's fame made his political opinions newsworthy. As he wrote in *A Comedian Sees the World*, he was surprised "to see how seriously my views were taken. Popularity . . . endowed my opinions with importance." One indication of this was an article that appeared in a rather unlikely section of the *New York Times*, the financial page, two weeks after his Vancouver comments. This piece reported the economic views Chaplin had expressed at another press conference. He suggested that the gold standard should be abolished as a basis of currency, that currency then be expanded, and that an international currency be established to help Germany pay off its war reparation debts. He also boasted that "leading economists" he had met on his tour could find "nothing wrong" with his plan. Though these prescriptions for economic ills may seem eccentric or cranky today, it bears noting that the United States did, at Roosevelt's urging, go off the gold standard the following April, to the chagrin of many conservatives.[33] Chaplin's economic views thus reflected some of the current thinking of how to get out of the economic collapse.

Chaplin did not speak out on political issues as frequently between 1933 and the release of *Modern Times* in 1936 as he had during and immediately after his world tour, but most indications suggest that he became a Roosevelt convert publicly sympathetic to the New Deal. Alistair Cooke, who as a young English college student in America met Chaplin and spent considerable time with him in the summers of 1933 and 1934, notes that Chaplin was sympathetic to the Labour party in England and that he praised Roosevelt's New Deal measures. Chaplin's support of the New Deal and the Democratic party is reiterated directly and indirectly in a number of sources. In October 1933, Chaplin made a speech in support of Roosevelt's National Recovery Administration (NRA) over a CBS radio affiliate. He supported Upton Sinclair's EPIC campaign as the 1934 Democratic candidate for the governor of California. And in November 1934, he made the statement to reporters that his upcoming film would *not* satirize the NRA, because he was "a great admirer of President Roosevelt and in entire sympathy with his policy,"[34] though of course given Roosevelt's growing popularity, this position was not unusual.

Although his autobiography admittedly looked back three decades to this period, Chaplin's longest and most detailed political affirmation in the book praised the United States during Roosevelt's early years. Calling it "the most inspiring era in American history," Chaplin added that opponents of the New Deal called its reforms "socialism." Whether or not the New Deal was socialist, Chaplin recalled, "it saved capitalism from complete collapse. It also inaugurated some of the finest reforms in the history of the United States. It was inspiring to see how quickly the American citizen reacted to constructive government" (MA, pp. 379–80). The fact that Chaplin gave $500 to Roosevelt's 1936 reelection campaign also indicates his mainstream sympathy for the Democratic party in the mid-1930s.[35]

However, the popular artist in a mass art form like the movies takes a chance when he or she speaks out on current issues. By identifying himself with specific political opinions or economic prescriptions, Chaplin risked alienating some of his audience. Since the star image includes both the private person and the movie persona on the screen, if Chaplin gave some of his audience reason to dislike him, Charlie (and the box-office prospects of his films) could also suffer. Although the press did not often directly attack Chaplin's politics in these years, Chaplin's image was beginning to be associated with leftist politics. One indication of this is newsman Karl Kitchen's report on an evening he spent with Chaplin in March 1935. In a casual comment, Kitchen notes that Chaplin "has long had the reputation of being a 'parlor pink,' and during one of the earlier Red Scares, he was reported to have remarked that even if the country went Bolshevist he would not care, as he would become 'the people's artist.' " Such an observation, made when leftist views were more widespread, was not too damaging. After World War II and the shift in the political climate, however, such "evidence" was used against Chaplin. In assessing his discussion with Chaplin, moreover, Kitchen observed that it was dubious "whether Chaplin is sincere when he discusses certain phases of socialism."[36] Like the New York reporter in 1921, Kitchen minimized Chaplin's seriousness about politics.

In trying to pinpoint Chaplin's political views as they appeared in the early and mid-1930s, it is most accurate to say that he became an enthusiastic New Dealer after becoming alerted to the dilemmas of the depression by his world tour. It is also accurate to say that Chaplin was beginning to think of politics in Manichaean terms—"progressives" versus "conservatives" or "the common man" versus the "financiers"— and clearly sided with the former. However, as his political interests and allegiances grew in these years, he was faced with a dilemma. Given his view of art as something separate from politics, as was indicated by his comments in *A Comedian Sees the World*, as well as his increasing interest in politics, Chaplin had to grapple with the question of how aesthetics and politics related. Such an issue may seem vague when stated in the abstract, but it became very concrete indeed to Chaplin as he thought about his new film. How would this new political awareness affect the aesthetic contract he had forged with his audience? And how would the resulting film, *Modern Times*, affect his star image?

Modern Times: Production, Publicity, and Promotion

Modern Times, in many ways one of Chaplin's most interesting and fascinating films, can be most profitably examined here as a case study of ambivalence about the relationship between aesthetics and ideology. The ambivalence is evident in the finished film itself, but it is also apparent in the film's production, the publicity surrounding it, the promotional material Chaplin's staff created to market it, and even the critical response to it. It seemed that Chaplin, his staff, his audience, and the reviewers were unsure of the place of political concerns within Chaplin's personal genre and star image, even though the times seemed to encourage them. As he contemplated *Modern Times*, we have seen that there was some pressure on (and compulsion in) Chaplin the artist, like many other artists in the depression, to make a political commitment and to express that commitment through his art. However, this conflicted with Chaplin's earlier, averred belief that art and propaganda did not mix.

The information Chaplin provided the press about his new film suggests something of his uncertainty. As early as August 1933, even before *A Comedian Sees the World* began to appear, Chaplin's business manager Alf Reeves announced that Chaplin would begin production on a new film the next month. According to Reeves, Paulette Goddard was to play "a tomboy character in the picture, which will be laid in the lower part of any big city with factories." The following month a report came from Los Angeles that Chaplin had reopened his studios and planned to begin shooting on the new film in sixty days. Yet progress was very slow. Charles Chaplin, Jr., recalls that his father had begun working on the project shortly after returning from his world tour, but that even as late as the spring of 1934, "his dark moods became more pronounced, his flashes of anger more frequent" as he worked on the script. "Fear of failure," according to his son, "was plaguing him." Not only did Chaplin have to worry whether the public would accept another nondialogue film—he had decided to keep Charlie mute yet again—but the subject matter of the film and its political thrust also presented a perplexing dilemma.[37]

After shooting began in October 1934, the kinds of issues discussed in published reports about the film showed how much the "aesthetic discourse" about Chaplin had shifted from the 1910s and 1920s. Before 1920, film reviews were rarely much more than a brief plot description or statement of the reviewer's impression of the film. In such a context, the central question was, depending on the reviewer's orientation, either "was it funny?" or "was it vulgar?" In the 1920s, Chaplin began making longer films and receiving more attention from the intelligentsia. Movie reviews in general were beginning to appear more regularly in elite, intellectual journals. In such a context, reporters and others who wrote on Chaplin's films seemed primarily interested in whether Chaplin would make a purely comic film like the early shorts (as Seldes urged) or whether he would blend comedy and pathos, as in *The Kid* or *The Gold Rush*. Already what Jauss calls the "horizon of expectations" within which Chaplin's films were received had changed.[38]

But it is evident that changes in the social and political sphere, particularly a wrenching shift like the depression, can influence changes in the critical and aesthetic sphere, and thus can affect the way aesthetic works are received and the way star images evolve. By the time *Modern Times* was in production, the "horizon of expectations" had shifted again, and the central critical question was whether Chaplin would make a "purely entertaining" film or a "socially conscious" film. Reports during the making of the film conflicted, sometimes dramatically.

For example, one early article (30 August 1934) gave a fairly accurate overall description of the film: "Its locale will be the industrial quarter of a great city and its main action will be outlined against a varying background of factories, workshops, waterfronts, and dance halls." Within this setting, the description went on, Charlie would befriend a "waif" played by Paulette Goddard. Some months later, when Chaplin denied a rumor that the film would satirize the NRA, a second article quoted Chaplin as saying that it would be "a comedy picture with no endeavor to comment or satirize on social or political affairs." The following March, further along in the shooting, another reporter who spoke with Chaplin found the same thing: "It does not, he told me, contain any political inferences." Yet the same article reported that the working title of the film was "The Masses," which surely had political implications, given the fact that *New Masses* was the name of the newspaper of the American Communist party in the 1930s. (Chaplin later denied that this ever was the working title.) Furthermore, the plot description Chaplin gave mentioned a "high-pressure factory," an employee who gets fired, an arrest at a Communist parade, and a final rally.[39] Chaplin apparently wanted it both ways: he wanted to show in his work that his political sympathies were in the right place, but for those in his audience who didn't share those sympathies, he wanted to claim that the film was pure entertainment, without political implications.

Chaplin's dilemma intensified when he received a well-publicized visit in the summer of 1935 from Boris Z. Shumiatsky, president and general manager of the Soviet motion picture industry. Shumiatsky and a small Soviet delegation had visited Hollywood and received some publicity on their tour. Shortly before he returned to the Soviet Union, Shumiatsky summed up his attitude toward the American film industry by praising a number of its artists, including Chaplin, as well as its sophisticated technology. But he also criticized Hollywood films that dealt with "subjects of an ephemeral and seasonal nature." Film was such an important art form, Shumiatsky told the press, that more American filmmakers should make films that "represent the life of America" and "the serious problems facing the people of this country."[40]

Such ideas were already familiar to Chaplin; what made the visit significant was that Chaplin showed Shumiatsky a rough cut of *Modern Times*. Though this made no news in the American press at the time of the screening, some of Shumiatsky's subsequent writings about the film in *Pravda* found their way to the *New Masses* and the *Daily Worker*, and then to the *New York Times*, which caused Chaplin a good deal of worry and consternation. In November, the *Times* reported that Chaplin's new film "has been put down as a document that takes sides in the social struggle." The *Times* quoted Shumiatsky's claim in *New*

Masses that Chaplin's film showed "honestly and truthfully how the American working class is carrying on the struggle against capitalism although he himself, to be sure, does not believe in the successful outcome of this struggle." The *Daily Worker* carried translations of several articles by Shumiatsky. One of them quoted his view that *Modern Times* was "a sharp satire on the capitalist system in which he derides capitalist rationalization, crisis, the decrepit morality of bourgeois society, prison, and war." Shumiatsky claimed that his criticisms of the film led Chaplin to say at their parting, "I am very pleased we met. But this meeting will cost me many weeks of labor on my film." According to Shumiatsky, his comments encouraged Chaplin to change the ending. In its final form, Shumiatsky predicted, the ending would indicate "a stage in the ideological growth of a remarkable artist" in which Chaplin would present "the conviction that it is necessary to fight for a better life for all humanity, with a conviction of the necessity for active struggle."[41]

It is quite possible that Shumiatsky's discussions with Chaplin about the film did contribute to production delays. The film was originally scheduled for an October 11 release date, then expected in December, then in mid-January, until it was finally released the first week in February 1936. Nevertheless, any public report that a Soviet film authority had told Chaplin how to make his film was doubly unacceptable to Chaplin and his staff. Not only did Chaplin's ego demand that he be perceived as the sole creator of his movies, but the suggestion that a Soviet official dictated the changes would have been poison to the financial success of his film in the United States, even in the depression years.

So Chaplin and his staff struck back, boosted by a defense from the prominent Hollywood columnist, Terry Ramsaye, in *Motion Picture Herald*. Ramsaye noted in the opening of a December 1935 article that *Modern Times* was "becoming a subject of international discussion, by reason of the zeal of Reds and the red and pink press which would have us believe that the picture has by Russian influence been converted into a document for their cause." Speaking through Alf Reeves, Chaplin denied the charges. "The Russian story," Reeves told reporters, "reads deep, terrible social meanings to sequences that Mr. Chaplin considers funny." In a denial repeated in similar terms throughout the production of the film, Reeves continued, "I can assure you that this picture is intended as entertainment, and perhaps it might be said, too, that Mr. Chaplin's purpose in making this picture is to make money." Although admitting that the film's ending had changed, he concluded, "it is not true that anybody can ever tell Mr. Chaplin anything about such matters—he, as you know, has very much his own way and he has his own ideas—always."[42] Like Ramsaye, Chaplin and his people sensed that the *Daily Worker* aimed to make some political hay about the upcoming film, and Chaplin clearly wanted no part of it: anything that might jeopardize the box-office reception quickly set him on edge. If one weighs all this prerelease publicity from the early plot descriptions to the Shumiatsky visit and its aftermath, it is hard to avoid the conclusion that Chaplin was ambivalent: he both wanted and did not want to make a socially relevant film.

The promotion campaign designed for *Modern Times* played down the political implications of the film and concentrated instead on its "entertainment" value and the return of the familiar Charlie after a five-year absence. The opening instructions to theater owners in the pressbook presented Charlie as a valuable commodity in the finest capitalist tradition: "Remember that the most valuable theatrical property in the world is being entrusted to your care. Ordinary advertising and publicity campaigns should be dwarfed when arranged alongside your campaign on Charlie Chaplin."[43]

The pressbook also contained a variety of suggestions about how to market the film:

1. Hire a Chaplin look-alike to wear a sandwich sign saying, "I'm back again."
2. Put a false cardboard factory front on the theater.
3. Have coloring contests or dot puzzles, available to theaters for purchase in bulk from United Artists, for children.
4. Rent from United Artists banners, puzzles, a gilded Chaplin shoe, Chaplin doorknob hangers, derby hats, *Modern Times* tire covers (for rear spare tires), or a neon marquee figure of Charlie.
5. Publish in newspaper ads an article (enclosed in pressbook) in which great people pay tribute to Chaplin's genius (many of these statements came from the 1931 world tour).
6. Publish in newspapers five caricatures of Charlie (enclosed) by famous newspaper cartoonists.

The pictures on the posters and stills did have one innovation from earlier pressbooks: Charlie was often featured in the pictures *with* the gamin (Charlie alone had dominated the photographs and posters in earlier pressbooks). This sharing of attention in the promotion may be autobiographically significant, for Paulette Goddard, who played the waif, became Chaplin's third wife and was a close and stable companion, as well as the only Chaplin wife who had successful movie roles outside of Chaplin films. It could also be read as an indication that

BEGINNING TODAY
CONTINUOUS
DAILY 9 A.M.
FROM
POPULAR PRICES
50 C and $1.00
CHARLIE
CHAPLIN
in
"CITY LIGHTS"
A Comedy Romance in Pantomime
MIDNIGHT PERFORMANCE EVERY NIGHT BUT SUNDAY GEO. M. COHAN THEATRE Broadway Between 42nd and 43rd Sts.

14. Advertisement for *City Lights* (1931).

Chaplin's compulsion to receive sole credit for his productions was moderating, or even as a tempering of his individualism.

Though the pressbook's pictures and posters paired Charlie and the gamin at times, newspaper advertisements often concentrated solely on the familiar image of Charlie to market the film. In fact, some ads for *Modern Times* used a sketch of Charlie's face that was nearly identical to an ad for *City Lights* (see Figures 14 and 15). On the whole, the promotion of *Modern Times* downplayed any political significance in the film and instead suggested that Chaplin would again be fulfilling the aesthetic contract he established with his audience in *The Gold Rush* and even earlier. Chaplin's growing interest in politics, as well as the intelligentsia's pressures on him to produce socially relevant art, thus

15. This advertisement for *Modern Times* (1936) presents Charlie without the gamin, but with an expression nearly identical to a *City Lights* ad (Fig. 14).

did battle with the promotion material on the film and his public statements about the movie as it was in production. This relatively conservative promotional campaign may have been the safest way to lure conservative viewers into the theater, but what did they see, how did they respond, and what effect did the film have on Chaplin's star image?

Modern Times: Political Ambiguity and Critical Response

As already discussed, Chaplin's previous three feature films before *Modern Times* had each featured Charlie and blended comedy, romance, and pathos in a relatively similar way, establishing an aesthetic contract between Chaplin and his audience. *Modern Times* also contains these three elements. The comedy of the film often hearkens back to earlier Chaplin films. For example, Charlie's skating in the department store toy department and his antics as a waiter near the end of the film both recall *The Rink* (1916). Other comic scenes—as Charlie's disruptive dance around the factory after the assembly-line work has driven him mad, or his performance during the gibberish song at the film's conclusion—rank among the finest pantomime Chaplin ever achieved. Like the other films, *Modern Times* has a romance, here between Charlie and the gamin (played by Chaplin's protégé, Paulette Goddard). The film contains some pathos, too, but unlike other Chaplin films, most of the pathos that exists here involves the plight of the gamin, not Charlie. What makes *Modern Times* decidedly different from Chaplin's previous three films are the political references and social realism that keep intruding into Charlie's world. One could argue that this constitutes a violation of Chaplin's aesthetic contract.

These topical allusions to social disorder and the problems of the depression, however, are intermittent and sometimes uneasily juxtaposed with the more conventional elements of Chaplin's personal genre. The allusions could be considered Chaplin's attempt to provide variety within the regularities of his typical structure—a common strategy of popular genre films. But the ambiguity of the film's political implications could also be seen as rooted in Chaplin's own ambivalence about how to reconcile Charlie with the new social and political dilemmas of the time.

The background to the opening credits of *Modern Times* is a clock face whose hands are approaching six o'clock, which is followed by a new work shift heading toward a factory. The political ambiguities of the film begin with a title that precedes the first shots of the film itself: "A story of industry, of individual enterprise, of humanity crusading in the pursuit of happiness." Does "industry" refer to the quality of hard work or to a sector of the economy? The next two phrases both could have quite patriotic associations to some American viewers. "Individual enterprise" could suggest the kind of ambition or active energy that has often been associated with and prized by middle-class Americans. "The pursuit of happiness" alludes to the Declaration of Independence, as patriotic a reference as one could ask for. On the other hand, to a depression viewer with leftist political sympathies, both phrases could carry more critical implications. "Individual enterprise" could be seen as a negative reference to one of the ideological tenets that drove the United States into the depression and something that needed to be replaced by social solidarity. "The pursuit of happiness" could easily be read ironically, for Charlie's pursuit seems thwarted at nearly every turn.

After the opening title, Chaplin uncharacteristically introduces viewers to the setting by using a stylistic device that calls attention to itself. In fact, as would have been clear to many leftist viewers of the intelligentsia, Chaplin used what Eisenstein called an "intellectual montage," a juxtaposition of two shots that creates a third conception that would not exist if the two shots were not joined.[44] *Modern Times* associates workers and animals in its opening. The first shot is of a herd of milling sheep, which dissolves to a mass of workers walking up subway steps on the way to work. This is followed by another dissolve to workers heading toward a factory and another shot of the workers inside the factory itself.

Unfortunately, because the viewer is given little context at the beginning of *Modern Times*, it is hard to determine the significance of the intellectual montage. Is it a criticism of workers, who behave like mindless sheep? Is it a criticism of a political and economic system that treats workers as sheep? In Eisenstein's film, the meaning of an intellectual montage is generally clear from what has preceded it in the narrative and carries virtually no ambiguity. In *Modern Times*, however, the intellectual montage promises social significance without first establishing a clear perspective: it is intriguing without being precise. And given the varied, perhaps even contradictory, view of workers and unions presented in the film, the montage never comes clearly into focus.

The film moves on to depict the owner of the Electro Steel Company and the workers who suffer under him, a portrayal consistent with popular leftist stereotypes of wealthy capitalists and oppressed workers in the 1930s. Sitting alone in his office as his workers sweat on the assembly line, the owner plays with a picture puzzle, then turns to the funny papers. Besides being lazy, frivolous, and simple-minded, the owner is insidious in his desire to squeeze as much production as he can out of his workers. Significantly, the first recorded words in any Chaplin film are the owner's, when he gives an order via loudspeaker to a lackey on the factory floor: "Section Five. Speed 'er up." Later he says over another loudspeaker: "Attention foremen. Trouble on line five. Check on the nut tightener [Charlie]. Nuts coming through loose on line five." And later still, as the working day is almost over: "Mac. Section Five, more speed."[45] The owner's willingness to try the Bellows Feeding Machine as another way to enhance productivity also defines his character. His obsession with efficient, assembly-line productivity ultimately drives Charlie mad. This part of the film supports Shumiatsky's claim that *Modern Times* is an attack on capitalist rationalization of production. In general, the portrayals of the factory owner and of the harassed workers who toil under him are ones that leftists in the audience would have relished.

As the narrative develops, however, other political dimensions emerge. One of the most prominent is the social realism that critics had urged on Chaplin, which is evident in a number of scenes. One of the first is Charlie's walk past a closed-down factory just after he gets out of prison. He picks up a red flag that has fallen from a truck bed and, waving to return it, finds himself at the head of a demonstration of workers who have just rounded the corner (see Figure 16). Though Charlie's action is innocuous, the response of the police is not: they beat back the demonstrators with their billy clubs and jail Charlie as a Communist agitator. (Ironically, Charlie seems more at home in the secure prison than the chaotic world of depression America; with his picture of Lincoln on the cell wall and his daily paper, he seems quite satisfied with his fate.)

Other instances of social realism include more violent encounters between police and workers; the suggestion in the department store burglary that hard times drive the working class to crime in order to eat; the gamin's theft of bananas to feed her siblings and unemployed father; and her father's situation itself. When introducing the father, Chaplin grants him a sympathetic close-up; it indicates the frustrating toll that unemployment had on people living in a society where not working was an indication of personal inadequacy rather than societal failure. The father's death at a demonstration of unemployed workers represents a degree of social realism rarely seen on American movie screens in the depression. This depiction was a primary reason that a social radical critic like Kyle Crichton could write in his *New Masses* review, "I came away stunned at the thought that such a film had been made and was being distributed. . . . To anyone who has studied the set-up, financial and ideological, of Hollywood, *Modern Times* is not so much a fine motion picture as an historical event."[46]

In addition to the ambiguous prologue title, the intellectual montage, the stereotypic owner and workers, and the social realism, however, *Modern Times* contains hints of Chaplin's Victorian roots. This suggestion is clearest in the gamin's situation after her father's death. In an action reminiscent of *The Kid*, the county juvenile division issues a warrant for her arrest (because she is still a minor). The authorities' persistent threat to the budding relationship between Charlie and the gamin in the last phase of the film provides a melodramatic situation,

16. Charlie the inadvertent radical in *Modern Times*, 1936.

rooted in Chaplin's apprentice years in the English theater, similar to
the one he had used well for emotional effect in *The Kid*. Here Chaplin's aesthetic view that the intensification of emotion is important to
art is evident.

The film also guardedly affirms American middle-class values, particularly its optimism. When Charlie sits reading the newspaper in
prison, with headlines like "Strikes and Riots: Breadlines Broken by
Unruly Mobs," he looks toward the camera and shakes his head dis-
approvingly in a way that many Americans did during the depression,

153

trying to shake away the negative effects of the "news." A more specific but complicated affirmation of middle-class values comes in the dream Charlie and the gamin have as they sit outside a middle-class home. Chaplin here parodies the happy American household when a husband and wife kiss outside their house as he goes off to work, with the wife skipping back inside for another apparently joyous day of housework. When Charlie asks the gamin if she could imagine them in such a house, however, the ensuing dream suggests that their aspirations are remarkably similar to that of the parodied couple. And later, after Charlie gets his job as a department store night watchman, the gamin luxuriates in an elegant white fur coat and dreams dreams like any middle-class consumer of the depression.

One could argue that the film is trying to undercut these dreams as foolish and unrealizable for the lower classes in the depression: the contrast between the dream house and the shack in which the girl and Charlie later live supports such an analysis. Less consistent with such a leftist analysis, though, is the subtle criticism of unions throughout the film, particularly evident when a strike is called immediately after a factory has reopened and Charlie has obtained a job that would enable him and the gamin to have some means of support.

Even more clearly, the conclusion of the film seems tailored to please the middle-class optimist. After having successfully eluded the juvenile authorities at the café, but losing their secure jobs in doing so, Charlie and the gamin are sitting beside a road the next morning. She, weeping, asks in a title, "What's the use of trying?" Charlie's response would have pleased Horatio Alger: "Buck up—never say die. We'll get along." The reassured girl responds, "you betcha" (if my lip reading is accurate), and the two stand, then walk down the road in the early morning light. Although little in the film gives grounds for such optimism—one leftist critic mocked Chaplin's title as a "bromidic optimistic caption"—classical Hollywood tendencies toward a closed happy ending encouraged it.[47] Furthermore, one could even argue that this simple affirmation of effort amid difficult circumstances had become not only an essential element of Charlie's character and the "personal genre" but perhaps even a central tenet for Chaplin himself, who had been forced to cope with difficulties in his personal and professional life yet managed to keep forging on. Charlie's final sprightly steps in *The Circus* and his encouraging affirmation of life to the suicidal millionaire in *City Lights* are both closely related, in substance if not exactly in tone, to Charlie's final words of encouragement in *Modern Times*. Despite the greater political awareness and references central to

Modern Times, the conclusion brings the viewer back to the familiar, the safe, and the ordinary that popular films so often embrace.

The quiet and perhaps groundless optimism of the conclusion thus was thrown into the same pot with the other ingredients of the film to make an unusual political stew. The reactions of critics to the film suggest that they perceived many elements in it. But their reviews also demonstrate that although there were enough different flavors to please everyone at least to some extent, they were not blended well enough to satisfy anyone fully.

In general, the reviews of *Modern Times* reveal how the critical discourse about movies had shifted since Chaplin's earlier films. Critics now focused on two questions, one old, one new: (1) is the film funny; and (2) is it socially significant, and if so, what is its political line? The first question had been asked by critics since Chaplin appeared on the scene; the second was more recent, in part, as we have seen, a product of the stress on socially relevant art engendered by the depression. While some reviewers affirmed the humor and denied the social significance, others—generally those critics who could be associated with Lounsbury's social radical or modern liberal critical traditions—argued that the film was both funny and socially aware. Kate Cameron's review in the *New York Daily News* typified the first group: "It had been hinted that Chaplin had gone serious on us and that he had a message of serious social import to deliver to the world in *Modern Times*. No such thing has happened, thank goodness. . . . There is nothing of real significance in Chaplin's work except his earnest desire, and his great ability, to entertain." Predictably, those critics who denied the social significance of the film seemed generally more conservative, both politically and aesthetically, than those who did not. They tended to believe that films should be "entertaining" and that "social significance" had no place in such entertainments. They saw *Modern Times* as another contribution to Chaplin's established mode of filmmaking, a fulfillment of his aesthetic contract. To these reviewers Charlie the comic persona loomed much larger than Chaplin the filmmaker in their conception of Chaplin's star image.

But to the modern liberal and social radical critics, the relevant questions and discussion focused not so much on Charlie as on Chaplin, the serious artist. What attitude toward the current social crises would he take? Richard Watts, Jr., who wrote in his first *Herald Tribune* review that the film was a social statement, responded to conservative letters opposing his opinion in a second review: "The people I disagree with most heartily are those who insist that *Modern Times* is merely rough-and-ready farce and that we who see a certain sociological interest and significance in some of it are bleak fellows who insist on seeing sermons in stones." Elaborating, Watts continued, "Its suggestion of ideas is intermittent and rather vague, but they are definitely Left Wing in their sympathy and interest."[48]

Watts's assertion that Chaplin's politics were leftist is important, for this view was shared by the leftist press in general. Three good examples are Crichton's review in *New Masses*, Charmion von Wiegand's longer treatment, "Little Man, What Now?" in *New Theater*, and Edward Newhouse's "Charlie's Critics," published in *Partisan Review* two months after the picture opened. All three can be considered social radical critics. Von Wiegand's essay noted that the posh audience at the New York City premiere was fully amused with the film but did not identify as closely with Charlie in his moments of suffering as a less wealthy morning audience some days later. The review also argued that "as a creative genius," Chaplin "is so sensitive to his environment that he has acutely felt the impact of the changes which are occurring in the body of our society." Though praising Chaplin for grappling "with the fundamental problems of our times" in the film, von Wiegand charges that he could not really do so when his central character was "still the optimistic, lovable Charlie—a clown." Like much of the leftist press, von Wiegand was thankful that Chaplin had made his art more socially oriented but also wished that he had been more explicit in his affirmations. In addition, the review implies, as did others, that Chaplin the intellectual and artist ought be the focus of Chaplin's star image, and that Charlie, however amusing, was something of a political liability in the new, trying era.

In his *Partisan Review* essay, Newhouse agreed that the film was leftist but directly responded to von Wiegand's urgings that Chaplin become a revolutionary.

> That would not only be fine but miraculous, and I don't think he will ever make it. . . . Chaplin has had his chances to learn about the revolution and there is no evidence he took much advantage of them. For all that, we must look at *Modern Times* as something that came out of Hollywood. That is what makes Chaplin great and his picture a tremendous achievement. Chaplin is an individualist, he is a romantic, but not romantic enough to have closed his eyes to the most fundamental cruelties of bourgeois society. To film these things beautifully and bitterly is a contribution as important as that of Dreiser in literature.

Although the Left could not fully agree on *Modern Times*, it did respect Chaplin the artist and intellectual for facing up to and presenting contemporary social problems like hunger, unemployment, and police brutality.[49] To these reviewers, Chaplin was beginning to break his aesthetic contract, and this was in many ways to the good.

What the reviews indicate is that with the release of *Modern Times* Chaplin's star image had become inextricably associated in the public mind with politics. Whether the reviewers decried or welcomed this, and whether they accepted or rejected the film's political implications, they agreed it was an issue worth writing about: it had become a part of the critical discourse of the 1930s. From this point until Chaplin's exile and beyond, his political and social views were never separate from his star image, and Charlie the persona became a less dominant dimension of that image. The pressures of the depression had affected both Chaplin and the critics who wrote on films, and the horizon of expectations for those watching Chaplin films entered a new phase.

Chaplin's new film did not succeed at the box office as some might have expected. Although *Variety* predicted that *Modern Times* would be "box office with a capital B," *Modern Times* grossed only $1.4 million domestically, at least a half-million dollars less than each of Chaplin's previous three films. Even *City Lights*, released during a deeper part of the depression than *Modern Times*, fared much better. In fact, *Modern Times* did not even cover its production costs until it went into foreign distribution, something highly unusual for a Chaplin feature film up to that time.

Though it would be unfair to call *Modern Times* a box-office disaster, its disappointing performance seems linked to at least two factors. Even though the film fulfilled the central concerns of the aesthetic contract, its foray into social significance probably diminished its popularity. Chaplin's ambivalence about the place of political themes in his art had led to a confusing mixture in *Modern Times*. The film criticized the domination of humans by machines. It presented social realities with sometimes uncompromising directness. And it occasionally offered rather typical American optimism to help face those problems. Though the mixture was fascinating, *Modern Times* was also apparently threatening to viewers who wanted pure Hollywood entertainment, untainted by messages and politics, in their movies.

Another explanation for the disappointing reception of *Modern Times* is suggested by Otis Ferguson's grousing remark in the *New Republic* that "*Modern Times* is about the last thing they should have called the Chaplin picture."[50] Chaplin's refusal to make a dialogue film, nearly a decade after sound films were introduced, made *Modern Times* a stylistic anachronism. Though Ferguson was one of the few critics to complain about the style—Chaplin movies were so established a genre that they received special treatment by critics—some movie viewers probably passed up *Modern Times* because it was a "silent" film. By maintaining what seemed to be an old-fashioned film style and simultaneously venturing into previously unfamiliar areas of social significance, Chaplin was risking his preeminence as a star in Hollywood and America.

6

The Popular Front,
The Great Dictator, and the
Second Front, 1936–1942

The Popular Front and American
Antifascism

Although Chaplin's uncertainty about the relationship between politics and art generated, as we have seen, a certain ambiguity in *Modern Times*, his thoughts on the subject gradually became clearer after the release of the film, which led his political commitments to become a more significant aspect of his star image. A contributing factor to this change in his image was his decision, after much resistance and brooding, to capitulate fully to sound and make a dialogue film. Equally important was the shift of the political climate in America and Hollywood in the last half of the 1930s toward a greater awareness of the international threat of fascism, which gave Chaplin a cause he felt he could and must fully embrace. Antifascism became the most passionate and public political commitment of Chaplin's life, one that would have an inestimable effect on his star image.

In the middle and later years of the 1930s, the attention of Americans gradually turned away from the domestic concerns of the depression to international concerns about fascism. The popularity of President Roosevelt had something to do with this shift: even though the depression had not "ended" by 1936, most Americans felt that conditions had improved and that the future was more hopeful than the recent past. Perhaps more important to the shift in political attention were the international events that thrust themselves on Americans with accelerating urgency. From the time of Adolf Hitler's rise to power in 1933, the rearmament of Germany in the mid-1930s, and the systematic denial of civil and human rights for German Jews during the same period, the character of fascism and the threat it posed became increasingly apparent. Similarly, the Italian invasion of Ethiopia in 1935 was an early example of fascist expansionism. When both Italy and Germany provided arms and other support for Franco's attack on the Spanish Loyalists during the Spanish Civil War (1936–

1939), the threat became more concrete and the lines of division more clearly drawn. Although the Munich Pact of 1938 temporarily averted war, it also raised questions about the futility of appeasement. After the European political situation was thrown into disarray by the Nazi–Soviet Nonaggression Pact of 24 August 1939, Hitler felt confident enough to invade Poland at the beginning of September. By September 3, England had declared war on Germany, and a riveted American population sympathetic to the Allied cause (84 percent in favor, according to a Gallup poll) both concentrated on the international situation and debated whether America should intervene or isolate itself from the tragic struggles in Europe. Richard Pells has summed up the movement in the era well: "inexorably, the crisis in Europe and the Far East supplanted the depression as the decade's major concern."[1]

Another aspect of this shift in attention was a change in the Communist party's political strategy. In 1935 the Seventh World Congress of the Communist International, concerned about the growing threat that Hitler posed to the Soviet Union, officially called for a "Popular Front" to combat the fascist threat. This call had varying effects in different countries, but it led the Communist Party of the United States (CPUSA) to tone down its rhetoric. Instead of calling themselves "revolutionaries," Party members would more likely refer to themselves as "progressives," which placed them within a much larger group of antifascists. Instead of celebrating the "proletariat," a member would celebrate "the people." Instead of dismissing the New Deal as "social fascism"—just another disguised variety of the rotten capitalist system—a member might have even praised its willingness to fight for the interests of the common people. These shifts meant that the drama of social conflict, although still apparent, was couched in new terms: instead of "revolutionary socialists" doing battle with "oppressive capitalists," American Communists in the late 1930s found themselves engulfed in a struggle between "progressives" and "reactionaries."

As it moderated its rhetoric, the CPUSA also began to identify itself with various American traditions. Instead of quoting Marx, Engels, and Lenin, the Party was much more likely to cite Paine, Jefferson, or Lincoln. Earl Browder, general secretary, indicated something of the change when he asserted that the Party was "really the only party entitled by its program and work to designate itself as 'sons and daughters of the American revolution.' " One slogan used by the Party during the Popular Front period was "Communism Is Twentieth-Century Americanism," a theme put into symbolic action when in 1937, on the anniversary of Paul Revere's ride, a Young Communist League chapter in New York hired a man in colonial garb to ride a horse down Wall Street. He also carried a sign: "The DAR [Daughters of the American Revolution] forgets but the YCL remembers." To Communists, at least in America, the Popular Front clearly meant identifying with national traditions.[2]

This shift in rhetoric and attitude toward national traditions had a political effect. Although the Party kept its distance from Roosevelt in the 1936 presidential election and continued to urge the formation of a Farmer–Labor party while acknowledging its preference for Roosevelt over Landon, by the 1938 elections it had abandoned its hopes for a third party and argued that such a strategy could only serve to fragment the Left and aid the forces of reaction. By this time, it had committed itself fully to cooperation with other antifascists. This led to widespread cooperation and increasing unity among groups on the political left and center who agreed on the seriousness of the fascist threat. Although some advocates of the Popular Front also sought to counter the efforts of conservatives who wished to stifle unionism and social reform measures, this was not a primary thrust of the Popular Front: it rather tended to downplay domestic issues that, had they been emphasized, would likely have divided those who could otherwise cooperate against fascism. In the domestic sphere at least, the Popular Front thus had conservative political implications.[3]

Perhaps the most vivid and, for understanding Chaplin's next film, the most relevant way to discuss the political atmosphere of the Popular Front period is to examine one of its most active areas: Hollywood. Except for New York City, Hollywood was the most important center of international awareness and activism in the United States during the mid- and later 1930s—and with good reason. Not only was Hollywood already an unusually cosmopolitan community thanks to the many European filmmakers and artists who came to work there during the twenties, but the Los Angeles area in general became the destination of thousands of Jewish refugees fleeing from Hitler from 1933 on. The list of artists and filmmakers who escaped Hitler and came to Hollywood is impressively long. It includes such people as actors Peter Lorre and Luise Ranier; composers Max Steiner, Erich Korngold, and Hanns Eisler; directors William Dieterle, Billy Wilder, and Fritz Lang; and writers Thomas and Heinrich Mann, Lion Feuchtwanger, Franz Werfel, and Bertolt Brecht. Because so many of the arrivals after 1935 came for political reasons, and because a number of "international salons" regularly functioned to bring together the refugees with other Hollywood residents, the political awareness of fascism became more pronounced and thus the Popular Front activity more lively in Hollywood than in most other parts of the country.[4] Chaplin came to know a number of the emigrés and exiles—Salka Viertel, Eisler, Feuchtwanger, and others—and was influenced by their politics, as will be discussed in Chapter 8 (MA, p. 434).

Probably the most prominent manifestation of Popular Front antifascism in Hollywood was the Hollywood Anti-Nazi League, which flourished between 1936 and 1939. The first important anti-Nazi gathering in Hollywood was a hundred-dollar-a-plate banquet at the Victor Hugo Restaurant in April 1936 attended by many movie luminaries. Following more organizational activity by Dorothy Parker, Donald Ogden Stewart, Fritz Lang, and Frederick March, among others, the official establishment of the Hollywood League against Nazism (shortly after renamed the Hollywood Anti-Nazi League) was held at the Wilshire Ebel Theater on 23 July 1936. By the fall the League was buying full-page ads in *Variety* and other trade magazines, using such headlines as "The Menace of Hitlerism in America," and announcing a mass meeting at the Shrine Auditorium. The meeting was attended by over 10,000 people. It has been estimated that at its peak the League had about 4,000 to 5,000 members representing a wide range of political views. In its four years of existence, the League held meetings, demonstrations, banquets, and parties; raised money for the Loyalists in Spain; published a newspaper (*Hollywood Now*) that reported on the dangers of fascism, both at home and abroad; and even sponsored two radio shows each week: "Dots and Dashes from Abroad" and "The Voice of the League." Leni Riefenstahl, the director of *Triumph of the Will*, and Vittorio Mussolini, the dictator's son and the head of the Italian film studio, Cinecitta—both of whom had been invited to Hollywood by conservative producers, were snubbed by the group. The League generally helped set up an atmosphere of vigorous antifascism in Hollywood in the three years before the war broke out in Europe.[5]

Another antifascist organization to spring up in Hollywood during these years was the Motion Picture Democratic Committee (MPDC). This group grew up partly as a reaction against the actions of studio heads and other businessmen during the 1934 EPIC campaign. It became active again in June 1938 to work for the election of the progressive Democratic candidate for governor of California, Culbert Olson. Due in part to the considerable funds that it raised, the MPDC helped to elect Olson, despite the fact that 1938 state and local elections generally turned out to be quite anti-Roosevelt. During the next year the MPDC continued its support of Olson and spent considerable time affirming such national causes as the La Follette Committee on

Labor and challenging others, like the newly established House Committee on Un-American Activities. The MPDC was more willing to question the Soviet Union than the Anti-Nazi League was (the 1939 MPDC Declaration of Policy affirmed "categorical opposition to any and all forms of minority dictatorship," right or left) and was more actively involved in electoral politics. However, like the Hollywood Anti-Nazi League, the MPDC was faced with a serious intellectual challenge when the Nazi–Soviet Nonaggression Pact was announced on 24 August 1939.[6]

The pact had a profound and shocking effect on Communist party members, liberals, and everyone in between. Its ultimate effect, particularly after the Soviet Union attacked Finland in late November 1939, was to dismantle the Popular Front and drive a wedge between radicals and liberals in Hollywood who had been cooperating for several years. Party members and their sympathizers who defended the Soviet's actions as pragmatic generally began calling for peace and attacking Roosevelt's foreign policy as war-mongering. In defending an isolationist foreign policy for the United States, they suddenly found themselves aligned with conservatives of various stripes with whom they had little else in common. On the other hand, many liberals drew themselves even closer to Roosevelt and moved toward a pro-Allies, interventionist position. This division made groups like the Anti-Nazi League and the MPDC unworkable, and within a short time both organizations, shorn of their unity and effectiveness, vanished from the scene. Not until the Wehrmacht attacked the Soviet Union on 22 June 1941 did the CPUSA shift back to an antifascist, interventionist political line. At that point an uneasy resurgence of the Popular Front took place.[7]

After the war broke out—and during the time Chaplin was shooting *The Great Dictator*—American public opinion gradually began shifting from an isolationist to an interventionist position. This was partly due to German successes on the battlefield. Two weeks after the war broke out in September 1939 (and just after Chaplin began shooting his new film), 82 percent of Americans polled expected the Allies to win. Only 7 percent expected that the Germans would win. However, in July 1940, more than a month after the fall of France (and while Chaplin was editing *The Great Dictator*), only 43 percent believed that England would win; 24 percent thought a German victory more likely. Furthermore, that same month, 69 percent said they believed that a German victory would affect them personally, whereas the previous March, before the fall of France and Belgium, only 47 percent held such a view. Despite a strong yearning, rooted in the painful memories of World War I, to keep out of another large-scale war, the American public was moving in 1940 toward a feeling that some sort of action in favor of the Allies was becoming essential despite the often vociferous opposition by midwestern isolationists and members of the CPUSA to any involvement.[8]

Within this context of antifascism, an increased participation in the political process by many Hollywood figures, and growing support for interventionism, Chaplin was contemplating and then shooting his next film. We have already seen that Chaplin was generally favorable to Roosevelt and the New Deal from the early 1930s. Furthermore, he, like many other Hollywood figures with liberal political inclinations, was influenced by the antifascist atmosphere of the 1936–1939 era. He attended Anti-Nazi League meetings and became more aware of the fascist threat. After the outbreak of the war and the early successes of the Germans, he also attended meetings of the Committee to Defend America by Aiding the Allies, a group whose name indicates its position. But unlike his politicized Hollywood colleagues, Chaplin possessed a financial independence that enabled him to make a film on a controversial political issue if he chose. And such ideas were percolating in his mind as he began to plan a film to follow *Modern Times*.[9]

The Great Dictator: Preparation, Production, and Promotion

A number of eerie similarities make one wonder if Chaplin was fated to make a film about Hitler. The two were born within four days of one another in April 1889. They were raised in similar circumstances of childhood poverty. Both at times demanded strict control over their subordinates when, as adults, they achieved positions of power. Probably the most widely discussed similarity, the physical resemblance of Hitler and Chaplin's persona Charlie, centered on their mustaches. Since Chaplin's interest in creating overtly political films coincided almost exactly with Hitler's consolidation of power in Germany and growing international notoriety, it is understandable that Chaplin gradually decided that his next film after *Modern Times* would satirize the German leader. Throughout the reverses of fortune and the shifts in political alliances in those volatile years of 1938–1940, Chaplin remained firmly committed to his conception: in October 1940, *The Great Dictator* opened in New York City.

Before he decided to make a "Hitler film," Chaplin had to consider whether he would continue to resist dialogue films. Because nearly a decade had passed since sound films had been introduced, Chaplin was seeming more than ever like an anachronism in the film industry. Two Sundays after *Modern Times* opened in 1936, the *New York Times* carried an uncharacteristically critical article on him, titled "The Curious Mr. Chaplin." In addition to charging that Chaplin was parsimonious, contradictory, egotistic, and difficult—even unreasonable—to work with, the article suggested that Chaplin "clings tenaciously to youth" because "he resents and fears growing old." That resentment and fear, according to the article, "has caused him to fortify himself in the past and to refuse to concede anything to the contemporary medium." In comments that must have been disturbing to the comedian (the *Times* generally gave him a great deal of attention, praise, and advance publicity for his features), the article called him a "lone wolf" who, to the current film industry, represented only "the Hollywood that was."[10]

For the rest of 1936 and into the following year Chaplin apparently did little work on a new film project. From shortly after the opening of *Modern Times* until early June, he and Paulette Goddard took a trip to the Far East, during which, according to Chaplin, they were married (MA, p. 385). Upon returning, Chaplin again agonized about the question of whether to make another nondialogue film. "To continue with a feeling that the art of pantomime was gradually becoming obsolete," he recalled years later, "was a discouraging thought" (MA, p. 385). The decision to abandon the pantomime so central to the comic persona that had enriched him was a difficult one. On the other hand, Chaplin's growing desire to comment on current social and political issues made dialogue films seem much more attractive.

By September 1937, Chaplin announced that his next film would be a talking one. Shortly after the announcement Frank Nugent paid tribute in the *New York Times* to the "little tramp" who was "the colossus of the cinema." He also seemed a bit relieved at Chaplin's decision. After *Modern Times*, he wrote, "it was useless to pretend that the sound revolution had passed over his head leaving him as firmly enthroned as ever." To compensate, Nugent suggested, Chaplin was to become "a producer with certain politico-sociological messages to deliver," an observation that emphasizes how Chaplin's star image was becoming linked to politics. A *Times* editorial the next day commented that "a note of sadness sighs through the announcement that Charlot is no more."[11]

Though the editorialists did not know it at the time, Chaplin shortly thereafter began to work on a film that would pit a caricature of Hitler against a close relative of Charlie. At least two people, Ivor Montagu and Alexander Korda, seem to have influenced Chaplin's decision to make an anti-Hitler satire.[12] Before he decided to forge ahead with a Hitler story, however, Chaplin had cast about for a film that would star Paulette Goddard. At one point in 1937, he was enthusiastic about having her do a film version of the novel *Regency*, by D. L. Murray, but that idea came to nothing. When an impatient Goddard signed a contract with David O. Selznick, Chaplin decided he needed a change of scenery and in February 1938 left Hollywood to spend several months in Pebble Beach, California. There he worked on another story, this one about a young millionaire who takes a cruise to China and falls in love with a beautiful White Russian employed at a dance hall. It was to have starred Goddard and Gary Cooper, but it too fell by the wayside as the Hitler idea kept crossing his mind. "How could I throw myself into feminine whimsey or think of romance or the problems of love," Chaplin recalled, "when madness was being stirred up by a hideous grotesque—Adolf Hitler?"[13]

Chaplin as usual sought to keep the persistent press from learning much about his film, but some information about it leaked out even before shooting began. These leaks give us some indication of how the story evolved. A report in November 1938 said that Chaplin would play a prisoner in a concentration camp who would speak gibberish because he didn't speak the same language as the others. (Apparently Chaplin did for a time toy with the idea of using language in much the same way as he had with Charlie's song in *Modern Times*.) By February 1939, articles reported that the new film would be called *The Dictators* and that Chaplin would play a local dictator who would use "Teutonic speech." About the same time Frank Nugent came back to New York City from the West Coast and summed up a story Chaplin had written called "The Dictator: The Story of a Little Fish in a Shark-Infested World." In the story, two dictators—Hinkle and Mussemup—tangle, and another character played by Chaplin is mistaken for Hinkle, taken to the city of Vanilla in the country of Ostrich, and gives a speech calling for world peace. As the crowd becomes stirred by his words, the character, much like the soldier in *Shoulder Arms*, wakes up in a concentration camp: his actions have just been a dream.[14]

Making film satires about contemporary political subjects can be a hazardous preoccupation: when political currents shift, the filmmaker's attitude toward his subject (and the film's appeal to its audience) can change radically. Chaplin came to know these dilemmas. According to one newspaper account, he had completed the script by the start of April 1939, then did shooting of miniatures and sound tests starting in June.[15] However, the Nazi–Soviet Pact in August and the outbreak of World War II in September delayed shooting and confronted

Chaplin with serious questions. First of all, this film would be Chaplin's most expensive to make, because of the large cast, the elaborate sets, and the recorded, synchronized dialogue. If *Modern Times* failed to earn production costs in domestic rentals, and if most European markets were closed to Chaplin and South American markets were threatened as well because of the war, would *The Great Dictator* be a poor investment? Second, if the American government remained officially neutral on the European war, would government pressure be brought to bear against the production of anti-Nazi films? Third, if American public opinion remained radically divided between isolationist and interventionist positions, would a satirical attack on Hitler and Nazism risk alienating a large potential segment of the audience? And finally, what position would Chaplin himself take vis-à-vis the Nazis: if he loathed them, did he loathe them enough to urge Americans to take up arms against them? And if so, would that notion be incorporated into the film?

These were all difficult questions, particularly since no one could foresee the scope or duration of the war. Ten days after the Germans invaded Poland, the *New York Times* reported that, despite denials by Chaplin, "there are indications that he will postpone *The Dictators* until the future can be appraised with more assuredness."[16] After a brief delay, however, Chaplin went ahead with the shooting, which was essentially finished in late March 1940. During the time Chaplin was cutting and scoring the film, Hitler launched an offensive on Belgium and France. The same day that the fall of Belgium was reported in the *Times*, in fact, another article noted that several early antifascist films, including *Mortal Storm*, *Four Sons*, and *The Great Dictator*, were pending but that their release was uncertain. According to the article, several United Artists executives predicted that releasing Chaplin's new film in the present political situation could only result in "disaster for the screen." Chaplin, however, issued a statement: "The report that I have withdrawn the film is entirely without foundation. I am cutting it now and as soon as it can be synchronized, it will be released. More than ever now the world needs to laugh. At a time like this, laughter is a safety valve for our sanity."[17] Already financially involved in the film to the tune of at least $1.5 million, Chaplin had little choice but to go ahead with his plans. A September release was announced.

That release date was pushed back to mid-October, and as the film's release drew near, articles about its topicality began to appear. One of the most detailed was an interview with and profile of Chaplin in the *New York Times Magazine* on September 8. There Chaplin, the serious political intellect, emphasized his opinion of Hitler: "Leaders with

17. Plea to exhibitors in *The Great Dictator* pressbook:
Chaplin the social critic.

tenth-rate minds have captured the new instruments of propaganda
and are using these instruments to destroy good, civilized, kind, behavior," he told interviewer Robert van Gelder. "I'm the clown, and
what can I do that is more effective than to laugh at these fellows who
are putting humanity to the goose-step?" The article also contained a
description of Chaplin's working methods and, with the accompanying pictures of Chaplin from *The Great Dictator* and other films, generally prepared readers for the monumental upcoming opening.[18]

Chaplin and United Artists were also preparing promotional material as the opening neared. The pressbook for *The Great Dictator*, more
than any earlier Chaplin pressbook, announced the fact that the film
had a "message." Consider the opening appeal to the exhibitor on
page one: "Here is the picture that is actually a national event . . . the
picture with the greatest combination of star and theme in the history
of the screen." *The Great Dictator*, it added, is "a history-making comedy based on the most vital topic in the history of the world" (see Figure 17). The program that accompanied the pressbook stressed Chaplin's brilliance and his commitment. One statement, after noting that

Chaplin was born less than one hundred hours before Hitler and that Chaplin spent a childhood of "almost Dickensian destitution," asserted that Chaplin's features to 1936 "are all classics of cinematic comedy, the acknowledged masterpieces of the man whom George Bernard Shaw called 'the only genius in motion pictures.' " It added that in *The Great Dictator*, however, "Chaplin is more than genius. He is an institution, the idol of millions of all races and creeds, the champion of the pathetic and oppressed. And, at a time when the world is sore and sick at heart, the little man with the funny moustache is something of a saviour, bringing with him at a time we need it most the invaluable therapy of laughter." Note the transformations here. In the midst of hyperbole common in Hollywood publicity, both persona Charlie and Chaplin himself are portrayed as internationalist spokesmen for humanity.

Accompanying pictures and posters showed Chaplin as the Jewish barber posing with Hannah, Chaplin as the dictator playing with the balloon globe, and a somber and posed Chaplin, wearing suit and tie, shot from a low angle. This picture was accompanied by a text that gave Chaplin yet more extravagant praise and again stressed his progressive political commitment: "Admiration for the little tramp . . . . is confined to no race, class, or creed. Essentially, Charlie Chaplin belongs to the little guy—the men, the women, and the children who make up the overwhelming portion of the population of all the countries of the world." The pressbook and accompanying program emphasized not only that Chaplin would talk in the film (preparing audiences for a fundamental departure from previous Chaplin films), but also that he would have a progressive message to convey.[19]

The advance publicity evidently was successful, for massive crowds on opening night gathered at both the Capitol and the Astor theaters in New York City to get a glimpse of Chaplin and Goddard, who attended both premieres. Newspapers and trade journals reported on the extravaganza, with some using pictures of Chaplin and Goddard nearly crushed by the crowds as they made their way toward the theater entrances. Others, like *Motion Picture Daily*, printed a number of pictures of prominent figures who had attended. (These included such industry luminaries as Harry Warner, president of Warner Brothers; Adolph Zukor, board chairman of Paramount; and Spyros Skouras, head of National Theatres.)[20] Despite the risk of making such a film and the controversy it was sure to engender, the opening night, at least, was a genuine media event.

The Great Dictator and the
Aesthetic Contract

The Great Dictator is Chaplin's most overtly political and topical film. It involved itself with the times more than any other of his works, and explored a subject that was weighing heavily on the minds of most Americans when the film was released. One way to underline the film's relevance is to look at the books that were featured in the *New York Times Book Review* the Sunday before *The Great Dictator* opened in October 1940. Ernest Hemingway's antifascist novel of commitment, *For Whom the Bell Tolls*, was reviewed. So was Edmund Wilson's study of Marxism, *To the Finland Station*, which he concluded with a sense of disillusionment that contrasted with his enthusiasm for that tradition earlier in the 1930s. A contemporary report on political conditions in Europe, Claire Booth Luce's *Europe in the Spring*, was given prominent attention, as were two books that sought to define the democratic values that could be used to counter fascism: Eleanor Roosevelt's *The Moral Basis of Democracy* and the interventionist Lewis Mumford's *Faith for Living*. The same day that *The Great Dictator* opened, two headlines on page one of the *Times* indicated the state of the current crisis. "London Is Rocked by Heaviest Raid, RAF Keeps Berlin Awake Six Hours," wrote one. A second showed that the interventionist/isolationist division in America had not disappeared: "Lindbergh Assails Present Leaders—Asks Voters to Back 'Strength and Peace' Instead of 'Weakness and War.' "[21] Whereas the attention of the American people was focused primarily on domestic affairs when *Modern Times* was released, these books and headlines indicate how fully that attention had shifted toward international affairs and the fascist threat. *The Great Dictator*, with its satiric attack on fascism and its affirmation of an alternative set of values, was exploring issues of central concern to Americans at the time of its release.

The topicality of the satire in *The Great Dictator*, which would have been clearly evident to most informed viewers in 1940, manifested itself through references to people, places, and historical events. Adenoid Hynkel (Hitler), the Phooey (Der Führer), is aided by his loyal sycophants, Minister of War Herring (Goering) and Minister of the Interior Garbitsch (Goebbels). The appearance and demeanor of the actors emphasized the satirical references. Chaplin, of course, bore a close physical resemblance to Hitler. In addition, though, Billy Gilbert's bulk brought Hermann Goering to mind, while Henry Daniell's suave and sleek manner created an effective analogue for the German minister of propaganda. After Chaplin's performance, probably the

170

strongest satirical acting was by Jack Oakie as Benzino Napoloni, Chaplin's caricature of Mussolini, also referred to as "Il Digaditch" (Il Duce). His rivalry with "Hinkie" helps deflate the expanded egos of the two tyrants.

Hynkel is from Tomania, a blend of the word for food poisoning and the suffix "mania"—madness. Napoloni's country is Bacteria—another poison infecting the world's body politic. In the military review scene, Napoloni refers to the name of his capital city: "Aroma." The historical setting of the film is extremely clear—from near the end of World War I to the Nazis' invasion of Austria in 1938. To strengthen the specificity of the setting, Chaplin presents several documentary montages. They include headlines with specific historical references as well as documentary newsreel footage, some of Nazi party rallies. Early in the film, headlines move the film from the Armistice to the rise of Hitler by referring to the Dempsey–Tunney fight, Lindbergh's transatlantic flight, and the onset of the depression. Later, two headlines refer to the Nazi persecution of Jews: "Ghettoes Raided" and "Jewish Property Confiscated."

The film's topicality is also rooted in specific events. One is the Nuremberg Nazi party rallies of 1933 and 1938, which are called to mind during Hynkel's speech at the start of the film and the barber's speech at the end. Another reference is to Mussolini's visit to Germany in September 1937, when he cemented his friendship with Hitler thanks to Hitler's flattery and the impressive display of German military might at a military review. The Anschluss, Hitler's annexation of Austria (called "Osterlich" in the film) in 1938, is a final reference.

This last event is significant, for Chaplin was becoming deeply concerned about the fate of Jewish refugees while he was working on the film. In mid-1939 the *New York Times* reported that Chaplin instructed United Artists to pay his share of the European rentals earned by *The Great Dictator* to a Vienna Jewish organization aiding Jews emigrating from Central Europe. These monies never went to the organization, for by the time the film was ready, no European nation except perhaps Switzerland could have shown the film, and the Vienna organization was defunct. But Chaplin persisted. On 28 July 1940, it was reported that he was among a number of people who had collectively deposited $6 million in a Milan, Italy, bank to support Austrian Jews who were being forced from Austria by the beginning of August. When the film shows that Hannah's dream of escaping her persecutors by moving to Osterlich is delusory, Chaplin is basing the film on concrete historical circumstances.[22]

In its use of this pointedly topical satire, *The Great Dictator* was atypical for Chaplin. Many of his earlier films had, of course, scored satirical points against various targets. Except for *Shoulder Arms*, however, that satire had almost never been directed toward matters of prevailing public debate. After *The Great Dictator*, however, Chaplin was much more willing to include specific historical references in his films, as we shall see. This departure from his aesthetic contract would have distinct effects on his star image.

In what other ways did *The Great Dictator* either fulfill or depart from Chaplin's aesthetic contract? Of course, the most significant stylistic departure from previous Chaplin films was the inclusion of dialogue. For the first time, excluding the brief gibberish song in *Modern Times*, audiences heard Chaplin's voice and those of his fellow players. Although *The Great Dictator* still has its share of effective pantomime, as when Charlie's surrogate, the barber, shaves a customer or when Hynkel does his "globe ballet," dialogue is an integral part of the film. Audiences had to get used to hearing Chaplin speak, both as the blustering Hynkel and as the timid barber.

Concerning two other characteristics of Chaplin's aesthetic contract—romance and pathos—the film is equivocal. There is a romance of sorts between the Jewish barber and Hannah. Because Paulette Goddard played Hannah, many viewers would have noted the continuity between this film and *Modern Times*. Yet the romance is less central to the narrative than in the earlier Chaplin feature comedies. The same is probably true of pathos. Though some scenes are poignant— the scene of the barber and Hannah overlooking the burning ghetto is perhaps the best example—the pathos is not directed toward the Charlie persona (or his surrogate) the way it was in *The Gold Rush*, *The Circus*, and *City Lights*. The differences in the handling of both the romance and the pathos in *The Great Dictator* represent, if not a violation of the aesthetic contract, at least an attenuation of it.

On one hand, the topicality, the addition of dialogue, and the handling of romance and pathos in *The Great Dictator* all represented to audiences shifts from the Chaplin films many knew. On the other, perhaps the central similarity between *The Great Dictator* and the earlier comic features that had established the terms of the aesthetic contract was the clear contrast between a "good" moral universe and an evil one, embodied by a contrast between Charlie and another character (the county officials in *The Kid*, both Jack and Black Larsen in *The Gold Rush*, the ringmaster in *The Circus*, and the millionaire in *City Lights*).

The Great Dictator centers on such a contrast. The opening credits emphasize it, for there Chaplin groups the actors under two categories: "People of the Palace" and "People of the Ghetto." The narra-

tive structure is itself one of Chaplin's most balanced: it contains a prologue set in World War I that shows the Jewish barber fighting as a
patriotic albeit ineffective Tomanian soldier and an epilogue set after
the start of World War II that shows the barber again, but this time,
disguised as Hynkel, urging his countrymen not to fight. Within this
frame, the stories of the barber and Hynkel, of life in the ghetto and
life in the palace, are regularly intercut: Hynkel and his cohorts are
on the screen 47 minutes, the barber and the others of the ghetto 46
minutes.[23]

The settings in which the barber and Hynkel live help emphasize
the moral contrast. The barber has a shop on a modest city street. The
courtyard between his shop and the Jaeckels' home, as well as the mer-
chants who sell their wares on the sidewalks, give the city a European
feeling, but the furnishings in the Jaeckels' home and the costumes
and manner of the people in the ghetto give it a folk flavor, similar to
the flower girl's home in *City Lights* or Jean's flat in *A Woman of Paris*.
These settings all suggest a warmth and simplicity associated with positive (and often threatened) values in Chaplin's films. In contrast, the
dictator moves in a setting of opulence. When he gives a speech to the
sons and daughters of the Double Cross, he stands on a massive platform, prominently displaying symbols of propaganda, high above the
thousands who are listening. In his palace Hynkel has a huge office
that dwarfs anyone who enters. His surroundings suggest his egotism:
he has a bust of himself on his desk, his file cabinets are false-fronted
mirrors that he preens before, and he sometimes goes briefly into a
room and poses for a sculptor and painter who work simultaneously
on tributes to the Phooey. All in all, Hynkel's settings suggest a callous
and egotistical leader who lives in splendor, far removed from his people, whom he manipulates and for whom he shows consistent disdain
(see Figure 18).

The characterizations of Hynkel and the barber (both played by
Chaplin), as well as of those who surround them—particularly Garbitsch and Napoloni in Hynkel's case, and Hannah and Schultz in the
barber's—also develop the moral contrast. A central feature of the
film is what Paul Goodman called its "invective" against Hynkel's qualities: his megalomania, narcissism, compulsion to dominate, and disregard for human life.[24] But though villains in earlier Chaplin films
exhibited similar qualities, Hynkel is different in that he is clearly associated with a historical and specific ideology: fascism. Thus the core
of Chaplin's invective against Hynkel is a historical and specific antifascism. This progressivism, grown and nourished during the Popular
Front period and extending beyond it for most non-Communist anti-

fascists even after the Nazi–Soviet Pact, envisioned a polar political spectrum that placed "fascism" at one end and "democracy" at the opposite.

The ideology of fascism is expressed most clearly in the film by Garbitsch's brief address near the end.

> Victory shall come to the worthy. Today, democracy, liberty, and equality are words to fool the people. No nation can progress with such ideas. They stand in the way of action. Therefore we frankly abolish them. In the future each man will serve the interests of the state with absolute obedience. Let him who refuses beware. The rights of citizenship will be taken away from all Jews and non-Aryans. They are inferior and therefore enemies of the state. It is the duty of all true Aryans to hate and despise them.

This speech explicitly expresses Chaplin's understanding of the fascism that his film opposed.

Typical of Chaplin's aesthetic contract, a humane code of values provides an alternative. In contrast to the power-hungry Hynkel and his henchmen, the barber, Hannah, and the other citizens of the ghetto simply want to live and let live. Hannah, a victim of modern civilization—she is an orphan whose father was killed in World War I—enunciates this philosophy to the barber: "Life could be wonderful if people could be left alone." But the physical layout of the ghetto shows that Hannah's dream cannot be realized. When on the sidewalks, the Jews are vulnerable to attacks from Hynkel's storm troopers, depending on the whims of the Phooey's policies. Early in the film, they have some protection within the courtyard between the barber's shop and Mr. Jaeckel's house; however, even this sanctuary is violated as the film progresses. Shortly after Chaplin cuts to a shot of a caged bird hanging by the Jaeckels' front door, soldiers raid the courtyard, capture the barber and the "traitor" Schultz, and send them to a concentration camp. The others have no alternative but to emigrate to Osterlich. The innocent, the kind, the tolerant, and the compassionate seem endlessly victimized.

Described in this way, the conflicts in the film seem to lead to a dark conclusion. If, as the film suggests is the case, the good are weak and the evil are powerful, is the world doomed? A central aesthetic and political question raised by *The Great Dictator* is this: how ought the good, and the advocates of democracy who empathize with them, respond to the cruelties of the fascists? This was a very real dilemma for Americans when *The Great Dictator* was being shot and released, for in

18. Chaplin as Hynkel in *The Great Dictator*, 1940.

the late 1930s, many antifascists were also pacifists or at least extremely reluctant to support any American involvement in another European war. Like the people of the ghetto, many Americans, though much less directly affected, were agonizing about how to respond to the threats of the dictators.

Several details in *The Great Dictator* suggest an answer. Early in the film Hannah uses her frying pan to smash the heads of two storm troopers who have been harassing the barber. It gives her a feeling of release and catharsis. As the scene closes, she tells the barber, "That did me a lot of good. You sure got nerve the way you fought back. That's what we should all do: fight back. We can't fight alone, but we can lick 'em together."[25] Although an American viewer in October

1940 could take this as an affirmation that the Allies supported by the United States could counter the fascist threat, active resistance by Jews to Hynkel and his supporters in the context of the film itself seems futile: those forces of darkness are too organized, too well armed, and too powerful to overcome. What perspective and tactics, then, does Chaplin defend?

The famous ending—the part of the film that elicited the most debate when the film was released and that has drawn considerable critical attention since—suggests an answer.[26] Following Garbitsch's comments, quoted above, the disguised barber, at Schultz's urging, walks up to the microphones and delivers a speech of three and a half uninterrupted minutes that counters Hynkel's speech near the opening of the film. Chaplin, who had resisted dialogue long after the rest of Hollywood had accommodated itself to the new technology, here finally affirmed the power of the word. This was a turnabout, for both *Modern Times* (in the phonograph record sales pitch) and an earlier scene in *The Great Dictator* (when the inventor demonstrates his bullet-proof uniform), use the line, "actions speak louder than words," indicating Chaplin's aesthetic resistance to the dictates of dialogue in pictures. However, in this final speech, Chaplin resolved his dilemma about the relationship of politics and aesthetics, and in doing so broke the irksome bonds of silence imposed on him by Charlie's pantomime.

Although the speech contains contradictions and inconsistencies, when read closely, its essential kernel defends the democracy of progressive politics in its struggle with fascism. As he concludes, the barber appeals directly to the Tomanian soldiers and implores that they not fight for the dictator but rather take power from him and return it to "the people." The barber does not specifically beat the drums of war against the fascists—he is, after all, urging the Tomanian soldiers to abandon their dictator, in which case any war would be over. He does clearly imply, however, that if the perverted dictators can be stopped in no other way, it may be necessary to fight for the well-being of the world, so that the kindness and decency of the people of the ghetto can survive and flourish.

Ultimately, one word sums up Chaplin's strategy for concluding his most overtly political film: "hope." As Garbitsch is introducing him, the barber hears Schultz urging him to speak: "It's our only hope." Pensively, the barber repeats the word, "hope," then makes his way to the microphones. The speech is an expression of hope despite what Chaplin saw as a world gone mad. The fact that it is followed by the soldiers' cheers and the barber's comments, via radio waves, to Hannah about seeing a better world on the horizon only reinforces the point. Chaplin's political sentiments and message rang clear in the film: he had met the challenge of progressive politics.

Although the presentation of contrasting moral perspectives was integral to Chaplin's aesthetic contract, the manner in which the "good" universe was defended in the conclusion was not. The ending was a stark departure from Chaplin's general practice and from the classical Hollywood system of filmmaking in the 1930s in three ways. First, the ending explicitly defended a topical and controversial political position. It was much more explicitly ideological than any previous Chaplin ending and hastened the tendency of Americans to associate Chaplin's star image with a progressive political perspective.

Second, the ending was not "closed": it failed to resolve all the narrative conflicts. Through a steady diet of Hollywood films in the depression, audiences were taught to expect neatly presented plot conflicts that were clearly and unambiguously resolved. This Chaplin did not do. Though the convention of mistaken identity that made the ending possible was an old one, this error is never cleared up. Hynkel, dressed as a duck hunter, is arrested by storm troopers when he claims to be the dictator. The barber, with his dictator's uniform, fools the troops into believing he is Hynkel. Chaplin faced an extremely difficult task in convincing the audience in the theater that the barber's gentle speech will deceive, much less be accepted by, the assembled crowd. And by leaving the final expression of hope balancing precariously on the tightrope of unresolved mistaken identity, Chaplin violated his audience's expectations. This change in their typical experience of moviegoing made many viewers uneasy, as we shall see, though few would have been able to articulate exactly why this was so.

Third, and even more significantly, by having the barber deliver a long, uninterrupted speech with shots of unusually long duration, the film style violated stylistic conventions audiences were familiar with from many American films. Though long speeches were not unheard of in Hollywood films of the era, they were generally broken up by cutting to different camera angles and distances of the speaker or, more commonly, by using a shot/reverse shot (cutting back and forth between the speaker and the character who was listening to him). One analyst who has looked closely at the American film style in the 1930s has estimated that a typical film then averaged a cut every seven seconds.[27]

The barber's speech is shot in a way that deviates widely from these conventions. During the speech itself, which lasts three and a half minutes (followed by two and a half minutes focusing primarily on Hannah, with the barber's voice occasionally urging hope for the future), Chaplin uses only three shots:

1. Medium close-up shot of the barber: 78 seconds
2. Dissolve to full shot of Hannah: 9 seconds
3. Dissolve to medium shot of the barber, dollying after 60 seconds to medium close-up: 122 seconds

Juxtaposed with the typical 1930s cutting rhythm of one shot every 7 seconds, Chaplin's violation of convention becomes starkly evident. As a number of writers on the classical Hollywood film have noted, the aim of its style is to draw attention away from itself to the narrative, and to tell that story in as functional, efficient, and engaging a manner as possible.[28] By using such long takes, with nothing varied in the background to draw the audience's attention away from the barber's impassioned face, Chaplin interrupted the relatively smooth and rapid flow of images that characterized the classical style. Thus, not only did Chaplin deviate in a number of ways throughout the film from the aesthetic contract he had forged with his audience through his comic features, but his ending also, through a violation of the ideological, narrative, and stylistic conventions of Hollywood films, disrupted the satiric fiction he had been creating. The close of *The Great Dictator* was not simply an unsatisfactory ending for many contemporary viewers and critics. It was also, despite Chaplin's courage and conviction in presenting this conclusion, the beginning of the decline of his enormous public popularity in America.

Critical, National, and International Reaction to *The Great Dictator*

As one would expect when the world's most famous movie star made a film about the world's most infamous political figure, the reaction to *The Great Dictator* was enormous—in fact, the most widespread of any film Chaplin ever made. That is true whether one measures reaction by the film's box-office success, the number of critical reviews it generated, or the official responses to the film by governmental officials.

For all of Chaplin's worry during production concerning the box-office prospects of *The Great Dictator*, the film was an overwhelming financial success. Opening at two theaters in New York City, it enjoyed a fifteen-week run there, a good indication of its appeal to audiences. Although it was not released until after the end of World War II in many European countries, it earned over $5 million in rentals worldwide, more than any other Chaplin film, which generated its maker a profit of $1.5 million on an investment of $2 million. *The Great Dictator* was more than just a financial success in 1940: when Bosley Crowther did an article in 1942 on the top ten moneymaking films in the previous half decade, *The Great Dictator* was third on his list. When one recalls that *Gone with the Wind* was made during that period and that roughly 2,400 other American films were released during the same time span, the box-office appeal of *The Great Dictator* becomes even more impressive.[29]

The critical reviews generated by *The Great Dictator* are extremely interesting to read, and there are a lot of them: because the film was so topical, it was even reviewed in places where movies were normally not given much attention. The critic for the *New York Times* suggested how important the film was when, after the excitement of its premiere, he wrote that "for the first time within memory, the most eagerly awaited picture of the year was a comedy."[30]

Reading through the reviews, one gains two somewhat contrary impressions. The first is that Chaplin was approaching the high point of his career as a star and public figure: the young comedian who was surprised in 1915 that anyone would be interested in his opinions or take them seriously had matured into a fifty-one-year-old man who had come to see it as his responsibility to comment on the world's most pressing public issue, and he was being recognized for it. But one also senses in reading the reviews that Chaplin's star was beginning to fall. Although the critics respected and were intrigued by what he attempted in the film, many felt the film engaged too directly with politics. Because of the ideology and aura of "entertainment" deeply embedded in the classical Hollywood system of filmmaking, overt treatment of controversial political issues was taboo. When a filmmaker violated that taboo, even in order to attack an ideology like fascism that was being widely assailed in the country at the time the film was released, the filmmaker was certain to alienate a substantial number of critics and to make many viewers uneasy. The ending particularly disturbed reviewers, for there the ideological violation was accompanied, as we have seen, by a violation of narrative and stylistic conventions of the classical Hollywood system. Since in his previous features Chaplin had for the most part adhered to the conventions of the closed ending and the continuity style, his substitution of direct address for closed ending and of extremely long takes for the much more common shot/reverse shot made Chaplin even more vulnerable to attack from critics. Henceforth, no movie fan would be able to separate the dimension of politics from the star image of Charles Spencer Chaplin. Furthermore, the persona of Charlie, and all the engaging qualities that made him the object of identification and comment, began to weaken as an integral part of the Chaplin star image.

If anything like a critical consensus can be gleaned from the newspaper reviews, it is that although the film was an important one that ought not be missed, the ending was unsuccessful and a mistake. Generally, the more conservative the critic or newspaper, the more negative the review. For example, Archer Winston wrote in the *New York Post* that although he enjoyed the comedy in the film, "the speech is so completely out of key with all that has preceded it that it makes you squirm. Even if you understand perfectly well the noble motives for it. . . . nevertheless, it is an artistic boner of the first water." Two days later, also in the *Post*, Sidney Skolsky recommended the film but added, Chaplin "wrote the final speech himself, and this is where the picture failed completely." The *New York Sun* observed that "Mr. Chaplin, who has been going in more and more heavily for social significance during his last two pictures, now goes completely overboard. He turns his show into drama that is closer to tragedy than comedy. . . . a great disappointment." Hearst's *Journal-American* judged that the film was "at its best when Chaplin devotes himself to comedy," and Ed Sullivan, whose political conservatism would lead him to attack Chaplin often after 1940, dismissed the film in the *Daily News* by writing that "every comic wants to play Hamlet, but no clown should play Hamlet." The *Herald Tribune*, generally sympathetic to Chaplin's work, wrote that "the pattern of [Chaplin's] new motion picture is definitely disconcerting. *The Great Dictator* is aflame with Chaplin's genius but the flame flickers badly."[31]

Other critics, generally those who were more sympathetic to Chaplin's progressive politics, were gentler with the film but still critical at times. Given the situation in Europe, a thesis proposed in William Boehnel's review in the *World Telegram* was certainly arguable: "Hitler and all he represents are beyond the kidding stage. [*The Great Dictator*] is propaganda first and entertainment afterward." Yet Boehnel still defended the film: "If it falters now and again as entertainment, the things it says and does must be honored." In the *Philadelphia Record* Elsie Finn wrote that although the final speech "is delivered in too Hitlerish a manner, it's the film's logical conclusion." And in what might have been the two most important reviews—those in *Variety* and the *New York Times*—Chaplin was luckier. "The preachment is strong, notably in the six-minute speech at the finish," wrote *Variety*, "but the comedy, which Chaplin has woven around the dictators, at whose expense he makes fun (partly with a sneer), is extremely entertaining." With prescience, the reviewer added, "The box-office potentialities

180

are excellent." Bosley Crowther's sympathy for socially significant films led him to praise it as "a superlative accomplishment by a great and true artist . . . unquestionably the most significant—if not the most entertaining—film that Chaplin has ever made." To Chaplin's credit, wrote Crowther, "He is actually making a most profound and tragic comment upon a truly evil state of affairs."[32]

One of the most interesting reviews of *The Great Dictator* appeared in the *Daily Worker*, the CPUSA newspaper. The film was released well after the Nazi–Soviet Pact but before the Nazis attacked Russia: precisely during that period when Party members had abandoned the co-operative antifascism of the Popular Front period and were generally working against American involvement in the world war. Given his responsibility to defend that political line in his review, the *Daily Worker* reviewer, David Platt, had his work cut out for him. His review in the *Worker* was titled, "Chaplin in *The Great Dictator* Achieves a Triumph of Satire." The two subtitles reveal the tension built into the review: "Masterpiece of Comedy Lashes All Oppression" and "Picture Ends With Eloquent Plea for Peace." The astonishing element of the review is its argument that *The Great Dictator*'s conclusion is "a tremendous contribution to peace." The film has nothing for the "Roosevelts and Churchills and little Hitlers in industry" who are trying to plunge America into "the dark age of war," wrote Platt. Rather, it is "a genuine people's film against war and fascism." This is a most torturously twisting review of *The Great Dictator*. Platt had the unenviable responsibility of being antifascist (but not too much so) and antiwar at the same time. By distorting the film, he managed to accomplish this.[33]

Despite widespread attention, *The Great Dictator* was thus much less successful with reviewers than it was at the box office. This somewhat critical response by reviewers can be understood in at least two ways. First, because Chaplin's film had so much prerelease publicity, because it treated such a topical issue, and because of Chaplin's high status as a filmmaker, the expectations of reviewers were probably higher and their standards more critical. The higher the expectation, the more likely one is to be disappointed.

Reception theory provides another reason for the negative critical response to *The Great Dictator*. In Jauss's terms, the "aesthetic distance" between *The Great Dictator* and the critics was greater than for any Chaplin film at least since *A Woman of Paris*. Hence the hesitant, ambivalent, or outright negative responses: the unsettling new political dimension in the film was hard for many to bear. Whereas much of Chaplin's work could easily be considered the "entertainment art" (*Unterhaltungskunst*) that Jauss devalues, this film was in certain ways less predictable and more disturbing to viewers. The work initiated a change in the horizon of expectations through which viewers would encounter Chaplin's subsequent work, and those shifts would create difficulties for the sustenance of Chaplin's star image.[34]

In any case, the attack by reviewers on the film's ending was more than Chaplin expected or could tolerate. Just a week after the film's New York City opening, but before the film went into general release, Chaplin publicly responded to the reviews in a letter to the *New York Times*. Countering those who argued that Hitler was no longer funny, Chaplin writes that it is not only possible but necessary to laugh at Hitler during these troubled times, because laughter is "health-giving." To those who find the ending inappropriate, he adds: "To me it is a logical ending to the story. To me it is the speech the barber would have made—even had to make. . . . May I not end my comedy on a note which reflects, honestly and realistically, the world in which we live, and may I not be excused for pleading for a better world?" Such comments show how Chaplin's aesthetic views had changed during the depression decade. From a view that art and politics lie in distinctly different realms, Chaplin, like many American artists influenced by the 1930s, was arguing that it was an artist's right, if not responsibility, to "reflect" the problems of the world and to "plead" for a better one. (It is also worth mentioning that as well as defending his political views, Chaplin was trying to protect his film's economic prospects.)[35]

The reaction to the film by the weekly magazines and monthly journals, most of which came out after Chaplin's letter, reveal much the same response found in the daily newspapers. One of the only purely positive reviews appeared in *Catholic World*. Although it was quite short, it was filled with praise: in the reviewer's words, "More devastating than any bomb invented, his caricature of tyrants will long outlive their tyranny." Much more common were charges that although the film was funny, the comedy and the serious social comment did not blend successfully. In the *New Republic* Otis Ferguson gave a mixed review. On the positive side, it was "a good picture," containing not just laughter but also "warmth and grace" (the qualities Ferguson associated with previous Chaplin films and the Charlie of old). He also found, however, "the symbiosis of comedy and earnestness an unhappy state of union, detrimental to both." In his view, "for the world's first funny man to prove that he too can write a *New Republic* editorial" was not particularly impressive, since Chaplin's came "several years later": denouncing Hitler took more prescience and courage in 1937 than in 1940. And the ending? To Ferguson, the "exhortation to the downtrodden of the world . . . is not only a bad case of overwriting but dramatically and even inspirationally futile." Philip Hartung's review in *Commonweal* followed similar lines: "When the world's best comedian takes himself and the world's woes too seriously, he goes sour." Likewise, the *Nation* ("the picture leaves one . . . with a curious mixture of enthusiasm and disappointment") and *Newsweek* praised parts of the film but on the whole were, with most other reviewers, uneasy.[36]

Saturday Review, in an editorial, attacked Chaplin's topicality most vigorously of all. "The root problem in *The Great Dictator*," according to its author, "is simply that Hitler and his doings are no longer funny." By tying his film to a particular time and place, Chaplin gave up the "universality" so central to his earlier movies. The editorialist believed he saw a lesson in the Chaplin episode. Rejecting the 1930s notion of socially aware, committed art, he wrote: "Our comedians will render good service to the national morale if they can give us something to laugh at in the years ahead; but they had better pick out material that would have been just as recognizable, just as funny, before Hitler was ever born." The tone of American cultural life was beginning to shift in a direction that ultimately would challenge Chaplin's progressive politics in a fundamental way. Looking back from nearly a half century, it seems more than a little significant that even the liberal journals that would have been sympathetic to the film's politics were criticizing it in their film reviews.[37]

The film continued to generate controversy and gain publicity for a long time after its release. In March 1941, Fritz Hippler, head of the Cinema Department of the German Reich's Ministry of Propaganda, answered President Roosevelt's comment to the Motion Picture Academy a week earlier that dictators fear the propaganda effect of American movies. Scoffing at the notion, Hippler remarked that "if it is true that the American movie has carried 'the ideals of a free nation' throughout the world, then America's ideal must be light amusement, song hits and tap dancing." He added that Germany's ban on American films resulted from the recent release of a number of "provocative films" that included *The Mad Dog of Europe*, *The Mortal Storm*, and *The Great Dictator*. The controversy continued throughout 1941: in July the *Daily Mirror* reported that Paulette Goddard had become the target of a smear campaign by domestic Nazi and fascist groups. Reviewers who commented on the film in its second or third runs in 1941 and 1942—after American involvement in the war seemed likely or had even begun—were more willing than the earlier reviewers, however, to endorse the film. In May 1941 the *St. Louis Dispatch* wrote: "If the rages of Adolph Hitler at times go beyond the limits of burlesque and become genuinely frightening and insane, it is because Chaplin has that to say about Hynkel or Hitler." Early in 1942 the *Dallas Morning News*, noting that the final speech "was roundly condemned eighteen months ago," added that "now, with *The Great Dictator* assuming a new seriousness, the oration does not seem off key."[38]

The film also came to the attention of various governmental officials, in part because it was so clearly antifascist at a time when the government was still officially neutral. Isolationists did not like *The Great Dictator*. In mid-1941, Senators Burton Wheeler and Gerald Nye, both members of the isolationist America First Committee, expressed their indignation over Hollywood's antifascist films (though there were only a few) and argued that they were promoting America's involvement into the war. Wheeler accused the film industry and the Roosevelt administration of carrying on "a violent propaganda campaign intending to incite the American people to the point where they will become involved in this war." To counter the threat they perceived, Nye joined Bennett Clark in proposing a resolution approved by the Senate on 1 August 1941, which was to investigate "any propaganda disseminated by motion pictures and radio or any other activity of the motion-picture industry to influence public sentiment in the direction of participation by the United States in the present European war." This resolution established the Senate Subcommittee on War Propaganda. Its members accused a number of films of being "war mongering documents," among them *Pastor Hall, Foreign Correspondent, Blackout, That Hamilton Woman, So Ends Our Night,* and *The Great Dictator*. Chaplin himself was subpoenaed in September to testify on *The Great Dictator* in October. Senator Clark told the press that the subcommittee "wished to ascertain Chaplin's motives" in making the film. The *Washington Evening Star* published a cartoon shortly after the announcement satirizing the fears of the subcommittee and defending Chaplin (see Figure 19). Although the legal files of United Artists show that Chaplin's lawyers prepared some information about *The Great Dictator* requested by the subcommittee, Chaplin never was called to testify: after a delay, Pearl Harbor interrupted the subcommittee's activities, and soon after it disbanded.[39]

In part because its antifascism was so pronounced, *The Great Dictator* caused the Roosevelt administration considerable difficulty in its relations with Latin America, many of whose nations had sizable German immigrant populations. The issue of showing or not showing *The Great Dictator* became hotly contested in many of the countries as time went on. After Germany overran most of Europe, many believed that Latin America would be the next area of Nazi aggression. Chaplin recalled meeting with Roosevelt for forty minutes at the White House after the

19. *Washington Evening Star* cartoon (September 1941) on
Chaplin the "premature antifascist": FDR cited the cartoon
to help mock the Senate Subcommittee's position.

President requested a print of the film. According to Chaplin, Roosevelt's only response to him specifically about the film was: "Sit down, Charlie, your picture is giving us a lot of trouble in the Argentine" (MA, p. 405). All through 1941 and 1942 the *New York Times* carried brief articles about whether or not various Latin American countries were showing the film. To list only the *Times* references, in January 1941 a cut version of the film was shown in Chile while it was banned in Paraguay and shown in its entirety in Nicaragua. In February it was shown in Costa Rica over the protests of both Germany and Italy. In March it played in Ecuador. As late as March 1942 Paraguay lifted its ban on the film, and it finally played in May. While all this was going on in Latin America, the *Times* reported that the film was getting a very strong response in England in February 1941 and a rental was being negotiated by the Soviet Union after the Nazi invasion made the film politically acceptable.[40]

The Great Dictator remained newsworthy. Shortly after Rome was liberated in June 1944, *The Great Dictator* played there. Probably because the country's devastating experiences of war were so recent, the Italian audience had a hard time laughing during the film. After the film, according to an American observer, the audience left "the cinema subdued and, it seemed, stunned." A similar reaction greeted the first showing of the film to a selected group of Germans in 1946.[41] No previous Chaplin film had generated such controversy or elicited such a strong reaction, and the fact that even its foreign releases garnered U.S. publicity suggests that Chaplin's star image was increasingly becoming associated with a certain political stance. As America became more involved in the fight against fascism, Chaplin himself was moving toward an active involvement in politics that would make this link even stronger.

Chaplin and the Second Front

Having expressed his progressive politics on film, Chaplin also reaffirmed them in 1941 and 1942 through overt political activity. Even though he had long been uncomfortable as a public speaker and had rarely spoken to large crowds except during the Liberty Loan tour of 1918—which usually involved very short, often comic, exhortations—Chaplin's hesitance about public speaking diminished after *The Great Dictator*. This was in part because he had something he wanted to say and in part because after having said so much in *The Great Dictator*, he no longer felt compelled to protect the pantomime of Charlie. Furthermore, Chaplin was goaded by the hate mail he received from domestic fascist sympathizers while he was making and helping to promote *The Great Dictator*. After the Nazis attacked the Soviet Union in June 1941 and the United States entered the war in December, Chaplin was even more willing to contribute to the war against fascism. Though it has become customary over the years, even ritualistic, to dismiss Chaplin's politics as unformed or contradictory or superficial, Chaplin's activities in 1941 and especially 1942 suggest that he made a concerted effort to contribute to the war as a progressive antifascist. This activity, which supplemented his political affirmations in *The Great Dictator*, wedded progressive politics even more closely to his star image.[42]

One of Chaplin's first public addresses after the release of *The Great Dictator* was to read its final speech in Washington, D.C., the evening before Roosevelt's third inauguration. Scheduled as one of a number of artists to perform at Constitution Hall, Chaplin arrived at Union Station the afternoon of 19 January 1941, to perform that evening. Upon his arrival, he told reporters, "I feel everyone has given the Nazis' momentary victories too much importance. . . . We should all be made more cognizant of human decency." When asked his views on Roosevelt, Chaplin replied, "He is the hope of us all. He is the hope of the world."[43] That evening, to a packed audience, Chaplin appeared with Nelson Eddy, Mickey Rooney, Raymond Massey, Ethel Barrymore, and others.[44]

The following day Chaplin stood at the Capitol Plaza to hear Roosevelt deliver his inaugural address, in which the President promised that the torch of liberty would remain burning brightly. As Chaplin left and moved toward the entrance of the Senate Office Building, however, he heard a small portion of the large crowd shout, "Heil, Hitler." According to a report, Chaplin "obviously had a retort ready, but friends quickly took his arms and guided him—almost forcibly—through the crowd."[45]

Later that year Chaplin read the speech again, this time at the hall of the Daughters of the American Revolution in Washington for a radio hookup (MA, p. 161). The same day he met with Roosevelt and had the conversation about Argentina mentioned above. One could of course argue that reading this speech was not particularly dangerous for Chaplin's public reputation: after all, he had already firmly associated himself with the positions it articulated. Shortly after America entered the war allied with the Soviet Union, however, Chaplin began to leave his *Great Dictator* speech at home and deliver more extemporaneous public addresses, this time in favor of the opening of a second front in Europe.

Chaplin's first step in this direction was to join several groups that aimed to foster Soviet–American unity during the war or to send humanitarian aid to the Soviets after the Nazis invaded. One of the earliest pieces of evidence demonstrating such activity is a full-page advertisement paid for by Russian War Relief and appearing in the 10 October 1941 issue of the *New York Times*. The advertisement's headline was "Russia's 'Scorched Earth' Calls to America's Green Fields" (the "scorched earth" referred to the Soviet policy of burning any of their own houses and fields that had to be abandoned in the face of the oncoming Nazis). Below this was an announcement of a Russian War Relief benefit scheduled for Madison Square Garden on October 27, as well as a list of the organization's supporters, who, according to the ad, were "moved not only by their humanitarianism but actuated by their common-sense Americanism." Around three hundred names appeared on the list. In addition to Chaplin, it included many actors (among them, Dame May Whitty, Gale Sondergaard, Basil Rathbone, Nigel Bruce, Helen Hayes, Alfred Lunt), film directors (Rouben Mamoulian, John Huston, Frank Capra, Lewis Milestone), writers (Elmer Rice, Thomas Mann, Lion Feuchtwanger, Brooks Atkinson), and intellectuals (Robert Lynd).[46]

A headline in the *Times* the same day suggests how the second front policy would gradually, by the middle of 1942, gain a broad level of support among the American populace. The headline read "Nazis Claim Vast Victory." The accompanying articles discussed the furious battles as the Nazis attacked and moved even closer to Moscow. The articles reported that, according to Soviet radio, German forces had "been halted in the terrific drives on Moscow from the south and southwest." As newspapers reported daily on the carnage in Russia, the dogged resistance of the Soviet military and populace, and the ferocity of the battles with the Nazis, more and more people, including important U.S. government officials, began to believe that it would be sound military strategy to have Great Britain and the United States establish a second front in western Europe that would force the Nazis to split their forces.

On a national level, the drive to support a second front policy was strongest in the United States between May and November of 1942. In the opening months of the year, several prominent spokesmen delivered well-publicized speeches in favor of such a policy. On February 26 the popular Soviet ambassador to the United States, Maxim Litvinoff, made a plea in a speech to the Overseas Press Club for a second front to be established by the spring. On April 23 a prominent British statesman, Lord Beaverbrook, spoke to a meeting of the American Newspaper Publishers Association and also defended a second front policy. He argued that by opening the second front, the chances for a quick defeat of the Axis powers would be at hand. Among American statesmen, both Wendell Willkie, the 1940 Republican presidential candidate, and Joseph E. Davies, the former U.S. ambassador to the Soviet Union, also came out publicly for the policy in the spring.[47]

By summer, the policy seemed to be the U.S. government's as well. When the Soviet foreign minister Molotov visited Washington in June, he bluntly asked Roosevelt and his aides if the United States could undertake an offensive that would drive off forty German divisions. According to Cordell Hull, who attended the meeting, when General George C. Marshall answered that it could be done, Roosevelt "authorized Mr. Molotov to inform Mr. Stalin that we expect the formation of a second front this year." Although the Soviets were forced to wait until 1944 before the American and British forces invaded western Europe, the Allies did invade North Africa in November 1942. At this point, the American perspective changed, and headlines like the ones on the front page of the *New York Times*—"American Forces Land in French Africa; British Naval, Air Units Assisting Them; Effective Second Front, Roosevelt Says"—helped to mute calls for a second front after the end of the year.[48]

As Ralph Levering has shown, partly because of broad coverage in the media during that time, the second front policy—despite a tradition in the United States of antipathy toward the Soviet Union—was supported by a significant majority of the American public by the middle of 1942. In July a Gallup poll showed that 60 percent of the people who had opinions about the second front policy favored it. It seemed to many a pragmatic policy when the Nazis exhibited so much strength in eastern and central Europe. Support for the policy was strongest among people with leftist or middle-of-the-road political views, while few conservatives, according to Levering, "spoke out either for or against a second front in 1942." (These conservatives, though hesitant to come out publicly in favor of the Soviet Union on any issue, nevertheless did not want to seem unpatriotic by coming out against a second front.) A *Time* magazine cover of Dmitri Shostakovich on July 20, accompanied by an article supporting the policy, as well as the popularity during the summer of two books that supported the Soviet Union—Joseph Davies's *Mission to Moscow* and young James Reston's pro-interventionist *Prelude to Victory*—also helped through sales and reviews to spur pro–second front opinion in the country.[49]

Chaplin, of course, had ideological reasons for supporting the second front policy: its main aim was to help defeat the Germans, and his antifascism was well served by supporting it. But Chaplin had also over the years met and enjoyed the company of Soviet visitors to Hollywood. We have already mentioned Chaplin's friendship with Sergei Eisenstein when the Soviet director was in California in 1930 and Chaplin's acquaintance, while cutting *Modern Times*, with Boris Shumiatsky and his colleagues. It also seems that the Soviet national response to Chaplin blossomed after the visit with Shumiatsky. In April 1938 the Soviet film industry, with Shumiatsky as spokesman, sent an official letter of greeting to Chaplin on his fiftieth birthday.[50] After *Modern Times* and *The Great Dictator*, the Soviets generally became much more positive about the humanitarianism in his films, and Chaplin often became the recipient of official praise from the Soviet Union, as we shall see. Chaplin's second front activities stemmed at least in part from his fondness for some of the Soviet "celebrities" that he had met in Hollywood and from his gratitude for Soviet praise of his films.

Between May and December 1942, Chaplin was a featured or sole speaker for at least six rallies, most of which were fund-raisers for Russian War Relief. At a time when many figures in Hollywood were enlisting in the armed forces or contributing to the war effort in other ways, like visiting USOs, Chaplin made his contribution through speech making.[51]

He first became involved as a speaker in a way that was unusual for a star of his stature: as a second choice, a substitute. On 17 May 1942, he received a phone call from a Russian War Relief official in San Francisco, who asked if he could fill in for Joseph E. Davies, who was to have been the featured speaker at a rally on May 18 in San Francisco's Civic Center but had fallen ill. Chaplin agreed and took the train to San Francisco. In his autobiography, Chaplin recalled that because of his full schedule, he had little time to plan a speech. That evening, after hearing a number of short speeches that he felt were too tentative in support of the policy, he stepped up to give his allotted four-minute speech, but went on extemporaneously for forty minutes when the crowd became enthusiastic. If his memory is accurate, he urged the audience to embrace the alliance more fully as a way to overcome the fascist threat, and was greeted at the end of his speech by seven minutes of applause (MA, pp. 407–9). The leftist San Francisco newspaper, *People's World*, reported that "it was Chaplin whose warmth and sincere entreaty for military action in Europe evoked the deepfelt response of the audience." According to the article, Chaplin and the audience then drafted a mass telegram urging President Roosevelt to open a second front as soon as possible.[52]

After the meeting Chaplin remembers dining with Dudley Field Malone and John Garfield. According to Chaplin, Garfield praised him for his courage in giving the speech. This disturbed Chaplin, for as he put it later, "I did not wish to be valorous or caught up in a political cause célèbre. I had only spoken what I sincerely felt and thought was right" (MA, p. 409). Though the comment left a "depressing pall" over Chaplin for the rest of the evening, he recovered enough to give another speech at a Russian War Relief rally in the Los Angeles Shrine Auditorium on May 25.[53] Though no transcript or detailed descriptions of the speech are available, it seems reasonable to surmise that the central thrust of his comments in Los Angeles mirrored his speech in San Francisco.

Chaplin's next public address in favor of the opening of a second front was via telephone on July 22, transmitted from Los Angeles to Madison Square Park in New York City, where the CIO sponsored a "Support the President Rally for a Second Front Now," which drew 60,000 people. Since the CIO's Greater New York Industrial Union

Council later published the speech as a brochure, along with a brief description of the occasion, we have an accurate transcript, which Chaplin later reprinted in his autobiography.[54] The crowd, who gathered on a beautiful day to support Roosevelt's call for the immediate opening of a second front, heard such speakers as U.S. senators James M. Mead and Claude Pepper, New York mayor Fiorello LaGuardia, and New York CIO president Joseph Curran.

According to an eyewitness account, when Chaplin's speech began to be broadcast, "The great crowd, previously warned not to interrupt with applause, hushed and strained for every word. Thus they listened for fourteen minutes to Charles Chaplin, the great people's artist of America, as he spoke to them by telephone from Hollywood." Chaplin opened dramatically: "On the battlefields of Russia democracy will live or die. The fate of the Allied nations is in the hands of the Communists." He went on to say that the Soviet Union's back was to the wall—the wall of democracy. If the Nazis prevailed, Chaplin argued, they would turn to America and Great Britain with promises that would be attractive to appeasers, even as they tried to "take away our liberty and enslave our minds." If that were to happen, Chaplin predicted in a passage that recalled *The Great Dictator*: "Human progress will be lost. There will be no minority rights, no workers' rights, no citizen's rights." How could this dire future be prevented? By opening a second front immediately and aiming "for victory in the spring." With a stirring challenge—"Remember [that] great achievements throughout history have been the conquest of what seemed the impossible"—Chaplin ended his call for a second front that would preserve democracy in the face of Nazi tyranny. It is worth noting here that nowhere in the speech does Chaplin either endorse or criticize the Soviet system; rather, he calls for support of the Soviet Union to help defeat the Nazi aggressors.

Chaplin's next public appearance to speak in favor of a second front was at Carnegie Hall in New York City on Friday evening, 16 October 1942. Sponsored by the Artist's Front to Win the War, the dinner was attended by 3,000 people, who heard such people as Sam Jaffee, I. F. Stone, Joris Ivens, Carl Van Doren, and Lillian Hellman speak before Orson Welles introduced Chaplin as the featured speaker (see Figure 20). Chaplin opened his half-hour speech in a way that would come back to haunt him: "Dear Comrades. Yes, I mean comrades. When one sees the magnificent fight the Russian people are putting up, it is a pleasure and a privilege to use the word 'comrade.'" From there he made comments on a number of topics. He praised Roosevelt "for the wonderful job he is doing," comparing him to Washington, Jefferson,

20. Chaplin and Orson Welles meet before Chaplin's Carnegie Hall speech in favor of a second front, October 1942.

and Lincoln and saying that he had done more for the "little people" than any American president except Lincoln. Turning to the second front theme, he said that "every self-respecting citizen in the United States wants a second front now. . . . The American people want to get this bloody job done and get it done now." In another comment open to later criticism, Chaplin praised Roosevelt for releasing early from prison the former general secretary of the CPUSA, Earl Browder. Chaplin also, according to a report in the *Herald Tribune*, said that he "found it a privilege to pay Uncle Sam" his taxes and expressed a lack of concern about reports that "after the war Communism may spread over world" because "I can live on $25,000 a year." Finally, he pleased the assembly in an encore by returning to the podium, raising two fingers in a "V," and telling the cheering crowd that the gesture stood "for victory and for '2'—second front." Compared to the telephone broadcast in July, this speech, though similar in ideological thrust— support of the Soviet allies and a second front policy—also contained many more comments than the earlier talk that, when reported in newspapers, gave political conservatives a sense that Chaplin had really become a radical sympathizer of the Soviet system.[55]

A little more than a month after the Carnegie Hall speech, Chaplin traveled to Chicago to speak at Orchestra Hall for a "Salute Our Russian Ally" rally, held on the ninth anniversary of the establishment of Soviet–American relations. There an estimated 2,600 people paid from 55 cents to $1.10 to hear Chaplin speak, with funds going to Russian War Relief. The brief report on the speech by the conservative *Chicago Tribune* makes it sound similar in tone and approach to Chaplin's October message. After the "Star-Spangled Banner" and the Soviet national anthem were played, Carl Sandburg and Rear Admiral H. P. Taylor spoke. Then Chaplin opened his remarks with "Ladies, Gentlemen, Friends, and Comrades," once again stressing a word that for him indicated support of the Soviet–American alliance. According to the *Tribune*'s report, Chaplin criticized the head of the Boston American Legion for protesting labor leader Harry Bridges's speech at Harvard and also told the audience that "no longer is the world shocked at the word 'communism.' " Such a comment likely did, however, shock the *Tribune*'s editorial staff and more than a few of its readers.[56]

Chaplin's final speech in favor of the Soviet–American alliance against fascism was at a dinner in his honor on 3 December 1942, at the Pennsylvania Hotel in New York City. It was given by the "Arts to Russia Week" committee of Russian War Relief. Chaplin was lauded as an artist who was fighting "to keep culture and the arts alive in a world of free peoples." Among the greetings to Chaplin were cables from Moscow sent by Shostakovich, Eisenstein, and the writer Alexei Tolstoi. Another cable, from Soviet war correspondent Ilya Ehrenburg, read in part: "All your life on the screen you have defended the little man against the malevolent and soulless machine. We are glad to see you taking a stand against Nazism. It isn't humans who've fallen upon us but ersatz-men, brutal, repulsive automatons. We defend against them our lives, our right to smile, our right to freedom and happiness. We are glad that you, Dear Chaplin, are with us." In his own brief remarks, Chaplin asked the seven hundred listeners to abandon their prejudices against Soviet political and economic ideals, "since our Allies do not object to our own ideals and form of government." According to the report in the *New York Times*, he also said that "Communism happens to be what the Russians are fighting for and from the way they are fighting they must like it pretty well. I am not a Communist, but I feel pretty pro-Communist."[57]

This gathering made it clear that the Soviets had embraced Chaplin as a "people's artist," whether he sought the title or not, and that Chaplin himself was willing to praise publicly the Soviet effort against the Nazis. Throughout his six speeches in 1942, Chaplin gradually, perhaps imperceptibly to him, moved from a focus on the necessity to oppose the Nazi threat to a tendency to praise the Soviet allies and urge closer ties with them. In the context of the war effort in 1942, such praise was not uncommon; in fact, it was quite typical of those who held progressive political views at the time. But when the political climate changed, Chaplin would be called upon to answer for his actions.

Thus Chaplin concluded the most active political period of his life. We have seen that Chaplin's political views during this time cannot be understood without understanding the historical context in which they formed: the pressures placed on artists during the depression to commit themselves to a socially conscious art, the growth of the Popular Front, and the intricacies of political alliances during the second front period. Although Chaplin would stay interested and even sporadically active, when he was not working on a film, in American politics until he left the country in 1952, he would never again speak to the large and enthusiastic groups he spoke to in 1942, in part because of the changing climate of opinion, in part because his star image was beginning to take on political associations controversial to more conservative Americans. A foreshadowing of that change was a 21 December 1942 column by the conservative gadfly Westbrook Pegler. Responding to Chaplin's December 3 speech, Pegler, using a dichotomous logic that would become common during the Cold War, wrote that "Chaplin lately has said that he was pro-Communist which means only that he is anti-American." In Pegler's view, Chaplin, "after years of sly pretending, when an open profession of his political faith would have hurt his business, now that he has all the money he needs and has lost his way with the public, has frankly allied himself with the pro-Communist actors and writers of the theater and the movies, who call themselves artists, but who are mostly hams and hacks."[58] Pegler ignored the fact that *The Great Dictator* was Chaplin's most successful film at the box office (hardly an indication that he had "lost his way with the public"), and he practiced a kind of guilt by association that Chaplin's candid public comments about communism during the second front period encouraged. Darkly foreshadowing what was to come for Chaplin in the years ahead, Pegler remarked in his column, "in common, I am sure, with many other Americans, I would like to know why Charlie Chaplin has been allowed to stay in the United States about 40 years without becoming a citizen." As a Scripps-Howard columnist, widely syndicated in some six hundred newspapers, Pegler was writing for such a broad audience that one might fairly say this column began the assault on Chaplin's progressive politics that would within a decade result in his exile.

FOUR

Unraveling

7

Joan Barry, the Press, and
the Tarnished Image

The Affair

Because stardom depends on winning and maintaining the good graces of an audience, and because public taste and cultural values shift over time, nearly every star's career is a story of his or her rise and fall. Chaplin's career is no exception. Chaplin's fall—following what was, for the movies, an unprecedented period of popularity—may be the most dramatic in the history of stardom in America, related as it is to the vagaries of history, the complex impulses of the star's personality, and shifting ideological currents in the United States. Charles Chaplin, Jr., recalling how gratified his father was with the ovation he received after delivering *The Great Dictator* speech at Roosevelt's preinaugural concert in 1941, has written that "my father's appearance at the gathering, the heartfelt applause at his earnest words, might be called the pinnacle of his public success in this country. From then on the path led downward by subtle degrees until it ended in his self-imposed exile."[1] In a decline that was not even "subtle" at times, Chaplin's star image suffered badly in the 1940s and early 1950s. So badly, in fact, that when he left the country for the London premiere of *Limelight* in September 1952, the attorney general's office revoked his reentry permit and stated Chaplin would have to prove his moral and political worthiness before returning to the country in which he had lived for nearly forty years.

The third of June, 1943, was a turning point in the unraveling of Chaplin's star image. That day, nearly six months after his last speech urging the opening of a second front in Europe, a young aspiring actress named Joan Barry filed a paternity suit against him that claimed he was the father of the baby she expected in October. The story made front-page headlines and filled the Los Angeles papers and many others across the country throughout most of the month. This case fell within the jurisdiction of the California state courts, but by August the U.S. attorney's office in California had begun an investigation of the Barry–Chaplin relationship, assisted vigorously by the Los Angeles office of the Federal Bureau of Investigation. The subsequent trials, both federal and state, also generated widespread publicity and contributed to the tarnishing of Chaplin's star image.

In a sense, the story of Chaplin's affair with Barry begins with his separation and divorce from Paulette Goddard. The estrangement began as *The Great Dictator* was being completed, and Chaplin's son Charles remembers that although both Goddard and Chaplin attended the October 1940 premieres of the film at the Capitol and Astor theaters in New York City, they did not travel together: Goddard came from Mexico, where she had been visiting painter Diego Rivera for the second time in six months. By early December she had moved into the empty beach house of her agent, Myron Selznick, and then became extremely busy, appearing in eight films in 1941 and 1942 alone. With no fanfare and almost no press coverage (in contrast to Chaplin's second divorce), she and Chaplin mutually agreed upon a divorce, which Goddard eventually received in Mexico on 4 June 1942.[2]

In May 1941, some months after *The Great Dictator*'s success and Chaplin's performance at Roosevelt's preinaugural concert, a young woman named Joan Barry returned to Los Angeles from Mexico City, bearing a letter of introduction from A. C. Blumenthal—an associate of J. Paul Getty—to Tim Durant, a close friend of Chaplin's since the late 1930s (see Figure 21). In early June, a few days after they first met, Durant asked Barry if she would like to meet Chaplin. With another woman, Durant and Barry dined with Chaplin at Perino's Restaurant in Los Angeles. The affair began around this time.[3]

Barry had just turned twenty-two. She had been born Mary Louise Gribble on 24 May 1919 in Detroit, Michigan. Her father, Jim Gribble, whom Barry described as a veteran of World War I suffering from shell shock, committed suicide before she was born, and her mother later remarried a man named Berry. They moved to New York City, where she attended elementary and secondary school before moving to California in 1938, hoping to become a movie actress. She told the FBI that at various times she had used the names Mary Louise Berry, Joan Barratt, Mary L. Barratt, Joanne Berry, JoAnne Berry, and Joan Barry, trying out the variations at least in part to find a suitable name for the movies.[4]

Her record in Los Angeles had been a checkered one. Twice caught shoplifting dresses from department stores in 1938, she was released after the first theft but booked after the second, receiving a suspended ninety-day jail sentence and a year's probation. FBI files reveal that "a local businessman became acquainted with Berry in September, 1938,

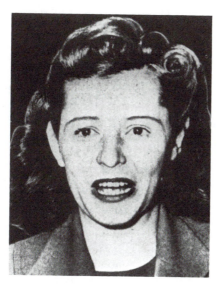

21. Joan Barry in March 1944.

and kept her in a local apartment house and hotel over a period of several years." Barry also told FBI agents that she knew J. Paul Getty before meeting Chaplin and had spent the early part of 1941 in Mexico City with Getty. According to her story, Getty persuaded A. C. Blumenthal to write letters of introduction for her to various people in Hollywood, including Chaplin's friend Tim Durant, in hopes of enabling her to break into the movies.[5]

After their first meeting at Perino's, Barry, escorted by Durant, attended one of Chaplin's tennis afternoons the following Sunday, and their relationship began to develop, though their versions of who pursued whom differ significantly. Chaplin claims that Barry called him the first two or three times after the Sunday party and made it clear that she was available to him. In his words, "Persistence is the road to accomplishment. Thus she achieved her object and I began to see her often" (MA, p. 414). In contrast, Barry later contended to FBI agents that Chaplin was the aggressor. After telling them that she and Chaplin first made love in his home, she added, "Chaplin's success in this regard was due to his verbal persuasiveness. I have been told, and from my personal experiences with him I know it to be true, that he is very proud of his success with women along these lines. This verbal persuasiveness of Chaplin's was his violent insistence that he was madly in love with me. He began calling me his favorite name for his lady loves, 'Hunchy.'"[6]

199

Both versions contain a degree of self-justification, and the truth probably lies somewhere in between. Barry, hoping for a movie career, did probably throw herself at Chaplin, and Chaplin, unencumbered and lonely following his separation from Goddard, likely played his part, too. In any case, Barry signed a movie contract with Chaplin on 23 June 1941 and read for the part of Bridget in a play called *Shadow and Substance*, to which Chaplin soon bought the rights. Barry's six-month contract paid her $75 a week and gave Chaplin the option to renew the contract after six months at $100 a week if he desired. He enrolled her in Max Reinhardt's acting school and began writing the script.[7]

The liaison continued intermittently through much of 1941 and into 1942, though Barry told FBI agents that she continued to see other men and even went to Tulsa in May 1942 to see Getty. That same month, Chaplin and Barry mutually agreed to cancel her contract (Barry hoped that a screen test with M-G-M would land her a job), though she continued on the payroll through September. Chaplin also made his first speech in favor of the second front that May, and much of his time over the next several months centered on his political commitments. Though the stories of what happened between Chaplin and Barry are widely contradictory, both parties agreed that Chaplin gave Barry and her mother train fare and some extra money to return to New York City. Chaplin later claimed that Barry had been negligent in her acting lessons and had decided she didn't want to be an actress, and that the money was a way of completely severing their ties. Barry said that "one day out of a clear blue sky" Chaplin told her she could go to New York. She and her mother left October 2. Toward the end of that month, a few days after Chaplin's second front speech at Carnegie Hall, Chaplin and Barry met one evening, apparently on Barry's initiative, and Barry went for a short time to Chaplin's suite at the Waldorf-Astoria, after which, she and Chaplin took a cab and he dropped her off at the Hotel Pierre, where she was staying. What exactly happened during this evening became a matter of great conjecture during the trials. It is clear that both returned separately to Los Angeles and that Barry made another trip to Tulsa to visit Getty for a week or ten days in November.[8]

The relationship had become extremely tenuous and sporadic, and by the end of December Chaplin wanted to be rid of the whole affair. At 1:00 A.M. on December 23, after her knocks and rings had gone unanswered, Barry forced herself into Chaplin's home by breaking two windows. Gun in hand, she went to Chaplin's second-floor bedroom, where she held him at gunpoint and threatened suicide. This incident—corroborated by Chaplin, Barry's courtroom testimony, and Chaplin's sons—was not settled until the morning, when Chaplin managed to get the gun from Barry and persuaded her to leave. At the end of the month, inebriated, she again tried to see Chaplin. On the morning of 1 January 1943, after having taken an overdose of barbiturates, she was arrested on the street by the Beverly Hills police department. (She was without money and had been evicted from her hotel because she could not pay her bill.) Charged with vagrancy, she was given a suspended sentence on the 2nd and placed on probation, the terms of which required that she pay some hotel bills and leave Beverly Hills. On January 5 she left for New York City by train, stopping first in Tulsa before going on.[9]

The affair seemed to be settled until Barry, pregnant, returned to Los Angeles in May. She tried to see Chaplin in order to claim that she was pregnant with his child. On 7 May 1943, following Chaplin's complaint, she was arrested by the Beverly Hills police for violating the terms of her probation and jailed. When the judge at her May 12 hearing learned that she was pregnant, he ordered her moved from the county jail to a sanitarium for health reasons. Later that month, after Barry's mother returned from New York to be with her daughter, Barry twice went uninvited to Chaplin's house—the second time around June 1—to discuss her plight. By her own admission she still hoped that she and Chaplin could be married. When Chaplin, by now deeply involved in a relationship with Oona O'Neill, refused to consider this, Barry and her mother decided to "go public." They asked two gossip columnists they had previously contacted, Hedda Hopper and Florabel Muir, to tell Barry's side of the story. When Barry filed the paternity suit naming Chaplin as the father of her child on June 3, the millstones of publicity had already begun grinding away at Chaplin's star image.[10]

Chaplin, Barry, and the Courts

Though Chaplin eventually became embroiled in federal charges, he first was faced with a civil violation that fell within the jurisdiction of the California state courts. Barry sued Chaplin on 3 June 1943. The following day Chaplin was served papers ordering him to appear in California Superior Court on June 17 to answer the charges. Chaplin denied the paternity charges and his lawyers worked out an arrangement whereby any trial would be postponed until after the birth of the child so Chaplin, Barry, and the baby (later born on October 3 and christened Carole Ann) could have blood tests. Through her lawyers,

Barry agreed to drop the paternity suit if blood tests proved that Chaplin could not have been the father of the child.[11] But in exchange Chaplin had to pay: for Barry's promise, he agreed to put up a sum of $2,500, plus $100 per week to support Barry; $500 more thirty days before the child was born; $1,000 when it was born; $500 monthly for four months after the child was born; $1,000 when the blood tests were taken; and $5,500 in attorney fees and court costs. Action on the paternity suit was then delayed until early 1944.[12]

However, in part due to the widespread publicity it was receiving, the Chaplin case soon came to the attention of federal authorities. Fred N. Howser, the U.S. district attorney of Los Angeles County, told the press that he was investigating two allegations: that Chaplin had paid for two abortions performed on Barry, and that the Beverly Hills police department was acting on Chaplin's behalf when Barry was arrested in January and May. By 24 June 1943, the FBI was also becoming involved, for that day R. B. Hood, the Special Agent in Charge of the Los Angeles office sent a memo to Hoover on "Information Concerning Charles Chaplin." This document contained information about Barry's dealing with Getty, the details of Chaplin's marriage to Oona O'Neill a week earlier, and an informant's denial that Chaplin was "Communistically inclined." The memo did not indicate, however, what charges would be investigated against Chaplin and Barry.[13]

By August, the abortion issue had been discarded, and the FBI, which often investigates cases handled by the U.S. Department of Justice, was beginning an investigation of Chaplin for possible violation of the Mann Act, which forbade paying for anyone's transportation across state lines for sexual purposes. Popularly known as the "White Slave Traffic Act," the law had been passed during the Progressive Era to stamp out organized prostitution but was sometimes used to threaten or harass wealthy or famous individuals. Trying to capitalize on the fact that Chaplin paid Barry's train fares both to and from New York City in October 1942, the FBI and the U.S. district attorney's office suspected that they might have a case. This was initiated after Special Agent Hood learned from the U.S. district attorney's office that Chaplin had paid for Barry's trip. He wrote a memo to Hoover on August 14, upon which Hoover wrote, "Shouldn't we run this down? If a White Slave violation, we ought to go after it vigorously." By August 17, FBI interoffice memos in Washington were referring to the case like this: "Charles Chaplin; Joan Barry, Victim—White Slave Traffic." And on August 20 Hoover ordered his communications section to telegram the Los Angeles office and ask them to report on developments and to "expedite investigation." The federal government was deeply involved in the case and would continue to be until the following May.[14]

Throughout the fall the U.S. district attorney's office in Los Angeles County and the FBI kept up their investigations. The FBI at first concentrated on obtaining evidence against Chaplin for violation of the Mann Act. Three reports from the Los Angeles office to Washington in October and November focused on that charge. Two were reports of the investigation by Agent H. Frank Angell (8 October 1943, 61 pages; and 9 November 1943, 45 pages); the third was a seven-page summary of Gerith von Ulm's biography of Chaplin (which contains considerable information about Chaplin's various affairs) by Special Agent Hood for the Washington office.[15] These reports, based on newspaper clippings, inquiries by FBI agents in Los Angeles and New York City, and the testimony of informants, began the attempt to provide the U.S. district attorney with evidence to use against Chaplin for Mann Act violations.

About the same time the November 9 report was filed, however, the investigation expanded. That day an interoffice memo in Washington reported on a telephone call from Special Agent Hood. He had met with the new U.S. district attorney, Charles Carr, who had taken over the Mann Act case in Los Angeles, and had learned that Carr was a little concerned about "the lack of a commercial angle" and about "Gribble's [Barry's] reputation." Both, he felt, could make it difficult to convict Chaplin for Mann Act violations. Carr was also interested, Hood continued, in Chaplin's role when Barry was arrested in early January and then ordered out of Beverly Hills, since one informant alleged that Barry's lawyer in the case was also Chaplin's. Carr thought that in this area "there may be a violation of the Civil Rights Statute."[16]

Soon thereafter, the FBI began to help Carr obtain information about the exact details of Barry's arrest on 1 January 1943, her suspended sentence the following day, and her whereabouts the next six months. The files from this part of the investigation contain some strange, almost paranoiac information. At one point, for example, the FBI speculates that Chaplin, through his lawyer, was trying to use his political influence in Washington to have the case dropped. This information was passed on directly from Hoover to Assistant Attorney General Tom Clark. Another set of memos discussed the possibility that Chaplin might flee the country, perhaps to the Soviet Union, if the investigations continued. When Hoover learned of this rumor, he wrote at the bottom of Hood's telegram: "Give immediate attention. Don't let this fellow do a run out." Hood responded by notifying FBI offices in San Diego, El Paso, Seattle, and Butte (!) to place stops at border stations in case Chaplin tried to leave the country. Looking for further negative information on Chaplin, another memo observed that Chaplin might have been buying black-market meat and having it delivered to his home.[17]

The central thread of FBI files from November through January concerns the possibility of a civil rights case to go along with the Mann Act charge. District Attorney Carr was hesitant about whether to go ahead with the civil rights charge; in fact, he slowed down the investigation of the case somewhat until Attorney General Biddle and Assistant Attorney General Clark told him to go ahead, adding that they thought chances of prosecution on this charge were pretty good.[18] By the middle of January Carr began presenting evidence to the grand jury. Among those testifying were FBI agents, gossip columnists Hopper and Muir, and Barry herself. On 10 February 1944 the federal grand jury handed down four indictments against Chaplin. The story made the front page of the next day's *New York Times*.[19]

The indictments all revolved around Mann Act charges or alleged violations of Barry's civil rights. The central indictment, and the only one to name Chaplin alone, alleged violation of Title 18, Section 398, of the U.S. Code (the Mann Act), and charged that Chaplin "did knowingly, wilfully, unlawfully, and feloniously transport and cause to be transported" Joan Barry "with the intent and purpose . . . of having [her] . . . engage in illicit sex relations with him." The indictment contained two counts: one for the train ticket to New York City and the other for the return ticket.

The remaining three indictments all named others with Chaplin and alleged that Joan Barry's right to due process, guaranteed by the Fourteenth Amendment to the Constitution, were violated in her January and May arrests. The first charged Chaplin, Beverly Hills police detective W. W. White, and municipal judge Charles Griffin of depriving Barry of her civil rights (violation of Title 18, Section 52 of the U.S. Code) when she was induced to plead guilty of vagrancy and taken to the train station in January. The second was similar: it alleged violation of Title 18, Section 51, and charged that Chaplin, his friend Robert Arden, and Detective White cooperated in denying Barry her civil rights in the same incident. Finally, in the longest and most complex indictment, alleging violation of Title 18, Section 88, seven people were accused of conspiring to deny Barry her civil rights both in the January incident and in May, when she was arrested for violating her probation and sentenced to thirty days in jail. The seven were Chaplin, Arden, Detective White, Judge Griffin, and three others: police sergeant Claude Marple, police matron Jessie Billie Reno, and

Chaplin's friend Tim Durant. If Chaplin were convicted on all four counts, he faced up to twenty-three years in prison and fines up to $26,000.[20]

After being fingerprinted (and photographed) on February 14, Chaplin was brought to trial under the Mann Act charges beginning on March 21. Both Barry and Chaplin testified. According to his lawyer, Jerry Giesler, Chaplin was excellent, "the best witness I've ever seen in a law court." Even when he was merely sitting at the counsel table, Geisler continued, "He looked helpless, friendless and wistful, as he sat there with the weight of the whole United States Government against him."[21] Apparently the jury was also impressed with Chaplin the witness and with Giesler's argument that Chaplin had no immoral intent when giving Barry train tickets. On April 4, after deliberating 6 hours and 58 minutes and going through four ballots, the jury returned a not guilty decision. Chaplin was acquitted.[22]

The three other federal indictments never came to trial. The civil rights and conspiracy charges were being prepared for trial in May, but both the Department of Justice in Washington and the U.S. district attorney's office in Los Angeles began to doubt the wisdom of bringing the case to trial because of flimsy evidence, particularly after Judge J.F.T. O'Connor, who also heard the Mann Act trial, dismissed all charges against Judge Griffin following a hearing. On May 5 Assistant Attorney General Clark directed District Attorney Carr in Los Angeles to drop all remaining charges against Chaplin and others not already cleared. Special Agent Hood, after talking with Carr, summed up Clark's justification for the decision in a May 11 memo to Hoover: "Carr said that the letter continued to the effect that he, Carr, knew the Department from the very beginning thought the cases against Subject [Chaplin] were weak, but had deferred to his judgment until the Department had a chance to go over all the evidence. Now that the evidence had been reviewed, the Department has decided that there is no case."[23] Thus Chaplin's problems with the federal court system over the Barry case were over.

Yet, the California paternity suit was not. Four months after the October 2 birth of Barry's daughter—and just after the indictments against Chaplin on federal charges had hit the newspapers—Chaplin, Barry, and Carole Ann had submitted to blood tests. Three doctors, one neutral, one hired by Barry, and one by Chaplin, analyzed the results. On 16 February 1944, the day after Chaplin's fingerprinting drew hordes of photographers, the doctors concurred that the blood tests proved Chaplin could not have been the father of the child. Chaplin, whose blood type was O (Barry's was A), could not possibly have fathered Carole Ann, whose blood type was B. Barry's lawyer, John Irwin, following the agreement he had reached with Chaplin's lawyers, was about to drop the charge. Barry, however, had other ideas. She decided to pursue the case and, after Irwin refused to continue as her lawyer, hired the rancorous seventy-seven-year-old Joseph Scott.[24]

Scott, a rangy, beetle-browed firebrand, decided that Chaplin must be brought to trial on the paternity charge and that he must be handled roughly. After Scott and Giesler took a week just to choose the jury, the case began December 19. Chaplin denied the paternity charges. Scott resorted to some name calling in the courtroom, and termed Chaplin a "pestiferous, lecherous hound," "a little runt of a Svengali" who lied "like a cheap Cockney cad," and more. The tactics, however, did not work. After deliberating four and a half hours on January 3 and nearly one more full day on January 4, the jury returned deadlocked, 7 votes to 5 in favor of Chaplin.[25]

Scott insisted on a retrial, which began 12 April 1945 and lasted through April 17. Chaplin again took the witness stand and denied the charges. In the course of the trial the prosecution called J. Paul Getty, among others, as a witness. He denied ever having sexual intercourse with Barry (he was suspected since Barry had visited Tulsa in November 1942 and in early January 1943). This jury voted 9 to 3 that Chaplin was the father and liable for child support, despite the findings of the blood tests, which at that time California did not accept as admissible evidence in paternity suit trials. Chaplin was clearly upset, but the next day Scott and Barry, who had been asking for $50,000 in fees and $1,500 per month for Carole Ann, had their turn to be disappointed. The court ordered Chaplin to pay Barry $5,000 in fees and $75 per week child support until Carole Ann reached the age of twenty-one.[26]

Chaplin and his lawyers immediately began to seek an appeal to reverse what they felt was a clear miscarriage of justice. The California state court system, however, disagreed. On June 6 Chaplin was denied a new trial on the paternity suit charges. The cases brought by Barry and by the federal government against Chaplin were finally closed. Because of the tempest of publicity Chaplin received from the time the paternity suit was filed in June 1943, however, the Joan Barry case was to lie close to the surface of the American public imagination for a long time and contributed to the decline in Chaplin's star image that would eventually separate him from the country he had called home since 1913.

Chaplin, Barry, and the
Gossip Columnists

Chaplin's legal difficulties in the Barry affair, however much they soured him on the American legal system, had little affect on his star image. However, the press coverage of those legal difficulties greatly affected his declining star image, for these reports presented Chaplin's problems in great detail to the American public. We have discussed Chaplin's first three divorces and seen that the Mildred Harris divorce received almost no press coverage; the divorce from Lita Grey, although treated prominently in the press, generated considerable sympathy for Chaplin in some quarters; and the quiet divorce from Paulette Goddard elicited no great publicity or criticism. In contrast, nearly all the press coverage of the Joan Barry affair, except for that of the small circulation left-wing press, was hostile to Chaplin. A look at coverage by the gossip columnists and the national mass press reveals how critically Chaplin was portrayed at this time.

Beginning in Hollywood as early as the 1910s, gossip columnists became particularly powerful in making and breaking movie stars. The essential function of the gossip columnist during the studio era was to chat to his or her readers about Hollywood: who would appear in a new picture, whose career was blossoming or withering, who was in love with whom, and so on. When a scandal hit, the columnist sought the "inside story" and often took sides while providing readers information about the course of events. The Barry-Chaplin situation was certain to draw the attention of the gossip columnists. Yet it also did more. To a surprising degree, not only did gossip columnists generate negative publicity against Chaplin in the Barry case, but two in particular even befriended Barry, enabling "her" story to be told, and provided the FBI with testimony that helped the federal government in its attempt to convict Chaplin on Mann Act and civil rights charges. The two primary gossip columnists to take up pens against Chaplin were Hedda Hopper (of the *Los Angeles Times*) and Florabel Muir (of the *New York Daily News*), both of whom were based in Hollywood and wrote columns widely syndicated in newspapers around the nation.[27]

Hopper, with Louella Parsons, was one of the two most prominent and powerful gossip columnists in Hollywood in the 1940s. A failed actress, she was also interested in politics and ran unsuccessfully for the Los Angeles County Central Committee in 1932 as a Republican. Her weekly column on Hollywood, which she began for the *Washington Post* in 1935, became more influential when, in 1938, the *Los An-*

geles Times picked it up in syndication. From that point on she became an important local outlet for the movie producers.[28]

Although Hopper did print friendly squibs about Chaplin as late as 1939, she came to dislike him for two reasons. First, she disagreed with his progressive politics. An avowed isolationist (even for a time after World War II broke out), she was suspicious of *The Great Dictator* and Chaplin's second front activities. As a political conservative who in her columns defended the right-wing Motion Picture Alliance for the Preservation of American Ideals, attacked the leftist Writer's Guild, and worried about the threats of domestic communism throughout the war, Hopper had little in common politically with Chaplin.[29]

Second, Hopper disliked Chaplin because he didn't truckle to gossip columnists, as so many stars and aspiring stars did. Though the fan magazines in the mid-1910s were, as we have seen, instrumental in helping to build the popularity of Chaplin's star image, by the 1920s his fame had become so widespread and his economic situation so independent that he didn't have to beat the bushes for publicity. Instead, the publicists came to him whenever he desired. For example, the *New York Times* movie columnists regularly gave Chaplin generous advance articles on all his upcoming films from *The Gold Rush* on, sometimes a year or more before the films were released. This enabled Chaplin to keep aloof in the era of gossip columnists. Since they liked power and recognition as much as many movie stars did, Chaplin's attitude easily stirred up their antagonism.

Given her distaste for Chaplin, Hopper jumped at the chance to attack him over the Barry case. She and Florabel Muir were in the thick of the case right from the beginning, not only through their columns but even through their personal interactions with Barry.

Sometime in May 1943, after Chaplin had Barry arrested for harassing him, Barry or her mother, seeking press coverage, contacted Hopper. Hopper showed great interest and won the trust of Barry and her mother so fully that by the end of the month Barry seemed to be in a three-party conversation with Chaplin and Hopper. In her long interview with FBI agents, Barry recalled that after Chaplin's attorneys put her off on Memorial Day, "I called home and they said that my mother had gone up to Hedda Hopper's, . . . and I called her there and Florabel [Muir] was there." Barry then had Chaplin's butler, Edward Chaney, drive her to Hopper's, and a few days later the paternity suit was filed. From the time of the Memorial Day visit Hopper and Muir became advocates in the press in support of Barry's case.[30]

The first key document in their case for Barry was Hopper's column of 3 June 1943: the same day Barry's lawyer filed the paternity suit.

Although the column purported to treat the "latest development on the Joan Barry–Charlie Chaplin situation," a "cozy little luncheon" at Chaplin's poolside, it also aimed to discredit Chaplin on a number of fronts. Some charges it made were entirely unrelated to the case: that Chaplin had never become a U.S. citizen; that Chaplin refused when asked to contribute to the Motion Picture Relief Fund Home; that Chaplin gave only $100 when asked to contribute to the Red Cross; that Chaplin called for a second front (presumably referring to his October 1942 appearance) when the policy "was already arranged by the American and British Governments." In a display of anti-Semitism, Hopper went on to criticize Chaplin for denying that he was Jewish. "Jews should be proud of their heritage," she wrote sanctimoniously. "Christ was a Jew." (Ironically, she was apparently unaware that Chaplin was not Jewish.) Hopper then quoted an earlier column, written when Barry's role in *Shadow and Substance* was announced, in which she congratulated Barry but warned her about Chaplin's proclivities: "There've been many Chaplin leading ladies before you. All got the same package with the same trimmings." The column concludes in a belligerent tone, asking a series of questions: "Will her child have a name? What is to become of that child and its mother, Joan Barry? Those are the questions Hollywood is asking today. Those are the questions Hollywood has a right to ask and not only hope for an answer but to demand one."[31]

Hopper struck again in her June 22 column. In it she noted that since "the Chaplin business has simmered down to a slow boil," she thought it useful to pass along the contents of a letter she received from "an important Chicago man." It read in part: "Chaplin should keep constantly in mind that he is not a citizen, merely a guest, and should conduct himself as a guest. Up to this point of exposure he had a right to become a citizen. But I doubt that he could now become one. I'm sure the laws of our country include moral turpitude as good and sufficient grounds for the deportation of an alien." The letter also criticized Chaplin's second front speeches, which involved him, according to the letter, in "matters for which he has neither been trained nor sufficiently well versed to talk intelligently." It concluded by doubting "if his native England would put up with an American guest in that country daring to be so bold." By quoting the letter at such length, Hopper was helping to establish a pattern that became more pronounced at time went by: the tendency to criticize Chaplin for both his politics and his alleged immorality, and to link the two. To increasing numbers of people after the Barry case broke, Chaplin's moral behavior was impolitic and his politics were immoral.[32]

Muir also defended Barry in her columns. Her 2 June 1944 column carried a story, like Hopper's, about Barry's luncheon with Chaplin. According to Muir, "Joan's momma is saying it would be nice—with a baby on the way—if Joan and Chaplin would wed." After the initial June publicity of the paternity suit died down, the case didn't get much coverage until Barry's baby was born in early October. Muir was at the forefront here. On October 10 she did an article called "Jane Doe Chaplin and Tests for Paternity." The article contained considerable information about the blood tests that would be done when the baby was four months old. But it also gave some prominence to the name of radio commentator Robert Arden when it outlined the Barry–Chaplin dealings the previous December and January. Muir wrote that Arden had used other names, including Rudolf Kleiger, a telling detail, for the same information later appears regularly in FBI files, which suggests that Muir was unknowingly or, more likely, knowingly providing information to the agency. Indeed, the FBI report from Los Angeles to Washington of 9 November 1943 contained in its section on Robert Arden some information from Muir given to the FBI through an unnamed "Source A."[33]

Hopper continued to criticize Chaplin in her columns in late 1943. She claimed in October, for example, that employees she visited at the Douglas Aircraft plant disliked Chaplin and, a few days later, she made veiled charges that Chaplin was guilty of casting-couch promiscuity. Just after Christmas Hopper commented that there was no truth to the rumor that Barry and Chaplin would settle the paternity suit out of court. Chaplin surely had a busy year, she added, struggling with the Barry case and "marrying a girl who just turned 18. . . . From things I learned, Charlie, who contributed $25,000 to the Communist cause and $100 to the Red Cross, soon will find himself involved with something about as serious as the Barry case." These imprecise charges about contributions would later end up in FBI files on Chaplin as a security risk, which will be discussed in Chapter 9. Hopper's final cryptic comment in this column suggests she had inside information about the Mann Act and civil rights charges that were soon to be taken before the grand jury.[34]

This was entirely likely, for both Hopper and Muir were involved in the legal proceedings against Chaplin. In early January 1944 Muir was interviewed by District Attorney Carr and FBI agents as they prepared the civil rights charges against Chaplin. When she told them that Chaplin's friends Tim Durant and Minna Wallis had secured a former lawyer of Chaplin's for Barry when she was dealing with the police in May 1943, Special Agent Hood telegrammed Hoover about the incident and said that Muir might "be used as a witness" because of that evidence. And indeed she was. On January 14 Muir, Hopper, and FBI agent Frank H. Angell, who had been writing the majority of the reports in Los Angeles for Hoover, all testified before the grand jury.[35]

Muir's support for Barry did not end here. At the end of January she was trying to help Barry control her drinking problem. Barry's lawyer, John J. Irwin, had asked Muir to talk with Barry and convince the young mother that appearing drunk in public could result in bad publicity and damage her chances in the upcoming trials. In the same meeting Muir discouraged Barry from making a trip to Mexico and then tried to get Barry's mother to take a short vacation, which Muir—aware of the tensions between Barry and her mother—thought might alleviate some of Barry's anxieties.[36]

Significantly, though Hopper criticized Chaplin once again in a January column, she did not mention him in February. On the one hand, the newspaper headlines made such references less necessary. On the other, it was also in February that the results of the blood tests, which established that Chaplin could not have been the child's father, were made public, thus perhaps quelling some of her public vitriol for Chaplin. In March, however, in a section of her column headed "Step Too Far," Hopper quoted from a "Beverly Hills scratch sheet" (Rob Wagner's *Script*, to be discussed below). "There are men and women in far corners of the world who have never heard of Jesus Christ," Wagner had written, "yet they know and love Chaplin." To which Hopper responded, "I'm wondering how the coupling of the buffoon's name with that of Diety [sic] will improve his standing with the public, whose good opinion he is assiduously courting for the first time." As the Mann Act trial was about to begin, Hopper sought to discredit Chaplin by suggesting that he was trying to manipulate the press to help him win his trial. In the same column she countered Wagner's assertion that "the Fascist clique is hounding" Chaplin. She asked, "Lord love us, Eddie Hoover, isn't that a new role for you and your FBI?"[37]

After the Mann Act trial began and Chaplin was eventually acquitted, Hopper wrote twice more on Chaplin. The first occasion was after a visit to the courtroom. Here she subtly attacked Chaplin's cause by stressing how slick his attorney was; the only way Chaplin could wriggle out of the charges, she implied, was to hire a famed Hollywood trial lawyer. After Chaplin's acquittal on April 4, Hopper waited nearly a week before responding. When she did, it was to charge again that the only way Chaplin could get off the hook was through deception. "Charlie Chaplin did a complete about face to members of the press during his trial," Hopper wrote. "He's always been the least cooperative star. . . . At night clubs he tells snapshot boys when to shoot and how often but at the trial he and Jerry Giesler hired a press agent. Charlie was ready, willing, and posed for everything."[38]

In one sense, of course, Hopper was right. Chaplin and Giesler had hired a press agent for the Mann Act trials, Giesler surmising accurately that Chaplin's star image was rapidly tarnishing and that it would have to be polished during the trials or Chaplin could be in for serious problems. But Hopper's treatment, coming as it did after a verdict was reached, was also an attempt to undermine the decision and persist in her attacks on Chaplin's reputation despite his acquittal.

Perhaps the most bizarre chapter in the story of Hopper's vendetta against Chaplin is contained in a four-page letter from Agent Hood to his chief, Hoover, in April. Hood takes up several topics, one particularly relevant here. Evidently a columnist for the *Hollywood Reporter* had called an FBI agent and reported the following story. Hopper had allegedly told Buddy Rogers, Mary Pickford's husband, that Chaplin's jury had been bought off, and Rogers asked for evidence. Hopper then told Rogers of a call she had received from a woman who had experienced a vision in which she had seen members of the Chaplin jury discussing a payoff from Chaplin. The woman also told Hopper that although she wasn't able to identify any of the jury members individually, she would give it more thought. On the basis of this call, Hopper was spreading the rumor. Even the zealous FBI agents in Los Angeles were skeptical: in his understated FBI prose, Hood told Hoover, "It is contemplated that no further inquiry will be made along this line unless more specific information is obtained."[39]

The same letter also provided evidence that Muir was continuing her investigation of the Barry–Chaplin case and feeding information to the FBI. Hood reminded Hoover that Muir "has followed this case from the beginning, and . . . has previously been referred to in previous communications to you." In this instance, Muir had called Agent Angell and reported to him that "rumor among the press representatives here in Los Angeles was to the effect that the government was going to dismiss the remaining charges against Chaplin, et al. because of the acquittal Chaplin received under the Mann Act charges." In this case, of course, Muir proved prophetic, for charges were dropped, but the letter also offers firm evidence that the gossip columnists were providing the FBI with information in the Barry–Chaplin investigations.[40]

Though Muir and Hopper ran out of steam concerning the Barry–

Chaplin case after Chaplin's federal charges were dropped, Hopper visited the courtroom again after the California state paternity trial began. Her resulting story, the lead in her column of December 22, typified her distaste for Chaplin. The brief reference described Chaplin as "no longer suave, simple and appealing but overacting frightfully" and contrasted him with "the center of attraction," Carole Ann: "a little innocent baby, cooing because she didn't know what it was all about."[41]

It is striking how influential Hopper and Muir were in the Barry–Chaplin situation, and not simply because of their writings. Not only did they befriend Barry, helping to put her plight before their reading public and seeking to help her control her behavior, but they also testified in her defense before the grand jury and shared information on her behalf with the FBI. Chaplin's star image, which at one time seemed unassailable, was under attack. It was also coming to be dominated much more by Chaplin the man—his views and his private activities—than by the lovable Charlie.

The Press and the Barry–Chaplin Story

The rest of the press gave the Barry–Chaplin story widespread coverage at certain crucial points. This gave it even greater prominence—often front-page headline coverage—and thus placed Chaplin's name and face before more people than the gossip columnists reached in their syndicated columns. The coverage significantly affected Chaplin's star image, for what was reported was largely negative toward Chaplin in the mass circulation press, though generally sympathetic in the small circulation leftist press. We will focus here on how a major daily newspaper, the *Chicago Tribune*, and the two most prominent U.S. mass magazines, *Time* and *Newsweek*, treated the case, in contrast to the treatment found in the leftist press.

Owned by the politically conservative McCormick family, the *Chicago Tribune* was a staid, conservative newspaper in the 1940s in both its editorial stance and its format. Of the two mass magazines, *Time*, edited by Henry Luce, had the larger circulation and was generally considered conservative in its presentation of the week's news. *Newsweek* generally tended to be more middle of the road.

It must be stressed that the *Chicago Tribune* was by no stretch of the imagination a sensationalist purveyor of yellow journalism. This being the case, one might expect that its treatment of the Barry–Chaplin story would be somewhat restrained. It is also true, however, that since Chaplin's politics contrasted sharply with the editorial line of the pa-

22. *Chicago Tribune* headline on 11 February 1944. Copyright
© 1987, Chicago Tribune Company, all rights reserved,
used with permission.

per, it had some reason to play up the story in hopes of discrediting Chaplin. Of these two contrary impulses, the latter won out.

News treatment of the Barry–Chaplin case in the *Tribune* and the two magazines peaked four times: (1) the indictment, fingerprinting, and blood-test stages in February 1944; (2) the Mann Act trials in late March and early April; (3) the first paternity suit trial in December 1944 and early January 1945; and (4) to a lesser extent, the second paternity suit trial in April 1945. Even though the coverage took place during the war years, when news from battle zones demanded press attention, the Chaplin case very often dominated the front page in the *Tribune* and figured prominently in weekly news magazine stories.

This was certainly the case when the indictment story first broke. On February 11 the lead headline in the *Tribune*, covering the entire top of page one, was "U.S. Jury Indicts Chaplin" (see Figure 22).[42] The brief story summarized the indictments, listed the penalties Chaplin might receive if convicted, and referred to Chaplin as the "white haired English alien." Four days later an equally large headline dominated page one: "Fingerprint, Book Chaplin in Barry Case." The subtitle was also conspicuous and was subtly critical: "Nervous and Testy on Appearance." For the first time, Chaplin's picture appeared in the

214

23. Chaplin fingerprinted after indictment, 1944. Wide World Photo.

photograph section, located on the back page of section one. In it, an obviously stressed Chaplin was shown being fingerprinted (see Figure 23). The photograph was the first of a number of shots used in the *Tribune*'s picture section throughout the case.

Although the weekly mass magazines, of course, wrote fewer articles than the newspapers on the Barry–Chaplin situation, *Newsweek* printed a devastating story following the indictment. The article, "Chaplin as Villain" (21 February 1944), was supplemented with five pictures: Barry on the witness stand, presumably during her grand jury testimony; an unflattering picture of Chaplin, looking inebriated while dining with Oona Chaplin; and three smaller pictures of Chaplin's previous three wives. The article called the Barry case the "biggest public relations scandal since the Fatty Arbuckle murder trial in 1921." Besides noting that Chaplin, if convicted, faced up to twenty-three years in jail, fines of $26,000, and even possible deportation, *Newsweek* revealed that Barry's situation had been publicized by Hedda Hopper and "veteran sob sister" Florabel Muir. The essay biased its audience against Chaplin when it wrote that the film industry collectively "felt no personal love for Chaplin—because of his egotism, intellectual pretensions, niggardliness, and failure to take part in Hollywood entertainment plans for the [armed] services." Appearing less than a month before the Mann Act trials were about to begin, this article boded ill for Chaplin's star image.[43]

Almost as damaging as the coverage of the indictment was the coverage of the Mann Act trials, which seemed designed to create sympathy for Barry and antipathy for Chaplin. The *Tribune*'s first article covering the trial typified this bias. The headline covering the top of the front page on March 22 read, "Chaplin Begins Nervous Role at Bar of Law." The physical description of Chaplin in the accompanying text painted an unattractive picture. His face, according to the reporter, was "heavy jowled, lined, and dissipated." His eyes were "small" and his figure "stocky." In addition, the article stressed something that Hopper had mentioned: that Chaplin had hired a press agent to help control his client's public image. The job of Casey Shawhan, according to the article, was "to feed, wine, and placate members of the press covering the trial." By mentioning Chaplin's strategy, the *Tribune*'s reporter blunted its effectiveness.

From then to the end of the trial, the *Tribune* continued to use large headlines that spanned the top of the front page each day after testimony was given. Those headlines included "Barry–Chaplin Tryst Told" (March 24); "Judge Shields Joan's Past" (March 25); "Denies Chaplin Blackmail" (March 29); "Chaplin Takes Stand Today" (March 30); "Joan Tells Chaplin Threat" (April 1); and "U.S. Jury Acquits Chaplin!" (April 4). The only exception to this headline size came on the day after Chaplin testified. In this case, the *Tribune* printed a front-page story with a headline smaller than the rest—"Chaplin Tells His Story, Denies All." It also undercut Chaplin in the accompanying story. It mocked Chaplin's "performance" on the stand and commented ironically after describing his testimony: "Ah. The sorrow of it!" The negative bias against Chaplin in the daily accounts of the trial was accentuated by the breadth of the coverage: front-page stories, huge headlines, pictures in the photo section a number of times, and relatively long transcripts of sometimes sensationalistic testimony on the inside pages.

Though *Newsweek* ran only one article about Chaplin's testimony during the Mann Act trial, it called the testimony "the most important performance of his life," subtly suggesting that he would not be telling the truth but rather simply acting to sway the jury. *Time*'s first reference to the Barry–Chaplin affair came shortly after the Mann Act trial began, and its treatment, like *Newsweek*'s, denigrated Chaplin. According to *Time*, Barry's affair with Chaplin "fitted into a familiar pattern," which, *Time* implied, was that Chaplin pursued and later abandoned women at will. The article also described Chaplin as "a dapper grey multimillionaire of 54, widely envied in Hollywood for his unassailable arrogance and for his affairs with a succession of pretty young 'proteges.' "[44]

After Chaplin's acquittal on the Mann Act charges, the *Tribune* was relatively quiet about Chaplin until the jury was selected for Chaplin's first paternity trial in December, which, of the whole Barry affair, generated the most vituperative comments about Chaplin. The press covered it closely. During the trial, the *Tribune* gave the story front-page coverage on six of seven days, sometimes with large, full-width headlines. Again, the *Tribune* regularly reprinted testimony on inside pages during this trial, some of which was particularly juicy because of the florid, accusatory rhetoric of Barry's lawyer, Joseph Scott. One notable bias in the *Tribune's* coverage of this case was the report on the hung jury. After consistent front-page coverage throughout the trial, the *Tribune* buried the outcome—a hung jury tipped 7–5 in Chaplin's favor—on page six.

Newsweek did not run a report on the first trial and its outcome, but *Time* carried two articles in consecutive weeks. The first, titled "Just a Peter Pan," aimed directly at Chaplin. With his "platinum hair damp against his perspiring forehead," Chaplin, it wrote, felt himself an "ill-used man." Calling the affair a "kind of profane love story the Hays Office has not allowed Hollywood to film for years," *Time*—blending the political with the sexual—reported that Chaplin had sought to inculcate in Barry proper antifascist attitudes. Then it quoted from one of Barry's letters to Chaplin: "Right you are, Charles. We should destroy soulless, unimaginative, money-mad hypocrites who boast of breeding but are more ill-mannered than the lowest serf." From the context, it is evident that *Time* believed Chaplin deserved this denunciation as much as any fascist. The next week *Time* carried a second piece, which concentrated on Scott's colorful criticisms of Chaplin. One notable quote was his assertion that Chaplin "goes around fornicating . . . with the same aplomb that the average man orders bacon and eggs for breakfast."[45] Such articles, so widely distributed, were key in helping to shape the image of Chaplin as an immoral womanizer.

The second paternity trial received less coverage in the *Tribune*. Fortunately for Chaplin—since the outcome went against him—this trial fell victim to a major story: the death of Franklin D. Roosevelt. In fact, the first two days of the retrial in April 1945 escaped notice in the *Tribune* because of Roosevelt's death. The second trial was also shorter and less flamboyant than the first. The only front-page story in the

Tribune was the April 19 report on the trial's outcome. There, a small-ish headline announced: "Rule Chaplin Must Pay $75/Week to Baby."

Much the same was true with *Newsweek* and *Time*. Just after the second trial, *Newsweek* carried just one rather straightforward report on both trials. It summarized the outcome of each, then listed the terms of the final settlement. It only strayed from this when it quoted some of Scott's denunciations of Chaplin in the first trial (repeating the "Picadilly pimp" accusation, among others). *Time*'s final word on the matter was a short report on 30 July. The article also seemed designed to portray Chaplin in a negative light. It noted that the court had ordered Chaplin to pay his $75 per week child support payment while the case was being appealed, and also mentioned that Chaplin had estimated his net worth at $3 million but was still balking at the payments. *Time* thus reinforced the picture of Chaplin's cheapness that they had explicitly commented on in their first article.[46]

Several points can be made about the press coverage of the Barry–Chaplin story. First, its prominence in the *Chicago Tribune* was striking: the story not only received almost constant front-page coverage but even earned the day's lead headline with surprising frequency. Second, both the newspaper and especially the mass magazines tended to highlight charges and testimony and downplay the results of the trial, particularly when the outcome favored Chaplin. (Chaplin was taught a lesson learned by many public figures in America: an indictment lingers in the public mind long after an acquittal.) Third, Chaplin's star image was affected most strongly and negatively by the story of the indictments and the charges leveled against Chaplin in the trials, particularly in the first paternity suit, when Scott skewered Chaplin with his pointed language.

One can gauge how strongly the dominant press came out against Chaplin by looking briefly at the way that the leftist press understood the issues involved. Two examples will suffice: an article in *Script* and an editorial by Mike Gold in the *Daily Worker*.

Script, a small Beverly Hills publication on movies that came out twice a month, was edited by Rob Wagner, a friend and former employee of Chaplin's who held leftist political sympathies. Shortly before the Mann Act trials began, *Script* published a lead article entitled "The Press: Its Own Worst Enemy," the article Hopper responded to when she talked about the fascist charges in a "Beverly Hills scratch sheet."[47] The essay sought to demonstrate how Chaplin had become a victim of "character assassination by the press." Among other things, it pointed out how the influential *Variety* carried "a lengthy editorial in effect asking the industry to boot Chaplin out," while the same day "the newspapers carried the news that exonerated the actor of the paternity charges." The essay also inquired why federal officials would choose Chaplin as a target for civil rights charges after the paternity suit was filed, when so many paternity suits are filed with no federal involvement. The answer, it said, was that "Chaplin is a shining target for the Fascist clique in America. He is an artist, a liberal artist who also is articulate. When he apeaks, through the medium of films, his audience numbers in the hundreds of millions." In making *The Great Dictator*, Wagner argued, Chaplin made himself a threat to the fascists, even those in America "who have leanings toward Fascism, under no matter what name." And in the Barry case, these domestic fascists and fascist sympathizers found a convenient situation that enabled them to discredit Chaplin's name. The essay thus placed the federal case against Chaplin in a political perspective and suggested a link between the moral and legal attacks against Chaplin on the one hand and ulterior political yearnings to discredit him on the other. It concluded by calling on its readers to "withhold judgment of Charles Spencer Chaplin. For decency's sake."

A similar interpretation was expressed in a *Daily Worker* editorial by Mike Gold, the same critic who had excoriated Thornton Wilder and urged a politically radical art in the early 1930s. His article, "Charge It," was published after the first paternity trial had returned with a hung jury and a retrial was scheduled.[48] Gold was briefer and blunter than the *Script* essay. The Barry charge, he said, "fits into the campaign for Chaplin's destruction running for years in the Hearst, McCormick fascist press of America." Though Chaplin as the lovable tramp had alienated no one, Gold argued, as soon as he made *The Great Dictator*, he alienated the right wing in America and abroad, so that by 1945 they "hate him bitterly from Berlin to Los Angeles." The Barry trials and the press coverage of it were, for Gold, simply manifestations of this political attack on Chaplin.

This tendency to see Chaplin's problems as a result of domestic political machinations was a keynote of the leftist interpretation of the Barry case, and a view far removed from the analysis and coverage offered by the dominant press. Instead of portraying Chaplin as a moral menace, the Left was beginning to look at him as a political victim.

To say that the press coverage of the Barry case damaged Chaplin's star image is no startling news. It is significant, however, that the story's prominence in major newspapers and mass magazines, as well as the consistently negative (or at best neutral) portrayal of Chaplin in them, was very different from the press coverage of the Harris divorce, the Goddard divorce, and even the divorce from Grey, over which the press was much more split, with many columnists and reporters coming to Chaplin's defense, even though the Grey divorce, too, received widespread coverage.

One more important outcome of the trial and the press coverage of it has been for the most part overlooked. Chaplin, a proud and stubborn man, suffered great humiliation for nearly two years during the Barry charges and trials; for some of that time he was even threatened with the possibility of imprisonment. Having become an active antifascist a relatively short time before, Chaplin was prone to believe interpretations, like those in the leftist articles discussed above, that portrayed him as a victim of domestic fascist activities. In his autobiography he mentions being disappointed that his lawyer Jerry Giesler failed to follow up a letter from a Catholic priest in San Francisco who claimed to have evidence that Barry was being used by a domestic fascist group (MA, p. 426). People who see themselves as victims of political pressures often tend to become more firmly attached to their views, even to the point of martyrdom. There is considerable evidence that Chaplin's political opinions became more rigid—and perhaps more simplistically Manichaean—as a result of the Barry trials and press coverage. To understand Chaplin's political views and activities during and immediately after World War II and the effect they had both on his work and, ultimately, on his unraveling star image in America, we must examine his next film, *Monsieur Verdoux.*

8

Monsieur Verdoux and the Cold War:
Irreconcilable Differences

The Hollywood Emigrés

Though the Barry affair generated a great deal of public hostility toward Chaplin, he did get support from one group of personal friends as he battled in the courts. "During the trial," he wrote in his autobiography, "we had been surrounded by many dear friends—all of them loyal and sympathetic. Salka Viertel, the Clifford Odetses, the Hanns Eislers, the Feuchtwangers and many others" (MA, p. 434). Chaplin goes on to describe the prominent literati who often gathered at Viertel's salon in Santa Monica: Thomas Mann, Bertolt Brecht, Lion Feuchtwanger, Stephen Spender, and others. The fact that most of these people were exiles, and a number of them German refugees forced to flee by Hitler's policies, is significant: a strong case can be made that Chaplin's progressive, antifascist political and social views during the 1940s were shaped through and solidified by his interactions with this immigrant community in Hollywood and with domestic American leftists like Clifford Odets and Donald Ogden Stewart. Furthermore, though these associations may not have been widely known around the country, they certainly were in the movie community, and they gave gossip columnists like Hopper more reason to attack Chaplin's star image on political grounds. By examining Chaplin's relationships with four of this emigré group—Salka Viertel, Lion Feuchtwanger, Bertolt Brecht, and Hanns Eisler—and the general political perspective they shared during this period, we can more fully understand the shape of Chaplin's world view as he conceived, thought about, and developed the film that became *Monsieur Verdoux*.

The hegira of political refugees from Europe to America in the 1930s, and the story of the part played by these refugees in American culture since that time, has been the subject of considerable attention in the past several years.[1] One can hardly imagine the course of American intellectual life in the postwar era, for example, without the contributions of Erik Erikson, Bruno Bettelheim, Erich Fromm, Hannah Arendt, Paul Lazarsfeld, Hans Morgenthau, Erwin Panofsky, Erich

Auerbach, Roman Jakobson, and Paul Tillich. The group with which Chaplin associated in Hollywood was different from the larger refugee community in two ways: it was made up primarily of artists, and the politics of the group in general emphasized a more distinctively leftist and activist antifascism.

Of the emigrés Chaplin knew best (and mentioned in his autobiography), nearly all—understandably, given Chaplin's orientation and profession—were involved in the arts. Salka Viertel, for example, was an actress who became a screenwriter best known for a number of Greta Garbo films, including *Queen Christina* and *Anna Karenina*. She had come with her husband Berthold to California in 1927, when F. W. Murnau asked him to collaborate on a script. Before directing a number of films in Hollywood, Berthold Viertel had established himself in Germany as a poet, playwright, and novelist. Hanns Eisler, one of Chaplin's closer associates, was a composer who later wrote the national anthem of East Germany. Bertolt Brecht, the noted playwright and poet who is today the best known of this group, also collaborated with Eisler on some musical pieces. Lion Feuchtwanger, though not much remembered now, was a novelist whose work was widely read in the 1930s.

Not every German refugee in America or in the Los Angeles area was a dedicated political leftist. In fact, some Germans preferred to remain silent on political matters after arriving in the country they willingly or unwillingly had adopted. Some were even politically conservative: one right-wing group in Los Angeles, an assemblage Otto Preminger called "the FBI group," often met at the home of the wealthy Lady Elsi Mendl, for example. Nevertheless, those forced from their homelands due to the raging racial policies of Hitler were on the whole actively antifascist. And as Anthony Heilbut has observed, the artists and radicals among the refugees "saw themselves as vanguardists, anticipating a future that would transcend the cultural and political limits of the present." Heilbut called the Viertel home in Santa Monica—just up the street from the ocean—the "real salon" in Hollywood, the place peopled by "the same group of left-wing bohemian filmmakers and writers that had come together at the Romanische Café" in Berlin in the 1920s.[2] That this group of refugee artists admired the director of *Modern Times* and *The Great Dictator* was no surprise.

The leftist, antifascist political inclination of Feuchtwanger, Brecht, and the Viertels was well established. Feuchtwanger had become known in Europe and America in part for his novel *The Oppermanns* (1934), an early antifascist work that dealt with a wealthy German Jewish family forced into political awareness and opposition to Hitler. While living in France from 1933 to 1940, Feuchtwanger was, according to one scholar, "one of the chief Socialist propagandists" against the Hitler regime. Brecht and Eisler, who knew one another well, were both Marxists whose political views were established in the 1920s, with Brecht involved in trying to incorporate his political views into drama and Eisler, into music. Salka Viertel, though probably less systematically radical than the other three, was nevertheless an ardent antifascist. Not only was she active with Donald Ogden Stewart in the founding of the Hollywood Anti-Nazi League in 1936, but she also was a driving force in the establishment of the European Film Fund, a group established in 1940 that pressed studio heads to hire refugee writers on one-year contracts so they could escape Europe. In her memoir of the period, *The Kindness of Strangers*, Viertel described, somewhat tongue in cheek, the political diversity in her family: "Berthold had his own personal kind of socialism, Peter was a New Dealer, I was a 'premature anti-Fascist,' Thomas a Democrat and Hans a Trotskyite." As a whole, this group was considerably more sympathetic to the Soviet Union and more enthusiastic about the Soviet–American alliance during World War II than the group surrounding Thomas Mann, which tended to combine its antifascism with a political liberalism that was skeptical of socialist ideology.[3]

Except for the Viertels, who had lived in the Los Angeles area from the late 1920s, these Germans all arrived in Los Angeles in the early 1940s: Feuchtwanger and his wife Marta in January 1941, Brecht in July 1941, and Eisler in April 1942.[4] It was Salka Viertel who helped bring the emigrés and Chaplin together. She had first met Chaplin in the late 1930s when seated next to him at a dinner. He was then working on *The Great Dictator*, and she recalls that "he was possessed by his work, and it was captivating to watch his never-ceasing absorption, his constant improvising of situations." After Barry's paternity suit was filed, Viertel saw Chaplin "quite often," and during this period Chaplin met and also became close, in varying degrees, to Feuchtwanger, Brecht, and Eisler. Chaplin learned in this period to analyze his legal problems and his problems with the press in political terms, or even to attribute them to political causes, much as leftist journalists like Mike Gold did. As Viertel herself describes the hoopla surrounding the paternity case, "For the patriots of the Right it was the occasion to punish Chaplin for having remained a British subject, and for his flirtations with the Left."[5] (The issue of Chaplin's citizenship came up frequently in the late 1940s and 1950s; it will be treated in chapters 9 and 10.)

Feuchtwanger's biographers also stress the friendship between the Feuchtwangers and Chaplin (and Oona O'Neill Chaplin as well after she became part of Chaplin's life), which began soon after Feuchtwanger and his wife arrived in the country. A close affinity developed between the two couples and they visited one another's homes frequently. The affinity stemmed partly from Feuchtwanger's admiration for Chaplin's films (Chaplin often liked those best who liked his films most), and Chaplin's admiration for Feuchtwanger's work. (According to a *New York Times* report in 1930, Chaplin considered buying the rights to and playing the lead role in Feuchtwanger's *Jew Suss*.) But their friendship also grew, according to the biographers, because of their similar political inclinations. Feuchtwanger supported Chaplin through all his ordeals in the 1940s and 1950s and then maintained a correspondence after Chaplin exiled himself to Switzerland. Chaplin himself remembers that during a private showing of *Monsieur Verdoux*, Feuchtwanger, Thomas Mann, and several more "stood up and applauded for over a minute."[6]

Chaplin and Brecht, who had been an admirer of Chaplin's films since 1918, "saw each other frequently at Eisler's home, at Salka Viertel's salon, in Chaplin's own home, and at Hollywood gatherings." They shared an interest in politics: Brecht recalls that he and Chaplin were the only two people at a large Hollywood party in 1944 listening to a radio broadcast of the presidential election results. Nevertheless, Brecht and Chaplin never grew really close and comfortable with one another. Hanns Eisler described Brecht's manner toward Chaplin as one of "cordial, attentive respect," something like that of a devoted student toward an admired mentor. According to Eisler, Chaplin wondered at Brecht's tendency to theorize systematically but at times obtusely about art. He was also mystified when Brecht, after reading a draft of the script for *Monsieur Verdoux*, commented only that Chaplin wrote the script "Chinese fashion" (MA, p. 434). When both Chaplin and Brecht were having political problems, however, Chaplin showed his loyalty to his friend by attending the Los Angeles opening of Brecht's *Galileo* in July 1947.[7]

Brecht and Chaplin were mutual friends of composer Hanns Eisler, whom Chaplin calls a "great musician" in his autobiography (MA, p. 452). Eisler had admired and written about Chaplin before they met. During a tour of the United States in 1935, for example, he reported on the controversy surrounding *Modern Times* and Boris Shumiatsky's comments on the film: "The reactionary Hearst press hastened to open an attack on Chaplin, claiming he was making a Communist film." Eisler went on to say, inaccurately and somewhat illogically, that

Chaplin expressed his support of communism in an interview "because under Communism he will be recognized as the greatest actor in the world." After they met in the early 1940s, Chaplin and Eisler became close friends and often saw one another. Eisler believed that he and Brecht radicalized Chaplin. Although Chaplin tended to dominate the discussion when Eisler and Brecht saw him, Eisler told an interviewer, Chaplin soon learned that Eisler and Brecht laughed loudest and longest when his jokes had a strong social thrust. It is not unreasonable to suggest that the sharply ironic and satiric comedy that emerged in *Monsieur Verdoux* was influenced by the humor Brecht and Eisler enjoyed. This kind of humor was, according to Heilbut, one of the central and distinguishing characteristics of the German emigrés in America. "Witty, impious, quite unlike any other, Jewish or American," Heilbut writes, its tone was "sharp and biting"—an almost perfect description of some of the humor in *Monsieur Verdoux*.[8]

Thus during the difficult period in which Chaplin was struggling with the Barry case, and then with the changing and increasingly hostile political climate in the United States, he and his new wife Oona O'Neill Chaplin, who was sympathetic to his political views, found themselves isolated from most of Hollywood but gaining companionship and support from this group of leftist emigrés, outsiders in a new land. They viewed Chaplin's problems as a manifestation of fascist forces at work in America to discredit him for his political activities and views.[9]

If one sought to sum up the political views of this group, the following would be central. First, the group was avowedly and actively anti-fascist. Second, they were in general enthusiastic supporters of the Soviet Union (Feuchtwanger wrote a book in 1937, based on a visit there that year, in praise of the Soviet system) and thus were sympathetic to the cause of Allied unity.[10] Third, partly because they were living in an alien culture, they were ambivalent about the United States: though America had granted them asylum, it also seemed unreasonably materialistic and hypocritically intolerant. (Two German emigrés, Fritz Lang and William Dieterle, like Chaplin, ran afoul of the House Subcommittee on Un-American Activities [HUAC], headed by Martin Dies, for the "anti-American" or "prematurely anti-fascist" ideas expressed in films they directed in the late 1930s. After the war, as we shall see, a number of others had similar and more serious problems.) In an era of patriotic fervor, systematically marshaled during World War II and perpetuated after the war, this genuine ambivalence about America was out of step with dominant ideological currents. And fourth, the group tended to understand conservative opposition to their views as fascist; thus Chaplin's legal problems, particularly the federal charges brought against him, were perceived as motivated by fascist forces who hoped to punish Chaplin for his "dangerous ideas."

It is a truism of social psychology that human beings come to understand who they are and what they believe through their interactions with "significant others"—their family and closest friends. As Chaplin emerged from the Barry trials and moved toward his next film, his significant others included Salka Viertel, the Feuchtwangers, Brecht, and the Eislers. The political perspective they collectively reinforced—strong antifascism, sympathy to the Soviet allies, and skepticism about the hypocrisies of American democracy—was becoming increasingly tenuous as American views shifted in the early postwar years.

The Cooling of Progressivism in Early Postwar America

Chaplin's association with the German emigrés is significant in part because of the influence of their progressive, antifascist world view on Chaplin's first film following the Barry case, *Monsieur Verdoux* (1947). The film is for Chaplin a fascinating departure, a work of social criticism and bitter irony shaped by his experiences and associations in the first half of the 1940s. As we shall see, it elicited extreme hostility from some quarters, making it Chaplin's first real box-office failure. Many American reviewers attacked the film, although it received high critical praise when it was rereleased in 1964 and again in 1973.[11] That rejection was in part, as we shall see later in the chapter, related to the film's departure from Chaplin's aesthetic contract. But this initial critical rejection can also be explained by reference to American cultural history: *Monsieur Verdoux* is a "progressive" work (in the 1930s sense of the term) released in a different era, hostile to that political position. What had changed?

The Communist party's official policy of Popular Front cooperation with other antifascist groups ended abruptly with the Nazi–Soviet Nonaggression Pact of August 1939, and this led to a break between the CPUSA and many American liberals. However, the Nazi invasion of the Soviet Union in June 1941 and the American entry into the war the following December helped partially and temporarily to mend that rift. The Americans and Soviets became allies, and if that made many American conservatives uncomfortable, it also renewed the hopes of some American leftists. For the Left, between 1941 and 1944 there was a tempered renewal of the Popular Front spirit, and liberals and

Communists alike cooperated to support the war effort. Chaplin's speeches during 1942 promoting a second front were just one manifestation of this spirit. Besides favoring the second front policy, American liberals in this period were also generally in favor of close military cooperation among the United States, Great Britain, and the Soviet Union (the so-called Big Three); moral and material support for resistance movements in occupied countries; and the hope for "One World"—or at least the need to preserve the "grand alliance"—after the war was over.[12]

These positions all primarily related to foreign affairs: for the duration of the war, domestic reform took a back seat to the conduct of the war effort. When liberals discussed American society, they most often presented it positively as the democratic alternative to fascism. The typical liberal view was that though the Soviet Union and the United States were different, both were "good" societies fighting against an evil one. Henry Wallace, Roosevelt's Vice-President, downplayed the differences between the Soviet Union and the United States when he wrote in the pages of the *New Republic* in 1942 that Russia, an "economic democracy," and the United States, a "political democracy," were unified in their desire "for the education, the productivity and the enduring happiness of the common man."[13] Such statements exemplify how cooperation between Communists and liberals, so common in the late 1930s had revived.

The Allied victory in 1945 led to optimistic expectations not just among American liberals but among Americans generally. The United States emerged from the war confident, powerful, and vigorous. It was, after all, the major power that suffered least during the war. No battles had been fought on its soil. None of its mainland cities had been bombed. Its economy, thanks in no small part to war-time production, was booming, well recovered from the crisis of the 1930s. It even had sole possession of the devastating and terrifying atomic bomb. The United States seemed in an ideal position to reshape the postwar world according to its own purposes. To progressive liberals this meant a world in which fascism was abolished, domestic New Deal reforms were pushed forward, and cooperation between the United States and the Soviet Union would foster a cooperative and peaceful, even united, world.

Historical events often dash hopes, and so it was with this American buoyancy after 1945. By 1950 the United States had experienced a number of shocks that shifted the cultural and political climate and made it much less comfortable for progressive liberals who, like Chaplin, had publicly called during the war for cooperation between the

United States and the Soviet Union. For most Americans the Soviet Union, having enlarged its sphere of influence and tightened its grip on Eastern Europe, had come to be considered America's bitter adversary. As early as March 1946, in a famous speech in Fulton, Missouri, Winston Churchill warned that "an iron curtain has descended across the continent" with the Soviet side subject "to a very high and in many cases increasing measure of control from Moscow."[14] The following year President Truman, much less popular with American liberals than his charismatic predecessor had been, articulated a get-tough containment policy and vowed to go anywhere on the globe to help contain the spread of communism. The same year HUAC began its infamous investigations of Communist influence and infiltration in the United States, including Hollywood, and many Americans were asked to take loyalty oaths if they wished to retain old jobs or get new ones. In 1949 two more blows stunned those who hoped for postwar international cooperation: Mao Tse-tung's Communists took control of China and the Soviet Union successfully detonated its first atomic weapon. To cap it off, by 1950 the United States found itself engaged in yet another war after only a half decade of respite, this time in far-off Korea.

This distinct shift in the political climate led to a crisis in American liberalism. Historian Mary McAuliffe has shown that American liberals after 1946 became divided over the issue of how to respond to the Soviet Union and Stalin. To understand the change, one might draw on William O'Neill's *A Better World*, a study of the reaction of American liberal intellectuals to Stalin. O'Neill uses the term "progressives" to describe those on the left who refused to denounce Russia and the term "anti-Stalinists" to describe those who actively opposed Stalin's brand of communism, even though they considered themselves liberals (in the American sense) on other issues. O'Neill distinguishes both groups from the "anti-Communists," conservatives who made blanket denunciations of the Communist government in the Soviet Union, regardless of who was leading it.[15]

These distinctions enable one to see the crisis and direction of postwar American liberalism more clearly. The progressive attitude toward the Soviet Union dominated American liberalism in the late 1930s, but its appeal gradually lessened for a number of reasons: news of Stalin's purges in the late 1930s, the 1939 Nazi–Soviet Pact, and—after the reprieve from 1942 to the end of the war—a growing belief that Stalin's aggression in foreign policy and his ruthlessness in Soviet domestic affairs betrayed the democratic socialist ideal that many leftists had embraced during the depression. As a result, progressivism declined and anti-Stalinism grew among American liberals. Henry Wallace's Progressive party campaign in 1948 was the last hurrah of the progressive position, and that campaign steadily lost steam through 1948 as the election approached: Wallace ultimately garnered just over a million votes (less than 2 percent of the ballots cast). Truman, by defining himself as a New Deal liberal in domestic affairs and a firm anti-Stalinist in foreign affairs, managed to stage his famous narrow victory.[16]

To define this decline in progressivism another way, between 1938 and 1948 the spectrum of American political ideology shifted radically. In 1938 a dichotomy existed, weighted toward and made up of a large and ecumenical progressive Left, united by its antifascism, at one end, and a smaller political Right, often isolationist, at the other. On the left Communists, socialists, New Dealers, and other antifascists could cooperate by minimizing their ideological differences and stressing their opposition to Hitler.

By 1948, the spectrum of American political ideology began to look quite different: tripartite rather than dichotomous. To borrow from the title of Arthur Schlesinger's influential book of 1949, liberals of the Americans for Democratic Action variety began to see the United States as a "vital center," poised between the left- and right-wing totalitarianisms of communism and fascism. In essence, a Cold War ideological consensus—a paradigm of assumptions and beliefs, which Geoffrey Hodgson has usefully called "the ideology of liberal consensus"—was beginning to solidify, and its main assumptions would dominate American intellectual life until its breakdown in the early 1960s.[17]

The two cornerstone beliefs of this ideology of liberal consensus cast light on the fate of *Monsieur Verdoux* and, ultimately, of Chaplin himself. The first belief centered on domestic issues. It held, roughly, that the American economic system had evolved, softening the brutalities of late-nineteenth-century capitalism and thus becoming more democratic and offering abundance to a wider segment of the population than ever before. The growth of the economy during and after the war led many to believe that the key to democracy was productivity and technology: in this view, by enlarging the economic pie, class conflict would be defused and blue-collar workers brought into the middle class. Social problems so evident and pressing in the depression thus seemed more manageable and less threatening. In short, the ideology of liberal consensus held that the structure of American society was essentially sound, needing only minor reform to keep it fine tuned.

Concerning foreign affairs, the ideology of liberal consensus held that the only serious threat to American harmony and progress was the spectre of communism, both within American society and abroad. The United States, as leader of the "free world," must brace itself for a long struggle against communism and fight it around the world while simultaneously promoting the economic and political virtues of the American system. Truman's containment policy was a logical outgrowth—or better, a central enunciation—of this dimension of the emerging paradigm of consensus. As Hodgson sums it up: "confident to the verge of complacency about the perfectability of American society, anxious to the point of paranoia about the threat of Communism—those were the two faces of the consensus mood."[18]

Ironically, the tendency of Americans after World War II to view the Soviet Union as an unalterable enemy reflected a frame of mind rooted in the late 1930s. Progressive antifascism encouraged people to think of international politics in Manichaean terms: us (antifascists; the Allies) versus them (fascists; the Axis). After the war, particularly given Soviet conduct in Eastern Europe, it was easy for many Americans mentally to change the name of their adversary from the Nazis to the Soviets: though the villain was different, the frame of mind was almost identical.[19] Simultaneously, the economic prosperity during and after the war defused most radical criticism of capitalism, so that social criticism of American and West European societies began to seem unnecessary to some, imprudent to others, and even "un-American" to an increasingly large number. Thus many progressives followed their fellow citizens and shifted the focus of their suspicions or hatred to the Soviet Union while simultaneously embracing American society.

To some progressives, however, Chaplin included, this new Cold War mentality seemed unnecessarily belligerent in foreign affairs and too complacent in domestic affairs. Chaplin and other progressives held out an optimism about the possibilities of peace with the Soviet Union and remained doubtful that American society was achieving a harmonious utopia. Having committed himself to progressive politics in *The Great Dictator* and his second front speeches, feeling himself a victim of fascist forces in the way he was treated during the Barry trials, Chaplin set out to make a film that expressed a progressive critique of capitalist society just as the Cold War was setting in with a vengeance. The result, as one might expect, did his star image no good.

Lashing Out: *Monsieur Verdoux*

Monsieur Verdoux (1947) constituted an extreme deviation in a number of ways from the kind of feature films Chaplin had been making. As we shall see later in this chapter, both the promotion and reception of the film contributed to the unraveling of Chaplin's star image, but so, too, did the film itself. The film can best be understood in the context of Chaplin's progressive antifascism and his public humiliation during the Barry trials. These two factors led to two central themes in the film: a social critique of capitalist society and a clear (though perhaps unconscious and unintended) disparagement of women bordering on misogyny.

Briefly, *Monsieur Verdoux* is set in France during the mid-1930s, from after the onset of the depression to 1937, following the outbreak of the Spanish Civil War. The central character, Henri Verdoux (played by Chaplin), has served faithfully as a bank clerk for thirty years but has been fired from his position because of the depression. To support his crippled wife and his son, Verdoux has become a Bluebeard—using his considerable charm to marry wealthy women for their money and then killing them. In the course of the film he murders two of his wives, fails to murder a third (the lucky Annabella, played by Martha Raye) after some comic misadventures, and just misses marrying another. Ultimately, his schemes catch up with him. After he learns that the police are on his trail (he manages to poison one detective), he also loses both the fortune he has accumulated in a stock market collapse and, subsequently, his family. Turning himself in to the authorities, he is tried, found guilty of murder, and sentenced to be hanged. At the trial he argues in his own defense that "numbers sanctify": that his efforts to survive led to minimal destruction when compared to the mass wartime murders of the state, and that it is unjust for him to be tried as a criminal while a murderous soldier is honored as a hero. The final shot of the film shows Verdoux walking away from the camera as he is led by prison guards to his execution.

Even this short description suggests how far *Monsieur Verdoux* strayed from Chaplin's aesthetic contract. First, its comedy is less evident and different from Chaplin's earlier films. Except for Verdoux's ability to count bills with amazing rapidity, his backward tumble out of a window, and his escapades in the rowboat trying to murder Annabella, slapstick or visual humor is at a minimum. Instead, the humor is macabre, very often emerging from Verdoux's attempts to carry out his murderous plans.

Second, the film is essentially devoid of romance and pathos. Although Verdoux is ostensibly happily married, the two sequences in which he returns to the sunlit country cottage to visit his crippled wife and his son are lifeless and stilted. It is clear that Verdoux is much more fully alive when he is out in his business world, marrying and murdering women. Whereas the pathos in most of Chaplin's earlier comic features was evoked when Charlie was disappointed in his romantic aspirations, the viewer is given no pathetic character with whom to identify in *Monsieur Verdoux*.

Third, Chaplin departs from his practice of presenting two moral universes, one good and one evil, through the central narrative conflict, a tendency that was clear through *The Great Dictator*. Instead, he establishes two sets of disturbing moral perspectives. The first set of values is society's, which is dominated by wartime destruction, economic chaos, and the primacy of profit over human needs. Counterpoised to and emanating from this set of values are Verdoux's. A victim of the depression and a ruthlessly competitive society, he becomes ruthless and murderous himself, all the while justifying his public actions on private grounds. The audience is left with no comfortable, comforting moral perspective, unlike all previous Chaplin features starring Charlie.

Related to these deviations from Chaplin's aesthetic contract is the most significant one: a new central character. In Chaplin's own apt description, the charming, loquacious, dapper, smartly dressed Verdoux is "a paradox of virtue and vice" (MA, p. 435). He adores and provides for his invalid wife but has murdered thirteen women and plans to kill more. He will carefully avoid stepping on a caterpillar, while behind him one of his victims burns in an incinerator. He has been a gentle and law-abiding citizen for fifty years but becomes first a systematic murderer and ultimately an accusing social critic. As with the character of Alex in Stanley Kubrick's *A Clockwork Orange*, audiences simultaneously abhor Verdoux and empathize with him because his society seems even more corrupt than he is. Verdoux is a far cry from the tender, gentle, resilient Charlie that was so important in building Chaplin's star image to the heights it achieved in the 1920s. Charlie was an ideal character for the creation and sustenance of Chaplin's star image; Verdoux immediately sets up a barrier between himself and an audience expecting Charlie.

One can also go beyond the observation that Chaplin broke his aesthetic contract with his audience. As in *The Great Dictator*, he also violated conventions of the classical Hollywood cinema. In *Monsieur Verdoux* these violations related more to narrative than stylistic norms. Principally, Chaplin strayed from the Hollywood tendency to treat individual characters, not social forces, as the causal agents in a narrative.[20] Absolutely central to the narrative of *Verdoux* is the conception that larger social and economic forces, particularly economic depression and war, determine the fates of individual people. Twice in *Monsieur Verdoux* these larger social forces pressure Verdoux to alter his life significantly. First, a depression forces him out of work, which leads him to a career as a Bluebeard to support his family. Second, a stock market panic wipes out his fortune, and, also grieving over the deaths of his wife and son of unspecified causes, he loses his desire to live. He then turns himself in to the police. Viewers of Hollywood films were accustomed to see the desires of their individual heroes opposed by individual villains, with the heroes generally realizing their goals and the villains foiled. In this film, though, social forces determine the fate of the hero, who himself is both villain and hero in certain ways and who at the end of the story is led to his execution. Such a narrative method distanced much of Chaplin's potential audience from the film.

Thus Chaplin violated both his aesthetic contract and the narrative conventions of classical Hollywood cinema. Why did Chaplin discard Charlie, trading him in for the urbane, polished Verdoux? It is tempting to answer this question autobiographically: Charlie, whose essential appeal was based largely on pantomime, could not express what Chaplin felt compelled to say after committing himself to progressive politics and experiencing loneliness, acrimony, and public humiliation during the Barry affair. Chaplin's disgust with the course of civilization and his discouraging relationships with women propelled him even further away from the world of his tender resilient screen persona than he had strayed in *The Great Dictator*. He needed a Verdoux to add a more explicit dimension of social realism and criticism to his films. This new persona enabled Chaplin to express his political denunciation of contemporary Western society and to exorcise the ghosts of his failures with women. However those two aims might hurt his star image, Chaplin had deeply felt, personal reasons for the social vision he presented through *Monsieur Verdoux*.

How did the film contribute to the state of Chaplin's star image in the mid-1940s? As we have already seen, even before *Verdoux*, Chaplin's star image was becoming less associated with Charlie the persona and more linked to Chaplin the man. Chaplin the man, furthermore, was becoming endowed with different traits. In the 1920s and early 1930s he was the "genius" filmmaker of astonishing versatility or the serious intellect, sensitive to true art and sympathetic to the plight of common people. As a result of *The Great Dictator* and the publicity surrounding his second front activities and the Barry trials, however, Chaplin's star image was becoming associated with progressive politics and questionable sexual morality.

These two traits invited viewers already upset with Chaplin to make an autobiographical reading of *Monsieur Verdoux*. The film's assault on women was easily linked to Chaplin's experiences during the Barry case, and the film's political critique recalled the progressive world view that Chaplin had embraced at least since *The Great Dictator*. It is clear, however, that these lashing attacks on women and on capitalist society were not designed to soothe and satisfy a mass audience. Chaplin had been one of the most consistently popular figures in American film history up through *The Great Dictator*. But for several reasons, he did not make *Verdoux* with a careful eye on the box office. In abandoning the comic persona Charlie after being associated or even identified with him for over thirty years, Chaplin was immediately risking the greatest source of his box-office appeal. But in substituting for Charlie a Bluebeard character—and particularly in doing so not long after Chaplin himself had been portrayed by bold headlines as a despoiler of young women—the director was further risking a dangerous identification of the actor with the new character he played. Finally, in having that central character justify his murders by articulating a progressive critique of capitalism, and then releasing the film at the very time that the dominant American ideology was increasingly defending its capitalist system as the only viable alternative to communism, Chaplin was asking for trouble.

A number of analysts, including Richard Dyer, have argued that stars exist in a culture in part because they embody within their characters certain prevailing cultural values and attitudes. Stars thus may serve two ideological functions: to reinforce the dominant ideology of the culture in which the star is popular or to conceal important cultural tensions and contradictions, a process that Dyer calls displacement.[21] At least two elements of Chaplin's Charlie persona may be cited in this regard. First, Charlie's ability to maintain his human dignity and resilience in spite of his lower-class status and minimal power in society clearly touched a deep chord among the American (and world) moviegoing public. This aspect of Charlie's character functioned to displace the tension in American society between the myth that anyone working hard can make it in America and the reality that very few move from the bottom to the top of the economic pyramid.

Second, Charlie's constant yearning for romance despite the factors working against him (his size, his lack of status) also appealed to an audience conditioned to expect romance in films, even if the romances in the Chaplin films were not always worked out in the end. (A content analysis of one hundred Hollywood films made in 1941–1942 found that most leading characters—68 percent—desired romantic love over all else.)[22] This element of Charlie's character reinforced the myth of romantic love, long a staple in American and much of Western culture.

But in *Monsieur Verdoux* Chaplin's persona fulfilled neither of these star functions. Verdoux, albeit driven by circumstances, becomes a financially successful businessman/murderer, so successful that he invests in the stock market, something that could and would never have occurred to Charlie. In creating an enterprising and successful bourgeois hero, Chaplin disgarded one of the most powerful reasons for his central character's appeal in previous films. And though Verdoux, under his aliases, does engage in some manipulative "romancing," the audience knows that his ulterior motives are always murder and money, a far cry from the tender and deeply felt longing Charlie exhibited when in the presence of his beloved. Moreover, Verdoux's love for his wife shows none of the intensity or enthusiasm of feeling Charlie directed from a distance toward Georgia or Merna or the blind flower girl. Such violations of his aesthetic contract of stardom, when combined with the negative publicity he suffered during the Barry affair, made it inevitable that Chaplin would antagonize the audience that had previously worshipped him as a star.

Monsieur Verdoux: Initial Promotion and Reception

When discussing a film's production history, it is usually appropriate to consider first its promotion and then its critical and popular reception. In the case of *Monsieur Verdoux*, however, it is much more useful to consider the promotion and reception simultaneously. Not only did the promotion of the film at United Artists begin very late, largely because Chaplin refused to lift the veil of secrecy from his production, but after the bad reviews the film garnered during its New York City opening and the press-conference grilling Chaplin endured the next Monday, United Artists was forced to withdraw the film and reconceive its promotion campaign in hopes of salvaging the film. This section will discuss the checkered promotion and reception history of *Monsieur Verdoux* until the film was withdrawn after the New York City run, and the next section will consider the fate of the film after that.

Compared to the tremendous advance publicity given films like *City Lights, Modern Times,* and especially *The Great Dictator, Monsieur Verdoux* remained shrouded in mystery almost to the day of its release (11 April 1947). The other three films were all the subject of a number of articles in the *New York Times* during the production and postproduction periods, which helped to ready the audience in advance. In the case of *Monsieur Verdoux,* however, the only *Times* article of any significance preparing the way for the film was a brief report and picture spread in the March 30 magazine section. After alluding to the secrecy surrounding the project, the article quoted Chaplin's description of the film:

> I am a mass killer. I start out as a bank clerk, a respectable, dapper, middle-class Frenchman. Then the depression of 1930 costs me my job. I have a wife and child whom I love and must support. And so I turn to the business of marrying women and killing them for their money. Actually, I am a very moral man; I never let these women touch me and I hate my new job, I hate the women. I am in business and I must do my duty after the classic heroic mode.

This terse and rather misleading description is accompanied by seven production stills over a two-page spread, but the photos suggest that Chaplin did not show the film to the *Times* reporter. One caption refers to Verdoux's "periodic weddings" in the film, although in fact only one is presented—and even it isn't carried out. Another caption says that Martha Raye's character ends up dead like the rest of Verdoux's victims, which is not true.[23]

Correspondence of the United Artists publicity staff in New York City confirms that Chaplin and his studio employees failed to give the film adequate advance publicity. In an April 3 cable to United Artists executive Paul Lazarus, about a week before the film's New York opening, Tom Waller of the publicity staff in New York complained that his office was having a difficult time developing any campaign since of the entire office, only he had seen the film. Waller continued in an ominous tone: "Chaplin today requested mass meeting of press. . . . I am setting up such a mass meeting for Monday April 14. Chaplin expects this will be controversial and understands we can do nothing to protect him or picture him once he submits to mass questioning."[24] Dutifully but reluctantly, the staff announced Chaplin's first extensive press conference for publicity in his career in a press release dated April 8, followed by an April 9 release stating that the conference would be restricted to accredited members of the press.[25]

Chaplin's lack of concern about promoting his film is somewhat surprising, given how shrewdly he had handled the press at other times in his career. As we have seen, he was particularly skillful at cultivating intellectuals like Stark Young, Gilbert Seldes, Waldo Frank, and Edmund Wilson in the 1920s, relationships that bore fruit in praise-filled articles in intellectual journals and a consequent raising and broadening of his star status. Yet his inattention to promoting *Monsieur Verdoux* is explicable. In the 1920s Chaplin was still in the business of solidifying and raising his reputation; he had not yet fully shaken the image of a vulgar music-hall comedian who entertained only unsophisticated audiences. By the 1940s, he had long been a darling of both the masses and the intelligentsia, accustomed to having the press at his beck and call. His behavior before the opening of *Monsieur Verdoux* suggests two explanations. Perhaps unaware of how much the Barry affair had strained his relations with the press, Chaplin seemed to believe—at least until he arrived in New York—that when his new film was ready, the audiences and reviewers would come flocking to him as they had since the 1920s. Another, darker, explanation is that Chaplin was driven by a subconscious wish to strike back at his attackers, even if it meant that his film would fail at the box office.

Whatever Chaplin's motivations, the lack of advance publicity for *Monsieur Verdoux* and the impending press conference even merited a column in the trade publication *Motion Picture Daily* on April 11, the day the film premiered. In it columnist Red Kann reported on United Artists' "initial difficulties with Chaplin" over publicizing the film. Chaplin had apparently hoped to open the film a week earlier, on Good Friday, but United Artists officials convinced him that the film would need more buildup. Kann also reported that Chaplin had first planned to talk only with the *Times*, the *Herald Tribune*, and a representative of one wire service. When United Artists officials objected to such minimal publicity, Kann continued, "Chaplin is the one who insisted upon a general press interview. . . . UA officials did what they could to discourage the en masse cross-fire, pointing out Charlie would have to take on all comers including those who might be after answers as to why he never became an American citizen and his version of his alleged lack of cooperation in the war effort." In reply to these worries, Kann reported, Chaplin replied only, "I can handle it."[26] One wonders how much Chaplin was unconsciously assuming the role of Verdoux, whose fast-talking charm usually enables him to extricate himself from the most difficult of circumstances.

Chaplin was not as persuasive as his fictional counterpart. Had he scheduled a press conference to promote the premiere of almost any other of his feature films—except perhaps *The Circus*, which followed closely on the heels of his divorce to Lita Grey—Chaplin would likely have been warmly received. But when he stepped forward on Monday, April 14, to answer questions from the press in the packed Grand Ballroom of the Gotham Hotel, he received a frosty reception.[27] Chaplin's opening comment, tinged with apparent irony, shows that he expected trouble: "Thank you, ladies and gentlemen of the press. I am not going to waste your time. I should say—proceed with the butchery" (p. 35).

And in many ways a butchery it was. Though the press conference was purportedly designed to help promote *Monsieur Verdoux*, most of the questions concerned Chaplin's political views and activities. If one does not count restatement or elaboration of questions, about 60 percent dealt with political issues, with no reference to films at all. Of the remaining 40 percent, about half asked Chaplin specifically about *Monsieur Verdoux* and the other half asked him about films in general. The political questions were generally hostile, peppering Chaplin on a range of issues and charges. Was he a Communist? Was he a Communist sympathizer? Why hadn't he become an American citizen? Why hadn't he contributed more prominently to the recent war effort? Why wasn't he more patriotic or nationalistic? Did he know Hanns Eisler and was Eisler a Communist? Wasn't postwar Soviet expansionism comparable to prewar German expansionism? And so on.

The most insistent and vituperative reporter there was James W. Fay, who represented a publication called *Catholic War Veterans*. Fay asked Chaplin thirteen questions, none of which had anything to do with *Monsieur Verdoux* or with films in general. Fay was particularly upset that Chaplin had not become an American citizen and that he had said publicly that he was not a nationalist. In the increasingly frigid atmosphere of the Cold War, Fay represented a considerable sector of the American public when he scolded Chaplin: "I'm objecting to your particular stand that you have no patriotic feelings about this country or any other country" (p. 36).

In his responses to the political questions, Chaplin consistently defended progressive views. He stated that he was not a Communist and had never belonged to any political party but said that he did "sympathize very much with Russia" during World War II because they were "holding the front" (p. 36). He explained his second front activities in progressive terms: in the speeches he had called "for the unity of the Allied cause—which at that time was being disrupted. . . . It was very obvious to see that [the Nazis] were trying to disunite us in this country" (p. 38). When asked if Eisler was a Communist, he replied,

"I don't know whether he is a Communist or not. I know he is a fine artist and a great musician and a very sympathetic friend." To the reporter who asked him to equate German and Soviet expansionism, Chaplin declined: "Now, when you're getting my opinion on political matters and on military matters, I'm not going to be embroiled" (p. 38). To Chaplin, the times were bad ("there is a lot of hate in the world and I think these are very troublesome days," p. 41), and the only way to counter the political atmosphere was to search for the kind of world unity envisioned by the Allied cause in World War II. This progressive outlook prevented him from denouncing the Soviet Union and joining the increasingly fashionable tendency to celebrate America unconditionally.

Just as Verdoux defended actions that were sure to be denounced by audiences, Chaplin refused to cut his conscience to fit the fashion of 1947, which gave considerable material to those in the press who opposed his views. The press conference thus promoted neither *Monsieur Verdoux* nor Chaplin's public reputation; the worst fears of United Artists press representatives were realized.

One can, however, overestimate the degree to which reviewers and critics attacked *Monsieur Verdoux* on the film's initial release. At the time of the premiere, American liberals were still deeply engaged in the debate over progressive and anti-Stalinist views of foreign policy. The day *Monsieur Verdoux* opened in New York City, for example, the *Times* carried advertisements both for Henry Wallace's progressive column in the *New Republic* (he had recently become editor) and for Churchill's anti-Stalinist article in *Life* headed, "It is barely a year since I spoke in Fulton." The same issue also contained a headline: "Churchill Says Britain Saved Greece from Communism," and on the day of the press conference, a small group in the U.S. House of Representatives—angry about Wallace's public criticism of the containment policy—demanded that his passport be revoked.[28] Progressives and anti-Stalinists were still debating, and in a similar vein Chaplin and his films had both critics and defenders, with those on the left more apt to defend him.

In the press conference, for example, a number of questions implied a civil and even a sympathetic attitude toward Chaplin. Most prominent among his defenders was James Agee—author of *Let Us Now Praise Famous Men*, "Comedy's Greatest Era" (an essay that highly praised Chaplin), and *The African Queen* screenplay—who was clearly outraged by Fay and others. Sitting in the balcony, he had to be handed a microphone so Chaplin could hear his trembling voice. In his comment, Agee wondered how the questioners could "congratulate themselves upon this country as the finest on earth and as a 'free country' " while they "pry into what a man's citizenship is, try to tell him his business from hour to hour . . . and exert a public moral blackmail against him for not becoming an American citizen, for his political views, and for not entertaining troops in the . . . way they think he should." Chaplin, gratified by the support after so much antagonism, replied, "Thank you very much" (p. 41).

Just as some defended Chaplin at the press conference, so did an articulate minority defend the film, though the negative reviews dominated. One of the few laughs Chaplin got during the press conference came when he was asked for his reaction to the reviews of *Verdoux* in the New York papers. "Well, the one optimistic note," he replied, "is that they were mixed" (p. 38).

The film surely had its detractors. Reporters at the press conference and many of the reviews of the film criticized it for its "message" and for not being like Chaplin's early Charlie films. At the press conference Chaplin received comments and questions like the following:

> "You have stopped being a good comedian since you've been bringing messages."
>
> "Are you going to make any more pictures for children?"
>
> "Are you going to make any more tramp pictures?"
>
> "Is there any possibility that some of your old pictures like *Modern Times* will be released?"

All such questions indicated a longing for an earlier (and less threatening) Chaplin whom the questioners clearly admired, and perhaps also a sense of regret concerning the new Chaplin who was emerging in the difficult present.

The negative and mixed reviews of *Monsieur Verdoux* convey much the same attitude. Perhaps the most hostile review in the New York City daily papers was Howard Barnes's in the influential *Herald Tribune*, which opened: "In *Monsieur Verdoux* Charles Chaplin has composed what he likes to term a 'comedy of murders' with a woeful lack of humor, melodrama, or dramatic taste." In the review Barnes made a mistake common among commentators on Chaplin: he equated Chaplin with the role he was playing and assumed that Chaplin justified or even approved of Verdoux's actions. If part of a reviewer's job is to recommend or steer his or her readers away from a film, there is no mistaking Barnes's attitude toward *Monsieur Verdoux*: "It has little entertainment value, either as somber symbolism or sheer nonsense."[29]

Such unequivocal denunciation was unusual. Of the negative and mixed reviews, it was much more common for reviewers to criticize

Chaplin's message and to yearn for a return to his earlier comic style. One might say that the "aesthetic discourse" surrounding the Chaplin films was changing again. In the 1910s reviewers asked if Chaplin's films were funny and some asked if they were unacceptably vulgar. In the 1920s they tended to ask whether the blend of pathos and comedy was successful. In the 1930s they asked if Chaplin was committed to a cause, and often hoped he was. Now in the late 1940s they were asking if he had a message, and hoped he did not. The tendency of critics in the 1930s to urge artists to commit themselves politically was diminishing rapidly in the 1940s, as the shift in the political climate affected the tastes and commentary of some reviewers.

Philip Hartung's review in *Commonweal* was typical. Titled, "Unusual—To Say the Least," the review asserted that "when he goes in for pantomime . . . Chaplin is at his best" but criticized the film's "spurious social philosophy."[30] John McCarten's *New Yorker* review, "Chaplin and a Murky Message," held that when Chaplin relied on his old "antics"— presumably scenes like the one when Verdoux falls backward out of a second-floor window—"one is tempted to forgive him for having got himself involved in a film full of cloudy observations on the cosmos." The only genuine success of the film comes "along sartorial lines," wrote McCarten. "Personally I preferred him when was baggier, humbler, and funnier." McCarten wished, in Jauss's terms, for a film of much less striking "aesthetic distance," a work of "entertainment" or "culinary" art.[31]

A related criticism—that a comedian should not try to do serious roles—came from *Variety* and *Newsweek*. *Variety* wrote that "Comedians who yen to do *Hamlet* usually wind up with neo-tragic results, and *Monsieur Verdoux* runs according to form," and opened its review with this terse box-office prediction: "Chaplin will have to carry this one. And how."[32] *Newsweek*'s review, "Little Man, What Now?" was supplemented with a picture of Raye and Chaplin, captioned "Better in Pantomime." It found the funny spots "too few and much too far between," and judged firmly: "Jean Gabin, famous for his heavy roles, would never try to be a commic juggler; there is no reason why Chaplin should take it upon himself to play straight."[33] The reviewer for the *Christian Science Monitor*, in "An Assault from Mr. Chaplin," frequently used the words "sardonic" and "bitter" to describe the "keenly disappointing" film. As in many other reviews, the message came under sternest attack: "his broadsides of indictment against society (particularly the ruthlessness of business) become merely petty and meaningless, expressions of hatred, contempt, and personal bitterness."[34] This chorus of negative criticism indicates how Chaplin's star was falling, just as it indicates that most American movie reviewers were becoming much less likely to encourage or even accept social criticism in films.

Other reviews, usually from more leftist, prestigious, or elite publications, were more positive. In the *New York Times*, Bosley Crowther, usually sympathetic with realist or "message" films, gave *Monsieur Verdoux* a generally positive review. More than most reviewers, Crowther caught the paradox of the Verdoux character: "As Mr. Chaplin plays him he is both a satan and a faun—a devil in elegant clothing and a charming innocent with the manners of a dude." With this character at the center, Chaplin created a film with a message: "Mr. Chaplin . . . believes in using his talent for socking hard—socking, that is, at the evil and injustice he sees in the world and aiming directly at the midriff of general complacency." While other critics were ready to write Chaplin off as a has-been, Crowther asserted that "Mr. Chaplin is still in the game—and hitting hard."[35]

The *New Republic*, more sympathetic to progressive politics than most newspapers, also gave *Monsieur Verdoux* some positive, albeit guarded, attention. Shirley O'Hara's review of the film, while polite, was generally negative ("I am bewildered by it and disappointed"). However, in a column two weeks later, on the press conference, she defended Chaplin and criticized the behavior of her press cohorts. O'Hara wrote that Chaplin "couldn't have expected the shockingly rude, sustained impertinence of the attack" during the press conference, and that Chaplin's "patience and courtesy were astounding." She and a few others "could only be ashamed at what ugly hostile liberties can be taken in the name of freedom of the press."[36] Though panning the film, the *New Republic* defended the comedian's political liberty.

The reviews that gave Chaplin almost unqualified praise came from journals firmly associated with the Left: the *Nation*, *Partisan Review*, *PM*, and the Communist magazine *Mainstream*. The *Nation* reviewer was Chaplin's most vocal defender in the press conference, James Agee. He devoted three entire columns to his review of *Monsieur Verdoux*, and his words still convey the enthusiasm and seriousness with which he wrote them. To Agee, *Monsieur Verdoux* was Chaplin's "most ambitious film." Likewise, his theme, "the greatest and most appropriate to its time that he has yet undertaken, is the bare problem of surviving in such a world as this." Though Agee argued that Chaplin could have expressed more clearly the root causes for Verdoux's murders, he still felt that *Verdoux* was "one of the few indispensable works of our time," a work whose "grim central spirit" was conveyed with "cold nihilistic irony," a "great poem" from a "great poet."[37] To Agee,

Chaplin was neither the rakish womanizer nor the naive leftist; he was rather a major twentieth-century artist exploring issues of profound importance.

Another long and serious treatment of the film appeared in *Partisan Review* and was written by the young Robert Warshow, a perceptive analyst of popular culture who later would write influential essays on the gangster and western film genres, as well as a tribute to Chaplin's *Limelight*. Warshow's essay, which has subsequently left its mark on our contemporary understanding of Chaplin, placed *Verdoux* as the culmination of a series of films that began in the early 1930s, when the pressure of the times forced Chaplin's screen persona to "be for or against the society," a decision that would become "the determining factor in his life and the defining element of his character." Ultimately, this led Chaplin to abandon the tramp character, conclusively, in the final speech of *The Great Dictator*. The new character, Verdoux, though not as great a character as Charlie, nevertheless continued the line of development in Chaplin's art begun in the early 1930s. By 1947, "Chaplin's view of society has taken on a new savagery," which can easily be linked to Chaplin's humiliation during the Barry trials and to the increasing pressure being placed on his progressive political views. Like Agee, Warshow found the film complex and important, one that "must" be approached with a willingness to understand and enjoy it as a shifting pattern of ambiguity and irony, made up of all the complexities and contradictions not only of our society but of Chaplin's own mind and the mind of the spectator."[38]

Although Agee and Warshow were leftists, neither toed the progressive line so fully and consistently as reviewers for *PM* and *Mainstream*, which both found much to praise about *Verdoux*, especially its criticism of modern capitalist societies. *PM* twice came to Chaplin's defense after the press conference, once in an editorial by Max Lerner and once in a transcription of some of Chaplin's comments from the press conference itself.[39] In his editorial, Lerner suggests that "Chaplin has given us as elaborate and satiric 'theory of business enterprise' as Thorstein Veblen ever dared." In an attempt to deflect the growing tendency to denounce Chaplin's art because of his politics—a tendency that culminated in reactions to Chaplin's next film, *Limelight*—Lerner countered, "As for myself, I am content to take him as an artist, and to face the criticisms of our institutions that his art implies. . . . Where he makes his money and how he spends it, what he did or did not do about the war, what he thinks of Russia or Communism: these are his affairs, not ours. This hounding of him is unclean." The progressive Left in America was not yet willing to give up criticism of American

243

life, as Lerner's discussion showed. A few days later, *PM* defended Chaplin again. Whereas the *Chicago Tribune* had found Chaplin stocky and jowly in the Barry trials, *PM* found him "a short white-haired man with small kindly wrinkles around his eyes" when he held his press conference. Noting that only three of the New York City papers carried stories after the press conference—despite the hundreds of reporters who attended—*PM* went on to quote approvingly many of Chaplin's press conference comments on political affairs, some of which would seem dangerously leftist to an increasing number of Americans as the Cold War worsened.

The longest and most thoughtful defense of *Monsieur Verdoux* was Arnaud d'Usseau's "Chaplin's *Monsieur Verdoux.*" It appeared in a new journal called *Mainstream*, a Communist publication. The essay discussed what d'Usseau saw as the film's central achievements and analyzed why it had been so savagely attacked. In d'Usseau's view, the film's chief accomplishment was Chaplin's social analysis, which placed "the moral burden" of Verdoux's murders "entirely on society." Here he quoted Shaw approvingly: "Not only does society commit more frightful crimes than any individuals, King or commoner; it legalizes its crimes, and forges certificates of righteousness for them, besides torturing anyone who exposes their true character." To d'Usseau, Verdoux is the "completely integrated" bourgeois citizen, shaped by capitalist society to behave as he does. Yet in Chaplin's hands he becomes a "tragic figure capable of evoking our profoundest sympathy." In his analysis of the critical response to the film, d'Usseau suggests at least three reasons why critics reacted to it with such hostility. First, Chaplin did not honor his star persona, Charlie, hence disappointing those seeking the familiar. Second, Chaplin parodied the success ethic by making a mock rags-to-riches story, thus challenging cherished American beliefs. And third, some critics, in d'Usseau's view, made the valid criticism that Chaplin's dialogue was at times weak and his film style at times mediocre. More than anything else, however, *Monsieur Verdoux* disturbed the critics because the central character's "behavior is a comment on those values our society celebrates." Since d'Usseau also objected to the values the film focused on—individualism, the profit motive, and the success ethic—he was sympathetic to Verdoux's analysis and concluded: "We are grateful to be alive in Chaplin's time. He is indeed our greatest artist."[40]

Regardless of these defenses, *Monsieur Verdoux* was a disappointment at the box office in its five-week run at the Broadway Theater in New York City. *Variety* reported during the third week of the run that the film was "falling back rapidly in the current frame," and the next week it reported that the third week's receipts were $6,000 less than it had predicted, with the box office "slipping badly" in the fourth week. According to *Variety*'s figures, the film drew $27,000 in the shortened first week, $28,000 the second, then $18,000, $15,000, and $12,000 in the last three weeks of the run.[41] In contrast to the immediate and long-running success of *The Great Dictator*, the box-office response of New York City audiences to *Monsieur Verdoux* shocked Chaplin, for it was even more dismal news than the critical reviews. Part of the failure of *Verdoux* at the Broadway Theater undoubtedly had to do with inadequate publicity buildup, but Chaplin also had to face two more unpleasant facts: without Charlie, he had no guaranteed large audience, and if he continued to insist on inserting progressive messages into his films in the changed political atmosphere, he would have to face the financial consequences. Before doing anything else, however, he agreed with United Artists officials to withdraw the film from release and try to give it a second, and better, start.

The Campaign That Failed

It was unprecedented, indeed nearly unthinkable, that Chaplin would be forced to pull a feature film from distribution and redesign its publicity campaign. Given the initial response to *Verdoux*, however, he had little choice. Fortunately for those interested in the evolution of Chaplin's star image, the United Artists Collection at the Wisconsin Center for Film and Theater Research contains considerable material on the redone publicity campaign for *Monsieur Verdoux*. Located in the files of Paul Lazarus, Jr., and Alfred Tamarin, two United Artists publicity executives, this material provides insight into Chaplin's combative mood in 1947. The reception of the film after the campaign began gives us a firm indication of the status of Chaplin's star image as the Cold War set in.[42]

As noted, Chaplin and officials at United Artists, who also had an economic stake in the film, decided to withdraw the film after its New York run ended in May 1947. They hoped to regroup and develop a new advertising campaign for a rescheduled national release in August. Even before the new campaign was prepared, however, ominous signs of pressure group resistance to the film began to appear. On May 12 *Motion Picture Daily* reported that a group in Ohio was urging theater exhibitors not to book *Monsieur Verdoux* because Chaplin had never become an American citizen. In Memphis the local censorship board decided to ban the film. Such grassroots resistance worried United Artists so much that it placed an ad disguised as an article in the July 23 issue of *Hollywood Reporter* that predicted that *Monsieur Verdoux* would do $20 million of business.[43] Soon after, however, they realized that the time was not ripe for a national release and the August date was postponed.

The new publicity campaign for *Monsieur Verdoux* began when, in late June, publicist Russell Birdwell signed a six-month contract with the Chaplin Studios to direct the publicity campaign for United Artists, in which he was assisted by Jane Turner. Birdwell wasted no time. On June 24 he wrote a letter to the editor of the *Hollywood Reporter* saying that *Monsieur Verdoux* was a controversial film that needed defending. The disputes over the film, he hoped, would "sweep *Verdoux* into a vortex of fiery condemnation and enthusiastic approval." The same day he announced the challenging, combative slogan that would provide a focus for the new campaign: "Chaplin Changes! Can You?" By June 27 Birdwell had asked Arthur Kelly to send out six thousand broadside ads using this approach to potential exhibitors.[44]

The ensuing pressbook prepared to promote the film nearly assaulted the viewer. Since Chaplin had traded his most marketable character, Charlie, for Verdoux, the publicists, in consultation with Chaplin, decided to emphasize the change and hope to sell the film at least partly on that basis. One 8½ by 11 inch advertising picture in the pressbook exemplified this approach: it showed Verdoux in medium close-up accompanied only by the campaign's theme as its caption: "Chaplin changes. Can you?" (see Figures 24 and 25). Such an overt challenge to the viewer at a time when Chaplin's public reputation had been slipping for several years seems, in retrospect, to have been a questionable approach.

Another ad in the pressbook indicated the difficulties United Artists had in selling a Chaplin film without Charlie or a close relative. It showed another medium close up of Verdoux at the center of the ad surrounded by close-up cutouts of four women who appeared in the film. The headline at the top of the page described the film as "A Strange Love Story That Hurts," and below the pictures was a more detailed description: "In *Monsieur Verdoux* there is a peculiar intensity of drama . . . an even more peculiar hysteria of laughter—and a strange love story that hurts." This appeal, like the previous one, suggested that Chaplin was doing something new but was hardly likely to generate much viewer enthusiasm.[45]

Nevertheless, this was the campaign that Birdwell, working for Chaplin, prepared for the anticipated August release. Corporate records indicate that though the film did get a few scattered August playdates in the hinterlands (in South Dakota, for example), the release was generally pushed back to September. This delay stemmed at least in part from complications arising over Chaplin's status with the House Subcommittee on Un-American Activities. Its investigators had been in Hollywood in the late spring and summer talking with a number of people, including Chaplin's friend Hanns Eisler, and it began to look as if Chaplin might be called upon to testify. Birdwell, in a decision consistent with his notion that the controversial nature of the film should be emphasized (he apparently felt that there was no such thing as bad publicity), decided to open the film in HUAC's home court—Washington, D.C. It became even easier for Birdwell to stress the controversial when Chaplin was indeed served with a subpoena to appear before HUAC—in the same group of people that included the Hollywood Ten (see Chapter 9)—and was originally scheduled to testify in late September. Birdwell responded by capitalizing on the headlines and tailoring the release around them. First, he scheduled the film to open on Thursday, September 25, the day after the HUAC probe was scheduled to open (when HUAC moved its date to October, he did not follow suit, however, but did move the opening a day to the more convenient Friday). Second, he decided to make use of the telegram Chaplin sent to all members of HUAC. It read: "I am opening my comedy, *Monsieur Verdoux*, on September 26th in five Washington, D.C. theaters and it indeed would be a pleasure to have you as my guest on opening day. Respectfully, Charlie Chaplin." United Artists sent out the telegrams September 19 and also informed the press. Finally, Birdwell decided to revise the ad campaign to portray the film as under siege by unreasonable censors.[46]

Beginning several days before *Verdoux* opened and then continuing after the premiere, Birdwell placed ads from the pressbook in the Washington papers, and added a new headline: "The Picture That Couldn't Be Stopped."[47] Instead of planning an exclusive showing of the film in one large downtown theater—as was customary with Chaplin films—he scheduled it for five theaters—the Nix, Apex, Atlas, Naylor, and Senator. Four of these were neighborhood theaters, and one a small midtown theater. By the day of the opening he exultantly cabled Chaplin that three of the four daily papers would carry rave reviews and predicted, "we will top a two and a half million gross."[48]

In Washington, at least, the strategy seemed to work. *Monsieur Verdoux* enjoyed a much better response from reviewers there than it had received in New York City. The best example was Richard Coe's *Washington Post* review, "Philosophical Clown." "*Monsieur Verdoux*," Coe wrote, "is a bold, brilliant, and bitterly amusing film"; he went on to give it one of its best newspaper reviews.[49]

24. Original ad for *Monsieur Verdoux*, 1947.

25. New, combative ad from second
Monsieur Verdoux ad campaign, 1947.

Verdoux also did much better than expected at the box office in Washington. On September 28 Birdwell telegrammed United Artists executive Paul Lazarus, Jr., that both the Pix and the Apex had broken their previous opening day and Saturday box-office records. In fact, by 3:00 P.M. the first day, the film had already garnered $12,876 in the two theaters—another record and 10 percent of what *Verdoux* had drawn in its entire five-week New York run.[50] By the end of the week, the film had earned $41,118, encouraging enough for United Artists officials to hold it over for two more weeks. What's more, Washington's interest in the film was sustained. *Variety* reported in its second week that the film was "still going strong," and in the third week that it was still holding, which was a "surprise to all."[51] It seemed that things were looking up.

Following the Washington run, however, the film slowed down. Its next play dates came around October 21 in Chicago, New Orleans, San Francisco, Seattle, Toronto, and Portland. But as the news of the first-day receipts came in, United Artists appeared to give up on the film. On October 22 Lazarus cabled Birdwell that Arthur Kelly had halted ads for the film because the grosses were so bad. By October 28, Lazarus cabled Birdwell again, this time to announce that "the picture is not going well." Birdwell fought to keep the film moving: on October 29 he cabled Kelly that he and Chaplin agreed that the film

249

should open at all dates and not be withdrawn or it would certainly be considered a genuine flop. Kelly and Lazarus, however, had made up their minds. That the film was indeed a flop in the United States is hinted at by the fact that the next correspondence between Birdwell and Lazarus in his file is on the final day of Birdwell's contract: his December 15 cable to Lazarus thanks him for "all of your help."[52]

What happened? For several reasons—a combination of the public pressure, the difficulty of selling what was for Chaplin such an unusual film, and the growing HUAC pressure on studio executives after the Hollywood Ten trials to quell "subversive" propaganda in their pictures—*Monsieur Verdoux* received virtually no more releases in the United States in 1947 and only a modest number in 1948. At the end of 1947 United Artists tallied up the total domestic receipts for their various releases of the year: *Body and Soul* had earned $2,035,800; *Red River*, $1,584,800; Olivier's *Henry V*, $383,000; and *Monsieur Verdoux*, $162,000. The company's most profitable filmmaker in 1941 (the year of *The Great Dictator*) had created its biggest disappointment of 1947.[53] In his history of United Artists, Tino Balio notes that two years after *Monsieur Verdoux* was first released, it still had grossed only $325,000 in the United States. According to Balio, "even though the picture grossed more than $1.5 million abroad [an indication of *Verdoux*'s more positive reception outside the United States], Chaplin felt that the UA sales force was responsible for its poor domestic showing, with the result that he lost confidence in his company."[54]

It seems much more likely, however, that Chaplin was searching for a scapegoat when he castigated the United Artists sales force. He had, after all, hindered the publicity staff by withholding information before the New York release. He had insisted on a press conference. And he had approved the hiring of Birdwell to direct the second publicity campaign and had agreed to an approach whose tone was haughty, almost belligerent, nearly daring the audience to change along with the great artist Chaplin. Surely Chaplin deserves a good part of the blame for the film's publicity.

But just why did *Monsieur Verdoux* fail so badly in its domestic release? Part of the reason relates to the social structure of stardom. We have already noted the framework provided by Richard Dyer, which proposes that a star's image is created out of a variety of media documents: promotion, publicity, films, and criticism/commentary.[55]

In each of these four areas *Monsieur Verdoux* failed to sustain Chaplin's star image in positive ways. The promotion and publicity for the film were almost nonexistent until the film's New York premiere, and then the primary promotion event—the press conference—worked more against than for the film and its star. Except for the Washington promotion campaign, which stressed the controversy surrounding the film and its difference from earlier Chaplin films, the promotion and publicity of the film were almost complete failures. The film itself, by breaking Chaplin's aesthetic contract with his audience in a number of ways (especially by presenting a new central persona different in class and interests from the familiar Charlie), also undercut Chaplin's star image. And as we have seen, the reviews and commentary on the film generally rejected the film, often for that very reason: for breaking his aesthetic contract, for failing to provide what he had provided in his previous films (and what the reviewers had grown to expect). The few passionate critical defenses of *Verdoux* came from leftist critics who, in Jauss's terms, were able to bridge the "aesthetic distance" between *Verdoux* and the audience because they were much more interested in Chaplin the serious artist and progressive social commentator than in the comedy and pathos of Chaplin's pantomimic alter ego, Charlie. Chaplin dared his audience to change, and these few reviewers did. Most, however, did not.

This leads to yet another reason for the failure of *Monsieur Verdoux* in the United States. It should be noted that the London and Paris openings of the film were much more successful than the one in New York City. Upon its mid-November opening at the New Gallery and Tivoli Theatres in London, *Monsieur Verdoux* garnered very positive reviews and did quite well at the box office. The public response in Paris was even stronger: it opened there in mid-June of 1948, breaking house records that had been held by *The Best Years of Our Lives* and *For Whom the Bell Tolls*.[56]

This more positive response to *Monsieur Verdoux*, particularly in Paris, suggests how a star image is intimately related to cultural values and historical change and thus helps us to understand a broader historical reason for the failure of *Monsieur Verdoux*. American culture, which lacked any established, strong socialist tradition, embraced the assumptions of the Cold War more quickly and fully than most West European countries. Many of the Americans who saw the film (and even many who only read about it) understood Chaplin's social critique as a leftist denunciation of his host country, even though the film was set in France. This understanding emerged at a time when the tendency to celebrate American society and to disapprove of criticism of it was becoming increasingly prevalent. This tendency was demonstrated by the public efforts in various areas of the country to ban the film and by the pressures put on Hollywood studio executives to eliminate "subversive content" (too often translated as "criticism of the

United States") from their films after the HUAC investigations. Both these pressures affected United Artists officials as they decided not to give *Monsieur Verdoux* more general release after the fairly successful Washington run.

When these cultural and historical factors are combined with the negative publicity surrounding Chaplin in the American press during the Barry trials and the unsatisfactory promotion, publicity, and commentary on *Monsieur Verdoux*, it is no wonder that the rift between Chaplin and the American public was steadily widening. It was not about to close. Chaplin's progressive political activities had continued after his second front period and would continue through 1949, and both congressional denunciations and FBI investigations of his politics would continue to chip away at his declining star image. The reputation that once had seemed a pillar of marble now seemed composed of sandstone.

9

Chaplin's Politics and American
Culture, 1943–1952

Chaplin the Progressive
Activist, 1943–1949

Just as *Monsieur Verdoux* contributed to the image of Chaplin as a leftist social critic, so did his public political activities in the latter part of the decade, many of which were publicized in the press. Although Chaplin's active involvement in politics had waned after his second front speeches of 1942—largely because until the middle of 1945 the Barry trials consumed so much of his time—he did not entirely halt his political activity. In fact, contrary to those commentators who downplay or disparage his interest, Chaplin's involvements in politics between 1943 and 1949 were nearly all consistent with the position we have termed "progressive." These clustered around two sorts of activity: interactions with Soviet artists and diplomats, and involvement in domestic political issues from a progressive perspective.[1]

Chaplin's relationship with Soviet artists and diplomats from World War II on resulted in part from his second front speeches and his support for various Soviet-American friendship groups that grew up during the war. Chaplin was, for example, one of the sponsors when the founding of the National Council of American-Soviet Friendship was announced in April 1943. Similarly, when an "American–Soviet Friendship Rally" was held in Madison Square Garden on 16 November 1944, a number of Hollywood movie stars—including Chaplin, John Garfield, Rita Hayworth, Orson Welles, James Cagney, Katherine Hepburn, Gene Kelly, and Edward G. Robinson—signed a message in a gesture of support for it. The statement said that the artists added their voices in favor of the bond that existed between "our great country and our great Allies." The message added: "In this friendship lies not only the hope but the future of the world."[2] In both these cases and in other such instances, Chaplin acted consistently with his desire to encourage Soviet–American cooperation and to defeat fascism.

As a result of his public support of the Soviet–American alliance, Chaplin was invited to functions by Soviet consulate officials in Los

Angeles and honored as an artist in the Soviet Union. In May 1943, while Soviet–American relations were still in full bloom, the *New York Times* commented on Chaplin's popularity in the Soviet Union.[3] This was formally recognized in 1944 when on April 26 and 27, a Soviet cultural organization called voks sponsored a tribute to Chaplin in Moscow. On the first evening a large audience made up of Soviet artists, public figures, and journalists, including foreign journalists, viewed selections from Chaplin's films at the Moscow Cinema Club. On the next day film actress Vera Maretskaya opened by reading a message of greeting from Chaplin, which was followed by tributes to Chaplin's life and work by people like director Vsevolod Pudovkin, Dmitri Shostakovich, and journalist Ilya Ehrenburg. The festival closed by sending Chaplin a collective telegram, wishing him "new successes assisting in our common struggle against Hitlerism, as well as many years of work for the good of the world and also of mankind." The event was reported by the *New York Times* and *Newsweek*. Such coverage in U.S. publications of large circulation affected the evolution of Chaplin's star image, for it gave him attention that would be seen as suspicious to many Americans after the political climate changed in the late 1940s.[4]

Chaplin returned the praise in 1946 to Soviet director Sergei Eisenstein, whom Chaplin had known since Eisenstein visited Hollywood in the late 1920s. In 1946 Chaplin saw Part One of *Ivan the Terrible* and was so enthusiastic about it that he sent a telegram congratulating Eisenstein on "the greatest historic film ever made."[5] The film made such a strong impression on Chaplin that he even praised it in his autobiography as "the acme of all historical pictures," one that "dealt with history poetically" (MA, p. 323).

Of gatherings at the Soviet consulate or other events honoring Soviet artists, perhaps the most publicized and damaging to his star image was a party Chaplin attended in late May, 1946, aboard a Soviet ship in Long Beach Harbor. The evening, arranged by Soviet consul Konstantin Simonov and Soviet trade representative Alexander Graachev, included a banquet and the showing of a Soviet film called *The Bear*. Charles and Oona Chaplin attended, along with director Lewis Milestone, actor John Garfield, and their wives. The event would probably have created no stir except for an incident that took place as the Chaplins were leaving. Apparently U.S. Customs agents, checking to be sure no dutiable articles were brought ashore after the banquet, were waiting as the guests left the ship. News photographers overheard Chaplin say, in reference to the Customs officials, "Oh, I see we are under the power of the American Gestapo." Though it is quite possible the comment was made in jest, the newspapers splashed their front pages with negative Chaplin publicity. The Hearst-owned *New York Journal-American*, for example, used a headline spanning half of the front page: "Chaplin at Red Ship Revel; Slurs U.S. Customs Men." A subtitle added, "Calls Agents 'Gestapo.' " The lead sentence provides a good example of the article's anti-Chaplin slant: "Tingling with champagne, a select group of Hollywood film luminaries applauded a Russian movie about a water-drinking revolutionary at a weekend revel aboard a Soviet ship in Long Beach harbor." An accompanying photograph, which showed Chaplin greeting an unidentified man, was captioned, "And One Saw Red!"[6] This "Simonov incident," which later turned up in Chaplin's FBI internal security file, raises at least two relevant issues. First, even if he was joking, Chaplin revealed his progressive assumption that American society had its own tendencies toward fascism as he understood the term. Second, the incident reiterated how certain factions of the press could turn an innocuous event into an opportunity for negative publicity about Chaplin's politics.

Besides these interactions with Soviet officials and artists, Chaplin engaged in considerable progressive political activity after World War II. One of the first occasions was a personal act with political implications: reading Theodore Dreiser's poem, "The Road I Came," at Dreiser's funeral on 3 January 1946. The novelist, long known for his progressive political sympathies, had joined the Communist party during World War II and had become acquainted with Chaplin after meeting him at a reception held at the Soviet consulate in Los Angeles in 1943. In her memoirs, Helen Dreiser notes that she and her husband subsequently came to know the Chaplins quite well and that Dreiser "had a deep regard for Chaplin as an artist, intellectual, humanitarian, world citizen, and comedian." Chaplin apparently also spent some evenings in the last years of the war with Dreiser, Clifford Odets, and John Howard Lawson, all political progressives. Lawson, a Communist screenwriter and later one of the Hollywood Ten, eulogized Dreiser at his funeral, and Chaplin read the poem, the end of which was later inscribed on Dreiser's memorial.[7]

Participating in an acquaintance's funeral is hardly a bold political act, but Chaplin also became something of a champion of progressive causes in the late 1940s, often in defense of the civil liberties of those holding unpopular leftist views. One such act was to protest the legal proceedings against Communists Eugene Dennis, Leon Josephson, and Gerhart Eisler (brother of Hanns Eisler). The three were about to be tried in federal court on contempt of Congress charges because they had refuesed to testify before HUAC, and in June 1947, two months after the devastating opening of *Monsieur Verdoux* in New York, Chaplin joined a group of notables who urged that the trials of these three men be postponed "in order that they may have proper time to prepare their case and in order to avoid undue prejudice against them at a time when red-baiting hysteria is so violent." Ultimately, both Dennis and Josephson were given one-year prison terms after being cited for contempt of Congress, and Gerhart Eisler left the country in 1949 with deportation proceedings hanging over his head.[8] By defending these figures as the political climate was becoming increasingly uncomfortable for domestic radicals, Chaplin was sticking out his neck and endangering his already slumping star image. Although it was certainly his right to express his views about these proceedings, Chaplin was either naive about how, given the change in political climate, his actions might affect his star image, or else he was beginning to feel that his political commitments were more important to him than his stardom.

Chaplin's encounters with HUAC also showed his progressive political sympathies. In addition to being subpoenaed to testify before the committee (as will be discussed in the following section), Chaplin confronted HUAC in at least two other ways. He added his signature to an *amici curiae* brief that challenged HUAC's contempt citations against the Hollywood Ten, and he supported his friend Hanns Eisler, who testified before HUAC in May and September 1947 about his alleged Communist political leanings (at the hearings he was called, among other things, "the Karl Marx of Communism in the music field"). Eisler denied being a member of the Communist party and concluded his testimony by charging that "the Committee hopes to create a drive against every liberal, progressive, and socially conscious artist in this country."

When it began to appear in November 1947 that deportation proceedings would be instituted against Eisler and his wife, Chaplin telegrammed Pablo Picasso and asked him to organize a group of fellow artists to protest at the American Embassy in Paris against the "outrageous deportation proceedings against Hanns Eisler." Chaplin also asked Picasso to send a copy of the protest statement so he could use it for publicity in Los Angeles. In December he joined thirteen other prominent artists and scientists, including Albert Einstein and Thomas Mann, in sending a petition to Attorney General Tom Clark, that urged him to drop the deportation proceedings. When the warrant for deportation was issued in February 1948, Chaplin again interceded, promising to provide the Eislers financial support if the U.S.

government would allow them to leave the country voluntarily. They ultimately did so, leaving for Czechoslovakia on 26 March 1948.[9]

In 1948 Chaplin became enthusiastic about the presidential campaign of Henry Wallace: Wallace's call to cooperate with rather than contain the Soviet Union was as attractive to Chaplin as Wallace's desire to extend the New Deal. Although Chaplin's name is not listed in the *New York Times Index* for 1948, his first absence since the 1920s, his political involvements with the Progressive party were prominently reported in the Los Angeles press. For example, on 29 March 1948, Wallace's running mate, Senator Glen Taylor of Idaho, addressed a "Rally for Peace" in Gilmore Stadium in Los Angeles, with 12,000 attending. The *Los Angeles Times* reported that Chaplin attended and contributed $500 to the campaign. An even more enthusiastic crowd of 24,000 gathered again at the stadium in mid-May to hear Wallace himself minimize the threat posed by the Soviet Union and attack America's support of reactionary dictators. Charles and Oona Chaplin met Wallace at the home of William Wyler during this visit, and the next day the *Los Angeles Times* gave first-page coverage to the story, including a picture of the smiling Chaplin writing a $1000 check for Wallace's campaign.[10]

Wallace lost, and lost badly. Chaplin found other ways to continue his political activities, however, and in 1949 he publicly supported two peace conferences, at a time when progressivism was clearly a waning political position in the United States. From March 27 to 29, the Cultural and Scientific Conference for World Peace was held in New York City. The State Department denied visas to many West European leftists, which left primarily American progressives and Eastern bloc Communists able to attend. A number of anti-Stalinist liberals attended in order to challenge the dominant progressive viewpoint. The harsh reception given the anti-Stalinists led many Americans, even (perhaps particularly) the anti-Stalinist liberals, to perceive such peace conferences as dominated by Communists.[11] Despite the controversies swirling around the peace conferences, Chaplin made a public statement on April 5 in support of the World Congress for Peace, to be held in Paris that month, and in September the *New York Times* reported that both Chaplin and Henry Wallace had sent messages of support to the American Continental Congress on World Peace, held in Mexico City.[12]

Chaplin also lent his name to protest the Peekskill incident, which has achieved prominence in the annals of Cold War repression in the United States. The incident involved the disruption of a picnic held by leftists at Lakeland Acres picnic grounds outside Peekskill, New

York, on 27 August 1949. Prominent black athlete, actor, singer, and political activist Paul Robeson was scheduled to sing that Saturday evening, but insults by American Legionnaires and other demonstrators led to a riot that prevented him from appearing. The performance was rescheduled for Sunday, September 4, and though Robeson was able to sing that afternoon, he did so with the epithets of demonstrators ringing in his ears. Then, as the huge crowd of 25,000 was disbanding, demonstrators threw stones, broke hundreds of car windows, overturned at least eight cars, burned a cross, and threw a woman over a hedge after taking her baby from her. When Robeson sent a letter to President Truman in October demanding a federal investigation of the incident and prosecution of the guilty, Chaplin signed it and indicated his support.[13] As with so many of his activities in the 1940s, Chaplin here demonstrated both his progressive political views and his belief that domestic leftists should be allowed to hold and express their views without interference or censorship. Such a consistent and firm political position made Chaplin vulnerable to challenges and attacks by government officials and agencies, and also by conservative voluntary associations like the American Legion, as the 1940s wore on.

Chaplin and the U.S. Congress

In the later 1930s, Robert Sklar has argued, American filmmakers like Walt Disney and Frank Capra, aware of the powerful cultural myth-making capacities of the movies, helped through their films to reaffirm traditional American cultural mythology. After America entered World War II, the film industry, with government encouragement and support, broadened this effort by going systematically into the business of affirming the American war effort and "the American way" in its pictures.[14]

In part because of the government's cooperative efforts with filmmakers, exemplified by fictional war films or such documentary films as the "Why We Fight" series, elected officials also came to believe in the power of movies. In addition to being pleased that films could affirm traditional American values, however, some officials became concerned that the opposite could also be true: that films could contain disruptive or "subversive" material that could erode dominant values. Just as the Legion of Decency placed pressure on the film industry from a religious perspective in the early 1930s, the U.S. Congress placed political pressure on the film industry to exercise care in the "content" of its films and to rid itself of anyone perceived as leftist, especially as the Cold War set in. Due to his consistently progressive stance throughout the 1940s, Chaplin became a frequent target of such congressional attacks. Since these criticisms were often publicized, they too contributed to the politicization of Chaplin's star image in the 1940s. They also indicate the pattern of hostility toward Chaplin and his star image that was developing throughout the decade.

As was noted earlier, Chaplin's politics first came under close congressional examination in the late 1930s and then again in 1941. In the late 1930s his name was mentioned, along with many others, by Martin Dies, then chairman of HUAC, as one with Communist sympathies, but nothing came of it. In 1941 the Senate's Subcommittee on War Propaganda, chaired by Senator D. W. Clark of Idaho, investigated Chaplin's *The Great Dictator* and a number of other films for their "prematurely anti-fascist" sentiments. This investigation was cut short, however, by America's entry into the war.[15]

During the war, publicity about the Barry affair certainly made Chaplin a more vulnerable and popular target for certain political factions. Two congressmen willing to make political hay by attacking Chaplin's morality were Senator William Langer of Missouri and Representative John Rankin of Mississippi. In February 1945, Langer introduced a bill on the floor of the Senate that would, if passed, have instructed the attorney general to investigate Chaplin and could have possibly led to his deportation. Although the bill was never passed, it indicated a trend. By July, Rankin joined the chorus of Chaplin denouncers. On the floor of the House that month, he criticized the Hollywood community for buying and hanging so many "loathesome" paintings and illustrations from the radical magazine *New Masses*, then added: "I am sure that some of them got into the home of Charles Chaplin, the perverted subject of Great Britain who has become famous for his forcible seduction of white girls."[16]

This was followed by more denunciation of the comedian by members of the Congress in 1947, the year of *Monsieur Verdoux*'s release and the Hollywood Ten trials. The attacks began when in a Senate hearing on 7 March 1947, Senator Langer commented that the U.S. policy of deportation was inconsistent. Why, he asked, should some people be deported when "a man like Charlie Chaplin, with his communistic leanings, with his unsavory record of lawbreaking, of rape, or the debauching of American girls 16 and 17 years of age, remains?"[17]

The hostile reaction to the release of *Monsieur Verdoux* provided some Congressmen with more ammunition for their anti-Chaplin arsenals. Rankin again attacked in June, when he announced how pleased he was that the "rotten picture by Charlie Chaplin" was being banned in Memphis. At the same time, he almost gleefully inserted into the *Congressional Record* an anti-Chaplin editorial from the *Shreveport Journal*, along with a hostile letter to the editor from a Shreveport businessman. But then his challenge to Chaplin became more concrete: "I am today demanding," announced Rankin, "that Attorney General Tom Clark institute proceedings to deport Charlie Chaplin. He has refused to become an American citizen, his very life in Hollywood is detrimental to the moral fabric of America. In that way he can be kept off the American screen, and his loathesome pictures can be kept from before the eyes of the American youth. He should be deported and got rid of at once."[18] As we shall see, Rankin's suggestion did reach Clark, who passed it on to J. Edgar Hoover, head of the FBI, who in turn incorporated the issue into the ongoing investigation of Chaplin as an internal security risk. The same call to deport Chaplin was heard again in 1949, when Senator Harry P. Cain urged that Chaplin be deported because of his Communist ties.[19] In the Cold War atmosphere, such public denunciations of the declining star's unpopular political views apparently played well to the constituents back home.

Although senators sometimes attacked Chaplin, his name was heard more often in the House of Representatives, for when HUAC was revived in 1947 under Chairman J. Parnell Thomas, Hollywood quickly became a key focus and remained one through the early 1950s.[20] Chaplin's name came up frequently, and in several contexts. He was among the initial group subpoenaed in 1947 to testify before HUAC; his name was mentioned regularly in the testimonies of witnesses who willingly or unwillingly appeared before the committee; and his name appeared in the special congressional reports written under HUAC auspices.

On 21 September 1947, five days before *Monsieur Verdoux* was released in Washington for its short but relatively successful run, HUAC subpoenaed forty-three Hollywood figures to testify as a part of its investigation of subversive content in Hollywood movies. Half of the group was made up of cooperative ("friendly") witnesses—people like Adolphe Menjou, Gary Cooper, Ronald Reagan, Walt Disney, Ayn Rand, and Sam Wood—and many of these had expected to be called. Some of the others were leftists who were at first called the Hollywood Nineteen, and ultimately the Hollywood Ten. This group of avowed progressives, some of whom were also Communists, opposed on constitutional grounds the committee's inquiries into their political opinions, were cited for contempt of Congress, and were sentenced to a year in prison on those charges. Chaplin was acquainted with or had met a number of the original Nineteen, including Bertolt Brecht, Lewis Milestone, Herbert Biberman, and John Howard Lawson. Because of his progressive political views and his association with some of the Nineteen, Chaplin, given HUAC's political aims, was in a vulnerable position.

Despite his subpoena, however, Chaplin never testified. He had most likely expected the call, for at least two reasons. First, in December 1946 the *Washington Post* reported that Chaplin would be subpoenaed to testify when HUAC reopened hearings in January. At that point the committee's chief counsel said the committee wanted to know more about "reports that motion picture money is financing a third party tentatively named the People's Front, which has an eye on running Henry Wallace for President." An article in such a prominent paper on such a subject undoubtedly came to Chaplin's attention. Second, Chaplin's friend Hanns Eisler was interrogated by FBI staff in Los Angeles in the summer of 1947 (and testified before a closed HUAC session in Los Angeles in May and then in a Washington public hearing September 24 and 26), and Chaplin probably felt that his own testimony would be inevitable, given his publicly affirmed friendship with and defenses of Eisler.[21]

After expecting to be called in the summer of 1947, Chaplin sent a telegram to committee chairman Thomas. It said, in part: "In order that you be completely up-to-date on my thinking I suggest that you view carefully my latest production *Monsieur Verdoux*. It is against war and the futile slaughter of our youth. I trust you will find its humane message distasteful. While you are preparing your engraved subpoena I will give you a hint on where I stand. I am not a Communist. I am a peace-monger." The combative tone of the telegram continued when Chaplin and United Artists decided to open *Monsieur Verdoux* the day after Hanns Eisler was scheduled to testify before HUAC in Washington. As mentioned in Chapter 8, a few days before that scheduled opening, publicist Birdwell sent a telegram in Chaplin's name to each member of HUAC that invited them to attend the premiere on September 26. None accepted Chaplin's invitation, yet for whatever reason— perhaps Chaplin's reputation, however much it was fading—HUAC decided not to call him and, according to Chaplin, sent him a courteous reply telling him that he could consider the matter closed.[22]

The reply was, however, far from the last time Chaplin's name came up in the HUAC investigations. It appeared a number of times in HUAC testimony. Several prominent anti-Communists leveled charges against him. In March 1947, at HUAC's early hearings, both Jack B.

Tenney and Walter S. Steele brought up Chaplin's name. Tenney, a California state senator, had chaired since 1941 the Joint Fact-Finding Committee on Un-American Activities, California's counterpart to HUAC, and enthusiastically shared his information.[23] When Representative Karl Mundt asked him about communism in Hollywood, Tenney answered: "We do know that many of the so-called stars in Hollywood permit their names to be used by Communist front organizations. . . . We have Garfield, John Garfield; Charlie Chaplin. Both of these gentlemen attended a party given by a Soviet writer in San Pedro harbor, and entertained him, we understand, at their homes, and in every way have given aid and comfort to Communist-front organizations."[24] Though Tenney mixed up his harbors (the ship was anchored in Long Beach Harbor), he did bring to the Committee's attention an incident that had already, as we have seen, appeared in the press and gave it a most sinister appearance.

Walter Steele was chairman of the National Security Committee of the American Coalition of Patriotic, Civic, and Fraternal Societies, a confederation of over a hundred patriotic organizations. He had first appeared before HUAC on 16 August 1938, when he branded 640 organizations, including the American Civil Liberties Union, the Boy Scouts, and the Camp Fire Girls, as "Communistic."[25] At the March hearings, Steele charged that Chaplin was a "charter member" of an organization called the People's Radio Foundation. According to Steele, the group's stated goal was to make the public aware of "worthy American civic and cultural traditions and achievements and like contributions made by nationality groups." Steele told HUAC that it was a Communist organization.[26] The story later made it into the newspapers—Ed Sullivan was one columnist who slurred Chaplin after the testimony. When Chaplin was asked about the organization in a 1948 interview with the Immigration and Naturalization Service (INS), he denied any involvement with it.[27]

A third witness to mention Chaplin in 1947 was Howard Rushmore, a former Communist who had served for a time as film critic for the *New York Daily Worker*. Converted to anticommunism after breaking with the Party, Rushmore was asked if he knew Chaplin or if Chaplin had sent articles to the *Daily Worker*. He answered no to both questions. But when asked if the *Worker* had any policy toward Chaplin, Rushmore replied, "He was what we call in the business a 'sacred cow.' . . . That is a newspaper phrase which—well, loosely, would mean that you always give favorable publicity to and a lot of it."[28] These three testimonies, given when guilt by association was a common practice, all damaged Chaplin, however false or distorted the testimony may have been and however much the testimony disregarded Chaplin's right to free association.

Chaplin's name also came up occasionally when leftists testified. For example, in 1950 Edward G. Robinson explained his contribution to the Committee for the First Amendment (a group that supported the Hollywood Ten) by saying that at one time "it was stated that Charlie Chaplin and I would be the first to receive subpoenas." Naturally, Robinson continued, he then contributed money to support others who did receive subpoenas. The following year John Garfield affirmed his presence with Chaplin at the infamous Simonov harbor party, and musician Artie Shaw explained that he signed a card allowing his name to be used as a supporter for the World Peace Congress in 1949 after he saw a number of names, including Chaplin's, on the letterhead of the request. Bishop G. Bromley Oxnam defended his involvements with the National Council of American–Soviet Friendship (he had spoken at the same "Salute to Our Russian Ally" meeting in 1942 as Chaplin had) by listing some of the sponsors, who included Chaplin, Van Wyck Brooks, Albert Einstein, Justice Learned Hand, Fiorello LaGuardia, Thomas Mann, Robert Lynd, and Ralph Barton Perry. These references reiterated Chaplin's progressive involvements during the 1940s. In addition, the testimonies by Shaw and Oxnam suggested that Chaplin, like many others during the war years, was sometimes influenced to support a cause because he saw names of other acquaintances or celebrities on the list of sponsors.[29]

Chaplin's name also came to HUAC's attention in the reports on various subjects that were prepared by aides at the behest of the committee and then made available to the public. Two in particular stand out. The first was HUAC's 1950 report on the Cultural and Scientific Conference for World Peace, held in New York City in March 1949.[30] The report opens by claiming that the conference "was actually a super-mobilization of the inveterate wheelhorses and supporters of the Communist Party and its auxiliary organizations" (p. 1). Chaplin was named twice. The first reference indicated that the French atomic scientist Frédéric Joliot-Curie had announced that Chaplin would be one of the American delegates to the World Peace Conference in Paris in April 1949 (p. 10). (Though the HUAC report was released a year after the Paris conference, it failed to note that Chaplin had not actually attended.) The second reference to Chaplin names him as one of the New York conference sponsors, a list that included an ecumenical group of leftists: Marlon Brando, Leonard Bernstein, Aaron Copland, W.E.B. DuBois, Albert Einstein, Judy Holliday, Robert and Helen Lynd, Linus Pauling, Muriel Ruykeyser, Studs Terkel, Henry Wallace, and a large number of Hollywood figures. Both Norman Mailer and F. O. Matthiessen were listed among the expected speakers (pp. 57–60). The HUAC report intimates that having one's name on such a list nearly constituted disloyalty to America.

The 1949 peace movement was a favorite target of HUAC, and in April of the next year it released its "Report on Communist 'Peace' Offensive."[31] The report's subtitle ("A Campaign to Disarm and Defeat the United States") and opening sentence ("the most dangerous hoax ever devised by the international Communist conspiracy is the current world wide 'peace' offensive") indicate its attitude. The report makes four claims about Chaplin's involvement:

1. That Chaplin was listed as a sponsor for the Cultural and Scientific Conference for World Peace, held in New York City, March 25–27, 1949 (p. 104).
2. That he was listed as one of "Americans sponsoring the World Peace Conference" in Paris in April 1949 (p. 110).
3. That he was a member of the Committee for U.S. Participation in the American Continental Congress for World Peace, held September 5–10, 1949 (p. 21).
4. That Chaplin and Henry Wallace sent greetings to that Congress, held in Mexico City (p. 23).

We have already noted Chaplin's willingness to lend his name in support of these peace conferences, in part because their general thrust coincided with his internationalist, "One World" sympathies. It is important to remember what involvement in such activities meant to most members of HUAC and to many other Americans in the Cold War era. Much like conservative critics of the nuclear freeze movement in 1984, HUAC investigators—in spite of the constitutionally guaranteed freedom of speech and assembly—tended to think of those who supported the 1949 peace conferences as dupes (at the very least), as naive instruments of Soviet foreign policy, as dangerous subversives, or worse.

Chaplin and the FBI: The Internal Security File

With all this attention paid in the U.S. Congress to Chaplin's progressive politics, it is no surprise that another organization vigilant in its attempt to ferret out what it termed Communist influence in America, the FBI, should pay some attention to Chaplin in these years.[32] Like other stars whose leftist political views have become public, including, more recently, people like Jane Fonda and John Lennon, Chaplin was closely observed by the FBI. As we have seen, the Bureau had already expended considerable time and resources in exploring Chaplin's involvement with Joan Barry. Their interest in Chaplin's politics went through two long phases, the first lasting from 1946 to 1949, the second from 1951 to Chaplin's banishment/exile in 1952. This section will trace the investigation through early 1952; the FBI's role in Chaplin's "banishment" will be discussed in Chapter 10. A summary of the Bureau's activities relating to Chaplin will highlight how this organization—one small but influential part of American culture—significantly affected Chaplin's fortunes and, more subtly, helped damage his star image.[33]

The subject of Chaplin's politics shows up very early in FBI files. The first known reference is a report from the Los Angeles field office to the Washington headquarters, dated 14 August 1922. The report indicated that Chaplin had held a reception at his home for William Z. Foster, a leader of the American Communist Party, when Foster was visiting Los Angeles. It added that the party had been attended by many of the Hollywood "parlor Bolsheviki." Copies of the report were sent by Director William J. Burns to Will Hays (the recently named head of the MPPDA), and to the Bureau's assistant director, J. Edgar Hoover. An accompanying memo to Hoover reported that "numerous movie stars are taking more than an active part in the Red movement" and evidently "endeavoring to organize a program for placing propaganda before the public via the movies."[34] One suspects that Hoover never forgot the connection between Chaplin and communism made in the letter's carelessly worded list of allegations.

During World War II, the FBI devoted little attention to investigating Chaplin's politics, except to the extent that his political views came up during the Barry investigations. Hoover did receive one report from a confidential informant in the New York office that summarized Chaplin's second front speech at the Hotel Pennsylvania on 3 December 1942, along with Russian War Relief press releases about the event. The informant's political views are clear from his comment that the speeches expressed "the usual pro-Soviet 'cultural' propaganda," a notion that was passed along in a memo summarizing the report two weeks later. It described Chaplin's speech by saying that he "defended Communism and eulogized Russia" in it.[35] This report and memo were exceptions to the rule, however; Chaplin's politics did not become the focus of FBI attention until after the war was over and the Cold War beginning.

In 1946, the Special Agent in Charge of the Los Angeles office received from Hoover a terse directive dated September 9: "It is requested that you review the references to Charles Chaplin in the films of your office and give consideration to recommending the preparations of a Security Index Card." (The security index card was filed for those who were under an active FBI investigation related to internal security matters.) This directive began a large investigation that continued off and on until 18 May 1953, some weeks after Chaplin turned in his reentry permit and decided to settle in Switzerland. At that point, Hoover directed the Los Angeles office to place Chaplin's card in the "unavailable" section.

Up through 1949 the investigation took place largely in Los Angeles, where FBI agents researched press clippings, magazine articles, and even Gerith von Ulm's biography of Chaplin; kept Chaplin periodically under observation; and interviewed a variety of informants and witnesses (whose names are most often blacked out in the released files, but who appear to include some members of the press and some of Chaplin's domestic staff) about Chaplin's political views, associations, and activities. In addition to the Los Angeles field office, others—including those in San Francisco and New York City—also played smaller parts in the investigation.

At first, however, the Los Angeles office seemed to drag its feet in responding to Hoover's September 1946 letter, for on 14 March 1947, Hoover, apparently piqued at their delay, wrote them again: "It is requested that the instructions contained in the Bureau's memorandum of September 9, 1946, be given attention at an early date."[36] Evidently the Los Angeles office knew when it had displeased its director, for the next item in the file is a fourteen-page report—the first report in the Chaplin internal security file, number 100–127090.[37]

The account contains little striking information, but it sets the tone for later reports: straightforward and factual, even when they contain unsubstantiated claims, questionable claims from informants, or downright falsehoods. One such detail that also shows up in a number of subsequent FBI reports is the claim that Chaplin was the "son of a family named THONSTEIN," which came from eastern Europe to London in 1850 (p. 1). The report implies that Chaplin is of Jewish descent, an implication later asserted as fact in a description of Chaplin at the end (p. 13). There it claims that Chaplin's "Descent" is "Jewish" and his only "Peculiarity" is that he "speaks with a Jewish accent." Despite the falsehood of these details, Chaplin is made to seem a more suspicious or secretive character in later reports because the opening page of most lists "Thonstein" as one of his aliases.

This initial piece served as the basis of a twenty-four-page, typed, single-spaced report prepared for Hoover himself by the Washington office. Completed 6 August 1947, this second report was longer in part because Chaplin had released *Monsieur Verdoux* in the intervening months and had had a number of run-ins with the press over his political sympathies. Preceding the August 6 report in the files are a number of press clippings concerning the controversy over *Monsieur Verdoux*, including positive reports from the *New York Daily Worker* and two Ed Sullivan columns that attack Chaplin's progressive politics (e.g., "During the war, instead of entertaining the troops or our wounded, Chaplin delivered nothing but political speeches for Russia, demanding a second front").[38]

The August 6 report, after a brief background introduction, was divided into eleven categories that with variations served as a basis for later reports:

1. Evidence of Membership in the Communist Party and Association with Known Communists [this section mentions that he read a poem at Dreiser's funeral]
2. Evidence of Financial Contributions to the Communist Party by Chaplin
3. Chaplin's Contacts with Russian Officials and Representatives of the Soviet Consular Service [this section mentions the Simonov incident]
4. Assistance Given by Chaplin to American–Soviet Relations
5. Additional Evidence of Pro-Soviet Activities on the Part of Chaplin [this section mentions a gossip-column squib that Chaplin was invited to a Soviet New Year's Party]
6. Affiliations with Russian War Relief
7. Affiliations with the Artists Front to Win the War
8. Activities on Behalf of a Second Front [the previous three sections detail some of Chaplin's 1942 and 1943 political activities]
9. Affiliations with the People's Radio Foundation
10. Associations with Miscellaneous Communist Front Organizations [these include a number of antifascist organizations]
11. White Slave Traffic Violation and Civil Rights and Domestic Violence Violations by Chaplin [this section includes results of FBI investigations in the Barry case on charges that Chaplin either was acquitted of or were dropped for lack of evidence]

Though it is clear that the FBI assiduously scoured press accounts and quizzed informants about Chaplin's political views in order to gather a great deal of information that establishes his progressive activity between 1942 and 1947, the report is devoid of any evidence that would suggest subversive activity.

Nevertheless, the Bureau was quite willing to share information, however inconclusive, circumstantial, or false, that could damage Chaplin's reputation. One way it affected Chaplin's public image was by providing information to gossip columnists. We have already seen in Chapter 7 how the FBI and gossip columnists Hopper and Muir worked in tandem during the Barry trials. All were investigators of sorts, and it appears that between 1943 and the early 1950s the FBI shared information with a number of gossip columnists, including Hopper, Muir, Parsons, and Sullivan.

The system seems to have worked like this. If the gossip columnists were able through their contacts to obtain information concerning Chaplin, they may have passed it along to FBI agents. It is not unlikely that some of the named and unnamed informants in the FBI reports were gossip columnists or their contacts. A 24 March 1944 FBI memo from Agent Nichols to Agent Tolson, for example, does report that columnist Florabel Muir provided a Los Angeles agent with the information that Chaplin hired a press agent during the Barry trials. (It is often difficult to determine with certainty if a columnist was an informant because informants' names are usually blacked out in the released files.)

Evidence is firmer that the FBI, in exchange, would provide information to the columnists that could be leaked through their gossip columns. For example, a memo of 14 August 1947 from Agent Nichols to Agent Rosen (both in the Washington office) shows that this practice of leaking information to gossip columnists was used. It opened: "The following might be an excellent item for Louella Parsons." "The following" turned out to be some extremely circuitous information: a report of a San Francisco FBI agent, dated 3 February 1922, that quoted a press dispatch from Berlin concerning an article in the Soviet newspaper *Pravda*, which praised Chaplin as a great comic actor and hailed him as a "Communist friend of humanity." The leak to Parsons was not an isolated case, for by August 24, another FBI memo from Assistant Director Ladd to Hoover referred to the "material prepared for Hedda Hopper" and described the same article from *Pravda*. Hoover, who often reveals hard-headed pragmatism in his memos and notations, jotted at the bottom of the memo: "Certainly a much labored effort brought forth a miserable product." Regardless of Hoover's skepticism, however, it seems apparent that the FBI was providing information to gossip columnists in 1947 that could be used to damage Chaplin's star image. And the FBI reports show conclusively that the FBI used information from gossip columns as evidence damaging to Chaplin, as when, in the August 6 report, under "Chaplin's Contacts with Russian Officials," Ed Sullivan's 6 April 1944 column was used as evidence. It claimed that the Soviet consul in Los Angeles had been authorized to turn over a Russian plane to take Chaplin to Moscow if he lost the Mann Act trial and that the Chaplins were studying Russian (p. 12).

FBI internal security files on Chaplin also show that the FBI shared its information on Chaplin with other governmental agencies. When the Immigration and Naturalization Service, responding to the calls for Chaplin's deportation by Congressman Rankin and others, wrote the FBI to ask if their investigation would conflict with the FBI's, Hoover replied that the INS inquiry "would in no way interfere with our investigation concerning him." The letter also referred to a request by John Boyd, the executive assistant to the commissioner of the INS, for information on Chaplin. In response, Hoover sent the INS a seventeen-page report that contained much of the same questionable information included in the August 6 report, and in exchange he received from Boyd the transcript of an interview Boyd conducted with Chaplin in 1947, an extremely interesting document.[39] Sharing information about Chaplin, even weak information, seems to have been a frequent practice of the FBI, and it did Chaplin's star image no good.

The Los Angeles office worked too slowly for Hoover a second time, and in February 1948 he wrote again, reminding them that he had asked nearly a year and a half earlier whether they thought it advisable that a security index card be prepared for Chaplin. In addition, he asked them to update their 13 March 1947 report. Though it is unclear what prompted Hoover's letter, it may be that a seven-page document from the Department of State, withheld in the material released to me but placed immediately before Hoover's letter in the FBI files, either requested information about Chaplin or reminded Hoover to continue the FBI's investigation of the comedian.[40]

Between February and early June 1948 the Los Angeles office responded with two letters and a short report, which primarily treated two issues: Chaplin's *Monsieur Verdoux* press conference and his November 1947 telegram to Picasso in support of Hanns Eisler. In addition to summarizing the details of the two situations, the letters and report surveyed the press response to each.[41] These three documents were followed by more activities. The Los Angeles office, after some difficulty, persuaded Hoover to ask the Treasury Department for Chaplin's income tax returns between 1941 and 1947: they hoped to find some evidence of contributions to Communist causes. They also wrote a longer report of thirty-two pages, dated 10 August 1948, and sent it to Hoover.

The August 10 report, similar in some ways to previous reports, is

significant for at least two reasons.[42] First, it shows that surveillance of
Chaplin's private activities was going on with some regularity and intensity. Although large portions of the released report are blackened
out or withheld, usually for reasons of national security ("b1" in FOIA
code), what remains does list a significant number of Chaplin's personal contacts and activities. These contacts include such minutia as
dinner invitations the Chaplins exchanged with Salka Viertel and the
number of telephone calls—five—Lion Feuchtwanger made to Chaplin's home in August and October 1945 (pp. 24, 26). Second, in a listing of leads to follow, the report suggests that the Washington office
request a transcript of the interview Chaplin had with INS commissioner John Boyd in April 1948 (p. 31), in which Chaplin specifically
defends his progressive and internationalist views.[43]

The investigation continued through 1948 and 1949. By November
a security index card had been prepared for Chaplin (two years after
Hoover had asked that this be considered), with the aliases of "Charlie
Chaplin" and "Thonstein" included on the card. When Hoover asked
Los Angeles in April 1949 to submit a report "showing the current
status of this investigation," the office responded with the 5 July 1949
report, the bulk of which contains Chaplin's interview with Boyd.
About a month later, Hoover responded to the report with this evaluation: "A review of this file at the Bureau reflects that no substantial
information has been developed to date which would indicate that the
subject has been engaged in espionage or other intelligence activities."[44] Hoover went on to ask the Los Angeles office to "submit your
observations concerning further investigative steps to be taken in this
case." On October 7 the office wrote Hoover to tell him that nearly all
the leads had been pursued and "no new information of value has
been obtained." If no significant new information were discovered
after two more interviews, they recommended that the Chaplin internal security case be closed.[45]

In November 1949 pressure was placed by the U.S. attorney general's office on Hoover himself, and his Washington office, to determine whether they had a case against Chaplin. In a November 10 letter to Hoover, Assistant Attorney General Alexander M. Campbell
asked to have "copies of all of the Bureau reports on Charles Chaplan
[sic]," particularly those related to "the field of subversive activities, any
Communist connections, associations or information concerning Communist Party activity, or front organization membership and/or activity."[46] The reports were sent, and on December 21, one of Hoover's
assistants sent him a memo saying that the attorney general's aide
asked the Bureau to "check its files to see if there is any information

therein which could be used in a trial to establish that Chaplin was a member of the Communist Party or had donated funds to the Communist Party itself."[47] Hoover immediately telegrammed the Los Angeles office to see if they knew of any witnesses who could testify against Chaplin on either of those issues.[48] They replied on December 27, and on the basis of that telegram, Hoover wrote to Peyton Ford, the assistant to the attorney general: "It was determined that there are no witnesses available who could offer testimony that Chaplin has been a member of the Communist Party in the past, is now a member, or that he has contributed funds to the Communist Party."[49]

Throughout this correspondence, the national fear, bordering on hysteria, of internal Communist subversion is evident. All this attention paid to Chaplin suggests how profoundly his star image was becoming associated with progressive politics. After several years of extensive FBI investigation of Chaplin, however, it appeared that the FBI's interest in Chaplin as a security risk was waning. They simply could not find what they wanted to undermine Chaplin.

An FBI memo of 7 February 1950 supports this conclusion. It noted that Chaplin had been investigated since November 1946 and that considerable information concerning his "pro-Communist sympathies and activities" had been discovered, but that "no information . . . indicating that Chaplin has engaged in espionage activities" had been found. Accordingly, the memo recommended that the Chaplin internal security investigation be closed.[50] Thus despite the FBI's vigorous efforts during an increasing Cold War atmosphere, this investigation of Chaplin as a security risk seemed to be winding down.

The investigation was not over, however. In the middle of 1950 two reports based on information obtained from confidential FBI informants helped to keep the file active. The first was an interoffice memo from Agent Turner to Agent Hennrich summarizing a conversation about Chaplin that the informant, a double agent, reportedly had with Petr Fedotov, the Soviet acting minister of state security. Fedotov told the informant that if Chaplin would move to Moscow he would receive anything he wanted, including a villa, for life and that Stalin, an admirer of Chaplin, was "interested in the prestige and reputation of the USSR in the world and if Chaplin would move to Russia, it would be good propaganda."[51] Although no FBI action was taken other than filing the memo, it did suggest that Chaplin's name and star image was becoming a pawn in the chess game of international Cold War politics.

The second document containing information on Chaplin was more instrumental in keeping the file open. On 21 June 1950 Louis F. Budenz, former managing editor of the *Daily Worker*, told New York FBI agents who had been interviewing him that Chaplin was a "concealed Communist." Budenz, a zealous anti-Communist following his withdrawal from the Party and his 1946 HUAC testimony, later claimed to have testified more than 3,000 hours to FBI agents.[52] The comments on Chaplin were part of a much longer testimony over several months that Budenz carried out in cooperation with the New York FBI office, resulting in the naming of some four hundred "concealed Communists" in the show business community. Budenz claimed that two Party members told him in 1936 that Chaplin was "the equivalent of a member of the Party" and alleged that he had submitted *Modern Times* to the "Moscow Board of Censorship in Russia." (This fantasy likely evolved from the screening of *Modern Times* for Shumiatsky in 1935.) He also claimed that Earl Browder suggested in the early 1940s that Chaplin should not apply for citizenship because it might generate problems that could lead to his deportation. (Budenz never explains why this made Chaplin a Communist.) Finally, he alleged that Chaplin was a member of various Communist-front organizations and had contributed money to some of them, something long known to FBI agents, because progressive groups like the National Council of American–Soviet Relations and the Progressive Citizens of America were on the attorney general's list of such organizations.[53]

On the basis of this memo, Hoover instructed the Los Angeles office in January 1951 to reopen the case and bring Chaplin's activities up to date. In March he prodded the office again, giving them an April 10 deadline to submit their report because Budenz was to testify again before HUAC, possibly about Chaplin. In response the Los Angeles office sent Hoover a fourteen-page report dated 5 April 1951, certainly one of the most feeble documents in Chaplin's FBI files. It contained a report by an informant "of unknown reliability"—a catering service employee—who said that Chaplin had attended a party at the house of Clifford Odets that was also attended by Gerhart Eisler. It also claimed that Chaplin had received three books on Czechoslovakia "from Moscow, Russia, through the Progressive Book Shop" in Los Angeles. Perhaps the wildest point in the report was an allegation by an informant whom the Bureau did not consider "to be very reliable." He claimed that Chaplin and another person whose identity has been blacked out in released files were "purchasing all types of arms, including revolvers, machine guns, and rifles" and that the two had "six airplanes that they are presently utilizing to fly these arms and other war materials in and out of Mexico."[54]

Apparently Hoover agreed with what was patently obvious from the report: that the Los Angeles office had to grasp for straws in compiling the April 1951 document. Or so it seems, at any rate, for nothing of consequence appears again in the FBI files until a letter from Hoover to Los Angeles in 1952. Because it deals with events leading up to the revocation of Chaplin's reentry permit, it will be discussed in Chapter 10.

What can we conclude about the FBI's investigation of Chaplin as a security risk through mid-1952? Chaplin's political views and private activities had been subject to severe—and many would say, unconstitutional—examination for over six years without any damaging information being accumulated, even by the extreme standards of the time. In addition, the FBI and the gossip columnists were apparently sharing information that could be used to harm Chaplin's reputation. Reading these files is a sobering experience. Not only do they underline how public even the most private activities of a star can become, but they also reveal how various institutions in American culture—in this case, the press, the FBI, Congress, and other administrative agencies like the IRS and INS—can cooperate formally and informally to discredit someone like Chaplin. The FBI investigation of Chaplin's politics constitutes one more step in the decline of Chaplin's star image that had begun in a serious way during the Barry trials, even though, as we shall see, Chaplin began to downplay and moderate his political views between 1950 and 1952 as a way to seek a truce, if not a reconciliation, with American culture.

Backing Away from Politics, 1950–1952

Following the Barry trials, the box-office failure of *Monsieur Verdoux*, and the negative associations resulting from his progressive political activity, Chaplin found himself in a bind. As a popular artist whose success depended on satisfying a large audience, he seemed to have two choices: either stop making films or reconcile himself with his audience by making a film more palatable to public taste than *Monsieur Verdoux*. As he began to plan the film that became *Limelight*, he seemed to be choosing the second path, even though this meant becoming more circumspect in public about the progressive political positions that he had firmly embraced through the 1940s.

One major reason for Chaplin's turnabout was economic. United Artists, the company he had helped found and through which he had released all his films from *A Woman of Paris* on, was for several reasons on the verge of economic ruin. The foreign market, which had provided a bonanza for Hollywood studios immediately after World War II, had begun to diminish by 1948 as European countries started to set up import quotas, high taxes, and other restrictions to keep too much currency from flowing out of their countries. The domestic market was also shrinking: between 1946 and 1948, movie attendance in the United States had declined between 15 and 25 percent, and this trend continued throughout most of the 1950s. And independent production, which United Artists had been almost the only company to encourage and cultivate before World War II, was becoming increasingly commonplace after war, so that talented producers and directors who would have previously come to United Artists were making deals with other studios. All these factors meant economic difficulties for Chaplin and Mary Pickford, the major United Artists stockholders. When the company's 1948 losses totaled $517,000, the worst it had ever recorded, Chaplin had good reason to aspire to making a film more popular than *Monsieur Verdoux*.[55]

The continuing pressure of the Cold War in the United States was a broader factor that encouraged Chaplin to become more discreet about his political activities from 1950 on. In foreign affairs, after the Soviet Union successfully detonated an atomic bomb and China "fell" to the Communists in 1949, and after the Cold War became hot in Korea in May 1950, any public statements in favor of more benign relations with the Soviet Union would have alienated the speaker from large portions of the American public.

Domestically, 1949 and 1950 saw the rise of Joseph McCarthy's virulent strain of anticommunism. After redbaiting an ex-Communist journalist in November 1949, McCarthy charged Communist infiltration of the State Department in a speech to a group of Young Republicans in November and, in a more famous speech of February 1950, to an audience in Wheeling, West Virginia, at which he held up a sheet of paper that he claimed listed 205 Communists in the State Department's employ. The year 1950 also witnessed strong fears of espionage: Klaus Fuchs was sentenced to fourteen years in prison for espionage in March, the same month that Harry Gold was arrested to begin the chain of events leading to the trial and execution of Ethel and Julius Rosenberg. And after the first Alger Hiss trial ended in a hung jury in 1949, Hiss was convicted of espionage in 1950 and given a five-year jail sentence. Amid this hostile atmosphere, large numbers of formerly leftist intellectuals either revised their progressive views or decided the wiser course was to remain silent on political issues. Chaplin's political activity (or inactivity) between 1950 and 1953 must be understood in this context.[56]

Thus Chaplin had good reasons to strive for reconciliation with his American moviegoing public, not the least being that his public reputation was in a shambles. The star image that had been so widely admired up to World War II had shifted radically. If we recall the assumption that a star image is a complex of meanings and effects that changes over time, we could say that as the 1940s progressed, Chaplin the man, and an increasingly controversial Chaplin at that, came to dominate the star image to a much greater extent, with a consequent decline in the centrality of the lovable, struggling, resilient Charlie. Chaplin's gradual capitulation to sound and subsequent abandonment of Charlie undoubtedly had much to do with this shift, but so did his active engagement in progressive politics and the publicity surrounding the Barry trials. Although Chaplin didn't seem to realize before the release of *Monsieur Verdoux* how badly his stardom had slipped, he appparently did understand his miscalculation afterward. But what could he do about it? Gestures of reconciliation seem to have been his answer.

One way Chaplin tried to mend the rift with his audience was by rereleasing *City Lights* in April 1950. We might recall that one suggestion Chaplin received during his *Monsieur Verdoux* press conference was that he either make more "Charlie" films or bring back the old ones. Chaplin chose the latter when in December 1949 he allowed the private school his daughter Geraldine was attending to show *City Lights* as a fund-raiser. It was a sellout; and patrons had to be turned away. Chaplin was pleased to see both young and old in the audience loving the film. That response prompted Chaplin and United Artists to open *City Lights* in Manhattan on 8 April 1950, and as late as May 21 the *New York Times* reported that the film was still "packing in satisfied customers."[57]

Rereleasing such a quintessential "Charlie" film as *City Lights* was a good way for Chaplin to reestablish ties with his audience: the film starred Charlie, it blended comedy and pathos with extreme skill and control, and its narrative omitted the overt progressive politics found in his subsequent features. Chaplin thus not only reminded his old fans of the star image they had so fully embraced but also introduced young viewers to the image of Charlie, one they would never have expected in the era of paternity suits and political harassment.

It is not unlikely that Chaplin hoped to mend fences with the public by systematically presenting his old features, in a sense creating his stardom afresh for a new generation. This is precisely what he did with the American rerelease of his films through RBC Films in the early 1970s, when the political climate in the country had changed enough to make the culture receptive to Chaplin's stardom again. But in 1950 it wasn't that easy. First of all, not that many screens were available for revivals of classic films. Granted, the Museum of Modern Art had established a Film Department a decade earlier, and other art museums were beginning to show an interest in classic films. In addition, the number of "art houses" and college film societies was beginning to grow; however, that number was certainly not large enough to affect many viewers outside a few large cities. Even more important, the political climate was still too hostile. One indication of the resistance to the rerelease of Chaplin's films occurred in December 1950, when the *New York Times* reported that the fledgling television station WPIX canceled its scheduled showings of Chaplin shorts after a protest, on political grounds, by the Hudson County, New Jersey, branch of Catholic War Veterans, the same group that James Fay had represented at the *Monsieur Verdoux* press conference.[58]

Yet there is good evidence that by 1950 Chaplin was seeking to distance himself from domestic communism in a way he had not throughout the 1940s. In July, the *Daily People's World*, a San Francisco–based leftist newspaper, announced that Chaplin's *The Circus* would be shown two nights as a fund-raiser for the paper. Chaplin, apparently sensitive to the negative publicity that could arise if one of his films were associated with the leftist group, put his foot down. He ordered his lawyers to halt the unauthorized showing of the film, a refusal that was even noted in the *New York Times*.[59] Although such an action was not surprising from a business standpoint, given the care with which Chaplin and his associates controlled his features and especially the revenues that flowed from them, it also contained political significance, for it was one of the rare instances after Chaplin's second front days that a newspaper report about him stressed his separation from, rather than his association with, a leftist organization.

This decision to deny a leftist group permission to show *The Circus* suggests that Chaplin was trying to tone down his progressive politics. In fact, I have been unable to find any references in the American press from 1950 to 1952 in which Chaplin defends the Soviet Union, even the Soviets' conduct in fighting fascism during World War II. This must be understood at least partly as consistent with the growing disillusionment with Stalin and the Soviet Union among American liberals that began to be widespread after the beginning of the Cold War. Yet even when Chaplin *could* be coaxed into talking about his political views, his tone was not belligerent, as it had sometimes been during the 1940s. For example, the *Hollywood Reporter* of 9 March 1950 (a month after McCarthy's Wheeling speech) quoted Chaplin's position on citizenship: "As a believer in 'One World,' I wish to respectfully state that my position is unaltered and that I have not made any request, officially or unofficially, for citizenship." Though Chaplin did not compromise his progressive position in this statement, he did—with the word "respectfully"—couch it in terms more conciliatory and hence more palatable to his audience, even for some of those who would have rejected his views.

Another indication of a thaw in the freeze that had developed between Chaplin and moviegoers was the appearance of several laudatory pieces on Chaplin in American mass magazines in 1949 and 1950. These articles came after several years when almost the only items that praised Chaplin were in the leftist, relatively small circulation press. Of these new mass-magazine pieces, the two most significant were by James Agee and Al Capp. Agee's "Comedy's Greatest Era," which appeared in a September 1949 issue of *Life*, probably reached the largest audience. Agee surveyed American silent film comedy in his essay but reserved his highest praise for the character of "the tramp." In Agee's words, "the finest pantomime, the deepest emotion, the richest and most poignant poetry were in Chaplin's work. He could probably pantomime Bryce's *The American Commonwealth* and make it paralyzingly funny in the bargain." Several months later Capp, best known for his "Li'l Abner" cartoon strip, published his essay. Although Capp was known as a political satirist, he argued here that Chaplin's work transcended politics. "When the ideological passions of our time are laughable curios," he wrote, "the greatest artist that our time has produced will be recognized as Charlie Chaplin." In this *Atlantic* cover article, Capp located the roots of humor in man's inhumanity to man, which he judged one basis of Chaplin's success, but he also pinpointed the pathos that often surrounded Charlie's relationship with women. "No confused, despondent lover ever saw a Chaplin picture," Capp wrote, "who didn't come away feeling considerably cheered up."[60]

Both Agee and Capp contributed ideas that in a more receptive political climate could help salvage Chaplin's star image. Agee emphasized the Charlie persona and the brilliant pantomime in the Chaplin films, both key aspects of the aesthetic contract that had cemented Chaplin's relationship with his audience in the 1910s and 1920s. Similarly, Capp, by emphasizing the intensity of Charlie's romances and the depth of pathos evoked when the romances went unrequited, brought to the fore elements that had played important roles in popularizing Chaplin's star image. It seemed that perhaps the worst was over for him.

In addition to these articles, which reached large audiences, three books on Chaplin were published in English in 1951 and 1952: Theodore Huff's *Charlie Chaplin*, Peter Cotes and Thelma Niklaus's *The Lit-*

tle Fellow, and Robert Payne's *The Great God Pan*. Although these books were not best-sellers when released and probably had little immediate effect on Chaplin's star image, they did look forward to a time when the *auteur* approach, to be discussed in Chapter 11, would come to dominate the history and analysis of film. Huff's biography, which was reprinted in paperback in the 1960s, eventually reached a relatively wide audience and thus had some effect on Chaplin's star image.[61]

By mid-1952 Chaplin had been quiet about his progressive politics for two years, quite a contrast to the vigorous political activity he had been involved in during the 1940s. As we have seen, the Barry trials and his political involvements had generated much controversy in the press during the 1940s, which had brought Chaplin the unwanted attention of elected government officials and the FBI. Nevertheless, with positive articles and books appearing and a nonpolitical film in the works, Chaplin may have thought that his preeminent star status was reviving.

10

Limelight and Banishment: The Futility of Reconciliation

Chaplin, the U.S. Government, and Banishment, 1952–1953

We know that stars have often been manufactured by publicity and promotion departments with little regard for the wishes of the contract actor who embodied the role. In such cases the actor has had little control over the star image. Chaplin, however—because of his personal charm, because of his enormous early success, and because he soon owned his means of production and then wrote, directed, and produced his work—was able to shape and control his star image to a significant degree between the World Wars.

Yet even with this much creative independence and business acumen, Chaplin was unable to control his star image fully, as he would learn most graphically in 1952 and 1953. We have seen in Chapter 9 how Chaplin, aware that publicity about his politics was endangering his career, began to retreat from his progressive commitments around 1950. Around the same time he was busily at work on a film tentatively titled *Foot Lights*. As Chaplin himself recalled, "I was optimistic and still not convinced that I had completely lost the affection of the American people" (MA, p. 456). Evidence suggests that the film, which was eventually released as *Limelight* in the fall of 1952, constituted Chaplin's attempt to reconcile himself with the American moviegoing public, in part by making the film more overtly autobiographical. Yet he learned that his desires for reconciliation were not easily realized. By 1952 and 1953 his star image had become a source of controversy in Cold War debates. The situation had become so serious that by the end of 1953, Chaplin had—following the attorney general's revocation of his reentry permit—sold his studio and his Hollywood home and, severing his ties almost completely from his adopted country of nearly forty years, moved permanently into a manor in Switzerland.

Because the release and reviews of *Limelight* occurred after Chaplin's departure for Europe, we must first look at Chaplin's decision to uproot himself from the United States. I am calling what occurred a

279

"banishment" in two senses of the word: both in the general sense of driving someone away from a country and the specific sense of a governmental action that forces one from a country or makes it extremely difficult for one to return.

Because so many misconceptions exist about the events of 1952 and 1953, and because the opening of the FBI files makes it possible to explore what kind of case the government had against Chaplin, it is important to outline what actually did transpire. In the summer of 1952, while he was finishing postproduction work on *Limelight*, Chaplin decided to travel to Europe for a family vacation and to attend the Paris and London openings of his new film. He applied to the INS for a reentry permit, which as a resident alien he would need to return to the United States following his trip. This was granted him on July 16.[1]

After setting sail from New York City aboard the *Queen Elizabeth* on September 18, however, Chaplin and his family received bad news: a spokesman for Attorney General James McGranery announced on September 19 that Chaplin's reentry permit had been revoked and that Chaplin would have to answer INS questions about his political views and moral behavior before he would be allowed to reenter the country. McGranery's spokesman told the press that his office had "a pretty good case" against Chaplin. Ten days later McGranery told the press that Chaplin "is in my judgement an unsavory character," and charged him with "making statements that would indicate a leering, sneering attitude" toward the country whose hospitality enriched him.[2] In his first public response to the situation, Chaplin told reporters that he still intended to return to America.

In contrast to the hostile treatment he had received from various government agencies and some quarters of the press in the United States, Chaplin was celebrated in England, France, and Italy in the last months of 1952. *Variety* reported that at the October 16 premiere of *Limelight* at the Odeon Theater in London, the ovation for Chaplin was "far greater than that accorded" Princess Margaret.[3] Five days later he and Oona were presented to Queen Elizabeth at a royal command performance of the film. Arriving in France in November and Italy in December, Chaplin drew equally enthusiastic crowds and, as on his world tour in 1931–1932, was celebrated by politicians and artists in both countries.

Some of the comments Chaplin made in interviews during these months also indicate that he was reformulating his political views away from his progressive tolerance of the Soviet Union to a position different and somewhat more palatable to his audience in the days of the Cold War. In his statement to the press upon his arrival in Cherbourg,

France, he said: "I am not political. . . . I am an individualist and believe in liberty. That is as far as my political convictions go." In a November interview with the Belgian newspaper *Le Peuple*, he commented, "I don't believe in any dogma. . . . It is the man, the individual who counts above all, more than anything. . . . In modern times where everything is being regimented the artist must more than ever think of the internal life of the individual, of this unique phenomenon which is a human being, the artist must create for man."[4] In both these statements Chaplin reverts to a defense of the individual against the massive institutions of modern society, a position he reasserts in his autobiography when he tries to "sum up the state of the world as I see it today": "The accumulating complexities of modern life, the kinetic invasion of the twentieth century, find the individual hemmed in by gigantic institutions that threaten from all sides, politically, scientifically, and economically. We are becoming the victims of soul-conditioning, of sanctions and permits" (MA, 470).

This defense of the individual over social institutions is similar to the anarchism that the young Marxist critic Lorenzo Rozas had perceived in Chaplin's work in his 1934 analysis and provides grounds for the assertion of some later critics that a sort of anarchism is the center of the Chaplin's sociopolitical world view.[5] The defense of the underdog against authority figures and powerful institutions had long been a trademark in his films; however, it became subordinated in his political activities during his progressive involvements from 1942 on. Only in 1952 did this resurface as a central part of Chaplin's political beliefs. Given his personal situation at the time, as he found himself caught in the cogs of bureaucratic machinery as tightly as Charlie ever was in *Modern Times*, his view was understandable.

In his autobiography Chaplin recalls having to bite his tongue when he first met the press after learning of McGranery's actions. "I would have liked to tell them that the sooner I was rid of that hate-beleaguered atmosphere the better, that I was fed up with America's insults and moral pomposity," he wrote, "but everything I possessed was in the States and I was terrified they might find a way of confiscating it." Therefore, "I came out with a pompous statement to the effect that I would return and answer their charges" (MA, p. 465). Even at this juncture Chaplin opted for reconciliation rather than denunciation: the once peerless star was hoping to halt the decline of his public reputation and protect his financial interests.

By April 1953, however, Chaplin decided that enough was enough. He had, after all, been celebrated across the European continent, feted by the wealthy, the famous, and the powerful as a (perhaps *the*) genius of the cinema. In such circumstances, the prospect of returning to America to face more interrogations about his political views and moral worth was clearly unappealing. To break ties with the United States, Chaplin had to get his assets out of the country. In January and February of 1953 Oona Chaplin accomplished this in a trip back to Los Angeles. At the same time, Chaplin acquired an estate called Manoir de Ban in Corsier-sur-Vevey, Switzerland, which would be his permanent residence until his death on Christmas morning of 1977. With these tasks completed Chaplin visited the American embassy in Switzerland on 10 April 1953 and turned in his reentry permit, thus officially giving up plans to return to the United States. The long and stormy love affair between Chaplin and America seemed to be over.

Since Chaplin did not return to the United States to answer the charges leveled against him by the attorney general's office, it has never been made clear whether he would have been refused entry had he chosen to fight the charges. However, documents from the FBI, INS, attorney general's office, and the State Department can help us answer that question, just as they provide a good picture of how actively these organizations worked on the Chaplin case in 1952 and 1953. Although, as we have seen, the FBI was the most active governmental agency investigating Chaplin through early 1952, the INS became more involved after he applied for a reentry permit. After he left the country, his case moved to the jurisdiction of the State Department, which began to provide information concerning his activities and the European response to him throughout the remainder of 1952 and 1953.

As we have seen, the April 1951 report on Chaplin as a security risk by the Los Angeles office of the FBI contained so little that Hoover apparently saw no need for further investigation. Or so it seems, at least, for nothing of consequence appears again in the FBI files until a letter from Hoover to Los Angeles in July 1952. It noted that Chaplin had recently applied for a reentry permit and had asked government officials if the permit would guarantee the right to return to the United States. With Chaplin's possible trip in mind, Hoover asked the Los Angeles office to forward any information they could accumulate "concerning the subject and his activities in relation to moving or taking a trip."[6]

On August 25 a Bureau memo notes that it had received information from the INS that Chaplin had been issued a reentry permit on July 16. It also observed that Chaplin had moved back his departure date from September 4 to "about September 10."[7] On September 9, a meeting took place between McGranery and Hoover. McGranery stated that he was thinking about how Chaplin's return to the United States could be prevented. Chaplin's planned trip abroad provided the opportunity, said McGranery, "of taking steps which would prevent his re-entry . . . because of moral turpitude." Hoover then drafted a memo dated September 11 to three of his aides instructing them to prepare immediately "a memorandum of all information in our files concerning Charlie Chaplin . . . [to] be transmitted to the Attorney General for his information."[8]

The idea of deporting Chaplin or preventing him from returning to the country was not new in September 1952. In the last chapter we noted that at least two members of Congress publicly called for Chaplin's deportation in the late 1940s. Similarly, *Variety* reported in February 1951 that Chaplin had abandoned plans to shoot some of *Limelight* in London, apparently because he could receive no firm guarantees that he would be permitted to return to the country after he left, even if he had a reentry permit.[9]

After Hoover's request, however, the preparation of material for the attorney general was given priority in the Washington office. The FBI effort was immediate and large scale. Agent Belmont's September 16 memo to Agent Ladd noted that they received Hoover's directive to write a report on Friday afternoon, September 12. Two agents immediately began to review the seven-volume Barry files and the six-volume internal security files. By Tuesday, the day of Belmont's memo, three more agents were laboring full time in the preparation of the document for McGranery. By September 18 the twenty-page summary was completed and sent out to the Attorney General. The following day Chaplin's reentry permit was revoked.[10]

But did the government have adequate grounds on which to exclude Chaplin? The evidence suggests it did not, at least as of the week following the revocation of the reentry permit. A key FBI document supports this. An FBI memo from Belmont to Ladd, dated September 30, recounts a meeting on the 29th attended by FBI Supervisor John E. Foley (the FBI's liaison representative to the INS) and three INS officials: Commissioner A. R. Mackey, Deputy Commissioner Benjamin Habberton, and Assistant Commissioner Raymond Farrell.[11] After thanking the FBI for its offer of assistance in the case, Commissioner Mackey asked Deputy Commissioner Farrell to brief Foley on the INS's progress in the case. According to Belmont's memo, "Mr. Farrell stated bluntly that at the present time INS does not have sufficient information to exclude Chaplin from the United States if he attempts to re-enter" (p. 2). Mackey broke in to say that the INS could make it difficult for Chaplin to reenter "but in the end, there is no doubt Chaplin would be admitted." Furthermore, he added, if the INS attempted to delay Chaplin's reentry, the case "might well rock INS and the Department of Justice to its foundations" (p. 2).

During the same meeting Farrell informed Foley that the INS hoped Chaplin would not attempt to return before December 24, when the recently passed Immigration and Nationality Act, which gave the State Department and its various agencies much broader powers in dealing with radicals, would go into effect.[12] "If Chaplin's lawyer was astute," Farrell told Foley, "he would have Chaplin return to the United States before the effective date of the new law." The meeting concluded with plans for the INS to press forward in trying to obtain information, perhaps via an interview with Chaplin's maid or butler, that would exclude Chaplin on a charge that he "conspired to cause one of his girl friends [Joan Barry] to abort." The INS officials feared that there could "be a great great deal of unfavorable publicity if attempts were made to exclude Chaplin on security grounds alone"—hence their interest in the abortion issue.

Thus at the end of September the INS believed they had no evidence, either on an abortion conspiracy charge or on a security charge, that could deny Chaplin reentry had he attempted to return. In a letter to Hoover on October 1 the INS officially requested the assistance of the FBI in its investigation of Chaplin, and for the next several months it tried to obtain such evidence in cooperation with the FBI. The FBI's internal security files on Chaplin between October 1952 and April 1953 contain a large number of documents, the longest of which is a 124-page report prepared by six Los Angeles FBI agents at Hoover's request for other FBI offices and for the INS.[13] The report was essentially a summary of earlier reports from Los Angeles that dealt with both the Barry case and Chaplin's political views. After a summary and some background information on Chaplin, the report's other major headings are:

A. Information Pertaining to Question of Communist Party Membership of Charles Chaplin
B. Individual Associates of Chaplin Who Are Reported to Be Communist Party Members [this section includes sections on Hanns Eisler, Lion Feuchtwanger, and Theodore Dreiser]
C. Affiliation of Charles Chaplin with Groups Declared to Be Communist Subversive Groups or Reputedly Controlled or Influenced by Communist Party

This report, and other shorter FBI reports sent by Hoover to the INS, provided the INS with allegations that could possibly have been used for the expected Chaplin hearing.

The INS needed witnesses to proceed, however. This need for reliable substantiation of the allegations in the FBI files provided the basis for a constant stream of correspondence beginning in October between the Washington and Los Angeles FBI offices, and between Hoover and various other non-FBI agencies, primarily the attorney general's office and the INS. Hoover wrote often to the Los Angeles office, instructing them to help the Los Angeles branch of the INS in seeking out FBI informants who might provide the INS with interviews for their investigation. He also told his agents to search for informants who were quoted or cited in the FBI reports that had been given to the INS.

Reading over this correspondence, one cannot help but be struck by how unsubstantiated many of the allegations were. For example, the 14 October 1952 FBI report, and others before it, claimed that Chaplin was a member of the Independent Progressive party and regularly attended its meetings. When the Los Angeles office, on Hoover's instructions, tracked down the source of that information, however, the unnamed woman informant told the FBI that she had obtained the information from another woman who had overheard it when she was a patron in a beauty salon. The FBI then contacted the second woman, who didn't have "any recollection of the information furnished regarding Chaplin's membership and attendance at IPP meetings." Another example is the charge that Chaplin received books on Czechoslovakia from the Soviet Union, in itself an improbable reason for deportation. The source for this story was a Customs agent in Los Angeles who provided the information through inspection of the mails. When contacted, he said "he had no personal recollection of the above literature being received by Chaplin."[14]

These examples, though perhaps more bizarre than others, are typical in that they turned up no witnesses for the INS. Several times in the fall and winter Hoover wrote the INS with the news that specific informants they asked about were unable to testify. One letter, of 31 October 1952, listed six specific sources requested by the INS: all were unavailable to testify. A December 9 letter bore similar news. Although it did give the INS the name of one informant, it added that he "has proven to be unreliable in the past." On 19 February 1953 Hoover again wrote the INS, telling them that the source of yet another story was from another governmental agency. When contacted, that agency could not identify specifically who originated the story. One can only conclude that the FBI had spent a tremendous number of hours and massive amounts of paper preparing long reports about

Chaplin that were based on shaky, distorted, or even downright false information.[15]

Other government agencies were brought into the Chaplin case after he left the country. On 8 October 1952, Hoover wrote to the chief of the Security Division at the State Department and sent a copy of the letter to the director of the Central Intelligence Agency (CIA). The letter informed the recipients that Chaplin had left the United States on September 17 and could "possibly be denied admittance to this country upon return." Hoover specifically stated that the FBI was not requesting any investigation of Chaplin by the State Department or the CIA, but he asked them to send "any information concerning subject's activity that may come to your attention."[16] I have found no evidence that either organization conducted a detailed investigation of Chaplin after receiving this letter; however, the U.S. Embassies in Belgium, England, France, and Switzerland all monitored Chaplin at one time or another. A letter from Belgium translated an interview Chaplin did with a leftist newspaper; the embassy in London translated several pro-Chaplin Soviet reports. The embassy in Paris provided the longest report: it photocopied several articles on Chaplin from newspapers of various political slants, translated them, and commented on how enthusiastically Chaplin was generally received in Paris.[17] For the most part, however, the FBI and the INS did the most to prepare for Chaplin's expected INS hearing, and right up until the day Chaplin turned in his reentry permit, they were unable to find solid evidence that would have excluded him from the country.

On April 15, the Department of Justice sent out a press release, a copy of which made its way into the FBI files. It stated that Chaplin had surrendered his reentry permit to State Department authorities in Geneva on April 10. The previous flood of FBI activity in the investigation of Chaplin dwindled to a trickle. On April 20 Hoover suggested to the Los Angeles office that Chaplin's security index card be removed from his file since he had given up his reentry permit. On April 30 Hoover wrote again, this time telling the Los Angeles office to complete its remaining investigation and "submit recommendations concerning subject's status on the Security Index so that this investigation can be closed." That final report, dated 10 July 1953, reiterated Chaplin's friendship with Hanns Eisler and Lion Feuchtwanger and said that John Howard Lawson was hoping to organize a campaign to have *Limelight* shown throughout the United States. Finally, on August 12 the Los Angeles office wrote Hoover that since Chaplin had turned in his reentry permit, they felt his security index card should be cancelled.[18] Although the files released by the FBI through the Freedom of Information Act contain another eighty pages of information, the last item dealing with the theft of his corpse in 1978, Chaplin's battle with the FBI was over.

Limelight: Autobiography and the Aesthetic Contract

As Chaplin had begun to contemplate and plan his next film in the late 1940s and 1950, he was confronted with a number of problems. His previous film, his first comedy since the 1910s with no persona similar to Charlie, had been a failure at the box office and with most critics. The company of which he was a major stockholder, United Artists, was experiencing serious economic difficulties, as was much of the Hollywood film industry. And his star image, which in previous decades had been dominated by Charlie (the romantic, funny, resilient representative of common people) and by Chaplin (the versatile artistic genius, masterful pantomimist, and even at times serious commentator on public affairs), had shifted in the 1940s. The Barry trials and Chaplin's involvement in progressive politics had transformed his star image so that two traits—questionable sexual conduct and progressive (in the minds of some people, even subversive) political views—came to do battle with the others.

One obvious solution would have been to make another film featuring Charlie, but two circumstances militated against that. First, Charlie was a product of nondialogue films, and Chaplin, regularly criticized by reviewers for an old-fashioned or awkward film style since *Modern Times*, would have been taking a serious risk to make a nondialogue film twenty years after the industry had shifted to talking pictures. Second, Chaplin was sixty years old in 1949: to perform the antics of the inimitable Charlie, Chaplin had to be physically capable of doing so. Despite his vigor, Chaplin would have been hard pressed to perform as Charlie for an entire grueling shooting schedule.

The issue of Chaplin's age had been raised by a critic remarkably early in Chaplin's career. In his 1922 essay, "Dear Mr. Chaplin," Stark Young had urged Chaplin to broaden and evolve as an artist because the public "uses up for its own ends what it finds and then throws it aside" and because of "the hard biological fact" of Chaplin's inevitable "physical decline from perfection."[19] Young couldn't have predicted that the introduction of sound pictures would combine with Chaplin's aging to make the antics of Charlie less possible, yet his comments were prescient: much of Chaplin's audience did abandon him, and by 1950, Chaplin knew better, given his age and appearance, than to dust off the derby, cane, baggy pants, and mustache and give Charlie a rebirth.

What, then, was the solution? Near the end of the *Monsieur Verdoux* press conference, when a questioner expressed dissatisfaction that Chaplin's recent films subordinated comedy to message, Chaplin replied: "as one gets older we are not just satisfied to go along with the same old line. We have to get excited by something before we can arouse our energy to do something. And I suppose it is one of my indulgences. I'm sorry."[20] By 1948 Chaplin's new "indulgence" was a film featuring neither Charlie nor a progressive political issue. Rather, he had become excited by a story about an aging comedian who fears he is no longer funny. He had begun working on a novel between 1948 and 1951, which eventually reached about 100,000 words,[21] and the manuscript became the source of Chaplin's next film.

The public began to learn a few details about the film quite early. In the spring of 1950 Richard Lauterbach interviewed Chaplin for an article to appear in *New York Times Magazine*. Already Chaplin had the story for his new film pretty firmly worked out. Lauterbach described it for his readers: "The script is finished. It will have music, dancing, humor, pity—everything but the tramp. Tentatively titled 'Foot Lights,' the story concerns the attempted comeback of an aging English music hall comic who falls in love with a young dancer. He has been on the top, but feels he is losing his touch and is afraid he can no longer make audiences laugh." After hearing the plot description, Lauterbach immediately asked Chaplin whether the film was autobiographical. "Everything is autobiographical," Chaplin replied, "but don't make too much of that."[22]

More than two years before the film was ready, Chaplin had let the press know its plot outline. Furthermore, it was apparent that the film would likely draw more heavily on autobiographical elements than most of Chaplin's other films, however much those earlier films may have covertly touched on autobiography. Despite the hostility that had greeted *Monsieur Verdoux*, despite the continuing investigations by various governmental bodies, and despite the unraveling of his star image, Chaplin was going ahead with his new film and would even draw on his own star image for details of character and plot. Like his other activities in 1950 and 1951, however, Chaplin's work on his new film suggested that he was seeking a reconciliation with his audience. He did so partly by returning to particular aspects of the aesthetic contract that had helped establish and sustain his stardom and partly by drawing on his own autobiography in quite explicit ways.

Though the title of the film was changed to *Limelight*, the finished

26. Chaplin as Calvero in *Limelight*, 1952.

work resembled the description Chaplin gave Lauterbach in 1950 quite closely. An aging music-hall comedian, Calvero (Chaplin), has been driven to drink as his career deteriorates (see Figure 26). At the opening of the film, he saves a young woman named Terry (Claire Bloom), after she has attempted suicide. Taking her into his apartment, Calvero nurses her back to health and encourages her to resume her ballet dancing. Her career blossoms. His declines. When he observes that she is falling in love with the young composer Neville (Sydney Chaplin), Calvero disappears for six months. At the end of the film, Terry persuades Calvero to allow a benefit tribute to be held for him. Calvero agrees, performs his comic routines successfully at the benefit, and dies offstage at the end of the film after suffering a heart attack, while Terry is onstage, performing.

The film makes several gestures of reconciliation toward Chaplin's American audience. Three of these are related to the aesthetic contract that had established and sustained his star image. For the first time since *City Lights*, Chaplin made a film without an overt expression of progressive politics. Apparently he realized after the failure of *Monsieur Verdoux* that progressive messages were likely to antagonize a large number of his potential viewers, mired as they were in the atmosphere of the Cold War. Like the film industry as a whole, which had given prominence to such "social problem" films like *Gentleman's Agreement*, *Pinky*, and *Intruder in the Dust* in the half decade after World War II, Chaplin learned where it hurts producers most—the box office—that sizable portions of the audience had by 1950 become sensitive about if not hostile toward movies that criticized American society.

Omitting messages was a negative act of reconciliation: it left out something that Chaplin had begun to include from *Modern Times* on as he revised his aesthetic contract. But in *Limelight* Chaplin also made two positive gestures of reconciliation, both of which drew on key characteristics of Chaplin's original aesthetic contract. The first was to include a number of comic incidents that would remind the audience of Chaplin's gift at pantomime. In the film's first scene, the down-and-out comedian Calvero comes home drunk and creates considerable humor through pantomime as he fumbles with his key and, after getting into the hall of his boarding house, looks at the bottom of his shoes after smelling a foul odor (thus demonstrating the very "vulgarity" for which Chaplin's genteel critics had attacked him in the 1910s). Although the film also includes several of Calvero's music-hall routines, the only other genuine moments of comic pantomime come when Calvero imitates several objects (like a pansy or a Japanese tree) for Terry, and when he and Buster Keaton perform together (for the only time in their careers) as a comic violinist and comic pianist in the film's conclusion. This latter scene, played without dialogue, almost brings the audience back to the tradition of American silent comedy that flourished in the 1920s and that Chaplin and Keaton did so much to establish.

Second, in *Limelight* Chaplin returned to another convention: the focus on a romance, often unfulfilled, between the Chaplin persona and a woman. As in so many other Chaplin features, the woman in *Limelight* is flawed or vulnerable. Here Terry, the young aspiring ballerina, has a history of rheumatic fever; her temporary paralysis aligns her with the other Chaplin heroines with physical flaws, especially the blind girl in *City Lights* and Mona, Verdoux's invalid wife. As an orphan, she is similar to the gamin in *Modern Times* (and not inappropriately, given Calvero's paternal concern for her, with Jackie Coogan's character in *The Kid*). When Calvero mistakes her for a prostitute early in the film, she is even linked with the streetwalker whom Verdoux spares.

In addition to Terry's similarities to earlier women characters, the contours of the romance in *Limelight* remind one of other Chaplin films, especially *The Circus*. In both films the character played by Chaplin comes to admire the heroine and yearn for her attention. In both the heroine falls in love with someone else, after which the Chaplin persona overhears her in a discussion that leads him to believe that his love affair is doomed. And in both films the Chaplin character sacrifices his longing to love the heroine for what he believes is her well-being and happiness. Thus Chaplin provided in *Limelight* another gesture of reconciliation: a romantic dilemma that had at least the potential for that which had made Charlie so endearing in *The Kid*, *The Gold Rush*, *The Circus*, and *City Lights*.

However, both the comedy and the romantic pathos in *Limelight* were at best partial gestures for audiences who wished Charlie were back. Except for the scene with Keaton and a few of Calvero's gestures, *Limelight* is not a very funny film. In fact, Chaplin is several times faced with the problem of a story that requires performing comic scenes that the audiences in the film do not think are funny. It doubtless takes a special talent to act out an ostensibly comic scene that is not funny, but it still doesn't yield comedy.

Similarly, the handling of the romance in *Limelight* is different in one key way from that in *The Circus*. In the "overhearing" scene in *Limelight*, Neville tells Terry on her doorstep that he loves her and that her feeling for Calvero is really pity, not love. She protests, but Calvero, lying half-drunk inside the door, overhears and, having predicted earlier that she would fall in love with Neville, leaves Terry voluntarily so that the young couple's relationship can blossom. When Terry sees Calvero again six months later and tells him that she still loves him, he replies, "I know." Since Calvero controls the relationship, the pathos resulting from unrequited love is muted compared to the feelings we experience when Charlie overhears Merna declare her love for Rex in *The Circus* or when Charlie awakes from his "Oceana Roll" dream in *The Gold Rush* to find that Georgia has stood him up on New Year's Eve. The empathy Charlie almost pleads for (and very often gets) in those two films—based on our common fear of being vulnerable, lonely, and rejected—is dulled in *Limelight*, for Calvero rarely appears as vulnerable in his relationship with Terry as Charlie almost always was in the presence of a woman to whom he was attracted. Though some pathos is generated when Calvero fails in his comic routines, almost none emerges from the romance.

Clearly something new is at work in *Limelight*, something besides a return to aspects of Chaplin's old aesthetic contract. In many of his earlier comic films, particularly from *The Kid* on, Chaplin had practiced "submerged autobiography": drawing subtly and indirectly on details of his life to create his characters. In *Limelight*, the submerged becomes explicit: Chaplin makes overt autobiographical references and creates parallels to his main character that are central to the film.

This movement from submerged to explicit autobiography began with *Monsieur Verdoux*. There the central character's critique of capitalist society and his murder of women loosely paralleled Chaplin's own political views and the public's perception of his problems with women; in fact, some of the audience actually connected Verdoux's politics and attitude toward women with Chaplin's, which did his star image no good. In reflecting on the film Chaplin admitted to Lauterbach that he made a mistake by not getting audiences to feel pity and understanding for Verdoux.[23]

In *Limelight* Chaplin, aware that his private life and public activities had increasingly come to dominate his star image in the 1940s, decided to use autobiographical elements so much a part of his "biographical legend" (the term is Boris Tomashevsky's).[24] However, he would be even more explicitly autobiographical than he was in *Verdoux* and would carefully select those details so that audiences would identify both with Calvero and with Chaplin himself. He would turn autobiography to his advantage and create an aging comedian afraid of losing his audience rather than a Bluebeard with progressive politics.

Calvero and Chaplin are indeed similar in a number of ways, and these similarities constitute the most obvious and important autobiographical level of the film.[25] To list only a few, at the opening of the film Calvero has begun to fail as a comedian so much that he even dreams of performing before an empty theater. In much the same way Chaplin was coming off a film, *Monsieur Verdoux*, that many in his audience thought far from funny. Compared to Chaplin's previous box-office successes, it too played to relatively empty theaters. A second similarity between Calvero and Chaplin is the relationship each has with a young woman. Just as Calvero and Terry develop a loving bond, so did the aged Chaplin and the young Oona O'Neill marry.

Calvero even makes a joke of his relationship with Terry that acts as Chaplin's ironic reference to his own relationships with women. When Terry protests about feigning marriage, Calvero responds, "I've had five wives already. One more or less won't matter to me." Throughout the film Calvero's philosophical comments on life remind one of the intellectual Chaplin that constituted a part of his star image from the 1920s on. One could even say that Calvero's last performance at the benefit is analogous to the film; *Limelight* thus becomes Chaplin's own swan song, his own last attempt to leave his audience entertained and enlightened.[26] To underline the similarity between Calvero and Chaplin visually, a poster on Calvero's wall promotes him as the "Tramp Comedian," and over his mantel is a posed photograph of Chaplin from the 1920s, wearing a double-breasted suit, the only photograph of Chaplin to appear in one of his films.

Chaplin also encouraged an autobiographical reading of *Limelight* by his casting. Chaplin's two sons from his marriage to Lita Grey both appear in the film. Sydney has the largest role, as Neville, while Charles, Jr., appears briefly (along with Chaplin's half brother Wheeler Dryden) as the policeman in the first part of the ballet sequence. In the film's opening shots, the three oldest children of Oona O'Neill Chaplin and her husband also appear briefly. Charles, Jr., explains these appearances when he writes that Chaplin "had a very sentimental reason for making *Limelight* what he called a family affair. He said he fully expected it to be his last as well as his greatest picture."[27]

The promotion campaign for *Limelight* reinforces the view that *Limelight* was a more overtly and consciously autobiographical film than any other Chaplin had made. On the day *Limelight* opened in New York City, the large ads in both the *New York Times* and the *New York Herald Tribune* centered on something no other ad for a Chaplin film had ever done: Chaplin's own face, minus the mustache. The *Herald Tribune* ad is most direct. Four columns wide, the ad's largest letters are at the top: "Charles Chaplin." The film's title is below and to the right of center, and below that, in the center, is a large picture of Chaplin's face without makeup and without mustache. Surrounding the head are four smaller pictures and captions promising comedy, slapstick, ballet, and romance, but the looming presence of Charles Chaplin dominates. The *Times* ad also features Chaplin's face, though in a slightly more complicated fashion (see Figure 27). Below the text at the top of the ad is a picture of Chaplin looking into a mirror and putting makeup on his eyebrows. Like the *Herald Tribune* picture, Chaplin is without a mustache, but here, the artifice of the theater is suggested: Chaplin clearly is preparing himself to take on another

27. Newspaper advertisement for *Limelight* (1952), promoting Chaplin.

role.[28] For the first time since he donned Charlie's costume and began overseeing his own publicity, Chaplin himself is in the limelight—the actor, director, producer, and human being Charles Chaplin, rather than the character he plays. That this element was central to *Limelight* is reinforced by another unusual aspect of the film's promotion: for the first time ever, Chaplin allowed *Life* magazine to roam his sets while he was shooting and to come into his home and photograph him interacting with his family. The resulting eleven-page spread included both candid shots from the shooting and pictures, formal and informal, of Chaplin and his family.[29] Showing Chaplin as the happily married family man surely presented an alternative picture to the embattled man fighting a paternity suit in 1945. But it also showed that Chaplin was preparing the publicity campaign for *Limelight* very carefully after the fiasco of *Monsieur Verdoux*. *Limelight* would clearly aim at reconciliation through a return to elements of Chaplin's aesthetic contract and a conscious use of autobiography. It would remain for the reviewers and the public to judge how successful Chaplin's attempt had been.

Critical Response to *Limelight*

How did American reviewers respond to *Limelight*? The critical response reflected in part a new, emerging aesthetic discourse about movies. If the discourse of the depression decade, at least among some reviewers (those we termed "social radical" and "modern liberal"), encouraged filmmakers to make films that were realistic, dealt with socially significant subject matter, and revealed the filmmaker's devotion to progressive politics, the aesthetic discourse emerging in the 1950s was different for at least two significant reasons.

First, the expansion of the Soviet Union and the growing fears about internal subversion in the early Cold War years both helped to break down the intellectual dominance of the progressive paradigm. To critics of narrative art, this meant that judging a book or film by the degree to which it elicited a sympathy for common people or articulated a progressive "message" was a thing of the past.[30] Chaplin himself found this out, with a vengeance, in the response to *Monsieur Verdoux*. Of course, this does not mean that writers influenced by the progressive aesthetic discourse stopped writing or totally shifted their perspectives. The influential Bosley Crowther of the *New York Times*, for example, long maintained his interest in and defense of "socially significant" movies, though he was more circumspect about directly criticizing American society in his reviews of the 1950s than social radical critics like Harry Alan Potamkin had been in the 1930s. Most reviewers were less drawn to social and political analyses of movies in the 1950s than they had been in the 1930s.[31]

Second, as cultural critics in the 1940s and 1950s generally began to worry less about defending progressive art, they began to worry more about the possibly deleterious effect of "mass culture." To many important critics in this period, Richard Pells has noted, "the rise of the media was associated with the decline of a traditional elite that once dominated the arts."[32] Although television and comic books bore the largest brunt of attacks, the movies also garnered their fair share.

In this new context, characterized by a suspicion of mass culture, how were movie reviewers and critics likely to approach films, particularly one by someone as well known and as established as Chaplin? One appealing focus for reviewers and critics was the "great artist" approach, a kind of pre-auteurist auteurism that drew on the Romantic literary tradition. (The auteur approach will be discussed in Chapter 11.) It suggested that a society's greatest artists possessed heightened perceptions and a special ability to explain and comment on society through their works—and in the case of a "mass art" like film, to "rise above" the alleged limitations of the medium. The responsibility of the reviewer of a film by a great artist was to identify what insights and truths the artist was imparting and how a new work fit into the larger body of work that the artist had created throughout his or her career.

Within this context (as well as a hostile political context, discussed in the next section) emerged the reception of *Limelight*. The reviews show first that Chaplin successfully communicated to reviewers the personal dimensions of the film. Whether reviewers liked or disliked it, they noted its autobiographical elements. William Barrett wrote that Chaplin "is the real subject of the movie" (the title of his review is "Chaplin as Chaplin"). To Crowther, *Limelight* was "an extraordinarily personal film." In a fully developed exploration of this dimension, Robert Warshow's *Partisan Review* article claimed that the film was Chaplin's "apology and, so far as he is capable of such a thing, his self-examination." Philip Hartung, less enthused, suggested in *Commonweal* that "the whole picture has the effect of being a kind of Chaplin apologia." *Newsweek* asserted that the film "crackles with comments it is difficult not to regard as autobiographical." In the *New Republic* Eric Bentley observed that "the film is at best a glorious failure about a glorious failure. The name is Calvero; the portrait on his mantelpiece is that of Chaplin, young. Symbolic autobiography: an amazing conception for a movie man." Chaplin clearly succeeded in this aim.[33]

How did the reviewers judge Chaplin's new, more explicitly autobiographical, mode? Barrett's review dwelt most fully on the film as autobiography. He confessed to being perplexed about the film because Chaplin himself remained an enigma. Chaplin portrayed a character who was "almost hypnotic in its fascination," but there remained "something unexpressed and mysterious about it." Barrett was left wondering "how much of the real personality is conveyed and how much held back." Though he did not think it Chaplin's best film and certainly not his funniest, Barrett believed it Chaplin's most powerful film, evoking a feeling that was "due in good part to the fact that here, more than any of his other pictures, Charles Chaplin has come the closest to playing Charles Chaplin." Barrett reaffirmed Chaplin's status as a great, versatile artist: "not since the days when Richard Wagner flourished . . . has such a display of universal genius been attempted."[34]

In *Saturday Review* Arthur Knight was equally absorbed by the autobiographical elements and even more positive about the film. To Knight, *Limelight* was "an artistic testament" in which Chaplin summed up his "fundamental philosophies and attitudes about life, about love, about audiences, about comedy." The experience of hearing such direct expression on film of an artist's philosophy, wrote Knight, was "something unprecedented except for the movie versions of a few Shaw plays and Chaplin's own *Monsieur Verdoux*." As the film develops, it becomes "the voice of a great comedian, a great spirit, giving cinematic shape to his own ripe experience." One could hardly imagine higher praise for the film.[35]

Some of those disappointed with the film noticed that Chaplin included elements of his old aesthetic contract but wished that it had been followed more fully. The *New Yorker* was pleased with the "rewarding flashes of the sort of comedy and pathos that distinguished Mr. Chaplin's work in the past." However, the film as a whole was "furiously loquacious," so much so that "it is sometimes hard to remember he is master of pantomime, able to put more into a shrug than most actors can put into a soliloquy." Hollis Alpert's review in *Saturday Review* also endorsed the "celebrated juxtaposition of comedy and pathos" in *Limelight*, as well as the comic routine with Buster Keaton ("a pure and utter gem"). But the film had too many faults, which showed "Chaplin in his present phase, with less to say than he had before, and with less assurance in the saying of it."[36]

Bentley's somewhat negative review in the *New Republic* is a good one to conclude this discussion, because Bentley himself was writing to some extent from within the progressive paradigm, unusual in

1952. Placing the film in the historical context of a great artist, Bentley compares *Limelight* unfavorably to *Monsieur Verdoux* and *City Lights*: "If *City Lights*, for example, says all that the Chaplin of the early period had to say, *Verdoux* sums up the Chaplin of the later period, the period when he had begun to think and to lose popularity, when his love of women, laughed at in the twenties, had come to be linked, by the logic of the intellectual underworld, with his political leanings." In contrast, *Limelight* "is a return to the bosom of the bourgeoisie," expressed through the bourgeoisie's favorite form: "sentimental domestic drama." Although Bentley agreed that the film might be too talky and pretentious, his review challenged those who longed for Charlie of the good old days. "The most inept thing is to wish he would 'just stick to the Tramp' for this is to forget that an artist must develop." Bentley's review is laced with the pre-auteur auteurism noted above, and he shows how much he respected Chaplin's work by writing that despite his criticism of the film, it was still "better than 999 out of 1000 films."[37]

Overall, these mixed to good reviews—most of which were written after McGranery revoked the reentry permit but before the scheduled (January 1953) nationwide release of *Limelight*—suggest several conclusions about Chaplin's attempted reconciliation. First, a good number of the reviews clearly longed for an earlier Chaplin, for more comedy and more intense pathos, and maybe even for Charlie himself. Second, a surprising number found Chaplin's new autobiographical mode interesting and sometimes even deeply moving. Third, Chaplin the filmmaker fared well when judged by the emerging critical discourse that emphasized the "great artist" approach. Even the negative reviews expressed a strong sense that Chaplin was an important and interesting artist, one who had played a large role in the history of American movies.

Thus, by toning down his progressive politics and trying to reconcile with his audience through autobiography and a return to some of the elements of his aesthetic contract, Chaplin's star image was at least partially sustained by the reviews of *Limelight*. Their focus throughout was on several characteristics of his star image: Chaplin's versatility, his acting skill, his philosophizing mode, and the creativity of comedy and pathos that were so much a part of his films. Given the fact that most of these reviews were written a month or less after Chaplin's reentry permit had been revoked but well before he turned it in, the reaction seems quite positive. However, as we turn from the reviews of *Limelight* to the reaction in the press to Chaplin's banishment, and then to the pressure group boycotts of Chaplin and *Limelight*, another story—the politicization of Chaplin's star image—predominates.

The Press and Banishment

Despite Chaplin's gestures of reconciliation in his actions and in his new film, and despite these relatively good reviews of *Limelight*, the response of the American press to Chaplin's "banishment" was affected by (and exemplified) the popular mood in the United States in the early 1950s. Although HUAC had not directly harassed Hollywood much since the Hollywood Ten contempt citations of October 1947, several events stimulated HUAC to renew its Hollywood investigations in 1951. Between 1947 and 1951 the trial of Alger Hiss, Mao Tsetung's victory in China, the Soviet Union's detonation of an atomic bomb, the arrest of atomic spy Klaus Fuchs in England and of Julius and Ethel Rosenberg in the United States, the passage of the McCarren Act (requiring registration of all members of the Communist party), the outbreak of the Korean War, and above all, the rise of Joseph McCarthy's vigorous brand of anticommunism (beginning with his February 1950 speech in Wheeling) all contributed to an intensified and often xenophobic anti-Communist sentiment in the United States. In the midst of this climate, HUAC, led by a new chairman, John S. Wood of Georgia, resumed its political inquisitions, sending subpoenas in March 1951 to eight film industry radicals, including Larry Parks, Howard da Silva, and Gale Sondergaard. This second wave of HUAC investigations of Hollywood ran intermittently through 1953.[38]

Furthermore, *Limelight* was released after Chaplin's reentry permit was revoked in September 1952. It premiered in New York City on 23 October 1952, then played in other cities beginning in January 1953. Given the heightened anti-Communist feeling in the United States, the renewed association of Hollywood and communism, and the revocation of Chaplin's reentry permit for unspecified reasons related to politics and morality, *Limelight* generated political controversy, despite the fact that Chaplin had not included any suggestion of progressive politics in the film. In fact, Chaplin's star image itself became highly politicized in 1952–1953, more than at any other time in his career, before or after. The reactions to Chaplin's banishment and new film became a kind of litmus test of a writer or group's own ideological leanings and identifications.

The conservative press had a field day with the news of Chaplin's woes. The *Chicago Tribune* not only gave the story front-page coverage but covered the top of the front page with a bold headline, "MOVE TO

28. *Chicago Tribune* headline on 20 September 1952. Copyright
© 1987, Chicago Tribune Company, all rights reserved,
used with permission.

BAN CHAPLIN IN U.S.," as in its handling of several stories in the Barry case (see Figure 28). The accompanying article recounted the details of the attorney general's actions, then slanted the story against Chaplin. It wrote that he had "scorned citizenship in this country" even though he had "amassed millions" in it; that he had been denounced in Congress as "left wing and radical"; that he supported "Communist-organized" peace conferences; that he had been declared father of Joan Barry's illegitimate child (but not that blood tests had proven he could not have been); and that he had once settled out of court after being accused of plagiarism. The front-page story leaves the reader no doubt about the *Tribune*'s attitude toward Chaplin: how could one feel about a dishonest, scheming, scornful, lewd radical?[39]

Westbrook Pegler, who had targeted Chaplin as a distasteful radical back in the second front days, went after the comedian again, even before hearing the news of McGranery's actions, upon learning that Chaplin was going abroad. His September 19 column was subtitled: "He Doesn't Care If Chaplin Never Comes Back." The crux of the column was contained in one sentence: "He has lived among us and imposed upon us by flouting our ideals and degrading our morals and standards in entertainment for almost half a century." To Pegler,

Chaplin was "never more than a custard-pie comedian." The following Sunday, he lauded McGranery's decision, calling it "the first honest show of initiative against the Red Front of Hollywood by the Department of Justice." Terming Chaplin a "filthy character who is a menace to young girls," Pegler helped to stir up public opinion against the departed star.[40]

Hedda Hopper, Chaplin's conservative gossip columnist nemesis, wasted no time in passing on the news. She headlined her "Looking at Hollywood" column in the same issue, "Screen Folk, Big and Little, Hail Action Against Chaplin." The opening sentence read, "There are hundreds of people in Hollywood, perhaps thousands—stars, directors, producers, and all those wonderful people we call little people, workers behind the camera, electricians, cameramen, props—who are dancing in the street for joy over Attorney General McGranery's statement that before Charlie Chaplin can return to the United States he will have to pass the board of immigration." The attack continued. Chaplin may be a good actor, "but that doesn't give him the right to go against our customs, to abhor everything we stand for, to throw our hospitality back in our faces." Forgetting Chaplin's Liberty Loan tour and discounting his second front speeches, Hopper stated: "he did nothing for either World War I or World War II." Then she closed: "I've known him for many years. I abhor what he stands for, while I admire his talents as an actor. I would like to say, 'Good riddance to bad company.' " This vituperative attack, playing on the era's anti-Communist phobias, was one of the worst press lashings Chaplin ever received. Given the fact that Hopper mentioned she'd had a "very close check" on his reentry permit situation "for months" and that the column appeared the same day as the news of the revocation, it is likely that Hopper was again being fed government information that she could use to discredit Chaplin.[41]

Hollywood's other major gossip columnist, Louella Parsons, who was less conservative politically, also publicized Chaplin's departure. Beginning on September 22, she syndicated a five-part series on the story of Chaplin's problems with the attorney general.[42] On one hand, since she had long been known as a friend of Chaplin's, having first met him when he worked briefly in Chicago at the start of his Essanay contract, one might have expected her to defend him. On the other hand, the prevailing political atmosphere (and the fact that her employer was the Hearst newspaper chain) put pressure on her to criticize Chaplin.

The articles are an important contribution to the star image of Chaplin as it solidified in 1952. They essentially paint him as a "charming, gracious" man who lost his way sometime in the 1940s. Although much of what appeared in the second, third, and fourth installments was positive regarding Chaplin, Parsons also criticized him, particularly in the fifth installment. Attacking Chaplin for his "smug statement" about being a citizen of the world, she also attributed his political views to his obstinacy and his feeling that he was a "law unto himself." She criticized him for the Simonov incident (in which he made his "American gestapo" statement), his affiliations with second front and peace organizations, and the alleged pro-Soviet inscriptions on the back of pictures he had given to the children of Maxim Litvinov, Soviet ambassador to the United States. To Parsons, Chaplin showed "nothing less than insolence" when he announced his work on *Limelight* about the time he also lent his name as a sponsor of the World Peace Congress. She also told of her final meeting with Chaplin, a cold visit to the set of *Limelight*. Of the film itself, Parsons wrote that she was "bitterly disappointed," for it had "too little comedy and I wasn't moved once." Parsons ultimately refused to defend Chaplin, saying for example that she had often urged him to become a citizen but that his "innate stubbornness" kept him from doing so.

Parsons concluded by portraying a king fallen due to his own hubris: "How very, very sad that the fantastic success story of Charles Spencer Chaplin is destined to end on such a tragic note." The series shows that Parsons was far more generous to Chaplin than Hopper. Nevertheless, it also enabled Parsons to establish a political distance from Chaplin while at the same time presenting a rise and fall morality tale, satisfying to audiences because they were not implicated in their hero's demise: he had brought his fate on himself.

If conservatives pictured Chaplin as an arrogant or stubborn comedian who showed nothing but ingratitude and scorn for the country in which he had become a wealthy and famous man, the progressive Left—what little remained of it—portrayed the banished Chaplin as a humane victim of American repression. This is best exemplified by the treatment of Chaplin's banishment in the *Daily Worker*. It first mentioned Chaplin's dilemma on September 22, and quoted from the *London Observer*'s editorial defense of Chaplin. The article's headline: "Britons Back Chaplin, Attack 'Smears' in U.S." The next day the *Worker* gave a sympathetic account of Chaplin's press conference upon arriving at Cherbourg, and on September 24 it began a three-part series on Chaplin and the reasons for his problems by David Platt. Collectively, these three articles give us a precise picture of the *Worker*'s understanding of Cold War politics, and of how its image of Chaplin could be used to further its own ideological ends, just as the conservative press had used another image of Chaplin for its purposes.[43]

The first, "Why Gov't Wants to Bar Charles Chaplin," opened by implicitly calling the U.S. position "fascist": whereas Hitler and Mussolini banned Chaplin's films, "Truman and McGranery have gone one step further. They want to ban Chaplin." The government action, wrote Platt, "climaxes a witchhunt by cultural illiterates against leading figures in the arts, sciences and professions, such as the world has not seen since the dark days of fascist dictatorships." The rest of the article recounted Chaplin's "persecution" in the United States, and was not above distortion, hyperbole, or even outright lying to make its case. It claimed that the press ganged up on him for his social satire in *The Immigrant*, though no such evidence has ever been turned up. It asserted with no specifics that "a year or two later Chaplin joined the ranks of artists and professionals who hailed the world-shaking Russian Revolution," a strained interpretation of Chaplin's 1921 comment to reporters that he had to be interested in Bolshevism, since it was a part of life and artists must be interested in life. It concluded that "the attempt to ban Chaplin is clearly a step toward depriving the American people of a vital segment of democratic culture."

The next two articles followed in the same vein. The first, "Chaplin's Films are Directed against Humbug and Injustice," accounted for Chaplin's popularity by noting his films "are on the side of the underdog and are directed against humbug, snobbery, social injustice," while also revealing "poverty and hunger in the midst of plenty." It also distorted, this time by misquoting Chaplin's 1918 comment on comedy, substituting "bloated capitalist" where Chaplin used "rich."[44] The final article, "Chaplin's *The Great Dictator* Appealed for Peace and Human Decency," argued that this film had been criticized because Chaplin was an advocate of peace in a country that wished war. To Platt, "behind the gang-up on Chaplin and *The Great Dictator* was a resentment that the film could not be used for war propaganda," which was abominable, for the film, "because of its suberb art and solid core of truth, is one of the few American films whose importance grows with the years." Grounding the Chaplin dilemma in the present, Platt concluded: "That its maker is now being barred from the U.S., which has been his home for more than 40 years, because of his antifascist convictions, shows how badly conditions have deteriorated in our country since the defeat of the fascist dictators so ably satirized in Chaplin's great film." The *Worker* thus used Chaplin's image to convey its view that Cold War America was war-mongering, undemocratic, and cruel to its greatest artists and that Chaplin was among its foremost progressive victims.

Ultimately, except for the Communist press, Chaplin had few outright defenders, even among liberals. Chaplin's case was the subject of a large number of newspaper articles and magazine "think pieces" in the liberal press, but nearly everyone who wrote anything sympathetic about him was very careful to criticize or at least keep a distance from his political beliefs, thus, like Parsons, protecting him or herself against the charge of being a Communist sympathizer.

The first and perhaps the least qualified defense of Chaplin appeared in the *New York Times*. Its editorial, "Is 'Charlot' a Menace?" appeared just two days after McGranery's action was announced.[45] After noting Chaplin's achievements and worldwide popularity, as well as the irony that he became wealthy by entertaining the common man and "puncturing the pretensions of the proud," the editorial judged that "those who have followed him through the years cannot easily regard him as a dangerous person." Although it granted that it possibly "will be shown that he has in some way been connected with or deceived by what have been described as Communist fronts," the *Times* stated that "unless there is far more evidence against him than is at the moment visible, the Department of State will not dignify itself or increase the national security if it sends him into exile."

The following Sunday Chaplin made the *Times* in three parts of the paper. The first was Crowther's defense, "Under Suspicion." Noting that Chaplin had been "perennial victim of gossip mongers and howlers of hate," Crowther wrote that "it is hard to imagine anybody less deserving of being an enemy of this country than this famous and accomplished man." The second reference was an article about how the INS would proceed if Chaplin came back to face his charges. The third was a cartoon called "The Old Routine," first published in the *Omaha World-Herald*, which showed Charlie slipping on two banana peels labeled "Left-wing Activity" and "Morals Charge," landing on his backside on a sidewalk labeled "Immigration Inquiry." Although the attitude of the cartoonist toward his subject is ambiguous, the cartoon certainly perpetuated the habit of blending the creator and his creation—an integral element of Chaplin's star image—and of associating left-wing politics with both.[46]

In the *New York Herald Tribune*, columnist Dorothy Thompson also came to Chaplin's defense, albeit in a somewhat strange way. She decided to play along with the anti-Communists and praise Chaplin for being one himself. Chaplin's central theme, Thompson argued, was "the tragic-comic fate of man, lonely against the organized mass."

Whereas communism exalted "the mass against the individual," Charlie was "the eternal nonconformist. . . . the champion not only of our rights, but of our human, individual follies." In Thompson's view, exiling Chaplin from the United States would simply aid the Communists: they would get fodder for anti-American propaganda, while the United States would lose an artist who was one of the "most effective anti-Communists alive." This conclusion may have puzzled a lot of readers, but Thompson's fear that the Chaplin affair would have international repercussions was borne out by subsequent events.[47]

Time gave the matter attention as the lead and longest story in the "People" section of its September 29 issue.[48] It reported on McGranery's action, then speculated about the grounds on which Chaplin would be charged. He had, said *Time*, "been cited as a sponsor for some Communist-front groups," and the Barry case could "leave him open to a charge of 'moral turpitude.' " Following these speculations, *Time* contrasted a defense of Chaplin from the London *Observer* to Hopper's "good riddance" attack, cited above. The brief account left one feeling that there may well have been good reasons to keep Chaplin out of the country.

Irving Kristol's "McGranery and Charlie Chaplin" was a typical antiStalinist liberal response to the charges against Chaplin. Appearing in *Commentary*, which Kristol edited, the essay criticized Chaplin's behavior and praised his art: "It is true that Mr. Chaplin, as an alien, is a guest in this country and that he has shown himself to be both rude and ungrateful. On the other hand, it is worth remembering that, alien though he be, Mr. Chaplin is one of the glories of *American* culture." Liberals in the early 1950s often seemed more worried about the American image abroad than almost anything else, and Kristol, writing that "according to one observer who has just returned from Europe, . . . Mr. McGranery managed with one stroke to erase a year's work by the Voice of America," was no exception. Though criticizing defenses of Chaplin in the European press as having "a sunny air about them," Kristol hoped that with a new attorney general taking office (Eisenhower had just won the presidential election, with Nixon as his running mate), the damage to the American reputation could be minimized. Instead of attacking the government's action as thought control and political repression, as a leftist in the late 1930s would likely have done, here an anti-Stalinist liberal wrung his hands about the U.S. reputation overseas and ignored the fact that Chaplin's reputation was being besmirched and his livelihood threatened for political reasons.[49]

The *Nation*, another liberal journal, also worried about the negative

AMERICAN WAY-OF-LIFE

29. Cartoon from the *Nation* (1952), which first appeared
in the *London Daily Herald*, bemoans the propaganda value
to the Soviet Union of the Chaplin banishment.

publicity the case would generate for the United States. In October it
suggested that "by threatening to bar Charlie Chaplin from coming
back to the United States the Department of Justice has gone several
leagues out of its way to invite ridicule and contempt of sensible people." The editors of the *Nation* warned that Chaplin might make
McGranery and his aides look "like a pack of fools," much as Charlie
had make the Kaiser look in *Shoulder Arms*.[50]

The negative foreign publicity that several commentators predicted
did occur: the banishment generated considerable anti-American publicity abroad. A cartoon in the *London Daily Herald*, later reprinted in
the *Nation*, suggests the international implications of Chaplin's woes
(see Figure 29).[51] By depicting a rotund, smiling Soviet cameraman in
the lower right corner, the cartoon suggests that the Soviets were happily recording the spectacle for their own purposes.

One final, rather quirky, article responding to Chaplin's banishment, William Bradford Huie's "Mr. Chaplin and the Fifth Freedom,"
appeared in the *American Mercury*.[52] Asserting that "our only real enemy is any form of tyranny over the human mind," Huie defended
Chaplin's freedom of speech and freedom of expression and criticized
the government for its action. But his defense was qualified. The article was subtitled "The Sovereign Right to Be a Fool," and a fool is
what Huie believed Chaplin to be: "a genuine twenty-four-carat, ring-
tailed stinker." The article distorts or misstates Chaplin's positions on

such subjects as citizenship, patriotism, lechery, and communism, but concludes that if all McGranery "can prove is that [Chaplin] is a stinker, they are only repeating what has been common knowledge for thirty years, and they should leave the man and his family alone." Such a "defense" was unlikely to do Chaplin's public image much good, but Chaplin could take solace in the fact that the *Mercury*'s circulation was small.

One could sum up the press's initial treatment of Chaplin's banishment by reiterating that though Chaplin's star image had become a pawn in the ideological chess game of Cold War America, it was not an even match. The Left, because the rift between liberals and progressives was widening as the Cold War intensified, was split. Liberals, unwilling to play whole-heartedly, for the most part sat out and left the game to the few remaining radicals. Those radicals, however, held far fewer pieces than the Right, and, as we shall see, the Right easily captured Chaplin's star image—at least for a time.

The *Limelight* Boycott and Chaplin's Star Image

If Chaplin's star image was somewhat harmed by the conservative press in 1952–1953, much more damaging to it and to the box-office fortunes of *Limelight* were the boycott efforts of conservative voluntary organizations that began in October 1952. Although national political figures like McCarthy and Nixon played a considerable role in generating anti-Communist feeling in America in the late 1940s and early 1950s, they were not alone. As one historian of American anticommunism in the postwar decade has argued, "Voluntary organizations played a crucial role in the development of the Red Scare. They responded to the Scare . . . by attempting to limit Communist expression in the general society."[53] Of these organizations, none was as damaging to Chaplin's public reputation as the American Legion.

The Legion, numbering 2.5 million members and another million auxiliary members, was the most influential anti-Communist pressure group to affect the movie industry in the early 1950s. Its interest in exposing Communist influence in Hollywood dated back at least to May 1949, when *American Legion Magazine* published an article, "How Communists Make Stooges out of Movie Stars," but its activity became more organized when its 1951 national convention called for the establishment of a "public information program" on the subject.[54]

Chaplin became the focus of the Legion's wrath during its next convention, held in early October 1952.[55] There a resolution was passed on October 12 urging theater owners not to show any Chaplin films (and Legion members not to attend Chaplin films if they were shown) until the matter of Chaplin's political and moral fitness to return to the country was cleared up. After the convention adjourned, it remained for local chapters to decide what actions to take if a Chaplin film were scheduled to be shown.[56]

United Artists officials were worried. According to James F. O'Neil, director of publications for the Legion, two United Artists executives, Arthur Krim and Robert Benjamin, visited him in his office on October 20 concerning the Legion's anti-Chaplin resolution. They told him that they were "stuck" with *Limelight* (Chaplin being a principal stockholder in the company) and had to seek distribution for the film. O'Neil nonetheless promised to take action against *Limelight* and even threatened to take action against United Artists itself.[57]

One of the first steps taken by the Legion thereafter was an article—Victor Lasky's "Whose Little Man?"—that appeared in the December issue of *American Legion Magazine*. Its vicious portrayal of Chaplin probably did much to fuel Legion zealotry in the boycott. The six pages included an opening photograph of Chaplin fingering a half-filled champagne glass. Admitting that Chaplin had become a universally popular figure, Lasky also pointed out that he had made an "inordinate" number of enemies, primarily because of Chaplin's "extreme megalomania, his total lack of interest in anything except himself—and his art." Besides displaying a "studied disinterest in personal ethics," wrote Lasky, Chaplin "added one especially unfortunate ingredient; he became a fellow-traveler of communism." He probably never became a party member, continued Lasky, for "it would be difficult even to imagine this supreme egotist submitting to the de-personalized, rigid discipline which Party members are forced to accept."[58]

The essay's contents suggest that Lasky had access to FBI files. He may have obtained them from the Bureau itself or perhaps had seen reports in the hands of gossip columnists Hopper and Muir, who are both prominently mentioned in the article. The topics covered in the article also frequently appeared in Bureau files: "pro-Soviet" second front speeches; failure to entertain at USO events; the Simonov incident; friendship with and defense of Hanns Eisler; support of Wallace's presidential campaign; defense of Gerhart Eisler, Josephson, and Dennis; support of various Peace Congresses; and Rushmore's "sacred cow" allegation. The article also included a wide variety of allegations relating to the Barry trials. A strong case was created against

Chaplin by playing on the anti-Communist assumptions of the day and neglecting information (such as Chaplin's Liberty Loan tour during World War I) that would give a more complex and rounded picture of Chaplin. The article was a catalyst for and harbinger of widespread anti-Chaplin activity by individual Legion posts.

This local pressure was most pronounced in January and February 1953, and then into the spring, when *Limelight* was being scheduled for a more general nationwide release. The first bombshell came on January 15, when Fox West Coast Theaters, the largest West Coast chain of theaters, announced its cancellation of a January 21 opening of *Limelight*. President Charles Skouras made the decision after Ward Bond and Roy Brewer, two members of the Motion Picture Alliance for the Preservation of American Ideals (a Hollywood anti-Communist group that opposed the Hollywood Ten), discussed the American Legion's resolution with Skouras.[59] Two days later it was announced that Loew's, which normally distributed United Artists films, had not chosen to do so with *Limelight*, partly as a result of Legion pressure, and RKO picked it up.

Shortly thereafter, the Legion found a powerful supporter in Howard Hughes, then principal stockholder of RKO Theaters Corporation and board chairman of RKO Pictures. Hughes wrote the Hollywood Legion Post no. 43 in late January that although he had no legal control over the theater operations, he would urge the management to "take the necessary legal measures to cancel all bookings of *Limelight*."[60] This industry pressure on distributors and large theater chains set the stage for more local efforts on the part of the Legion and allied groups like the Veterans of Foreign Wars and the Catholic War Veterans.

Protests began springing up around the country and often had a significant effect on the distribution of the film. For example, in the first half of February, the Ritz Theater in Newburgh, New York, canceled a scheduled run of the film after an American Legion protest, the World Theater in Philadelphia withdrew the film four weeks before the end of its run because of Legion protests, and fifteen Legionnaires picketed two RKO theaters in the Bronx (at the Marble Hill and Fordham theaters). At the time of the Bronx picketing, *Limelight* had just begun a week-long run at sixty-seven New York City area theaters, but it was withdrawn after only three days at most of them. *Variety* reported on February 4 that Legion officials in Washington, D.C., had announced boycotts of *Limelight* when it opened at the Little and Plaza Theaters and had released a statement criticizing "Chaplin's long record of association with Communist Fronts and causes, and his openly expressed contempt for the United States." The film was also withdrawn in Columbus, Ohio, and New Orleans. One contemporary journalist writing on the boycotts contended that normally a Chaplin film would have played at about 2,500 theaters by the end of February but as of February 15 it had only played at about 150. After examining how broadly and systematically the Legion protested and picketed against *Limelight* because of questions raised about its maker, one begins to understand Chaplin's statement to the London press after he turned in his reentry permit that he had been the victim of "reactionary" forces.[61]

Given the positive and mixed national reviews of *Limelight*, there is little doubt that the boycott had a considerable effect on the box-office fortunes of *Limelight*. This is particularly evident when one looks at how the film did in its fall 1952 New York City run—before the Legion's boycott activities were organized. These initial box-office figures from *Variety* suggested that *Limelight* would make a lot of money. In their review of the film two weeks before the New York opening, *Variety* had predicted that despite the length, "It's all Chaplin and deserving of stout b.o." *Limelight* then opened at the Astor and Trans-Lux 60th theaters in Manhattan and did strong business the first week ("Sock 45½G at 2 Locations," according to the *Variety* headline). The run continued through October and November, and the film brought in around $35,000 per week for at least three more weeks. Though receipts sagged in early December, they bounced back to nearly $50,000 the week of Christmas. Ultimately, *Limelight*, perhaps buoyed by some good reviews, ran twelve weeks in its initial run and did extremely well given the political and social climate.[62]

After Legion pressure began to be applied in January and February 1953, however, the door slammed shut. Although *Limelight* did manage to get some bookings in cities like Toronto, Seattle, and Chicago, the overall performance was extremely disappointing for Chaplin and United Artists. After ranking a lowly eleventh in *Variety's* box-office receipts for January—and never higher than eighth for any individual week—the film did not even make the top twelve in February, when the nationwide release occurred and the highest grosses were expected. The disappointing February performance in the New York City neighborhood theaters, where the film was withdrawn from most after three days, led *Variety* to predict that *Limelight's* total take for distributors would be no higher than a million dollars. Considering the fact that the film made some $5 million worldwide, its U. S. box-office performance, influenced by the Legion's campaign, was very weak.

Relatively few viewers were even given the opportunity to see Chaplin's gesture of reconciliation.[63]

These pressure tactics did not go unnoticed in the press. Some liberal publications evinced a sympathy that had been evident in some of the reviews of *Limelight*. This sympathy can be best understood by placing it in a broader context of opposition to the tactics of HUAC and McCarthy. In the early 1950s a minority opposition did exist, however quiet or aberrant it might have been considered at the time. When many intellectuals were celebrating America for its democracy and freedom and tolerating or even embracing McCarthyism, some refused to go along with the tide. In the words of Richard Pells, intellectuals like Dwight Macdonald, Henry Steele Commager, Lillian Hellman, Arthur Miller, Mary McCarthy, and I. F. Stone "resisted not simply the tactics of but the rationale for McCarthyism"—sometimes by publicly denouncing the rationale in print, sometimes by refusing to name names before HUAC.[64]

Though none of these figures spoke out concerning the Legion's actions against *Limelight*, its tactics did raise the anticensorship hackles of other writers and journalists. These defenses of Chaplin reflected different degrees of dissent, but together they formed a nucleus of sympathy that later helped to regenerate Chaplin's star image in the 1960s and 1970s. For example, *Commonweal* quoted Justice Learned Hand: "I believe that that community is already in process of dissolution where each man begins to eye his neighbor as a possible enemy, where non-conformity with the accepted creed, political as well as religious, is a mark of disaffection." Even though *Commonweal* covered itself by admitting that Chaplin had "no doubt" said "some things which are, perhaps deservedly, unpopular in the country" and that his conduct "has shocked many people," it did take the Legion to task in an era when such a challenge made one vulnerable to harsh criticism. Even more unusual than these defenses was the position taken by a veteran's organization. On February 7 the *Times* published a letter from Bernard Storder, chairman of the Motion Picture Section of the American Veterans Committee. It read in part: "As citizens and as veterans we condemn this latest attempt at thought control by the Legion as a gross violation of the basic democratic principle of the freedom of the arts from interference by pressure groups." To counter the Legion pressure, his group urged *Times* readers to request that theater owners show the film. The position of the AVC, however, was the exception among veterans' groups rather than the rule; most were sympathetic to the Legion campaign.[65]

Chaplin's decision to turn in his reentry permit was the last phase of the 1952–1953 controversy and returned editors and journalists, on the right and left, to their typewriters. The *New York Times*, which had defended Chaplin since the day after the revocation of his reentry permit, was a little harder on the comedian in its editorial, "Mr. Chaplin Bows Out." Reminding its readers of its earlier support of Chaplin, the *Times* stated that "Chaplin's evident unwillingness to return deprives him of the opportunity to fight the charges against him . . . and, unfortunately, will give great encouragement to those who believe in the 'purge' technique for American artistic and cultural life." As in *Commonweal*'s attack on the Legion tactics, the *Times* editors also distanced themselves from Chaplin, writing that "we hold no brief for Mr. Chaplin's private life or public views" and coming close to implying that he might have had trouble with the immigration officials had he chosen to return.[66]

The conservatives also commented. Representative is Robert Ruark's syndicated column, entitled "Chaplin's Worst Sin," which appeared after Chaplin's decision. The "worst sin" was failing to become a citizen of the United States after residing so long in the country. Had Chaplin done so, Ruark believed, he would have been spared many of his problems, and surely the reentry issue would have disappeared or at least have been framed in different terms. Yet Ruark's distaste for Chaplin is clear; referring to the Barry case, Ruark called him "a bounder of the worst sort" and "a little blighter." Of Chaplin's refusal to face an INS hearing Ruark judged that "tacitly he must stand as convicted" of the Communist charges. The conclusion belittled the artist who had been a public figure, and often a public idol, for many of the almost forty years he had lived in the country: "I think the loss is small, any way you figure it. And that no great injustice has been done anybody."[67]

Such small-minded commentary is perhaps a fitting way to conclude this look at the state of Chaplin's star image as he decided to settle abroad. In the midst of the charges and countercharges, the attacks and the defenses, one quality came to dominate Chaplin's star image: the progressive political activism. Chaplin's alleged moral turpitude played a minor role. Except for a few reviews, Chaplin the great filmmaker and actor was neglected, and Charlie was forgotten. The star image was out of Chaplin's hands. Despite his gestures of reconciliation in the early 1950s—both his relative temperance in political matters and his appeals in *Limelight*—American culture rejected him. Although the liberal community did some ineffectual hand-wringing, organized pressure-group activity on the right, particularly by the American Legion, made it certain that Chaplin—the man whom Shaw had called the only genius the movies had produced, and the man who had created the mythic persona so profoundly central to the movies— would receive no hearing. Since the Left was declining and in disarray, radical support of Chaplin had little influence on the cultural debate— and what effect it had was negative. By the early 1950s, the Right was in the saddle in the United States, and Chaplin, both the real human being and the star image that surrounded his name, became one of its victims.

FIVE

**The Exile and
America**

11

The Exiled Monarch and the Guarded
Restoration, 1953–1977

Running Battles: Chaplin, American Culture,
and the Later 1950s

Between 1953 and his death in 1977, Chaplin lived outside the United
States, and his star image affected American culture considerably less
than it had during the years he lived and worked in the country. However, during that period his star image also recovered from its nadir
in the late 1940s and early 1950s until, by the early 1970s, it enjoyed
a guarded restoration. Chaplin's star image evolved from one associated with the qualities of "dangerous radical" and "womanizer" to one
much more positive, which emphasized Chaplin the virtuoso filmmaker and aging family patriarch, as well as, once again, the adorable
Charlie. Some of the reasons for the change include an evolving political climate in the United States, shifts in the "aesthetic discourse"
about movies (in particular, the dominance of auteurism), and Chaplin's careful management of both his star image and his business interests through rereleases, the publication of his autobiography, and his
1972 return visit to the United States.

This change did not, however, happen overnight. In Chaplin's first
years away from the United States he did little to endear himself with
the American press and public, and the press particularly played its
part in perpetuating his reputation as a misguided radical. One of
Chaplin's first public statements after he turned in his reentry permit
set the hostile tone for relations between Chaplin and the press
through much of the 1950s. In April 1953, Chaplin visited London
and issued a press release. This scathing statement, quoted in *Newsweek* a week later, enabled Chaplin to vent the frustrations that he had
been harboring at least since the days of *Monsieur Verdoux*:

> It is not easy to uproot myself and my family from a country
> where I have lived for 40 years without a feeling of sadness. But
> since the end of the last war, I have been the object of vicious
> propaganda by powerful reactionary groups who by their influ-
> ence and by the aid of America's yellow press have created an

unhealthy atmosphere in which liberal-minded individuals can be singled out and persecuted. I have therefore given up my residence in the United States.[1]

As the American Legion boycott activities and the response of the conservative press to Chaplin and his exile demonstrated, Chaplin's allegations contained large doses of truth, however inflammatory his rhetoric. Yet to most Americans, increasingly self-satisfied about the essential goodness of their institutions as the 1950s wore on—and, as a legacy of the McCarthy era, becoming intolerant of views that offered criticism of those institutions—Chaplin's comments simply supported the widely shared image of Chaplin the radical.

Neither Chaplin nor the American press seemed much concerned about mending the rift in the next several years. Chaplin himself was involved in three publicized events that hurt his reputation in America. The first was the announcement in May 1954 that Chaplin and Dmitri Shostakovich were the winners of the Soviet-sponsored World Peace Council award. The other two were meetings with Communist officials: with Chinese prime minister Chou En-lai in Geneva in 1954 and with the Soviet leaders Nikita Khrushchev and Nikolai Bulganin in London in 1956.

In each of these situations, Chaplin affirmed his commitment to world peace, a position that conservatives and anti-Stalinist liberals in the United States considered naive and dangerously left-wing. When Chaplin accepted the $14,000 peace prize in June (he later donated it to several charities), for example, he told reporters, "To promulgate a demand for peace, whether from East or West, I firmly believe is a step in the right direction."[2] In his autobiography Chaplin remembers drinking "many toasts" with Chou En-lai during their 1954 dinner. In one of them, he recalled, "I toasted the future of China and said that although I was not a Communist I wholeheartedly joined in their hope and desire for a better life for the Chinese people, and for all people" (MA, pp. 485–89). The meeting with the Soviet officials came when Chaplin received an invitation to the Soviet embassy following a goodwill address Khrushchev made in London. Chaplin recalls complimenting Khrushchev on the speech: "It had come like a ray of sunshine, and I told him so, saying that it had given hope for peace to millions throughout the world" (MA, p. 482).[3]

The American press reaction to Chaplin's continued commitment to progressive causes was mostly critical. Responding to the peace prize, the *New York Times*, which had in general defended Chaplin through his career, editorialized unequivocally against him. Titled

"Little Man, Farewell," the editorial claimed that if Chaplin "knew more about Russia, or if he were perhaps less bitter, he would be well aware that the 'peace prize' is not a peace prize at all but a prize offered to those in Russia or outside of Russia who serve the purposes of a brutal and tyrannical imperialism." Chaplin should know, the *Times* wrote, that his little tramp "could not survive and prosper in today's Russia." By accepting the prize, Chaplin "has allowed himself to be used by a sinister conspiracy of which the little man he so touchingly represented is the victim. . . . He shuffles off leftward, toward Moscow, perhaps not calling himself a Communist or a fellow traveler—but there he goes and the sag of his back, the flap of his coattails, the set of his little derby over the ears and the sadly reminiscent twirling of his cane move us almost to tears."[4] The editorial's only positive comment related to Chaplin's early films. As so often happened after *The Great Dictator* and especially after *Monsieur Verdoux*, Chaplin the aspiring social commentator was negatively compared to Charlie the silent film comic. Thus a contradiction grew up in the Chaplin star image: though dominated by the present Chaplin—an arrogant radical sympathizer—the star image also included the faded image of funny little Charlie. This subordinate dimension provided a seed for Chaplin's renaissance in the 1960s and 1970s. But in the mid-1950s Chaplin the Red dominated.

In September 1954, the *Saturday Evening Post*, the conservative family-oriented magazine with a huge circulation, lambasted Chaplin in an editorial titled "Double Play: Chaplin to Robeson to Malenkov."[5] Its opening charge is a strong one, claiming that Chaplin was "doing all he can to make the world weep bitterly and worry its head off. After living in the United States forty years, Chaplin has openly joined our enemy, the Soviet slave masters." The basis for this charge was first, that he had "dined at Geneva with Chou-en-Lai, Red gauleiter in China"; second, that he had accepted a prize from the World "Peace" Council [their quotation marks], the "foremost Soviet front in the world"; and third, that he had sent a telegram to a "Culture Salute to Paul Robeson" held in New York City. To cap its argument, the *Post* quoted the Kremlin's public praise for Chaplin after he received the peace prize: "He came into our camp as simply and naturally as a tributary falls into a river, as a river falls into the ocean." The editorial makes use of the guilt by association tactics that victimized Chaplin in the late 1940s: if the Soviets like something, the logic went, it must be bad. The editorial also demonstrates the degree to which Chaplin's image was still at the mercy of Cold War politics.

Partly because of this continued press hostility, Chaplin and his films continued to be the occasional targets of pressure groups. Early in 1955 Muhlenberg College scheduled four Chaplin films to play in its "Films of Yesterday" series. When the American Legion protested, however, the college quickly buckled under the pressure and the four films were canceled.[6]

The anti-Stalinist liberal intelligentsia, however, despite its disapproval of Chaplin's progressive politics, was beginning to make itself heard after McCarthy and his tactics fell from favor. The day after the ban on the Chaplin films was announced, the American Committee for Cultural Freedom, an organization of prominent American intellectuals formed in 1951, attacked the Legion's tactics and the college's action. Within a week the college had reversed its position and decided to go ahead with the films.[7] The Legion was blocked. Though it is evident that the Legion's activities against Chaplin were not nearly so prominent in the late 1950s as they had been during the *Limelight* release, it still was able to bring some influence to bear. In fact, as we shall see, Chaplin believed that the sentiment against him in America was so powerful that he did not even attempt to release any of the films he controlled (the First National and United Artists films) until 1963.

The years from 1953 to 1957 were thus generally years of tension in the relationship between Chaplin and American culture. For most of that period, Chaplin was either contemplating or actively working on a film that would allude to the treatment he received in the United States in 1952 and earlier. Although that film, *A King in New York*, did not play in the United States in its initial run, the American press coverage of the French and British openings of the film in 1957 also contributed, generally in a negative way, to Chaplin's star image.

After beginning to script the film in the middle of 1953, Chaplin shot the film in London between May and July 1956, edited and scored it in Paris, and released it in 1957.[8] The film's narrative focuses on King Igor Shahdov (Chaplin) who, after being dethroned during a revolution in his country of Estrovia, travels to New York City with his valet, Jaume, carrying blueprints for a project that could harness atomic energy for peaceful ends. After a night on the town, he learns that his untrustworthy prime minister has stolen his securities, which leaves him in a financially precarious position. This leads him to accept invitations from New York socialites and to endorse various consumer products for money. On a visit to a progressive school, King Shahdov debates, then later befriends, a prodigy, Rupert Macabee (played by Chaplin's son, Michael), whose parents are Communists in conflict with the HUAC. When the press gets wind of the association between

Rupert and Shahdov, the former king also comes under the suspicion of HUAC and is subpoenaed to testify. En route to the hearing, Shahdov's finger is caught in a water hose. Bringing it along with him to the HUAC chambers, he gets his finger out only when water pressure builds, after which the hose showers the entire committee. Though he clears himself of any Communist associations, Shahdov decides, after a final visit to Rupert—who is devastated after having "named names" to secure his parents' release from prison—to return to Europe.

As in *Limelight*, Chaplin encouraged an autobiographical reading of *A King in New York* by playing a character far different from Charlie and similar in a number of ways to Chaplin himself. Like Chaplin, King Shahdov has to flee his country of residence and become an exile. Like Chaplin during the Barry trials, the king is surrounded by the press when he is fingerprinted upon his arrival in the United States. Like Chaplin, he is an idealist interested in promoting the cause of world peace. Like Chaplin, he is subpoenaed to testify before HUAC because of his associations with alleged Communists. Like Chaplin (in the comedian's earlier years, at least), he shows considerable interest in young women. The former king of American film comedy and the exiled king had much in common.[9]

If these autobiographical associations were unlikely to endear the film to American critics, neither did its cultural critique of the United States find favor. Although detailed analysis of its social criticism is not necessary here, the film satirized at least four aspects of American society: popular culture, progressive education, advertising, and the behavior of the press. Even though much of the film's social critique is based on a rather traditional perspective—the satirical jibes at rock music, wide-screen movies, and "creativity" in progressive schools, for example—American society in the mid-1950s was not receptive to criticism from abroad.[10] Chaplin guessed as much, for he chose not to release the film widely in the United States until 1973, a year after he returned to be honored in New York City and Los Angeles.[11]

Even without showing the film in the United States, Chaplin managed to generate negative commentary. The titles of articles reporting on the British response give an indication of the American press's hostility to Chaplin. Four reports from large circulation U.S. newspapers and magazines, all of which appeared within two weeks of the film's London press screening, are representative: "Critics Are Cool to Chaplin Film," "Unfunny Charlie Chaplin," "Critics Find Chaplin's Anti-U.S. Movie a Flop," and "The Unfunny Comic."[12] A number of these early reports wrote that the foreign, particularly British, press disliked the film. For example, the *New York Times*, which subtitled its essay, "Fails to Impress London Writers," quoted three negative reviews from British newspapers and charged that Chaplin used the film "to ridicule many aspects of American life." *Time* reported that the film "impressed most critics as being less a labor of love than one of hate." The *Nation* held that "critical response has been almost unanimous in its disappointment." In the *New York Herald Tribune* Art Buchwald wrote a column from Paris on a screening he had of the film with a French journalist and a potential U.S. independent distributor. In addition to quoting a negative review from the *London Daily Express*, Buchwald reported that the French journalist laughed just three times, that the exhibitor said only, "it stinks," and that all three left the screening room "sadly deflated."[13]

This early negative response, particularly the reports that the British press panned the film, seems at least partly a case of American journalists searching for the worst response. Although disappointment was expressed in some British reviews, *A King in New York* was also highly praised in some quarters. In the influential *London Times*, for example, Dilys Powell made the extravagant claim that "the very fact that [*A King in New York*] occurs enables the cinema . . . to take its place without question among the seats reserved for the major arts." Admitting that Chaplin's satire was characterized at times by "a dash of malice," Powell pointed out with some relish the film's paradox that "a monarch is more democratic on some of his political thinking than a republic."[14] David Robinson's recent assertion that "the British press was largely favourable and at worst respectful" to *A King in New York* may be too generous, but the British response was surely more positive than the American press granted at the time.[15]

The reviews in American newspapers and periodicals reveal some interesting similarities, which suggest that the prevailing critical discourse for discussing Chaplin films had regressed. Shunning the tendency of critics in the 1930s and early 1940s to encourage "progressive" political concerns in films, the American critics of *A King in New York* reverted to critical questions that were more characteristic of the 1910s and the 1920s. Partly because the economic prosperity of the war and postwar years had muted the calls for the restructuring of the American economy that had been more prevalent in the depression years and partly because radical critics were frequently attacked or summarily dismissed during the most frigid years of the Cold War, most American audiences and reviewers were less enthusiastic about, or even openly hostile to, the "progressive" films that earlier critics like Harry Alan Potamkin or Lewis Jacobs had called for and praised during the 1930s. The 1950s were, as noted earlier, dominated by an ideological consensus that considered American society fundamentally sound and equitable. Working within this sociopolitical consensus, few U.S. critics and reviewers would respond favorably to a film overtly critical of American institutions, and fewer still would agree that a film's political position was the standard upon which one would base an evaluation of the film.[16]

This does not mean that American reviewers were hesitant about attacking the film because it criticized the United States. In fact, some were happy to do so. *Time*, for example, opened its review by telling its readers that Chaplin was a "bitter man" and a "self exile" settled in Switzerland: "Convinced that he had been persecuted by Mc-Carthyism, Red-liner Chaplin decided to deprive the U.S. of one of the few authentic geniuses produced by the movies." *Time* then prefaced a plot summary with a sharp critique of its politics: "Intended as satire, *King's* few funny spots are outweighed by shrill invective and heavy-footed propaganda." The *Nation*, whose editors could have been sympathetic to the film's political satire, noted that the film had a "political plot" but commented that "the really good parts of the film were strung on a line that had nothing to do with" it. Similarly, the *New Republic* minimized (or side-stepped) the validity of the political critique by finding fault with the presentation of the material: "Chaplin leads us clumsily towards the point of the film—McCarthyism—by introducing a repugnant little schoolboy, played by his son." The same review also disparaged the film's political dimension by referring to the "incredible inaccuracy of the satire." And even when a reviewer accepted the validity of some of the satire—as Marvin Felheim did in his *Reporter* review—he followed the admission by writing that "most of these evils have been much more blatantly condemned in American films" like *Storm Center*.[17]

Reviewers of *A King in New York* tended to ask whether the film was funny, as had their counterparts in the 1910s, or if the film successfully blended pathos and humor, as in the 1920s. In both cases, the reviewers generally answered no.

Saturday Review: "This film is not funny enough and not often
  enough"
Nation: "It is not very funny" (p. 310)
New Republic: "For about 90 seconds he is very funny. But that is the
  beginning and the end" (p. 22)
Newsweek: "The Unfunny Comic" (title)
Time: "Unfunny Charlie Chaplin" (title)[18]

Some reviewers did find funny incidents in the film—Felheim, for example, was pleased with the satire on American movies. The point to be stressed, however, is that the reviewers seemed to be judging a film that had no intention of being a Keystone comedy by the very standards of slapstick.

Similarly, some reviewers looked for the blend of pathos and romance Chaplin perfected between *The Kid* and *City Lights*. To Robert Fulford in the *New Republic*, "*A King in New York* . . . is dismaying from any position you choose to take. If you look for comedy, it is almost entirely missing: and when it turns up it is usually inept. If you look for pathos, you look in vain: Chaplin tries for the pathetic a dozen times, but he never comes close" (p. 22). *Saturday Review* took the same position, arguing that "Chaplin attempts to use the boy for pathos as he used a little boy in *The Kid* and the blind girl in *City Lights*. But it doesn't come off, chiefly because there are not enough gags or comic sequences to carry the serious parts" (p. 27). Thus, while Chaplin was more concerned with blending political satire and a critique of American commercial culture in the 1950s, the reviewers were measuring the film by standards applied to his films of the 1920s.

The resulting mismatch was another blow to Chaplin's star image. A number of the reviewers even turned nostalgically back to the Chaplin of earlier years and lamented the decline of an artist of genius. "There are flashes of the old Charlie Chaplin," wrote Felheim, "but at the center is Mr. Chaplin. . . . Unhappily he is a sadder and an older man: the real punch is gone. His dethroned king is an ironically apt image." Similar, but perhaps harsher and thus more representative, was the *New Republic*'s analysis:

> So long as Chaplin took black-and-white subjects (like the kind tramp versus the vicious millionaire in *City Lights*), his childlike, though never childish, approach invariably worked. . . . It was only when he turned to a sort of half-baked philosophy that he began to bore his audience.
>
> Now Chaplin has put that kind of comedy behind him. He is facing . . . a world that is too big and too confusing for him. The difference now is that it is the artist, and not the character, who is lost and helpless. (p. 23)

Though one could argue that this yearning for the Charlie of earlier days contained the seeds for the eventual restoration of Chaplin's public reputation, the reviews of *A King in New York* did not indicate this. Because Chaplin's earlier feature films were not available for viewing, they remained at best vague shadows in the memories of reviewers and audiences. And although the auteur theory was flourishing as "les politique des auteurs" among the renegade French group of *Cahiers du cinema* critics by the mid-1950s, the approach had not yet taken root in the United States. Both factors would later help to restore Chaplin's public reputation, but two titles best describe the state of Chaplin's star image in the United States after the reviews of *A King in New York*. In one review, Chaplin was "a monarch in exile." In another, he was "a king in decline."

These labels continued to describe the state of Chaplin's reputation in the United States through the late 1950s, for following the European release of *A King in New York* and the generally negative reviews of it that appeared in the American press, Chaplin's name did not cease generating controversy. Probably the most prominent and widely distributed criticism of Chaplin to appear in the American press shortly after *A King in New York* was James O'Donnell's three-part essay, "Charlie Chaplin's Stormy Exile," in the widely circulated and conservative *Saturday Evening Post*.[19] Apparently in March 1958, the opening piece clearly set out to paint a negative portrait of America's fallen clown. The top left-hand corner of the article's first page, for example, contained an unflattering, jowly picture of Chaplin frowning and looking down, his double chin folded; beneath was a caption that described Chaplin as "a tragi-comedian with 'furious and hidden' grievances." The subtitle of the essay read, "Poor Charlie, once the funniest man alive, is now a stuffed shirt who has destroyed the peace of a dreamy Swiss village" (1: 19). Such details set the tone for all three articles, which complained about Chaplin's failure to pay back taxes, his parsimony, his rudeness to employees and to Vevey city officials, and his acceptance of the peace prize. Collectively, the widely read articles portrayed Chaplin as an unreasonably arrogant man, criticized his recent work (*A King* is described as "a reckless satire of not much of anything," 1: 96), and generally perpetuated the star image of the politically unwise monarch in decline.

One other incident in the late 1950s epitomizes the state of Chaplin's star image in America. Early in 1958 the Hollywood Chamber of Commerce announced a list of 1,500 celebrities whose names were to be inscribed on brass plaques and embedded in local sidewalks. Chaplin's name was absent from the list, and no official explanation was offered. After this early announcement, it took some time for the project to get under way. In 1960 it was reported again that Chaplin's name was left off the list of those who would be included in the "Walk of Fame" along about a mile of Hollywood Boulevard. This time, however, the Chamber of Commerce told reporters that some of the local property owners, who were footing the bill for the project, objected to

Chaplin's inclusion.[20] Latent hostilities against Chaplin still smoldered in the movie community, as they did in the wider culture.

Shifting Winds: The 1960s

In the 1960s, particularly between 1960 and 1964, Chaplin's star image began to take on more positive associations in the United States. At least five factors contributed to this renewal. On the broadest plane, the ideology of liberal consensus that had dominated American intellectual and political life since the late 1940s began to break down. Many came to question its basic assumptions and, increasingly, to accept those who, like Chaplin, challenged them. Second, on a more specific legal and economic level, Chaplin's representatives worked through the federal courts to clarify his ownership of his First National and United Artists films, and thus to secure his legal right to distribute them. Third, when that was completed, Chaplin arranged to show a series of his feature films in New York City. Fourth, the publication of Chaplin's autobiography in September 1964 brought the shape of his career—told from his own perspective—to the attention of readers and reviewers. Fifth, the 1967 release of Chaplin's disastrous final feature film, *A Countess from Hong Kong*, though a critical and financial failure, stressed to viewers through contrast how good his earlier films were. These factors combined to mute the negative image of Chaplin the radical and to bring Charlie—a central ingredient in the creation of Chaplin's stardom in the first place—back into the calculus of Chaplin's star image in America.

The key contextual factor to understanding the shift in Chaplin's reputation from the Eisenhower years to the election of Lyndon B. Johnson as President in 1964 was the waning intensity of anti-Communist zealotry in the United States and the growing tendency among some Americans to admit that the United States itself faced such difficult domestic problems as poverty and civil inequality. Perhaps the first important indications of the shift came in 1954, when the Supreme Court handed down its school desegregation decision, the Democrats regained control of Congress in the fall, and the Senate officially condemned the actions of Joseph McCarthy. In 1955, the Montgomery bus boycott was the first important protest of the civil rights movement.

In foreign affairs, Stalin's death in 1953 and the Soviet Union's partial condemnation of him in 1956 led many intellectuals to reassess their tendency to divide the world into simple categories of good and evil. Though the Soviet involvement in Hungary in 1956 served as a reminder that the Soviets would act decisively to protect its "sphere of influence," the Kremlin also frequently commented on the necessity for "peaceful coexistence" in a split world. Especially in the late 1950s, the Cold War seemed to experience a thaw as both Eisenhower and Khrushchev began to call for summit conferences, reciprocal visits, a curbing of the arms race, and cultural exchange programs. Although problems intensified again between 1960 and 1962, as evidenced by the Gary Powers spy plane incident, the Berlin Wall crisis, the aborted Bay of Pigs invasion, and the Cuban missile crisis, by September of 1963 (about two months before Chaplin's films began their New York rerelease run) the U.S. Senate ratified a nuclear test ban treaty that ushered in a period of relative stability in U.S.–Soviet relations.

That the monumental civil rights march on Washington, D.C., took place in August 1963 and that President Kennedy was assassinated three months later only accentuated the shifting focus of national attention from foreign to domestic affairs. As Richard Pells has described, "an increasing number of Americans were questioning, if not discarding, many of the assumptions and practices of the previous fifteen years."[21] The decline of Chaplin's public reputation and the growing tendency to regard Chaplin the star as an unwise radical had been closely related to these "assumptions and practices," now beginning to be challenged.

Chaplin also used the courts to help lay the groundwork for improvement of his star image. After settling with the IRS in late 1958 over back taxes owed for 1953,[22] thus clearing any liabilities he had in the United States, Chaplin was free to begin rereleasing his films in the United States without worrying about having the profits held up or confiscated. Rereleasing the earlier features was an attractive possibility. Doing so would present the Charlie persona to a new generation. And the number of theaters willing to present foreign films and older film "classics" was growing: according to one industry count, the number in the United States grew from 83 in 1950 to 644 in 1966.[23] This growth was creating a market for films like Chaplin's silent features.

But to tap that market, Chaplin needed to establish conclusively his sole legal ownership of the films and his right to distribute them. Since he did not own the rights to the Keystone, Essanay, and Mutual films, they had been frequently revived and even made available for sale for decades. This made it tempting for entrepreneurs, particularly after Chaplin left the country and was out of favor, to obtain and even distribute prints of other Chaplin films to which he did own the rights.

In June 1959 Chaplin, through Roy Export Company (his European-based distributing company) and Lopert Films (the company authorized by Chaplin to distribute his films in the United States), filed suit in federal district court against the International Art Production Management Company. The suit sought an injunction against International to stop its distribution of *The Gold Rush*, which they had rented to a New York City theater for the previous six weeks. The suit alleged unfair trade practices and the unlawful ownership of prints. In July the courts found in favor of Chaplin and awarded Roy Export a permanent injunction against the showing of any Chaplin First National or United Artists film in the United States with the exception of one version of *The Gold Rush*.[24] Chaplin's control of these films was thus secure.

Chaplin, sensing lingering hostility within certain segments of American culture, did not immediately schedule rerelease of the films. In the early 1960s, though, some indications of a more positive treatment of Chaplin in the American press began to appear. One of the earliest was Bosley Crowther's interview and feature in the *New York Times Magazine* in 1960, titled "The Modern—and Mellower—Times of Mr. Chaplin."[25] The article helped to revive his U.S. reputation in several ways. First, it indicated that his attitude toward the United States for the treatment he had received in the late 1940s and 1950s had softened. Crowther quoted Chaplin on his current attitude: "I cannot help but be bitter about many things that happened to me. But the country and the American people—they are great, of course." Second, Crowther outlined Chaplin's entire career, and in his summary he refused to dwell on details of Chaplin's private life that alienated him from so many Americans and focused instead on Chaplin the actor, particularly on his persona Charlie, who "represented the ever-hopeful average man in the eternal and usually hopeless struggle of the individual against the mass." A number of stills visually supported this return of Charlie. Finally, Crowther, writing that "many close investigations" failed to turn up any evidence that Chaplin was a Communist, implicitly defended Chaplin's political views (p. 59). In the article Chaplin the man thus emerges more as a victim of repressive political times than as a dangerous radical.

Chaplin's star image also benefited from Oxford University's decision in 1962 to award the aging comedian an honorary degree—a ceremony that made the front page of the *New York Times*. In an interview afterward, he told reporters that he felt no bitterness toward the United States. The *Times*'s editorial staff apparently took notice and found the changing tone significant, for a few days later they brought up the subject in an editorial titled, "Re-enter the 'Little Tramp.'"[26] In addition to noting that Chaplin had been awarded the honorary degree (along with Secretary of State Dean Rusk), it comments on the lasting image of the "little tramp": he "lives, and will live until the last of the films that show him in action have turned to dust." The editors do not fail to establish their credentials as Cold War liberals in the piece; they write that the Communists "tried to use [Chaplin] for their purposes" but that "he insisted that he never had belonged and never would belong to their humorless fraternity of the Left." However, the climax of the editorial is its conclusion, which urges the Kennedy administration to lift the ban imposed on Chaplin in 1952: "We do not believe the Republic would be in danger . . . if yesterday's unforgotten little tramp were allowed to amble down the gangplank of a steamer or plane in an American port." The imagery is significant: in defending Chaplin, the *Times* stressed Charlie, sympathetically revised Charles, and kept Chaplin the woman chaser out of the picture.

Articles like Crowther's and honors like the Oxford degree helped set the stage for the next three key events: the rerelease of Chaplin feature films in New York, which played continuously for eleven months beginning in November 1963; Chaplin's autobiography, published in 1964; and Chaplin's final film, *A Countess from Hong Kong*, released early in 1967. Although Chaplin did receive some negative response from critics and audiences concerning these events, particularly *Countess*, the tendency of each was to enhance his star image "retrospectively." That is, all three encouraged viewers and readers to look back over Chaplin's whole career and not simply to dwell on his films and activities during the years when his reputation was sliding. By looking at the entire sweep of Chaplin's work from the more favorable historical context of the mid-1960s, viewers and readers helped to revise the negative star image of Chaplin inherited from the late 1940s and 1950s. This occurred in large part by returning the factor of Charlie to the polysemy of Chaplin's star image.

Perhaps heartened by the conciliatory tone of the *Times* editorial and other positive responses from the United States, Chaplin and his business representatives arranged the first systematic rerelease of Chaplin's features, limited to one theater in New York City. From the opening of *City Lights* in the last week of November 1963 until mid-October 1964 (well past the September publication date of Chaplin's autobiography), six Chaplin programs had a successful and continuous run at the Plaza Theater. After *City Lights*, the Plaza showed the Chaplin Revue (*Shoulder Arms*, *A Dog's Life*, and *The Pilgrim*), *The Great Dictator*, *Modern Times* (double featured with *The Gold Rush* in all but the first two weeks), *Monsieur Verdoux*, and *Limelight*.[27]

Note the pattern of release: Chaplin chose to present audiences first with his Charlie persona, the trademark that did so much to establish his star image. If we accept the barber in *The Great Dictator* as a kind of surrogate Charlie, viewers were not confronted with Chaplin's later personae, Verdoux and Calvero, until the last two films of the run. If we recall the excoriation Chaplin received from nearly every quarter when *Verdoux* was released in 1947, it is remarkable to note that *Monsieur Verdoux* not only enjoyed the longest (with *City Lights*, nine weeks) and most financially successful run in the series but also received widespread critical acclaim. Something was happening to Chaplin's star image.

Opening on Friday, July 3, *Monsieur Verdoux* set a weekend box-office record for the 525-seat Plaza, garnering $13,500 in receipts for the three-day weekend. (At the ticket prices of $1.50 and $2, this indicates more than thirteen sellouts for the three days.) The film continued to do a strong business, grossing $12,500 in the seventh week, compared to $11,500 in the seventh week for *The Great Dictator*, whose gross was the second biggest of the series.[28]

The critical response, such as it was (it was not customary in 1964 for reviewers to write about revivals), was positive. In the *New York Herald Tribune* Judith Crist, praising the film's "fantastic comedy, its biting ironies . . . , and its crushing social satire," told her readers that *Verdoux* was a "classic that we are at last privileged to appreciate after its abortive debut 17 years ago." Crowther recommended the film highly and used two reviews in the *New York Times* to praise and to chide those who initially gave it a hostile reception. One of the few who had given *Verdoux* a relatively good review in 1947, Crowther was more enthusiastic in 1964, calling it "a superior sardonic comedy" and "an engrossingly wry and paradoxical film, screamingly funny in places . . . and devoted to an unusually serious and sobering argument." In a follow-up article a week later in the Sunday *Times*, Crowther told his readers that seeing *Monsieur Verdoux* was "a rare and rousing privilege that no one should miss." He also wrote about the "almost faded notoriety that was unjustly fomented against it at the time of its release" and lamented "the melancholy memories [the film] stirs of the outrage and abuse so cruelly heaped on Mr. Chaplin, who caused it to be withdrawn."[29] The article suggested that Chaplin had been a victim of the times.

In July, a *Newsweek* article seconded that view. Entitled "Charles the Great," it contained four stills of Chaplin playing Verdoux and reported on the huge gap between the film's reception in 1947 and in 1964. To *Newsweek* the enthusiastic reception of *Verdoux* was a comment on the times as much as on the film: "What has changed—at least in New York, and probably throughout the country—is the atmosphere. *Chaplin is no longer a villain.* A new generation has grown up, receptive to his artistry and eager for his gift of laughter. This very change affects the way we now view the film."[30] Chaplin's star image was evolving, distinctly taking on the image of victim instead of villain, of a man and performer unjustly attacked during the years of excessively zealous anticommunism.

This new and more positive response to *Monsieur Verdoux* provides an almost perfect case study for key assumptions of Hans Robert Jauss's aesthetic of reception. For Jauss, "a literary work [or in our case, a work of cinema] is not an object that stands by itself and that offers the same view to each reader in each period." Instead of being a kind of "monument" revealing its "timeless essence," a work is more "like an orchestration that strikes ever new resonances among its readers" as time passes.[31] The stark contrast between the reception of *Monsieur Verdoux* in 1947 and its reception in 1964 vividly illustrates Jauss's principle. In 1947 the character of Verdoux deeply offended reviewers for at least two reasons. First, Verdoux's occupation of marrying and murdering women for money almost inevitably reminded reviewers and audiences of Chaplin's own unhappy experiences with women, particularly Joan Barry. Second, Verdoux's overt social criticism of capitalist society during the depression found little sympathy in a society that had just fought a world war to defend that way of life and was swiftly moving into a Cold War climate that considered any criticism of domestic institutions misguided if not treasonous.

Jauss's concept of "aesthetic distance"—the disparity between what the initial audience of a work expects (its "horizon of expectations") and what the new work actually presents—can help us explain this vast difference in the reception of *Monsieur Verdoux*. When the aesthetic distance is large, Jauss posits, the work will disturb, puzzle, or shock the expectations of the initial audience, but it may also help change the horizon of expectations so that eventually, the aesthetic distance between the work and a later audience will diminish.[32]

Just such a process was at work during this reevaluation of *Monsieur Verdoux*. By 1964, the details of the Barry case and of Chaplin's other escapades with young women had faded from public memory and thus played no more than a minuscule role in the audience's response to the film. Chaplin had been a happily married man for twenty years. Few remembered Chaplin's political activism from the 1940s. More recalled the circumstances that drove him from the country in 1952 as a victim of the McCarthy era. Given the shifting political climate, characterized by a greater willingness to criticize American institutions, audiences in 1964 were more inclined to understand and sympathize with the social criticism in the film. The often bitterly ironic satire found in *Monsieur Verdoux* had defied audience expectations in 1947: such humor was unusual in that era not only for Chaplin but also for American film comedy in general. But sophisticated New York City audiences were more prone to accept such satire in 1964, as is evidenced both by the popularity of *Dr. Strangelove* during its New York run early in 1964 and by the attention the "black humor" novelists (Vonnegut, Southern, Friedman, Heller) were receiving at roughly the same time. The moviegoer who was interviewed by a *New York Times* reporter after having seen *Monsieur Verdoux* may have been right: he said that the film was released "seventeen years before its time."[33]

If the 1964 response to *Verdoux* indicated that American audiences were becoming more responsive to Chaplin and his films, the entire rereleased series also contributed to the shift in his star image. By running three of Chaplin's best First National films and all of the comic features through *The Great Dictator* except *The Circus*, the schedule brought to the fore the Charlie persona who originally did so much to establish Chaplin as a star in Hollywood. Then, by playing the controversial *Verdoux* and the autobiographical *Limelight*, the series enabled viewers who saw all the films to examine them as examples of how Chaplin the director and actor evolved after he felt compelled to abandon the Charlie persona. The fact that the "auteur theory," popularized by Andrew Sarris (and to be discussed below), was fast becoming an influential approach to the study of film meant that the Chaplin rereleases were well timed: they allowed *cinéastes* in New York to survey much of the director's career and identify his preoccupations and his evolution as an artist. Times had muted the political and moral objections to Chaplin the man rooted in the 1940s, and this extended series of his mature work helped to begin restoring Chaplin the serious artist and Charlie the persona to the center of Chaplin's star image.

The publication of Chaplin's autobiography in September 1964 also contributed to this shift. The publishing history of *My Autobiography* was itself news; *Time*'s review called it "one of the richest publishing coups of the century." The book was released simultaneously in eight languages and Chaplin was reportedly guaranteed a minimum royalty of $500,000 for the English-language editions alone.[34] *Publishers Weekly* announced that just in the United States, the book had accumulated advance sales of over 47,000 copies before the official publication date. Within a month it was already in its third printing, and by

Thanksgiving it was tied for first (with Douglas MacArthur's *Reminiscences*) on *Publishers Weekly*'s list of best-selling nonfiction books. By December 1964, 100,000 hardcover copies were in print, and the book remained in the top ten on the best-seller list through the middle of March 1965.[35] These figures apply only to the hardcover edition published by Simon and Schuster. The book was also a main selection of the Book-of-the-Month Club, and it remains in print even today in paperback.

That is not to say, however, that the reviews of the book were unequivocally positive. On the contrary, nearly all the reviews were mixed, with the same complaints cropping up repeatedly. One of the most common criticisms was that the last half or more of the book was a listing of famous people Chaplin had met. Aligned with that objection was the complaint that Chaplin had almost nothing of consequence to say about the films that made him famous. Reviewers also regularly attacked Chaplin's writing style, particularly his apparent tendency to leaf through a thesaurus in search of obscure vocabulary (among the most frequent targets were Chaplin's use of "esurient" and his references to the "intellectual subcutaneous texture of Greenwich Village" and to an "affluent potpourri" of celebrities). One reviewer summed up the book as "stupendously verbose"; Brendan Gill clucked at the "gross solecism" of the "my" in the title.[36]

Two reviewers for more conservative publications, *Time* and *National Review*, included political stabs at Chaplin and his book. *Time* described Chaplin as "notoriously vain, snobbish, difficult to know and to work with" and charged that he left the country "in a sneering rage." For *Time*, the book was "uneven and uncommunicative about his many loves and his vociferous left-wing politics." The reviewer for *National Review* objected to Chaplin's assertion that the New Deal years constituted "the most inspiring era in American history," and he too criticized Chaplin's brevity in discussing his leftist politics and his love life. These reviewers seemed to want Chaplin to provide evidence that would corroborate the political and moral charges against him that had flown so thick and fast in the press during the late 1940s and early 1950s.[37]

This sort of attack and innuendo was, however, the exception. One of the most striking elements about the remaining reviews is how often they chide American institutions for their mistreatment of Chaplin during the McCarthy era. To *Newsweek*, Chaplin's exile was "disgracefully, sneakily perpetrated by his adopted nation." To John Houseman, Chaplin was one of the victims of the "Red purge" that "reached a virulent and spiteful climax in Hollywood during the late forties." In a second *New York Times* review, Brooks Atkinson lamented the "squalid paternity suit brought by Joan Barry and the United States Government's cowardly revocation of his re-entry permit." Perhaps no reviewer was as direct as Robert Hatch, writing in *Harper's*: "The persecution of Chaplin in the name of American patriotism and public decency is a scandal this era is saddled with forever."[38] To the extent that the reviews give an accurate indication of the state of Chaplin's star image, it is clear that Chaplin the political victim had by 1964 superseded Chaplin the dangerous Red.

As well as presenting a more generous attitude toward Chaplin's political views, the reviews, like the rereleases, brought Charlie the tramp back to the center of the Chaplin star image. *Newsweek* included a shot of Charlie from the 1910s. The titles of the reviews often mentioned the tramp:

Newsweek: "The Tramp"
Commonweal: "Real Life of the Tramp"[39]
National Review: "Only the Little Tramp Matters"
Time: "The Little Tramp: As Told to Himself"
New York Times: "Chaplin, the Biographer, Is Not So Eloquent as the Silent Little Tramp He Created"

Just as important, the reviews often centered on the significance of the Charlie persona and even quoted the passage in which Chaplin described the origin of the character. To Atkinson, "the little tramp was one of the great myths, like Pierrot or Harlequin." For Hatch, Charlie "was the most beloved folk image the world had ever known." To Gill, "Chaplin the actor and Chaplin the deviser of gags" are characterized by "genius." This theme is well summed up in Charles Poore's initial *New York Times* review. After quoting the best part of Chaplin's long description of Charlie, Poore concludes, "But why go on? The characteristics the world has seen in him cover all humanity. And that's enough to ask, this side of paradise."[40]

Paradoxically, Chaplin's final film—a critical and financial failure—also helped rebuild Chaplin's star image. Less than a year after the publication of *My Autobiography*, news began to circulate about Chaplin's preparation of another film. Gradually word came out that the movie, about a White Russian countess who falls in love with an American ambassador, would star Marlon Brando and Sophia Loren. By January 1967 *A Countess from Hong Kong* was given its world premiere in London and on 16 March 1967, its New York City benefit premiere, attended by such luminaries as Henry Fonda, Lynda Byrd Johnson, and Jacob Javits.[41]

The publicity about the film contributed to the rebuilding of Chaplin's star image, especially two photo essays in *Life* magazine, whose 1967 circulation was 7.4 million. "A Passionate Clown Comes Back" appeared during the shooting schedule in 1966; "Ageless Master's Anatomy of Comedy" came out about a week before the film's opening in New York.[42] Both articles roughly follow the format of the *Life* spread on *Limelight* in 1952. All of them included some plot description, some comments by Chaplin about the film or about filmmaking and comedy in general, and a good number of photographs. All three included pictures of Chaplin with his wife and children, which stressed his role as a happy family man. By 1966 Chaplin was more than twenty years away from the Barry affair and more than twenty years into his apparently happy marriage with Oona O'Neill Chaplin. The 1966–1967 articles also emphasized Charlie, both in pictures from *City Lights* and *The Tramp* and in Chaplin's comments about him: "I never thought of the tramp in terms of appeal. He was myself, a comic spirit, something within me I must express." Chaplin the proud patriarch and "ageless master"; Charlie the tender comic spirit: these were key dimensions in the revaluation of Chaplin's star image in the 1960s.

Nevertheless, *A Countess from Hong Kong* was an unmitigated disaster, both with the critics and at the box office, despite the fact that Chaplin directed the picture and that two of the era's top box-office draws, Brando and Loren, starred. The reviews were surely the most negative Chaplin ever received. To *Time*, the film was "a substandard shipboard farce . . . the worst ever made by Charlie Chaplin." The *Newsweek* reviewer wrote that Chaplin's "old techniques are not simply crusty and conventional but stiff and clumsy." In the *National Review*, Hugh Kenner judged the film "one long prolix fumble, like a freshman theme," and asked, "how did Charlie get trapped inside this turkey?" "I wish I could say some nice things about the new Chaplin movie," wrote Philip Hartung in a brief paragraph in *Commonweal*, "but *A Countess from Hong Kong* is so old-fashioned and dull that one can hardly believe it was made now."[43]

The box-office figures were similarly dismal. Though the Sutton Theater tried in a *Times* advertisement to promote the film by picturing people standing in long lines by the theater marquee, *Countess*—a new film—probably grossed less, in this much larger theater, than the rereleased *Monsieur Verdoux* had grossed in 1964.[44] After its run was completed around the country and *Variety* listed its 1967 box-office grosses, *Countess* was sixty-second on its list, with just $1.1 million in rentals. In comparison, *The Dirty Dozen* topped the list with $18.2 million, *Georgy Girl* was seventh with $7.3 million, and *Blow-Up* fourteenth with $5.9 million.[45]

Yet despite the negative reviews and the poor box-office showing, when one examines the reviews closely and considers the context, it seems that the reviews probably didn't much hurt Chaplin's star image, for at least two reasons. First, the film did not really get that much critical attention. The reviews of *My Autobiography* were much longer and more numerous in American mass periodicals than the reviews of *Countess*. Second, the film was a considerable departure from the kind of films that had helped to create and sustain Chaplin's star image. Except for *A Woman of Paris*, this was the only Chaplin film that did not feature Chaplin in a lead role (though he did have a Hitchcockian walk-on as a nauseated ship steward). Because Chaplin did not star in the movie, reviewers could distinguish between Chaplin the aging director and Chaplin the performer/actor/director/composer/producer—that is, Chaplin the auteur—who had made such a mark on the history of American film.

And that is to some extent what the reviewers did. Whereas hostile reviewers of Chaplin's three previous films had seemed at times to review Chaplin's political views and sexual history as much as the films themselves, the reviewers of *Countess* appeared almost anguished at having to tell readers that the film was a bomb. Hartung, for example, expressed in *Commonweal* his desire to find something good in Chaplin's new film "because I think he is one of the greatest movie makers of all times." *Newsweek* contrasted the failure of *Countess* with the previous achievement of Chaplin: "[his] vision was the poetry of an age—the age of the underdog and of poetic justice, of innocent romance and innocent beauty, of clowns and orphans and lyrical anarchy, a post-Victorian age where love conquered all." The world had changed, the reviewer went on, and Chaplin's vision stayed the same—hence the regrettable failure. In *National Review*, Hugh Kenner attributed the failure of *Countess* to the fact that Chaplin's genius was as a performer, not as a director.[46] With that perspective, one could throw out the bath water but not the baby—dismiss the film without discarding the artist. Whether the reviewers focused, like *Newsweek*, on the director Chaplin's "vision" or, like Kenner, on the performer Chaplin's artistry, they made it clear to their readers that their harsh view of *Countess* did not diminish their admiration for Chaplin's previous achievements.

Chaplin's star image in America had changed considerably from the days of *A King in New York*. The increasingly leftist political climate, characterized by a greater willingness to criticize American domestic policy, helped curb the attacks on Chaplin's politics rooted in the 1940s and 1950s and encouraged the public to think of Chaplin as a political victim instead of a political villain. Just as important, the revival of the Chaplin films in New York City, the publication of Chaplin's autobiography, and even the release of *Countess* encouraged people to think back to the beginnings of his career (instead of back only to the 1940s) and to consider again the importance of the Charlie persona in Chaplin's star image. As the 1960s drew to a close, the Chaplin cult was again growing.

A Guarded Restoration: The 1972
Return Tour

In April 1972, as the twentieth anniversary of his exile from America approached, Charles Spencer Chaplin, accompanied by Oona O'Neill Chaplin, returned to New York City and then to Los Angeles to receive accolades and an honorary Oscar. The trip elicited enormous press coverage, by far the most attention Chaplin had received in the United States for at least two decades. Coupling this visit with a widespread rerelease of his films, Chaplin and his associates helped generate a huge interest in his films and his star image. The dangerous leftist of the 1950s had become the wronged genius of the 1970s.

Interestingly, economic considerations played a large part in Chaplin's decision to break the vow he made in early 1953 never to return to the United States. The story begins in May 1971 at the Cannes film festival. There the French government awarded Chaplin with its highest public recognition, making him a Commandeur de la Légion d'Honneur. As a part of the festivities, *City Lights* was screened before an enthusiastic audience. The Charlie that the critics longed for in their reviews of *A Countess from Hong Kong* had returned—to great acclaim.

One member of the audience was a film distribution executive for Columbia Pictures, Mo Rothman, who upon leaving the theater bumped into Oliver Unger, an American independent film producer. The two agreed that distributing a package of Chaplin's films would be a wonderful and potentially profitable idea. Calling Chaplin shortly thereafter, they soon met with him and his wife in Cap d'Antibes to discuss the idea, and managed to overcome Chaplin's reluctance by pointing out that it would be a perfect way for his children to know what a great motion picture star he had been. By the fall of 1971, Chaplin and Rothman had signed an agreement. Rothman advanced Chaplin $6,000,000 against 50 percent of the income derived from the film rentals in exchange for the exclusive right to distribute nine Chaplin films. The Chaplins, along with their eight children, attended the world premiere of the rereleased films in Paris in November, and by January 1972 the series had already been scheduled to play in twenty-eight cities in the United States.[47]

Rothman, however, hoped for some special promotion. He reasoned, and Chaplin agreed, that one of the best ways for Chaplin to gain public exposure and hence to generate interest for his rereleased films was for him to visit the United States. Managing the visit, Rothman planned for Chaplin to be shielded from journalists but to be available for a series of "balcony appearances," in which still and movie photographers could capture his image and relay it to the public.[48] Given Chaplin's unfortunate experience with press conferences, particularly during the release of *Monsieur Verdoux*, the choice seemed a wise one.

The return became a major media event. On January 13 Motion Picture Academy president Daniel Taradash announced that Chaplin would attend the Oscar ceremonies in April to receive a special Oscar. Chaplin helped to defuse some possible resistance to his visit by telling an interviewer in February that the press had exaggerated his pique over the criticism he had endured in 1952 and that he was eagerly anticipating his return visit.[49] By mid-February the itinerary was planned: the Chaplins would arrive in New York City, spend several days there while attending various festivities, and then move on to Los Angeles, where the special Oscar would be awarded.

The reception in New York was all that could have been expected and more. The Chaplins arrived on April 3, where a hundred members of the press awaited them at Kennedy Airport. The next evening the Film Society of the Lincoln Center sponsored a "Salute to Charlie Chaplin." Over 2,800 people jammed Philharmonic Hall to see *The Kid* and *The Idle Class* and to catch a glimpse of Chaplin himself. Celebrities and luminaries from Paulette Goddard and Leopold Stokowski to Dick Cavett and Norman Mailer attended. When the eighty-two-year-old Chaplin first swept into the hall, Zero Mostel, high up in a tier, broke a few moments' silence by shouting, "Bravo, Charlie, bravo," and soon the entire gathering was shouting "bravo" and "*Charlie, Charlie, Charlie!*" After the screenings, Chaplin said a few words: "Thanks for the wonderful applause. . . . It's so gratifying to know that I have so many friends." Chaplin later said that the occasion made him feel like he was being "reborn."[50]

But New York was not finished with Chaplin. On April 6 Chaplin received the Handel Medallion, the city's highest cultural award, from Mayor John Lindsay. In his introduction, the mayor described Chaplin as "this compassionate man, this most decent human being, this skilled artist, this great citizen of the world"—quite a change from the terms political figures were using to describe Chaplin in 1952.[51]

The following day the Chaplins flew to Los Angeles. Arriving at 3:00 P.M., they were escorted past dozens of photographers and reporters to a waiting limousine, where two representatives of the Academy, President Taradash and Howard Koch, welcomed them. At crowded gatherings in Los Angeles, Chaplin had reunions with many friends and associates from the past, including Jackie Coogan (the kid in *The Kid*), Georgia Hale (of *The Gold Rush*), and Tim Durant.

The Oscar ceremony on April 11 was the final high point. Chaplin, reportedly afraid no one would show up for "his" night, watched the ceremonies backstage on a television monitor and showed great pleasure at recognizing old friends in the audience. Taradash presented the special award, which honored Chaplin for his "incalculable effect in making motion pictures the art form of the century." Nearly overcome by the reception, Chaplin delivered a brief speech: "I thank you so much. This is an emotional moment for me, and words are so feeble, so futile. I can only say thank you for inviting me here. You're sweet people." Thereafter Jack Lemmon, one of the emcees, handed Chaplin a hat and cane. Chaplin, giving the audience a taste of the comedy and pathos he had generated for so many millions of viewers over the years, fumbled for a moment with the familiar derby, then departed. After the ceremony Chaplin was more verbal: "It was all so *emotional* and the *audience*—I felt *their* emotion. I thought some of them might hiss, but they were so *sweet*—all those famous people, all those artists. You know, they haven't done this to me before. It surpasses everything."[52] By April 12 the Chaplins were returning to Europe.

Just how was Chaplin's public reputation in the United States affected by these ten days in 1972? One might begin answering that question by placing the visit in the context of the times. We have seen that Chaplin began in the 1960s to be looked at more as a victim of McCarthyism than as a violator of American morals and manners. The shifting political climate, which led to an increasing willingness on the part of many Americans to grant the weaknesses of their social institutions, made Charlie's nose-thumbing antics and Chaplin's progressive politics seem much more acceptable than they had been in the decade after World War II.

Even though American society in the late 1960s and early 1970s became polarized over the issues of Vietnam and urban disorder, and even though the old cold warrior Richard Nixon had been elected President in 1968 and was about to be reelected six months after

Chaplin's visit in 1972, the prevailing attitude toward communism and the Soviet Union had changed since 1952. Ironically, Nixon and his advisor Henry Kissinger would soon come to be identified with a policy advocating détente with the Soviet Union, and Nixon himself visited China and opened up a dialogue that would lead to normalized relations between the two countries. This new view of relations between the United States and leading Communist nations provides a useful framework for understanding the context of Chaplin's return in 1972 and the press's generally enthusiastic reportage of it. The culture that had sought to expunge leftist politics in the early 1950s had become more tolerant of those views by the early 1970s.[53]

Chaplin's return visit created an avalanche of publicity in the American press, the most concentrated and pervasive since the Barry case and perhaps even since his rise to stardom in 1914 and 1915. Between April 1 and May 6 alone, twelve important mass magazines and journals of opinion carried feature articles on Chaplin.[54] Unlike the coverage of the Barry trial, however, this publicity was on the whole favorable. For example, *Time*, *Newsweek*, and *Life* (in two separate articles) all carried generous stories, amply illustrated with photographs, about the New York and Los Angeles festivities.[55] The title of one of the *Life* articles, "Love Feast for Charlie," gives a good indication of how these articles presented Chaplin.

This positive treatment was typical, but Chaplin's restoration was nevertheless guarded. Another *Time* article, a two-page preview of Chaplin's visit on April 10, "Re-Enter Charlie Chaplin, Smiling and Waving," illustrates how a conservative magazine dealt with Chaplin's return. The piece was almost classic in its ambivalence, a kind of welcome mat before a closely guarded door. After describing and praising the "mute grace" of Chaplin's Tramp, the essay surveyed the "ambivalent skirmish" between Chaplin and the United States that led up to his exile and mentioned his marriage and divorce to Lita Grey, as well as the opposition of "industrialists" to *Modern Times* and of isolationists to *The Great Dictator*. Discussing Chaplin's politics, the essay called Chaplin a "fan of sentimental collectivism, of revolution seen through a scrim," but excused the views by saying they originated in the actor's childhood of poverty. Then it discounted his opinion, describing him as "a political naif who would only fellow-travel in first class." Though the government's decision to withdraw the reentry permit was "a classic in xenophobia," Chaplin's *King in New York* was a "labor of hate, a film entirely without humor" and his autobiography a work "of benign evasion" in which the "bitterness was cloaked." The article, arguing that the reconciliation between the United States and

Chaplin has been too long in coming, concluded with a kind of paean to the United States: "America of the '70s has become a better region for the artist."

Although the text of the essay refused to condone many of Chaplin's past activities, its visual imagery drew one away from Chaplin the man and toward Charlie the persona. Of the nine photographs, seven were stills from Chaplin films. The remaining two were of Chaplin as a younger man doing acrobatics and of the elderly, white-haired Chaplin smiling, thumbs in his ears and fingers waving. The pictures thus presented Chaplin as an unthreatening entertainer. This stress on Charlie was reiterated by the final sentences of the article, in which Chaplin's Oscar ceremony was called a Chaplinesque gesture, "like an entire nation shaking off its bygone disappointments and its tragic errors, kicking out its legs and setting off once more on that long and hopeful road."[56]

Newspaper editorials and editorial cartoons joined in welcoming Chaplin back to the United States. A *New York Times* editorial, "Charlie's Happy Return," appeared in February after the details of the trip were released and set the stage for Chaplin's welcome. "If a nation could collectively blush," it opened, "the United States had good reason to do so when its officialdom ruled two decades ago that Charles Chaplin could not come back to these shores until he offered proof of his 'moral worth.' " Chaplin's return, the editor concluded, signified a "welcome if long-delayed victory of art and humor over bureaucratic rigidity."[57] Consistent with shifts that began in the 1960s, the presentation of Chaplin here was as the victim of political and bureaucratic machinations.

The *Los Angeles Times*, generally much less sympathetic to Chaplin than the *New York Times* during his difficult days, nevertheless paid double editorial tribute to Chaplin on the day he was to receive his Oscar. The first was a cartoon of an Oscar statuette wearing a derby, captioned "Academy Award's Finest Hour!" (see Figure 30). The accompanying editorial, "Charlie Chaplin Returns," noted Chaplin's worldwide reputation and observed that the government's actions in 1952 were "widely and correctly interpreted as a shabby cover to bar Chaplin from the country for political reasons." Another newspaper that had often treated Chaplin harshly, the *Chicago Tribune*, featured Chaplin in an editorial cartoon on April 10. In it, Charlie wore his regular Tramp costume with the sole exception that the derby had been replaced with an Uncle Sam top hat of stars and stripes (see Figure 31). Though the lack of a caption or of any distinctive expression on the cartoon figure's face made the cartoonist's point of view un-

Academy Award's Finest Hour!

30. Frank Interlandi's April 1972 cartoon in the *Los Angeles Times* celebrates Chaplin's special Oscar.

clear, it seems most likely that the cartoon simultaneously observed Chaplin's new softened comments about the United States and the country's celebration of the artist.[58]

While these more conservative publications were making fresh accommodations with Chaplin, those on the left, the *Nation*, for example, saw Chaplin's return through more jaundiced eyes and used it as an opportunity to recall the unsavory McCarthy years and comment more skeptically on the present—however sympathetic they may have been to Chaplin himself. In its editorial, "Modern Times," the *Nation* commented that Chaplin's homecoming "has been a triumph—but a very melancholy one, because all the auspices were wrong. Chaplin's moral worth is not being vindicated by this visit; there is merely a conspiracy to pretend that some of that unsavory nonsense never occurred." The editorial further commented that Chaplin had returned not "because the people loved him" but because "there is a lot of money to be made out of him"—an allusion to his $5 million distribu-

31. *Chicago Tribune* editorial cartoon acknowledges
Chaplin's 1972 return trip. Copyright © 1987,
Chicago Tribune Company, all rights reserved,
used with permission.

tion contract with Rothman. All in all, "it has been a sad return—years too late and for shabby motives. We hope it has not hurt the old man in body or heart, and wish him a safe journey back to Switzerland."[59]

If that editorial demonstrated that the political controversies surrounding the Chaplin image were still alive—however diminished—other evidence reinforced that suspicion. Although, the *Los Angeles Times* published a positive editorial on April 10, the day before it chose to print an article entitled "They Haven't Given Up—Letter Writers Assail Chaplin." Subtitled "Bitterness Survives 20 Years," it reported that "hundreds of letters" had "poured in" to the paper and that most of them appeared "to have been written by elderly people and mentioned Chaplin's alleged leftist leanings."[60] Some of the letters quoted called Chaplin a "traitor," "Comrade Charlie," and an "insane Revolutionary Zionist."

A second indication that Chaplin's name was still controversial centered on the old debate in Hollywood about whether Chaplin should be memorialized by placing his name and a bronze star on the Hollywood Boulevard Walk of Fame, an action that, after pressure group activity, had been refused in 1959 by the Hollywood Chamber of Commerce. But about a month after Chaplin's return visit had been announced, the Chamber of Commerce reversed itself and announced that Chaplin's name would be put on "Star Boulevard." At the dedication ceremony on April 10 (the same day Chaplin received his Oscar), however, several older women passed out a sheet of paper that purported to describe "Charlie Chaplin's Red Record." Though Chaplin did not attend the dedication, it was clear that his day of triumph and celebration was not shared by all Americans. Such a conclusion was reinforced when on April 17, the former movie actor and then governor of California, Ronald Reagan, told reporters that although Chaplin may have been a "genius" filmmaker, American officials acted correctly in 1952 when they revoked his reentry permit.[61]

Despite these misgivings, however, the response of the press to Chaplin's return was, if never as consistently high as the treatment Chaplin received during the halcyon years in the 1920s, predominantly positive. Two of the longest articles from that time illustrate this well: Richard Schickel's cover essay for the April 2 New York Times Magazine, and Father George H. Dunne's long memoir in Commonweal, "I Remember Chaplin."[62] As two of the longest and most informed explorations of Chaplin and his achievements to appear in the popular press in 1972, they deserve more detailed treatment.

Schickel's article, which appeared the Sunday before Chaplin arrived in the United States, constituted a kind of prestigious prologue to his visit. Not only was it the cover article of the issue, but it also contained generous stills of Charlie from films like One A.M. and A Night Out, of Calvero from Limelight, and of Chaplin rubbing elbows with such notables as Winston Churchill and George Bernard Shaw.

Schickel began by observing that because Chaplin had already been so highly regarded by his peers, critics, and the literary intelligentsia, "praise, at this point, seems superfluous" (p. 12). He also pointed out how impossible it was to find an article that criticized Chaplin or even treated his work objectively without somehow apologizing for the criticism. "No entertainer in history," Schickel argued, had "so imposed himself on the consciousness of his times for so long a time" (p. 13).

Nevertheless, Schickel's essay sought to review both the strengths and the limitations of Chaplin's art. In doing so, he did much to summarize some of the most significant commentary on Chaplin by prominent American critics since the 1920s. As he examined the intelligentsia's response to Chaplin over the decades, Schickel both acknowledged the growing historical awareness of the movies in the 1970s and revealed his adherence to auteurism. From the 1920s he alluded to Gilbert Seldes's enthusiasm for *The Pawnshop* and Edmund Wilson's view that though Chaplin was a consummate actor, he was a lackluster director. From the 1930s Schickel cited Otis Ferguson's observations on the stylistic primitivism of *Modern Times*. He also referred to Robert Warshow's analysis from the 1940s concerning the inevitable destruction of the tramp after *City Lights* and James Agee's paean to Chaplin in "The Golden Age of Comedy" (1950). The general thrust of Schickel's treatment was that Chaplin's greatest years were the early ones. The later films, in his view, were seriously flawed. The ending of *The Great Dictator* was a "desperate preachment"; the ending of *Verdoux* was "bitter." *Limelight* was filled with "self-pity" and *A King of New York*, "reportedly" (Schickel apparently had not yet seen the film), with "savagery." That left only the "sheer emptiness and lack of energy" of *A Countess from Hong Kong* (p. 49).

The essay was ultimately a concise statement of an influential view of Chaplin's work that had been developing among certain segments of the public since the 1940s and among critics since the early 1960s: that Chaplin was a great comic actor whose work began to sour after *City Lights*, primarily because he wanted to deal with "big themes" in his work. Such a view was at least in part an example of how fully the progressive critical principles prevalent in the 1930s and into the 1940s had been rejected by American reviewers and critics. In Schickel's words, "One could see that [Chaplin] was increasingly bewildered by the world, increasingly unable to encompass his feelings about (and prescriptions for) it in the metaphors he employed in lieu of The Little Fellow in his films" (p. 49). Schickel did mention despising those who harassed Chaplin about his political views and his morality; he also wrote that "guilt well[ed] up" in him as he criticized Chaplin. Nonetheless, Schickel placed the zenith of Chaplin's achievement before 1935—the era of Charlie—before Chaplin's capitulation to dialogue in films and before more overt social themes entered his work.

George Dunne's "I Remember Chaplin," subtitled "a nostalgic retrospect," complemented Schickel's article. Although Dunne did not concentrate on Chaplin's films, he did briefly praise, as did Schickel, Chaplin's films before World War II. Having seen *Modern Times* again shortly before writing the article, Dunne described the experience as "a sheer delight and a moving reminder of how much the world is indebted to the unique genius of this man" (p. 303).

However, Dunne's essay is much more concerned with defending Chaplin from his political detractors by describing his meetings with

Chaplin in the late 1940s. A Catholic priest, Dunne had written what he described as an "interracial documentary play," *Trial by Fire*, which was about to open in Hollywood at a theater on Sunset Boulevard. On the evening of the dress rehearsal, Chaplin attended, probably on the recommendation of a union head who knew both Chaplin and Dunne. Chaplin gave Dunne and the rest of the group some advice about the play, and after the rehearsal, Dunne and Chaplin dined with two others at the Players Club and talked well into the evening. The following night both Charles and Oona Chaplin attended the play's opening.

The Chaplin depicted in Dunne's article was a victim of the age. Himself a liberal engaged in union and civil rights activities, Dunne recalled how he was visited by Ronald Reagan, George Murphy, and Jane Wyman during the late 1940s and warned about the Communist control of the unions he was defending. He also depicted Joseph Scott, Joan Barry's lawyer, as a "superpatriot and a militantly loyal Catholic" whose "patriotic sensibilities" were offended by Chaplin's failure to become a citizen (p. 306). These conservative Chaplin foes are the villains of Dunne's memoir.

In contrast, Chaplin, despite his fame, showed Dunne and the rest of his group an "easy, informal and friendly manner" that was "totally without affectation" (p. 307). Dunne admitted that his estimation of Chaplin might be colored by the fact that Chaplin considered *Trial by Fire* a good play. But his account of their postrehearsal discussion depicted Chaplin's politics as reasonable and humane. On the question of citizenship, Dunne recalled Chaplin's comments:

> I have been in nearly every country. . . . And I have found people everywhere, regardless of color, race or nationality, to be pretty much the same, all human beings with the same desires, the same impulses. I feel a bond with all of them. Were I to take citizenship anywhere it would be here. This is where I have made my home. This is where I have made my career and my money. I am grateful to America. . . . But the swearing of allegiance to any country seems to me a rejection of all other people in the world. And this I cannot bring myself to do. (p. 308)

Nor, in Dunne's view, should he be forced to.

Dunne concluded by trying to explain, on the basis of his evening with the comic, his understanding of Chaplin's sympathy for the Soviet Union. Noting Chaplin's "nostalgia for the pre-mechanical age," Dunne speculated that Chaplin opposed "not so much capitalism as the mechanical age." Since Chaplin lived in capitalist nations as he saw the world become more mechanized, however, he equated the two. "The flaw in his reasoning," wrote Dunne, was that the Soviet Union, however opposed to capitalism, was by no means opposed to mechanization. Chaplin, when asked why he had never visited the Soviet Union, replied, "Because . . . I am afraid I might be disillusioned" (p. 309).

This comment provided Dunne a key to understanding Chaplin:

> That said everything that needed to be said about the nature of Chaplin's interest in Communism and the Soviet Union. It grew out of an act of hope that there was an alternative to the dehumanizing kind of society organized under capitalistic auspices which threatened human values and issued in an act of faith that the Soviet experiment contained the promise of realizing such an alternative. If he lost that faith what would be left of hope? And so he refused to run the risk. (p. 309)

The evening was a memorable one for Dunne, capped only by the attendance of the Chaplins on opening night and their kind words for the author. Reflecting on the significance of his experience, Dunne can only comment on Chaplin's exile: "The loss—and the shame— were America's" (p. 309). Perhaps as well as any, this comment sums up the press's view of Chaplin's 1952 departure during his triumphant return to the United States twenty years later. Schickel and Dunne helped create the image of Chaplin as a significant and humane artist who became a victim of his age.

Rereleases and Chaplin's Star Image in the 1970s

In addition to generating monumental press coverage during his 1972 trip to the United States, Chaplin contributed to the revival of his star image in the 1970s through the rerelease of his films. Thanks to his agreement with Rothman, Chaplin's films began to show in retrospectives around America beginning late in 1971. The rereleases were extremely important in perpetuating Chaplin's star image, for Chaplin himself made no new films after 1967 and had not appeared in any significant role since 1957. The history of Hollywood films is filled with stories of faded stars, and Chaplin could have become one himself, had his films not been made available. In fact, although the return trip drew the most concentrated attention to Chaplin in the 1970s, one could easily argue that the rereleases contributed more to Chaplin's star image because they provided so much opportunity for commentary. This came from newspaper reviewers, magazine journalists, and academic critics, and all of them shaped and solidified Chaplin's star image.

Until the films' systematic rerelease, few Americans outside of New York City (where the 1963–1964 Chaplin retrospective was held) had seen any of Chaplin's feature films for twenty years, except perhaps mediocre prints of *The Gold Rush*. And almost no one had been able to see the films chronologically, in the order of their creation. But beginning in late 1971, dozens of revival theaters and campus film societies began scheduling Chaplin film series for weekly showings or even longer runs.

This provided viewers with what was then a unique chance to see much of Chaplin's work in a relatively concentrated time. As one reviewer noted, in these retrospectives "a lifetime of work can be seen over a period of a few months, not jammed together, as it might be at a film festival, not caught piecemeal over the years."[63] Such an opportunity was relished by many *cinéastes*, because it gave them a chance to examine firsthand how Chaplin developed as an artist and to weigh the strengths and limitations of his work. Given the assumptions of the auteur theory, then a prevailing critical perspective, such showings were ideal.

But before the commentary could be generated, it was necessary to get viewers into the theaters to see the films. The enormous coverage of Chaplin's return visit helped to generate an interest in the films, as Rothman and Chaplin had surmised it would. But newspaper advertisements for the rereleases also helped promote the movies, in large part by featuring Charlie's image. Two examples appeared in the 5 April 1972 *New York Times* in an ad whose headline also tied in with Chaplin's return visit to the city. One half announces the showing of *City Lights*. It contains the famous closeup of Charlie holding a rose with his mixed expression of joy, fear, and expectancy. The other half announces *Modern Times*, and is dominated by a large image of the sprightly Charlie. Next to a quote from Canby's rave review, Charlie strides briskly, cane in hand, toward the viewer (see Figure 32).[64] Some versions of the ad for *Modern Times* included six identical smaller images of Charlie set beside the theater names. Rothman and Chaplin knew that the persona Chaplin had created was a valuable commodity, and the promotion stressed this.

Reviewers in newspapers also helped to stir up enthusiasm for the films with their positive reviews. One of the most enthusiastic critics was Vincent Canby in the *New York Times*. *The Idle Class*, he wrote, "has

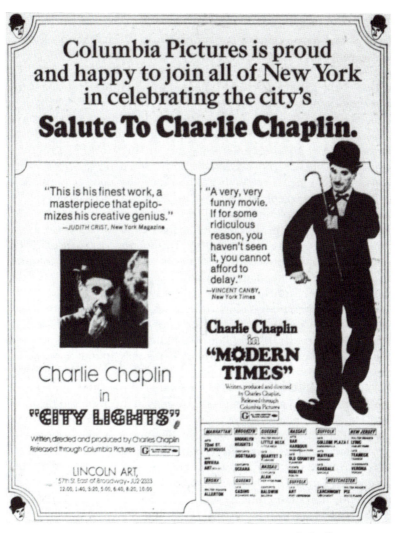

32. Newspaper ad during 1972 rerelease: the return of Charlie to
center stage of the Chaplin star image.

the density of content and much of the comic resonance of the later
features." *City Lights*, his favorite of the films, was "perfectly conceived
as a single entity." *The Great Dictator* was, in his view, the "most passionate of low farces," a film that had taken on a "special eloquence." Although the much-criticized final speech was "still awkward," it could
also "be understood as part of the development of an artist whose life

349

has always been so much a part of his work." Even *Monsieur Verdoux* was a comedy "of the highest order," both "rigorous and demanding."[65]

Gene Siskel in the *Chicago Tribune* was also enthusiastic about the rereleased films, calling *City Lights* "more elemental and elegant than today's movies." In contrast to the "ill-considered dialogue" and music that "comes across as just so much noise" in contemporary films, he found that *City Lights* used its "romantic, stirring score" as a counterpoint for its physical comedy. Siskel also appreciated *The Great Dictator*. Here, Siskel judged, Chaplin broke his silence for good reasons: "It is to his everlasting credit that he gave up his artistic principle of silence for a moral principle that compelled him to speak against Hitler and Nazism." Although the film was not, in his view, as strong as *City Lights* or *Modern Times*—largely because the slapstick was not particularly inventive—Siskel defended the often-criticized ending. He not only called it "a great humanitarian sermon" but also quoted excerpts from the final speech for nearly the last half of his review.[66]

Another representative daily reviewer to praise Chaplin was Kevin Thomas in the *Los Angeles Times*. The titles of two of his reviews indicate his perspective: "Still a Lot of Candlepower to *City Lights*" and "*Limelight* in L.A.—at Last." Although Thomas found that *Modern Times* had "the same grace and poignance" as *City Lights* but "considerably more substance," he called the ending of the latter film "one of the most affecting, justly famous conclusions in the history of the movies." He also praised *Limelight* as "an incomparable, profoundly moving portrait of the artist as an old man." Thomas marveled at Chaplin's ability "to create a world of his own on film" so successfully that in his various roles as star, director, writer, and composer, Chaplin was "sublime in his artistry." As with Canby and Siskel, Thomas filled his reviews with admiration for Chaplin.[67]

One can make several points about the image of Chaplin that emerged from the commentary of newspaper reviewers and the journalists like those who contributed to the special *Film Comment* issue on Chaplin in the fall of 1972.[68] First, they tended to look at the films as expressions of Chaplin's inner self and world view. As Canby put it, "Despite the overlay of social consciousness, all of Chaplin's movies— and not just the later ones—have been to some extent emotional autobiographies." Similarly, in the *Film Comment* issue, Emily Sieger discussed *Limelight* as Chaplin's attempt to continue developing as an artist after the aesthetic and ideological conclusions of *Monsieur Verdoux* had closed a number of options available to him. The dominance of the auteur approach in the 1960s and 1970s, the opportunity to see the rereleases systematically, and the availability of Chaplin's autobiography (Siskel and others seemed to use it for reference material in their reviews) all encouraged journalists to read the films as expressions of Chaplin's psyche and world view, as his "emotional autobiographies."

Related to this stress on an auteurist approach was the critics' tendency to discuss the development of Chaplin's "vision" by dividing that evolution into various stages. For example, in *Film Comment* William Paul, writing on *The Gold Rush*, argued that Chaplin's "vision was expanding" as he made the feature films: the "emotional expressiveness of his works" grew deeper (p. 16). The later films thus contained "a more spiritual quality," for they had progressed from the earlier stress on "the basic hungers of physical existence . . . to the expression in art of man's need to transcend these hungers" (p. 18). As one reads through the commentary, though, most of the *Film Comment* critics hold that the apogee of Chaplin's art was located sometime in the 1930s or early 1940s, after which Chaplin created complex, interesting, but less successful films. This would be consistent with Canby's view that Chaplin's greatest films began with *The Kid* and continued through *Modern Times*: these are in large part the feature-length films starring Charlie. Such attention helped create the image of Chaplin as a serious artist whose work, much as Shakespeare's or Tolstoy's, grew and evolved through time.

Perhaps most important, there was a decided tendency to stress two aspects of Chaplin's star image: the Charlie persona and Chaplin's versatility and "genius" as a filmmaker. In the *Film Comment* special issue, the most singularly positive analyses were of the films in which Charlie appeared. Films from *Monsieur Verdoux* on did not fare as well. When William Paul wrote that "the one unifying force in all Chaplin films is simply Charlie himself," he expressed a view that was explicit or implicit in nearly all the essays (p. 16). In the comments on Chaplin as filmmaker, some objections were raised. Hirsch, writing about *Monsieur Verdoux*, and David Robinson, writing from memory about *A King in New York* (it had not yet been rereleased when he wrote the piece), both criticized the stylistic primitivism or lack of attention to detail in the films. However, in general, these observers tended to reject the earlier view, expressed by people like Wilson and Ferguson, that Chaplin's style was awkward and old-fashioned. They did so not by detailed defenses of Chaplin's style but rather, as in Paul's reference to "Chaplin's unfairly criticized visual style," by briefly suggesting that Chaplin's style was suitable for his aesthetic aims. Chaplin's intuitive artistry, in their view, enabled him to present narrative concerns with appropriate stylistic means.

The stress on the Charlie persona in the *Film Comment* issue was reinforced by the illustrations. The articles were accompanied by seventeen stills, sixteen of which were of Chaplin playing his various roles. Included were one still of Chaplin as Hynkel, one as Verdoux, two as Calvero, and one as King Shahdov. The other eleven were of the Charlie persona, peering around a corner with the kid, doing a David and Goliath mime sermon in *The Pilgrim*, waving a red flag in *Modern Times*, and so on. At least as far as the *Film Comment* articles and the newspaper reviewers were concerned, the return of Chaplin to the United States in 1972 was as much a return of the symbolic power of the Charlie persona as it was of the aging, tottering comedian.

Yet another factor contributed to the evolution of Chaplin's star image: the growth of academic interest in film. Before the mid-1960s, college courses on film as an art form were nearly as rare as courses on the novel in universities before 1900. In the mid- and late 1960s a dramatic proliferation of film courses occurred. More widespread American release of European art films by directors like Bergman, Antonioni, Godard, and Fellini demonstrated that films could be as complex and ambitious as other narrative art forms. American movies (within limitations) also became more able to experiment in subject matter and film style, as television became the dominant medium of mass entertainment and film began to aim at more specialized audiences. Furthermore, college enrollments expanded dramatically as the baby boom generation came of age and as a college degree became a required credential for more and more jobs. And the social and political climate included a sense that education ought to be "relevant" to students' lives. Since moviegoing was often a regular part of those lives, film courses seemed to meet that demand for relevancy. Combined, these factors contributed to the rapid growth of film classes. Although only about 200 institutions offered film courses as late as 1969, the American Film Institute reported that by 1978, over 1,000 colleges and universities around the country were offering over 9,000 courses in film and television studies. Over 40,000 students were pursuing degrees in the field. Those figures, moreover, were probably conservative, based only on the institutions that had responded to the AFI survey.[69]

By the 1980s, a large number of people had been introduced to Chaplin's work through courses that asked them to watch his films, read about him, listen to lectures about his work and place in film history, and even write about him. In a general sense Chaplin's contemporary star image has thus been shaped in part by the academic discourse about Chaplin in the past two decades. A brief look at some of that work gives a sense of the various ways Chaplin and his films have been approached.[70]

It is most useful to begin by looking at Andrew Sarris's views on Chaplin. Sarris was in the 1960s the most influential American advocate of the auteur approach to film study. Beginning more as a journalist than as an academic, Sarris's influential "Notes on the Auteur Theory in 1962" set off a cultural debate when Pauline Kael lambasted the central conceptions of the "theory" in an article called "Circles and Squares."[71] Sarris's central notion was that film history ought to be organized by examining the films of a particular director as a coherent body of work. That group of films could then be explored to define its stylistic, narrative, and thematic patterns and preoccupations. The critic/historian could also evaluate the quality of the work and compare the director's work with that of other directors. In 1968 Sarris put this approach into practice with *The American Cinema: Directors and Directions, 1929–1968*, which became for many the reference book of auteurism in the late 1960s and early 1970s.[72]

The auteur approach was an ideal springboard for Chaplin's reputation. The auteurists tended to approve most highly of two kinds of directors: those who, during the American studio years, managed to place a "personal stamp" on their films in spite of the homogenizing pressures of the studios; and European directors who, like Renoir or Bergman or Murnau, seemed to express a distinctive style and world view through their films. The most highly valued auteurs were independent creators in the best Romantic tradition. What better candidate for laurels could there have been than Chaplin, whose stormy life personified independence, whose films featured the unique and mythic Charlie, and whose creative independence was ensured by his versatility and by his sole ownership of a movie studio?

Sarris's thumbnail sketch of Chaplin in *The American Cinema*—appearing in the "Pantheon," Sarris's section on the greatest directors—was understandably filled with praise. The reasons for this praise have helped shape the way we presently think about Chaplin. Sarris, echoing Canby, praised Chaplin first for the personal quality of his films: "Viewed as a whole, Chaplin's career is a cinematic biography on the highest level of artistic expression" (p. 41). Second, Sarris connected Chaplin's film style to the Charlie persona. Because, Sarris said, Chaplin's "other self on the screen has always been the supreme object of contemplation," he tended toward a film style that minimized heavy editing in favor of long takes that focused on Charlie and on the objects that surrounded him.

Third, Sarris minimized the significance of the ideas and social criticism in Chaplin's later features: "Chaplin dabbled in Marxian (*Modern Times*) and Brechtian (*Monsieur Verdoux*) analysis, but the solipsism of his conceptions negated the social implications of his ideas." Sarris's discounting of Chaplin's ideas was consistent with much early auteurist criticism, for at least in part, auteurism was a reaction against the kind of socially oriented film criticism rooted in the 1930s and personified in the 1940s and 1950s by the reviews of Crowther in the *New York Times*.[73] Sarris admitted as much in his introduction to *The American Cinema* by criticizing what he called the "forest critics," who wanted every movie to deal "Realistically with a Problem in Adult Terms" (p. 22).

Sarris continued to write about Chaplin and to review rereleases of his films in the years after the publication of *The American Cinema*. After his sketch there, Sarris's article on Chaplin in *Cinema: A Biographical Dictionary*, is probably his most important in developing an auteurist interpretation of Chaplin's significance.[74] In the dozen years that had elapsed since the publication of the earlier analysis, Sarris's approach to cinema had evolved. He had become less dogmatic about the auteur approach and more interested in the relationship between politics and the cinema.[75] This shift is apparent in his more recent treatment of Chaplin.

If anything, the entry views Chaplin even more favorably than the earlier piece. It opens: "Charles Chaplin is arguably the single most important artist produced by the cinema, certainly its most extraordinary performer and probably still its most universal icon" (p. 201). One reason for such high praise, especially for a dictionary of cinema, is that Sarris had come to place more value on the later, more political and autobiographical, Chaplin films. Admitting that Chaplin advocates could often be divided into those who favored the early shorts and those who favored the later, more overtly ideological, films, Sarris suggested that "it would seem that time is more on the side of his features than of his shorts." Chaplin was able, Sarris continued, to "communicate emotionally with the troubled masses through all the convulsions of War, Revolution, Inflation, Depression and Disillusion that passed blindly across his pantomimic path" (p. 202). And even though Chaplin abandoned his tramp and lost much of his audience after World War II, those who remained "gained in appreciation as they contemplated an artist who for more than half a century had used the screen as his personal diary" (p. 211). Benefiting from Chaplin's rereleases of 1972 and thereafter, which gave Sarris and others the opportunity of seeing the Chaplin films—even *A King of New York*—as a whole body of work, the later features began to seem more understandable. Some, especially *The Great Dictator* and *Monsieur Verdoux*, also began to seem more important than the earlier films, even though they are less funny. Auteurism thus combined with the rereleases and a more liberal climate of opinion to elevate the latter part of Chaplin's career.

In addition to the work of Sarris, the writings of Gerald Mast have done much to shape the academic perspective on Chaplin in the past fifteen years. On the broadest and most basic level, Mast's treatment of Chaplin in *A Short History of the Movies* has been influential.[76] Mast offered a more thoughtful, detailed, and probably more influential analysis of Chaplin, however, in *The Comic Mind* (1973).[77] His treatment of Chaplin appears in chapters 6 through 8: "Chaplin: From Keystone to Mutual," "Chaplin: First Nationals and Silent Features," and "Chaplin: Sound Films." Throughout, Mast devoted considerable attention to analyses of individual films and a cross-referencing analysis of stylistic, narrative, and thematic motifs in Chaplin's films.

For our purposes, however, the center was located in an early section, "The Chaplin Career and Chaplin Clichés," of chapter 6. In it, Mast posited a set of four clichés that he opposed about Chaplin's work:

1. "Chaplin is a funny man without a real idea in his head."
2. The structures of Chaplin's films are flawed.
3. Chaplin's films are " 'bad' cinematically . . . Chaplin didn't understand composition, editing, lighting, and sound; many of his best bits would be as good on the stage as on a screen."
4. "Chaplin . . . reached brilliant perfection in the Mutuals and then got longer, duller, more banal, less unified, less funny, more saccharine in the later films." (64–66)

Mast countered each, and in doing so helped to shape our current understanding of Chaplin.

Mast admitted that Chaplin often had trouble expressing ideas with words (they "were not his medium"), but said that he did have "complex ideas about human conduct and social organizations" and "could express them brilliantly." He generally did so not with words but with "his face, his hands, his body" (p. 64). Examples abounded in Mast's subsequent analysis.

Concerning structure, Mast countered that *Remembrance of Things Past*, *Waiting for Godot*, and *Ulysses* could also be attacked for not telling a neatly structured story. For Mast, such criticism was beside the point:

"Chaplin's structures are not stories but thematic investigations—putting the wandering *picaro*, the homeless tramp ... in juxtaposition with a particular social and moral environment" (p. 65). Instead of being structured primarily around the goal of telling a story—the usual "dominant" of classical Hollywood films—Chaplin's films investigated a theme implied by the film's title. The structures flowed from that aim.

Mast also defended Chaplin's film style. Giving examples of Chaplin's composition (Charlie in the house of mirrors in *The Circus*), camera movement (Charlie and the red flag in *Modern Times*), editing (the globe balloon scene in *The Great Dictator*), lighting (the audition scene in *Limelight*), and other stylistic elements, Mast argued that Chaplin's style, though not flashy or obtrusive, was functional, "exactly right for Chaplin" (p. 66).

Regarding the comparative worth of the shorts and the later features, Mast argued a position similar to Sarris's later article (in fact, he may have influenced Sarris). This view admitted that the most effective Mutual shorts were "flawless gems of comic business in a comic structure." However, though the longer features did occasionally lapse into "sentimentality, slow pacing, or overstated moralizing, they are far more impressive expressions of the human spirit" because they "work with more complex emotional and intellectual material," flawed though they may otherwise be (p. 67). To prefer the Chaplin shorts to these later films, Mast suggested, is to opt for the perfection of *The Comedy of Errors* over the complexity of *Hamlet*. Chaplin's paramount importance in film history, the centrality of the Charlie persona and his relationship to Chaplin himself, and the value and significance of Chaplin's later feature films were thus among the emphases expressed by Sarris and Mast. Because their work has been so widely read, their perspectives have shaped our current image of Chaplin.

During the 1970s, however, other approaches to the study of film challenged, proposed alternatives to, and even denounced the auteur approach to film study. One common alternative approach to film study is the formalist or neoformalist approach, which emphasizes close textual examination of the individual film. In the words of a widely used introductory film text, "form is a specific system of patterned relationships we perceive in any artwork." The task of the formalist film analyst is to examine the patterns of narrative form and cinematic style in any individual work, as well as to evaluate the film according to such criteria as originality, intensity of effect, and complexity.[78]

The neoformalist approach, and most others that propose close attention to the cinematic style of individual texts, has lowered Chaplin's reputation, particularly in relation to the films of Keaton. Formalism often prizes films in which the cinematic style calls attention to itself in interesting and original ways. Whereas Chaplin's films rarely do so (perhaps with the exception of the use of the sound track in Chaplin's three films after *The Circus*), Keaton's sometimes do, as when Keaton's title character in *Sherlock, Jr.* falls asleep in his projection booth, and his double-exposure alter ego walks through the theater and up into the screen. As the character stands immobile in the frame, the environment around him constantly changes, calling attention to the nature of cinematic form and illusion. Keaton's interest in cinematic style and his allegedly tighter narratives have led to judgments like Dwight Macdonald's: "I think he was much greater than Chaplin. He made half a dozen long films that are absolutely superb, and really work better than Chaplin's long films."[79]

A second approach that has probably dented Chaplin's reputation in the academy is, broadly speaking, one that blends an interest in semiology (the study of the way signs create meaning) with attention to ideology. Although this "approach" exists in many variations, it evolved from the work of French theorists like Christian Metz and Louis Althusser and found its strongest articulation in English on the pages of *Screen* magazine during the 1970s. Rooted in the political divisions of the late 1960s, radical dissatisfaction with capitalist society, and an awareness of the theoretical flaws of auteurism, this approach turns away from the focus on directors and the listing of film masterpieces to questions of how meaning is created in the cinema, how the industrial and economic context of commercial cinema determines its products, and the way in which ideology in films "constructs" the desires and perceptions of viewers. Some advocates of this approach denounce all commercial cinema as irrelevant and prefer to devote attention to avant-garde cinema. Others, while retaining interest in commercial films, reject the auteur approach as too Romantic, too theoretically imprecise, or too traditional to be of any assistance in answering their most pressing questions about the cinema. To the extent that these semiological and ideological approaches have found advocates in academia, Chaplin's reputation has declined not so much from attacks as from indifference.[80]

Others, however, have retained a fascination with Chaplin's life and career, and have contributed new insights or perspectives on Chaplin. Julian Smith, for example, in a critical biography of Chaplin, adopts a somewhat traditional psychoanalytical approach.[81] Though critics have long pondered the relationship between Chaplin and Charlie,

Smith proposes, rather, that Chaplin expressed various sides of his personality through different characters in the same films: in Pierre, Jean, and Marie in *A Woman of Paris*; in Charlie and the ringmaster in *The Circus*; in Charlie and the millionaire in *City Lights*, and so on. In effect, Smith examines Chaplin's films, even that do not seem overtly autobiographical, as Chaplin's elaborate attempts to work out psychological conflicts through the various characters in his films. This approach leads one to speculate that Chaplin was much more self-conscious about and perhaps even sensitive to his own compulsions to control and dominate others. Such a view would help to alter Chaplin's star image should it become widespread.

Historical film research and scholarship, which works to uncover, study, and assess the significance of various documents in an attempt to reach a fuller understanding of a subject, has also contributed to Chaplin's public reputation in the past fifteen years. One recent area of research likely to shape the evolving view of Chaplin in the United States relates to the production histories of Chaplin's films.[82]

Two books and a documentary film series have contributed considerably to our understanding of Chaplin's production methods. Although Gerard Molyneaux did not have access to Chaplin's papers, he does a thorough production history of *City Lights* in his monograph *Charles Chaplin's "City Lights"*. Through careful research and interviews with those involved, Molyneaux reconstructs the troubled production history of the film. He clearly shows his admiration for *City Lights* in his subsequent analysis, but after examining the evidence, his conclusion about Chaplin's organizational ability is nevertheless compelling: "Chaplin's skill as a director is undistinguished and unenviable. At worst, his methods are counter-productive."[83]

One suspects that Chaplin's unplanned, intuitive method of filmmaking, rooted in his early days at Keystone, is responsible for his problems and delays in production. That suspicion is reinforced by the three-hour documentary, *The Unknown Chaplin*, compiled by Kevin Brownlow and David Gill. Consisting of outtakes and home movies from Chaplin's own archives and interviews with Chaplin associates like Lita Grey and Georgia Hale, the film gives a vivid picture of Chaplin's working methods. It contains some rich material for those interested in Chaplin, such as an entire comic scene originally meant to open *City Lights*, and also, as Anthony Slide puts it, depicts Chaplin as "overindulgent in his filmmaking," shooting scenes "with total disregard as to the amount of film he is using or even, presumably, the wear and tear on his fellow workers."[84]

A more generous interpretation of this overindulgence would posit, as Slide does at one point, that Chaplin had "a dedicated, relentless search for perfection" (p. 9). The argument would hold that because Chaplin's final results were at times so unforgettable and because he was spending his own money when shooting so much footage, criticism of Chaplin's directorial methods are beside the point. David Robinson's recent biography of Chaplin takes this more sympathetic point of view. One of the book's most valuable contributions is its production history of Chaplin's films. Blessed with Oona Chaplin's cooperation and access to Chaplin's papers, Robinson affirms Chaplin's extreme methods for many of his films (the ratio of film shot to film used for *The Great Dictator* was 41:1, for *City Lights*, 38.8:1). Yet like Slide, Robinson in the end admires Chaplin for what he terms his "indefatigable application to the quest for perfection." He also shows that Chaplin worked in a much more organized and regimented fashion in some of his later films than he had in *City Lights*.[85] If access to Chaplin's working records are extended to other scholars, it will be interesting to see what effect the resulting information will have on Chaplin's public reputation.

Thus the work of scholars and critics has continued to keep Chaplin's life and career in the public eye and has helped to shift and alter the image Americans have of Chaplin and Charlie. Several questions are raised by this recent scholarship. They lie at the center of the critical/aesthetic discourse about Chaplin in the 1970s and 1980s. Was Chaplin an inferior stylist or does his style perfectly carry out its function? Were Chaplin's features or shorts greater achievements and why? Of what quality and significance are Chaplin's later features (from *The Great Dictator* on)? To what extent are Chaplin's films indications of his psychological makeup? Were Chaplin's huge shooting ratios a manifestation of his quest for perfection or an indication that he too often had no idea of what he wanted in his films?

Though these questions are still being debated, one thing is certain: Chaplin's star image went through a drastic transformation between 1952 and the late 1970s. A complex set of factors made the shift possible. The changing political climate, which tolerated and even encouraged criticism of the United States, transformed Chaplin from a political villain to a victim of repressive times. It also encouraged critics and viewers to value more highly films like *Monsieur Verdoux* and *A King of New York*, which overtly engaged in social criticism. A shift in the prevailing critical discourse to auteurism also benefited Chaplin's star image, for his versatility, his tendency to center on a comic persona he played himself, and the increasingly autobiographical characteristics of his later features all seemed tailor-made for auteurist critics. However, Chaplin's own actions played a role. His presentation of himself as a family patriarch helped diminish the image, rooted in the 1940s and before, of Chaplin the womanizer. His business decisions, which included his rereleased films, the publication of his autobiography, and his 1972 return tour, also played a key role. Politics, economics, critical discourse, presentation of self through the filters of the media: all help to make and break stars. All helped in this case to return the exiled monarch to his throne. It remains only to examine what has happened to this star image after the death in 1977 of the person who embodied, created, and constituted it.[86]

12

Epilogue

In his elegy to the memory of William Butler Yeats, W. H. Auden wrote that when Yeats died, he "became his admirers." The line is an eloquent one, suggesting that the achievements of artists survive them when their admirers discuss and thus perpetuate the vitality of their work and the memory of their lives. In the case of stars, however, the line is incomplete. When they die, stars do in a sense become their admirers. But they also become their detractors and even, in some instances, become those who wish to "commodify" the images—that is, use the image to sell something else.

Whether through the efforts of admirers, detractors, or commodifiers, a star image very often outlives a star. We know this to be true from the stories and legends still circulating about the great nineteenth-century Shakespearean actors. In the age of mechanical and electronic reproduction, this survival is especially pronounced, for some arts can be frozen in time, the physical presence of the star preserved for future generations. It is still possible in the 1980s, for example, to observe the sprightly twenty-eight-year-old Chaplin as Charlie cleaning up Easy Street or the weathered sixty-two-year-old Chaplin as Calvero musing about the perplexities of art, aging, and declining fame. Though the person is dead, the image survives.

That the evolution of Chaplin's star image in the United States is intimately related to the shifts in American political and cultural history since World War I is as true today as it was in the 1910s and 1920s. During the 1980s, the presidential administration of Ronald Reagan has promoted an ethic that hearkens back to the 1920s. That ethic opposes increased taxation and the expansion of government in the social sphere and counters by celebrating individualism and the entrepreneurial spirit of capitalism. Most political analysts agree that the liberal coalition forged during the New Deal had fragmented by the first half of the 1980s and left the Democratic party with no unifying sense of purpose. President Reagan's polished media presence and uncanny knack of telling the public what it wanted to hear, however contradictory the stories, filled the political void left by the collapse of the New Deal coalition.

Oddly enough, when Chaplin was alive, he defended in different ways and at different times both New Deal liberalism and entrepreneurial capitalism. His progressive political positions in the 1940s were shaped by the ethos of the New Deal. On the other hand, from his early years in the movie industry and throughout his career, Chaplin, assisted by his business and legal advisors, jealously guarded the rights to his films in the best capitalist spirit.

It is not surprising, therefore, that immediately after Chaplin's death, representatives of Roy Export, owned by the Chaplin family, moved to protect the copyrights to the Charlie image and to all Chaplin movies from the First National period on. Although there was (and is) some legal disagreement concerning what happens to the rights to a character after the death of the actor who created and portrayed that character, Roy Export was upheld in its first legal test. It sued CBS News for using film clips from Chaplin features in its obituary of the comedian and was awarded $700,000 in fines by a federal district court. Despite CBS's argument that it was exercising its First Amendment right to report on a newsworthy event, the U.S. Court of Appeals allowed the decision to stand. The decision explicitly supported Roy Export's ownership of the Charlie character and implicitly endorsed the right of its Swiss-based licensing company, Bubbles, Inc., to lease that image to businesses that desired to use it for commercial or promotional purposes.[1]

It is both ironic and somehow appropriate that Chaplin's star image in the 1980s was most actively perpetuated, other than by the films themselves, by the "Big Blue"—IBM, the model of corporate America. In fact, even more than the Chaplin films, IBM's advertising campaign for its personal computers, begun in 1981 and continuing until 1987 (when the actors of the M.A.S.H. television program took over), kept the image of Charlie before the eyes of the American public. The IBM advertising campaign provides an interesting picture of one way, and for what purposes, Chaplin's star image is outliving its creator.

Before 1980, IBM was known primarily as a reliable yet staid company that provided high-quality office machines to businesses. Although it was hesitant to try the untested, mass consumer market of personal computers, in 1980 it decided to enter the fray and sent a crew of engineers to Boca Raton, Florida, to create a machine that could compete with Apple and the other computer manufacturers. By August 1981 the IBM-PC was ready to be sold to customers.[2]

But the product had to be marketed as well as engineered and manufactured. As the engineers were working in Florida, advertisers at the New York agency of Lord, Geller, Federico, Einstein (LGFE) were thinking about advertising campaigns as early as January 1981. One of LGFE's executives, Bob Tore, recalls a meeting with his colleague, Bob Mabley: "We were talking about the problems of big computers and their unfriendliness. We had the idea of showing the history of the computer shrinking—a big white box in a white, sterile room, that would get smaller and smaller. We wanted to have a person reacting to it, and with all that white background, we obviously needed a character in a black suit to stand out. That became Charlie." Mabley, who had just joined the firm in February 1981, adds his recollections:

> We wanted a figure to represent us, but with Dick Cavett doing Apple and Bill Cosby doing Texas Instruments, the field was getting a little cluttered. We knew we wanted a single, friendly person who would represent Everyman. But we didn't really see a need for on-camera dialog. That pointed to mime.
>
> We talked about Marcel Marceau for about 10 minutes and considered a few other ideas. We quickly developed criteria for who this mime should be and ended up with the conclusion that it could only be Charlie Chaplin. After that, Bob Tore and I were on a roll, and everything began to work.[3]

The idea was planted. Before it could grow to fruition, however, IBM had to secure the rights to use the Charlie image from Bubbles, Inc. Bob Mabley conceded to a reporter in 1983 that the law was inconclusive about rights to an image like Charlie's after Chaplin died. "But IBM," he added, "being who they are, wanted to be absolutely sure."[4] After negotiations, IBM signed a one-year licensing agreement with Bubbles, renewable each fall, that gave the company the exclusive right to use the Charlie image and the title "Modern Times" for advertising personal computer and office products. Bubbles retained the right to review the advertising material that used the image. IBM officials refuse to divulge how much the rights cost them, but it is known that by 1983, IBM was spending an estimated-$25 million on its PC advertising budget alone. The contract was renewed into 1987.[5]

After auditioning over thirty candidates, the agency hired an actor named Billy Scudder, born in 1940, to play the Charlie character. Scudder had been impersonating Charlie at amusement parks like Knotts Berry Farm and at parties for nearly a decade. By September 1981, the first IBM television spot using the Charlie image, "House," was aired, beginning a long and successful collaboration that soon would expand to print and radio advertisements.[6]

The campaign was by several standards remarkably successful. If success is measured by IBM-PC sales, there is no doubt: in 1983, IBM sold 850,000 units, as much as Apple had sold in four years.[7] Although subsequent sales of the PCjr were disappointing and although by 1986 IBM-compatible machines—the "clones"—were gaining a greater share of the personal computer market, there is no doubt that IBM attained a strong foothold in the market almost immediately after its PC was available and the advertising campaign had begun. Indeed the speed with which many companies began to develop and sell IBM-compatible machines indicates how fast it was becoming the industry standard.

If success is measured by what advertisers think about the campaign, the IBM–Charlie collaboration receives similarly high marks. An IBM official noted that the campaign was extremely successful at getting the public to associate a character (Charlie) with the product (personal computer): when marketing researchers asked people what character they associated with the personal computer, the answer very often was the "little tramp." This "top-of-mind awareness" or "unaided recall," the official added, was one sign of a very effective campaign.[8]

Although it is not surprising that IBM officials would praise the campaign, it has also been praised by other advertising organizations. The campaign won a number of awards in 1981, including an Andy Award, an International Broadcasting Award, and awards from the Art Directors Club and the International Film and Television Festival. "Bakery," the third of the television spots featuring Charlie, won one of *Advertising Age*'s Best Commercial Awards for 1982.[9] And by 1985 director Stuart Hagman had directed nine IBM–Charlie commercials, had been nominated five times for Directors Guild of America television commercial awards, and had won twice.[10]

Just as Charlie spawned imitators in the 1910s, IBM competitors quickly began to use the Charlie image in ads to promote their own products—perhaps the surest indication of the campaign's success. Seequa, for example, advertised its computer by showing Charlie with his pockets turned inside out: buying a Seequa, the ad promised, would cost a lot less than buying an IBM (see Figure 33). Another company, Fortune Systems, used Charlie to attack the capabilities of the IBM-PC and promote its own. The ad pictures Charlie from behind. His right hand is behind his back with fingers crossed. The accompanying caption reads, "and trust me, when your information needs grow, you can always connect all your PCs together." Here the ad alleges that Charlie is IBM's corporate liar in terms of the network-

33. One of countless computer ads making unauthorized use of Charlie's image after the IBM "Little Tramp" ad campaign.

ing capabilities of its product. Even Apple suggested Charlie's presence in a TV commercial: the ad compared the Apple IIc and the IBM-PCjr. At the end of the commercial the narrator asks viewers which machine is preferable, and a cane appears from the side of the screen and chooses the IIc. The imitation was so widespread that in one issue of *PC Magazine*, for example, twelve ads for software or peripherals directly or indirectly alluded to the IBM–Charlie campaign.[11]

As expected, however, IBM challenged the rights of other computer companies to use the image. The licensing agency that leased the image of Charlie to IBM also went into action. In mid-1984, Herbert Jacoby, a New York lawyer representing Bubbles, Inc., told a reporter,

"Almost everybody in the industry seems to want to use the tramp. . . . I must have written to 75 companies about this." Asked about what influence his letters have had, Jacoby replied, "Ninety-five percent of the companies I talk to are cooperative. . . . Only rarely does anybody tell me to go to hell."[12] For that 5 percent, Jacoby and his firm were likely to go to court. Through 1986, the relationship between IBM and Charlie remained harmonious.

Why did IBM choose Charlie? How did the ads portray his image? What qualities did the advertisements associate with Charlie, and how were they related to the selling strategy?

Those involved in creating the advertisements offer some answers to these questions. To Scudder, Charlie's essential quality is his vulnerability: "That's the key to Chaplin. He did all those tricks and mischief, but he was still vulnerable." This enables people to identify with and respond so easily and fully to Charlie, in Scudder's view. Arlene Jaffee, an LFGE writer on the campaign, stresses how the character helped to create an unthreatening mood: "I think its secret was that the whole gestalt of the campaign was so friendly, human, and communicative."[13]

It is easy to see how this quality proved attractive to IBM. One marketing analyst has observed that the Chaplin campaign "operates as a foil to the large intimidating monolith called IBM. Chaplin's antics not only allay fears about using a personal computer but about IBM itself."[14] By his very demeanor, Charlie can help reduce the computer to human scale and break down the public's fear of it. If Charlie can use one, the unarticulated logic goes, then I certainly can. In computerese, Charlie makes the computer seem "user-friendly."

A few examples of the ads themselves illustrate how Chaplin's image has been used. The first television spot, "House," emerged very much as Mabley and Tore conceived it. In the course of the ad, a gigantic box shrinks. When it becomes a manageable size, Charlie takes out an IBM-PC, scans a "how-to" book, then sits at a white table with a rose on it and begins to work on the computer. As he does so, the voice-over narrator concludes, "IBM made its personal computer to help a person be more productive, to help a person be more creative, and those are good reasons for a person to feel good." By moving from the forbiddingly large computer of the old days to the manageable PC of the present, and by associating the PC with productivity, creativity, and feeling good, IBM creates an environment in which Charlie's vulnerability and ultimate resilience can thrive. The rose, which was used frequently in later ads, is entirely consistent with the Charlie image in films like *The Bank* and *City Lights*. And by having Charlie master the

34. Charlie operates a computer: the IBM "Little Tramp" ad campaign. Note the association of Charlie and flowers, which derives from films like *City Lights*. Courtesy IBM.

PC so effortlessly, the advertisement underlines to its audience how nonthreatening and simple an IBM computer really is.

This was not the only commercial to refer to specific Chaplin films. Another put Charlie on roller skates, much as he had done in *The Rink* and later in *Modern Times*. And the term "modern times," which IBM had also leased rights to, appeared regularly. Two examples are print advertisements for the IBM-PCjr, which emphasized how a home TV can be connected to the computer, and the IBM Portable PC, which stresses its mobility. Both used the phrase in their titles: "How to Plug Your Family into Modern Times" and "How to Move with Modern Times and Take Your PC With You." Both also used the rose introduced in the first television commercial, as did ads for the IBM-PC (see Figure 34).

Though the Charlie of the IBM ad campaign resembles Chaplin's Charlie, he also differs in certain ways. As in most of Chaplin's films, Charlie wears a derby, floppy shoes, and a dark suit. For IBM, however, Charlie is cleaned up. He usually wears a pressed striped tie and pinstriped pants, and he seems to have the same tailor as the wealthy man Chaplin portrayed in *The Idle Class* (see Figure 35). Apparently the down-and-out, frazzled, threadbare Charlie of films like *A Dog's Life* was not appropriate for the corporate giant.

The commercials also very often make Charlie a small businessman (who is saved by a computer) or a hustling entrepreneur. One ad stresses how IBM computers can grow with a business by showing Charlie's success as a furniture store owner. Another print ad appropriated a phrase common about the time of the 1984 Los Angeles Olympics: "How to Go for the Gold." In it Charlie is clearing a hurdle and wears a number 6 over his suit coat; the ad goes on to plug a software game called Decathalon, which would allow an IBM-PC user to "experience the thrill of victory."[15]

Throughout the ad campaign a curious (and apparently conscious) transformation of Charlie's image took place. In 1936, Chaplin's *Modern Times* presented technology as an impersonal, harmful force. The speed of the assembly line turned Charlie into a physical wreck. A television monitor operated by the owner invaded Charlie's privacy in the rest room. The Bellows feeding machine tried to mechanize eating in the interest of factory productivity. In perhaps the most famous symbolic image, Charlie was nearly swallowed up by the cogs of a gigantic machine. One of Chaplin's themes was that technology victimized Charlie. It was an imprisoning, not liberating, force in *Modern Times*.

Though the IBM commercials have often used the title "Modern Times" to accompany Charlie's image in its advertisements, at some points their purposes obviously contradict the thrust of Chaplin's *Modern Times*. One angry computer executive for an IBM competitor, peeved when Bubbles told his company to stop using the image in its ads, charged that "Charlie would roll over in his grave if he knew they were siding with IBM." But Bob Mabley is straightforward in admitting that Charlie's frustration with technology shifts in the IBM ad campaign. "By bringing Charlie into real modern times," he commented, "we were able to show how he is finally able to conquer that frustration. It is clear that technology is now on his side." An article in *PC Magazine* states the counter-argument to Chaplin's *Modern Times* in its most blithely optimistic terms: "As many of the early PC ads and

35. To market computers, Charlie is spruced up in pinstripes
for the "Little Tramp" campaign. Courtesy IBM.

commercials implied, the Personal Computer, like a 16-bit Moses, can help to set us free."[16]

Critics could easily argue that although a personal computer enables one to store and manipulate large quantities of information, it is not necessarily a liberating force for people like data processors who "input" information eight hours a day. Critics can legitimately complain that the IBM commercials distort the image of Charlie garnered from the Chaplin films. The fact remains, however, that Roy Export has sold the image to IBM and that in doing so, the image is subject to transformation through the way it is manipulated by people other than the original creator. Chaplin, the man widely denounced as a dangerous leftist and exiled from the United States in part because of those perceived commitments in the 1940s and early 1950s, is after his death enriching his survivors through the sale of that image, in the best capitalist tradition, to one of the most massive of corporate enterprises. To compound the irony, the image is being used to sell what has become a central icon of high technology: the microcomputer.

Was IBM concerned that the allegations about Chaplin's politics might be dredged up to damage its own corporate reputation? An article in *PC Magazine* suggests that his suspect past was taken into account by IBM (the article calls *Modern Times* Chaplin's "springboard for his increasingly public socialist sentiments," which "would cause him to be hounded during the McCarthy era"). To inquiries about this issue, an IBM spokesperson replied with the official company position: IBM was confident that the public could distinguish a fictional character from the man who created that character. If that distinction were made, Chaplin's past, which IBM admitted might be suspect, should have no effect on the campaigns.[17] No available evidence suggests that details of Chaplin's past had any significant negative influence on the IBM–Charlie collaboration to sell personal computers.

As WE REACH the centenary of Chaplin's birth, what conclusions can be drawn about the evolution of Chaplin's star image in American culture? It is clear, due in part to IBM, that Chaplin's star image is still alive and evolving over a decade after his death. One direction of its evolution is also somehow characteristic of a dominant trend of the period: as the Reagan era has celebrated capitalist enterprise, so has the image of Charlie helped market the computer, a product so representative of the 1980s that *Time* named it "Man of the Year" in 1985.

Yet it would be too pessimistic—and a distortion as well—to suggest that IBM's Charlie has *become* the Chaplin star image. Those who commodify the image to sell products are joined by other admirers and detractors of the image. Other texts besides the IBM advertisements contribute to Chaplin's star image in the 1980s. Chapter 11 suggested that Chaplin and his work still draw the interest of writers and readers, as David Robinson's recent biography, *Chaplin: His Life and Art*, demonstrates. College film courses often include examinations of Chaplin's work on their syllabi. Chaplin's films are still being shown by revival houses and college film societies. And the films appear on cable channels, most prominently the Disney channel, which in the mid-1980s ran a full series of the United Artists features and some of the First National shorts. Video shops rent the films. A documentary series like *The Unknown Chaplin* even presents us with more of Chaplin's work. IBM had no monopoly on Chaplin's star image in the 1980s, however secure its license to use Charlie for selling computers.

This book has traced the evolution of Chaplin's star image in America by exploring the interactions between Chaplin and various public institutions, especially the press, the government, and pressure groups. These interactions have been placed in their historical context, which includes not only the history of the film industry and film criticism and reviewing but also the more specific history of Chaplin's relevant personal and political involvements and the broader cultural and political history of the United States. In the case of Chaplin, it seems self-evident that the evolution of his star image and the changing reception he and his films received were closely bound up with these historical currents.

After examining how Chaplin's star image has evolved in the United States since the heady days of "Chaplinitis," it is apparent that Chaplin's star image is a product of history for at least two different reasons. First, Chaplin himself lived in a historical context, both shaped by and shaping that context through his public actions and his films. His Liberty Loan and second front activities; his films and his shifting conception of character in them; his divorces and affairs; his exile and return—all took place within and were influenced by historical context. The histories of the American film industry (both its technological and its signifying practices), American society, and even international politics inform the ways in which Chaplin's star image has evolved and is evolving in the twentieth century. But Chaplin was not a passive subject fully determined by those histories, however much they constrained him or limited his choices. The evolution of Chaplin's star image also suggests that, through his actions and films, Chaplin played an important role himself in shaping that image. Whereas many stars in the studio era had minimal control over their star images, Chaplin, because he owned his means of production after 1918 and participated in so many aspects of filmmaking (including of promotion campaigns), was able to help control his star image to a degree unthinkable for most other stars. Despite the legitimate skepticism in some critical circles since the late 1960s about auteurism and romanticization of the individual artist, Chaplin clearly contributed in important ways to the shaping of his star image.

Second, the star image is a product of history because the reception of Chaplin and his films, including the prevailing critical discourse about films, is rooted in history. Those who read about Chaplin, write about Chaplin, or watch his films also function in a specific historical context. The qualities that Chaplin's admirers and detractors discover in his life and films have changed over time. The vulgarity or hilarity of Charlie, the persona, struck audiences in the 1910s. The filmmaker

Chaplin's blend of pathos and comedy seemed prominent in the 1920s and early 1930s. From the mid-1930s through the 1950s, the man's political perspectives, whether in his films or in his public activities, as well as his associations with women, seemed to dominate public attention. Thanks to Chaplin's lower, more accommodating public profile and the shrewd rerelease of his films in the past two decades, the character of Charlie began to reassume a larger role in Chaplin's star image. Simultaneously, due in part to the dominance of auteurism, Chaplin himself was again regarded as a talented artist rather than as a man with questionable political views and morality. Chaplin's star image has evolved in certain ways partly because the critical discourse about movies and their place in American culture has shifted significantly since Chaplin's career began. But to bring the argument full circle, these shifts in the critical discourse (think of the 1930s, for example) were themselves often related to the same broad social and economic forces that influenced Chaplin. Chaplin's star image can only be understood within the web of culture and history.

Further research is needed to examine how individual viewers have read and responded to Chaplin films and the ways in which groups of different social classes, genders, and ages receive him in different, patterned ways. However impossible it is to identify all the ways that Chaplin and his movies have affected Americans, people have used Chaplin's movies and his star image for a variety of purposes. To some, the movies have offered compensation: even though their lives were frustrating and bounded, Charlie offered an image of how the physically small and powerless could survive with dignity and resilience. To others, some of his movies have reinforced a sense of alienation from modern society: for them, *Monsieur Verdoux*'s sustained examination of an impersonal and ruthless society elicited a powerful response. To some, Chaplin even became a reified political position. Whether such people denounced or celebrated Chaplin depended on whether they were, in the American sense, political liberals or conservatives. Chaplin then became the victim or the villain, depending on one's views. Doubtless an exploration of individual responses to Chaplin's life and films would demonstrate that the star image has been meaningful to people in many other, and often culturally patterned, ways.[18]

Chaplin's star image thus is, as Richard Dyer suggested in his book on stars, a "structured polysemy." That is, his star image is made up of many, sometimes contradictory, qualities and meanings that evolve as the culture converses about his life, his films, and his worth. As Auden would have it, Chaplin has, since his death, become his admirers. But he has also become his detractors and his commodifiers. The future shape of his star image will depend on the quality of the cultural conversation about Chaplin, Charlie, and the films that brought both to stardom. Let the conversation continue.

Notes

PREFACE

1. Film historians have often cited the *Olympic* as the ship on which Chaplin arrived, but since that ship had been sent to Belfast for refurbishing on 21 September 1912, they have made a mistake. Documents from the U.S. Immigration and Naturalization Service verify that Chaplin arrived on the *Oceanic*. See Harold Manning and Timothy J. Lyons, "Charlie Chaplin's Early Life: Fact and Fiction," *Historical Journal of Film, Radio, and Television* 3, no. 1 (1983): 35–41.

2. Timothy Lyons, in his invaluable *Charles Chaplin: A Guide to References and Resources* (Boston: G. K. Hall, 1979), lists over 1,700 books and articles about Chaplin, yet concludes that "the literature has not fully explored Chaplin's life and work in the context of American culture and society" (p. 19). Although here I focus on the relationship between Chaplin and American culture, my research has led me to believe that it would be interesting and worthwhile to examine the evolution of Chaplin's star image in a number of countries, especially Great Britain, France, and the Soviet Union.

3. Throughout the book, "Charlie" will refer to Chaplin's most familiar screen persona, often called "the tramp" or "the little fellow." "Chaplin" will refer to the real person, Charles Spencer Chaplin.

4. A recent work on American film history that skillfully delineates the relationship between popular films and such internal and external historical developments is Robert Ray, *A Certain Tendency of the Hollywood Cinema, 1930–1980* (Princeton: Princeton Univ. Press, 1985). See especially the introduction and pp. 28–29. Such attention to historical factors is consistent with the neoformalist approach, to which I am indebted. As David Bordwell has observed in his brief exegesis of the neoformalist approach ("Lowering the Stakes," *Iris* 1, no. 1 [1983]: 15), "the historical emphasis of [Russian] Formalism does not exclude consideration of economics, ideology, technological change, or other historical factors."

5. Richard Dyer, *Stars* (London: British Film Institute, 1979), p. 1.

6. Dyer, *Stars*, pp. 69–72. Examining this broad variety of media texts in addition to Chaplin's films is absolutely central if one is to get a firm sense of how Chaplin's star image evolved. Tony Bennett, a scholar interested in the James Bond phenomenon, has recently drawn on Pierre Macherey's work to argue that "incrustations" which shape and do much to define the evolution of Bond, have grown up around the Bond novels and films. Bennett goes so far

as to propose that the Bond text (film or novel) "does not have any existence that is separable from such incrustations." Similarly here, Chaplin's star image evolved not simply because of his films, but also because of such "incrustations" as movie posters and press kits; feature articles about films; reviews; publicity about Chaplin's private and public activities; and the broader shifts in the social and political climate. On "incrustations," see Bennett's "Text and Social Process: The Case of James Bond," *Screen Education*, no. 41 (Winter/Spring 1982): 3–14.

7. "Literary History as a Challenge to Literary Theory," in Hans Robert Jauss, *Toward an Aesthetic of Reception*, trans. Timothy Bahti (Minneapolis: Univ. of Minnesota Press, 1982), p. 20.

8. In *Speaking of Soap Operas* (Chapel Hill: Univ. of North Carolina Press, 1985), Robert Allen observes that even though Jauss is interested in the relationship between literary history and broader historical currents, his "model of literary history is largely insular" (p. 99). He also cites (p. 182) Robert Holub's survey of German reader-response criticism, in which Iser and Jauss are strongly criticized "for their lack of sociological grounding with respect to the reader." Greater attention to the broader sociohistorical currents is necessary if we are to understand the evolution of Chaplin's star image.

9. F. O. Matthiessen, *American Renaissance* (New York: Oxford Univ. Press, 1941), p. xv.

1. CHAPLIN, THE EARLY FILMS, AND THE RISE TO STARDOM

1. The account of Chaplin's entry into the movies comes from Chaplin's *My Autobiography* (New York: Simon and Schuster, 1964), pp. 137–39; the date of his departure from the Karno company is found in Theodore Huff, *Charlie Chaplin* (1951; reprinted New York: Pyramid Books, 1964), p. 3, and corroborated by John McCabe, *Charlie Chaplin* (Garden City, New York: Doubleday, 1978), pp. 46–47. David Robinson, in *Chaplin: His Life and Art* (New York: McGraw-Hill, 1985), pp. 102–7, also treats Chaplin's introduction to the movies and reprints a part of his first contract. These three are presently the most reliable of the Chaplin biographies in English and can be supplemented by Georges Sadoul, *Vie de Charlot* (Paris: Lherminier, 1978). Hereafter, Chaplin's autobiography will be cited as MA and the Robinson biography as CHLA.

2. See Robert C. Allen, *Vaudeville and Film, 1895–1915: A Study in Media Interaction* (New York: Arno, 1980), esp. pp. 23–92.

3. On the struggles for control of the film industry from 1908 on, see Tino Balio, ed., *The American Film Industry*, 2nd ed. (Madison: Univ. of Wisconsin Press, 1985), pp. 103–251. The transformation of the film industry from the "primitive" phase to the "classical Hollywood" phase is treated most fully in David Bordwell, Janet Staiger, and Kristin Thompson, *The Classical Hollywood Cinema: Film Style and Mode of Production to 1960* (New York: Columbia Univ. Press, 1985), esp. parts. 2, 3. Hereafter, this work will be cited as CHC. Background on Keystone can be found in Mack Sennett, *King of Comedy* (New York:

Doubleday, 1954) and Kalton C. Lahue and Terry Brewer, *Kops and Custards* (Norman: Oklahoma Univ. Press, 1968).

4. Janet Staiger, "Seeing Stars," *Velvet Light Trap*, no. 20 (Summer 1983): 13; CHC, ch. 9, esp. pp. 101–2.

5. Though the persona portrayed by Chaplin in so many films has been called a number of different things—the tramp, the little tramp, the little fellow, and others—I will in this study regularly refer to the persona as "Charlie." (See the Preface, note 3.)

6. *Moving Picture World* 19 (17 February 1914): 678. The subsequent references in this paragraph come from volumes 19–22 of the same periodical. Dates and page numbers are cited parenthetically in the text.

7. *Motion Picture Magazine* 13, no. 7 (August 1914): 126. The subsequent references in the next few paragraphs come from the same volume. Issues and page numbers are cited in the text.

8. Charles Spencer Chaplin, *Charlie Chaplin's Own Story*, ed. Harry Geduld (1916; reprinted Bloomington: Indiana Univ. Press, 1985), p. 140. This book, actually written by a journalist named Rose Lee Wilder after interviews with Chaplin in 1915, was published by Bobbs-Merrill in Indianapolis but never released . See Chapter 2, below, and CHLA, pp. 180–85, for further information on the book.

9. Charles J. McGuirk, "Chaplinitis," *Motion Picture Magazine* 9, nos. 6–7 (July and August 1915): 85–89 and 121–24. The quotation is from part 1, p. 87.

10. *Motion Picture Magazine* quoted in Raoul Sobel and David Francis, *Chaplin: Genesis of a Clown* (London: Quartet Books, 1977), p. 144; *Cleveland Plain Dealer*, 9 June 1915; *New York World*, 19 June 1915 (both newspaper articles are in the Robinson Locke Collection, vol. 110, within the Billy Rose Collection, Lincoln Center Branch, New York Public Library, New York); Wes Gehring, *Charlie Chaplin: A Bio-Bibliography* (Westport, Conn.: Greenwood, 1983), p. 62. The books by Sobel and Francis and by Gehring both contain useful information about the Chaplin craze. The Robinson Locke Collection will hereafter be cited as RLC.

11. Discussions of Ritchie are found in Sobel and Francis, *Chaplin: Genesis of a Clown*, pp. 143–44, and McCabe, *Charlie Chaplin*, p. 89. McCabe also comments on another Chaplin imitator, Charles Amador, who changed his name to Charles Aplin.

12. Howard Philip Rhoades, "Who Is This?" *Motion Picture Magazine* 10, no. 10 (November 1915): 115.

13. An example of the comic strip can be found in Chaplin, *My Life in Pictures* (New York: Grosset and Dunlap, 1975), p. 16. The RLC, vol. 110, contains one such cartoon from the 5 April 1915 issue of the *Cleveland Leader*.

14. McGuirk, "Chaplinitis," part 1, p. 87.

15. Dyer, *Stars*, pp. 48–49.

16. E. V. Whitcomb, "Charlie Chaplin," *Photoplay* 7 (February 1915): 35–37; "A Real Film ABC," *Moving Picture World* (6 February 1915), both in RLC, vol.

110. The point here is not whether Chaplin actually was humble—and evidence suggests that his pride did grow as he aged—but that he was being presented as humble by the press.

17. The quotations come from the articles by Whitcomb, McGuirk, and "A Real Film ABC." See also, in RLC, vol. 110: Victor Eubank, "The Funniest Man on the Screen," *Motion Picture Magazine* (March 1915); "Charlie Chaplin, Cheerful Comedian," *Picture-Play Weekly* 1, no. 3 (24 April 1915): 1; *Chicago Tribune*, 25 April 1915.

18. Santayana's essay is included in *Winds of Doctrine* (New York: Scribner's, 1913).

19. Charles Alexander, *Here the Country Lies* (Bloomington: Indiana Univ. Press, 1980), p. 9. On the Genteel Tradition, see ibid., pp. 1–27; Henry F. May, *The End of American Innocence* (New York: Knopf, 1959); and Stow Persons, *The Decline of American Gentility* (New York: Scribner's, 1973).

20. Both quotations appear in Lary May, *Screening Out the Past* (New York: Oxford Univ. Press, 1980), pp. 59, 53.

21. Review of *The Property Man* in *Moving Picture World* 21 (15 August 1914): 961.

22. *New Orleans American*, 9 September 1915, RLC, vol. 110.

23. *Detroit News*, 13 April 1916, in RLC, vol. 110.

24. J. B. Hirsch, "The New Charlie Chaplin," *Motion Picture Magazine* 10, no. 12 (January 1916): 115–17. Page numbers for citations of this article in subquent paragraphs are given in the text.

25. Though two recent studies of movie theaters in Boston and New York dispute the traditional view that moviegoing before 1915 was almost exclusively a working-class entertainment, they do agree that by the mid-1910s, the audience was growing and much of it was middle class. See Russell Merritt, "Nickelodeon Theaters, 1905–1914," in Balio, *American Film Industry*, pp. 59–82, and Robert C. Allen, "Motion Picture Exhibition in Manhattan, 1906–1912," in *The American Movie Industry*, ed. Gorham Kindem (Carbondale: Southern Illinois Univ. Press), pp. 12–24.

26. *Motion Picture Classic* 3 (September 1916): 41–44.

27. See CHC, pp. 177–83.

28. Quoted in Gerald D. McDonald et al., *The Films of Charlie Chaplin* (New York: Bonanza Books, 1965), p. 99.

29. Janice Radway, *Reading the Romance* (Chapel Hill: Univ. of North Carolina Press, 1984), pp. 10, 147–49.

30. McGuirk, "Chaplinitis," part 1, p. 89.

31. McCabe, *Charlie Chaplin*, p. 78. Apparently, Chaplin also shot footage during the early 1920s for another film dealing with the flophouses he saw in his childhood. Kevin Brownlow's fascinating compilation film, *The Unknown Chaplin*, includes some of that footage.

32. Chaplin's request to Ramsaye is reported in the *Toledo Blade*, 10 March 1916, RLC, vol. 110.

1. Chaplin's Mutual contract negotiations and the Hippodrome evening are discussed in Robert Grau, "The More People Laughed at the Idea of Chaplin's Salary, the More They Had to Pay," *Motion Pictures Magazine* (May 1916), RLC, vol. 110; and Terry Ramsaye, *A Million and One Nights* (1926, reprinted New York: Simon and Schuster, 1964), pp. 731–36.

2. CHLA, pp. 180–85. Harry Geduld, in his introduction to the recently reprinted edition of *Charlie Chaplin's Own Story*, argues that, although there is a good deal of invented detail in the book, it does provide some useful insight into some aspects of Chaplin's life to 1916, if used judiciously. Geduld's introduction corrects some of the errors found in the book, but one wonders if he would have been more critical of the book had he had access to the information Robinson recounts in his biography.

3. Huff, *Charlie Chaplin*, p. 58; MA, p. 188.

4. *Photoplay* (March 1916), RLC, vol. 110.

5. Sobel and Francis discuss this March 1916 article in *Chaplin: Genesis of a Clown*, pp. 149–50.

6. "Newspapers Aided Chaplin to Fame," *New Orleans Daily States*, 23 July 1916, RLC, vol. 110.

7. *Harper's Weekly* 62 (6 May 1916): 494. Benjamin McArthur (p. 176) called Fiske "a leading box-office attraction from the 1890s to the 1920s."

8. *New Republic* 10 (3 February 1917): 16–18.

9. Wes Gehring, "Chaplin and the Progressive Era: The Neglected Politics of a Clown," *Indiana Social Studies Quarterly* 34 (Autumn 1981): 10–18, at 10, 11, 18. Ivens is quoted by Gehring.

10. Walter Kerr, *The Silent Clowns* (New York: Knopf, 1975), p. 88.

11. See John Cawelti's "typology of literary formulas" in *Adventure, Mystery, and Romance* (Chicago: Univ. of Chicago Press, 1976), ch. 2, and esp. pp. 41–42. Cawelti's concept of "formula" is an extremely rich one and, I would argue, useful in understanding the body of Chaplin's work: in a sense, Chaplin created, then later in his career deviated from, his own unique formula.

12. Quoted in *Moving Picture World* (21 July 1917), RLC, vol. 110.

13. Quoted in Mabel Condon, "In Chaplin's House of Glass," *Picture-Play Magazine* (December 1916), RLC, vol. 110.

14. This move to a tighter narrative structure is consistent with the general trend of Hollywood films through the 1910s. By the end of the 1910s, according to Kristin Thompson (CHC, p. 193), Hollywood narratives "came to place more emphasis upon character, and to construct tightly organized causal chains." These characteristics stemmed partly from the tendency to make longer films, which Chaplin himself began with *A Dog's Life* and continued with *The Kid* (1920).

15. Lewis Jacobs, *Rise of the American Film* (1939; reprinted New York: Teacher's College Press, 1971), pp. 251, 253. Jacobs discusses movies during World War I in considerable detail in chapter 14.

16. The fate of civil liberties during World War I is treated in Harry N.

Scheiber, *The Wilson Administration and Civil Liberties, 1917–1921* (Ithaca: Cornell Univ. Press, 1960) and William Preston, Jr., *Aliens and Dissenters: Federal Suppression of Radicals, 1903–1933* (Cambridge: Harvard University Press, 1963). The Committee on Public Information is treated in James R. Mock and Cedric Larson, *Words That Won the War* (Princeton: Princeton Univ. Press, 1939).

17. Kevin Brownlow, *The War, the West, and the Wilderness* (New York: Knopf, 1979), pp. 38–40.

18. " 'No Chaplin Here,' Say English Signs; Sore at Comedian," *New York Star*, 28 June 1916, RLC, vol. 110.

19. Huff, *Charlie Chaplin*, pp. 74–75; *Variety*, 22 June 1917, p. 20.

20. Huff, *Charlie Chaplin*, p. 75; Brownlow, *War*, p. 40; *Variety*, 22 June 1917, p. 20.

21. Burton Ormesby, "*The Weekly Dispatch* Gets Another Craving to See Chaplin in Khaki," *New York Telegraph*, 22 July 1917, RLC, vol. 110.

22. Beally quoted in *Moving Picture World* (18 May 1918, RLC, vol. 111; Chaplin letter in *Pictures and Picturegoer* (23 February 1918): p. 241.

23. *Washington Post*, 7 April 1918, p. 8.

24. "20,000 Throng Wall Street to Hear Movie Stars Tell How to Win War," *New York Herald Tribune*, 9 April 1918, p. 8; "Stirring Celebrations Help Speed Loan Drive," *NYT*, 9 April 1918, p. 4.

25. "8,000 People Buy Bonds from Charlie Chaplin," *Atlanta Constitution*, 18 April 1918, p. 1.

26. "Chaplin Sells Liberty Bonds; Meeting at Ryman Proves Grand and Glorious Success," *Nashville Banner*, 19 April 1918, p. 7; *Memphis Commercial Appeal*, 21 April 1918, pp. 1, 10.

27. Huff, *Charlie Chaplin*, p. 75.

28. *Moving Picture World* (18 May 1918), RLC, vol. 111.

29. *Memphis Commercial Appeal*, 21 April 1918, p. 10.

30. Corporal J. Stuart Blackton, "Chaplin Holds the Rhine," *Photoplay* (June 1918), RLC, vol. 111.

31. Review of *The Immigrant* in *Photoplay* 12 (September 1917): 99.

32. David Auerbach, "Charlie Chaplin: Of Crime and Genius—A Psycho-Portrait," *Encounter* 60 (May 1983): 86–92.

33. McCabe, *Charlie Chaplin*, p. 35; MA, p. 108.

34. MA, pp. 178, 267. Kelly's brother, Arthur, later became a prominent executive in the foreign offices of United Artists.

35. See Sadoul, *Vie de Charlot*, pp. 229–32 for a chronology of their relationship.

36. Marjorie Daw, "A Little Journey to the Home of Mr. and Mrs. Charles Chaplin," *Detroit Journal*, 31 January 1920, RLC, vol. 111.

37. Huff, *Charlie Chaplin*, p. 78; *NYT*, 3 August 1920, p. 14; *NYT*, 4 August 1920, p. 14.

38. *NYT*, 11 August 1920, p. 8.

39. One of the few critics who likes the film, Gerald Mast, places it in the cat-

egory of Chaplin's ironic comedies, culminating in *Monsieur Verdoux*, in which Chaplin takes "cynical, unpleasant material" and makes it funny. Mast argues that "in the course of the film, Chaplin has booted the rural idyll itself in the pants, particularly in the breach between what it supposedly believes and what it actually does." See Gerald Mast, *The Comic Mind*, 2nd ed. (Chicago: Univ. of Chicago Press, 1979), p. 92.

40. Julian Smith, in *Chaplin* (Boston: Twayne, 1984), p. 46, has perceptively suggested that Purviance's portrayal of the gullible farmer's daughter is a projection of Chaplin's recent bride: both seem to be somewhat foolish and fickle, a far cry from the characters Edna had played in the initial two First Nationals. Just as Mildred was wooed into a contract shortly after her marriage by Louis B. Mayer, Smith points out the farmer's daughter is swept off her feet by a city slicker in town for a day. Robinson (CHLA, pp. 248–50) also suggests that Chaplin's difficulties during the long production of *Sunnyside*, as well as the romantic triangle in the film, seem drawn from Chaplin's unfortunate marriage.

41. "A Letter to a Genius," *Photoplay* 17 (April 1920): 27; *Variety*, 20 June 1919, p. 53; *Variety*, 12 December 1919, p. 45.

42. *Ladies' Home Journal*, August 1918, p. 82.

43. *Photoplay* 14 (September 1918): 81.

44. Ibid., pp. 83, 117.

45. "Appeals to Brows High and Low," *Moving Picture World* (23 March 1918), RLC, vol. 111.

46. *Toledo Times*, 16 May 1918, RLC, vol. 111.

47. "Some First Impressions of Charlie Chaplin," *Pictures and Picturegoer* (11 October 1919): 444, RLC, vol. 111. Emphasis in original.

48. Charles Spencer Chaplin, "What People Laugh At," *American Magazine* 86 (November 1918): 34, 134–37.

49. *Theatre Magazine* 30 (October 1919): 249; the essay is also reprinted in *Focus on Chaplin*, ed. Donald McCaffrey (Englewood Cliffs, N.J.: Prentice-Hall, 1971), pp. 71–73.

50. *Photoplay* 17 (April 1920): 27.

3. FROM *THE KID* TO *THE GOLD RUSH*

1. Chaplin's portrayal of artists in his films is intriguingly varied. An artist saves Charlie and Edna from the waiter in *The Immigrant*, is the rival for Edna's affections in *The Vagabond*, a cad in *The Kid*, and as we shall see later in this chapter, a rather romantic but doomed character in *A Woman of Paris*.

2. A nondiegetic insert is a shot showing an object not part of the space of the narrative, which is cut into the narrative sequence.

3. Chaplin deleted this shot from the rerelease, perhaps because he felt its sentimentality too obvious and forced.

4. See Huff, *Charlie Chaplin*, p. 106; CHLA, p. 265.

5. *Exceptional Photoplays* 3 (January-February 1921): 2, 6–7; reprinted in *American Film Criticism*, ed. Stanley Kauffman (New York: Liveright, 1972), pp. 115–18.

6. *New Republic* 26 (30 March 1921): 136–37; reprinted in Kauffmann, *American Film Criticism*, pp. 118–21.

7. *Variety*, 21 January 1921, p. 40; *NYT*, 22 January 1921, p. 9; *Theatre Magazine* review quoted in *The Films of Charlie Chaplin*, ed. Gerald D. McDonald et al. (New York: Citadel, 1965), p. 167.

8. CHLA, p. 295.

9. As Julian Smith notes, Chaplin explores in *The Idle Class* "more intensely than any other the split between his person and his persona"—in other words, between Chaplin and Charlie (*Chaplin*, p. 56). From Smith's perspective in the 1980s, Chaplin increasingly began to invest his own psyche in more than one character after 1920, sometimes by playing two roles, as in *The Great Dictator*, and sometimes by expressing two sides of his complex personality through two different characters. See Chapter 11.

10. Robinson (CHLA, p. 296) notes that this is the first Chaplin film for which much written script and gag material has survived in Chaplin's records. Because the production itself was stopped for work on the story much less often than in previous films, Robinson suggests "that Chaplin was moving away from his earlier method of creating and improvising on the set and even on film, towards a greater degree of advance planning on paper." Though he would still have some huge production problems, particularly on *City Lights*, Chaplin seems somewhat belatedly to have begun moving toward the production practices that had been common in Hollywood for nearly a decade.

11. See Anthony Channell Hilfer, *The Revolt against the Village, 1915–1930* (Chapel Hill: Univ. of North Carolina Press, 1969).

12. Benjamin De Casseres, "The Hamlet-Like Nature of Charlie Chaplin," *NYT*, 12 December 1920, sec. 3, p. 5.

13. See Sobel and Francis, *Chaplin: Genesis of a Clown*, p. 79. Robinson (CHLA, pp. 131–33) transcribes a 1914 letter from Chaplin to his brother Sidney which, besides providing a fascinating picture of Chaplin's state of mind at Keystone, shows that Chaplin was not a highly educated man.

14. Charles Chaplin, *My Trip Abroad* (New York: Harper, 1922.

15. See R. K. Murray, *The Red Scare* (Minneapolis: Univ. of Minnesota Press, 1955), and Louis F. Post, *The Deportations Delirium of Nineteen-Twenty* (1923; reprinted New York: DaCapo, 1970). Post was the assistant secretary of labor who halted the wholesale deportations.

16. *Literary Digest* 72 (28 January 1922): 48; *Collier's*, 11 November 1922; reprinted in Gehring, *Charlie Chaplin*, pp. 108–14.

17. The context for the founding of United Artists is well described in Tino Balio, *United Artists* (Madison: Univ. of Wisconson Press, 1976), ch. 1. My discussion here is indebted to Balio's work.

18. A. H. Giebler, *Moving Picture World* (1 February 1919): 619. Quoted in Balio, *United Artists*, p. 3.

19. Balio, *United Artists*, p. 12; MA, pp. 221–23.

20. Balio, *United Artists*, pp. 12–13, takes this account from Giebler's article (cited in note 18).

21. Balio, *United Artists*, p. 24.

22. See CHC, esp. chs. 12–13, and George Mitchell, "The Consolidation of the American Film Industry," *Cine-Tracts*, nos. 2 (1976): 28–36, and 3/4 (1976): 63–70.

23. *NYT*, 23 February 1923, p. 16.

24. De Casseres, "The Hamlet-Like Nature of Charlie Chaplin," sec. 3, p. 5.

25. Interesting background and production information on *A Woman of Paris* can be found in Adolphe Menjou and M. M. Musselman, *It Took Nine Tailors* (New York: McGraw-Hill, 1948), ch. 14, esp. pp. 104–6.

26. "What Chaplin Thinks," *NYT*, 7 October 1923, sec. 9, p. 4.

27. Menjou and Musselman, *It Took Nine Tailors*, p. 118.

28. By mise-en-scène, I mean those elements of film style that film shares with the theater: sets and props, costumes, lighting, and acting styles. See Bordwell and Thompson, *Film Art*, 2nd ed. (New York: Random House, 1986), ch. 5.

29. There is even an oblique reference to Chaplin's childhood in *A Woman of Paris*. Marie cares for orphans at the end of the film, much as Charlie cared for the boy in *The Kid* and as Chaplin himself may have wished for when he and Sydney were in the Lambeth workhouse.

30. The following is indebted to Smith, *Chaplin*, particularly pp. 63–65.

31. *NYT*, 2 October 1923, p. 7.

32. *NYT*, 7 October 1923, sec. 9, p. 4.

33. *New York Herald Tribune*, 3 October 1923, p. 12.

34. Quoted in *Selected Film Criticism, 1921–30*, ed. Anthony Slide (Metuchen, N.J.: Scarecrow Press, 1982), p. 320.

35. *Photoplay* 25 (December 1923): 73; reprinted in Slide, *Selected Film Criticism, 1921–30*, p. 318.

36. "The Death of Zeus," *New Republic* 36 (7 November 1923): 283.

37. *Variety*, 27 September 1923, p. 25. The *Variety* reviewer's comment about the bigger houses points out that American movie audiences were not identical throughout the country. In general, the taste of viewers who attended first-run showings in the major cities was more sophisticated and less moralistic than viewers in small-town America. As we shall see in subsequent chapters, Chaplin's star image often became a subject of considerable controversy in the press, partly because of these different orientations of American viewers and writers.

38. Balio, *United Artists*, p. 45. Though this was a considerable box-office return for an average picture, one can get an idea of how disappointing it was for a Chaplin film by noting that the gross for Fairbanks's *Robin Hood* was $1.4 million the same year and for *The Gold Rush*, Chaplin's next film, $2.07 million in its first year. See United Artists Balance Sheets and Work Papers, box 1, folders 5 (1923) and 7 (1925), United Artists Collection, the Wisconsin Center for Film and Theater Research in the Wisconsin State Historical Library, Madison (hereafter cited as UAC).

39. *NYT*, 7 October 1923, sec. 9, p. 4.

40. *NYT*, 16 October 1923, p. 23.

41. Pressbooks on Chaplin's United Artists films are available in two places: the UAC, and, from *The Circus* (1928) on, the Billy Rose Collection (hereafter BRC) at the New York Public Library, Lincoln Center Branch. *The Gold Rush* pressbook is found in UAC, UA pressbook 448, reel 13.

42. C. F. McGlashlin, *History of the Donner Party* (San Francisco: A. Carlisle, 1922), p. vi. Chaplin also discussed the genesis of the film in his autobiography, pp. 304–5, though he exaggerated how many survived. See also Timothy Lyons, "The Idea in *The Gold Rush*: A Study of Chaplin's Use of the Comic Technique of Pathos-Humor," in McCaffrey, *Focus on Chaplin*, pp. 113–23.

43. Lita Grey Chaplin, with Morton Cooper, *My Life with Chaplin: An Intimate Memoir* (New York: Grove, 1966), ch. 5, discusses the shooting at Truckee, much of which was discarded after Grey was replaced as Georgia.

44. Apparently Chaplin had this scene in mind early in the conception of the film, for Lita Grey, Chaplin's second wife and the person originally cast to play Georgia, tells how proudly Chaplin showed her this particular set when he was first considering her for the role. See Grey, *My Life with Chaplin*, pp. 53–54.

45. Joan Mellen, *Big Bad Wolves: Masculinity in American Film* (New York: Pantheon, 1977).

46. See Morin, *Stars* (New York: Grove, 1960), pp. 111–12.

47. One could argue that presenting the wealthy Charlie as unhappy is another manifestation of what Robin Wood has called "the Rosebud syndrome," the ultimately conservative notion that because the rich are necessarily unhappy, we should all be satisfied being poor or of moderate means. Unlike Charles Foster Kane, though, Charlie, deprived of love for much of the film, is also unfulfilled when he is poor. Also, unlike Kane, he apparently achieves both wealth and happiness in the film's ending.

48. UA pressbook 448, reel 13, UAC.

49. Chaplin cut the ending short in his 1942 rerelease of *The Gold Rush*. In it—the version most readily available today—the final shot of the film is of Charlie and Georgia walking arm in arm up a stairway, away from the camera, a more purely "happy ending." Dennis DiNitto and William Herman have discussed the original ending in *Film and the Critical Eye* (New York: Macmillan, 1975), p. 101. One might add that this self-referentiality in Chaplin's films was more evident to reviewers in *The Circus* and *Modern Times* than in *The Gold Rush*. And it was not widely commented upon until, in our postmodern era, self-referentiality in art became widely practiced by artists and widely praised by critics. See Garret Stewart, "Modern Hard Times: Chaplin and the Cinema of Self-Reflexiveness," *Critical Inquiry* 3 (1976): 295–315.

50. A discussion of the place of advertising in the film industry is found in CHC, pp. 97–102.

51. A copy of the program is available in the RLC. This account of the promotion of *The Gold Rush* comes from this program and the pressbook of the film (UA pressbook 448, UAC).

52. *Variety*, 1 July 1925, p. 32.

53. *Variety*, 19 August 1925, p. 36.

54. *Photoplay* 28 (September 1925): 50.

55. "Here and There with Chaplin," *NYT*, 11 November 1925, sec. 7, p. 3.

56. Although this study is concentrating on Chaplin and the United States, it is worth noting that the first book-length study of Chaplin, *Charlot*, by poet, journalist, and *cinéaste* Louis Delluc, was published in France in 1921. (An English edition was published in 1922.) Delluc had been a co-founder of the world's first film society in 1920. An opening challenge in the preface of his book likely encouraged young American intellectuals who read the book to take Chaplin's work seriously: "To the creative artist of the cinema, the mask of Charlie Chaplin has just the same importance as the traditional mask of Beethoven has to the musical composer."

57. Max Eastman, *Great Companions* (New York: Farrar, Straus, and Cudahy, 1959), p. 209.

58. Edmund Wilson, *The Twenties* (New York: Farrar, Straus, and Giroux, 1975), p. 158. Chaplin posed for a photograph with the *Vanity Fair* group, sans Wilson, which is reproduced in MA, p. 247. Gorham Munson, in *The Awakening Twenties* (Baton Rouge: Louisiana State Univ. Press, 1985), ch. 13, writes that the evening Chaplin spent with Crane and Frank was in October 1923, when Chaplin was in New York to promote *A Woman of Paris*. Munson recalls missing the meeting because he was already in bed in his Greenwich Village apartment when the three came by and rang the doorbell, and he also quotes from several of Crane's letters from that period discussing the meeting. From his more detailed account, it seems clear that this is another instance of inaccuracy in Chaplin's autobiography, even though Frank and Chaplin may also have met in 1920. Munson, does, however, agree with the point being made here when he recalls "Chaplin's sympathetic interest in the intelligentsia who were speaking out against reaction in the early postwar years" and when he recounts that Chaplin contributed in 1919 to the founding of a little magazine called *The Modernist* that Munson was working on (p. 233).

59. Among others, Eastman later wrote extensively on Chaplin in *Love and Revolution* (New York: Random House, 1964), *Heroes I Have Known* (New York: Simon and Schuster, 1942), and *Great Companions*.

60. See Chaplin, *My Trip Abroad*, chs. 2, 15.

61. Both comments are taken from "Hollywood and Chaplin," in *Memoirs of Waldo Frank*, ed. Alan Trachtenberg (Amherst: Univ. of Massachusetts Press, 1973), pp. 147–54.

62. Frank, *Memoirs*, p. 154.

63. *New Yorker* 1 (23 May 1925): 9–10; the essay was reprinted in *Time Exposures* (New York: Boni and Liveright, 1926), pp. 87–92.

64. *New Republic* 31 (23 August 1922): 358–59. The ensuing quotations are from this article.

65. Letter to Julian Huxley, 2 December 1923, in *Stark Young, A Life in the Arts: Letters, 1900–1962*, ed. John Pilkington (Baton Rouge: Louisiana State

Univ. Press, 1975). Young was alluding in the letter to Eleonora Duse, the noted Italian dramatic actress who used an extremely naturalistic acting style.

66. Gilbert Seldes, *The Seven Lively Arts* (New York: Harper's, 1924).

67. Wilson, *The Twenties* p. 157.

68. Letter to Alyse Gregory, 17 April 1924, in Edmund Wilson, *Letters on Literature and Politics, 1912–1972*, ed. Elena Wilson (New York: Farrar, Straus, and Giroux, 1977), p. 114; review of *The Seven Lively Arts* (1924), collected in Edmund Wilson, *The Shores of Light* (New York: Farrar, Straus, and Young, 1952), p. 156. The review originally appeared in the *Dial*, where Seldes had served for a time as editor.

69. Wilson, *Shores of Light*, pp. 158–59.

70. The review appeared in the 2 September 1925 issue and is conveniently reprinted in Kauffmann, *American Film Criticism*, pp. 162–65.

71. Balio, *United Artists*, p. 57.

72. Both this review and the other, "Sex Appeal in the Movies," are reprinted in *The Collected Essays of John Peale Bishop*, ed. Edmund Wilson (New York: Scribner's, 1948), pp. 210–21.

73. This attitude, and the resulting desire of American studio heads to hire "artistic" directors from Europe to enhance the prestige of their films, is discussed by Allen and Gomery in *Film History: Theory and Practice* (New York: Knopf, 1985), pp. 91–105.

4. STRUGGLING THROUGH THE TWENTIES

1. Chaplin, *My Life in Pictures*, p. 228.

2. A close analysis of Chaplin's relationships with, attitudes toward, and cinematic portrayals of women would make a fascinating study. Anyone interested in his relationships with women in the early 1920s would want to look at Anita Leslie's biography, *Claire Sheridan* (New York: Doubleday, 1977); Pola Negri's autobiography, *Memoirs of a Star* (New York: Doubleday, 1970); Max Eastman's treatment of Chaplin's affair with Eastman's lover, Florence Deshon, in *Love and Revolution*, pp. 184–211 passim; and, most important, Lita Grey Chaplin's *My Life with Chaplin*.

3. Grey, *My Life with Chaplin*, p. 186. Huff, *Charlie Chaplin*, p. 166, and a number of other lesser biographers accept the altered date. Charles Chaplin, Jr.'s insightful *My Father, Charlie Chaplin* (New York: Popular Library, 1961), seems implicitly to substantiate his mother's story, for instead of writing, "I was born on June 28, 1926," he writes, "June 28, 1926, my birth certificate reads" (p. 9).

4. *NYT*, 2 December 1926, p. 1; 3 December 1926, p. 1.

5. Grey, *My Life with Chaplin*, pp. 252–55, discusses the complaint and quotes a number of the most juicy passages from it. The entire complaint and Chaplin's cross-complaint, along with a number of court orders and commentary by an old Chaplin nemesis, Ed Sullivan, were published as *Chaplin vs. Chaplin*, ed. Ed Sullivan (Los Angeles: Marvin Miller Enterprises, 1965).

6. The story of the legal tussle between Chaplin and Tully is summarized in

NYT (all 1927), 8 January, p. 19; 9 January, p. 8; 14 January, p. 15; and 3 February, p. 25. The articles themselves appeared in four installments in the January-April issues of *Pictorial Review*.

7. *NYT*, 18 January 1927, p. 1; 20 January 1927, p. 1; 23 January 1927, p. 1; 28 January 1927, p. 7; 10 February 1928, p. 26.

8. *NYT*, 16 January 1927, p. 5.

9. *NYT*, 23 August 1927, pp. 1, 8.

10. *Chicago Tribune*, 11 January 1927, pp. 1, 14.

11. Quoted in Grey, *My Life with Chaplin*, p. 260.

12. *NYT*, 12 January 1927, p. 1; *NYT*, 13 January 1927, p. 27; *Boston Advertiser*, 14 January 1927, RLC, vol. 111. The UAC contains a letter from Chaplin to the United Artists Legal Department telling them not to sue the city of Lynn in an attempt to lift the ban. He did not want more publicity at that point.

13. Grey, *My Life with Chaplin*, p. 260.

14. *NYT*, 15 January 1927, p. 1; *NYT*, 26 January 1927, p. 9; *New York Herald Tribune*, 30 January 1927; *NYT*, 11 February 1927, p. 2; *NYT*, 14 February 1927, p. 15. The Cooper quotation is taken from Sumner Smith, "The Spotlight Turns Yellow," *Moving Picture World* (22 January 1927): 252.

15. Hays was president of the Motion Pictures Producers and Distributors of America The "Hays Office" was the industry's self-censorhip body. *New York Morning Telegraph*, 15 January 1927, p. 4; "The Level Head of Will Hays," *New York Morning Telegraph*, RLC, vol. 111. The *Telegraph* seemed to be a strong defender of Chaplin; its film columnist, Herb Cruikshank, in "The Screen in Review" on January 15, offered Chaplin first-page space to give his version of the story. Cruikshank's open letter says, "The dignity of your silence has been impressive."

16. "Something More about the Much-Discussed Chaplin," *New York Herald Tribune*, 23 January 1927, sec. 6, p. 3; "A Sage Once Said, 'It Takes All Kinds to Make a World,' " *New York Herald Tribune*, 30 January 1927, sec. 6, p. 3.

17. "The Spotlight Turns Yellow," p. 252.

18. Quoted in Huff, *Charlie Chaplin*, p. 169.

19. *New Yorker* 3 (23 January 1927): 17–18.

20. *Boston Evening Transcript*, 9 April 1927, p. 3.

21. Dyer, *Stars*, pp. 52–53. Emphasis in original.

22. *NYT*, 29 November 1925, sec. 7, p. 5.

23. Quoted in *Literary Digest* 96 (24 March 1928): 41.

24. *New Republic* 38 (8 February 1928); reprinted in Kauffmann, *American Film Criticism*, pp. 201–4.

25. Kerr, *Silent Clowns*, pp. 339–43, argues in considerable detail that *The Circus* is "a comedy about the consciousness of being funny." See Smith, *Chaplin*, pp. 79–84, both on that notion and on more autobiographical issues, to which my discussion is indebted. Though both give fruitful readings of the film, I believe both undervalue it.

26. Tully, *Pictorial Review*, January 1927, p. 8.

27. Grey, *My Life with Chaplin*, p. 323.

28. Tully, *Pictorial Review*, January 1927, p. 8.

29. See Smith, *Chaplin*, pp. 82–83.

30. Tully, *Pictorial Review*, February 1928, p. 75.

31. "Bonnie Prince Charlie of the Custard Pies," *Literary Digest* 96 (24 March 1928): 36.

32. "Bonnie Prince Charlie," p. 42.

33. Bakshy's review, which appeared in the *Nation* on 29 February 1928, and Young's, which appeared in the *New Republic* on 8 February 1928, both are reprinted in Kauffmann, *American Film Criticism*, pp. 200–204.

34. O'Brien file, box 209, files 1–2, UAC. Since both films were through their initial release by this time, these figures provide a relatively accurate comparison.

35. The film industry's transformation to sound is treated in Harry Geduld, *The Birth of the Talkies* (Bloomington: Indiana Univ. Press, 1975); Douglas Gomery, "The Coming of Sound to the American Cinema: A History of the Transformation of an Industry" (Ph.D. diss. Univ. of Wisconsin, 1975); Alexander Walker, *The Shattered Silents* (New York: Morrow, 1979); and CHC, ch. 23. Balio, *United Artists*, ch. 4, treats the response of United Artists to the challenge and threat of sound films.

36. *NYT*, 14 July 1929, sec. 9, p. 4.

37. "Movie Stars Give Big Radio Program," *NYT*, 19 March 1928, p. 23.

38. *Variety*, 4 April 1928, p. 9.

39. Ibid., p. 2.

40. *NYT*, 25 November 1928, sec. 11, p. 22.

41. *NYT*, 10 February 1928, p. 26.

42. Chaplin, Jr., *My Father, Charlie Chaplin*, p. 36.

43. Gladys Hall, "Charlie Chaplin Attacks the Talkies," *Motion Picture* 37 (May 1929): 29. Three months later, the August issue of *Motion Picture* carried Al Jolson's response to Chaplin's defense of silent films. Jolson, noting that Chaplin was energetically talkative at parties they had both attended, challenged that "if Charlie wants to keep what he calls 'the great beauty of silence,' let him go lock himself in a room—become a nun's brother, or something. . . . Charlie goes on record as loathing talkies. . . . I think he'd better get to like 'em—or he'll find out the public don't like him."

44. *NYT*, 14 July 1929, sec. 9, p. 4. As *City Lights* was about to open, Chaplin again articulated his reasons for spurning dialogue in an article, "Pantomime and Comedy," *NYT*, 25 January 1931, sec. 8, p. 8.

45. A sampling of the negative response to talking pictures in 1928–1929 can be found in Geduld, *Birth of the Talkies*, app. A. See, for example, comments by George Bernard Shaw, Luigi Pirandello, Thomas Edison, and Aldous Huxley.

46. On the interplay of convention and invention in narrative formulas, see Thomas Schatz, *Hollywood Genres* (New York: Random House, 1981), esp. chs. 1–2, and Cawelti, *Adventure, Mystery, and Romance*. See also Stephen Neale,

Genre (London: British Film Institute, 1980), esp. ch. 3. His term "regularized variety" capsulizes well this dimension of genre films (p. 48).

47. This information is related in the third part of Brownlow's fascinating documentary film, *The Unknown Chaplin.* See also Gerard Molyneaux's production history of the film in *Charles Chaplin's "City Lights"* (New York: Garland, 1983), ch. 1, and CHLA, ch. 12.

48. This information on the pressbook of *City Lights* is taken from the UA pressbooks, microfilm no. 448, reel 13, UAC.

49. See Smith, *Chaplin*, pp. 93–94, on submerged autobiography in *City Lights.*

50. For a similar but more fully developed analysis on this theme, see Molyneaux, *Charles Chaplin's "City Lights,"* pp. 210 ff.

51. Looked at more pragmatically, Chaplin's decision not to root the film too securely in time and place also made the film more appealing to a wider audience, both in the United States and abroad. This lack of specificity thus served much the same purpose for Chaplin as avoiding dialogue.

52. Molyneaux provides a helpful breakdown of scenes in an appendix to *Charles Chaplin's "City Lights,"* pp. 242–48.

53. Molyneaux, *Charles Chaplin's "City Lights,"* p. 221.

54. The running times for *City Lights* are listed, among other places, in an ad in the *New York Herald Tribune*, 7 February 1931, p. 8. Balio, *United Artists*, pp. 91, lists the total grosses of the Cohan run, where he also notes that *City Lights* eventually earned Chaplin over $5 million worldwide; Balance Sheets and Associated Records, 1931 volume, UAC.

55. *NYT*, 7 February 1931, p. 11.

56. *New York Herald Tribune*, 7 February 1931, p. 8.

57. *New Republic* 66 (25 February 1931): 46–47.

58. *Variety*, 11 February 1931, p. 14.

59. *Nation* (4 March 1931): 250–51. Two other somewhat guarded reviews, one by Rob Wagner, a former Chaplin associate, the other in *Life*, are reprinted in *Selected Film Criticism, 1931–40*, ed. Anthony Slide (Metuchen, N.J.: Scarecrow, 1982), pp. 48–51. The *Life* review suggested that moralist critics of Chaplin's "vulgarity" had not disappeared: it thought "the scene in which Charley acts effeminate while a pugilist is undressing" was in "bad taste and entirely out of step with the picture" (p. 51).

5. THE DEPRESSION, THE WORLD TOUR, AND *MODERN TIMES*

1. Andrew Sarris, "Charles Spencer Chaplin," in *Cinema: A Critical Dictionary*, ed. Richard Roud (London: Secker & Warburg, 1980), 1: 208, 203.

2. A relatively detailed chronology of the trip is provided in Sadoul, *Vie de Charlot*, pp. 243–44.

3. Though first announced in the London press, the *NYT* reported it on 5 May 1931, p. 2.

4. Chaplin's quotation, the cartoon, and the comments of several American

editors, are included in "John Bull Hit by a Chaplin Pie," *Literary Digest* 109 (23 May 1931), p. 10.

5. Ibid.

6. According to Robinson (CHLA, p. 453), Chaplin wrote the memoir himself between June 1932 and February 1933. It was published in five monthly installments between September 1933 and January 1934 in *Woman's Home Companion*, vol. 61. Subsequent references to these articles will include only the month and page number of the citation.

7. January, p. 86; September, p. 87.

8. September, p. 88.

9. October, pp. 15, 17; December, p. 22. It is entirely likely that Chaplin's conversation with Gandhi had some effect on his imagination as he contemplated his next film, which is much less optimistic about machines.

10. See Richard Pells, *Radical Visions and American Dreams* (New York: Harper, 1973), p. 334.

The term "progressive" will be used regularly to describe Chaplin's political views in this and succeeding chapters. As Raymond Williams has noted in *Keywords* (London: Fontana, 1976), pp. 205–7, "progressive" emerged in the nineteenth century as a term of political position, the antonym of "conservative." Williams points out that today the term has a built-in complexity, for it is used two ways: (1) by the left to describe its position (as in "progressive-minded person") and (2) by leftists and others to distinguish advocates of moderate and orderly change from advocates of more radical and sudden change. In this second sense of the word, even a conservative could call him or herself a progressive—an advocate of gradual social evolution.

Chaplin used the term "progressive" to describe himself at times; when he did, he generally used it in two ways: to mean the opposite of conservative or to describe himself as a leftist (as we shall see, in 1947 and 1948 he also at times aligned himself with Henry Wallace's Progressive party, a more specific usage). When I use the term in this book, it will refer to a political position that is consistent with both of these implications, but it will also refer to something more specific and historically rooted. When the term became used more frequently in the United States in the second half of the 1930s, it was associated with three political issues, in descending order of importance: (1) antifascism; (2) a belief in domestic reform that benefited the "common people" or the "working class"; and (3) a sympathy for the Soviet Union. In this study, "progressive" will be used in this sense, except when it obviously refers to Wallace's party, the Progressive Citizens of America.

11. November, p. 100; January, pp. 21, 86.

12. September, p. 10. This position reiterates the one he had expressed to Flora Merrill in a February 1931 interview that appeared in the *New Work World*, which he gave the month *City Lights* opened and just before he began the world tour: "I am always suspicious of a picture with a message. Don't say that I'm a propagandist" (quoted in CHLA, p. 458).

13. September, p. 8; October, p. 104; January, p. 86.

14. P. W. Wilson, "Ten Men Who Stand as Symbols," *NYT*, 10 January 1932, sec. 5, p. 10.

15. These details, and others, come from "Sealing Wax, Cabbages, and Kings," *NYT*, 30 September 1934, sec. 9, p. 5.

16. The standard one-volume social and political history of the Roosevelt era is William E. Leuchtenburg, *Franklin D. Roosevelt and the New Deal* (New York: Harper, 1963). The economic statistics are taken from this work, pp. 1–2. Leuchtenberg's history contains a good bibliography for works published up to 1963; a more updated bibliography appears in Pells, *Radical Visions*. See also Arthur M. Schlesinger's pro–New Deal, three-volume history of the thirties, *The Age of Roosevelt* (Boston: Houghton Mifflin, 1957–60).

17. Leuchtenberg, *Franklin D. Roosevelt*, pp. 7–17 passim.

18. Ibid., chs. 3–4.

19. In *The American Film Industry* (Madison: Univ. of Wisconsin Press, 1976), editor Tino Balio briefly sketches the effects of the depression on the movie industry. See also Douglas Gomery's essay on how the NRA benefited the movie producers: "Hollywood, the National Recovery Administration, and the Question of Monopoly Power," *Journal of the University Film Association* 31, no. 2 (Spring 1979): 47–52.

20. The producers' salary reduction plan, and the political atmosphere in Hollywood generally during the classic sound era, is treated in Larry Ceplair and Steven Englund, *The Inquisition in Hollywood: Politics and the Film Community, 1930–1960* (New York: Doubleday, 1980), pp. 19–20. Nancy Lynn Schwartz, *The Hollywood Writers' Wars* (New York: Knopf, 1982), pp. 9–12, also treats the salary cuts as a crucial incident leading to a unionization move in Hollywood.

21. 23 October 1934, quoted in Leon Harris, *Upton Sinclair: American Rebel* (New York: Crowell, 1975), p. 305.

22. Harris, *Upton Sinclair*, p. 172; Upton Sinclair, *The Autobiography of Upton Sinclair* (New York: Harcourt, 1962), p. 273; Ceplair and Englund, *Inquisition Hollywood*, pp. 92–93.

23. Malcolm Cowley, *Exile's Return* (New York: Viking Press, 1951), pp. 113–31; see also Alexander, *Here the Country Lies*, p. 154.

24. *New Republic* 64 (22 October 1930): 267; for a broader treatment of the Gold-Wilder controversy and the responses it generated, see Daniel Aaron, *Writers on the Left* (New York: Harcourt, 1960), pp. 237–243.

25. Myron Lounsbury, *The Origins of American Film Criticism* (New York: Arno, 1973), chs. 4, 5, and pp. 484–86. Lounsbury ends his useful survey of American film criticism with a reading of Lewis Jacobs's *Rise of the American Film*, but it seems clear that the social film criticism of Bosley Crowther, influential *NYT* film critic from 1940 to 1967, is closely aligned with the "modern liberal" approach and more loosely related to the "social radical" position.

26. Harry Alan Potamkin, Introduction, *The Compound Cinema: The Film Writings of Harry Alan Potamkin*, ed. and intro. Lewis Jacobs (New York: Columbia Univ. Press, 1977), p. xxxi.

27. Potamkin, "Motion Picture Criticism," in *Compound Cinema*, p. 49 (originally in *The New Freeman*, 4 March 1931); "Film Cults," in *Compound Cinema*, p. 228 (originally in *Modern Thinker and Author's Review*, November 1932).

28. Lorenzo Turrent Rozas, "Charlie Chaplin's Decline," *Living Age*, no. 396 (June 1934): 319–23.

29. The importance of commitment in the 1930s has been discussed in a number of works, among them Warren Susman's "The Culture of the Thirties" (1970) and "Culture and Commitment" (1973), collected in *Culture as History* (New York: Pantheon, 1984), pp. 150–210; Pells, *Radical Visions*, ch. 4, esp. 158–69; and Charles Maland, *American Visions: The Films of Chaplin, Ford, Capra, and Welles, 1936–1941* (New York: Arno, 1977), pp. 5–9.

30. *NYT*, 30 August 1921, p. 10.

31. John Diggins, *The American Left in the Twentieth Century* (New York: Harcourt, 1973), p. 17 and passim; Eastman, *Great Companions*, p. 215; MA, pp. 242–43; Frank Harris, *Contemporary Portraits*, 4th series (New York: Brentano's, 1923), pp. 56–76.

32. *NYT*, 14 June 1932, p. 26.

33. *Women's Home Companion*, December 1933, p. 23; *NYT*, 28 June 1932, p. 26; Leuchtenberg, *Franklin D. Roosevelt*, pp. 50–51. On the international fate of the gold standard during the early years of the depression, see Gustav Cassel, *The Downfall of the Gold Standard* (New York: Oxford Univ. Press, 1936).

34. Alistair Cooke, *Six Men* (New York: Knopf, 1977), pp. 25, 27; CHLA, p. 458; *New York Herald Tribune*, 22 November 1934, p. 14.

35. *New York American*, 29 January 1937, RLC, vol. 110. Paulette Goddard, Chaplin's third wife and female lead in *Modern Times* and *The Great Dictator*, shared Chaplin's enthusiasm for the New Deal. She told a *NYT* reporter (18 October 1936) that she believed in the New Deal but that many Hollywood figures were "falling easy victims to fascism," which was "fast outdistancing communism in the film colony."

36. NYT, 17 March 1935, sec. 8, p. 4; the article was also discussed in the *Motion Picture Herald*, 23 March 1935, p. 49.

37. *NYT*, 29 August 1933, p. 20; *NYT*, 20 September 1933, p. 16; Chaplin, Jr., *My Father, Charlie Chaplin*, p. 81. Though Chaplin consistently told the press that Charlie would not talk in the new film, Robinson notes (CHLA, p. 466) that Chaplin and Paulette Goddard did do some sound tests in late November 1934, more than two months after shooting had begun.

38. Robert Allen and Douglas Gomery discuss the useful concept of the prevailing critical or aesthetic discourse and apply it to Murnau's *Sunrise* in *Film History: Theory and Practice*, pp. 89–108. Jauss discusses the "horizon of expectations" in "Literary History," in Jauss, *Toward an Aesthetic of Reception*, esp. pp. 25–28.

39. *NYT*, 30 August 1934, sec. 9, p. 3; *New York Herald Tribune*, 22 November 1934, p. 14; *NYT*, 17 March 1935, sec. 8, p. 4.

40. "Mr. Shumiatsky on American Films," *NYT*, 4 August 1935.

41. Boris Shumiatsky, "Charlie Chaplin's New Picture," trans. Leon Dennen,

New Masses (24 September 1935): 29–30; *NYT*, 17 November 1935; the *Daily Worker* articles are quoted in Terry Ramsaye, "Chaplin Ridicules Reds' Claim Film Aids 'Cause,' " *Motion Picture Herald*, 7 December 1935, p. 1.

42. Ramsaye, "Chaplin Ridicules," pp. 1, 2. One might augment Reeves's final comment by noting that people who worked with Chaplin often recalled that he would never immediately accept a suggestion from someone else, though he often would use such an idea later, claiming it as his own.

43. *Modern Times*, microfilm pressbooks, BRC. The New York promotion campaign, engineered by Monroe Greenthal of United Artists, followed many of the suggestions in the pressbook and was successful enough to earn praise in *Box-Office* 28 (15 February 1936): 7. According to the article, among Greenthal's other contributions were a display window in Macy's of the "original Chaplin hat, shoes, and cane" and a neon sign reading "CHARLIE CHAPLIN" on the theater marquee instead of "ROXY."

44. A good example of intellectual montage in Eisenstein's work are the cross-cuts between the massacre of the workers with the slaughter of an ox at the end of *Strike!*: the workers are being treated like animals. Chaplin undoubtedly was aware of developments in Russian cinema in the 1920s. Eisenstein frequently visited Chaplin's home in the summer and fall of 1930 when he was in Hollywood, for a time under contract with Paramount, and for a time seeking financing for a film to be made in Mexico. Eisenstein first gained entry into Chaplin's company thanks to letters that his companion, Ivor Montagu, had obtained from H. G. Wells and Shaw. In his autobiography, Eisenstein recalled Chaplin's first words of greeting when they met by Chaplin's tennis court: "Just saw *Potemkin* again. You know, in five years it hasn't aged a bit; still the same." See Sergei Eisenstein, *Immoral Memories*, trans. Herbert Marshall (Boston: Houghton-Mifflin, 1983), p. 81. Another account of the Eisenstein–Chaplin friendship, including some pictures, is provided in Montague's *With Eisenstein in Hollywood* (New York: International Publishers, 1969).

45. The facts that the owner's voice is heard only via a loudspeaker and that the sales pitch for the Bellows Feeding Machine (designed for "keeping ahead of the competition") is on a phonograph record are also significant. One important dimension of *Modern Times* not stressed here is Chaplin's implicit critique of the tyranny of sound in motion-picture art. Just as the owner's words tyrannize the workers, the technology of sound reproduction tyrannizes the makers of films. But Chaplin has the last word (no pun intended): Charlie's gibberish song and pantomime at the end of *Modern Times* communicates far more effectively and pleasingly than all the other words in the film. On Chaplin's self-reflexiveness in *Modern Times*, see Stewart's excellent essay, "Modern Hard Times."

46. *New Masses*, 18 February 1936, reprinted in Kauffmann, *American Film Criticism*, pp. 329–31. Crichton was the pen name Robert Forsythe used when writing for *New Masses*; under his own name he was an editor for *Scribner's* and *Collier's*.

47. Charmion von Wiegand, "Little Man, What Now?" *New Theater* 3 (March 1936): 36.

48. All these reviews are included in the Chaplin clippings file, BRC: *Daily News*, 6 February 1936; *Herald Tribune*, 16 February 1936; *Variety*, 12 February 1936.

49. Von Wiegand, "Little Man," pp. 6–8, 35–37; Edward Newhouse, "Charlie's Critics," *Partisan Review* 3 (April 1936): 26.

50. *New Republic* 85 (19 February 1936); reprinted in Kauffmann, *American Film Criticism*, pp. 331–34.

6. THE POPULAR FRONT, *THE GREAT DICTATOR*, AND THE SECOND FRONT

1. The Gallup Poll results were published in *Public Opinion Quarterly* 4 (1940): 102; Pells, *Radical Vision*, p. 293. American response to the international situation is treated in Leuchtenberg, *Franklin D. Roosevelt*, Chs. 9, 12, 13.

2. Daniel Bell, *Marxian Socialism in the United States*, rev. ed. (Princeton: Princeton Univ. Press, 1967), pp. 135–36; Irving Howe and Lewis Coser, *The American Communist Party* (Boston: Beacon, 1957), p. 341, and more generally, 319–55.

3. See, for example, the contrasting attitudes toward Roosevelt expressed in Joseph Freeman, "The Middle Class and the Election," *New Masses* 20 (11 August 1936): 28, and A. B. Magill, "Still Time to Unite," *New Masses* 27 (10 May 1938): 5–6. See also Pells, *Radical Vision*, ch. 7.

4. On the cosmopolitanism of Hollywood, see John Baxter, *The Hollywood Exiles* (London, 1976) and the more rigorous and specific book by John Russell Taylor, *Strangers in Paradise: The Hollywood Emigrés, 1933–50* (London: Faber & Faber, 1983). Ceplair and Englund, *Inquisition in Hollywood*, esp. pp. 94–104, also discuss Hollywood's internationalism and its effect on the politics of the Popular Front.

5. Ceplair and Englund, *Inquisition in Hollywood*, pp. 107–8.

6. Ibid., pp. 117–24.

7. See Leo Rosten, *Hollywood* (New York: Harcourt, 1941), pp. 139–44; Ceplair and Englund, *Inquisition in Hollywood*, pp. 139–99 passim; Pells, *Radical Vision*, pp. 347–51.

8. See Robert Endicott Osgood, *Ideals and Self-Interest in American Foreign Relations* (Chicago: Univ. of Chicago Press, 1963, 1953), pp. 407–10.

9. Philip Dunne, the son of the famous humorist and a screenwriter active in liberal politics from the 1930s on, recalls first meeting Chaplin at an Anti-Nazi League meeting and also later encountering him at a meeting of the Committee to Defend America by Aiding the Allies. See Philip Dunne, *Take Two* (New York: McGraw-Hill, 1980), pp. 139–40.

10. *NYT*, 16 February 1936, sec. 9, p. 1.

11. *NYT*, 15 September 1937, p. 27; 19 September 1937, sec. 11, p. 5; 20 September 1937, p. 22.

12. Montagu, who spent considerable time with Chaplin in 1930 when he was in Hollywood with Sergei Eisenstein, recalls (*With Eisenstein in Hollywood*,

p. 94) that sometime during the 1930s he sent Chaplin a Nazi propaganda book of photographs of Jews, *Juden Sehen Dich An* (Jews Are Looking at You). Though Chaplin was not Jewish, the book included a portrait of Chaplin with a caption, "Dieser ebenso langweilige wie widerwärtige kleine Zappeljude" (this little Jewish tumbler, as disgusting as he is boring). Chaplin recounts Korda's suggestion in MA, pp. 392–93.

13. Chaplin, Jr., *My Father, Charlie Chaplin*, pp. 128, 140–46; MA, p. 391.

14. Jack Oakie, who plays Napolini in the films, recalls how secret Chaplin kept the set in his memoir, *Jack Oakie's Double Takes* (San Francisco: Strawberry Hill Press, 1980), pp. 71–80; *NYT*, 6 November 1938, sec. 9, p. 5; 26 February 1939, sec. 9, p. 4.

15. *NYT*, 18 August 1940, sec. 9, p. 3.

16. *NYT*, 10 September 1939, sec. 9, p. 3.

17. *NYT*, 26 May 1940, sec. 9, p. 3.

18. *NYT*, 8 September 1940, sec. 7, pp. 8–11.

19. *The Great Dictator*, microfilm pressbooks and programs, BRC. On the use of the term "progressive" in this study, see Chapter 5, note 10.

20. *Motion Picture Daily*, 16 October 1940, p. 7; *NYT*, 16 October 1940, p. 29.

21. *NYT*, 13 October 1940, sec. 9, passim; *NYT*, 15 October 1940, p. 1.

22. On the Nuremberg Nazi party congresses, the Mussolini visit to Germany in 1937, and the details of the Austrian Anschluss, see, e.g., William Shirer, *The Rise and Fall of the Third Reich* (1959; reprinted New York: Simon and Schuster, 1980), pp. 230, 264, 382–83, and ch. 11; *NYT*, 15 June 1939, p. 11; *NYT*, 28 July 1938, p. 6.

23. Smith, *Chaplin*, p. 114.

24. Paul Goodman, "Chaplin Again, Again, and Again," *Partisan Review* 7 (November/December 1940): 58–64.

25. This speech resembles the endings of two other important American films released after the war began but before the United States entered: Steinbeck/Zanuck/Ford's *Grapes of Wrath* (1940) and Capra/Riskin's *Meet John Doe* (1941). All three express the progressive's faith that "the people" can survive adversity and even triumph in the name of democracy.

26. Among the critics who have focused on the final scene are Smith, *Chaplin*, pp. 117–89; Robert Warshow, *The Immediate Experience* (Garden City: Doubleday, 1962), p. 210; André Bazin, "Defense de *Monsieur Verdoux*," *Les Temps Modernes* (3 December 1947): 1115–22; and Maland, *American Visions*, pp. 89–94.

27. Barry Salt, "Film Style and Technology in the 1930s," *Film Quarterly* 30 (Fall 1976): 19–32.

28. See Bordwell and Thompson, *Film Art*, pp. 57–59, 163–71; CHC, chs. 1–7 passim; Noël Burch, *To the Distant Observer* (Berkeley: Univ. of California Press, 1979), pp. 61–66; Ray, *A Certain Tendency*, esp. pp. 25–65.

29. Balio, *United Artists*, p. 165; *NYT*, 22 March 1942, sec. 6, pp. 12–13.

30. *NYT*, 20 October 1940, sec. 9, p. 3.

31. *Post*, 16 October 1940; *Post*, 18 October 1940; *Journal-American*, 16 Oc-

tober 1940; *Journal-American* and *Daily News*, cited in *Daily Worker*, 19 October 1940; *Herald Tribune*, 20 October 1940; all unpaginated in Chaplin press clippings file, BRC.

32. *World Telegram*, 16 October 1940; *Philadelphia Record*, 24 October 1940; *Variety*, 16 October 1940; *NYT*, 20 October 1940, sec. 9, p. 3: all in Chaplin press clippings file, BRC.

33. *Daily Worker*, 16 October 1940. The *Worker* followed up this review with an October 19 article, "Those Peculiar Reviews," which lambasted the daily newspaper reviewers. According to the *Worker*, the critics from other newspapers attacked *The Great Dictator* "because of its peace message."

34. Jauss, "Literary History," in Jauss, *Toward an Aesthetic of Reception*, p. 25.

35. *NYT*, 27 October 1940, sec. 9, p. 5.

36. *Catholic World* 152 (December 1940): 333; *New Republic* 4 (4 November 1940), reprinted in *The Film Criticism of Otis Ferguson*, ed. Robert Wilson (Philadelphia: Temple Univ. Press, 1971), pp. 314–16; *Commonweal* 33 (November 1940): 80; *Nation* 131 (26 October 1940): 401; *Newsweek* 16 (28 October 1940): 60.

37. *Saturday Review* 23 (9 November 1940): 8.

38. *NYT*, 9 March 1941; *Daily Mirror*, 7 July 1941; *St. Louis Dispatch*, 16 March 1941; and *Dallas Morning News*, 14 February 1942: all unpaginated articles in Chaplin press clippings file, BRC.

39. The Reich protest was reported in *NYT*, 22 December 1938, p. 14. On the Senate Subcommittee on War Propaganda, see Ceplair and Englund, *Inquisition in Hollywood*, pp. 159–62, and *NYT*, 14 September 1941, p. 41. The resolution establishing the subcommittee was S.R. 152 (77th Cong., 1st sess.), introduced by Senators Clark of Missouri and Nye of North Dakota. Chaplin and United Artists' response to the subcommittee is detailed in correspondence in the O'Brien legal files, box 186, folders 6 and 7, UAC.

40. *NYT* (all 1941), 5 January, p. 34; 28 January p. 22; 30 January, p. 18; 1 February, p. 2; 16 February, p. 39; 10 March, p. 20; 24 June, p. 6; 15 March, sec. 8, p. 3; 3 May, sec. 8, p. 3.

41. *NYT*, 23 October 1944, p. 6; *NYT*, 10 August 1946, p. 16.

42. Alistair Cooke's portrait of Chaplin in *Six Men* provides a good example of how observers have minimized or downplayed the seriousness of Chaplin's political perspective.

43. *NYT*, 20 January 1941, p. 7; *Washington Post*, 20 January 1941, pp. 1, 4.

44. *NYT*, 21 January 1941, p. 1.

45. *Washington Post*, 21 January 1941, p. 1.

46. *NYT*, 10 October 1941, p. 15. On 25 September 1941, *People's World* named Chaplin as one of the original sponsors of Russian War Relief, Incorporated, though in the *Times* advertisement he is not listed as any kind of officer, honorary or otherwise.

47. Ralph Levering, *American Opinion and the Russian Alliance, 1939–1945* (Chapel Hill: Univ. of North Carolina Press, 1976), pp. 63–70.

48. *The Memoirs of Cordell Hull*, 2 vols (New York: Macmillan, 1948), 2: 1264; *NYT*, 8 November 1942, sec. 1, p. 1.

49. Levering, *American Opinion*, pp. 70–84 passim.

50. *NYT*, 23 April 1938, sec. 4, p. 2. One might note that Chaplin did not allow his United Artists films to be released in the Soviet Union until the 1930s because the Soviets were unwilling to pay the money Chaplin and United Artists thought would be fair for such a large country. Nevertheless, as early as 1930 retrospectives of Chaplin's films, using old prints, were being shown in Moscow. See *NYT*, 13 April 1930, sec. 10, p. 4.

51. One might note that both of Chaplin's sons, Sydney and Charles, Jr., enlisted in the U.S. armed forces in October 1943.

52. *People's World*, 20 May 1942, p. 1.

53. *Los Angeles Times*, 26 March 1941.

54. The Museum of Modern Art Film Department, in its "Chaplin, 1940–49" folder, has a copy of the brochure. It is reprinted in MA, pp. 410–13.

55. *New York Herald Tribune*, 17 October 1942, p. 4; *NYT*, 17 October 1942, p. 16.

56. *Chicago Tribune*, 26 November 1942, p. 23.

57. The Ehrenburg cable is included in a clipping in the "Chaplin, 1940–49" folder, Museum of Modern Art Film Department; *NYT*, 4 December 1942, p. 15.

58. Westbrook Pegler, "Fair Game," *New York World-Telegram*, 21 December 1942.

7. JOAN BARRY, THE PRESS, AND THE TARNISHED IMAGE

1. Chaplin, Jr., *My Father, Charlie Chaplin*, p. 192.

2. Ibid., pp. 187–90; Lyons, *Charles Chaplin: Guide to References and Resources*, p. 30; MA, p. 406.

3. The details of the relationship between Chaplin and Barry are impossible to recount with absolute confidence. Ironically, the files of the FBI's investigation of Chaplin surrounding the Barry case, available through the Freedom of Information Act, file no. 31–5301, probably constitute the best source. Much of the information in this section is from that file, particularly from the 11 November 1943 report of the Los Angeles office to Director J. Edgar Hoover in Washington, D.C., which runs 43 pages, and a second report from the office to Hoover, dated 25 February 1944 (66 pages). Of course, the information contained in the FBI files must be looked at critically and sifted carefully, since the aim of their investigation was to obtain information that could be used against Chaplin by the U.S. district attorney's office and since Barry's interviews with them contain inconsistencies and contradictions. But used cautiously, the files shed light on the Chaplin–Barry affair.

4. FBI report, L.A. office to Washington, 9 November 1943, p. 10.

5. FBI report, 9 November 1943, p. 11.

6. FBI report, L.A. office to Washington, 25 February 1944, p. 4.

7. FBI report, 25 February 1942, pp. 5, 9; MA, pp. 414–15. Barry and Chap-

lin differ about the timing of the *Shadow and Substance* reading. Chaplin claims the reading took place before he put her on contract; Barry remembers that Chaplin didn't even know of the play until the fall of 1942, after which he arranged the reading. Chaplin apparently exaggerated what he paid Barry, claiming that her salary was $250 a week (MA, p. 414); Barry showed FBI agents her salary check stubs to substantiate the $75 figure.

8. FBI report, 25 February 1944, pp. 13–14, 18; MA, pp. 415–18.

9. FBI report, 25 February 1944, pp. 20–21; MA, p. 419; Chaplin, Jr., *My Father, Charlie Chaplin*, pp. 204–9; Jerry Giesler, *The Jerry Giesler Story* (New York: Simon and Schuster, 1960), p. 187.

10. FBI report, 25 February 1944, pp. 23–24.

11. Although blood tests cannot prove someone *is* the father of a child, they can prove about 15 percent of the time that someone is *not* the father of a child, since parents with certain blood types cannot possibly produce a child with a third blood type. Because such a high percentage of people have one of two blood types, however, the percentage of men who can prove that they are not the father of a child is relatively low.

12. *NYT*, 11 June 1943, p. 22.

13. FBI memo, Hood to Hoover, 24 June 1943.

14. FBI memo, Hood to Hoover, 24 August 1943; FBI memo, Pennington to Rosen, 17 August 1943; FBI telegram, Hoover to SAC (special agent in charge) Los Angeles, 20 August 1943; FBI memo, SAC Los Angeles to Hoover, 25 August 1943.

15. Gerith von Ulm's biography, *Charlie Chaplin: King of Comedy* (Caldwell, Idaho: Claxton, 1940), was written partly through the cooperation of Chaplin's longtime valet and chauffeur, Kono. This cooperation makes the biography seem more like an "insider's" look at Chaplin's private life than most biographies of Chaplin.

16. FBI Memo, Pennington to Rosen, 9 November 1943.

17. FBI Memo, Davis to Rosen, 9 November 1943; memo, Hoover to Assistant Attorney General Clark, 7 December 1943; FBI memo, SAC Los Angeles Hood to Hoover, 22 December 1943; FBI teletype, SAC Los Angeles to Washington, date blacked out but apparently around 10 December 1943.

18. A telegram from Washington to SAC Los Angeles, probably about December 27 (the date is blacked out), reported on the Carr/Clark interchange on this issue and ordered that future Los Angeles investigation include the civil rights angle.

19. *NYT*, 11 February 1944, p. 1.

20. SAC Hood in Los Angeles sent copies of all four indictments to Agent Rosen in Washington on February 14; they are included in the FBI files on the case, and my quotations are taken from them.

21. Giesler, *Jerry Giesler Story*, pp. 187–88.

22. *Chicago Tribune*, 5 April 1944, p. 1.

23. FBI memo, Hood to Hoover and Rosen, 11 May 1944.

24. *NYT*, 16 February 1944, p. 19; *Chicago Tribune*, 18 February 1944, p. 1.

25. *Time* 45 (8 January 1945), p. 36; *Chicago Tribune*, 5 January 1945, p. 6.

26. *NYT*, 14 April 1945, p. 13; 18 April 1945, p. 25; 19 April 1945, p. 29.

27. An interesting biographical treatment of Hollywood's two most powerful gossip columnists, Hopper and Louella Parsons, is George Eells's *Hedda and Louella* (New York: Putnam's, 1972). Eells notes that in general, Parsons was more sympathetic to Chaplin: she repaid Chaplin for giving her the "scoop" on his marriage to Oona O'Neill by reporting in an article that the blood tests *proved* Chaplin was not the father of Barry's child. Hopper never mentioned this in her writing on Chaplin.

28. Eells, *Hedda and Louella*, pp. 130, 171.

29. Ibid., p. 173. The Motion Picture Alliance, founded in 1944, later numbered Hopper as one of its officers—see Ceplair and Englund, *Inquisition in Hollywood*, p. 211.

30. Barry's testimony is included in the FBI report, Los Angeles office to Washington, 25 February 1944; the interview took place in early January 1944.

31. *Chicago Tribune*, 3 June 1943, p. 22.

32. The FBI files include Hopper's column from the *Pittsburgh Press*, 22 June 1943. The column was apparently sent unsolicited to the FBI: an envelope addressed to Hoover and postmarked Pittsburgh, June 25, is the second photocopied page of the FBI file on Chaplin.

33. *New York Daily News*, 2 June 1943, p. 4; 10 October 1943, pp. 22–23. FBI report, Los Angeles office to Washington, 9 November 1943, pp. 36–37.

34. *Chicago Tribune*, 4 October 1943, p. 18; 6 October 1943, p. 26; 27 December 1943, p. 14.

35. FBI telegram, SAC LA Hood to Hoover, date blacked out (probably about January 5–8); FBI telegram, Hood to Hoover, 14 January 1944.

36. FBI telegram, Hood to Hoover, 31 January 1944, p. 1.

37. *Chicago Tribune*, 18 January 1944, p. 18; *Los Angeles Times*, 13 March 1944, p. 10.

38. *Chicago Tribune*, 28 March 1944, p. 15; 10 April 1944, p. 18.

39. FBI letter, Hood to Hoover, 14 April 1944.

40. In her column of April 28—two weeks after Muir's conversation with the FBI but three weeks before charges against Chaplin were dropped—Hopper wrote that the remaining federal charges against Chaplin would likely be dropped upon Attorney General Biddle's request.

41. *Chicago Tribune*, 22 December 1944, p. 15.

42. *Chicago Tribune*, 11 February 1944, p. 1. In the following paragraphs on the *Tribune*'s coverage of the Barry–Chaplin story, the dates of the articles will be cited in the text.

43. *Newsweek* 23 (21 February 1944): 46, 48.

44. *Newsweek* 23 (10 April 1944): 29; *Time* 43 (3 April 1944): 24–25.

45. *Time* 45 (1 January 1945): 15–16; 45 (8 January 1945).

46. *Newsweek* 25 (30 April 1945): 41; *Time* 45 (30 July 1944): 52.

47. *Script* 30 (4 March 1944): 1–2. Hopper's article is discussed in the previous section, above.

48. Mike Gold, "Charge It," *Daily Worker* (19 January 1945), Chaplin clippings file, BRC.

8. *MONSIEUR VERDOUX* AND THE COLD WAR

1. On the contributions of these refugees to scholarship, science, and the arts in America since their arrival, see especially Lewis A. Coser, *Refugee Scholars in America* (New Haven: Yale Univ. Press, 1984), which does not limit itself to *German* refugees, and Anthony Heilbut, *Exiled in Paradise: German Refugee Artists and Intellectuals in America, from the 1930s to the Present* (New York: Viking, 1983), which does.

2. Heilbut, *Exiled in Paradise*, pp. 108, viii.

3. Ibid., p. 35; Salka Viertel, *The Kindness of Strangers* (New York: Holt, Rinehart, 1969), p. 211; Taylor, *Strangers in Paradise*, p. 146. Another more general book on the contribution of Europeans to American cinema is Baxter, *The Hollywood Exiles*, esp. chs. 11, 12. While Brecht's political views are well known and have been much discussed, Eisler's are less so; *A Rebel in Music*, ed. Manfred Grabs (New York: International Publishers, 1978), is an interesting collection of his essays and lectures. A key theme of his writings is contained in an interview from June 1935, in which Eisler calls for "an alliance between the music intellectuals and the working class" (p. 100).

4. See Taylor, *Strangers in Paradise*, ch. 9, "The New Weimar," for a discussion of the arrival and settlement of the German refugees in Hollywood. See also James K. Lyon, *Bertolt Brecht in America* (Princeton: Princeton Univ. Press, 1980), pp. 28–31. Another treatment of Brecht's experiences in the United States is Bruce Cook, *Brecht in Exile* (New York: Holt, Rinehart, 1982).

5. Viertel, *Kindness of Strangers*, p. 290.

6. See Hilda Waldo, "Lion Feuchtwanger: A Biography," in John M. Spalek, ed., *Lion Feuchtwanger: The Man, His Ideas, His Work* (Los Angeles: Hennessey and Ingalls, 1972), p. 15; Wilhelm von Sternburg, *Lion Feuchtwanger: Ein deutsches Schriftstellerleben* (Königstein: Atheneum, 1984), pp. 300–301, 305 ff.; Volker Skierka, *Lion Feuchtwanger: Eine Biographie* (Berlin: Quadriga Verlag, 1984), pp. 242–43; *NYT*, 24 January 1930, p. 26; and Harold von Hofe, ed., *Feuchtwanger–Zweig: Briefwechsel, 1933–58* (Berlin and Weimar: Aufbau Verlag, 1984), 2: 202; MA, p. 450.

7. Lyon, *Bertolt Brecht*, pp. 84, 196; interviews with Eisler in Hans Bunge, ed., *Fragen Sie Mir über Brecht: Hanns Eisler in Gesprach* (Munich: Rogner & Bernard, 1970), pp. 58–59.

8. Eisler, *Rebel*, p. 102; Bunge, *Fragen Sie Mir ber Brecht*, pp. 58–59; Heilbut, *Exiled in Paradise*, p. ix.

9. One leftist, screenwriter Bess Taffel, remembers that when leftists in Hollywood like Eisler and Chaplin were becoming isolated after the start of the Hollywood Ten trials, the formerly large groups that gathered at the Eislers' home had dwindled to Taffel, Salka Viertel, the Feuchtwangers, the Chaplins, and their hosts. Ceplair and Englund, *Inquisition in Hollywood*, pp. 379–80. Taffel, who joined the Communist party during the height of its patriotic rhetoric

in 1943, became disillusioned when its idealism declined around 1946, and she eventually broke with the Party entirely. She saw her friends at the Eislers' as "non-Party left-wingers." Another leftist, though not a German refugee, who knew Chaplin and was sympathetic to this political perspective was screenwriter Donald Ogden Stewart, who was blacklisted in the 1950s. His memoirs, *By a Stroke of Luck* (New York: Paddington Press, 1975), particularly pp. 264 ff., provide another picture of the shape of progressive antifascism during and after World War Two.

10. Feuchtwanger's favorable book on the Soviet Union, *Moskau 37*, was published in Amsterdam in 1937.

11. Among the major reviewers who praised *Verdoux* during these rereleases were Bosley Crowther, *NYT*, 4 July 1964; Andrew Sarris, *Village Voice*, 23 July 1964; and Vincent Canby, *NYT*, 8 July 1973. In his review Canby wrote that *Playtime* (directed by Jacques Tati) and *Monsieur Verdoux* were "two of the greatest comedies of all time."

12. Ceplair and Englund, *Inquisition in Hollywood*, p. 186, call the period between 1941 and 1944 "Popular Front Redivivis." On this spirit, see also Richard Pells, *The Liberal Mind in a Conservative Age* (New York: Harper and Row, 1985), pp. 32–40.

13. "Beyond the Atlantic Charter," *New Republic* 107 (23 November 1942): 667.

14. The text of the speech is found in *Churchill: Complete Speeches*, ed. Robert Rhodes James (London: Chelsea House, 1974), 7: 7283–93.

15. Mary McAuliffe, *Crisis on the Left* (Amherst: Univ. of Massachusetts Press, 1978); William O'Neill, *A Better World* (New York: Simon and Schuster, 1982).

16. On the decline of progressive liberalism through 1948, see McAuliffe, *Crisis on the Left*, ch. 3.

17. Geoffrey Hodgson, *America in Our Time* (New York: Doubleday, 1976), esp. chs. 1–4. On the emergence of the American consensus, see also Robert Skotheim, *Totalitarianism and American Social Thought* (New York: Holt, Rinehart, 1971); Lawrence S. Wittner, *Cold War America* (New York: Praeger, 1974); and Pells, *Liberal Mind*, esp. chs. 1–3.

18. Hodgson, *America in Our Time*, pp. 75–76.

19. Pells (*Liberal Mind*, p. 97) makes almost the same point: that American intellectuals, used to "taking sides" since the Depression, found it easy to shift villains after the war. "The identity of the combatants had now changed," Pells writes, "Russia having supplanted both the 'bosses' and the Nazis as embodiments of everlasting villainy. But the intellectuals' frame of mind remained the same."

20. See CHC, esp. ch. 2.

21. See Dyer, *Stars*, pp. 28–32. See also William R. Brown, *Image Maker: Will Rogers and the American Dream* (Columbia: Univ. of Missouri Press, 1970), and Charles Eckert, "Shirley Temple and the House of Rockefeller," *Jump Cut*, no. 2 (July-August 1974): 1, 17–20. Brown argues that Rogers's image reinforced certain dominant American values at a time when they were under threat. Eck-

ert also believes that stars reaffirm dominant values, though in part through this complex process of displacement.

22. Dorothy B. Jones, "The Quantitative Analysis of Motion Picture Content," *Public Opinion Quarterly* 16 (1942): 411–28.

23. Thomas F. Brady, " 'Bluebeard' Chaplin," *NYT*, 30 March 1947, sec. 6, pp. 24–25.

24. Cable, Tom Waller to Paul Lazarus, Jr., 3 April 1947. Alfred Tamarin papers, file 6, folder 6, UAC.

25. United Artists press releases, 8 April and 9 April 1947, Alfred Tamarin papers, file 6, folder 6, UAC. The publicity staff was worried about the conference right up to the day it was held. That day Tom Waller sent a note to Paul Lazarus, Jr., which said that UA executive and old Chaplin associate Arthur Kelly had told him to downplay the press conference. To this Waller added tartly: "I reminded Mr. Kelley that twice when I saw Mr. Chaplin I advised strenuously against any mass press meeting."

26. Red Kann, "Insider's Outlook," *Motion Picture Daily* 61 (11 April 1947): 2.

27. We are fortunate that a transcript of the Chaplin press conference, with notes by George Wallach, who attended the meeting and did the taping, has been published (the article mistakenly says the press conference was held on April 12). See George Wallach, "Charlie Chaplin's *Monsieur Verdoux* Press Conference," *Film Comment* 5 (Winter 1969): 34–42. The page numbers for quotations from the press conference are cited parenthetically in the text.

28. *NYT*, 11 April 1947, pp. 1, 17, 18; 14 April 1947, p. 1.

29. *New York Herald Tribune*, 12 April 1947, p. 8.

30. *Commonweal* 47 (2 May 1947): 68.

31. *New Yorker* 23 (19 April 1947): 42; Jauss, "Literary History," in Jauss, *Toward an Aesthetic of Reception*, pp. 25–26.

32. *Variety*, 16 April 1947, p. 8.

33. *Newsweek* 29 (28 April 1947): 98.

34. John Beaufort, "An Assault from Mr. Chaplin," *Christian Science Monitor*, 19 April 1947, Chaplin clippings file, BRC.

35. *NYT*, 12 April 1947, p. 11.

36. *New Republic* 116 (21 April 1947): 38–39; 5 May 1947, p. 39; *Theater Arts* gave the film a guardedly positive review much like that of the *New Republic* in Hermane Rich Isaacs' "Expectations: Great and Small," *Theatre Arts* 31 (June 1947): 47–48.

37. James Agee, *Agee on Film* (Boston: Beacon, 1964), 1: 252–62.

38. Appearing in a journal that prized the complexity, ambiguity, and irony of writers like Kafka and Céline at the same time that it pulled away from the easy pieties of progressivism, Warshow's essay found a proper home. "*Monsieur Verdoux*" first appeared in *Partisan Review* 14 (July-August 1947): 380–89, and is collected in Warshow's *The Immediate Experience*; see pp. 208, 215, 222.

39. Max Lerner, "Chaplin—Art and Politics," *PM*, 17 April 1947, p. 2; "The Essential Quality of Civilization," *PM*, 20 April 1947, Chaplin clippings file,

BRC. The United Artists press staff even corresponded about Lerner's editorial the day before it appeared, which shows how worried they were about generating positive response to the film. See memo, Larry Beller to Tom Waller, 16 April 1947, Alfred Tamarin file, box 6, folder 6, UAC.

40. Arnaud d'Usseau, "Chaplin's *Monsieur Verdoux*," *Mainstream* 1 (Summer 1947): 308–17.

41. *Variety*, 30 April 1947, p. 13; 7 May 1947, p. 15; 14 May 1947, p. 11.

42. On the redesigned publicity campaign, see particularly the files of Paul Lazarus, Jr., box 16, folder 14, and box 17, folder 8; and of Alfred Tamarin, box 6, folder 6, all UAC.

43. *Motion Picture Daily*, 12 May 1947, p. 3; d'Usseau, "Chaplin's *Monsieur Verdoux*," p. 316; *Hollywood Reporter*, 23 July 1947, p. 5.

44. This information comes from box 16, folder 14 of the Lazarus files, UAC.

45. Chaplin clippings file, BRC.

46. United Artists publicity papers, Alfred Tamarin file, box 6, folder 6, UAC; "Moral: Chaplin Should Heckle Congress More," *Variety*, 1 October 1947, p. 4.

47. See, for example, *Washington Post*, 27 September 1947, sec. B, p. 8.

48. Cable, Birdwell to Chaplin, September 26, 1947, Paul Lazarus, Jr., file, box 16, folder 14, UAC.

49. *Washington Post*, 27 September 1947, sec. B, p. 8.

50. Telegram, Birdwell to Lazarus, 28 September 1947, Alfred Tamarin file, box 6, folder 6, UAC.

51. *Variety*, 8 October 1947, p. 4; 15 October 1947, p. 12.

52. All cables in the Paul Lazarus, Jr., files, UAC.

53. Domestic earnings, 1947, Paul Lazarus, Sr., sales correspondence, UAC.

54. Balio, *United Artists*, p. 214.

55. Dyer, *Stars*, pp. 68–72.

56. United Artists press releases, November 1947 and June 1948, Alfred Tamarin file, box 6, folder 6, UAC.

9. CHAPLIN'S POLITICS AND AMERICAN CULTURE

1. Alistair Cooke's observation, in *Six Men*, p. 27, provides a good example of this tendency: Chaplin's "much-abused 'radical philosophy' was no more than an automatic theme song in favor of peace, humanity, 'the little man,' and other desirable abstractions—as humdrum politicians come out for mother love and lower taxes."

2. See *Daily Worker*, 6 April 1943, p. 2; 29 September 1943, pp. 2, 5; 21 November 1944, p. 11.

3. *NYT*, 9 May 1943, sec. 6, p. 10.

4. *Moscow News*, 29 April 1944, p. 4; the event was also reported in *NYT*, 28 April 1944, p. 4, and, in an insinuating tone, in *Newsweek*, 15 May 1944 (just after Chaplin's acquittal on Mann Act charges and the Justice Department's order not to continue prosecution of Chaplin on the civil rights charges). See

Grigori Alexandrov, "Chaplin's Art is Weapon in Fight against Fascism," *Moscow News*, 29 April 1944, pp. 4–5.

5. Yon Barna, *Eisenstein* (Boston: Little, Brown, 1973), p. 257.

6. *New York Journal-American*, 28 May 1946, p. 1. Garfield discussed the affair in his testimony before HUAC on 23 April 1951. According to Garfield, Simonov was a screenwriter and novelist who visited Hollywood; he gave the party on the ship as a gesture of thanks to Chaplin, Milestone, and Garfield. See Garfield testimony, HUAC hearings, Communist Infiltration of the Motion Picture Industry, vol. 2, 82nd Cong., p. 354.

7. Helen Dreiser, *My Life with Dreiser* (New York: World, 1951), pp. 281, 319–22 (the latter is an account of the funeral; it also quotes the poem). See also W. A. Swanberg, *Dreiser* (New York: Scribner's, 1965), p. 509.

8. *Daily Worker*, 4 June 1947; Gerhart Eisler, a prominent Communist before he came to the United States in the early 1940s, lived a quiet life in the United States, occasionally contributing articles to the Communist press. In 1946, however, he was charged with being a "top Communist International Agent" in the United States, and he finally left the country in April 1949, stowing away in a Polish vessel, the *Batory*. See Joseph R. Starobin, *American Communism in Crisis, 1943–1957* (Cambridge: Harvard Univ. Press, 1972), esp. pp. 304–5.

9. David Caute, *The Great Fear* (New York: Simon and Schuster, 1978), p. 503; Eisler, *Rebel in Music*, p. 152; Ceplair and Englund, *Inquisition in Hollywood*, pp. 379–80. On the Picasso telegram and the appeal to the attorney general's office, see Sadoul, *Vie de Charlot*, p. 149; Heilbut, *Exiled in Paradise*, p. 374; and *Daily Worker*, 18 January 1948, sec. 2, p. 3. In its 11 December 1947 issue, the *Hollywood Reporter* ran an article quoting the November 27 telegram. It also carried an editorial by W. R. Wilkerson that indicates how badly Chaplin's reputation was slipping. It read in part: "The wonder to us is that Washington hasn't long ago relieved Chaplin of his privilege of living in this country, working among us, banking millions of dollars while, at the same time, it becomes quite obvious that he is not satisfied with the conduct of our government and continually criticizes its actions." As we shall see, such sentiments mirrored views being expressed by members of Congress at around the same time, which fueled the FBI investigation of Chaplin's politics in the late 1940s. Indeed, Wilkerson's editorial is quoted in an 8 May 1948 letter from the FBI's Los Angeles field office to Director J. Edgar Hoover. Hanns Eisler himself eventually settled in East Germany in 1950 where he resided until his death in 1962.

10. *Los Angeles Times*, 30 March 1948, sec. 1, p. 10; 17 May 1948, sec. 1, p. 1.

11. O'Neill, *Better World*, pp. 163–69, provides an account of the Waldorf Conference sympathetic to the anti-Stalinists and critical of the progressives. More recently, anti-Stalinist Sidney Hook has described his attempts to participate in the conference in "The Communist Peace Offensive," *Partisan Review*, *50th Anniversary Edition*, ed. William Phillips (New York: Stein and Day, 1985), pp. 210–29.

12. *NYT* 5 April 1949, p. 7; 12 September 1949, p. 5.

13. On the Peekskill incident and Chaplin's involvement in it, see Philip S. Foner, *Paul Robeson Speaks* (New York: Brunner-Mazel, 1978), pp. 543–45; Dorothy Baker Gillim, *Paul Robeson: All-American* (Washington, D.C.: New Republic Books, 1976), esp. ch. 16; and Howard Fast, *Peekskill* (New York: New Century, 1950).

14. Robert Sklar, *Movie-Made America* (New York: Random House, 1975), pp. 196–97; see also Garth Jowett, *Film: The Democratic Art* (Boston: Little, Brown, 1976), ch. 12, "Hollywood Goes to War."

15. On the Dies Committee and the Clark Committee, see Ceplair and Englund, *Inquisition in Hollywood*, esp. pp. 109–11 and 155–65, passim.

16. Langer's bill, which was never passed, was reported in *Variety*, 15 February 1945; Rankin's remarks are found in *Congressional Records*, 79th Cong., 1st sess., 19 July 1945, p. 7377.

17. *Congressional Record*, 80th Cong., 1st sess., 7 March 1947, p. 1792.

18. *Congressional Record*, 80th Cong., 1st sess., 12 June 1947, p. 6895.

19. *NYT*, 14 May 1949, p. 19.

20. The literature on HUAC and the Hollywood Ten—one of HUAC's most famous cases—is enormous, but one of the best places to start is with Walter Goodman, *The Committee* (New York: Farrar, Straus, 1968). Also indispensable are the transcripts of testimonies before HUAC, some of which appear in Eric Bentley, ed., *Thirty Years of Treason* (New York: Viking, 1971), pp. 482–95. See also the *Cumulative Index to Publications of the Committee on Un-American Activities, 1938–1954* (Washington, D.C.: U.S. Government Printing Office, 1962).

21. *Washington Post*, 6 December 1946, p. 3; Ceplair and Englund, *Inquisition in Hollywood*, pp. 379–80.

22. On Chaplin's HUAC interactions, see Balio, *United Artists*, pp. 211–13; and MA, pp. 447–49. In his autobiography, Chaplin gives a shorter and less argumentative version of the telegram, but it too contains the assertion, "I am not a Communist. I am a peace-monger."

23. See Edward L. Barrett, Jr., *The Tenney Committee* (Ithaca: Cornell Univ. Press, 1951).

24. "Hearings on H.R. 1884 and H.R. 2122, Bills to Curb or Outlaw the Communist Party of the United States," HUAC 24–28 March 1947, testimony of Jack B. Tenney, p. 264.

25. Goodman, *The Committee*, pp. 29–30, 198. p. 13. Steele's testimony to the Dies Committee in 1939 and 1940 is published in "Executive Hearings Made Public," HUAC, vols. 1 and 2, pp. 278–428 and 455–706.

26. "Hearings on H.R. 1884 and H.R. 2122," pp. 107–8.

27. In his "Little Old New York" column in the *Washington Times Herald* on 16 April 1947, Sullivan accused Chaplin of "always pitching for the Kremlin": "Chaplin has been a prominent member of at least five Communist-front organizations, one of which tried desperately to get an FM broadcasting station to spread their doctrines in the New York area." Chaplin's denial of association with the group is included in the transcript of the INS interview, pp. 31–32, included in FBI report, SAC Los Angeles to Hoover, 5 July 1949.

28. "Hearings Regarding Communist Infiltration of the Motion-Picture Industry," HUAC, 20–24, 27–30 October 1947, p. 179. See Chapter 10 below for a discussion of the degree to which Chaplin was a "sacred cow" to the *Daily Worker*.

29. Robinson testimony, HUAC Hearings and Reports, 81st Cong., p. 3332; Garfield testimony, HUAC Hearings, "Communist Infiltration of Hollywood Motion-Picture Industry, Part II," 82nd Cong., p. 354; Shaw testimony, HUAC Hearings, "Investigation of Communist Activities in the New York City Area, Part I," 83rd Cong., p. 1185; Oxnam testimony, HUAC Hearings, "Testimony of Bishop G. Bromley Oxnam," 83rd Cong., p. 3599.

30. "Review of the Scientific and Cultural Conference for World Peace," 81st Cong., 26 April 1950, House Report no. 1954. Page numbers for references given in the text.

31. "Report on Communist 'Peace' Offensive," 82nd Cong., 25 April 1951, House Report no. 378. Page numbers for references given in the text.

32. The FBI was established in 1908 by Attorney General Bonaparte under the name "Bureau of Investigation." It underwent a reorganization after J. Edgar Hoover was named director in 1924 (a position he held until his death in 1972) and took its present name in 1935. Its investigative jurisdiction relates to federal cases in two areas: general investigation (as with their involvement in Chaplin's Mann Act charge) and domestic investigative intelligence (as in the present case). Thanks to the Freedom of Information Act, the FBI files on Chaplin have become available to scholars upon request. The files I have obtained concerning the investigation of Chaplin as a security risk between 1946 and 1953 contain hundreds of pages. They include such documents as letters between government agencies, interoffice memos, clippings from newspaper and magazine articles, summaries of testimony and information gathered from informants, and formal reports prepared by FBI staff for Director Hoover or for other administrative agencies. It should be stressed that the files are not complete. Many reports and letters have words or even entire sections blacked out, while at times entire pages are withheld (and a form noting this is inserted), for varying reasons, the most common of which are to protect the identity of an informant or to preserve national security.

33. For a fuller account of Chaplin's interactions with the FBI and other governmental agencies, Timothy Lyons's forthcoming *The Case against Mr. Chaplin* promises to be an important and fundamental work. Lyons has published a brief article on the subject, "The United States vs. Charlie Chaplin," *American Film* 9 (September 1984): 29–34. Robinson's recent biography also contains a brief appendix discussing the FBI investigations of Chaplin (CHLA, pp. 750–56).

34. FBI report, Los Angeles to Washington, 14 August 1922; FBI memo, "GFR" to Hoover, 28 August 1922.

35. FBI report, New York to Washington, 4 December 1942; FBI memo, Welch to Ladd, 23 December 1942.

36. FBI memo, Hoover to SAC Los Angeles, 14 March 1947.

37. FBI report, SAC Los Angeles to Hoover, dated 13 March 1947, received in April. Page references cited parenthetically in the text.

38. FBI clipping of Sullivan column in *Washington Times Herald*, 12 April 1947.

39. FBI letter, Hoover to commissioner, INS, 2 October 1947. The transcript of the INS interview is included in FBI report, SAC Los Angeles to Hoover, 5 July 1949.

40. FBI letter, Hoover to SAC Los Angeles, 21 February 1948.

41. FBI letter, SAC Los Angeles to Hoover, 25 February 1948; FBI letter, SAC Los Angeles to Hoover, 8 May 1948; FBI report, Los Angeles office to Washington office, 9 June 1948.

42. FBI report, SAC Los Angeles to Hoover, 10 August 1948. Page numbers of references cited in the text.

43. Although the interview took place in 1948, it was not made public until the late 1970s and hence had no bearing on Chaplin's star image until then. This is in contrast to some of the information accumulated by the FBI and shared with the press.

44. FBI letter, Hoover to SAC Los Angeles, 7 April 1949; FBI letter, Hoover to SAC Los Angeles, 3 August 1949.

45. FBI letter, SAC Los Angeles to Hoover, 7 October 1949.

46. Letter, Assistant Attorney General Campbell to Hoover, 10 November 1949.

47. FBI memo, Agent D. W. Ladd to Hoover, 21 December 1949.

48. FBI telegram, Hoover to SAC Los Angeles, 22 December 1949.

49. FBI telegram, SAC Los Angeles to Hoover, 27 December 1949; FBI letter, Hoover to Peyton Ford (assistant to attorney general), 29 December 1949.

50. FBI memo, Agent Turner to Agent Whitson, 7 February 1949.

51. FBI interoffice memo, Turner to Hennrich, 4 May 1950.

52. See Kenneth O'Reilly, *Hoover and the Un-Americans* (Philadelphia: Temple Univ. Press, 1983), p. 236. According to O'Reilly, Budenz, who also taught at Notre Dame and Fordam universities, earned a hefty supplementary income as a professional anti-Communist writer and lecturer: $61,000 until his retirement for health reasons in 1957.

53. FBI letter, SAC New York to Hoover, 14 July 1950, p. 4.

54. FBI report, SAC Los Angeles to Hoover, 5 April 1951, pp. 3, 5, 12.

55. On the state of United Artists and the film industry in the late 1940s, see Balio, *United Artists*, pp. 219–29. On the rise of independent production, see Janet Staiger, "Individualism versus Collectivism," *Screen* 24, nos. 4/5 (July-October 1983): 68–79, as well as her chapter on the "package unit system" of production in CHC, pp. 330–37.

56. See Caute, *Great Fear*, chs. 2, 3, and passim, and Pells, *Liberal Mind*,, esp. chs. 2, 5. In a section on three intellectuals who had been socialists in the 1930s—Dwight Macdonald, William Phillips, and Philip Rahv—Pells sums up the direction of their views: "by the end of the 1940s, their minds and their

essays were filled less with the dream of a social democracy than with the harrowing imagery of totalitarianism" (p. 83).

57. Richard Lauterbach, "The Whys of Chaplin's Appeal," *NYT Magazine*, 21 May 1950, p. 24. Lauterbach, a former editor of *Life* magazine, was preparing a biography of Chaplin but died before completing it.

58. The growth of art house screens between 1950 and 1965 is noted by Douglas Ayer et al., "Self Censorship in the Movie Industry," in *American Movie Industry*, ed. Kindem, p. 223; *NYT*, 7 December 1950, p. 52.

59. *NYT*, 31 July 1950, p. 19. The incident surrounding *The Circus* even became a focus of FBI attention: see FBI letter, SAC Los Angeles to Hoover, 2 August 1950, which reported that Chaplin "was incensed about the unauthorized use of his film" and instructed his lawyers "to take all legal steps to prevent such an exhibition and to prosecute the proposed exhibitioners to the fullest extent of the law."

60. *Life* 27 (5 September 1949): 77; "The Comedy of Charlie Chaplin," *Atlantic* 185 (February 1950): 26. Other articles during this period treating Chaplin positively include the following: *New Yorker* 26 (25 February 1950): 24; *Saturday Review* 33 (6 May 1950): 46–47; *NYT Magazine*, 21 May 1950, p. 24.

61. Huff, *Charlie Chaplin*; Peter Cotes and Thelma Niklaus, *The Little Tramp* (New York: Philosophical Library, 1951); Robert Payne, *The Great God Pan* (New York: Hermitage House, 1952). Huff's book was reprinted by Pyramid in 1964 and by 1972 had gone into its fourth printing. Arthur Knight reviewed all three of these books in two book reviews: see *Saturday Review* 34 (7 April 1951): 10–11, and 35 (26 April 1952): 13–14.

10. *LIMELIGHT* AND BANISHMENT

1. See FBI letter, Hoover to SAC Los Angeles, 16 September 1952.

2. *NYT*, 20 September 1952, pp. 1, 16; 3 October 1952, p. 1.

3. *Variety*, 22 October 1952, p. 61.

4. *NYT*, 23 September 1952, p. 21; the second passage and some other Chaplin comments are included in a letter from the American embassy in Brussels to the U.S. Department of State, 17 November 1952.

5. See Rozas, "Charlie Chaplin's Decline," and Philip G. Rosen, "The Chaplin World View," *Cinema Journal* 9 (Fall 1969): 2–12.

6. FBI letter, Hoover to SAC Los Angeles, 8 July 1952.

7. FBI memo, Foley to Keay, 25 August 1952.

8. These details are recounted in an FBI memo, Belmont to Ladd, 16 September 1952.

9. *Variety*, 14 February 1951, p. 3.

10. FBI memo, Belmont to Ladd, 16 September 1952, p. 2; FBI summary report, Washington office to McGranery, 18 September 1952.

11. FBI memo, Belmont to Ladd, 30 September 1952.

12. The act, Public Law 414, 82nd Cong., provided the INS with a powerful tool to deprive leftist citizens of their citizenship and to revoke the residence

permits of leftist aliens and deport them. In *The Great Fear*, Caute says the act "set the Congressional seal on wide-spread xenophobia" (p. 225).

13. FBI report, SAC Los Angeles to Hoover, 14 October 1952.

14. FBI letter, SAC Los Angeles to Hoover, 7 November 1952, pp. 2–3.

15. See FBI letters, all from Hoover to the commissioner and assistant commissioner, INS, 31 October and 9 December 1952 and 19 February 1953.

16. FBI letter, Hoover to chief, Division of Security, U.S. Department of State.

17. Letter, legal attaché, American embassy in London, to Hoover, 31 October 1952; letter, legal attaché, American embassy in Paris, to Hoover, 6 November 1952. (The letter from the embassy in Brussels was sent on 19 November 1952 to the Department of State and a copy was forwarded to the FBI.)

18. FBI letters, Hoover to SAC Los Angeles, 20 April 1953 and 30 April 1953; FBI report, SAC Los Angeles to Hoover, 10 July 1953; FBI letter, SAC Los Angeles to Hoover, 12 August 1953.

19. Young, *New Republic* 31 (23 August 1922): 358–59.

20. Wallach, "*Monsieur Verdoux* Press Conference," p. 39.

21. Robinson, *Chaplin: His Life and Art*, p. 550.

22. Richard Lauterbach, "The Whys of Chaplin's Appeal," *NYT Magazine*, 21 May 1950, p. 24.

23. Lauterbach, "Whys," p. 26.

24. On "biographical legend": see Boris Tomashevsky, "Literature and Biography," in *Readings in Russian Poetics*, ed. Ladislav Matejka and Krystyna Pomorska (Ann Arbor: Univ. of Michigan Press, 1978).

25. Robinson (CHLA, pp. 550–58) emphasizes how consciously autobiographical Chaplin was in preparing the film. Chaplin's unfinished novel told the story of Calvero and Terry much as it was presented in the film but supplemented it with more information about the past lives of both characters. Robinson, who calls the novel a "complex series of autobiographical reflexions," convincingly argues that Chaplin was not only reflecting on his own personal situation in the film but also on his father, his mother, and a number of other family relationships from his earlier years.

26. This analogy becomes more convincing when we learn from Charles Chaplin, Jr., that during the shooting of *Limelight*, his father told him, "I think your father is going to quit after this one. He's getting old." See Chaplin, Jr., *My Father, Charlie Chaplin*, p. 253.

27. Chaplin, Jr., *My Father, Charlie Chaplin*, p. 253.

28. *Herald Tribune*, 23 October 1952, p. 31; *NYT*, 23 October 1952, p. 39.

29. See "Chaplin at Work," *Life* 32 (17 March 1952): 117–27.

30. On the breakdown of the progressive paradigm in the postwar years, see Pells, *Liberal Mind*, esp. ch. 3, and Gene Wise, *American Historial Explanations: A Strategy for Grounded Inquiry*, 2nd ed., rev. (Minneapolis: Univ. of Minnesota Press, 1980), ch. 8.

31. See Frank Beaver, *Bosley Crowther: Social Critic of the Film* (New York: Arno, 1974). As noted in Chapter 5, note 25, Crowther is a good example of

a "modern liberal" reviewer; after 1950 the "social radical" perspective of the 1930s had almost disappeared.

32. Pells, *Liberal Mind*, p. 220. A convenient sampling of postwar writings on mass culture can be found in Bernard Rosenberg and David White, eds., *Mass Culture* (Glencoe, Ill.: The Free Press, 1957).

33. William Barrett, "Chaplin as Chaplin," *American Mercury* 75 (November 1952): 90; Crowther, *NYT*, 24 October 1952, p. 27; Warshow, in *Immediate Experience*, p. 225 (originally in *Partisan Review* [November-December 1954]); Hartung, *Commonweal* 57 (31 October 1952): 102; *Newsweek* 33 (27 October 1952): 112; Bentley, *New Republic* 127 (17 November 1952): 31. These are only a few of the many reviews that comment on *Limelight's* autobiographical elements, on which even non-American reviewers commented. See the comments by the British reviewer Gavin Lambert ("At 63 Chaplin has executed an imaginative portrait of the artist as an old man and shown his creative powers to be at their height") and André Bazin (*Limelight* is "confessional," a "portrait of the author"). See Lambert, " 'The Elegant Melancholy of Twilight': Impressions of 'Limelight,' " *Sight and Sound* 22 (January-March 1953): 123–27, and Bazin, "*Limelight*," in *What Is Cinema?* vol. 2, trans. Hugh Gray (Berkeley: Univ. of California Press, 1971), pp. 124–27.

34. Barrett, "Chaplin as Chaplin," pp. 90–95, passim. Quotes at pp. 90, 91, 95.

35. Knight, *Saturday Review* 35 (25 October 1952): 29, 30.

36. *New Yorker* 28 (25 October 1952): 141; Alpert, *Saturday Review* 35 (25 October 1952): 31–32. See also Manny Farber's review in the *Nation* 175 (25 October 1952): 393–94.

37. Bentley, *New Republic* 127 (17 November 1952): 30–31.

38. On second wave, see Ceplair and Englund, *Inquisition in Hollywood*, ch. 11.

39. *Chicago Tribune*, 20 September 1952, pp. 1, 9.

40. *New York Journal-American*, 19 September 1952, p. 3; 21 September 1952, p. 4.

41. *Chicago Tribune*, 20 September 1952, sec. 2, p. 2.

42. Though the articles appeared throughout the country, I am referring to those that appeared in the *San Francisco Examiner*, 22–26 September 1952. All the quotations in this paragraph and the next are taken from this series.

43. *Daily Worker* (all 1952), 22 September, p. 6; 23 September, p. 3; 24 September, p. 5; 25 September, p. 7; 1 October, p. 7. Quotations in the next two paragraphs are taken from the last three articles.

44. The correct statement, in Chaplin's "What People Laugh At," reads, "people as a whole get satisfaction from seeing the rich get the worst of things." Chaplin's article is excerpted in *Focus on Chaplin*, ed. McCaffrey, pp. 48–54. It originally appeared in *American Magazine* 86 (November 1918): 34, 134–37.

45. *NYT*, 21 September 1952, sec. 4, p. 10. The *Nation* editorialized almost identically in its 4 October 1952 issue (p. 287): "Whatever his political views

may be—and he says he has never been a Communist—Charlie Chaplin can hardly be regarded as an overt threat to American institutions."

46. *NYT*, 28 September 1952, sec. 2, p. 1; sec. 4, p. 10.

47. "Chaplin's Art Proclaims Him Anti-Communist," *New York Herald Tribune*, George W. Demott scrapbook, BRC.

48. *Time* 60 (29 September 1952): 34.

49. Irving Kristol, "McGranery and Charlie Chaplin," *Commentary*, 24 November 1952, p. 9. Emphasis in original. See also Pells, *Liberal Mind*, pp. 130–47, which treats the increasing celebration of American society among liberals in the early 1950s and their attendant rejection of the progressive critique of American society. Kristol's article contains seeds of both attitudes. A radical in the late 1930s and early 1940s, Kristol moved right in the 1940s and even came to defend McCarthy in a qualified way. See Alan Wald, *The New York Intellectuals* (Chapel Hill: Univ. of North Carolina Press, 1987), pp. 350–54.

50. *Nation* 175 (4 October 1952): 287.

51. Ibid., p. 288.

52. William Bradford Huie, "Mr. Chaplin and the Fifth Freedom," *American Mercury* 75 (November 1952): 123–28.

53. James Truett Selcraig, *The Red Scare in the Midwest, 1945–1955: A State and Local Study* (Ann Arbor: UMI Research Press, 1982), p. 87.

54. On the American Legion's campaign against Hollywood in the early 1950s see Selcraig, *Red Scare*, pp. 90–92, and Caute, *Great Fear*, pp. 502–4.

55. One local Legion post succeeded in getting a college showing of Chaplin shorts canceled a week *before* the convention. See *Knoxville Journal*, 6 October 1952, p. 4; 7 October 1952, pp. 1, 3; 8 October 1952, p. 10.

56. See William Murray, "*Limelight*: Chaplin and His Censors," *Nation* 176 (21 March 1952): 247. The Legion's attitude toward McGranery is indicated by its California branch, which gave him a plaque of commendation in late October for his stand against Chaplin. See *NYT*, 29 October 1952, p. 32.

57. Murray, "*Limelight*," p. 247.

58. Victor Lasky, "Whose Little Man?" *American Legion Magazine*, December 1951, pp. 28, 46–50.

59. *NYT*, 16 January 1953, p. 18. Brewer was also head of IATSE, the dominant film industry craft union. His anti-Communist strategy during the long film industry strike in 1945 is detailed in Sklar, *Movie-Made America*, pp. 256–62.

60. *NYT*, 28 January 1953, p. 23; Murray, "*Limelight*," p. 247.

61. Murray, "*Limelight*" surveys the censorship campaign of the Legion, but see also *NYT* (all 1953), 26 January, p. 15; 28 January, p. 23; 3 February, p. 21; 5 February, p. 15; and 13 February, p. 17; and *Variety* (all 1953), 21 January, p. 3; 4 February, p. 23; and 11 February, p. 5.

62. See *Variety* (all 1952), 8 October, p. 6; 29 October, p. 9; 5 November, p. 9; 12 November, p. 11; 19 November, p. 11; 26 November, p. 13; 3 December, pp. 8–9; 10 December, p. 9; 17 December, p. 9; 24 December, p. 9; 31 December, p. 9.

63. *Variety*, 4 February 1953, p. 5; 11 February 1953, p. 5; 4 March 1953, p. 4.

64. Pells, *Liberal Mind*, p. 265. In chapter 5, Pells discusses in considerable detail the varied responses of American intellectuals to the loyalty oaths, HUAC, McCarthy, and other issues that raised questions about the character of and threats to civil liberties in the United States in the late 1940s and early 1950s.

65. *Commonweal*, 6 February 1953, p. 441; *NYT*, 7 February 1953, p. 14. In the same issue (pp. 451–53), *Commonweal* also included a sympathetic and thoughtful review of *Limelight* by J. L. Tallenay, editor of a French journal, *La vie intellectuelle*, in which the review originally appeared.

66. *NYT*, 17 April 1953, p. 24.

67. Ruark's column is included in the George W. DeMott scrapbook, BRC.

11. THE EXILED MONARCH AND THE GUARDED RESTORATION

1. *Newsweek* 41 (27 April 1953): 37.

2. *Newsweek* 43 (14 June 1954): 48. A 1958 article on Chaplin in the *Saturday Evening Post* 230 (8 March 1958) reported that Chaplin refused to accept the award publicly in Berlin or London and preferred to accept it at his home, perhaps to avoid some of the negative publicity in the West that a more public ceremony could have generated.

3. See *London Times*, 25 April 1956, p. 10; and *NYT*, 25 April 1956, p. 3. In his autobiography Chaplin mistakenly reverses the visits with Chou En-lai and the Soviet leaders.

4. *NYT*, 5 June 1954, p. 16; for a similarly negative response, see also *Newsweek* 43 (14 June 1954): 48.

5. *Saturday Evening Post* 227 (4 September 1954): 10, 12. One of the few articles sympathetic to Chaplin appearing in the mid-1950s was "The Great Chaplin Chase," by Ernest Callenbach, which appeared in the *Nation* 83 (4 August 1956): 96–99. After surveying Chaplin's career, the article attributed American hostility for Chaplin to his politics, his escapades with women, and what Callenbach termed the "folk anarchism" of Chaplin's screen persona.

6. *NYT*, 7 January 1955, p. 16.

7. *NYT*, 8 January 1955, p. 9; 13 January 1955, p. 31. A similar incident occurred at the Hicksville (N.Y.) Public Library in November 1958; after letting the situation cool for a month, the library's board of trustees lifted their ban and permitted the screening of four Chaplin short films. See *NYT*, 12 November 1958, p. 39; 13 November 1958, p. 36; 19 December 1958, p. 2.

8. For brief reports on the production in the American press, see *NYT*, 20 December 1953, sec. 2, p. 5; 16 October 1954, p. 12; 26 August 1955, p. 11; 28 October 1956, sec. 2, p. 5.

9. During the time of the film's British release, Chaplin admitted to Ella Winter the parallel between himself and the deposed monarch. "There was a time," he told Winter, "when they put out the red carpet, literally, on every platform when I went from Los Angeles to New York. The crowd adored me." But both the king and Chaplin were deposed. See CHLA, pp. 592–93.

10. The roots of this conservative cultural critique appear to be autobiographical. Chaplin himself had long been accustomed to celebrity status, clearly used to the attention a king or even an ex-king would enjoy. He also increasingly came to enjoy a quiet and rather conservative home life when he was not making films. Charles Chaplin, Jr., describes this side of Chaplin in parts of *My Father, Charlie Chaplin*. After Chaplin's marriage to Oona O'Neill, this personally conservative side became even more central: his last twenty-five years were spent living in Swiss baronial splendor. In his film Chaplin gives King Shahdov both of these characteristics: enough celebrity status to warrant the attention of others and enough conservative temperament to find certain aspects of American culture amusing or even repugnant.

11. Chaplin apparently planned and budgeted the film knowing it would not be released in the United States. Robinson (CHLA, p. 590) notes that shooting took only twelve weeks, the shortest for any Chaplin feature. And given the enthusiastic welcome Chaplin received in Europe after his departure from the United States, he was probably right in assuming that he could recoup his expenditures via the European market alone.

12. *NYT*, 11 September 1957, p. 29; *New York Herald Tribune*, 11 September 1957; *Newsweek* 50 (9 September 1957): 108; *Time* 70 (23 September 1957): 48.

13. *NYT*, 11 September 1957, p. 29; *Time*, 70 (23 September 1957), p. 48; *Nation* 185 (2 November 1957), p. 310; *New York Herald Tribune*, 15 September 1957, sec. 4, p. 1.

14. "Chaplin Satirizes McCarthyism," *London Times*, 11 September 1957, p. 3.

15. CHLA p. 591; see also David Robinson, *Chaplin: The Mirror of Opinion* (Bloomington: Indiana Univ. Press, 1984), pp. 158–61.

16. Hodgson, *America in Our Time*, pp. 67, 75–76. One critic who did appreciate films with sociological or political "messages," *NYT* critic Bosley Crowther, did not attend the London premiere and consequently did not review the film. Of all the influential American critics in the mid-1950s, he was the one most likely to have responded positively to the film.

17. *Time* 70 (23 September 1947): 48; *Nation* 185 (2 November 1957): 310–11; *New Republic* 137 (7 October 1957): 22; and *Reporter* 17 (17 October 1957): 43. The commentators who criticized the film because its production values were low and its satire out of date did have a point. When the king is about to leave for his night out, for example, Chaplin cuts to some stock footage of movie marquees: one theater is playing *Three Little Words*, another is playing *Pretty Baby*, both American films released in 1950. Only the theater Shahdov walks into is playing a more recent film, *The Baby and the Battleship* (British, 1956). Though all three titles are consistent with Chaplin's satirical picture of the thinness of popular culture, the inclusion of out-of-date or foreign titles reveals a lack of concern for production values that the classical Hollywood cinema prided itself in. Similarly, since McCarthy had been censured by the Senate nearly three years earlier and HUAC was much less prone to issue con-

tempt citations than it had been between 1947 and 1953, Chaplin's satire was less topical than it was, say, in *The Great Dictator*.

18. *Saturday Review* 40 (28 September 1957): 26; *Newsweek* 50 (9 September 1957): 108. The subsequent reviews have already been cited in note 17; their page numbers are cited in the text.

19. *Saturday Evening Post* 230, part I (8 March 1958): 19–21 ff.; part II (15 March 1958): 44–45 ff.; part III (22 March 1958): 38 ff. Further references to these articles will be cited in the text with the part and page numbers in parentheses.

20. *NYT*, 21 February 1958, p. 19; *NYT*, 26 April 1960, p. 40.

21. Pells, *Liberal Mind*, p. 346. Pells treats this shifting mood of the late 1950s in chapter 6. On the circumstances leading to the downfall of Joseph McCarthy, see Eric F. Goldman, *The Crucial Decade and After, 1945–1960* (New York: Vintage, 1960), pp. 271–79.

22. *NYT*, 30 December 1958, p. 7, reported that Chaplin agreed to pay $425,000 in 1953 taxes. He claimed that since he was not in the country after September 1952, he was not liable for 1953 taxes. Though the IRS in 1956 announced that they would seek $1.1 million, the settlement was ultimately for $330,000 with interest. See CHLA, p. 593.

23. Ayer et al., "Self Censorship," in Kindem, *American Movie Industry*, p. 223.

24. *NYT*, 11 June 1959, p. 37; 24 July 1959, p. 14. *The Gold Rush* was not fully included in the decision. Chaplin had rereleased *The Gold Rush* with a recorded musical score in 1942, and his organization—perhaps partly due to the political pressures Chaplin found himself facing—failed to renew the copyright to the original film in 1952. Chaplin's organization thus still retains the copyright to the 1942 version of *The Gold Rush* but does not have rights to the 1925 version. That is one reason for the variant endings often found in that film.

25. Bosley Crowther, "The Modern—and Mellower—Times of Mr. Chaplin," *NYT Magazine*, 6 November 1960, pp. 52–60.

26. *NYT*, 28 June 1962, p. 1; 29 June 1962, p. 12; 2 July 1962, p. 28 (editorial).

27. An examination of *Variety*'s box-office grosses and the *Times* movie ads during this period establish the continuous run; generally, the Plaza ran a large ad in the *Times* at least the day before and the day of a new program's opening, then ran much smaller ads as time passed.

28. *NYT*, 7 July 1964, p. 25; *Variety*, 22 April 1964, p. 10; *Variety*, 26 August 1964, p. 13.

29. *New York Herald Tribune*, 26 July 1964, p. 26; *NYT*, 4 July 1964, p. 8; *NYT*, 12 July 1964, sec. II, p. 1.

30. *Newsweek* 64 (27 July 1964): 78. Emphasis added.

31. Jauss, "Literary History," in Jauss, *Toward an Aesthetic of Reception*, p. 21.

32. Ibid., pp. 25–26. Jauss argues that the "aesthetic distance" of a work also "provides a criterion for the determination of its aesthetic value" (p. 25): the

greater the aesthetic distance, the greater the work. Such an aesthetic seems clearly to derive from a modernist stress on originality and is problematic when applied to a commercial medium like the movies. If one accepts this tenet of Jauss's aesthetic, it is hard to avoid concluding that *Monsieur Verdoux* is Chaplin's greatest film.

33. *NYT*, 7 July 1964, p. 25. On the reception of *Strangelove*, see Charles Maland, "*Dr. Strangelove*: Nightmare Comedy and the Ideology of Liberal Consensus," in *Hollywood as Historian*, ed. Peter Rollins (Lexington: Univ. of Kentucky Press, 1983), pp. 208–10. The black humorists are treated perceptively by Morris Dickstein in *Gates of Eden* (New York: Basic, 1977), ch. 4.

34. *Time* 84 (2 October 1964): 132.

35. *Publishers Weekly* 186 (5 October 1964): 132; (26 October 1964): 74; (23 November 1964): 98; (14 December 1964): 106; 187 (15 March 1965): 98.

36. John Houseman, "Charlie's Chaplin," *Nation* 199 (12 October 1964): 223; *NYT*, 1 October 1964, p. 33; Brendan Gill, "Total Strangers," *New Yorker* 40 (12 December 1964): 237.

37. *Time* 84 (2 October 1964): 132; *National Review* 16 (December 1964): 1068.

38. *Newsweek* 64 (5 October 1964): 112; Houseman, "Charlie's Chaplin," p. 224; *NYT*, 16 October 1964, p. 36; *Harper's* 229 (October 1964): 131.

39. *Commonweal* 81 (16 October 1964): 104. Other reviews cited in notes 37 and 38.

40. Atkinson, *NYT*, 16 October 1964, p. 36; Hatch, *Harper's* 229 (October 1964): 129; Gill, *New Yorker*, 12 December 1964, p. 238; Poore, *NYT*, 1 October 1964, p. 33.

41. *NYT*, 23 July 1965, p. 19; 2 November 1965, p. 28; 17 March 1967, p. 35.

42. *Life* 60 (1 April 1966): 80–86; 62 (10 March 1967): 80–94.

43. *Time* 89 (31 March 1967): 95; *Newsweek* 69 (3 April 1967): 90; *National Review* 19 (30 May 1967): 599, 600; *Commonweal* 86 (1 April 1967): 128. It is unlikely that the negative reviews surprised Chaplin, for he had already suffered through a similar set when the film premiered in London in January. According to the *NYT*, Chaplin told reporters that the London critics who didn't like *Countess* were "bloody idiots." See *NYT*, 7 January 1967, p. 22.

44. *Monsieur Verdoux* and *Countess* both ran just over two months and grossed slightly over $20,000 in their first two weeks. At the end of two months in 1964, however, *Monsieur Verdoux* was still grossing $11,500 per week at the Plaza; *Countess* was down to about $8,500 per week at the Sutton. See *Variety*, 10 May 1967, p. 10.

45. *Variety*, 3 January 1968, p. 25.

46. Hartung, *Commonweal* 86 (1 April 1967): 90; Kenner, *National Review* 19 (30 May 1967): 600.

47. *Chicago Tribune*, 11 January 1972, sec. 2, p. 1; *NYT*, 7 April 1972, p. 24; CHLA, pp. 620–21.

48. *NYT*, 7 April 1972, p. 24.

49. *NYT*, 14 January 1972, p. 18; 9 February 1972, p. 44.

50. *NYT*, 5 April 1972, p. 38; *New Yorker*, 15 April 1972, pp. 36–37.

51. *NYT*, 7 April 1972, p. 24.

52. *NYT*, 12 April 1972, p. 9; *Los Angeles Times*, 12 April 1972, sec. 4, p. 13; *Life* 72 (21 April 1972): 90. Emphasis in original.

53. See Hodgson, *America in Our Time*, pp. 384–85, 421–28.

54. See *Reader's Guide to Periodical Literature*, vol. 32 (1972), s.v. "Chaplin, Charlie."

55. *Time* 99 (17 April 1972): 71; *Newsweek* 79 (17 April 1972): 94; Richard Meryman, "Love Feast for Charlie," and Candace Bergen, " 'I Thought They Might Hiss,' " *Life* 72 (21 April 1972): 86–90..

56. *Time* 99 (10 April 1972): 65–66.

57. *NYT*, 8 February 1972, p. 24. The *Times'* followup editorial, "Tramp's Triumph" (7 April 1972, sec. 1, p. 34), appeared after the Lincoln Center affair and was, if anything, even harder on the officials who banned Chaplin in 1952. It noted that Chaplin's admirers were on hand to greet him, but the faded officials responsible for his exile were not. "Chaplin knows the difference between the morals of a country and the moralizing of its passing politicians," wrote the editors. "We can only be grateful that he does, for otherwise we would not have had the pleasure of his return."

58. *Los Angeles Times*, 10 April 1972, sec. 2, p. 6; *Chicago Tribune*, 10 April 1972, p. 16.

59. *Nation* 214 (24 April 1972): 518–19.

60. *Los Angeles Times*, 9 April 1972, sec. 1B, p. 1.

61. *NYT*, 11 February 1972, p. 36; *Los Angeles Times*, 9 April 1972, sec. 1B, p. 1; *Los Angeles Times*, 11 April 1972, sec. 1, p. 3; *Los Angeles Times*, 18 April 1972, sec. 4, p. 18.

62. Richard Schickel, "Hail Chaplin—The Early Chaplin," *NYT Magazine*, 2 April 1972, pp. 12–13, 47–48; George H. Dunne, "I Remember Chaplin," *Commonweal* 96 (2 June 1972): 303–9. Subsequent references to these articles will be made parenthetically in the text.

63. *NYT*, 18 June 1973, p. 5.

64. *NYT*, 8 April 1972, p. 16; 7 April 1972, p. 29.

65. *NYT*, 16 April 1972, sec. 2, pp. 1, 26; 23 January 1972, sec. 2, p. 12; 18 June 1973, sec. 2, p. 5; 8 July 1973, sec. 2, p. 1.

66. *Chicago Tribune*, 25 February 1972, sec. 2, p. 13; 17 March, sec. 2, p. 1.

67. *Los Angeles Times*, 2 April 1972, Calif., p. 12; 13 December 1972, sec. 4, p. 28.

68. *Film Comment* 8 (September-October 1972): 11–26. Page numbers for quotations from this issue will be cited in the text. The *Film Comment* articles probably had a somewhat larger influence on Chaplin's image than they normally would have, because Chaplin's American distributor in the mid-1970s, RBC Films, sent out photocopies of this issue, along with a 1970 *Film Comment* article on *The Circus* by David Bordwell, to those who ordered a Chaplin series.

69. Sam L. Grogg, Jr., and Dennis R. Bohnenkamp, *AFI Guide to College Courses in Film and Television* (Washington: American Film Institute, 1978).

70. A detailed bibliographical essay on Chaplin criticism is available in Wes Gehring, *Charlie Chaplin: A Bio-Bibliography* (Westport, Conn.: Greenwood, 1983), ch. 4. See also Timothy Lyons, *Charles Chaplin: A Guide to References and Resources* (Boston: G. K. Hall, 1979).

71. The articles by Sarris and Kael are included in Gerald Mast and Marshall Cohen, *Film Theory and Criticism*, 3rd ed. (New York: Oxford Univ. Press, 1985), pp. 527–52. The articles have appeared in this widely used anthology since its first edition. See also Edward Murray, "Andrew Sarris and *Auteur* Criticism," in his *Nine American Film Critics* (New York: Ungar, 1975), pp. 38–66.

72. Andrew Sarris, *The American Cinema: Directors and Directions, 1929–1968* (New York: Dutton, 1968).

73. See Beaver, *Bosley Crowther*.

74. Richard Roud, ed., *Cinema: A Biographical Dictionary* (New York: Viking, 1980), 1: 201–12.

75. This shift is most apparent in Sarris's more recent collection of film criticism, *Politics and Cinema* (New York: Columbia Univ. Press, 1978); see esp. pp. 1–22 .

76. Gerald Mast, *A Short History of the Movies*, 2nd ed. (New York: Dutton, 1976), chs. 5, 6, and 11.

77. Mast, *Comic Mind*, pp. 61–124.

78. Bordwell and Thompson, *Film Art*, 2nd ed., pp. 34–35. In this second edition, Bordwell and Thompson have added two other possible criteria for evaluating films: coherence and intensity of effect (p. 34). It could easily be argued that some of Chaplin's films would fare considerably better if evaluated by those standards than by the standards of originality and complexity.

79. Quoted in Roud, *Cinema: A Biographical Dictionary*, p. 201.

80. For an attempt to discuss the historical context and describe the critical agenda of this semiological/ideological approach, see Sylvia Harvey, *May '68 and Film Culture* (London: British Film Institute, 1980). Some of the challenges to the auteur approach, some from semiological or ideological perspectives, are discussed or reprinted in John Caughie, ed., *Theories of Authorship* (London: Routledge and Kegan Paul, 1981), pp. 199–291.

81. Smith, *Chaplin*, passim.

82. Chaplin himself helped stimulate interest in the production history of his films when he published *My Life in Pictures*, a kind of photo album summarizing his career. The book was published in England in 1974 and in the United States in 1975.

83. Molyneaux, *Charlie Chaplin's "City Lights,"* p. 57.

84. Anthony Slide, "The American Press and Public v. Charles Spencer Chaplin," *Cineaste* 13, no. 4 (1984): 9.

85. CHLA, pp. 746, xiv.

86. Chaplin's death on Christmas Eve in 1977, and the subsequent bizarre

story of his disinterment and demands for ransom to return the body, are discussed in CHLA, pp. 627–31.

12. EPILOGUE

1. Martin Porter, "That's Why the PC Is a Tramp," *PC Magazine* 2 (July 1983): 329–34.

2. Verne Gay, "Charlie Chaplin is Alive and Well," *Marketing and Media Decisions*, 19 April 1984, p. 89; Porter, "That's Why," pp. 329–34.

3. Daniel Burstein, "Using Yesterday to Sell Tomorrow: How the Unlikely IBM–Charlie Chaplin Marriage Came to Be," *Advertising Age* 54 (11 April 1983): sec. 2, p. 4; Porter, "That's Why," p. 333.

4. Burstein, "Using Yesterday," p. 5.

5. Telephone conversation with IBM, Montvale, N.J., 11 August 1986; Gay, "Charlie," p. 94.

6. Burstein, "Using Yesterday," p. 5.

7. Gay, "Charlie," p. 88.

8. Telephone conversation with IBM, Boca Raton, Florida, 11 August 1986.

9. Burstein, "Using Yesterday," p. 5.

10. Bob Marich, "Hagman Has DGA Top Spot for His TV Work," *Advertising Age* 56 (14 March 1985): 3.

11. Paul Richter, "Estate Zealously Guards Chaplin's Little Tramp," *Los Angeles Times*, 12 June 1984, sec. 4, pp. 1, 3; Porter, "That's Why," p. 331; *PC Magazine* 1, no. 2 (1983), passim.

12. Richter, "Estate," pp. 1, 3.

13. Porter, "That's Why," p. 330; Burstein, "Using Yesterday," p. 5.

14. Gay, "Charlie," pp. 88–89.

15. The ad is reprinted in Burstein, "Using Yesterday," p. 4.

16. Porter, "That's Why," pp. 332, 334, 330.

17. Ibid., p. 330; telephone conversation with IBM, Montvale, N.J., 11 August 1986.

18. On stardom and the ideological functions of compensation, reinforcement of values, and displacement of values, see Dyer, *Stars*, pp. 22–34. An interesting collection focusing on gender and reading response is Elisabeth Flynn and Patrocinio P. Schweickart, *Gender and Reading: Essays on Readers, Texts, and Contexts* (Baltimore: Johns Hopkins Univ. Press, 1986). See particularly the essays by Crawford and Chaffin, Bleich, and Flynn. Another useful essay on reader response criticism and its application to television viewing is Robert C. Allen's in *Channels of Discourse*, ed. Robert C. Allen (Chapel Hill: Univ. of North Carolina Press, 1987), ch. 3.

Select Bibliography

This bibliography lists a selection of the works most useful in the researching of this book and is divided into four categories: newspapers and periodicals; works by or about Chaplin (including memoirs and parts of books); works on film history, film theory, and literary theory; and works on twentieth-century American cultural history. Archives consulted are listed in the Acknowledgments. My search for secondary sources dealing with Chaplin has been considerably assisted by two very useful bibliographies: Timothy Lyons, *Charles Chaplin: A Guide to References and Resources* (Boston, 1979), and Wes Gehring, *Charlie Chaplin: A Bio-Bibliography* (Westport, Conn., 1983).

NEWSPAPERS AND PERIODICALS

This listing includes only the newspapers and periodicals I consulted most systematically in my attempt to gauge the character and evolution of Chaplin's public reputation in America.

Chicago Tribune	*Motion Picture Magazine*
Daily Worker	*Moving Picture World*
Los Angeles Times	*Nation*
New York Herald Tribune	*New Masses*
New York Times	*New Republic*
Variety	*Newsweek*
Washington Post	*Photoplay*
Commonweal	*Saturday Evening Post*
Life	*Time*

WORKS BY OR ABOUT CHAPLIN

Auerbach, David. "Charlie Chaplin: Of Crime and Genius—A Psycho-Portrait." *Encounter* 60 (May 1983): 86–92.

Bishop, John Peale. *The Collected Essays of John Peale Bishop.* Edited by Edmund Wilson. New York, 1948.

Burke, Thomas. *City of Encounters.* Boston, 1932.

Callenbach, Ernest. "The Great Chaplin Chase." *Nation* 83 (4 August 1956): 96–99.

Chaplin, Charles. *Charlie Chaplin's Own Story*. Edited by Harry Geduld. Indianapolis, 1916. Reprinted Bloomington, 1985.

———. "In Defense of Myself." *Collier's*, 11 November 1922, reprinted in Gehring, *Charles Chaplin*, pp. 108–14.

———. "What People Laugh At." *American Magazine* 86 (November 1918): 34, 134–37.

———. *My Trip Abroad*. New York, 1922.

———. "Pantomime and Comedy." *New York Times*, 25 January 1931, sec. 8, p. 8.

———. "A Comedian Sees the World." *Woman's Home Companion* 61 (September 1933–January 1934). Five-part memoir.

———. *My Autobiography*. New York, 1964.

———. *My Life in Pictures*. New York, 1975.

Chaplin, Charles, Jr. *My Father, Charlie Chaplin*. New York, 1961.

Chaplin, Lita Grey, with Morton Cooper. *My Life with Chaplin: An Intimate Memoir*. New York, 1966.

Cooke, Alistair. *Six Men*. New York, 1977.

Dreiser, Helen. *My Life with Dreiser*. New York, 1951.

Dunne, George. "I Remember Chaplin." *Commonweal* 96 (2 June 1972): 303–309.

d'Usseau, Arnaud. "Chaplin's *Monsieur Verdoux*." *Mainstream* 1 (Summer 1947): 308–317.

Eastman, Max. *Heroes I Have Known*. New York, 1942.

———. *Great Companions*. New York, 1959.

———. *Love and Revolution*. New York, 1964.

Eisenstein, Sergei. *Immoral Memories*. Translated by Herbert Marshall. Boston, 1983.

Film Comment 8 (September-October 1972). Special issue on Chaplin.

Frank, Waldo. *Memoirs of Waldo Frank*. Edited by Alan Trachtenberg. Amherst, 1973.

———. *Time Exposures*. New York, 1926.

Gehring, Wes. "Chaplin and the Progressive Era: The Neglected Politics of a Clown." *Indiana Social Studies Quarterly* 34 (Autumn 1981): 10–18.

———. *Charlie Chaplin: A Bio-Bibliography*. Westport, Conn., 1983.

Giesler, Jerry. *The Jerry Giesler Story*. New York, 1960.

Harris, Frank. *Contemporary Portraits*. 4th series. New York, 1923.

Huff, Theodore. *Charlie Chaplin*. 1951. Reprinted New York, 1964.

Kerr, Walter. *The Silent Clowns*. New York, 1975.

Lyons, Timothy. *Charles Chaplin: A Guide to References and Resources*. Boston, 1979.

———. "The United States vs. Charlie Chaplin." *American Film* 9 (September 1984): 29–34.

McCabe, John. *Charlie Chaplin*. Garden City, N.Y.: Doubleday, 1978.

McCaffrey, Donald, ed. *Focus on Chaplin*. Englewood Cliffs, N.J., 1971.

Macdonald, Dwight. "On Chaplin, Verdoux, and Agee." *Esquire* 63, April 1965.

MacDonald, Gerald et al., eds. *The Films of Charlie Chaplin*. New York: Citadel, 1965.

Maland, Charles J. *American Visions: The Films of Chaplin, Ford, Capra, and Welles, 1936–1941*. New York, 1977.

———. "A Documentary Note on Charlie Chaplin's Politics." *Historical Journal of Film, Radio and Television* 5, no. 2 (1985): 199–208.

———. " 'Are You Now or Have You Ever Been?': An INS Interview with Charles Chaplin." *Cineaste* 14, no. 4 (1986): 10–15.

Manning, Harold, and Timothy J. Lyons. "Charlie Chaplin's Early Life: Fact and Fiction." *Historical Journal of Film, Radio, and Television* 3, no. 1 (1983): 35–41.

Mast, Gerald. *The Comic Mind*. 2nd ed. Chicago, 1979.

Menjou, Adolphe, and M. M. Musselman. *It Took Nine Tailors*. New York, 1948.

Molyneaux, Gerard. *Charlie Chaplin's "City Lights."* New York, 1983.

Montagu, Ivor. *With Eisenstein in Hollywood*. New York, 1969.

Moss, Robert F. *Charlie Chaplin*. New York, 1975.

Munson, Gorham. *The Awakening Twenties*. Baton Rouge, 1985.

Negri, Pola. *Memoirs of a Star*. New York, 1970.

Newhouse, Edward. "Charlie's Critics." *Partisan Review* 3 (April 1936): 25–26.

Oakie, Jack. *Jack Oakie's Double Takes*. San Francisco, 1980.

Ramsaye, Terry. "Chaplin Ridicules Reds' Claim Film Aids 'Cause.' " *Motion Picture Herald* 7 December 1935, p. 1.

Robinson, David. *Chaplin: The Mirror of Opinion*. Bloomington, 1984.

———. *Chaplin*: His Life and Art. New York, 1985.

Rosen, Philip. "The Chaplin World View." *Cinema Journal* 9 (Fall 1969): 2–12.

Rozas, Lorenzo Turrent. "Charlie Chaplin's Decline." *Living Age* 396 (June 1934): 319–23.

Sadoul, Georges. *Vie de Charlot*. Paris, 1978.

Sarris, Andrew. "Charles Spencer Chaplin." *Cinema: A Critical Dictionary*. Edited by Richard Roud. Vol. 1. London, 1980.

Schickel, Richard. "Hail Chaplin—The Early Chaplin." *New York Times Magazine*, 2 April 1972, pp. 12–13, 47–48.

Seldes, Gilbert. *The Seven Lively Arts*. New York, 1924.

Sinclair, Upton. *The Autobiography of Upton Sinclair*. New York, 1962.

Shumiatsky, Boris. "Charlie Chaplin's New Picture." *New Masses*, 24 September 1935, pp. 29–30.

Slide, Anthony. "The American Press and Public versus Charles Spencer Chaplin." *Cineaste* 13, no. 4 (1984): 6–9.

Smith, Julian. *Chaplin*. Boston, 1984.

Sobel, Raoul, and David Francis. *Chaplin: Genesis of a Clown*. London, 1977.

Stewart, Donald Ogden. *By a Stroke of Luck*. New York, 1975.

Stewart, Garret. "Modern Hard Times: Chaplin and the Cinema of Self-Reflexiveness." *Critical Inquiry* 3 (1976): 295–315.

Sullivan, Ed, ed. *Chaplin vs. Chaplin*. Los Angeles, 1965.

Tyler, Parker. *Chaplin: Last of the Clowns*. New York, 1972 (reprint), 1947.

Viertel, Salka. *The Kindness of Strangers*. New York, 1969.

von Ulm, Gerith. *Charlie Chaplin: King of Comedy*. Caldwell, Idaho, 1940.

von Wiegand, Charmion. "Little Man, What Now?" *New Theater* 3 (March 1936): 6–8.

Wallach, George. "Charlie Chaplin's *Monsieur Verdoux* Press Conference." *Film Comment*, 5 (Winter 1969): 34–42.

WORKS ON FILM HISTORY, FILM THEORY, AND LITERARY THEORY

Agee, James. *Agee on Film*. Vol. 1. Boston, 1964.

Allen, Robert C. *Vaudeville and Film, 1895–1915: A Study in Media Interaction*. New York, 1980.

———. *Speaking of Soap Operas*. Chapel Hill, 1985.

———, ed. *Channels of Discourse*. Chapel Hill, 1987.

Allen, Robert C. and Douglas Gomery. *Film History: Theory and Practice*. New York, 1985.

Balio, Tino. *United Artists*. Madison, 1976.

Balio, Tino, ed. *The American Film Industry*. 2nd ed. Madison, 1985.

Baxter, John. *The Hollywood Exiles*. London, 1976.

Beaver, Frank. *Bosley Crowther: Social Critic of the Film*. New York, 1974.

Bennett, Tony. "Text and Social Process: The Case of James Bond." *Screen Education* 41 (Winter/Spring 1982): 3–14.

Bennett, Tony, and Janet Woollacott. *Bond and Beyond: The Political Career of a Popular Hero*. London, 1987.

Bordwell, David, and Kristin Thompson. *Film Art*. 2nd ed. New York, 1986.

Bordwell, David, Janet Staiger, and Kristin Thompson. *The Classical Hollywood Cinema: Film Style and Mode of Production to 1960*. New York, 1985. Abbreviated in notes as CHC.

Brownlow, Kevin. *The War, the West, and the Wilderness*. New York, 1979.

Burch, Noël. *To the Distant Observer*. Berkeley, 1979.

Caughie, John, ed. *Theories of Authorship*. London, 1981.

Cawelti, John. *Adventure, Mystery, and Romance*. Chicago, 1976.

Ceplair, Larry, and Steven Englund. *The Inquisition in Hollywood: Politics and the Film Community, 1930–1960*. New York, 1980.

DiNitto, Dennis, and William Herman. *Film and the Critical Eye*. New York, 1975.

Dunne, Philip. *Take Two*. New York, 1980.

Dyer, Richard. *Stars*. London, 1979.

Eckert, Charles. "Shirley Temple and the House of Rockefeller." *Jump Cut* no. 2 (July-August 1974): 1, 17–20.

Eells, George. *Hedda and Louella*. New York, 1972.

Eisler, Hanns. *A Rebel in Music*. Edited by Manfred Grabs. New York, 1978.

Ferguson, Otis. *The Film Criticism of Otis Ferguson*. Edited by Robert Wilson. Philadelphia, 1971.

Geduld, Harry. *The Birth of the Talkies*. Bloomington, 1975.

Gomery, Douglas. "The Coming of Sound to the American Cinema: A History of the Transformation of an Industry." Ph.D. dissertation, University of Wisconsin, 1975.

Haralovich, Mary Beth. "The Social History of Film: Heterogeneity and Mediation." *Wide Angle* 8, no. 2 (1986): 4–14.

Harvey, Sylvia. *May '68 and Film Culture*. London, 1980.

Jacobs, Lewis. *Rise of the American Film*. New York, 1939.

Jauss, Hans Robert. *Toward an Aesthetic of Reception*. Translated by Timothy Bahti. Minneapolis, 1982.

Jowett, Garth. *Film: The Democratic Art*. Boston, 1976.

Kauffmann, Stanley, ed. *American Film Criticism*. New York, 1972.

Kindem, Gorham, ed. *The American Movie Industry*. Carbondale, Ill., 1982.

Lounsbury, Myron. *The Origins of American Film Criticism*. New York, 1973.

McArthur, Benjamin. *Actors and American Culture, 1800–1920*. Philadelphia, 1984.

Mast, Gerald. *A Short History of the Movies*. 2nd ed. New York, 1976.

Mast, Gerald, and Marshall Cohen. *Film Theory and Criticism*. 3rd ed. New York, 1985.

May, Lary. *Screening Out the Past*. New York, 1980.

Mellen, Joan. *Big Bad Wolves: Masculinity in American Film*. New York, 1977.

Mitchell, George. "The Consolidation of the American Film Industry." *Cine-Tracts* nos. 2 (1976): 28–36; and 3/4 (1976): 63–70.

Morin, Edgar. *The Stars*. Translated by Richard Howard. New York, 1960.

Murray, Edward. *Nine American Film Critics*. New York, 1975.

Neale, Stephen. *Genre*. London, 1980.

Potamkin, Harry Alan. *The Compound Cinema: The Film Writings of Harry Alan Potamkin*. Edited by Lewis Jacobs. New York, 1977.

Poteet, George H. *Film Criticism in Popular American Periodicals, 1933–67*. New York, 1977.

Radway, Janice. *Reading the Romance*. Chapel Hill, 1984.

Ray, Robert. *A Certain Tendency of the Hollywood Cinema, 1930–1980*. Princeton, 1985.

Rosten, Leo. *Hollywood*. New York, 1941.

Sarris, Andrew. *The American Cinema: Directors and Directions, 1929–1968*. New York, 1968.

———. *Politics and Cinema*. New York, 1978.

Schatz, Thomas. *Hollywood Genres*. New York, 1981.

Schwartz, Nancy Lynn. *The Hollywood Writers' Wars*. New York, 1982.

Sklar, Robert. *Movie-Made America*. New York, 1976.

Slide, Anthony, ed. *Selected Film Criticism, 1921–30*. Metuchen, N.J., 1982.

———. *Selected Film Criticism, 1931–40*. Metuchen, N.J., 1982.

Staiger, Janet. "Seeing Stars." *Velvet Light Trap* no. 20 (Summer 1983): 13–17.

———. "Individualism versus Collectivism." *Screen* 24, nos. 4/5 (July-October 1983): 68–79.

Taylor, John Russell. *Strangers in Paradise: The Hollywood Emigrés, 1933–50*. London, 1983.

SELECT BIBLIOGRAPHY

Tomashevsky, Boris. "Literature and Biography." In *Readings in Russian Poetics*, ed. Ladislav Matejka and Krystyna Pomorska. Ann Arbor, 1978.
Walker, Alexander. *The Shattered Silents*. New York, 1979.
Warshow, Robert. *The Immediate Experience*. New York, 1962.
Williams, Raymond. *Keywords*. London, 1976.

WORKS ON TWENTIETH-CENTURY AMERICAN CULTURAL HISTORY

Aaron, Daniel. *Writers on the Left*. New York, 1961.
Alexander, Charles. *Here the Country Lies*. Bloomington, 1980.
Barrett, Edward L., Jr. *The Tenney Committee*. Ithaca, 1951.
Belfrage, Cedric. *The American Inquisition*. New York, 1973.
Bell, Daniel. *Marxian Socialism in the United States*. Rev. ed. Princeton, 1967.
Bentley, Eric, ed. *Thirty Years of Treason*. New York, 1971.
Caute, David. *The Great Fear*. New York, 1978.
Cook, Bruce. *Brecht in Exile*. New York, 1982.
Coser, Lewis. *Refugee Scholars in America*. New Haven, 1984.
Cowley, Malcolm. *Exile's Return*. Rev. ed. New York, 1951.
Diggins, John. *The American Left in the Twentieth Century*. New York, 1973.
Foner, Philip S. *Paul Robeson Speaks*. New York, 1978.
Gillim, Dorothy Baker. *Paul Robeson: All American*. Washington, D.C., 1976.
Goldman, Eric. *The Crucial Decade and After, 1945–1960*. New York, 1960.
Goodman, Walter. *The Committee*. New York, 1968.
Harris, Leon. *Upton Sinclair: American Rebel*. New York, 1975.
Heilbut, Anthony. *Exiled in Paradise: German Refugee Artists and Intellectuals in America, from the 1930s to the Present*. New York, 1983.
Hilfer, Anthony Channell. *The Revolt against the Village, 1915–1930*. Chapel Hill, 1969.
Hodgson, Geoffrey. *America in Our Time*. New York, 1976.
Howe, Irving, and Lewis Coser. *The American Communist Party*. Boston, 1957.
Leuchtenberg, William. *Franklin D. Roosevelt and the New Deal*. New York, 1963.
Levering, Ralph. *American Opinion and the Russian Alliance, 1939–1945*. Chapel Hill, 1976.
Lyon, James K. *Bertolt Brecht in America*. Princeton, 1980.
McAuliffe, Mary. *Crisis on the Left*. Amherst, 1978.
Manchester, William. *The Glory and the Dream*. New York, 1974.
May, Henry F. *The End of American Innocence*. New York, 1959.
O'Neill, William. *A Better World*. New York, 1982.
O'Reilly, Kenneth. *Hoover and the Un-Americans*. Philadelphia, 1983.
Pells, Richard. *Radical Visions and American Dreams*. New York, 1973.
―――. *The Liberal Mind in a Conservative Age*. New York, 1985.
Skotheim, Robert. *Totalitarianism and American Social Thought*. New York, 1971.
Starobin, Joseph R. *American Communism in Crisis, 1943–1957*. Cambridge, 1972.
Susman, Warren. "The Culture of the Thirties" and "Culture and Commitment." In *Culture as History*. New York, 1984. pp. 150–210.

Wald, Alan. *The New York Intellectuals*. Chapel Hill, 1987.

Wilson, Edmund. *The Shores of Light*. New York, 1952.

———. *The Twenties*. New York, 1975.

———. *Letters on Literature and Politics, 1912–1972*. New York, 1977.

Wise, Gene. *American Historical Explanations: A Strategy for Grounded Inquiry*. 2nd ed., rev. Minneapolis, 1980.

Wittner, Lawrence S. *Cold War America*. New York, 1974.

Young, Stark. *Stark Young, A Life in the Arts: Letters, 1900–1962*. Edited by John Pilkington. Baton Rouge, 1975.

Index